COLLECTED WORKS OF ERASMUS

VOLUME 67

COLLECTED WORKS OF
ERASMUS

SPIRITUALIA and PASTORALIA

EXOMOLOGESIS

ECCLESIASTES 1

edited by Frederick J. McGinness

translated by Michael J. Heath and James L.P. Butrica

annotated by Michael J. Heath and Frederick J. McGinness

contributing editor Alexander Dalzell

University of Toronto Press

Toronto / Buffalo / London

The research and publication costs of the
Collected Works of Erasmus are supported by
University of Toronto Press.

© University of Toronto Press 2015
Toronto / Buffalo / London
Printed in the U.S.A.

ISBN 978-0-8020-9948-8 (2 vol. set)

Printed on acid-free paper

Library and Archives Canada Cataloguing in Publication

Erasmus, Desiderius, –1536
[Works. English]
Collected works of Erasmus.

Includes bibliographical references and indexes.
Contents: v. 67–68. Spiritualia and Pastoralia
ISBN 978-0-8020-9948-8 (v. 67–68)

I. Title.

PA8500 1974   199'.492   C74006326X

University of Toronto Press acknowledges the financial assistance
to its publishing program of the Canada Council for the Arts
and the Ontario Arts Council, an agency of the Government of Ontario

Canada Council   Conseil des Arts
for the Arts   du Canada

ONTARIO ARTS COUNCIL
CONSEIL DES ARTS DE L'ONTARIO
an Ontario government agency
un organisme du gouvernement de l'Ontario

University of Toronto Press acknowledges the financial support
of the Government of Canada through the Canada Book Fund
for its publishing activities

Collected Works of Erasmus

The aim of the Collected Works of Erasmus
is to make available an accurate, readable English text
of Erasmus' correspondence and his
other principal writings. The edition is planned
and directed by an Editorial Board, an Executive Committee,
and an Advisory Committee.

In memory of James Lawrence Peter Butrica

Contents

Foreword

Volumes 67 and 68 of the *Collected Works of Erasmus*, comprising the introductions and annotated translations of *Exomologesis sive modus confitendi* (1524) and *Ecclesiastes sive de ratione concionandi* (1535), have been made possible through the generous dedication of a number of scholars whose exemplary work it is fitting to acknowledge at the outset. It has been many years ago now since Michael Heath completed the introduction, translated, and annotated Erasmus' principal treatise on confession, *Exomologesis*, and eight years since James Butrica brought forth the first English translation of books 1–4 of Erasmus' next-to-last and lengthiest treatise, *Ecclesiastes*. As the final stages of his first complete draft were being revised in early 2005, while working through various questions and difficulties presented by a number of passages of Erasmus' text, James Butrica, after months of struggle with a debilitating illness, passed away on 20 July 2006, leaving the English text all but complete in its final form. With his passing the University of Toronto Press and Memorial University lost an amiable colleague, translator, and superb classicist.

Two years after James Butrica's death, James McConica and Ron Schoeffel at the University of Toronto Press enlisted Professor Emeritus Alexander Dalzell, well known for his work as translator of many volumes of CWE, to collaborate with me on James Butrica's translation in order to emend a number of passages and resolve many remaining questions raised by the Latin text that he and I had not yet settled. The final translation of book 1 of *Ecclesiastes* appearing here in volume 67 and books 2–4 in volume 68 therefore owes a vast debt to Alexander Dalzell, contributing editor, who after James Butrica's untimely death graciously assumed responsibility for the final edition of the English text and worked diligently to complete it on schedule. Alexander Dalzell's polished emendations, with the collaboration of Ann Dalzell, gracefully advance James Butrica's workmanlike rendering of Erasmus' Latin text in a way he no doubt would have commended as meticulous, elegant, and fully in tune with Erasmus' sensitivities. Special thanks go as well to Daniel J. Sheerin who went over the complete earlier draft of this treatise and offered copious helpful comments and suggestions. This work is also deeply indebted to the late Jacques Chomarat, who established the final Latin text of *Ecclesiastes* that was used for this edition and appeared as volumes v-4 (1991) and v-5 (1994) in the North Holland edition (ASD) of *Opera omnia Desiderii Erasmi Roterodami.*[1] Jacques Chomarat passed away on 9 June 1998, not long after completing this edition, but his exhaustive efforts in establishing an authoritative Latin text with full critical apparatus, introduction, and ample footnotes have been of immense help to those of us who now bring to light the English translation and annotations of this singularly important treatise of Erasmus. Volumes 67 and 68 are based on Chomarat's Latin text and in consultation with the Leiden edition (LB). Erasmus himself apparently added an *erratum* to the *editio princeps,*[2] which was incorporated into Chomarat's Latin edition of the text. Fortunately only a very few modifications occurred between the *editio princeps* and the second edition, which appeared in March 1536 (B: Basel).[3] These few differences have been noted in the footnotes by the translator.

We are also grateful to Michael J. Heath, James K. McConica, John O'Malley, the late John H. Munro, Carole Straw, Wendy Watson, John Varriano, Angelo Mazzocco, T. Frank Kennedy, Margaret Liggett, Lyn Minnich, Sarah Wilson, Kathryn Kirby, Robert Doran, Holly Sharac, David Myers, Eugene Hill, Frank Brownlow, Carlin Barton, Andrew Feldherr, Mark Peterson, Benny Grey Schuster, Katharine Maughan, Calvin Payne-Taylor,

* * * * *

1 Desiderius Erasmus *Ecclesiastes sive de ratione concionandi* ed Jacques Chomarat in ASD v-4 *Ecclesiastes* (Libri I–II); v-5 *Ecclesiastes* (Libri III–IV) (Amsterdam 1991 and 1994)

2 See Chomarat's discussion of the very minor changes in the successive editions of *Ecclesiastes* from 1536–40 in ASD v-4 22–7. Fortunately for Chomarat very little emendation of the text was called for, thanks largely to The Royal Library at Copenhagen's possession of an autograph of a substantial portion of the first book of *Ecclesiastes*. An examination of this work shows that very few minor changes were added, and those mainly to clarify or enrich the sense of the text, correct the Latin, etc. Chomarat's edition of *Ecclesiastes* incorporates those emendations that have appeared in successive editions of the work, and at times, but rarely, he emends the text himself to re-establish the order and sense. See Butrica 'Translator's Note' 239. For the 'Copenhagen Manuscript,' see 'Appendix XIII: The Copenhagen Manuscript' Allen III 630–4; see also Kleinhans I–II.

3 See Chomarat's introduction ASD v-4 28 for abbreviations to the various editions of this work.

Natalie Kulikowski, Bryan Goodwin, Ann Drury, Jennifer Chien, Rozelynn Douglas, Ajay Menon, and to Carla DeSantis, Philippa Matheson, and Mary Baldwin and the editorial staff of the University of Toronto Press.

Finally, the editors must acknowledge the sad loss of Ron Schoeffel, University of Toronto Press editor, who did so much in making these volumes possible, whose gracious, unflagging assistance to everyone collaborating in the CWE project over the years has been an admirable testimony to his great and generous spirit.

FJM

THE MANNER OF CONFESSING

Exomologesis sive modus confitendi

translated and annotated by
MICHAEL J. HEATH

Exomologesis sive modus confitendi was published by Froben at Basel in March 1524. With it were printed Erasmus' short paraphrase on Psalm 3, his letter to Joost Vroye concerning sudden death, an exchange of correspondence with Pope Adrian VI on Erasmus' disputes with the Louvain theologians, and the *Conclusiones* of Diego López Zúñiga followed by Erasmus' *Apologia*.[1] These pieces were well chosen to accompany Erasmus' contentious discussion of the sacrament of penance. The psalm commentary, though relatively uncontroversial and unspecific,[2] does evoke the troubles of the faithful beset by enemies, the temptations of sin, and the consoling abundance of God's mercy and forgiveness, while the letter to Vroye includes a polemical passage on deathbed confessions.[3] The other pieces relate to the controversies in which Erasmus had recently been embroiled, not least over the sacrament of penance; in a sense the *Exomologesis* is merely the longest contribution to a debate in which Erasmus was involved for more than a decade.[4]

In the psalm commentary Erasmus gives a clear and traditional description of the object of the sacrament. It is essentially a re-enactment of the paschal mystery, in which a Christian dies to sin, through contrition, and rises again with Christ into newness of life.[5] The controversy had arisen over Erasmus' views on the origins of the sacrament as practised in the contemporary church and on the details of its operation.

There are many references in the New Testament to the confession of sins and to the imposition of penalties for sin, but there are no precise instructions on the procedure to be followed. The church had adopted two distinct methods. The austere discipline of public penance leading to absolution in the early church[6] had been superseded gradually by the familiar 'private' penitential system involving auricular confession, absolution, and

* * * * *

1 See, respectively: CWE 63 147–68; Ep 1347; Epp 1310, 1324, 1329, and 1338 (the latter pair first published with the *Exomologesis*); LB IX 381B–392C. Erasmus had been at work on the *Exomologesis* since the previous November (Ep 1397:15).
2 There is a brief passage (CWE 63 159–60) condemning the 'mockers of the church's sacraments' and the 'heretics' who belittle penance.
3 Ep 1347:82–104
4 The work is comparable in this sense to the *Institutio christiani matrimonii* of 1526 (CWE 69 203–438), another attempt by Erasmus to resume and clarify a long-standing controversy over one of the sacraments.
5 CWE 63 164
6 This kind of penance could be performed once only, according to the famous dictum of St Ambrose: 'As there is one baptism, so there is one penance' (*De poenitentia* 2.10 PL 16 [1845] 520). This is cited (as outmoded) by Peter Lombard *Sententiae* book 4 dist 14 c 3 and by most subsequent medieval commentators.

penance or satisfaction.[7] Penance was not universally recognized as a sacrament until the twelfth century, but it was made an annual obligation by decree of the Fourth Lateran Council in 1215 and became, under the scrutiny of canon lawyers and scholastic theologians, subject to a dense complex of regulations and conditions.[8]

In the fifteenth century some humanists began to emphasize the essentially inward character of the sacrament and the need for individual responsibility, presenting repentance as the most essential of moral virtues.[9] More radically still, Luther's *Sermon on the Sacrament of Penance* (1519) reduced the priest's role in granting absolution to a purely declaratory function, though Luther recognized the utility of the sacrament as a pastoral instrument. In the following year he denounced the schoolmen's regulations in *A Discussion on How Confession Should Be Made*, and declared roundly, in *The Babylonian Captivity of the Church*, that the institution could not be considered a sacrament since it lacked the necessary visible sign, divinely instituted.[10]

* * * * *

7 The new system may have evolved from Celtic and Anglo-Saxon practices codified in the 'penitentials,' some of which date from the sixth century. The evolution of the private system is still a matter of controversy; the various cases were fairly put by R.C. Mortimer *The Origins of Private Penance in the Western Church* (Oxford 1939). See also the introduction to McNeil (3–22), which is followed by surviving fragments of early documents.

8 The most accessible guide to these developments is Tentler *Sin* (see 3 n1 for his predecessors), complemented by Myers *Sinning* 15–103. See also the historical survey in Spykman 17–83; Jean Delumeau *Sin and Fear: the Emergence of a Western Guilt Culture* trans Eric Nicholson (New York 1990); Rahner; and the background material in Payne 'Penance and Extreme Unction' in *Erasmus: His Theology of the Sacraments* (181–216). For a more detailed but more controversial account, see B. Poschmann *Penance and the Anointing of the Sick* trans F. Courtney (Freiburg and London 1964). On the evolution in Germany, see Susan C. Karant-Nunn *The Reformation of Ritual: an Interpretation of Early Modern Germany* (London and New York 1997) 91–137. For articles on practices throughout Christendom, see *Penitence in the Age of Reformations* ed K. Jackson Lualdi and A.T. Thayer (Aldershot and Burlington, Vt 2000).

9 See Myers 'Humanism' 364 and the example of Bartolomeo della Fonte in Charles Trinkaus *In Our Image and Likeness: Humanity and Divinity in Italian Humanist Thought* (London 1970) II 616–33 ('Humanists on the Sacraments: On Penance'). Humanists also found relief from the guilt culture of the Middle Ages in the attitude of the ancient Greeks, who held that sin derived largely from ignorance.

10 *Eyn Sermon von dem Sacrament der Pusz* (LW 35 9–22), *Confitendi ratio* (LW 39 35–7), and *De captivitate Babylonica* (LW 36 124). See Spykman 90–113; Rahner 153–62; P. Palmer in NCE 11 76–7 on the Reformers' attacks on the schoolmen's analysis. The latter argued that the 'matter of penance' (the penitent's acts) was

When Luther burned the papal bull excommunicating him, he also cast into the fire one of the most popular confessors' manuals, the *Summa angelica* of Angelus de Clavasio.[11]

Erasmus first became embroiled in the controversy because in the *Annotationes* of 1516 and 1519 he had 'raised in passing'[12] the question of the divine institution of the sacrament as at present practised, for which he could find no precise scriptural authority.[13] It seemed to Erasmus' critics that such doubts also called into question the necessity of the sacrament and endorsed Luther's attempts to abolish the majority of the sacraments. Erasmus was first attacked on these grounds by Jan Briart and Edward Lee at Louvain,[14] and his reply to Lee's detailed criticism was published in March or April 1520.

The lengthy passage on penance in this *Responsio* was a reply to Lee's attack on the annotation on Acts 19:18.[15] Here Erasmus adopted his most extreme position, from which he was gradually to retreat over the next decade. He repeated his conviction that most modern penitential practices were of human institution, demolishing in particular appeals to Matthew 8:4. He complained, as Luther was to do, that the church's requirement that

* * * * *

given form by absolution, and that together these made the sign of the sacrament. Luther considered this dangerously close to Pelagianism; the Council of Trent reasserted the traditional position against him (Denzinger 1673–5 and 1704).

11 Tentler *Sin* 34–5; Myers 'Humanism' 365. For succinct accounts of Luther's views, see Myers *Sinning* 63–76; Karant-Nunn (see introductory note 3 n8 above) 94–9.

12 He used the phrase, rather ruefully, while writing the *Exomologesis*, in a letter of January 1524, probably to Lorenzo Campeggi (Ep 1410:34–9). For fuller treatment of the controversies involving Erasmus see Payne's chapter 'Penance and Extreme Unction' (3 n8 above) and Tentler 'Forgiveness.' Neither writer, however, knew of the *Manifesta mendacia* or of Erasmus' textual emendations to the *Exomologesis*, discussed later in this introduction (see introductory note 10 below).

13 On the medieval controversy on this point, see Tentler *Sin* 57–9; and on the continuing debate since the Council of Trent reaffirmed in 1551 the principle of divine institution (Denzinger 1670, 1683 and 1701), see Rahner 166–74.

14 Erasmus gives an account of the controversies in Louvain in Ep 1225:1–134. Lee's *Annotationes* were published in February 1520. On his relations with Erasmus generally, see Rummel I 95–120.

15 CWE 72 362–4; Erasmus' original annotation concerned public penance in the early church; in 1519 he added the hypothesis that modern auricular confession had developed later from the practice of bishops counselling informally those troubled in conscience (LB VI 507–8).

confession be complete made no allowance for human frailties, such as lapse of memory. He asked provocatively what harm would result from abolishing private confession, taunting Lee with underestimating and thereby undermining the church's authority; it would retain both the power of binding and loosing (Matt 16:19), through excommunication, and also the traditions of general public confession and absolution at mass. If confession enabled priests to know their flock, why did they so often abdicate the task to itinerant Franciscans or Dominicans? The germ of much of the *Exomologesis* lies in Erasmus' subsequent enumeration of the 'evils' that beset contemporary confession, in particular the bad character of many confessors; the satire here is sharper than anything in the *Exomologesis* itself.

Erasmus then gave Lee a history lesson (which, significantly, he did not repeat in later replies to critics) concerning the operation as well as the origin of the sacrament. He claimed that in the millennium from St John Chrysostom to the canonist Gratian, no theologian maintained that private confession as currently practised was necessary; on the contrary, all gave priority to spontaneous personal contrition leading to direct divine forgiveness, their model being St Peter (Luke 22:62). Erasmus is alluding to the ancient 'contritionist' tradition, revived in the Middle Ages by Abelard, Gratian, and Peter Lombard, where the accent was placed on sorrow and amendment rather than on acts of penance. In this tradition the best confession is one that leads to a change of life; shame before God is more salutary than shame before a priest. But the contrasting view that the consummation of penance lies in the absolution by the priest had gained ground in the thirteenth century under the aegis of St Thomas Aquinas and Duns Scotus, the latter going so far as to transpose the sacramentality of the whole process of penance exclusively into the priestly absolution.[16] Luther had again revived the essentials of contritionist theory.[17] Erasmus' conclusion did little to allay the suspicion that he sympathized with this theory; having reviewed the historical evidence, he offered, grudgingly, not to rebel against the church's authority if it insisted that he must conform to its opinions on the divine origin and the necessity of auricular confession.

* * * * *

16 See Rahner 157–70; Tentler *Sin* 105–6, 120–3 and, for the whole dispute, 233–300; Spykman 38–83.
17 Luther held that forgiveness is granted unconditionally to faith without the necessity for confession, still less for penitential works (Tentler *Sin* 358–60). Some modern Catholic theologians consider that it is grace that leads to contrition and that forgiveness is therefore guaranteed before penance (Rahner 164).

Naturally this far from conciliatory reply won Erasmus few friends among the theologians at Louvain. Briart, who had pressed him to acknowledge that auricular confession was instituted by Christ,[18] was now dead, but Nicolaas Baechem took over and taunted him with holding Lutheran views on confession; Erasmus protested that he had read very little of Luther.[19] Further damage was done when selected extracts from the *Annotationes* were published in pamphlets supporting Luther; they included Erasmus' complaint that the burden of confession had been increased by the traps laid by bad confessors.[20] Interestingly, Erasmus' shouting match with Baechem was held before the professor of theology at Louvain, Godschalk Rosemondt, who had recently published a traditional manual of confession; he seems, however, to have remained neutral in the debate.[21]

The controversy continued with the 1522 edition of the *Colloquia*. This included the *Confabulatio pia*, in which the boy Gaspar, a 'contritionist' who confesses daily to God, will not commit himself on the divine institution of modern confession, while his companion Erasmius criticizes the conduct of some confessors on grounds to be developed in the *Exomologesis*. Erasmus was soon defending these inflammatory remarks against Baechem, pointing out his own and the boys' orthodoxy and obedience to the church's decree ('confession I actually approve'), though repeating that his mind was 'not yet quite clear' on the origins of modern confession.[22]

From further afield Zúñiga twice attacked Erasmus' views on penance (and much else) in the *Annotationes*. In 1522 Erasmus replied briefly, reasserting his willingness to submit to the church's ruling. His second reply was published alongside the *Exomologesis* itself. In his *Conclusiones* Zúñiga had picked out four questionable propositions concerning confession, all to do with its disputed history. Erasmus refers his opponent to

* * * * *

18 Ep 1225:130–1
19 See for example Ep 1164:73–5 and Ep 1225:180–1.
20 See Ep 1202:253–5 and nn46 and 50. Erasmus repeated the point about traps in the *Apologia adversus monachos* (LB IX 1063E), adding that they condemned many to an unquiet death.
21 For the dispute with Baechem, see Rummel I 135–43; Epp 1153, 1162, 1164, and 1172; *Spongia* (CWE 78 69 n187). In Ep 1162:180–7 Erasmus insinuates that Baechem himself typified the 'bad confessor.' Rosemondt's *Confessionale* had been published in 1518.
22 See Rummel II 4–5; Epp 1299:66–74 and 1301:17–31. For the text at issue, see CWE 39 97. Erasmus also defended his views in *De utilitate colloquiorum* (CWE 40 1108). For other apparently less contentious passages on confession in the *Colloquia*, see Payne 192.

his replies to Lee, but also points out that his doubts were expressed before Leo x's bull *Exsurge Domine* (June 1520) had condemned Luther's stance. He remains open to persuasion but, on a new tack, doubts whether modern confession was instituted by the apostles: how could they have coped with the multitude of their converts? He also wonders whether confession of any kind was obligatory in the early church but, in a parting shot that reveals the context of the debate, advises Zúñiga to go off and read Luther in order to appreciate the difference between the two.[23]

It is clear from Erasmus' correspondence and other writings of this period that his 'passing remarks' on confession were constantly returning to haunt him, and his decision to devote a whole treatise to the subject, the *Exomologesis*, was in part the product of this unease. But he failed to placate his critics and in 1530 took the relatively unusual step, for him, of thoroughly revising an earlier work. This new edition of the *Exomologesis* is almost twice as long as the original.[24] The additional illustrations and clarifications somewhat obscure the simple structure of the 1524 work. It begins with an analysis of eight 'advantages' of confession, which highlight the moral as well as the spiritual benefits to be gained. There follow nine 'evils' or 'disadvantages,' five of them attributable to confessors and the rest to penitents. Erasmus then indicates how attitudes might be changed for the better, first addressing the confessors (and their ecclesiastical superiors) and then the penitents, before suggesting some procedural reforms and discussing briefly the technical questions of restitution and satisfaction. Throughout the work Erasmus uses the well-worn image of the priest as physician to the soul to emphasize the consolatory and curative functions of penance.

* * * * *

23 *Apologia ad Stunicae conclusiones* LB IX 389B–D; the 1522 reply is at 369C (*Apologia adversus Stunicae Blasphemiae*). On Erasmus and Zúñiga generally, see Rummel I 145–77 (172–3 on the *Conclusiones*).

24 In LB the 1530 additions make up roughly ten columns out of the final total of twenty-four. The additions are studied later in this introduction and in M.J. Heath 'Confession and Concession: the Texts of Erasmus's *Exomologesis*' in *Acta Conventus Neo-Latini Cantabrigensis: Proceedings of the Eleventh International Congress of Neo-Latin Studies, Cambridge, 2000* ed Rhoda Schnur et al (Tempe, Ariz 2003) 263–70. Jean-Pierre Massaut knew of the additions, but made little use of them in an article which posits the consistency of Erasmus' middle way between traditionalism and Lutheran reforms: 'La position "œcuménique" d'Erasme sur la pénitence' in *Réforme et humanisme: Actes du 4e colloque* ed Jean Boisset (Montpellier 1977) 241–81.

The title *Exomologesis* ('open declaration') echoes the Greek verb used in the New Testament to mean confession, to God or man, either of one's sins (Matt 3:6) or of God's greatness (Rom 14:11).[25] For Erasmus the word thus has desirable overtones of an act of worship as well as of contrition. The subtitle *Modus confitendi* (*The Manner of Confessing*) is perhaps ironical, since it is the title of a succinct and very popular manual of confession by Andreas de Escobar, which is not much more than 'a handy list of sins with some brief thoughts on forgiveness and repentance' – just the sort of book that Erasmus condemns for fostering anxiety or scrupulosity in the penitent.[26] He had pointed out to Lee that his real objections were indeed to the 'manner of confessing' rather than to the sacrament of penance itself.[27] This change of emphasis enabled subsequent critics to challenge Erasmus' views on matters of procedure as well as the other contentious topics.

The critics had some justification. In the *Exomologesis* Erasmus satirizes the extraordinarily compendious discussions of procedural questions by theologians and canon lawyers and the countless manuals for confessors, practical, conservative, and authoritative, which set out in detail the role of both confessor and penitent.[28] Erasmus' main target in the *Exomologesis* is the perceived inadequacy of the clergy; but that was also, explicitly or implicitly, the target of many of these manuals, and their advice is not so very different from Erasmus'. He echoes their complaints about the insecurity of the confessional, or the intimacy of the questioning, and joins them in condemning the greed of confessors seeking a rapid turnover. Sometimes they

* * * * *

25 For the range of meaning and the earliest use of the word by the Fathers Cyprian and Tertullian, see Crichton 23; McNeil 10–11; E.F. Latko 'Auricular Confession' NCE 4 131.

26 Tentler *Sin* 40. Escobar's abridgment of a full-length manual was among the most frequently printed books of the fifteenth century, and also appeared in even briefer form, sometimes as a one-page 'shopping list.' It claims on the first page to contain 'almost every sin.' Luther probably had it in mind in his attack on scholastic distinctions in *Confitendi ratio* (LW 39 36–7).

27 *Responsio ad annotationes Lei* CWE 72 369–72

28 They are exhaustively studied by Pierre Michaud-Quantin *Sommes de casuistique et manuels de confession au moyen âge* (XII–XVI siècles) (Louvain, Lille, and Montreal 1962). See also Tentler *Sin* 28–53. The notes to the text below give references to three manuals, already mentioned, which are characteristic of the genre: Escobar's brief enumeration, Clavasio's alphabetical encyclopedia of 'cases of conscience' and Rosemondt's contemporary yet traditional study of the sacrament in all its aspects.

go further than Erasmus: Rosemondt, for example, suggests remedies 'if the priest falls asleep or mishears.'[29]

We do not know how many of the manuals Erasmus had read. In the *Exomologesis* he names only one of his predecessors, Jean Gerson, whom he accuses of sowing unease in many a conscience with his book on nocturnal emissions. Erasmus is a little unfair: Gerson had earned the title of the Consoling Doctor, and frequently expressed reservations about the inflexibility of confessional practices.[30] He clearly shared Erasmus' views about the moral value of penance, since he took the most common medieval definition of contrition ('Contrition is sorrow for sins voluntarily assumed with the intention of confessing and doing satisfaction') and added 'and with the intention and desire of abstaining from sins.'[31] The contents of most of the manuals prove that if the system of penance were practised according to their principles, the primary subject of the exercise would be the individual's conscience; the sacrament would offer consolation at least as much as discipline. The medieval theorists seem to have been as aware as Erasmus of the damage done to these salutary principles by the human frailty of both confessors and penitents.

If Erasmus expected the *Exomologesis* to silence his critics, he was quickly disabused. His apparent willingness now to submit to ecclesiastical discipline earned him the contempt of some Reformers, including Johannes Oecolampadius and Guillaume Farel,[32] though he was heartened by the reaction from England, where his arguments endorsing those of Henry VIII's book against Luther had apparently helped to re-establish the proper practice of confession.[33] From Paris, however, came reproaches from Noël Béda, and from Antwerp indirect attacks by Jacques Masson (Jacobus Latomus) in his book *De confessione secreta*.[34]

* * * * *

29 Rosemondt f 133 verso
30 See for example Tentler *Sin* 145–7 and 308–11. Erasmus names Gerson only in an addition made in 1530. Luther was more sympathetic to Gerson in his *Confitendi ratio* (LW 39 40).
31 Tentler *Sin* 235 (citing no less than twelve authorities who quote this standard definition) and 238.
32 Epp 1523:118–26 and 1582:95–6 with n14. Oecolampadius thought that the *Exomologesis* was an attack on his own *De confessione* (1521), but Erasmus had not read it.
33 See Ep 1582:95–110.
34 See Rummel II 10–12; Epp 1579 and 1581:459–60 with n58. Ostensibly, Masson was attacking Oecolampadius, but the latter was convinced that the true target

But the most violent criticism of the *Exomologesis* came once more from the theologians of Louvain, four of whom (all Dominicans) seem to have contributed to a pamphlet that appeared at Antwerp in March 1525 under the fictitious name Godefridus Ruysius Taxander. Erasmus drafted a reply, *Manifesta mendacia* (*Manifest Lies*), which remained unpublished, perhaps because Clement VII and Charles V both responded at about this time to Erasmus' plea to intervene on his behalf with the Louvain theologians.[35] But Erasmus was clearly stung by the book and fumed about it to numerous correspondents.[36] *Manifesta mendacia* repeats much of Erasmus' earlier defence of his views on the origins and necessity of confession, which were still apparently too ambiguous for the theologians. The new element is a vigorous defence of his analysis of confessional procedure. The Dominicans took particular offence at the enumeration of nine 'disadvantages' and only eight 'advantages' of modern confession; in this case, at least, Erasmus was happy to redress the balance in 1530.[37] They also complained that Erasmus' scurrilous examples of bad confessors would contribute to bringing the priesthood and the sacrament into disrepute; Erasmus replied that on the contrary he considered such examples salutary.

Similar criticisms resurfaced in the next full-blown attack on Erasmus' book, this time from the 'Spanish monks.' In his reply, published early in 1528,[38] Erasmus makes the clearest possible statement of his personal acceptance of confession as now practised, with all its accessories, such as reserved cases, enumeration of the kind, species, and circumstances of sins, and 'anything else of this kind' – though perhaps this last phrase contains a hint of irony. He also states more forcefully than ever his willingness but

* * * * *

was often Erasmus. Erasmus refers to Masson again in *Manifesta mendacia* (see next note and CWE 71 116).

35 On Clement's role, see Myers 'Humanism' 372. The pamphlet, whose title page is reproduced in CWE 11 250, also attacks Erasmus' *De esu carnium*. *Manifest Lies* has been translated by Erika Rummel in CWE 71 114–31; see also her articles in *Renaissance Quarterly* 43 (1990) 731–43 and *Acta Conventus Neo-Latini Hafniensis* ed R. Schnur (Binghamton 1994) 179–86. I am grateful to Dr Rummel for supplying a draft of the Latin text prepared for publication in ASD and transcribed from the autograph manuscript in Copenhagen.

36 See for example, from 1525, Epp 1571:70–4, 1581A:132–72, 1582 passim, 1585: 71–7, and 1600:40–50. The insult still rankled as late as 1534 (Allen Ep 2956:32).

37 See *Manifesta mendacia* 122 no 25 and book 1 35–6 below. Erasmus returned to the fray in the *Responsio ad epistolam Alberti Pii* (CWE 84 71), arguing that he had enumerated the disadvantages to enable them to be remedied.

38 *Apologia adversus monachos* LB IX 1062E–1064B; see Rummel II 92–6.

inability to ascribe the institution of modern confession to Christ, and his conviction of its value if properly performed. His exposure of corrupt practices does no more, he claims, than confirm what everyone knows to be true; but he insists, somewhat disingenuously, that he has drawn attention to the evils surrounding confession, by which mortals thwart the good it can do, rather than to the intrinsic disadvantages of the institution itself.[39] Thinking of the news from England, he claims that his book, far from damaging confession, has reconciled many who were contemplating throwing off its yoke. He used this argument again in 1528, in reply to mild reproaches from Alonso Fernández; he pointed out to him the difficulty of writing a book on confession at Basel in 1524, in the midst of clamour for reform.[40] A little later he summarized the same arguments to assuage the doubts of John Longland, the friendly bishop of Lincoln, and also assured the archbishop of Cologne that his aim was to make confession 'more sincere and less anxious.'[41]

In his additions to the 1530 *Exomologesis* Erasmus went as far as he could to placate if not reconcile both sets of opponents. However, he stood by his original text to the extent that he made deletions only for stylistic reasons. At the outset he not only added, quite accurately, that even Lutherans considered confession salutary, but also stressed that he personally practised confession and upheld the tradition of reconciliation to God through a priest (20). He could only emphasize his attachment to the institution by attacking both those who would abolish it and those who besmirched it by corrupt practices. Here he came closer than ever to acknowledging the divine origin of the sacrament: 'I am more inclined towards the party that believes that it was instituted by Christ,' though he still lacks conclusive proof (22–3). He then made a very long addition to his discussion of the first 'advantage' of confession, its humbling of human pride. A lesson for his opponents, perhaps? But the detailed comparison here of public penance in the early church and solemn penance in the modern church suggests a new attempt to identify an historical continuity with more apostolic times; unusually, Erasmus admits the utility of 'certain external rites and ceremonies' as a path towards charity (26–7). Apart from a few extra illustrations, the next long addition is a measured attack

* * * * *

39 See 38–9 and n79 below on the unreliability of this claim.
40 Epp 1904 (from Fernández) and 1969; Erasmus had already used the last argument in a reply to the theologians of Louvain (Ep 1582:107–10). On Fernández see CEBR II 23–4.
41 Epp 2037 and 1976

on scrupulosity, exposing further a danger acknowledged by the manuals of confession (31). Erasmus now introduced the required 'ninth advantage' of confession but, as well as giving arithmetical balance, the passage injects a vibrant sense of the liberation and reconciliation to be found in the sacrament (35–6). Having answered the Dominicans, Erasmus next added a scathing portrait of the evil confessor clinging to his materialistic privileges in a passage that was more likely to gladden the Reformers (44–5). So too was a long addition on faith and charity, contrasted with external works of satisfaction, where Erasmus went so far as to include one of Luther's characteristic arguments against ritual confession (55–7).[42] The penultimate addition is a relatively anodyne passage of familiar social satire, illustrating the need for restitution by exposing the tricks of the retail trade (62–6). It has little theological content – except that it appears to conceal an attack on Erasmus' Catholic critics in the guise of crooked wine merchants.[43] Finally the rather abrupt conclusion of 1524, a brief complaint about pilgrimages, is expanded by a lengthy development on the pitfalls of satisfaction or reparation. In 1530 the treatise ended with a recapitulation, for the less experienced, of the remedies against the nine 'disadvantages'; like some other additions, it reinforces the pastoral aspect of Erasmus' treatise. In expanding his book, Erasmus was even-handed towards his opponents, but above all he continued to pursue a median line, acknowledging the discipline of the church whilst promoting the consolatory functions of the sacrament.

This modestly conciliatory tone may reflect a general calming of the controversy, since in the Augsburg Confession of 1530 Melanchthon asserted that the Lutherans had retained the sacrament of penance, along with baptism and the Eucharist. They had not abolished confession and the priest's absolution, though they had reduced their function to that of arousing in the sinner faith or confidence in God's mercy. It seemed that even convinced predestinarians, by retaining an ecclesiastical rite of forgiveness or reconciliation, assigned (for practical purposes) some kind of work for the penitent to do, however committed their theologies to human impotence and iniquity. Later, Calvin too acknowledged the pastoral value of private confession but denied it sacramental status.[44]

* * * * *

42 See n144 to the text.
43 See n168 to the text.
44 *Augsburg Confession* 11.12.15 and Calvin *Institutes* 3.14 and 4.19.16, cited by P. Palmer in NCE 11 76–7; for a full discussion of the Reformers' views and

Did Erasmus, after a decade of struggle, finally convince some of his Catholic critics? Agostino Steuco, writing in 1531 to commend him, albeit half-heartedly, for his recantation over confession, had perhaps read the new edition. Steuco's *Adversus Lutheranos* deals at length with confession, and he complains that his task has not been eased by Erasmus' blackening of confessors, even if the latter has now – apparently – abandoned his notorious opinions. Steuco still holds such inflammatory ideas responsible for the overthrow of monastic life in certain regions.[45] In the same year Maarten Lips wrote from Lens to say that he had not heard the *Exomologesis* decried for some time, though the *Moria, Colloquia,* and *De esu carnium* were still often reviled.[46] Although the Sorbonne kept up the attack on the portrayal of confession in the *Colloquia,*[47] by 1533 Erasmus could conclude one of his last reflections on confession with the expectation that both sides would await the decision of a general synod concerning the divine institution of confession.[48] Finally and fittingly, Erasmus returned to the pre-eminently consolatory function of the sacrament in the *De praeparatione ad mortem* of 1534.[49]

The decision of the general synod came of course at Trent, where it was decreed that confession is indeed of divine origin and necessary for salvation by divine law; an anathema was pronounced against anyone claiming that secret confession is a human invention. The power of the keys and absolution by the priest were upheld.[50] The decrees of Trent were maintained

* * * * *

practices, see Tentler *Sin* 349–63. The Augsburg Confession (1530) was the confession of faith, drawn up by Philippus Melanchthon and presented to the emperor Charles v, which stated the fundamental Lutheran position on the articles of the Christian faith and demanded the remedy of abuses in the church; among the demands was the abolition of compulsory confession. See 'Augsburg Confession' in *The Oxford Encyclopedia of the Reformation* ed Hans J. Hillerbrand (New York 1996) 1 93–7.

45 Ep 2513:394–455. Steuco's tone is suspicious; he wonders whether Erasmus has changed his mind – or just his language. See also Rummel II 136–7 on Steuco's hostility.

46 Ep 2566; on Lips see CEBR II 333–4.

47 Erasmus provides the by now familiar replies in his *Declarationes ad censuras Lutetiae vulgatas* of 1532 (CWE 82 1–326).

48 In *De concordia* CWE 65; see the analysis of the whole passage, which recapitulates familiar arguments, but now without passion, in Payne 209.

49 CWE 70

50 See Spykman 114–221; and Myers *Sinning* 107–13. The decrees and canons are in Denzinger 1668–93 and 1701–15. On the keys, see 34 n67.

until 2 December 1973, when a new *Ordo penitentiae* was issued by the Vatican, in which a clear shift in emphasis is evident from absolution towards reconciliation in a broader sense,[51] a move that Erasmus would surely have found congenial.

Exomologesis was written during a brief period when reform of the sacrament along humanist lines seemed possible and even imminent. The work advocates essentially the transformation of a judgmental and dogmatic institution, represented by 'innumerable labyrinthine questions' (18), into a flexible pastoral instrument, in which the conscience of the sinner is to be guided and consoled by a counsellor intent on moral improvement rather than retribution; the result for penitents is self-knowledge and a 'genuine hatred of their crimes' (74). Erasmus' insistence on the simile of the physician, at the expense of the equally traditional judicial imagery revived in particular by the decrees of Trent, found an echo in a number of attempts among reforming Catholics in the 1520s and 1530s to humanize the institution and to restore its usefulness in Christian life.[52] In one sense the work is aimed at Erasmus' Catholic critics, a defence against charges of Lutheranism; but in a wider sense *Exomologesis* was directed at all those, beginning perhaps with Pope Clement himself,[53] who might be persuaded of the immense pastoral and psychological benefits to be gained from reforms in procedure and in the training and attitude of confessors. For Erasmus mercy and consolation were always to be preferred to judgment and retribution, and a sacrament embodying these virtues was most likely to rescue penance from the Reformers' attempts to undermine it.

The *Exomologesis* was published in 1524 by Johann Froben at Basel and by Michaël Hillen at Antwerp; two further editions appeared at Basel, the

* * * * *

51 See Crichton's *Ministry of Reconciliation*; the book contains an English translation of the *Ordo* together with a commentary. The new Order maintains, as did the Council of Trent (Denzinger 1670), that the origin of the sacrament lies in John 20:21–3 (Crichton 92). For a contrasting commentary, highlighting continuity in the evolution of the sacrament into the present century, see Rahner.

52 See Myers 'Humanism' 378–82 on reforms in Cologne and Verona; W. de Boer *The Conquest of the Soul: Confession, Discipline and Public Order in Counter-Reformation Milan* (Leiden 2001), which deals also with other parts of Italy; V. Lavenia *Tributi, pene e confessione nella teologia morale della prima et à moderna* (Bologna 2004), which draws particular attention to Erasmus' use of the medical analogy.

53 Myers ('Humanism' 372) suggests ingeniously that the new text was designed to 'please the pontiff and flatter the Medici family,' not least by means of the medical similes.

first undated and the second the expanded edition of 1530. There was another printing at Paris in 1534. A French translation by Claudius Cantiuncula (Claude Chansonnette) was published at Basel on 26 April 1524, more
or less simultaneously with the Latin.[54] An anonymous English translation
of the 1530 text, printed in London by John Byddell, appeared in the 1530s.[55]

The text translated here is that of LB v 145–70, checked against the first
edition (Basel: Froben 1524), the revised edition (Basel: Froben 1530) and the
Basel *Opera omnia* of 1540. Significant differences between the texts of 1524
and 1530 are indicated in the notes. Translations of Scripture are my own,
as no English version exactly matches Erasmus' text.

I am grateful to the Leverhulme Trust for the award of a Senior Research Fellowship which enabled me to undertake this work.

MJH

* * * * *

54 The French text is in E. Droz *Chemins de l'hérésie* (Geneva 1970) I 10–41; it was
revised and republished, with a new epistle, by Etienne Dolet at Lyon in 1542.
On Cantiuncula, who also translated More's *Utopia* into German in 1524, see
Epp 852 and 1841 (eulogies by Dorp and Erasmus); CEBR I 259–61.
55 British Library C 110 b 31; *A lytle treatise of the maner and forme of confession,
made by the most excellent and famous clerke, M. Eras. of Roterdame* (London: Iohan
Byddell [1535?]). The translation is generally accurate if somewhat wordy, and
the translator identifies some scriptural references in the margins. For a study
of all the translations, see M.J. Heath 'Translation and Transmission: the Case
of Erasmus' *Exomologesis*' in *Court and Humour in the French Renaissance: Essays
in Honour of Professor Pauline Smith* ed Sarah Alyn Stacey (Oxford and New
York 2009).

DESIDERIUS ERASMUS OF ROTTERDAM TO THE REVEREND FATHER
FRANÇOIS DU MOULIN, BISHOP DESIGNATE OF CONDOM,
GREETING[1]

When he delivered your letter, most honoured prelate, which was full of a
rare sincerity and exceptional kindliness towards myself, my man Hilarius[2]
really brought me in full measure the cheerfulness that his name suggests.
And so, since you have been so kind as to tell me how things are in your
part of the world, it seemed right for me in my turn not to leave you in
ignorance of what I was engaged on here when your letter reached me. Horace, when pondering the things that pertain to living well, uses the words
'I put together and lay up in store what I may later use.'[3] I have a better
right to use these lines, for at that moment I was wholly engaged in prepa-
rations for a virtuous death. That is the most important chapter in philosophy, and the most serious. It is of course something that everyone should
be considering all their life long, but somehow or other we are most of us
Phrygians,[4] and nothing but blows will make us mend our ways. An affliction of the kidneys, from which I have often suffered before, attacked me
so severely last July that I had seriously to consider my departure hence;[5]
but around Christmas it set about me so severely that I despaired of living
and actually prayed for death.[6]

The stone is a merciless and rude remembrance, more cruel than death
itself. Even so I owe it a debt, or it would be truer to say I owe it through
the stone to the Lord Jesus, for making me now give careful thought to
the question how not to be overtaken by death in a state of unreadiness,
even if it has not given me space for my *Exomologesis*,[7] which I now send
you as a kind of appendix to my letter to you. If you think your letter well
repaid, I shall have good reason to be delighted, for I know that nothing

* * * * *

1 The dedicatory letter is Ep 1426. On Du Moulin, see Allen and CWE; CEBR I
   411. He had been nominated to the vacant see of Condom in 1521, but was
   in fact ousted after litigation by a rival candidate. He died in 1526. Erasmus
   added the word 'designate' in 1530.
2 Bertholf (Ep 1384 n31); the letter in question is not extant.
3 *Epistles* 1.1.12
4 That is, we learn wisdom too late; *Adagia* I i 28.
5 See Ep 1376 n4.
6 See Ep 1408 n2.
7 This is the text in Allen and CWE, but as Allen's variants record, the edition of
   1530 added the word *supremae* 'final' (maintained in the 1540 *Opera* and in LB),
   which implies that Erasmus had not had time to make his own final confession
   when he thought he was in danger of death.

I can do for you can ever requite your feelings towards me. Come then, most excellent prelate, let us in the meantime enjoy each other's company in the Lord after this fashion, until the days of peace return and allow a closer intimacy. Farewell.

Basel, 24 February AD 1524

EXOMOLOGESIS, OR
THE MANNER OF CONFESSING[1]

Alongside the innumerable labyrinthine questions[2] on which scholars also laboured years ago – the power of the keys, restitution, satisfaction, indulgences – I see that now a good many have begun to investigate whether this[3] confession of sins, by which nowadays each one of us annually lays bare the wounds of our conscience to a priest, and[4] which most people call sacramental while some make it part of a sacrament, was established by the Holy Scriptures or instituted by Christ in person – in which case it cannot under any circumstances be abolished by mere mortals – or whether it was established by our forefathers but has gradually acquired such strength that its authority is as great as if Christ had instituted it, especially since it has been backed by the authority of the Roman pontiff and the general approval of

* * * * *

1 LB V 145–70
2 An allusion to scholasticism. Many medieval theologians, including St Bonaventure and St Thomas Aquinas, debated *quaestiones* based on the *Sententiae* of Peter Lombard (d 1164), which inspired innumerable commentaries in the later Middle Ages; cf Erasmus' disparaging remarks in the prefatory letter to the *Enchiridion* CWE 66 9–10 (Ep 858:35–84). The four topics Erasmus cites are discussed at length by Lombard *Sententiae* book 4 dist 14–22 and Aquinas *Summa theologiae* III q 84–90 and *Supplementum* q 1–28. Erasmus discusses the last three towards the end of this tract; on the keys, see 34 n67 below.
3 Erasmus carefully uses the demonstrative to denote the modern form of confession, as he points out to his critics in the *Apologia adversus Stunicae Blasphemiae* (LB IX 389B) and in the opening lines of *Manifesta mendacia* (CWE 71 116).
4 and which ... in person] In 1524 Erasmus wrote 'and which they call sacramental, was instituted by Christ.' In 1530 he expanded the text to include his own view; later in this work he distinguishes between 'sacramental confession' (eg 30 below) and the 'sacrament of penance' (eg 43 below), of which confession is a part. He had established this position in *Manifesta mendacia* CWE 71 122 no 23 and *Apologia adversus monachos* LB IX 1062E.

the Christian people.⁵ Then, if one accepts that it was established by mere mortals, they ask whether it would be advisable to leave it alone, in view of the numerous and obvious advantages that are derived from it, or to abolish it, because of the numerous and manifest evils that we understand this practice brings, for which both penitents and confessors are to blame.

Reader, you can expect no such debate in this little book, both because these questions have already been carefully discussed by men of great learning, and because I have no wish at the moment to open up such fresh sores in areas that are already inflamed. It is no time to 'touch the untouchable,'⁶ but rather, as Plato advised, to 'make the best of what you have.'⁷ For however strongly one side may contend, with a plethora of weighty arguments, that this form of confession was not instituted by the Lord Jesus in person, and that such a heavy burden or⁸ heroic task (so to speak), should not have been imposed by a mere mortal on his fellows, at least it cannot be denied that someone who has confessed properly to a capable priest is safer than before.⁹

Even¹⁰ those who defend Luther's teachings admit that it is salutary and not at all to be despised. Although I can offer neither conclusive scriptural

* * * * *

5 This hesitation over the origins of confession was the main bone of contention between Erasmus and Catholic critics of the *Exomologesis*; see the introductory note 13. The Protestant Reformers universally denied that annual confession was instituted by Christ, making it a purely human law; Myers 'Humanism' 364.
6 Erasmus quotes in Greek a proverbial expression found in Herodotus 6.134.
7 Cf *Adagia* II v 1. Erasmus quotes in Greek a stock phrase found for example in Lucian *Menippus* 21; the exact words do not appear in Plato, though a similar idea found in *Gorgias* 449C is used in *Adagia* II ix 33 and IV ii 43 (see CWE 33 238 and n11).
8 or heroic . . . speak] Added in 1530. Luther condemned the 'heavy and unbearable burdens' placed upon penitents by mere mortals in his *Confitendi ratio* of 1520 (LW 39 46).
9 Erasmus insists on the utility of confession, but in a way that might not have displeased Luther, which is no doubt why he added the next paragraph in 1530. He had pursued the same line in defending his annotation on Acts 19 against Edward Lee, rejecting Lee's 'illogical' contention that one confessed 'more truly' as well as 'more safely' using this form; *Responsio ad annotationes Lei* CWE 72 362–4.
10 Even those who . . . the church] Added in 1530. This addition of 1530 could refer to Melanchthon's retention of the confessional and of absolution in articles 11 and 12 of the Augsburg Confession, published in that year; see Mark A. Noll *Confessions and Catechisms of the Reformation* (Leicester 1991) 90–1. But in 1520 Luther himself had described confession as 'most salutary' if stripped of corrupt practices (*Confitendi ratio* LW 39 40 and 46).

evidence nor irrefutable arguments to persuade the stubborn that this form of confession – I mean the one currently in use – was instituted by Christ or even by the apostles, I do think that it should be scrupulously practised by all the faithful, at the very least as a rite brought to its present state by the leading men of the church, not without the inspiration of the Holy Spirit.[11] The others, who teach that confession is not a necessity, must decide for themselves whether they are well advised to do so. But if my mind were burdened with a mortal sin, I should not dare to approach the Lord's table or to await my last day without being reconciled to God through a priest according to the long-accepted custom of the church.[12]

It is thus beyond dispute that this form of confession is for many reasons highly salutary, provided that it is performed properly by the two participants, both the one who seeks healing for the soul through confession, and the one who is consulted as a kind of spiritual physician.[13] But I thought it useful to discuss briefly some ways in which the greatest possible benefit can be derived from confession and the least possible evil be brought into it. Of course it is obvious that the evils arise not so much from the rite itself as from human mischief-making. There is almost nothing in human life so holy, pious, and (one might say) heavenly that people cannot turn it into a plague on themselves by their perverse misbehaviour.

* * * * *

11 Erasmus had used this retort against Lee in 1520, but had been more forthright then in his denial: 'We do not read that private confession was instituted by Christ' (*Responsio ad annotationes Lei* CWE 72 362). However, in the colloquy *Confabulatio pia* the boy Gaspar sidesteps this question and leaves it to the theologians to decide (CWE 39 97).
12 The last sentence of this paragraph echoes a remark in Ep 2136 to Ludwig Baer in 1529 (lines 110–16). Erasmus distances himself from Luther and replies to the allegation of 'Taxander' that he is undermining the church's authority (*Manifesta mendacia* CWE 71 124 no 31), as he had earlier to similar criticism from Lee (*Responsio ad annotationes Lei* CWE 72 368–9) and Zúñiga (*Apologia ad Stunicae conclusiones* [LB IX 389D], where he exhorts his opponent to 'go off and read Luther' to appreciate the difference!).
13 The medical simile is commonplace in writings on penance, though destined soon to lose ground to judicial language in official Catholic accounts (cf Rosemondt f 2; McNeil 44–6; Tentler *Sin* 157–8; Myers 'Humanism' 371–3). It goes back to the Gospels but was given particular point by Origen, one of the earliest advocates of spontaneous confession, who urged self-accusation 'since some are almost choked by their peccant humours' (*Homilia super psalmum 37* PG 12 1386). The image of Christ as physician was also developed by the Fathers; for a bibliography, see Carole Straw *Gregory the Great* (Berkeley, Los Angeles, London 1988) 153 n21.

In[14] truth I thoroughly disapprove of the kind of people who seek to abolish something that is good in itself simply because of human failings, when it would be better to try to cure them. Until now those who have discussed this question seem to have concentrated their efforts on explaining the most common species and kinds of sins,[15] and they have addressed themselves to penitents and not to confessors as well, although that would be particularly desirable, especially these days, when it is sadly obvious that the majority of monks and priests have sunk so low that they frequently outdo the ignorant people in their own ignorance and moral depravity. I have therefore attempted to advise both parties, those who hear confessions as well as those who make them, on how to perform their duty in order to derive abundant benefit from this excellent institution.

Now some believe that this form of confession was instituted by Christ, while others hesitate. Some, though considering it a purely human institution, still practise it no less scrupulously than if Christ had spoken the words that instituted it. Others think it arbitrary but still argue, as I have said, that it is not to be despised, since it can be salutary. I have prepared this little book for all of them. I disagree entirely with those who teach that it is arbitrary.[16] In this little book I neither agree nor disagree with those who contend that it was instituted by mere mortals, but I am more inclined towards

* * * * *

14 In truth I thoroughly disapprove ... better results] These two paragraphs were added in 1530.
15 A reference both to the penitentials, handbooks for confessors, which proliferated from the sixth century, when auricular confession became established, and to the more wide-ranging summae or manuals of confession which succeeded them. In both types of manuals penances were graded according to the nature of the sin and, usually, the station in life of the sinner. On their utility and the complaints about them, especially from Reformers, see Tentler *Sin* 134–40. An example of the scholastic classification of sins would be Peter Lombard's discussion of lying, in which he identifies three kinds (*genera*) or broad categories (the 'white' lie, the jocular lie, and the malicious lie), and eight species, subcategories that scrutinize intentions and results more closely; *Sententiae* book 3 dist 38 c 1, based essentially on St Augustine *De mendacio* 14. Rosemondt exemplifies the copiousness of these discussions; he has 24 pages (ff 8–19) on the species of pride and no less than 86 (ff 73–116) on those of avarice.
16 That is, optional. The sixteenth-century English translator glosses Erasmus' *arbitrariam*: 'that is to say, not of necessite, but standynge in man's wyll and pleasure to do it, or leve it undone' (A verso; see introductory note 15 n55 above). Erasmus underlines his dissent from Luther in this passage added in 1530 (see 22 n17 below).

the party that believes that it was instituted by Christ; I shall be ready and willing to defend that view when I have been equipped with the righteous armour of Scripture and authoritative proof, to avoid making the case worse if I do not succeed in my attempt.[17] For it is not much use merely to make assertions; the Catholic teacher must win the argument by using clear evidence from the Scriptures. 'Anyone who feared they might not win sat still.'[18] It is better to leave the case intact for others than to make it worse by handling it badly. Therefore I shall leave to others a task that requires a true champion and content myself with a mere foot-slogger's role; I shall just mention a few things that will ensure that confession produces better results.[19]

In the interests of clarity, I shall first outline the many advantages of this form of confession. Next[20] I shall show how it can on occasion blight true religion among us. Then I shall discuss some ways of reaping the benefits and avoiding the pitfalls. Finally, I shall deal with all the other matters relating to the duties of confessor and penitent. I[21] imagine that my efforts will seem less helpful to confessors than to penitents, but I expect both parties to take it in good part if, by the nature of the subject, certain things emerge that do little to soothe human sensitivities. You should expect sound advice, not pleasant conversation, from a doctor.

* * * * *

17 Erasmus reiterates (in 1530) his defence against critics who had reproached him for not asserting that the present form of the sacrament was instituted by Christ; see *Manifesta mendacia* 116 and *Apologia adversus monachos* LB IX 1063A and 1064A. But in 1520, replying to Lee, Erasmus had gone to some lengths to discredit such theories, being particularly hard on Lee's allegorization of Luke 17:14, though Lee was by no means the first to use it; see *Responsio ad annotationes Lei* CWE 72–8; Payne 182–3; Tentler *Sin* 57. In the *Apologia ad Stunicae conclusiones* (LB IX 389C) he pointed out the impracticality of auricular confession in apostolic times, when a single bishop and a few priests had to cater for a numerous congregation.

18 Horace *Epistles* 1.17.37. This and the two preceding sentences were recommended for deletion in the *Index expurgatorius* LB X 1820A.

19 Payne (189–90) finds the passage on the institution of confession unexpectedly conciliatory and 'not quite candid' in the light of Erasmus' other pronouncements in the 1520s, but it is in fact consistent enough with Erasmus' later views, as expressed for example in a passage from the *De concordia* (1533; CWE 205–6) cited by Payne.

20 Next I shall ... among us] This clause was recommended for deletion in the *Index expurgatorius* LB X 1820A, as was the passage on confessional practice (see 37 n75 below) to which it refers.

21 I imagine that ... doctor] This defensive passage was added in 1530.

Thus the first and principal advantage[22] to be derived from the confession of sins is, I think, that there is no better or more effective way to break down our intellectual arrogance, the stiff-necked pride[23] that makes us oppose God; unless we make great efforts to repress it, it will ultimately stand opposed to everything that is worshipped or spoken of as God. For the source of all impiety is, and has always been, that we think ourselves something when we are nothing. It was this that hurled down Lucifer and his wretched band, since he claimed as his own the gifts that God's goodness had freely bestowed on him. Rising up against the majesty of his creator, he was flung headlong to the depths as he plotted to scale the heights; after finding so much to admire in himself, he became the lowest of the low.[24] And it was through his prompting and example that the first founders of the human race, having tasted the fruit of the forbidden tree, tried to become like gods, and were expelled from Paradise. Lucifer was an intelligence at once noble, immortal, and incorporeal, endowed with gifts we can scarcely conceive. But since he would not bow to the one from whom he had received every blessing he enjoyed, and compared to whom he was nothing, he fell, irredeemably. How much less fitting is it that we humans, in our infinitely lower estate, should be stiff-necked and oppose God, by whom we were made and without whom we have nothing and can do nothing? Yet this canker is deeply implanted in the human mind, and the cunning serpent unceasingly exploits this disease[25] of ours to drag anyone he can to the spot from which he fell.

Just as arrogance and self-confidence have always been the first steps on the road to impiety, so the first steps towards recovery are total self-abasement and submission to God. Now there can be no more complete submission than for someone voluntarily to fall prostrate at another's feet and to divulge to him not only his deeds, but even his most secret thoughts.[26]

* * * * *

22 Here Erasmus begins the first part of *Exomologesis*, which consists of the nine advantages of confession (though he admits they are in fact 'innumerable') and nine 'evils that seem to arise from the practice of confession, although,' as he makes clear, 'the blame lies with us rather than the institution itself.' See 37.
23 *cervix erecta*, a phrase with biblical overtones (eg Jer 7:26, 17:23) though not a quotation
24 Cf Isa 14:12–13.
25 The 'cunning serpent' echoes Gen 3:1. A misprint in the 1524 edition reads *lucem* 'light' instead of *luem* 'disease.'
26 Erasmus appears to accept the requirement (Tentler *Sin* 153–6) to confess sinful thoughts, which Luther denounced as an innovation introduced by 'avaricious,

All the more so is submission necessary since some deeds and thoughts may be the sort that are deeply shaming to admit, whilst others are the kind that could put their life in grave danger when disclosed to a person who may one day, through folly, drink, spite, or illness, divulge what he has heard. Just think how arrogant and insolent some people are by nature! Again, think of all the pride that worldly success engenders in others, such as the rich or handsome, princes, scholars, actors, or anyone else rising above the rest of us by some mark of distinction. Such people must do great violence to their self-esteem when the fear of God and the desire for salvation make them swallow all their pride[27] and cast themselves at the feet of a priest, a person generally regarded by the world as lowly and contemptible; they must reveal to him, as to a spiritual physician, all the festering wounds in their hearts and the open sores in their consciences. But when, as humans and for God's sake, they humble themselves in this way before a man, they are raised up and magnified before God.

Unless the haughty spirit within us be broken, the gentle spirit of Jesus Christ cannot enter, since it dwells only with the humble and mild and those who tremble at his words. I have heard learned and godly men claim in casual conversation that they have often received more enlightenment and heavenly grace from making a full confession than from anything else, even though it were made to a humble and ill-educated priest, so[28] effective is self-abasement as a means of placating divine anger. The Ninevites were threatened with imminent destruction, but they submitted to the prophet who threatened them, betook themselves to sackcloth and ashes, and soon God's rigorous sentence was changed into mercy.[29] Similarly their barbaric king came down from his lofty throne and sat in the ashes, put on sackcloth

* * * * *

inquisitive or tyrannical prelates' and unknown to the early church (LW 39 32–3). See for example Escobar (a 2 recto), who places *cogitatio* first in his roll-call of sins, and the famous Latin poem on confession attributed to Peter of Blois, *Poeniteas cito*: 'Declare, besides your deeds, those that you wanted to commit' (PL 207 1154C); on the popularity of this very representative poem, see Tentler *Sin* 47–8.

27 Literally 'lower their crests'; cf *Adagia* I viii 69.
28 so effective ... Pride is demented] Added in 1530. The indictment of human pride and insistence upon the value of submission to the priest in this substantial addition to the discussion of the 'first advantage' (to 23–9 below) suggest a further effort by Erasmus to distance himself from Luther (eg *The Sacrament of Penance* LW 35 3–22 on the relatively minor role of the priest in confession).
29 The story is told in the book of Jonah.

instead of purple and, instead of the menacing noises that kings usually make, he uttered prayers to God, saying: 'Who can tell if God will turn and forgive us?'[30]

God opposes the proud, but he has never despised a humble and a contrite heart.[31] Being contrite, it will not stiffen or swell but, if mixed with a few moist tears, it can take on any shape, like damp clay or dough, beneath the guiding hand of its maker.[32] If you have humbled your heart before God, it will be no hardship to submit to a priest. By sinning you stiffened your neck against God and bowed to the devil's yoke; are you now reluctant to submit to a minister and vicar of God? When, lured by the attractions of sin, you put your head into Satan's noose, that was the time to remember your pride, not now, when, just in time, you are struggling free in order to be raised from the pit toward heaven. If you have a sore somewhere on your body, you obey the physician and uncover it, however embarrassing it may be; when your mind is reeling from so many wounds, is it so hard to have them examined briefly by a physician of the soul?

Those who minister to the poor do not say to themselves: 'How lowly is this person I am now serving.' No, they say: 'How great is the one for whom I am performing this duty.' Similarly, those going to the priest should take no heed of his status in the eyes of the world, but should say to themselves: 'How great is the one he represents, and how great the power entrusted to him, more exalted by far than a king's or an emperor's!' If some beggar[33] can relieve your fever, then no matter how distinguished you may be, will you not be more than willing to beg him to restore you to health? If you were captured by pirates, would you not gladly fall at the knees of anyone, however humble his station, if you knew that it was in his power to get you home? Suppose that you had committed some capital offence against the emperor, and that he gave one of his cooks the task of deciding whether you should be punished or restored to the prince's favour. Would you not eagerly fall at the cook's knees, press your cheek against them, and generally behave like the meanest of supplicants, thinking not of what he is, but of what he can do, and revering the emperor's majesty in his humble person?

* * * * *

30 Jon 3:9
31 Cf 1 Pet 5:5; James 4:6; Ps 51 (Vulg 50):17, one of the seven penitential psalms.
32 Cf Rom 9:21.
33 The text reads *mendicus* 'beggar,' but there is presumably a play on *medicus* 'doctor' as well as an allusion to the mendicant orders whose members often heard confessions: see 44 n97 below.

You would willingly and happily submit to the praetor's rod, since it would change your status from slave to freedman,[34] and yet you refuse the hand of a priest, who can change you from a slave of the devil to a child of God? To destroy your soul, you flung yourself gladly beneath Satan's hooves, and yet you shrink from approaching a priest to save your soul. What is this but inverted pride and perverse humility? As soon as you hoist yourself up, you are forced down again; to be raised up, you must abase yourself. Nothing is higher than God, but holding your own head high takes you further from him; to draw nearer, you must humble and abase yourself like the tax gatherer.[35] God hurls his thunderbolt upon the mountains that tower above the clouds, but he sends rain and streams of water into the valleys, which grow green with lush grass and abound in many fruits. This is of course what the Scriptures say: 'He gives his grace to the humble.'[36] Remember the accursed mountains of Gilboa, on which fall neither dew nor rain.[37] But there are also mountains in which the Lord takes delight. There was the mountain on which Abraham prepared to sacrifice his only son. The law was given on a mountain. Remember the renowned Mount Zion that trusts in the Lord, and the mountains to which the faithful lift their eyes, whence comes their help.[38] The Lord frequently prayed on the mountains. He was transfigured on a mountain. He ascended to heaven from a mountain.[39] To become a mountain that is pleasing to the Lord, you must cast out the high peaks from your heart and become a valley, that you may receive the Lord's blessing. The thistles and thorns that grow in soil subject to his curse will be rooted out, and you will abound with the many fruits of virtue.

Believe me, those whose minds rebel against submitting to a priest have not yet abased their hearts sufficiently before God or fully repented. Consider whom you offend, what terrible punishments you have earned, what indignity and shame you have brought upon yourself by sinning, how shabby and vile you make yourself in the eyes of God, the saints, and all

* * * * *

34 A reference to the Roman ceremony of manumission, in which the slave to be freed was touched with a rod, the *vindicta*
35 See Luke 18:13.
36 James 4:6; 1 Pet 5:5
37 Cf 2 Sam 1:21. For a similar development on scriptural mountains, cf *In psalmum* 2 (CWE 63 121–2).
38 See Gen 22; Exod 19–20; Ps 125 (Vulg 124):1; Ps 121 (Vulg 120):1.
39 Cf Matt 17, 28:16 and Acts 1:12.

the angels. When you spurn the stole and the ring,[40] you are banished from the fellowship of God's children and become a slave to the devil, an heir to hell. How can you find shame in an act that will raise you from these depths of infamy to the heights of bliss? Are you ashamed to be thought a sinner? Then, by the same token, are you ashamed to be thought human? And even if a measure of humiliation is involved, it is less shameful to have been a slave than to refuse your freedom. In the end, at least, one humiliation will drive out another, as one nail does another.[41]

Consider whether it is better to feel humiliation just once, here and now, in the presence of one single mortal, or to blush with shame hereafter, in the sight of God, the angels, and all the saints who have lived since the world began and will have lived before its end. Think what a scene that will be! Where will you find the nerve to look God in the eye, your creator, father, redeemer, and advocate, whom you have spurned despite all his encouragement, his kindness, his magnificent promises, and his gentle forbearance? How will you raise your eyes towards the most blessed fellowship of the heavenly host, from which you have chosen to banish yourself by plunging into such wretched company? Think of all the dishonour, the disgrace, the infamy, the shame, and you will find it easy to ignore a fleeting embarrassment that will spare you eternal infamy. 'Blessed are those whose sins are put away.'[42] For confession puts away our misdeeds; God will not recall them, nor will the devil recognize them.[43]

Now, since all who are in thrall to sin have stood up against God, it is right and proper that they should be humbled in body too; and just as the body often provides sin with its opening, so too it can frequently inspire or assist the mind towards virtue. That is why the church's early rulers introduced certain external rites and ceremonies, for use not only in administering the sacraments and in divine worship, but also in banishing those who had relapsed into wrongdoing and in receiving those who had made amends through penance. They intended to deter people from sin, to invite those still unabashed by their crimes to change their ways, and to inspire in those whose penance seemed inadequate a greater antipathy to

* * * * *

40 Cf Luke 15:22; the sense is that the unrepentant sinner rejects the gifts bestowed by his father on the prodigal son.
41 *Adagia* I ii 4
42 Ps 32 (Vulg 31):1
43 This paragraph echoes a commonplace subject of sermons and manuals of confession; see Tentler *Sin* 129; *Poeniteas cito* 1155A.

sin. For the human mind in its frailty requires much encouragement before the flame of charity is kindled there and begins to burn until, as the flame grows stronger, it is transformed and filled with love.[44]

In the past wrongdoers were rebuked by the bishop and banished from the society of the Christian flock; bareheaded, barefoot, dressed in sackcloth, and sprinkled with ashes, they would stand before the church porch, humbly beseeching the passers-by and those who entered to remember them in their prayers. They were ordered to fast, to drink nothing but water, to sleep on the ground, and to do other things that were hard on the human constitution but salutary – both for those who beheld them, in order to protect their innocence and for those who suffered, in order to expiate their guilt.[45] Some vestiges of these customs survive even today, especially in the church at Rome. Certain penitents are stripped to the waist and beaten with rods outside the church, sometimes until the blood runs, watched by huge crowds; but only the penitentiary knows the charge, though everyone is aware that some appalling crime has been committed.

But in places where piety has grown cold and wickedness overflowed, the prelates have made allowance for human frailty and remitted the greatest part of the humiliation and punishment, to avoid alienating too many by exercising their prerogative against everyone. But it is our duty to compensate for the erosion of these outward ceremonies by becoming humble in mind and contrite of heart. The more the discipline of the ancient church is relaxed for us, the less indulgent we must be towards ourselves. For example, the church has conceded that, with the exception of a few kinds of sin, we may be purged of all our sins, however heinous, by confession in secret

* * * * *

44 This paragraph, part of the long passage added in 1530, is cited by Payne (193–4) as evidence of Erasmus' unexpected acceptance of confessional practice. It is in fact in line with his later more conciliatory views, also evident in *De praeparatione* (CWE 70 389–450, cited by Payne). The last sentence reflects an Augustinian and Thomistic view of sin as an impediment to charity (Rahner 150–1).

45 Erasmus describes the 'public penance' of the early church, when after confession the sinner was enrolled in the order of penitents and excluded from the prayer of the faithful and the Eucharist; Erasmus seems to be alluding to the lowest grade of penitents, the 'mourners' or 'weepers,' who were actually excluded from the church building (McNeil 8). This was apparently the only form of penitential act performed in the early church; Augustine contrasts it specifically with prayer, the remedy for lighter sins (*De symbolo ad catechumenos* 7.15 PL 40 635–6). Erasmus describes next the 'solemn penance' of the contemporary church, one of three categories of penance identified by the schoolmen (see 69 n186 below).

without incurring any shame or damage to our reputation. But we must be wary that the church's indulgence here does not teach us to be lukewarm in hating our sins; they cannot be considered trivial when any one of them can earn us eternal torment in hell. Therefore we must abandon this useless, indeed dangerous, embarrassment, just as we must banish our foolish, godless pride. How can it be that we are afraid to share our thoughts with a single man, but are unafraid of God's all-seeing eye? Pride is demented.[46]

The second advantage of confession: many people, because of their age or inexperience, do not understand the nature of their illness. They think, mistakenly, that some mortal sin is no crime at all, or else that something is a sin when it is not.[47] Or perhaps they know what is wrong, but are so deeply enmeshed that they do not know how to escape. This[48] occurs in many a case concerning matrimony, vows, restitution, and other similar things, where sometimes even the learned theologians and lawyers get confused. Here absolution is not enough; such cases require someone upright, discreet, equipped with a knowledge of Holy Writ, and with experience in both kinds of law.[49]

Another point: just as the human body may harbour latent illnesses, all the more dangerous because they are concealed, so the human spirit often harbours hidden flaws, which go unnoticed or delude us because they are disguised as piety.[50] Here the priest can help, like a skilled physician, by diagnosing from the symptoms an unrecognized disease and correcting the error. Again, he can reassure someone who is needlessly frightened by a non-existent danger. Finally, he can offer learned and reliable advice to those who are helplessly entangled with evil, showing them how to root it out, whether it be some tendency ingrained in them by nature or something that constantly resurfaces, having become habitual and familiar over the years. For the medical profession finds no illness more difficult to treat than one which has established itself over a long period of time. Sometimes

* * * * *

46 The long addition made in 1530 (24 n28 above) ends here.
47 Only mortal sins had to be formally confessed, but it was acknowledged by the manuals (eg Rosemondt ff 144–58) that distinguishing them from venial sins was not a simple matter; see Tentler *Sin* 144–8.
48 This occurs ... as piety] Added in 1530.
49 That is, canon law and civil law. Erasmus discusses many of the intricate legal problems concerning marriage and vows in his *Institutio christiani matrimonii* of 1526; see 48 n111 below.
50 This second point seems to echo Luther's argument against the requirement (eg Rosemondt f 3) that confession be complete (*A Discussion on How Confession Should Be Made* LW 39 23–47 and *The Keys* LW 321–77).

such cases are quite hopeless, and the best that can be offered is not a cure but some relief of the symptoms; examples are chronic epilepsy, gout, or gallstones. But where disease of the spirit is concerned, we must never despair of salvation. Remember that Christ not only cleansed the lepers and the woman troubled for years by the issue of blood, but he also raised the paralytic who had lain for years by the pool, and finally revived Lazarus, dead for four days.[51] The learned and trusty physician can predict the onset of illness from physical symptoms and can forestall it with no great difficulty, though once established it is hard to dislodge without intensive treatment. The wise and trusty physician to the soul does the same: recognizing the danger signs of approaching trouble, he gives advice and shows how it can be avoided. And such advice is never more timely than during sacramental confession.

It will make no difference whether we consider what I am about to name as the third advantage of confession, or simply add it to the previous section: in confession the priest can cure two very great ills. One of them is a dangerous complacency or (more dangerous still) vanity about one's sins. The other is far more perilous than either – despair of God's forgiveness. The[52] first to experience this was Cain, the model for Judas Iscariot.

A mysterious cachet, you see, attaches to certain sins, such as debauching pretty girls, laying siege to rich and noble matrons, losing huge sums at dice, doing the dirty on one's enemies, or throwing an outrageously lavish feast. The way some people confess suggests that, far from being ashamed of these misdeeds, they would like to trumpet them as glorious achievements. Realizing this, the priest must endeavour to banish such foolish vanity from his penitent's mind. He must expose the wickedness of the sin and replace that dangerous vanity with salutary shame and grief.

By contrast, some sins are of such a kind that they revolt our natural feelings and even their perpetrators curse and hate themselves: for example, parricide, infanticide, monstrous and unspeakable sexual practices, common thefts that require no skill, sorcery, pacts with unclean spirits, blasphemy against God, and other similar crimes. The enormity of these crimes often brings people to the brink of despair, the most terrible of all afflictions. Someone who takes God's goodness for granted clearly offends him less than someone who, despairing of his forgiveness, denies that God is good and merciful, even though he is mercy itself; such people deny that

* * * * *

51 Matt 8:2–4; Matt 9:20–2 and Mark 5:25–34; John 5:2–9, conflated with Matt 9:2–7; John 11:1–44
52 The first ... Iscariot] Added in 1530.

God speaks truth, even though he promised forgiveness to every sinner, without exception, who undergoes a change of heart,[53] and will surely keep his promise, if he is true; they deny God's omnipotence, as if there were some human affliction he could not cure. In such a case the priest will therefore try by every means to arouse in the despairing and downcast penitent the hope of forgiveness and to fortify that hope against a relapse.

[The fourth advantage.] But there are some whose spirit is so irresolute and weak that they dare not promise themselves forgiveness, even of the tiniest misdeed, and whose consciences are not at ease until the priest has been through the prescribed ritual by which absolution is granted. Now Christian kindness requires, I think, that human frailties of this sort should be humoured until the people concerned have developed greater strength of character; it will be necessary to encourage them to do so time and time again.

I[54] have known people who could not be convinced that they had been absolved unless the priest confirmed it in writing. These days a great many people scrupulously confess even the most insignificant of venial sins, some of them quite trifling,[55] such as nocturnal emissions, which are caused entirely involuntarily by a mere physical reflex, with no consent involved. Jean Gerson wrote so anxiously on this subject that he sowed unease in many a conscience.[56] Similar are those who, when saying their prayers, are never easy in their minds and fret about the most insignificant details; very often a weakness of this sort contains an element of perversity. Their only anxiety

* * * * *

53 In 1530 the single adjective *resipiscenti* 'undergoing a change of heart' replaces a phrase meaning 'whenever one bewails his sin.' The adjective recalls Erasmus' suggested translation of μετανοεῖτε in Matt 3:2 (LB VI 17F), translated by Jerome *poenitentiam agite* 'do penance.' Erasmus considers that *resipiscite* conveys better the Greek sense of a change of mind, and avoids the ambiguity of *poenitentia*, which means both 'repentance' and 'penance'; cf Rummel I 140–1.

54 I have known people ... resist them] These following three paragraphs were added in 1530.

55 On the dangers of scrupulosity, well recognized by the medieval confessors, see Tentler *Sin* 156–62. Some Reformers concluded that it could lead to despair (Myers 'Humanism' 365), and the Council of Trent agreed that venial sins need not be confessed (Denzinger 1680).

56 Gerson *De pollutione nocturna et praeparatione ad missam* ('On Nocturnal Pollution and Preparation for the Mass') in *Oeuvres complètes* ed P. Glorieux (Paris 1973) IX 35–49, a work very frequently reprinted in the sixteenth century. Gerson was one of the most widely read and authoritative late medieval writers on confession; see Tentler *Sin* 45–6 and passim. It was usually considered that a mortal sin, which had to be confessed, must involve a measure of consent (eg Rosemondt ff 159–67).

is whether they have correctly enunciated every last letter and syllable; it is a matter of complete indifference to them whether they understand what they are reading, or whether they respect and are influenced by the holy words they say.

Similarly people confess sudden, fleeting thoughts, which do not lodge in their minds but merely skim across them, as if they had definitely decided to do what came into their mind, or even as if they had actually done it, though often these are things too abhorrent to put into words, like sudden doubts about the truth of Scripture or the articles of faith, or thoughts of incest and other unnatural lusts. To confess things like this, scrupulously, one after the other, is merely to burden the confessor with superfluities and afflict the penitent with groundless fears. It is the sign of good character, so they say, to fear guilt where there is no guilt.[57] Good, perhaps, but by no means perfect. Such a tendency in a boy or girl suggests a temperament suitable for religious instruction, but in adults it is inappropriate and useless, dangerous even, if these unnecessary efforts to avoid sin lead to some more serious sin, something that, thanks to Satan's wiles, we see happening to a good many people. Such perverse behaviour must be challenged, and foolish weakness corrected. A Christian conscience will be pained by such examples of human weakness and will do all in its power to counteract them and to strive for improvement.

The truly pious wish to keep their bodies quite unblemished, as they hope they will be at the resurrection, and thus are upset when their earthly vessel is polluted by lewd dreams; but not everything that troubles us is necessarily a sin. The pious are upset when the body, with its hunger, thirst, somnolence, or weariness, breaks their concentration on prayer, when the members rebel against the heart and the flesh desires against the spirit.[58] But so far from these weaknesses being sins, they provide the opportunity to be strong, if one does one's utmost to resist them.[59]

I think that the same methods should be adopted for people with a similar weakness, who try to confess the same sins over and over again, torturing themselves and wasting the priest's time.[60] Christian charity suggests

* * * * *

57 An allusion to a celebrated aphorism of Gregory the Great often cited in the debate over scrupulosity (Tentler *Sin* 156–7)
58 Cf Rom 7:23 and Gal 5:17.
59 The addition made in 1530 ends here; the following sentence thus refers back to those who seek formal absolution for the 'tiniest misdeed.'
60 'Taxander' read this as a suggestion that the same sin should never be repeated in confession and attacked it as 'wrong and scandalous'; *Manifesta mendacia*

that they be humoured sometimes, but in such a way that they are guided towards better things by admonition, and learn to love more and fear less.

The fifth advantage: there can be no remission of sins unless through the love of God penitents conceive an appropriate detestation of the sins they have committed, together with a firm and serious resolve to refrain in future from everything that offends God. All this will be considerably easier to achieve if one thinks carefully about one's confession beforehand. People about to testify before a judge will give the matter a lot of thought, weighing up all the attendant circumstances more carefully than if they were not obliged to testify.[61] In the same way, people who are thinking out what to say to the priest must give deeper thought to the magnitude and the gravity of their crimes. They will recall how often they have relapsed into sin, how long they have dwelt in this darkness and squalor, and in the meantime how many blessings they have denied themselves, estranged from God, separated from communion with the whole body of Christ, and exposed to eternal punishment in hell. Close scrutiny of all this will produce a dread of sin.

Sometimes this dread is caused by fear of punishment, which will engender despair unless, through contemplation of God's mercy and through trust in the Lord Jesus, who has once and for all paid the price for all our sins, it develops into a hope of forgiveness,[62] when servile fear is replaced by a love worthy of a son who is sorry for the offences he has committed, not because they drag him down to hell, but because they offend the best of fathers, who deserves our gratitude. For if any son who loves his parents with all his heart will not knowingly do anything to upset them, even without any fear of punishment, how much more will someone who loves God, who must be loved above all else, not only detest the past misdeeds that offended God, but also try to ensure that nothing similar occurs in the future? So this advantage would encourage people to confess to a priest, even if confession were not necessary; how much more should they embrace it if necessity forces them to take advantage of it!

* * * * *

CWE 71 121 no 20. The suggestion that such people be humoured up to a point was common in the medieval manuals (Clavasio f 48 and Tentler *Sin* 77–8; see also Payne 204 and n85).

61 Unusually, Erasmus resorts to a judicial analogy. On the competing images, see Anne T. Thayer 'Judge and Doctor: Images of the Confessor in Printed Model Sermon Collections, 1450–1520' in *Penitence in the Age of Reformations* ed K. Jackson Lualdi and A.T. Thayer (Aldershot and Burlington, Vt 2000) 10–29.

62 Erasmus is describing the transformation of 'attrition' into 'contrition'; see 35 n68 below.

The sixth advantage: the deep regret we feel in contemplating our sins helps to obtain God's mercy and forgiveness for our past misdeeds and strengthens our resolve to refrain from sin in future. Similarly the humiliation of baring our conscience to another removes much of the punishment and prevents us from backsliding too easily, just as children learn from beatings and humiliation not to repeat some piece of bad behaviour.[63] Now the great majority of us are weak and foolish and inclined to sin. But this kind of humiliation is so hurtful to more noble minds that many would prefer death to dishonour, were it not that they love God or fear hell.

The seventh advantage: as the old proverb has it, the greatest part of wisdom is to know oneself.[64] Nothing contributes more to self-knowledge than confession, which immediately sets before our eyes our entire existence; it shakes out every thicket of the mind, forcing us to consider where God's commandments should lead, and to ponder our own inclinations and the things that may tempt us to slide back. For true meditation upon the law of the Lord[65] means seeking to achieve the kind of life that we would wish to be leading if the last day of life were at hand.

The eighth advantage is that anyone who confesses to a priest is assisted not only by his counsel, comfort, and encouragement but also by his prayers. For he prays that the penitent should receive the grace of the Holy Spirit, along with the strength and courage to resist Satan. Given that any devout Christian's prayer has a role in obtaining God's grace, how much more effective will a priest's prayer be? This is of course James' theme when he says that here too the assiduous prayers of the righteous are the most powerful of all.[66] I shall say nothing at the moment concerning the power of the keys, on which the theologians have written so extensively that there is no need to pursue it here.[67] What is meant by 'attrition,' whether confession

* * * * *

63 Erasmus does not explain what he means by the 'punishment' that is removed by 'the humiliation of baring our conscience to another'; one might understand this as psychological self-punishment ('deep regret'), the punishment of penance, or perhaps eternal punishment. For 'The Shame of the Confessional,' see Tentler Sin 128–30.
64 Adagia I vi 95
65 Cf Ps 1:2.
66 James 5:16; 'here too' means in the confession of sins to one another, to which James' dictum refers.
67 The two keys entrusted to Peter in Matt 16:19 are vital to the theory of confession. The key of knowledge enables the priest to judge the penitent's sin, and the key of power enables him to pronounce absolution and determine satisfaction. See Tentler Sin 96–7; Myers Sinning 18; and especially P. Anciaux

changes 'attrition' into 'contrition,' whether confession ensures the instant remission of sins from the first moment – I shall leave the Scotists to argue about all that.[68]

The[69] ninth advantage: through baptism we are saved from Satan's tyranny and are made children of God, grafted to Christ's body, the church; we are admitted to the blessed fellowship of the angels and of all who are destined to inherit heaven, wherever on earth they live, have lived, or shall live. Through penance, similarly, we are formally restored to that company. Now those who have been inspired by God to hate their sins are already freed from guilt, given that confession to a mere mortal is not

* * * * *

La théologie du sacrement de pénitence au xiie siècle (Louvain 1949) 539–73. Elsewhere Erasmus minimizes the power of the keys (see Payne 210–11) and, for example, has Pope Julius make mock of them in Julius exclusus (CWE 27 168 and n2). Luther denied them to the priesthood altogether: 'The keys are yours and mine' (Eyn Sermon LW 35 16); he developed his thought in The Keys of 1530 (LW 40 325–77).

68 'Contrition' is usually defined as perfect sorrow for sin arising from love of God, whereas 'attrition' is a hatred of sins arising from a lesser motive, such as the wickedness of sin or the fear of punishment, human or divine (see, for example, the Council of Trent's definition in Denzinger 1678). On the whole question, up to and including the Council of Trent, see Spykman. Tentler (Sin 250–63) analyses the more subtle distinctions made by the schoolmen (eg Clavasio f 48 verso) on the basis of differences in formation by grace, degree of perfection, and intensity of sorrow. Erasmus obviously considered attrition to be dangerously conducive to despair, and at best merely a first stage towards contrition (see, for example, 33 above). On the controversies among the schoolmen (including Duns Scotus himself) over the conversion from attrition to contrition, see Payne 328 n95; Rahner 153–62; Tentler Sin 263–73; Myers Sinning 16–25. Discussion among the theologians as to whether sin was actually remitted through contrition, before the priest pronounced absolution, was based on Luke 5:14; Erasmus alludes to this in his reply to Béda (Apologiae aliquot in Natalem Beddam LB IX 611C). On the background, see Payne 318–19 n7; Tentler Sin 281–94.

69 The ninth advantage ... gospel freedom] Added by Erasmus in 1530. In these three paragraphs Erasmus counteracts the allegation of 'Taxander' that he had undermined confession by enumerating nine disadvantages but only eight advantages (Manifesta mendacia 122 no 25) and formally distances himself from the Reformers, answering accusations that the original Exomologesis supported Luther (Manifesta mendacia 117 no 3). Tentler ('Forgiveness' 116) points out that this 'advantage' makes clear what is most important for Erasmus, namely that confession restores the penitent to the society of the body of Christ. Payne (204–5) sees here Erasmus' 'traditionalism and concern for church unity' (which are indeed more apparent in some of these 1530 additions).

strictly necessary; though the opposite used to be taught and is still taught by some today,[70] I take the liberty of disagreeing. However, contempt for a widespread and long-standing custom, and stubborn resistance to the traditions of the church, do offend God and undermine the peace of the Christian commonwealth. At least someone who confesses to a priest cannot be accused of that. Moreover, even if one were free of sin beforehand, a confession properly made will bring much enlightenment and grace, benefits that no true Christian will spurn.

Again, some people have, or think they have, a clear conscience as long as they are in good health; but when their end is near, they see things very differently, either because danger is now close at hand or because it is now that the Tempter deploys all his wiles against them. The surest remedy against such disquiet is to confess to a priest in one's own time and in good faith. Finally, the church is more willing to accept someone who makes confession than someone who does not, just as the Jews were more willing to accept the circumcised than the uncircumcised. For it is part and parcel of true piety to fulfil all righteousness, to avoid the stumbling block, and, as St Paul says, to please all in all things.[71]

I have said all this not on my own account, but for the sake of those who are still not convinced that this form of confession, being a human institution, is strictly necessary for salvation. They who are spiritual judge all things and are judged by no one,[72] but since the common run of humanity is predisposed to shake off the Lord's yoke, I consider contempt for confession to be a slippery slope leading to paganism, down which we see a great many sliding at the moment, under the false banner of gospel freedom.[73]

* * * * *

70 The necessity of confession once a year was imposed by the Fourth Lateran Council in 1215 and reaffirmed by the Council of Trent (Denzinger 812 and 1683; see Tentler *Sin* 20–2 and 57–70; and Tanner I 245 and II 712). Luther calls this 'a diabolical and murderous doctrine' (*A Discussion on How Confession Should Be Made* LW 39 35), but some schoolmen had already argued that if one has no mortal sins to confess this is only a hypothetical necessity; cf Aquinas *Summa theologiae* III q 84 a 5 and *Supplementum* q 6 a 3. Erasmus makes much of the authoritative canonist Gratian's hesitations over the necessity of confession in his *Responsio ad annotationes Lei* (CWE 72 374–5).

71 Allusions to Matt 3:15; 1 Cor 8:9 and 10:33

72 1 Cor 2:15. Rosemondt (f 2 recto) asserts in his first sentence that the sacrament of penance is necessary for salvation, and the decrees of the Council of Trent insist on it, in opposition to Luther and Calvin (Denzinger 1672, 1683 and 1706).

73 Passage added in 1530.

Thus far I have been listing the principal advantages of confessing, which[74] I know are in any case innumerable. Now the time has come to deal briefly with the evils that seem to arise from the practice of confession, although the blame lies with us rather than the institution itself.[75]

First, the practice of communicating one's sins to other people seems likely to poison natural simplicity and innocence, such as we see in boys and girls as yet untouched by life's corruption. Such innocence depends largely upon being ignorant of sin and indeed having no idea that people exist who commit such and such a crime. Even learned priests, who have acquired a wealth of knowledge from books, frequently admit that they would never have suspected that such wicked deeds were committed in the world as those they hear from penitents.

The most infectious are those connected with sex or the forbidden arts. There are some sexual practices that no wise parents would allow to be mentioned before their sons and daughters, because nature, given the chance, is inclined to experiment with evil. It is safer that such things be unknown, as far as possible. Then there are the black arts, which seduce the inquisitive into experimentation; the vice of curiosity is naturally implanted in almost all of us, titillating our minds with the desire to find out.

Now priests are only human, often young, and sometimes wicked or at least weak. Minds like these are corrupted by hearing the monstrous misdeeds of others, and they are often prodded into committing the very crimes that they have heard about from others. And the infection spreads more widely each time that a priest, as often happens, reveals to others what he has heard from his penitents, though without mentioning their names, of course. Sometimes[76] in fact they do name names, but even if the names are kept very quiet, the deeds themselves will usually be enough to poison the listener's mind.

However, it is an even worse mistake to mention the unmentionable in public, in sermons. That is why the wisest secular magistrates, wanting

* * * * *

74 which ... innumerable] This clause was added in 1530 as a further riposte to the numerical nit-picking of 'Taxander.'
75 Erasmus had already briefly enumerated these 'evils' in his reply to Lee in 1520 (*Responsio ad annotationes Lei* CWE 72 369–71) and in the colloquy *Confabulatio pia* of 1522 (CWE 39 97). His critics considered that the mere fact of listing them would do the institution great disservice: see *Manifesta mendacia* 119 no 11 and 122 no 23; *Apologia adversus monachos* LB IX 1063A. The *Index expurgatorius* (LB X 1820A) recommends for deletion the entire critique of confessional practice from this point to 'life in heaven' 53 below.
76 Sometimes ... quiet] Added in 1530.

to keep their town healthy, will pronounce sentence of death on a felon, but without always specifying all his crimes, it being inadvisable for everyone to know that there are people who commit such crimes. Long ago in Deventer, when I was still a boy, I heard some women of doubtful virtue – there was a great army of them there in those days – applauding and congratulating one another on the fact that they could indulge themselves with their lovers because the parish priest in his sermon had said that certain shepherds had confessed that they had behaved unchastely towards their flock. It was during the Jubilee.[77] Could anyone be more foolish than that priest who, under no compulsion and for no possible useful purpose, blurted this out to the people and thus encouraged fornicators and adulterers in their vices? Recently, too, a certain Franciscan said, in a public sermon in a famous town, that if the old law that adulterers should be stoned were still in existence, a whole mountain of stones would not be enough for all the stonings.

The second evil is similar. Many people no doubt become complacent about their sins when they compare them with worse. For example, a man utterly defiled by fornication and adultery will consider himself an innocent if he hears via confession about foul couplings with incubi or animals, or else if he discovers that people whom he took to be learned, grave, and saintly are in fact staggering beneath terrible crimes. It is human nature to want to exaggerate someone else's faults and understate one's own. I heard a certain theologian, himself no stranger to ladies of easy virtue, say that he had heard that a certain spiritual director to a convent had confessed to debauching two hundred nuns.[78] The man telling the tale was so pleased with himself that apparently it would never have crossed his mind to consider practising chastity.

The third disadvantage[79] is that this form of confession makes a good many priests very haughty, though God appointed them to be fathers and

* * * * *

77 This passage is frequently cited in discussions of Erasmus' early life. Although the Jubilee was proclaimed in Rome at Christmas 1475, it was not celebrated in Deventer until mid-March 1478; see Allen I 579 (Appendix II Erasmus' Early Life) and H. Vredeveld 'Ages of Erasmus and the Year of His Birth' *Renaissance Quarterly* 46 (1993) 790–1.

78 This anecdote was condemned by 'Taxander,' but Erasmus replied that the subject required it 'lest the priest cast those confessing carnal sins into despair'; *Manifesta mendacia* 119 no 12.

79 The Spanish monks complained about Erasmus' use of the word *incommodum* 'disadvantage.' In his reply (*Apologia adversus monachos* LB IX 1063A) Erasmus states that he calls them 'evils' (*mala*) and not 'disadvantages' (*incommoda*),

not masters of the people. But anyone who knows another's secrets becomes the master. Anyone who has entrusted secrets to another is bound to be fearful, and the person who knows such things about another usually becomes contemptuous. Thus confession seems to take away Christian freedom, even though Christ wished there to be no masters among us,[80] and to put out the flame of charity, since if you fear someone, you also hate them,[81] and if you know all about another's guilty secrets, you can scarcely be expected to love them. At best, the priest will think less of his penitents, having a weapon with which he could frighten and ruin them. Even if the priest is too honest to abuse his conscience, things often come out by accident that will throw suspicion upon him. This explains why there can be no genuine friendship between penitent and confessor.

The fourth is that it is not uncommon for penitents to fall among wicked priests who, under the cloak of confession, will perpetrate unmentionable deeds, and instead of their healers become their allies, or masters, or pupils in wickedness. I wish that this warning were superfluous and that there were not plentiful examples to be found everywhere, which I cannot recall without pain and could not set down without feeling ashamed.

The fifth is that this form of confession endangers a lot of reputations and even lives because priests too often fail to keep silent. Which of our organs is more slippery than the tongue? Is there anyone who will not on occasion blurt out some secret in the bosom of a friend, to whom they will rashly confide everything that has been confided to them? Not to mention the many whose character is such that they will burst if they do not blurt out secrets entrusted to them; I wish that this defect were confined to the female sex. No doubt all too many examples will occur to everyone, so I am happy to refrain from giving any. But even allowing that a priest may know how to control his tongue, all too often hatred and jealousy spring up to break the bonds of silence; sometimes drunkenness, too, makes a secret concealed in the heart float up onto the tongue. Finally a fit of illness or frenzy can break the silence of the confessional. I saw this happen to a

* * * * *

though this is strictly true only of the first two. When he reviewed the remedies in the 1530 edition of the *Exomologesis*, Erasmus used *incommoda* throughout (70–4 below).

80 Cf Matt 23:10. In Ep 2037:291–2 Erasmus castigates monks who expect a 'rich harvest' from the wealthy families whose secrets they have learned via the confessional.

81 Cf *Adagia* II ix 62, a famous definition of the tyrant.

parish priest when I was young; becoming overheated during a sermon, he named a number of women and exposed their crimes. Again, there are several examples of people whose thoughts, confided to a priest, have later cost them their lives.[82]

Now there are certain exceptional cases in which it is lawful to betray a penitent.[83] But some priests pretend that anything that makes them blurt out a secret must be one of these cases. Others believe that there is nothing wrong in defaming a household or a community so long as they suppress the names of individuals. But will anyone be pleased to hear even his town or his country being brought into disrepute? I have heard so many of them recount, at some party or other, the things they learned from the confessions of people now dead, believing that they are allowed to do it, though no living person would want their memory to be besmirched for posterity. Finally, princes sometimes demand on oath that priests should betray the perpetrator of a crime. I should approve most heartily if a priest could serve his country without betraying an individual, but I would not consider him perjured if he swore that he knew nothing about it, if he were being asked questions that he should not be compelled to answer. It seems inhuman to expose anyone to such a peril, especially as there are so many examples of priests being endangered in this way. The burden seems as heavy on the confessor as on the penitent.

I will pass over how disagreeable it is for a good and learned priest to waste so much time listening to the sordid details of people's lives, while risking his honour, as I have said, and to be subjected to fetid breath stinking of garlic or infected with disease, especially when so many are suffering from leprosy, without being segregated, or from the French pox, which is a form of leprosy. There is no surer way to become infected than to breathe

* * * * *

82 *per jugulum rediere*, literally 'have returned through the throat'; Erasmus plays on the figurative sense of *jugulum* 'murder.' A more light-hearted version of these charges is found in the *Moria* (CWE 27 132).

83 Breaking the seal of confession could be punished with lifelong pilgrimage, according to Gratian (*Decretum* 2 dist VI 11) or lifelong incarceration in a monastery, according to canon 21 (*Omnis utriusque sexus*) of the Fourth Lateran Council of 1215; see Tanner 1 245 and 245 n4 for further bibliography on auricular confession. The schoolmen debated exceptions, including the possibility of preventing by disclosure grave evils to church or state, but post-Tridentine rulings reaffirmed the inviolability of the seal; see J.L. McCarthy in NCE 4 133–4 and, on the whole question, B. Kurtscheid *A History of the Seal of Confession* trans F.A. Marks (St Louis and London 1927).

an invalid's breath, so that no little danger is thus added to his general in-convenience.[84] How hard it is for a parish priest, in the flower of his age, and well equipped intellectually and morally to serve the community, to be constrained to enter, at dead of night, some bedroom where a plague victim has just emptied his bowels or vomited, or where the one suffering is sweat-ing, washed, smeared with ointment, and on fire with the so-called French pox; and he must risk sitting there until the patient has finished confess-ing. Nor is one visit enough: he is called back time after time, whenever the victim, dying and by now delirious, shouts out that he has forgotten some detail or other.

The theologians use such facts to argue that this form of confession was not introduced by mere mortals, but by Christ himself. For since Pe-ter, the first of the apostles, thought it unfair to yoke the Gentiles to the law of Moses (which the Jews themselves found hard to bear, like their fathers before them),[85] it would seem very cruel for mere mortals to impose on their fellows the burden of confession, which is more irksome, by itself, than the whole of Moses' law[86] (whose[87] rituals St Peter did not think should be im-posed on the Gentiles; he even lifted them from the Jews), since brotherly love seems rather to encourage us, as far as possible, to lighten one another's burdens.[88] Christ did not demand celibacy from anyone; would a mere mor-tal demand something so difficult from another? Paul allows for human frailty and remits some part of the Lord's command;[89] how much impu-dence, they ask, would it take for people, who cannot be compared to Paul, to impose such a burden over and above the Lord's command? Especially[90]

* * * * *

84 Richard DeMolen regards this passage as evidence that Erasmus himself heard confessions (*The Spirituality of Erasmus of Rotterdam* [Nieuwkoop 1987] 58), though there is no documentary evidence of this.

85 Acts 15:10

86 This argument was used by Duns Scotus and a number of his followers, in terms very similar to Erasmus' here (Tentler *Sin* 69). But they did not make the comparison with the law of Moses, and indeed 'Taxander' found it objection-able. Erasmus replied that the relative gravity of the two laws was a subject worthy of a debate (*Manifesta mendacia* 119 no 14), to which he had already contributed in the *Responsio ad annotationes Lei* CWE 72 369–70.

87 whose rituals . . . Jews] Added in 1530.

88 Cf Gal 6:2.

89 Payne (200) suggests that this refers to 1 Cor 7:15, where Paul relaxes some-what Christ's commandment concerning divorce.

90 Especially since . . . conscience] Added in 1530; Erasmus reiterates his distaste for the present ritual, with its preoccupation with form rather than results.

since auricular confession is at present so hedged around with doubts and obstacles invented by men that scarcely anyone leaves the priest with a tranquil conscience.

The sixth disadvantage is that this disclosure of secret transgressions, and even of secret thoughts, seems to encourage immodesty. When people have, several times over, 'wiped off their blushes'[91] sufficiently to risk confessing such things to the priest, it makes them progressively bolder, inciting them to act as they please. Modesty is the only sure guardian of innocence. And with some kinds of vice it is almost more dangerous to recall them than to indulge them in the first place.

The seventh: this recollection of secret crimes reduces many of the weaker sort to despair, and some even to madness, whereas the main aim should be to make sinners place their trust in Christ's promises and to love rather than fear him. For it is a waste of time to confess if you do not thereby conceive a feeling of love for God. But an excessively scrupulous recital of the kinds and species of your sins, and of the aggravating circumstances leading to other kinds of sin, distracts the mind from love for God and spawns hatred and despair, especially since some priests surround the business of confession with so many complications that it is hard to find anyone who leaves them with a completely easy conscience.[92] This evil particularly besets children, women, the aged, and people who are timid by nature; I know quite a few of those! And the danger increases if such people happen upon an intimidating and cantankerous priest.

The eighth: there are others who are just plain arrogant, giving little or no thought to changing their lives and having no serious regrets about their past; they consider it sufficient simply to tell the priest what they have done and for him to pronounce absolution. Nothing is more pernicious than this kind of overconfidence. But there is no shortage of priests who will pander to such people, or at least connive with them, because[93] they value

* * * * *

91 *Adagia* i viii 47
92 'Taxander' compares this to Luther's assertion that contrition based on discussion and consideration of sins is hypocritical, a position condemned by the Council of Trent (Denzinger 1705). Erasmus replies that he has often argued that contrition of the heart is enhanced by such things (*Manifesta mendacia* 121 no 21). The passage was also attacked by the Spanish monks: *Apologia adversus monachos* LB IX 1063D. To mollify his critics Erasmus added *nimis* 'excessively' in 1530. Medieval confessors were well aware of the dangers of scrupulosity; see Tentler *Sin* 76–8.
93 because they value ... of this kind] This satirical passage was added in 1530.

the income that the recital brings more highly than the salvation of souls, which engenders the love of God that drives out false beliefs.[94] Hence the joke you hear many people make as they return from the priest: 'I've got rid of that load; I dumped it all in a monk's cowl.' These people must be steered away from overconfidence of this kind.

The ninth is that the performance of confession seems to offer many the chance to play the hypocrite. Applying one's mind to making a true and proper confession is no easy matter, yet through fear of disgrace or excommunication many people make bogus confessions and thus make a mockery of the sacrament of penance. They would do less harm if they abstained from both the Eucharist and confession until, having grown to hate their past life, they were prepared of their own accord to seek the solace of confession. As it is, they add hypocrisy to sacrilege. These are just some of the things that people get up to. After weighing the whole question very carefully, one may ask whether these human failings do not result in confession doing more harm than good to piety.

It remains for me to suggest how best we may deal with an institution which, as some[95] teach, cannot be changed, in order to derive the greatest possible benefit and the least possible disadvantage from it. It would help if both parties, confessor as well as penitent, were to do their job properly. A priest must not take on the arduous task of hearing confessions unless he possesses the appropriate learning, moral probity, wisdom, and – above all – piety. Whatever his personal inclinations at other times, when he prepares to hear confession he must take on the role of priest and have nothing on his mind but God, whom he represents, to some extent, in this act. Even those whose lives are far from unblemished try to make themselves fit to participate before they receive the Eucharist.[96] Similarly a confessor should prepare his mind for so important and so sacred a task, lest he play the bad doctor, worsening his neighbour's illness and calling the wrath of God upon himself, with the result that each of them leaves the other worse off

* * * * *

94 A glancing allusion to the 'alms' that the confessor expected (Tentler *Sin* 71 and 87–8). Erasmus had been much more severe on the cupidity of confessors in the *Responsio ad annotationes Lei* CWE 72 369, even suggesting that the confessor should pay penitents a fee to encourage them to come to him. See also Allen Ep 2205:106–23 on confessors who pursue money, power, and sex.

95 Erasmus added *quidam* 'some' in 1530; previously this appeared to be the universal opinion.

96 *synaxis* (corrected from *syntaxis* in the first edition); probably a gibe at monks, since this rare Grecism was used to mean both the mass and an assembly of monks meeting for prayer; cf CWE 78 167 n28.

than before. These days it is most often the priests who are dirty, ignorant, frivolous, worthless – some of them not right in the head and many the worse for drink – who appropriate this task, and all for the sake of a few pence.

A good deal of the blame lies with the bishops, who have a duty to ensure that unworthy candidates are not accepted indiscriminately into the priesthood. It would be better to have a small number of capable priests than a whole flock who are useless, if not downright dangerous. The bishops should exercise greater foresight to prevent the care of the Christian flock from being entrusted to anyone unsuited to the task. The same should be urged upon the superiors of the Franciscan and Dominican orders, whose members are particularly eager to take on this task and will appropriate it whenever the extraordinary sloth of the parish clergy gives them an opportunity.[97] For this is a task that must not be delegated to just anyone.

These[98] days we see that no one is keener to hear confessions than priests who are young, ignorant, or immoral. The wise and honest ones, when faced with this task, make it plain that they will do it only if they are pressed into it by charity, if their superiors insist, or if the case is urgent.[99] Take a good look at the sort of people who will confound heaven and earth[100] should anyone warn against the over-eager practice of confession; you will see men who are ravenous, covetous, devoted to their bellies, and often frankly immoral. They would make less fuss were it not that confession fuels their extravagance, greed, and lust. The state will not allow just anyone to be a doctor and heal the body; is it enough, for the healing of souls, to sport a cowl or a shaven crown? In the courts, decisions about the

* * * * *

97 Under special privileges, the mendicant Franciscans and Dominicans had the power to hear the confessions of laymen not officially under their pastoral call. Many of them wrote manuals of confession, in view of this special interest; see Tentler *Sin* 64, 313–18 and Myers *Sinning* 31. The long-standing conflict between parish clergy and these orders is satirized in Erasmus' colloquy *Funus* cwe 40 763–95.

98 These days we see ... unfit for it] This satirical paragraph was added in 1530. The qualities of the ideal confessor are listed in the manuals; see for example *Poeniteas cito* 1155A and Rosemondt f 2 verso.

99 In his *Responsio ad annotationes Lei* (cwe 72 372–3) Erasmus attributed this reluctance to the anguish that confession causes to both parties. This rather Lutheran idea (cf *The Sacrament of Penance* lw 35 15–16) has been toned down in this 1530 addition to the *Exomologesis*.

100 That is, cause a great commotion; *Adagia* I iii 71.

most trivial matters are entrusted only to the most sober of citizens; should this holy work be done by a bleary-eyed drunkard straight after an orgy? It should therefore be the role of prelates, or even of state officials, to assign to this domain only those best suited to it by their age, lifestyle, learning, faith, wisdom, and humanity, and, conversely, to remove or, if they deserve it, to punish severely those who are unfit for it.

Again, anyone preparing to make confession must themselves be careful to choose a suitable priest and must be in no hurry to change when once they have found a good one. When physically ill we will look out for a capable doctor, but when the sickness is spiritual, we will send for anyone at all,[101] which is especially dangerous since it has not been unknown for inquisitive laymen to play the role of the priest. Now those who, through immaturity or inexperience, have not yet acquired the necessary discrimination will have to ask more experienced relatives or teachers to suggest a suitable person to whom to confess. At the moment one may observe many who, left to themselves, choose the worst possible confessor in order to be rid of an unpleasant chore with the least possible fuss. Such a confession is a confession in name only.

Nor is confession much more beneficial to those who go to the priest light-heartedly and more or less out of habit. When preparing to confess one must be mindful that it is an important undertaking, the most solemn of all, and one must endeavour to confess as though one might never confess again. For penance is like a second baptism. No one undergoes baptism without a determination to do nothing that would require a second baptism. Similarly, while the acknowledged frailty of human nature means that people who relapse and must constantly return to the remedy of penance are not turned away, those who undergo penance must hope and pray to face death ten times over rather than repeat the sins that they lament. At one time those who had reoffended after performing penance were barred by most churches from repeating public penance, so eager was the church that there should be, if at all possible, no returning to sin.[102] But in this, as in so much else, people's priorities are upside down. They torment themselves in their anxiety to list all their sins in good faith, to leave out no species of sin, to pass over no circumstance; and they were right to leave nothing out.

* * * * *

101 Doubtless a commonplace; exactly the same point is made in the manual of Jacobus de Clusa, printed in 1520 (Tentler *Sin* 126). On the choice of a confessor, see 72 and n194 below.

102 On public penance, see n45 above; it could not normally be repeated (52 n127 below).

But while they are absorbed in this, they miss the main point of the whole operation.[103]

In the first place, therefore, confessions must be made to God. Now it is no easy matter to confess to him, because he will hear nothing but the words of the heart; but once this is accomplished, it will be easy to confess to a man. Thus the first part of the process must be given as much attention as if it alone sufficed. Its main objective is that the penitent should conceive a deep hatred of sin – not merely of particular sins, but of everything that offends God, and not merely through fear of retribution, divine or human, but through the unfettered love that transports us toward God. For those who detest their sins only up to a point, but would repeat them if no punishment were involved, will not escape damnation. And anyone who, for instance, detests drunkenness but indulges in illicit lovemaking does not hate sin through love for God; otherwise everything offensive to God would be equally hateful. A vow to improve one's life will be neither firm nor effective unless it is inspired by love for God.

Moreover, it is beyond the power of sinners to grant themselves this feeling of love. It is a gratuitous gift of God, though it must be sought from him with tears, prayer, almsgiving, and other spiritual exercises. It is sometimes helpful to beg our fellow Christians to intercede for us with God. But if a request is not immediately answered, a good beginning must not be abandoned. Often God delays his gifts in order to give more abundantly. He is generous and will bestow his gifts freely, but not upon the lazy. Thus if people reflect on a life ill lived and on the terrors of hell and thereby conceive a measure of detestation for their crimes, they should not instantly run to the priest but continue their weeping. They must use prayer to seek, beg, and implore, until they are touched by another kind of fear, accompanied by a determined vow to change their lives and by a love that is full of hope. When they have been touched by this spirit, which Paul calls spirit of the children,[104] let them remember not to attribute it to themselves, but to acknowledge it as God's gratuitous gift. Falling at his feet, let them give thanks for his loving kindness and ask him to maintain forever this gift, freely bestowed of his goodness, and to make it grow forever stronger. They must not rely on their vow and imagine that their own efforts will keep them from sin; instead, filled with awe, they

* * * * *

103 Erasmus quotes the preceding two sentences in the *Manifesta mendacia* (121 no 21) to illustrate his constant concern with the drawbacks of over-scrupulous formal confession.
104 Rom 8:14–16

must implore heaven's aid and ask that he who inspired their vow will strengthen and sustain it. In addition, such a vow implies not merely the avoidance of sin itself but of all the things by which they are usually tempted to sin.[105]

Having advanced this far, one is already restored to the church, already transformed from a slave of the devil to a child of God, already free from sin and[106] even, it is to be hoped, from chastisement, if both one's suffering and one's love are profound. How little now remains to be done, compared with what has gone before! Anyone who has truly humbled himself before God need be no more than mildly embarrassed before a man; like one nail driving out another,[107] shame will drive out shame and suffering drive out suffering. It will be no hardship to disclose in good faith to a priest things that will be said just once, especially if one remembers that through the priest one is speaking to God. But it would be advisable for people to examine their conscience every day and to confess to God from the heart, renewing their resolve; or if business will not allow, then at least once a week, resolving to see a priest whenever time and opportunity permit – unless they are so weak willed that they cannot rest until they have confessed to a priest.

I shall not discuss here how much importance should be given to the complications with which we mortals have surrounded confession; I mean such things as the powers of the priest to whom you confess, reserved cases, and censures.[108] However, in the interests of easing penitents' consciences,

* * * * *

105 Erasmus here describes in detail the conversion of attrition to contrition to which he has already alluded more than once (see 35 n68 above). But, like his medieval predecessors Abelard and Peter Lombard (see Tentler *Sin* 18–23), he is careful to maintain the role of the priest in penance and avoid the anticlerical and anti-sacramental implications that Luther did not hesitate to draw from 'contritionist' theory (*The Sacrament of Penance* LW 35 11–13).

106 and even ... profound] Added in 1530. Erasmus underlines his doubts concerning formal satisfaction (see 66–70 below), perhaps echoing the view of Peter Lombard that intense contrition may remit all penalties: *Sententiae* book 4 dist 20 c 1 s 6 and book 4 dist 20 c 3 s 1. See Thomas Tentler 'Peter Lombard's "On those who repent at the end"' *Archivio italiano per la storia della pietà* 9 (1996) 297–9.

107 *Adagia* I ii 4

108 These topics are discussed, for example, by Pseudo-Augustine *De vera et falsa poenitentia* 10.25 (PL 40 1122); Aquinas *Summa theologiae* III q 84–90; and Luther *Confitendi ratio* LW 39 41–3. The controversies concerned the extent of the priest's personal power to remit sins, the nature of cases reserved for special absolution by bishops or the pope (Tentler *Sin* 304–18), and the role of

I wish that the bishops and pontiffs would grant to those whom they entrust with the authority to hear confession the authority to absolve all sins of whatever kind or magnitude, together with the power[109] to relax certain censures, at least in the forum of conscience,[110] and finally the power to grant dispensations in cases where the difficulty is caused purely by human regulations. Examples of this might be a marriage made between two people related by blood but not within the degrees which, according to Holy Writ, prevent a legal marriage from being contracted, a marriage between two people joined by spiritual kinship,[111] or the infringement of a vow, especially if the infringement were committed by mistake and not out of malice. They could be given the power to relax the usual rules in other cases for compelling reasons. Who better to judge whether this needs to be done than the confessor before whom a whole human life is laid bare?

All this could be expedited if the pontiffs would repeal, on practical grounds, certain regulations which they introduced originally on religious grounds, and at the same time make clear which of their regulations are intended to make us guilty of sin and which not (if[112] in fact any mortal can make another guilty of sin). For those who have absolute power to repeal a regulation must also have the power to ensure that it does not carry with

* * * * *

ecclesiastical disciplinary justice, 'censures' being the general term for disciplinary measures short of excommunication.

109 'Power' is omitted in LB.

110 As opposed to the 'external forum' in which, for example, financial restitution might be imposed

111 These are among the eighteen ecclesiastical impediments to marriage enumerated by Erasmus in the *Institutio christiani matrimonii* of 1526 (CWE 69 265–8 and 269–70). In that treatise Erasmus points out that the prohibited degrees of consanguinity had been increased by the church beyond the norms established in both Jewish and Roman law. He is very scathing about 'spiritual kinship' (relationship resulting from the administration of sacraments), regarding it as an unnecessary ecclesiastical obstacle added to the existing complications of matrimonial law. The reinforcing passage 'but not within ... contracted' was added in 1530.

112 if in fact ... sin] The sceptical parenthesis was added in 1530; the implication is that, like Luther (*A Discussion on How Confession Should Be Made* LW 39 31), Erasmus would define sin only as an offence against divine law, whereas in the early church, at least, sin was regarded as an offence against the church with which the sinner must be reconciled (Rahner 170). The Council of Trent acknowledged that the people tended to equate infringements of ecclesiastical law with offences against natural or divine law, but made this an argument for more precise confession of the kind, number, and circumstances of sins (Denzinger 1681; Crichton 7).

it an imputation of sin unless there is evidence of persistent wickedness. But while things remain as they are, I would advise penitents to seek out a priest endowed with learning and honesty but also with sufficient legal authority to ensure that no particle of doubt remains in their mind that might force them to repeat their confession later.

For the rest, I do not much approve of over-careful explanations of all the circumstances, since the opinions[113] of the theologians on this point are usually based on a book called *De vera et falsa poenitentia*, whose attribution to St Augustine is known to be false.[114] Similarly, I disapprove of the excessive trepidation of those who think that, as the proverb says, a scorpion sleeps under every stone,[115] and who will turn every little fault into a mortal sin. For example, I once knew a man who was fasting; the day before at dinnertime he had eaten something sugary. But when he stood up, ready to sing mass before the people and the local ruler, who was also present, he licked his lips and felt a slight taste of sugar from a grain that had, I imagine, lodged in a hollow tooth; he rushed up to me, half-dead with worry, to ask whether he should go on with the service. I laughed at the man's silliness, telling him to take courage and get on with the divine service.[116]

Scruples of this kind almost always result from human regulations. For the rule that a priest must fast before mass was established – though not without justification – by men alone. As a result of it, some priests are terrified if, when they wash out their mouths, a drop of liquid slips down

* * * * *

113 *sententiae*, probably a reference to the famous work of that name by Peter Lombard, the 'Master of the Sentences,' to whom the contemporary English translator refers in a marginal note in *A lytle treatise*, H iv recto (see 31 above, introduction n55). On Lombard, see n1 above.

114 PL 40 1113–30; chapter 14 (1124–5) deals with 'circumstances' that may extenuate – or aggravate – a sin and even determine whether it be mortal or venial, as Erasmus had pointed out with some misgivings in his *Responsio ad annotationes Lei* (CWE 72 370). The authenticity of Augustine's book was questioned, on philological grounds, at the end of the fifteenth century by Joannes Trithemius (*De scriptoribus ecclesiasticis* 17; for Trithemius, see ODCC 1643). Luther also condemned its nefarious influence (*A Discussion on How Confession Should Be Made* LW 39 38); it had been quoted *in extenso* by such important figures as Gratian, Lombard, and Aquinas. On 'aggravating circumstances' in general, see Tentler *Sin* 116–20, and for a compact example *Poeniteas cito* 1154D.

115 *Adagia* I iv 34

116 Erasmus' reaction was criticized by 'Taxander' who, however, misquotes him, alleging that Erasmus wrote: 'I laughed at the pious man's silliness' (*Manifesta mendacia* 120 no 15 and n29).

their throats, and they either refuse to say mass or do so in fear and trembling. But it was never the intention of those who introduced the rule that,
for example, if a priest was ministering to the sick and tasting their food for
them, and[117] happened to swallow a morsel before spitting it out, he should
refrain from saying mass as if he had broken his fast.

Here my opponents will croak that it is a mark of piety to fear guilt
where there is no guilt.[118] I hear them, and I see the point; but to spend
your whole life in a state of trepidation seems no less monstrous than to
remain a child or an infant all your life. I prefer fussy piety to unrestrained
criminal wickedness. But generally speaking those who are most fussy about
this sort of thing are astonishingly nonchalant about more important things.
How many I have known who would not have dared to say mass if they
had inadvertently nibbled a bit of ginger to calm a queasy stomach, but
would go ahead without a qualm while harbouring some implacable hatred
against their neighbour and plotting their revenge.[119] But true charity, which
opens up the heart, and staunch faith in Christ will easily dispel such minor
scruples.

Similarly, some torment themselves over the method and the extent of
preparation for confession, which those who wish to glory not only in the
flesh[120] but also in the consciences of men assert must be absolutely right.
I can accept without demur a modest amount of preparation, within our
limits, so long as it is accompanied by a thorough hatred of one's misdeeds
and a fixed and determined vow to change one's life for the better. But
preparation will be less of a trial if people follow my advice and get into
the habit of examining their lives and confessing to God every day, or at
least once a week.

Now penitents must take care that as far as possible they keep their
confession short and do not burden the priest's ears with superfluities. They
can do this by mentioning only things that justifiably[121] weigh on their conscience, meaning those that are certainly, or are strongly suspected to be,
mortal sins.[122] Of course, venial sins are not to be overlooked when it comes

* * * * *

117 and happened ... out] The parenthetical phrase was added in 1530 to clarify
     the example.
118 See 32 n57 above on this aphorism.
119 Luther denounces similar hypocrisy in his *Confitendi ratio* (LW 39 39–40).
120 Cf Gal 6:13, a passage on the redundancy of circumcision 'in the flesh.'
121 The adverb was added in 1530.
122 Erasmus' character Gaspar makes a similar remark in the colloquy *Confabu-
     latio pia* (CWE 39 97), which was attacked as 'Lutheran' by the theologians of
     Cologne, presumably on the grounds that Luther had little faith in the ability

to examining and improving one's life. For if they are overlooked, they can lead to worse and, if we believe Augustine, they will gradually accumulate until finally they swamp the ship of conscience like a mighty wave[123] that suddenly sinks a ship. But some people turn confession into a cosy chat and babble on about anything and everything; women are particularly prone to this fault, since they enjoy chatting like this to men and will pour out to them a stream of complaints about their husbands or neighbours. I have also come across people who confess according to a formula – and a very long one – that they have learned. They use it to run through all the things they might have done, not just what they have done. I can think of nothing sillier.

The priest, too, must not suggest or allow during confession any topic unless it concerns penance, nor must the penitent speak of anything else. Unfortunately,[124] the sort of talk that goes on under cover of confession is all too notorious. Some people thoroughly approve of frequently repeated confession – and a general confession,[125] at that – and argue that it should be repeated, however slight the excuse. I thoroughly disagree with them. I consider it important that a person should reveal their misdeeds to a priest in good faith once and wash them away with a flood of tears. Then people will not grow old in everlasting grief, but regain their confidence and set out happily and eagerly to build a better life. If they happen to relapse, they need only tell the priest what they have done wrong since their last confession. Otherwise confession becomes a habit rather than a cure; some even begin to take pleasure in constantly shovelling the dirt, which should in itself be unpleasant. At the same time modesty, which, as I have said, is the most sure guardian of innocence, is gradually unlearned.

* * * * *

of mere humans to distinguish between mortal and venial sins (*The Sacrament of Penance* LW 35 20). Reformers felt that this process allowed confessors excessive control (Myers 'Humanism' 365). Erasmus replied in Epp 1301:15–31 and 1301:53–97; see also Payne 325 n77.

123 *unda decumana* 'the tenth wave,' proverbially higher than the rest; cf *Adagia* IV ix 54. The reference to Augustine may be to *Enarratio in psalmum* LXVI 7 (PL 36 809); WSA II-17 307–23 or *De civitate Dei* 21.5, but Erasmus probably found it in Peter Lombard *Sententiae* book 4 dist 16 c 3. Augustine's remedy against light sins was, like Erasmus', daily prayer (*De symbolo ad catechumenos* 7.15 PL 40 635–6); NPNF 3 374–5.

124 Unfortunately ... notorious] Added in 1530. Rosemondt (f 132 recto) makes similar observations. Erasmus quotes much of the rest of this paragraph in the *Manifesta mendacia* (120 no 20) to support his argument that it is preferable to confess well than to confess often.

125 That is, involving repetition of all or many of one's past confessions; on the benefits to be gained, see P.E. McKeever in NCE 11 81.

It is characteristic of certain people that, once they begin to appreciate something, they can never get enough of it. For example, long ago it did not seem irreverent to have some daily commemoration of the Virgin Mother, who could never be sufficiently praised. A canticle was recited at vespers, but a short one; now, however, in some rites it is much longer – and attended by greater ceremony and greater crowds – than the actual liturgy of vespers handed down by our forefathers. Nor was this enough: the tolling of the morning bell was introduced on the grounds that it is uncertain whether Gabriel greeted the Virgin at dawn or at dusk; it seemed an important issue. Special prayers to the Virgin were added to the hours, as if she were too little praised in the daily praise given to her Son. Many recite them before the traditional prayers, in case the Son should appear to take precedence over his Mother. Even that is not enough. The thanks given to God after a meal are unsatisfactory unless they include many special tributes to the Blessed Virgin. Would that not be enough for anyone? But then a dawn service is introduced, sung with a polyphonic setting, especially[126] in Britain, and with organ accompaniment too – not to mention the chapels dedicated specially to her in our churches and the parading of her statues.

'What are you getting at?' you will ask. I am trying to show that human waywardness allows many customs, though introduced with the best of intentions, to get out of hand. It seems that the same thing has happened with confession. At first it was acceptable to make confession just once in a lifetime.[127] Then it had to be repeated once a year. That seemed reasonable enough.[128] Then it began to be expected twice in Lent, over and above

* * * * *

126 especially in Britain] Added in 1530. Erasmus made similar criticisms of the cult of the Virgin elsewhere, for example in the *Modus orandi Deum* CWE 70 224–5, Ep 2284, and the colloquy Ἰχθυοφαγία CWE 40 675–762. On Erasmus' somewhat ambiguous approach to the whole question, see Léon-E. Halkin 'La Mariologie d'Erasme' *Archiv für Reformationsgeschichte* 68 (1977) 32–55 (especially 47–8 on the topics here).

127 In the early church this was not merely *plausibile*, as Erasmus puts it, but mandatory: the public penance then in use could not be repeated (McNeil 14–15). On the consequences of this severe discipline, see Tentler *Sin* 6–7.

128 The custom of an annual ceremony of reconciliation for penitents on Maundy Thursday began in the fifth century, but the obligation on every Christian to confess once a year was laid down in the famous decree *Omnis utriusque sexus* (canon 21) of the Fourth Lateran Council in 1215 (Denzinger 812; translation in McNeil 413–14 and Tanner I 245; commentary in Tentler *Sin* 21–2, 61–2 and Myers *Sinning* 29–32). Erasmus cites this decree in his reply to Lee and remarks sardonically that those who profit from confession wish it could be enforced daily rather than annually (*Responsio ad annotationes Lei* CWE 72 364–5,

what the church had decreed. There are those who argue that it must be re-peated every time one relapses into sin.[129] Others[130] demand that the whole Iliad of woes[131] be repeated in its entirety, if one has by some oversight for-gotten a sin, unless one returns to the same priest who heard the earlier confession.Various other reasons have been found for repeat performances.

There is no end to the confessing. Before approaching the Lord's ta-ble, the priest will confess a first and then a second time to another priest. Again, coming down from the altar, he will make confession as a prelimi-nary to the service. This seems to be for the people's benefit. Then again, in Italy and perhaps in other countries too, after the gospel reading the parish priest will turn and, in place of a homily on the gospel text, he will pro-nounce the prescribed form of confession and absolution.[132] There is also the ancient custom of sprinkling those entering the church with holy water. The same happens as they go out. This too is a form of confession. More-over, the Eucharist is not given to lay people unless they are shriven. Again, confession is demanded of those already kneeling at the altar, at a moment when it would be better for the priest to say something that would inspire the communicants with love for the one whose body and blood they are tak-ing. Finally, when the last struggle with death is upon us, how often is con-fession thrust upon us? The soul is trembling on the lips, when along comes a priest or monk to ask if anything has been forgotten and to pronounce ab-solution on a corpse. Let no one think that this is said to inspire hatred of confession; but at that moment some other song would be more appropri-ate, recalling, for instance, Jesus Christ's love for the human race, our faith in his goodness, the promises made in the gospel, the calamities of this life, or the joys of life in heaven.[133]

* * * * *

369). He cites it again in Ep 1300:21–5 and Ep 1301:53–97 in defending the colloquy *Confabulatio pia* against the attack of Nicolaas Baechem.

129 For discussion of these points among late medieval writers on confession, most of whom warned against the dangers of habitual confession, see Tentler *Sin* 72–80 and 121–4.

130 Others demand ... earlier confession] Added in 1530. Scholastic writers usu-ally recommended reiteration if previous confessions could be considered for some reason invalid; see Clavasio f 48 and Tentler *Sin* 123–4.

131 *Adagia* I iii 26

132 References to the non-sacramental formulae of confession and absolution (*Con-fiteor ... Misereatur*) used in the mass; cf Rahner 162–3; Tentler *Sin* 79–80 and 111–13. Erasmus had mentioned the Italian custom in his reply to Lee (*Respon-sio ad annotationes Lei* CWE 72 365).

133 Erasmus was to develop these topics in the colloquy *Funus* (1526; CWE 40 763–95) and especially in *De praeparatione ad mortem* (1534; CWE 70 389–450); see Tentler 'Forgiveness' 119–33. Erasmus' letter to Joost Vroye (Ep 1347), which

But you have now been waiting some time, reader, to hear about a method of confessing that, when followed, will enable you to reveal all to the priest in a fitting way. A great many writers have published books on this, some even in the vernacular languages, listing every sin that we humans commit or may commit.[134] I will not deny that these books may safely be read by men who are forearmed by age and experience of the world, but in my opinion it is dangerous to spread them among ordinary people. Some priests make a similar mistake when they demand to know everything about everyone, without consideration for sex, age, and intelligence.

Now St Thomas wrote very fully on the genealogies of virtue and vice.[135] But I am writing this mostly for the benefit of lay people, and so some simpler method must be sought. To live the good life, a knowledge of the Creed and of God's commandments is necessary, even if there were no necessity for every one of us to confess. These are the things that the parish clergy ought briefly and clearly to pass on to their flock every year and even put into little books written in the vernacular. Although[136] it is quite true that frequent attendance at holy sermons will greatly help to prepare people for making proper confession, whether to God or to a man, reading holy books will have the same effect.

Now at the head of all the commandments stands faith, which works through love.[137] There are two kinds of love: love of God and love of one's neighbour. All who understand this will find it easy to see when they have turned aside from the paths of faith and charity. Now faith must not be lightweight, merely flitting about our lips, but deep-rooted in the heart, if what our mouths confess is to lead to salvation. Faith consists above all in believing what those Holy Scriptures, which all Christians unanimously accept, say about the past, promise for the future, or[138] instruct us to do, and in confidently placing in God all our hopes for the present and future life.

* * * * *

included a satirical passage on deathbed confessions (86–101), was printed with the *Exomologesis* in 1524. On the censure of this whole passage on confessional practice, see 37 n75 above.

134 On these books see 21 n15 above.

135 See for example Aquinas *Summa theologiae* II–I q 65 and q 73 and II–III passim.

136 Although ... same effect] This sentence was added in 1530. The 'little books' are clearly to be different in content from the penitentials and summae (n15 above); in fact, they sound remarkably like Luther's *Small Catechism*, published in 1529 in the wake of a dispiriting tour of Saxony during which he observed the ignorance of the laity.

137 Gal 5:6

138 or instruct us to do] Added in 1530.

What myriads there are who profess the name of Christian but disbelieve or at least doubt the resurrection of the body, and some even the immortality of the soul! The vast majority, especially those who have achieved high office or honours, can be seen leading lives that suggest either that they do not believe Holy Writ or else that they never think about it. If they were seriously to examine their lives from time to time, they would realize how far they have strayed from their duty as Christians. And indeed this is the source of all sinfulness. In fact it is a grave sin to have neglected this part of our duty as Christians. People generally are quite oblivious to this and think it enough just to list their drinking bouts, adulteries, and thefts.

We[139] must pray constantly that God will increase our faith,[140] far more than we should pray for good health or a good harvest. From time to time other methods must be used to strike the spark of faith: meditation on the Scriptures, conversation with good Christians, holy thoughts.

Some people confess that they do not believe the Creed. That is no sacramental confession unless their intention is either to be instructed and brought to belief by the priest or to satisfy the church by some form of penance. To have doubts or be lukewarm in one's faith is an acceptable subject for confession, but unbelief is not.

Faith and charity, therefore, are the two principal yardsticks[141] against which we must measure every aspect of our lives, and they are the springs from which flows every act that is pleasing to God. If the springs are muddied or have run dry, even ostensible virtues become vices, whereas nothing sinful can emerge from pure faith and true charity, even if it looks like a sin. By contrast, people to whom faith and charity are completely alien lead lives that are, so to speak, just one long sin. But the common run of humanity, busy with the branches and the leaves, neglects the roots, even though the first and closest examination should have been given to them.[142]

People set themselves goals, such as wealth, worldly glory, or prestige, and with their eyes on their particular target they do much that is superficially virtuous: they give alms, they build monasteries, they fight for their

* * * * *

139 We must pray constantly ... without cheating] This and the following five paragraphs of pastoral advice concerning faith were added in 1530.
140 Cf Luke 17:5.
141 Erasmus uses the Grecism *gnomon*, literally the pin of a sundial, or a carpenter's square, but frequently used metaphorically.
142 A familiar metaphor in manuals of confession. The well-known *Rosetum* of Jan Mombaer even illustrated the kinds and species of sin diagrammatically by depicting a tree; see Tentler *Sin* 137.

country. Let others decide if such philanthropy actually offends God; certainly it curries no favour with God. By contrast, for those enlightened by faith and afire with charity, every act of their lives is governed by the twin goals of faith and charity; even as they restore their bodies with food and drink and refresh their minds with play, indeed even as they sleep, they are serving Christ.

Again, there are people whose natural inclination is never to do good disinterestedly but to weigh everything against their own advantage. And yet they seem to have no terrible vices: they keep away from drink and loose women; they pray and have time for mass. In short, they consider themselves good Christians, and so does everyone else. No disease is harder to cure, and to deal with it the wise confessor will need to be all the more alert. It is no use for such people to deceive themselves that they love God for his own sake, since they do not love their neighbour; or if they do, it is not for God's sake but out of self-interest. It is vital that princes and prelates be made aware that these are the twin springs of virtue, because they cannot perform their duties properly unless it is for God and the state.

Thus faith drives out all the little excuses that wickedness inspires people to make up. 'If I give to the poor, I shall be worse off. If I carry on my business or my trade without cheating, I will end up with no profit but a loss.' Such people obviously mistrust God's promises: 'Cast your cares upon the Lord, and he shall sustain you,' and 'I have not seen the righteous forsaken,' and 'Seek first the kingdom of God, and all these things shall be given to you.'[143] Do you believe that God is false and will not fulfil his promises?[144] Do you imagine that he is powerless and cannot fulfil them? Or do you think that he is sleeping and thus neglectful of his people's needs? This same faith will console the godly when an ungrateful world greets all their good works with indifference. They have entrusted their fortune to one who is faithful, and he will return it with incalculable interest. But it is generally true that those who make these excuses waste more than enough money on luxury, sex, and gambling and thereby squander even the profits they could have made if they did not enjoy their leisure more than their lucre. They are the sort who will say, without blushing: 'I can't make a living without cheating.'[145]

Now charity, as I have said, has two objects: God and our neighbour. In the first, three persons meet, Father, Son, and Holy Spirit, one God, who

* * * * *

143 Ps 55:22 (Vulg 54:23); Ps 37 (Vulg 36):25; Matt 6:33
144 An argument frequently used by Luther to demonstrate the inutility of formal confession (*The Sacrament of Penance* LW 35 12–14; Tentler *Sin* 355).
145 The passage of pastoral advice inserted in 1530 ends here (see 55 n139 above).

is to be loved above all things, both visible and invisible.[146] People show him too little love when they mistrust his promises, neglect his commandments, or place anything beside or above him, for example by holding their lives more dear than God and being less afraid to offend him than to die a thousand deaths. Our 'neighbour' takes on many guises. Here we must consider whether we have fulfilled our obligations to wives, parents, children, tutors, pupils, pastors, ruler, officials, relatives, friends, and benefactors – in short, to all Christians. What is more, we are all our own neighbour – and a self-inflicted wound is more hurtful than any. If you have hurt your neighbour's reputation, confess it. But if drink or a loose tongue has made you blurt out your own guilty secret, weep and wail; you have again hurt your neighbour, but[147] twice over: you have hurt both yourself and the person you confided in.

Concentrate your thoughts on all these things, and any sins worthy of penance will quickly spring to mind. It may jog your memory if you can recall where you lived at the time, what business you were engaged in, and with whom you lived. One thing will remind you of another.[148] Some people also seek grounds for confessing within themselves. For every sin is lodged either in the mind or in one of the five senses. Faith and love for God and one's neighbour belong to the mind, as do the vices that oppose them, especially the spiritual ones: envy, hatred, the desire for revenge, pride, hypocrisy, malice. But although every sin springs originally from the heart, those that involve debauchery, lust, violence, and assault are attached to the senses and the organs of the body.[149] Many sins are committed by the eyes, many by the ears, many by the belly and gullet, many by the hands – but most of all by the tongue. For the tongue by itself can commit all the sins that the other organs do in their respective ways. The tongue pours out blasphemies against God, the tongue slanders our neighbour, the tongue destroys gentle peace and foments deadly war, the tongue arranges illicit affairs and breaks sacred friendships, the tongue uses flattery, calumny, and filthy stories to infect innocent minds, the tongue, without sword and without poison, murders brothers and friends. In short, the tongue teaches heresy and turns Christians into Antichrists.[150]

* * * * *

146 A reminiscence of Col 1:16.
147 but twice ... confided in] Added in 1530.
148 Such aids to recollection are also recommended by the manuals of confession; see Rosemondt f 2 verso; Tentler *Sin* 110.
149 This division into fleshly and mental sins is characteristic of manuals of confession; see the similar list in *Poeniteas cito* 1153D and Escobar a 6 verso.
150 See especially *Lingua* CWE 29 249–412.

This should suffice, I think, to enable lay people to examine their consciences, provided they know the Apostles' Creed and the essentials of the gospel's teaching. Now I shall say something about the matters discussed at great length by the theologians, such as circumstances, omission, and restitution, but more as advice than precept.

It is wrong for the confessor to try to discover the penitent's accomplices by prying into circumstances that will allow the people involved to be identified. No one is obliged to divulge other people's misdeeds to the priest, if it can possibly be avoided.[151] Sometimes, of course, one cannot avoid betraying the identity, for example, of a girl abused by her father or a man who has pitched his prince into unjust war. In this case the theologians suggest finding a priest to whom both parties, or at least the one whose identity must be protected, are unknown.[152]

Again, where sins have been committed out of lust, some priests ask irrelevant questions out of lustful curiosity.[153] It is right that a man who has seduced a woman should specify whether he has committed adultery with someone's wife or incest with a nun, or whored with a prostitute, fornicated with a single girl or ravished a virgin, but he has no need to describe all the details of the act, because they do not change the species of the sin.[154] But in such cases people will often pass over circumstances that are more relevant than these vulgar details. The theologians distinguish adultery from simple fornication, but often the circumstances make fornication a far more deadly sin than adultery. It is a lesser sin to commit adultery by chance, when an opportunity happens to arise, than to use wicked wiles over a long period to entrap and then to seduce a good, innocent girl, from a good family and destined for an honourable marriage, and then to shame her by boasting of the deed, and[155] even to prostitute her to others, which some courtiers seem to find very amusing. Again, it is a lesser sin if someone happens to

* * * * *

151 A long-standing principle 'unanimously' upheld by the medieval theologians (Tentler *Sin* 93–4); see for example the regulations of 1197 quoted in McNeil 412 section 14.

152 Gerson also gives this advice in connection with incest (Tentler *Sin* 94); on Gerson see 31 n56 above.

153 Most manuals of confession (eg Rosemondt f 132 recto) warn against this, but there were exceptions; see the remarkable examples in Tentler *Sin* 91–3 and 196.

154 The obsession of medieval confessors – and penitents – with such details is well illustrated by Tentler's chapter on 'Sex and the Married Penitent' 162–232. Fornication with a nun was considered 'spiritual incest.'

155 and even ... amusing] Added in 1530.

find something in a holy place and steals it away because he is poor, than if someone who is far from destitute enters a house by night, armed with a dagger, and plunders a layman's strongbox or robs a poor man who can barely support his wife and many children. For it is not only the time, the place, and the person that must be considered, but also the malice of the intent, the magnitude of the temptation, and the number of people harmed by a single sin. For example, if someone kills a man on whose counsel the whole state depended, that single crime harms a great many, as[156] does someone who incites a prince to play the tyrant.

Now most people identify sins of omission and also transgression according to human regulations: for example not attending mass on a Sunday or eating meat on a Friday.[157] But more serious are the sins of omission that break God's commandments, such as neglecting an opportunity to help one's neighbour. Again, it is a graver sin to hate one's neighbour than not to abstain from eating meat on a Friday. But a sin of omission is graver if failure to act at the same time inflicts great harm on one's neighbour. If a neighbour's life is in danger and one does nothing to save him despite having the chance, then it is murder. The same is true if evil replaces the good that has not been done. To take an example: the Lord's day was given to us so that at leisure we might examine our conscience, reconcile ourselves to God, and rekindle our love for God and our neighbour by pious meditation, by prayer, by attending sermons, and by reading or discussing religious matters. Thus it is a sin twice over to spend the whole day in silly games, whoring, drinking, telling dirty stories, or even in quarrelling and brawling.

This is a sin that is particularly prevalent among those who occupy positions of power or authority: princes, bishops, parish priests, abbots,[158] magistrates, heads of households. Just as these people do a lot of harm by their misdeeds, so they do great harm when they fail in their duty. It is not sufficient that the pope should not himself stir up wars between the princes; it will be considered a crime if he does not make strenuous efforts to settle existing wars. It will be laid to a prince's charge not only if he robs and oppresses the nation himself, but also if he does not use the power he

* * * * *

156 as does ... tyrant] Added in 1530. The two illustrative additions are suggestive of Erasmus' characteristic hostility towards courtiers and the courtly ambience.

157 Erasmus had developed this particular theme in the *De esu carnium* of 1522 (ASD IX 1–50).

158 The abbots were added to the list, provocatively, in 1530.

possesses to remove officials who are unjust or who in other ways subvert the liberties of the subject. His sin will be twice as great if, corrupted by money or some other inducement, he has deliberately entrusted an official position to someone he knows to be a scoundrel. A bishop is guilty twice over if, first, he makes no attempt to change his flock for the better and if, second, he actually teaches them corruption through unsound doctrine and his own perverse way of life; or[159] else, corrupted by greed, he knowingly entrusts the care of his flock to someone unworthy. This being so, the prince or bishop must be neither idle nor lazy, but always alive to any opportunity of doing good.

Every private individual must try to do the same, if possible, and seize every opportunity to do good; let the rich use their wealth, the learned their authority, the eloquent their skill with words, the old the respect they have earned, the court favourites their influence, and the young their energy. Young people will confess their involvement in brawling or whoring, but will not admit that they have allowed so many of their best years to slip by unprofitably, when they had the chance to learn things that would be useful for the rest of their lives. In such cases one realizes that the priorities of both penitents and confessors are often distorted. A prince may confess that he has killed with his own hand, and that is indeed a serious crime to confess; the life of a prince should be blameless in every respect. But the same man will perhaps not confess that the innocent are being slaughtered, the blameless plundered, and unspeakable crimes committed in a war sparked off by his ambition or anger. He will confess that he has perhaps exceeded his powers in confiscating someone's property, but he will not confess that he has knowingly and deliberately sold control of tax collection to someone patently rapacious and unjust, and is well aware that countless citizens will be robbed by him.

Consideration must be given here to the duties attached to any position, and sins of omission judged accordingly. It is the special task of the bishop to nourish his flock with holy doctrine. But perhaps[160] he does not feed them or take pains to appoint suitable shepherds, preferring, in exchange for money or favours, to entrust the cure of souls to the unworthy. Though he may not confess this, he may well confess to whoring or to missing evening prayers. Similarly, it is the prince's special duty to protect everyone and to defend the freedom and peace of the nation. But while he will keep quiet the many great atrocities committed on his orders, or at best

* * * * *

159 or else ... unworthy] Added in 1530
160 perhaps] Added in 1530

because of his negligence, he will confess that he failed to attend mass on a given day or did not say his hours. But these are not sins peculiar to a prince. Nowadays too a custom has infiltrated some princes' courts whereby every single day they run right through all the prayers that priests must say, and during that time they are free from interruptions. Who would dare to interrupt a prince at prayer? Now I do not condemn religion in a prince, if in fact religion is found in such things, but I do condemn it if princes make religious observance an excuse to neglect the special duties that pertain to their office: so many widows and wards unlawfully exploited, so many commoners suffering indignities. God will not be indignant if to deal with such matters a prince lets his prayers or even his mass be interrupted; for[161] human institutions must always yield before the higher obligations of charity.

Thus the priest's first concern must be to establish the station in life of his penitent.[162] Now since, as some have said, not unreasonably, penitents speak to God through the priest, the judgments made must of course be correct in the sight of God, who weighs everything by the intentions of the heart. These days many attach the greatest importance to what is fleshly and ritualistic, and the least importance to what is spiritual. Again, they place a high value on what has been established by mere mortals, and neglect what was commanded by God. For example, who will not execrate a priest if he appears with his head unshaven? But no one execrates him if he is caught in a drunken brawl in a brothel. Who will not revile a monk if he puts on layman's clothing?[163] But it is considered merely comical if a monk – still wearing his cowl – goes whoring and drinking, breaks up people's homes, or practises magic. It is a horrible crime for a priest to break his fast before mass or matins, but it is considered trivial if a priest approaches the Lord's table unreconciled with a brother he has wronged. There may be some good reason why mere mortals punish trifling offences more severely, but in confession, at least, the judgments should be commensurate with the offence.

Now the course of our discussion brings me to the subject of restitution. I admit that I have nothing new to say on this topic, given[164] that the

* * * * *

161 for human ... charity] This challenging clause was added in 1530.
162 This was generally recommended as a preliminary to confession by medieval writers; see Tentler *Sin* 84.
163 No doubt an allusion to Erasmus's own 'apostasy' in exchanging the habit of his order for the dress of a secular priest; see for example Ep 296:181–218 and Ep 1581A:3–19, 87–143.
164 given that ... discussing it] Added in 1530. For discussions of this topic, simply defined as 'any satisfaction that must be done to someone else,' see Tentler *Sin* 340–3.

theologians have devoted enormous tomes to discussing it. I shall merely give some advice on the mistakes that the less experienced may make.

People have an extraordinary obsession with restoring money or clothing. By contrast, those who have perverted innocent minds with poisonous words, or destroyed their neighbour's peace of mind with their virulent tongue, or damaged a reputation by slander, or incited princes or people to war by perverse counsel, all think little of repairing the damage they have done. But to many reputation is more precious than life, and nowhere could restitution be more necessary. But, people will say, this is an area in which restitution can hardly ever be made. All the more reason to try to do whatever can be done and to regret constantly that full reparation cannot be made. These days some empty-headed courtiers think that they have splendidly compensated a girl they have dishonoured – and often prostituted to others afterwards – if they finally farm her out with a little dowry to a husband; they almost seem to think that they themselves deserve a reward for finding the girl some sort of husband. She is married, but to some nobody, whereas she should have been married, unsullied, to a man of honour. Nor does the wedding expunge the damage to her reputation. Some compensation! And yet, fortified by this, they proceed to seduce more girls, and still more after that.

Again, when it comes to things that merely make us poorer, some practices are so regular and widespread that they are too commonplace to be considered theft. In this area most artisans who handle other people's goods, but especially millers and tailors, have a bad reputation, so much so that there is even a proverb: 'We are all thieves in our own trade.'[165] But the worst offenders among them are those who adulterate food and drink, for example diluting their wine with water or doctoring it with alum, lime, sulphur, salt, or other substances, because they not only steal people's money, but also damage their health and are little better than poisoners. How much disease and death have we seen caused by adulterated wine? But it is all,

* * * * *

165 A Dutch proverb not recorded in the *Adagia* but found in an anonymous collection published c 1495; see R. Jente ed *Proverbia communia* (Bloomington 1947) no 56, although the Latin translation is different. I am grateful to István Bejczy for supplying this reference. A German version, together with Erasmus' Latin wording, is cited in K.F.W. Wander *Deutsches Sprichwörter Lexikon* (Leipzig 1867–80) II 338–9 sv Handwerk nos 23 and 68; the Latin follows the *Viridiarium* of J.G. Seybold (Nuremburg 1677) 652 which, however, gives no source. Tradesmen and their wiles figure frequently in the contemporary practical literature of sin; see Tentler *Sin* 163–4.

apparently, part of the game. Moreover, their favourite victims are those who least deserve to be cheated. Brotherly love should insist that those who are prevented by ignorance from assessing goods properly should be assisted by the seller's sense of fair play. But these days you will not find many prepared to miss any chance to cheat and make a quick profit. And yet, though we all make a living by mauling one another, we still consider ourselves Christians. And since it has become routine, we do not even bother to confess it or, if we do, we think it quite sufficient simply to have told a priest what we have done.

Now who is more obligated to make full restitution than the ruling classes? And yet it appears that the rules of restitution do not apply to them. They take refuge in 'arrangements.' It is a kind of remedy, and I do not condemn it. But I am afraid that many of the arrangements made between mortals will not be ratified by God. They say[166] that there will be nothing left to feed their wives and children if they restore all that they have taken unlawfully, even though it was robbery that made them great men and advanced the family fortunes, enabling them to live in pomp and luxury. If they truly repent of their misdeeds, let them throw away the damnable dice, practise thrift not extravagance, and take up farming or some other honest calling; this will give them the means to make restitution. Let them guide their children into the same paths. If, after assiduously following this plan, they still lack the wherewithal, perhaps an arrangement will make up for it.

Some make the excuse that those they cheated are dead – but their heirs are still alive. Others say that they do not know exactly whom they have robbed but make no effort in the meantime to find out; they think they are completely in the clear if they have purchased title to the property for a few coins. If people can be entitled to keep their ill-gotten gains, why should they not also be entitled to commit adultery and murder? Even those who have robbed churches or monasteries can settle their conscience for a few coins. Do they really not know to whom they should make restitution? But they fear for their reputation. They should have thought of that when they embarked on their crimes. However, there is a kind of remedy available here too: let them make restitution through a third party who can be trusted implicitly. Or ultimately, if we are to accept this sort of

* * * * *

166 The rest of the discussion on restitution (to 66 'add their own') was added in 1530. Erasmus also attacked arrangements (*compositiones*) in the colloquies *Militaria* and *Funus* (CWE 39 58 and 40 773).

excuse, I think it would be safer to give the money to the poor rather than to intermediaries.

Now there are some species of robbery and theft that few people will confess, let alone consider making restitution for them, and most of these concern agreements and contracts. I was at a banquet where someone was boasting that he had sold a horse for six angels when he knew it was not worth six pence.[167] These days what wine merchant will not pretend to the uninitiated that wine from Auxerre or Spain is Beaune, or that Louvain wine is Rhenish,[168] and sell heavily diluted wine as full strength? Would it cross any of their minds to make restitution, even though what they do is sheer robbery? Is it not a mere game today to sell a dog's hide as Roman hide or to pretend that a bolt of scarlet cloth has been dyed with cochineal when it has not? Who will not extort four times the price from a naive customer, if they can? I know that the lawyers say that vendors are not always compelled to reveal the defects in their merchandise. But the gospel law does not absolve them: 'Do not do to others what you would not have them do to you.'[169]

Has any barrister ever confessed that due to incompetence or deceit on his part a plaintiff has suffered a material loss? What can I say about soldiers, who will justify any crime under the laws of war? But those are the laws of the devil, not of war. Again, carters and merchant seamen employed to transport wine will exercise their 'right' to drink as much as they like of it – and only the best, at that! They will top up fine wine with foul water, even if what they are transporting is destined for the sick. Will any of them confess this as theft? Will any think of making restitution? This kind of

* * * * *

167 The angel was an English gold coin worth 6s 8d, which means that the horse was sold for more than eighty times its worth; cf CWE 1 342; CWE 14 424–86 and appendix.

168 Beyond the literal sense, this passage, with its reminiscence of Matt 9:17 ('new wine in old bottles'), seems to contain a jibe at Erasmus' opponents, the theologians of Spain and Louvain. 'Auxerre' may possibly indicate Paris; the adjective *Altissiodorensis* (usually *Autissiodorensis*) 'Auxerrois' would bring to mind the church of St Germain L'Auxerrois opposite the Louvre (the French court was known as the 'cour de St Germain'). Less likely connections are the thirteenth-century Paris theologian William of Auxerre, whom Noël Béda admired (Ep 1579:29), and the humanist Germain de Brie of Auxerre (Ep 1597). It is doubtful that 'Beaune' and 'Rhenish' are used allegorically, since these were (and are) renowned wines. But perhaps the references to 'Roman hide' and 'scarlet' (the colour worn by cardinals) that follow shortly after may hint at doctrinal inadequacies among the prelates.

169 An echo of Tob 4:16; cf Matt 7:12 and Luke 6:31.

person, being stiff-necked,[170] must not be merely admonished in confession but severely rebuked and told to root out of their hearts the frivolous excuses they habitually use. 'Carters (or sailors) have their rights where food and drink are concerned,' they say, 'and everyone does it.' But these rights are written on Satan's tablets, not in Christ's laws.

The tailors, too, have found a colourful excuse. 'The cloth is placed with us,' they say, 'to be made into a suitable garment. The skilled craftsman will make one out of fewer lengths than the unskilled; anything left over is the reward for skill, and the client is still satisfied.' Thieves will never hang if the accused can pronounce their own sentences like this. Ask if the client is satisfied! I shall pass over the goldsmiths and jewellers who adulterate their materials with alloys, who shave the metals they are given, who sell paste gems as real ones. But it is remarkable how lax even the civil laws are in this area, though they will crucify some wretched petty thief who has lifted five drachmas from a carelessly guarded purse.[171]

In areas where it is the state that suffers most, it would be worthwhile to make an example of someone from time to time to deter the others. I shall say nothing here about the adulteration and revaluation of the coinage, since that is the business of princes and magistrates. I have already touched on it in my *Institutio principis christiani*.[172] So I come to those who hire out their services by the day. They do not consider it theft if they take four days to complete a job that could have been finished in one, living all the while at someone else's expense and taking the agreed payment for each day. Nor do they consider it lying to make promises they do not keep. But how do they excuse their deceitfulness? 'That is the rule of our trade,' they say. No, the rule of your trade is not to steal or lie but to use your skills to complete the job in good faith.

However, greater sinners even than these are the apothecaries and doctors, whose watchword is 'quid pro quo.' Sometimes apothecaries will sell one product as something else or instead of medicine supply stuff that is rotten, useless, and by now poisonous as well. You ask for rhubarb, but you get something that was rhubarb forty years ago. There is no spice, no amber, still less any root or herb, however strong and durable, that will not fade over a long period of time. 'But,' they say, 'unless we mix old

* * * * *

170 Exod 32:9, 33:3; cf 23 n23 above.
171 Five drachmas would amount to a trifling amount.
172 *Institutio principis christiani* 4 (CWE 27 262). Erasmus' ambiguity here is deliberate, since in the earlier work he had suggested that governments profited most from manipulation of the coinage.

stock with the new, we will end up starving.' It would be better to end up dead than to sell your sick brother, who should be treated for free anyway, something that will make the illness worse or perhaps hasten his death. The same sins are found among the doctors. Here it would also be a good idea to inquire into the public responsibilities of those who govern our cities.

Charity requires that in time of need we relieve our brother's poverty. And yet some, who consider themselves Christians, will increase the price of their goods in line with the urgency of their brother's need. Someone has a pomegranate bought for a few pence; the patient is in danger, and there are no others to be had; the pomegranate is worth its weight in gold.[173] Similarly, some will hide away their grain so that if there happens to be a shortage of grain, they can sell it for four or ten times the usual price – and they do not realize that this is sheer robbery. I have given a few examples; informed readers will add their own.[174]

Let me make an end by adding a few words about satisfaction.[175] There are two kinds, public and private. As concerns the public kind, I would wish any priest entrusted with the authority to hear confession to be given powers to moderate the penance according to the circumstances or even, if the case warrants it, to change it to a private penance. For if the Fathers who instituted public acts of satisfaction allow incumbent bishops the right to increase or decrease the prescribed penalty according to the station in life of the penitent,[176] why should not the same power be entrusted to those who stand in for the bishops in this most burdensome of tasks? If these functions have been entrusted to someone less than suitable, the blame must fall on the bishops anyway.

Now when it comes to penalties imposed in private, the priest must be like a skilful doctor who will not prescribe any medicine to any patient at

* * * * *

173 The medicinal qualities of the pomegranate, like those of the purgative rhubarb, were well known: 'Pomegranates be of good juyce, and profitable to the stomacke' (T. Elyot *The Castel of Helth* 2.7 2nd ed [London 1541] 21).

174 The inserted passage on restitution (see n166 above) ends here. Thus the majority of Erasmus' own examples was added in 1530.

175 Works of satisfaction, or external penance, followed contrition and confession to complete the procedure of penance. Traditionally (eg Clavasio f 305) they consisted of prayer (against pride), fasting (against concupiscence), or alms (against avarice), though others such as vigils and flagellation were available (Tentler *Sin* 320). Erasmus generally championed contrition at the expense of satisfaction, particularly since he found no scriptural basis for the latter; see Payne 211–13.

176 On public penance in the early church, see 28 n45 and 52 n127 above.

random but the one that he knows will be most effective, given the nature of the disease and the station of the patient. For the same illness he may prescribe one thing for a strong man and something else for a weaker one, one thing for someone brought up in a particular way and something else for someone of different background; indeed, he will often prescribe, for the same person and the same sort of disease, one remedy when they are young and another when they are old.[177] These days a good many priests prescribe nothing more than a few short prayers. 'Read the psalm "Have mercy on me, O God",' they say, 'with the collect "God to whom it belongs." In addition the *Salve regina*, with the collect "Grant us your servants." Plus the psalm for the departed *De profundis*, with the collect "God of the faithful".'[178] I do not condemn any of this, as I recognize the great value of obedience, but confessors do better to prescribe prayers containing a specific remedy against the evil by which they feel the penitent is threatened. For example, our forefathers picked out certain psalms as being particularly appropriate to certain kinds of prayer.

It would also be useful to prescribe, instead of prayers, some reading matter[179] that will inspire the penitent to hate the sin that troubles him. Let us say that someone is tempted by paganism or Judaism and has unsound views on the Christian faith, being led astray either by his inexperience or by reading poets and philosophers. He must be told to spend an hour or two every day reading Lactantius[180] or the books against pagans, Jews, and heretics bequeathed to us by Origen, Tertullian, Cyprian, Chrysostom, and others.[181] It is almost impossible that someone who has carefully read Origen's books against Celsus[182] should not develop sounder views on Christ's most holy teaching. There are various books by the holy Fathers in praise of chastity, in reprobation of slander, on the instruction of monks and

* * * * *

177 The same advice, using the same simile, is given in *Poeniteas cito* 1156A.

178 Respectively Ps 51 (Vulg 50), the antiphon *Salve regina*, and Ps 130 (Vulg 129: two of the seven penitential psalms), accompanied by liturgical prayers of contrition (ie collects), two of them used in the mass for the dead and the other (*Concede nos famulos tuos*) in several masses of the Virgin.

179 Erasmus' suggestion that appropriate reading be imposed is unusual – but characteristic of him.

180 No doubt Erasmus has in mind Lactantius' *Institutiones divinae*, a comprehensive defence of Christianity and attack on paganism completed in AD 313. Lactantius' style is praised in the *Ciceronianus* CWE 28 412 and *De contemptu mundi* CWE 66 170.

181 Erasmus cites the prominent pre-Augustinian Fathers (third to fourth centuries AD) involved in the struggle against heterodoxy.

182 PG 11 641–1632, a vast apologetic tract of AD 246, refuting the Hellenistic philosopher Celsus

clergy, on preserving widowhood, on the duty of bishops, on the duty of the prince, on the sanctity of marriage, on concord, and on countless other virtues and vices.[183] From among them a reading must be chosen for each individual that will do most to remedy the failing of which the penitent stands confessed. All must however be urged to read attentively and with the sincere desire to reform their lives. It is a good idea to prescribe a whole programme of study for the young, who are often at risk because they have too much time on their hands. I do not entirely approve of prescribing for youngsters, at a tender age that still has its playful side, fasting, vigils, or other trials that may lead to ill health in later years. It is preferable to reform the younger generation by teaching them respect for their elders and giving them useful things to do.

For the rich, it is correct to prescribe generosity to the poor, but I think they should be warned not to misplace their gifts. There is no reason to disapprove if someone endows a chapel, an altar, a monastery, a school, a college, or something similar. Yet alms are holiest when they relieve the present needs of our neighbours and disappear from sight, so to speak, when they pass from the hands of the giver to the recipient; their fame may perish in the eyes of humanity, but it is all the more secure in the eyes of God. Moreover, if the penitent's age and physical constitution seem to require the imposition of a fast, he should also be advised that if he has sufficient means, he should give to the needy whatever money he saves by abstaining from food. Some confessors prescribe long pilgrimages, which means that the penitent, equipped with an iron breast-plate, must beg the fare and set out for Rome to[184] visit Peter's portals, or Jerusalem, or James at Compostela, a kind of penance I would not wish to condemn entirely. However, it is not right to prescribe it for those who have spouses and children at home who will be exposed to hardship or danger by their absence.[185] It is also a hazardous prescription for adolescents or young women who are at an age when their honour and chastity are better protected by staying at home.

This kind of penalty is best left to secular magistrates, being rather similar to some of the punishments they impose: they can order a flogging,

* * * * *

183 These subjects are treated by the Fathers from Tertullian (*De pudicitia* 'On Chastity') to St Bernard (*De detrectatione* 'On Slander') but are not all titles of specific works.

184 to visit ... Compostela] Added in 1530. Despite the next remark, futile pilgrimages were a frequent target of Erasmus' satire; his views are encapsulated in the colloquy *Peregrinatio religionis ergo* CWE 40 619–74.

185 The rest of the treatise, apart from the brief valedictory passage, was added in 1530.

amputate a hand, cut off an ear, put out the eyes, perforate the tongue, or brand the forehead or hand. None too different were those solemn penalties that the church used to impose in public, less to satisfy God than men, though also to satisfy God.[186] However, even the secular magistrate would be better advised to punish certain kinds of theft, or those other crimes that are not serious enough to warrant capital punishment (especially among Christians), by making criminals undertake service to the community instead of burning or mutilating them. For example, in the past some were fettered and made to work for their creditors, while others were chained and made to dig the fields or cut down trees; those who knew some sedentary craft were more suited to the workhouse. This kind of punishment is useful in two ways: it rehabilitates the offenders instead of destroying them, and it serves the state or the victim of the crime.[187]

The priest will tell certain penitents that they must sincerely forgive the person who has done them wrong, attempt to overcome evil with good,[188] and seek his friendship with kind words and deeds. Even if this cannot be achieved, they must at least expel from their heart all desire for revenge and try to forget the wrongs they have suffered. The Lord Jesus himself recommended this kind of satisfaction to us, just as the Holy Scriptures commended almsgiving to us.[189] The priest will therefore ensure that, if he has prescribed some penance involving pain or toil, the toil will be a labour of love; it will not endanger the health of the penitent's body and make it less fit to obey the spirit's instructions, but will simply put a check on its waywardness.

On[190] this point I am not seeking a fight with those who say that satisfaction has no role to play in penance. 'God alone,' they say, 'can remit sins, and if he remits someone's guilt, he also remits the penalty. For the guilty

* * * * *

186 The schoolmen identified three kinds of penance: solemn, public, and private, of which the first was provided for those guilty of capital sins that hurt the church and required a special ceremony of absolution (Lombard *Sententiae* book 4 dist 14 c 3). The kind of ceremonies performed in both the early and contemporary church are described by Erasmus 27–8 above.

187 A similar proposal is made in More's *Utopia*, when Raphael Hythlodaye describes the customs of the mythical Polylerites; see *The Complete Works of St Thomas More* 4 (New Haven and London 1965) 74–8.

188 Cf Rom 12:21.

189 See for example Matt 6:1–4 and 14–15. In his annotation on 2 Cor 7:10 Erasmus had extolled works of satisfaction that are helpful to others, rather than painful and useless like the torments inflicted in the Underworld (LB VI 774D).

190 On this point ... primary importance] This paragraph and the next were recommended for deletion in the *Index expurgatorius* LB X 1820A.

party is released through charity and the Holy Spirit, and that release leaves them nothing to do except grow ever stronger in charity. This,' they say, 'is the only true satisfaction in the eyes of God.'[191] From this they conclude that papal indulgences cannot relax penalties, except those imposed, or potentially imposed, by a mere mortal, and then only for the most pressing of reasons.

I would not wish totally to condemn papal relaxations, but I think it would be safer to hope for full remission of our sins from charity and from Christ's compassion than from mere human documents. Where there is no charity, what use is a bull? Where there is enough, the document is superfluous. Where it is deficient to some extent, they say that the pope cannot grant pardon, which belongs to God alone. The Holy Scriptures are silent on indulgences, as indeed are the early Fathers of the church. Modern theologians have always differed in their opinions on this subject, writing about it tentatively and incoherently. They must make up their own minds, but it is undeniable that we have the gospel's guarantee, in that the woman's many sins were forgiven her because she loved much.[192] I shall not take up arms against anyone who maintains that indulgences are not to be ignored, so long as they do not make that an excuse to ignore the points that are indisputably of primary importance.

From what I have already said it is clear enough, I think, how we may avoid the disadvantages often entailed in the performance of this form of confession, which are partly the confessors' fault and partly the penitents'. However, for the sake of the less expert, I am quite willing to provide remedies for each of them in rough outline. Such is human life that everything we do is flawed in some way.

So, the first disadvantage will do less harm if the prelates, and others whose business it is, are on their guard and ensure that the power to hear confession is not handed out irresponsibly to just anyone, but only to men of mature years and proven integrity, who are also sober and capable of silence. Priests must be censured if in their cups they blab, for amusement, whatever they have heard in the privacy of the confessional. If they ever

* * * * *

191 This is the logical conclusion to the 'contritionist' theory of Abelard, Lombard, and others (47 n105 above) but, with its specific hostility to indulgences, obviously recalls Luther's stance, inspired originally by his opposition to that form of forgiveness (*The Sacrament of Penance* LW 35 9–10).
192 Luke 7:47; the underlying point is that the woman's sins were forgiven her unconditionally and without penance. On Erasmus' generally unsympathetic views on indulgences, see Payne 214–16.

require advice on these matters, they must confer in private with learned and responsible colleagues.[193] Similarly they must be rebuked if in their holy sermons they blurt out secrets of the confessional that would be better concealed. The confessor will be more reliable if he is sober, forearmed with a modicum of prayer, if he approaches his task with a sense of awe, and if his questioning goes no further than is necessary to establish the nature of the sin.[194] As for the penitent, although it is sometimes risky to recall one's sins, it is certainly more often riskier to ignore them. Thus the wise and faithful minister of God will so arrange things that he will not poison the minds of the inexperienced and weak, but will not allow them to ignore something that, if ignored, could not have been remedied or avoided.

For the second, similar remedies can be prescribed: silence and integrity on the part of the priest. For the true and holy shepherd will not be lulled by this into complacency about his own sins, but inspired to greater fear and love of God, and to more earnest prayers and greater vigilance on behalf of the Lord's flock, when he sees the monstrous sins that people fall prey to, if once they have thrown off the Lord's yoke through ignorance or malice. This sin could not have happened had their shepherd safeguarded them with teaching, advice, rebukes, and entreaties. For the rest, they should not publicly name the crimes of those who are punished by the law for unnatural intercourse, sorcery, or other such villainy.

The third, since it cannot arise unless the priest is at fault, must be remedied by appointing men who, rather than swelling with pride,[195] will weep for the woes of humanity; witness St Paul, who admits that he was humiliated and brought to tears because there were among the Corinthians some who deserved a severe rebuke.[196] And sometimes the sins of the people fall on the head of the priests because they do not give the attention they should to teaching them the straight ways of the Lord. When such priests remind themselves that the Lord will demand his sheep from the hand of the shepherd,[197] they should be stirred to repentance rather than pride. Any one of all the sins that have ever been committed by humanity

* * * * *

193 This notion of conference was enjoined by the decree *Omnis utriusque sexus* (canon 21) of the Fourth Lateran Council in 1215 (text in McNeil 414 and Tanner I 245; cf Tentler *Sin* 99).
194 On the medieval debate over the degree of questioning to be used, see Tentler *Sin* 88–95; most manuals give similar advice to Erasmus'.
195 Literally 'raising their crests'; cf 24 n27 above.
196 Cf 2 Cor 2:1–4 and 12:21.
197 Cf Ezek 34:10.

can be committed again by any individual, and if any are not committed, we owe it to God's goodness, not to our own powers. Therefore the nature we share should not fill us with pride, but move us to pity. The priest who does not harbour feelings of paternal tenderness towards his flock is unsuited to his task. Would any father whose son fell victim to some horrible disease treat him with more disdain than before and not hasten instead, with grief in his heart, to get him cured? Now, if freedom is dear to you, then freedom from guilt should be equally dear. A doctor has no hold over someone who makes the effort to stay healthy. If by your own fault you have succumbed to illness, you must take especial care so that you stand free before God. Finally, just as when you are ill you choose a doctor to cure you – and not to rebuke you – you should do the same when choosing a priest.

As for those who identify the fourth disadvantage, are they doing more than point out that there are some bad priests? I wish that I could gainsay them! But we have not dispensed with the art of medicine simply because we know that there are bad doctors. It just makes us more careful to ensure that there are good doctors; it makes us more circumspect in choosing whom to trust with our treatment. In the end, it is the duty of the prelates to deal with these priests who put the sacraments to shameful uses, in such a way that it acts as a warning to the rest.

Of the fifth I can say no more than that exceptional cases must not be forced to prove the general rule. How few do we actually know who have blurted out their secrets in a fit of fever or frenzy? And who is crazy enough to trust a madman? Here again it will help to choose a suitable priest, as I have already said several times. Ultimately, if your crime puts your life at risk, and you distrust the parish priest and your own clergy, you are allowed to go to a place where you are a stranger and to confess, in disguise or in the shadows, to a stranger.[198] But in the end your soul's health should be more precious than your body's. To heal your body, you will perhaps show a doctor the wound you received while committing a capital offence; are you afraid to do so to heal your soul?[199]

Let that be my reply to the penitent. As for the priest, I admit that it is a great and arduous task to visit, with obvious risk to their lives, people afflicted by the plague or similar diseases; but they must remember that

* * * * *

198 This solution, which was thought to imperil principles of jurisdiction and discipline (discussed at length by Clavasio ff 51–3), was allowed in exceptional circumstances; see Tentler *Sin* 61–4; McNeil 413.

199 Medieval manuals use the same image to stress the necessity of telling everything if one is to be healed; see Tentler *Sin* 116.

they have taken up an arduous profession, and if they wish to be good shepherds, they must whenever necessary expose their very lives for the well-being of their flock, especially when souls are at stake. It is splendid work that they do, but they may expect a splendid reward; in the meantime, however, they are allowed to take precautions to ward off infection. For they are not compelled to put God to the test. If a priest is indispensable to the people and entrusts himself in absolute faith to God, he will not die before his time, but the Lord will fulfil his promise: even though what they drink be fatal, it will do them no harm.[200]

A great many will dare to approach a plague victim in pursuit of a legacy; will they fear to do so when their neighbour's soul is in peril? However, it would be common courtesy to light a fire and fumigate the room the priest is to enter, to make it as clean and safe as possible. There is another specific remedy: whenever the plague strikes, everyone while still healthy should make confession and receive the Eucharist once a week (something that many people did, in days gone by, even in healthy times). And after confession they should make the most strenuous efforts not to relapse into mortal sin, which is not so difficult with the aid of Christ's grace. This ensures that the priest is in no danger, and the others will be in safety even if sudden death or some highly contagious illness overtakes them. It will also help if we place our principal hopes of salvation in love and in the mercy of God rather than in listing our sins, especially when death looms over us.

A word on the sixth: those who forget modesty while remembering their sins are not yet truly sorry for their misdeeds. It must be drummed into them whom they have offended and how vile sin is, so that the more often they relapse into sinfulness, the more they will be ashamed. They must also be warned that confession without heartfelt contrition is profitless; but when once it has filled their mind, it will bring shame but also remove shame. It will bring shame for the vileness of their misdeeds in the sight of God; it will remove shame because shame will not conceal what is cured by being revealed.

My response to the seventh is that many more people are imperilled by overconfidence brought on by ignoring their sins, rather than by despair brought on by examining them.[201] The priest will find it more difficult to

* * * * *

200 Mark 16:18
201 Erasmus appears to have said the opposite 30 above, but as Payne (203, via Tentler 'The problem of anxiety and preparation for death in Luther, Calvin, and Erasmus' [PhD diss, Harvard University 1961] 200 n30) points

transform people's overconfidence into fear of the Lord than to rescue them from despair. There is thus a middle path between the two: the examination of sins must be sufficiently rigorous but not excessively anxious, and if it does cause anxiety, perfect ease of conscience will follow and counterbalance it when charity begins to drive out fear.[202] For fear without hope and charity produces despair.

I have already amply demonstrated the remedy for the eighth disadvantage. As for the ninth: I admit that, of the two evils, the lesser is to abstain from the Eucharist if your thoughts are fastened upon some criminal act, provided that you have struggled with all your might against the feeling but cannot dislodge it. Otherwise, to give up the sacraments completely is a step towards paganism. The case of confession is not the same. It appears that people cannot be entirely impenitent if they approach a priest with the intention not to deceive and mock him, but partly to obey the church and partly to find a better way to hate their sins, which they are still unable on their own to hate as they should. There is some sort of penitence in being upset with oneself because one does not sufficiently repent one's crimes. And it often happens that someone who goes to the priest barely penitent at all will discover during confession a genuine hatred for his crimes. This recital of disadvantages is not therefore intended to put us off confession, but to help us derive the maximum benefit from confession.

I have thought it right, best of prelates, to offer some advice that goes beyond the traditions of the early Fathers concerning confession,[203] in order that it should bear us as much fruit as possible. If people think that some danger attaches to my advice, let them reflect on how much more dangerous it is to go round with a guilty conscience; if it seems difficult, let them reflect on the peace of mind that bitter medicine can bring. They must be all the more wary of relapsing and having to swallow the same bitter pill over and over again. But let them confess just once in such a way that they will never need to confess in the future, and let it suffice to be humiliated just

* * * * *

out, Erasmus seems to imply here that more people actually suffer from overconfidence, though despair is the more dangerous of the two states.

202 Cf 1 John 4:18. Erasmus had already quoted this in reply to the Spanish monks in 1528; see *Apologia adversus monachos* LB IX 1063E.

203 Erasmus had set out the opinions of the early Fathers, from Chrysostom to Ambrose, in his *Responsio ad annotationes Lei* (CWE 72 370–7), arguing that they considered confession a personal matter in which Christ acted as intercessor and in which the sinner voluntarily withdrew from the fellowship of the church.

once before a man. Those who have once conceived a deep and heartfelt hatred for all their sins will not easily relapse into sin. God will assist a holy purpose, so long as we give him thanks for whatever befalls, and, while relying on his protection and not our own powers, try every day to improve ourselves until we reach the completeness of our humanity as measured by the full stature of Jesus Christ.[204]

* * * * *

204 Eph 4:13

THE EVANGELICAL PREACHER
BOOK ONE

Ecclesiastes sive de ratione concionandi

translated by
JAMES L.P. BUTRICA

annotated by
FREDERICK J. MCGINNESS

In May of 1535, with civic peace restored in reformation Basel, Erasmus moved from Freiburg im Breisgau to his beloved city on the upper Rhein after a five-year absence to oversee the publication of Origen's *Opera* and his own long-awaited treatise on preaching, *Ecclesiastes sive de ratione concionandi*. [1] He would not live to see Origen's works come to light, but over the summer of that year he concluded the penultimate and the longest treatise of his career, *Ecclesiastes*, a 'massive work' (*vastum opus*)[2] that would crown the many achievements of his life.[3] The work would set forth a ground-breaking approach for instructing preachers in Christian eloquence that would draw upon Sacred Scripture, the writings of the Fathers of the church, the works of the best classical authors, and many of his own texts. His treatise would have a decisive impact on the course of sacred oratory for years to come and cross-confessional divisions. Next to St Augustine's *On Christian Teaching* (*De doctrina christiana*) the work would stand as a milestone in the history of Christian homiletics.

    Ecclesiastes, which comprises over 333 folio columns in the Leclerc edition (LB) of his Erasmus *Opera omnia* and two full volumes of the North Holland (ASD) edition, virtually recapitulates the entirety of the man's career.[4] Nearly every page of the work teems with allusions to his earlier writings,[5]

* * * * *

All classical references are to the Oxford Classical Text series.
1 On Erasmus' return to Basel, see Thompson 'Return'; Schoeck (2) 350–61; and Reedijk 33–45. Reedijk (44) puts him there on 27 May 1535, or very shortly before this date. Based on Allen Ep 3028 (Basel, 28 June 1535), Schoeck (2) says he 'arrived in Basel no later than 28 June' (359 n1). Reedijk's article offers an insightful interpretation of the data for Erasmus' additional reasons for returning to Basel at this time.
2 See Erasmus' dedicatory letter to Christoph von Stadion, 6 August 1535, 242–6 below.
3 Erasmus' final work is his exposition of Psalm 14 *De puritate tabernaculi* CWE 65 217–67, which he dedicated to Christoph Eschenfelder (dated 27 January 1536). See Allen Epp 3086 and 3081.
4 LB (1703–6 [7]). For studies on *Ecclesiastes*, see: Chomarat 'Introduction' and his *Grammaire* II 1053–5; Robert G. Kleinhans 'Ecclesiastes sive de Ratione Concionandi' in *Essays on the Works of Erasmus* ed Richard L. DeMolen (New Haven and London 1978) 253–66; Michael Grünwald 'Der "Ecclesiastes" des Erasmus von Rotterdam: Reform der Predigt durch Erneuerung des Predigers' (Diss. University of Innsbruck 1969); O'Malley 'Sacred Rhetoric'; James Michael Weiss '*Ecclesiastes* and Erasmus: The Mirror and the Image' *Archiv für Reformationsgeschichte* 65 (1974) 83–108; Hoffmann *Rhetoric* 39–60; Béné *Érasme* 365–425; Judith T. Wozniak *A Time for Peace: The 'Ecclesiastes' of Erasmus* (New Orleans 1966); McGinness 'Erasmian Legacy.'
5 For intertextuality and 'intertextual play' in Erasmus and some difficulties

with pedagogical, scriptural, patristic, and classical references, and with his customary criticisms, all the while imparting reverence for the church, urging consensus, concord, harmony, peace and tranquillity, and offering his and later generations the best instruction on sound preaching he could devise. Though much more might have been included for the benefit of readers, such as a table of contents, subdivisions, and a clearer statement of the treatise's overall structure,[6] *Ecclesiastes* nonetheless was the product of mature reflection, published nearly sixteen years after he first conceived of the project, and just after 'the heavy loss' of two dear friends, Thomas More and John Fisher.[7]

In his dedicatory letter to Christoph von Stadion, bishop of Augsburg, Erasmus underscores the importance of *Ecclesiastes* for training 'men to spread the word of God sincerely, fervently, and faithfully.'[8] Though he regards the work as not living up to his own standards, the result nonetheless is a masterly achievement of pastoral utility and theological learning for instructing future preachers[9] in the most important of the church's ministries; as he declares at the very start, 'Many and varied are the gifts which divine goodness, in its eagerness for our salvation, has provided to the human race to obtain eternal life; but none among these is more splendid or more effective than to dispense the Lord's own word to his flock, and there is no other office in the whole ecclesiastical hierarchy either more outstanding in worth or more difficult to perform or more fruitful in application than to act as a herald of the divine will to the people and as a steward

* * * * *

identifying 'the sources of numerous quotations, proverbs, and motifs,' see Ari Wesseling 'Twentieth Annual Roland H. Bainton Presidential Lecture: Intertextual Play: Erasmus' Use of Adages in the Colloquies' ERSY 28 (2008) 1–28; see especially Richard J. Schoeck '"In loco intertexantur." Erasmus as Master of Intertextuality' in *Intertextuality* ed Heinrich F. Plett (Berlin and New York 1991) 181–91, who observes that 'Erasmus was . . . the most intertextual of prose writers and perhaps also of poets, certainly of the Renaissance'; Schoeck calls attention 'to intertextuality within certain selected adages and between adages and his other writings' (182).

6 See O'Malley 'Sacred Rhetoric' 18.

7 Dedicatory letter to Christoph von Stadion, 6 August 1535, 244 below

8 Dedicatory letter to Christoph von Stadion, 6 August 1535, 245–6 below. Christoph von Stadion, bishop of Augsburg (1478–1543), CEBR III 274–6. Erasmus also dedicated to him the Froben five-volume edition of the works of John Chrysostom *Opera* (Basel: Froben 1530); see Allen Ep 2359.

9 As in *Ratio* Erasmus refers to the future preacher as *adolescens*, a young man training to preach (*adolescens concioni destinatus*); see eg *Ratio* 187.

of the heavenly philosophy.'[10] Throughout this treatise Erasmus will stress
the signal importance of the preacher for the life of the church and for carrying on Christ's mission of teaching the heavenly philosophy, for on this
depends the salvation of humankind.

Ecclesiastes draws upon Erasmus' life's work of pedagogy, biblical, patristic, and classical scholarship, philology, grammar, and rhetoric, devotional writing – the sum of his life's enterprise in bonae litterae and sacrae
litterae. And it draws especially on Erasmus' humanistic, theological method
of investigating the sources (fontes) of Christian godliness (pietas) for appro-
priating and teaching the philosophy of Christ.[11] Rightly does Charles Béné
call Ecclesiastes Erasmus' grand testament and the principal work of his final years: 'Nothing expresses like the Ecclesiastes the sum of a teaching that
never ceased to develop during an entire life of study and dedication to
culture in service of Christianity.'[12] Johann Huizinga sees it as 'the great
work, which more than any other represented for him the summing up
and complete exposition of his moral-theological ideas.'[13] Emile Telle observes it is 'probably his most finished production and intellectual testament . . . which crowned his life, his literary, philosophical, and theological

* * * * *

10 See 252–3. On the place of philosophy in the education of the free-born child
see also Plutarch De liberis educandis 7D: 'It is necessary to make philosophy
the foremost matter of all education.'
11 In this translation of Erasmus' work on preaching, the translators often employ
the word 'godliness,' used by the DV (Isa 11:2–3) to render Erasmus' pietas. In
this introduction both 'godliness' and pietas are used interchangeably. For a
discussion of recent scholarship on pietas in Erasmus see John W. O'Malley's
introduction to Erasmus' Spiritualia CWE 66 ix–li, especially xv–xxx; see also
his 'Grammar'; and Tracy (1) 104–15. For studies on the philosophy of Christ,
see Chantraine 334–62; Augustijn Erasmus 71–88; Schoeck (2) 28–40.
12 Béné Érasme 372: 'On peut dire que l'Ecclesiastes a été son "grand testament."'
Béné Érasme 373: 'Aucune n'exprime comme l'Ecclesiastes la somme d'un en-
seignement qui n'a cessé de se développer pendant toute une vie studieuse et
dévouée à la culture au service du christianisme.' See also Grünwald 67: 'Das
letzte und umfangreichste Werk ist so der Schlussstein in diesem Ganzen.'
13 Johann Huizinga Erasmus and the Age of Reformation repr (New York 1957) 181.
Later he states that 'Ecclesiastes is the work of a mind fatigued, which no longer
sharply reacts upon the needs of his time' (182). Other scholars make this
point; see eg Weiss 'Ecclesiastes and Erasmus' 90: 'Hence Erasmus' difficulty in
writing Ecclesiastes: a treatise on Christian eloquence necessarily called for a
recapitulation of the aim, the method, and the achievement of his life's work.'
See also 106–7, where he aptly calls the work 'a summary and a retrospective
of Erasmus' entire career' (107). Grünwald notes it is 'die letzte seiner großen
Schriften, ja sein umfangreichstes Werk überhaupt' (1).

output.'[14] As for its significance in homiletic tradition, John O'Malley hails it 'the great watershed in the history of sacred rhetoric.'[15]

Although a monumental work in so many ways, *Ecclesiastes* registers Erasmus' lament for the passing of a grand moment in his life that had promised positive change in the theological culture of Europe and bright prospects for a morally better world. Twenty years before its publication, before the turmoil of the Reformation and his involvement in theological *quaestiones disputatae*, Erasmus looked optimistically to genuine reform in church and society based upon his programme of education in *bonae litterae* and *sacrae litterae*.[16] It was an age when 'the minds of princes' seemed truly bent upon 'the pursuit of peace and concord under the leadership above all of Leo, pontiff supreme in more than name ...,'[17] and when enthusiasm for returning to the sources of Christian godliness energized a generation of capable biblical humanists to pursue Latin, Greek, Hebrew, and other oriental languages. It was an age when it seemed progress was being made daily with more accurate editions of the classical and Christian authors as neglected and once inaccessible works of antiquity came to light and passed into the hands of clergy and laity alike, eager for intellectual nourishment, social and ecclesiastical renewal.[18] By 1535, however, sensing his scholarly energies nearly spent, he would look back dispondently on his unrealized ambition of emending and editing the texts of the ancients: 'Indeed, we too, along with others, have striven with all our power in this regard; if only we had been able to accomplish all that we wanted!'[19] *Ecclesiastes* represents, as well, a lament for an era when one might criticize the foibles and

* * * * *

14 Emile V. Telle '"To every thing there is a season ...": Ways and Fashions in the Art of Preaching on the Eve of the Religious Upheaval in the Sixteenth Century' ERSY 2 (1982) 14. Hoffmann says the same: 'the crowning culmination of his lifework' (*Rhetoric* 31).

15 O'Malley 'Sacred Rhetoric' 13; see also 14: the *Ecclesiastes* is 'one of the best informed and most profoundly learned treatises on the subject ever produced, without any doubt far surpassing anything that had preceded it or that would be published for decades to come.'

16 See Albert Rabil Jr 'Desiderius Erasmus' in Rabil 2 216–64, especially 216–18.

17 Letter to Wolfgang Capito (Antwerp, 26 February 1517), Ep 541:11–65. Erasmus sees everywhere signs that the princes of Europe are 'tearing out by the roots the nurseries of war and binding peace in chains ...'; 'So it is to their piety that we owe the spectacle of the best minds everywhere rising ... as they set themselves in concert to restore the humanities' (Ep 541:36–53).

18 See Erasmus' *Paraclesis* for a similar expression of optimism in Olin *Catholic Reformation* 92–106. See also Augustijn *Erasmus* 71–2.

19 See book 3 973.

pretensions of pompous prelates and theologians, when freer and more col-
legial discourse took place among Christian scholars,[20] which might have at
last led to peace for Christian letters. Finally, it is perhaps Erasmus' lament
for his own passing glory, for a time when he once saw himself acclaimed in
European lands as the prince of humanists, who was sought out by rulers,
statesmen, bishops, and literati for his scholarship, illustrious wit, pedagogical wisdom, urbanity, and humanistic theological learning.[21] By 1535, however, the world of Europe – and Erasmus' own world – had changed dramat-
ically, and much for the worse.[22] His celebrated fame had lost much of its
lustre among the many Reformers angered at his opposition to Luther and to
other currents of the Reformation, and among many Catholics disappointed
in his doubtful orthodoxy and religious allegiance.[23]

By 1535 Erasmus also suffered from the sheer burden *Ecclesiastes* had
brought upon him. Wanting his customary diligence in getting works to
press in timely fashion, he had taken close to sixteen years to complete *Ecclesiastes*. In his dedicatory letter to von Stadion, Erasmus describes the work
as 'vast and complex,' the most agonizing work he ever undertook.[24] At the
same time we might infer that in his own estimation this treatise was also the
most important of his entire life; nothing greater could he offer the church

* * * * *

20 On criticism, see eg *Moria*; *Epigramma Erasmi in Julium* II in *Opuscula* 35–7. See
   also J.K. Sowards 'The Two Lost Years of Erasmus: Summary, Review, and
   Speculation' *Studies in the Renaissance* 9 (1962) 161–86, especially 178–81. On
   free discourse, see letter to Christopher Fisher (Paris, [about March] 1505), Ep
   182:46–97.
21 See eg letter to Servatius Rogerus (Hammes castle, 8 July 1514), Ep 296:99–180.
   See also Tracy (1) 74–86, 121–2 and especially part III 'Second Thoughts, 1521–
   1536' 127–208; Augustijn *Erasmus* 31–42; Schoeck (2) 349–59, especially 352,
   who speaks of the events after 1517 that 'shook Erasmus' optimism'; Wolfs,
   and Seidel Menchi *Erasmus als Ketzer* 21–32, 33–66.
22 For Erasmus' 'weariness with the world' after his return to Basel, see Schoeck
   (2) 350–61; Tracy (1) 127–208; and Augustijn *Erasmus* 183. See also Alan Per-
   reiah 'Humanist Critiques of Scholastic Dialectic' *Sixteenth Century Journal*
   13 (1982) 3–22; Christian Dolfen *Die Stellung des Erasmus von Rotterdam zur
   scholastischen Methode* (Osnabrück 1936) 5–6.
23 See Rummel *Catholic Critics* II passim and Seidel Menchi *Erasmus als Ketzer*. See
   also Augustijn *Erasmus* 119–33. For Erasmus' supporters in Rome, especially
   Tommaso de Vio (Cajetanus), see Paul Grendler 'Italian Biblical Humanism
   and the Papacy, 1515–1535' in *Biblical Humanism and Scholasticism in the Age of
   Erasmus* ed Erika Rummel (Leiden 2008) 227–76, especially 270–3.
24 See Erasmus' dedicatory preface to Christoph von Stadion (242). Allen III 631–
   2 notes: 'As to when he began to write the *Ecclesiastes*, there is no definite
   evidence to show ...'

than this much needed manual to guide future clergy in preaching Christ purely, simply, and sincerely.[25] *Ecclesiastes* would serve as a crucial resource for clergy when, Erasmus believed, good preaching by bishops and secular and regular clergy was in woefully short supply. Arguably, few were better capable of composing such a work than himself; certainly many contemporaries believed this, as his correspondence makes clear. His sentiment proved accurate: his final *opus* would justly count among the most influential of all his works; paradoxically, it would be among those least acknowledged by its readership.[26] Catholic quarters would not grant it a long public life. In 1559, with Pope Paul IV's Index of Forbidden Books (*Index librorum prohibitorum*), the public sale and circulation of Erasmus' *opera* in Catholic lands ceased.[27] This did not mean, however, that *Ecclesiastes'* use and influence ended.

Why Erasmus decided to compose *Ecclesiastes* is not altogether clear, nor is it easy to identify with precision the range of reasons for its composition and all the persons with whom some type of agreement was made to undertake it. The best account of the work's genesis and development is given in Erasmus' dedicatory letter to von Stadion. If we accept his words at face value, it started with a promise, though one given perhaps more in jest: 'Several years ago I promised a work on preaching. To tell the truth, I was not serious, and did not really mean it.'[28] But afterwards, urged by people to carry out what he 'had not seriously promised' and in response to these mounting pressures, Erasmus composed notes and ideas, hoping he might later 'find the will and the opportunity to tackle the subject.' Years passed, however, and with them his loathing grew ever greater at the prospect of undertaking such an ambitious project demanding so much labour.[29] Often he broke off his work, only to return to it, and each time he renewed his commitment to the project, he felt racked with deeper anguish. Through all

* * * * *

25 See eg letter to Jan Becker of Borsele (Louvain, 24 April 1519), Ep 952:51–2.
26 See McGinness 'Erasmian Legacy.'
27 See Paul F. Grendler *The Roman Inquisition and the Venetian Press, 1540–1605* (Princeton 1977) 117, 146. See also Seidel Menchi *Erasmus als Ketzer* for the characterization of Erasmus in Italy as wholly abhorrent: 'Der Erasmus, auf den man im Italien des Cinquecento traf, war ein verwerflicher Ketzer, ein Unruhe- und Unheilstifter' (6).
28 Letter to Christoph von Stadion, preface (242). For the history of the composition of *Ecclesiastes*, see especially Kleinhans 7–28.
29 Letter to Christoph von Stadion, preface (242); Erasmus' words about his difficulties in producing this work echo Quintilian's words to his friend Trypho in the *prohoemium* to book 1 of *Institutio oratoria* (1–23).

this Erasmus complains of ill health and pressing responsibilities of various kinds; still, at the end he would reveal his satisfaction in knowing that before his death he had made good on his word to complete what had once seemed unattainable and for years bled him of health and inner peace.

Arguably the strongest push to produce this work came from John Fisher, bishop of Rochester: Erasmus tells us that 'he, more than anyone else, encouraged me by letter to take up this task ...' (Ep 3036).[30] But it is not clear how often these epistolary stimuli occurred. Erasmus however makes explicit that he 'had made no promise to him but merely turned over the possibility silently in my mind.' It is interesting to speculate what Erasmus might have told Fisher about his intentions to compose the treatise, but lacking correspondence on this exchange we shall likely never know. Whatever his words to Fisher, they might have been spoken as early as 1511–12, when Erasmus resided at Queen's College in Cambridge, but far more likely between 1512 and 1519, and probably closer to the latter date.[31] Further support for Fisher as prime mover is given in Erasmus' letter to the bishop of Basel, Christoph von Utenheim (Basel, [early January?] 1523), when he tells him, 'If Christ grants me the strength, I shall finish a book on the principles of preaching, which I promised long ago and am frequently asked for in letters from that best of prelates, John, bishop of Rochester, who appeals to our ancient friendship and his unfailing and continual support of me.'[32]

* * * * *

30 Letter to Christoph von Stadion, preface (244); see 'John Fisher' CEBR II 36–9. See also Erasmus' letter to John Fisher (Basel, 1 [September] 1522), Ep 1311: 20–2.

31 John Fisher (1469–1535) was both bishop of Rochester (1504–35) and chancellor of the University of Cambridge (1504–35). It is likely Erasmus first met him on his second visit to London in 1505–6, when he stayed at the house of Thomas More to collaborate on translating the writings of Lucian; he resumed contact with Fisher in 1509 on his visit to England, and again in 1511–14, when he lived at Queen's College, Cambridge, teaching Greek and theology at Fisher's invitation. Already in September 1511 Erasmus writes Fisher from Cambridge expressing the wish to dedicate 'some literary gift that should be worthy of your Eminence ...' (Ep 229:6), but the work would likely be some translation of the Fathers; see Schoeck (2) 109–25. According to Erasmus Fisher wrote to him often; see Ep 457 to Johann Reuchlin (Calais, 27 August [1516]). For a study of Erasmus and Fisher's relationship, see Porter 'Fisher and Erasmus,' which looks at the tensions that grew between Erasmus and Fisher after 1519.

32 Letter to Christoph von Utenheim (Basel, [early January?] 1523), Ep 1332:40–5. Erasmus' wording is somewhat ambiguous and can admit the reading that he promised such a work to John Fisher ('... librum De ratione concionandi

On 4 September 1524, Erasmus wrote Fisher, 'I had made a start on the book [*Ecclesiastes*] you ask for (and others ask for it too); but my complaint, which threatened me with the worst, and certain other interruptions obliged me to break off.'[33] Despite later apparent disagreements with Fisher,[34] Erasmus obviously retained deep admiration for the prelate whom he regarded as 'a bishop of exemplary godliness,' 'a man of incomparable holiness and learning' and 'a true bishop in all the offices worthy of a prelate but especially in his zeal for teaching the people ...'[35] Fisher's life, apostolate, and administration as permanent warden, or 'chancellor,' of the University of Cambridge in many ways served as a model for Erasmus' reflections on the excellent *ecclesiastes* 'preacher.'[36] Erasmus tells von Stadion that as 'chancellor' of Cambridge Fisher sought to establish three colleges that would produce true 'theologians' (*theologi*) who were not so much armed

* * * * *

absolvemus: quem olim a me promissum crebris litteris efflagitat optimus praesul Ioannes Roffensis episcopus ...' Allen Ep 1332:36–8). The letters of Fisher to which Erasmus refers here are presumably not extant. See Porter 'Fisher and Erasmus' 85–6 and Erasmus' letter to Johann von Botzheim (Basel, 30 January 1523), Ep 1341A:1332–8: 'I still have by me several things which I started long ago; among them is a commentary on Paul's Epistle to the Romans, of which I had finished four books, if I mistake not, twenty-two years ago. For a work on the theory of preaching I had only jotted down some divisions of the subject-matter. And yet, if Christ grants me life and tranquillity, I have a mind to finish a work on preaching, which may do some good, especially as I am urged to do so by men whose opinion carries great weight.' For the Latin text, see Allen I [I] 34:19–22: 'In Opus de ratione concionandi tantum annotaveramus quaedam rerum capita. Et tamen si Christus dabit vitam ac tranquillitatem, est animus Opus concionandi [hoc anno utrumque hoc opus] in publicam utilitatem absolvere, praesertim huc adhortantibus magnis autoribus.' Allen's edition notes the emendation Erasmus made where he deleted the words *hoc anno utrumque hoc opus*. It seems Erasmus had the intention of finishing and publishing *Ecclesiastes* as early as 1523, but he deletes these words in his revision of this letter to Botzheim, which he then published in September 1524. See Allen I [I].

33 Letter to John Fisher (Basel, 4 September 1524), Ep 1489:368–70
34 Porter 'Fisher and Erasmus' 90–6
35 See book 1 354 below; letter to Archduke Ferdinand (Basel, 29 November 1522), Ep 1323:25.
36 See book 1 352–5 for Erasmus' comment on William Warham (b 1450–22 August 1532), who held Fisher in great esteem. See also his comments on Warham in Ep 384 to Leo x (Basel, 1 February 1516). Warham became lord chancellor and archbishop of Canterbury in 1503; see CEBR III 427–31 Erasmus portrays Warham as a model bishop. See also *Peregrinatio religionis ergo* (*Colloquia*) CWE 40 669 n155.

for the battle of words (λογομαχία) as trained for the sober preaching of the word of God.'[37] Like William Warham, archbishop of Canterbury,[38] and some other notable clergy, Fisher would have recognized Erasmus' talents as an educator, one eminently qualified to compose a preaching manual for the instruction of his clergy as he envisioned for his colleges at Cambridge. It is certainly conceivable too, as Erasmus' comment to von Stadion suggests, that at some point in their friendship he acceded to a request from Fisher at least to consider composing a treatise on preaching.

On the basis of firmer textual evidence we know that Jan Becker of Borsele, Erasmus' acquaintance from Louvain, also provided a crucial stimulus. Most scholars concur it was Becker, dean of the College of Zandenburg (or Zanddijk), near Veere, who in 1518 exacted from Erasmus a promise to write a work on preaching.[39] A year later, 28 March 1519, Becker urged Erasmus once again to 'devote a few days to writing a book on the theory of preaching for those who wish to preach the Gospel,' pleading with him to 'remember that you promised me you would do it, in the winter of last year, when I was constantly, perhaps even tiresomely, at your side.'[40] In 1521,

* * * * *

37 See the dedicatory letter to Christoph von Stadion, 244 below; also the letter to Alonso de Fonseca (Freiburg, [May] 1529), Ep 2157:124–30. See 1 Tim 6:4; cf *Ratio* 303.
38 On Warham see n36 above.
39 Béné, Kleinhans, and Chomarat identify Becker as the single individual responsible for giving Erasmus the idea for this work. Kleinhans (7–28) identifies Becker as the single source of Erasmus' motivation to compose *Ecclesiastes*, though he does acknowledge the numerous requests Erasmus received from others, including Fisher, for a work on this subject. See Chomarat 'Introduction' 3 and *Grammaire* I 1053; Béné *Érasme* 373; and Grünwald 4–14. On Jan Becker see CEBR I 115–6; cf Ep 932:19–22: 'But there is one request I wish to make of you: that when you get a little time to spare from your more serious researches, you should devote a few days to writing a book on the theory of preaching for those who wish to preach the Gospel ...' See also 43–5: 'If all this does not suffice to move you, remember that you promised me you would do it, in the winter of last year, when I was constantly, perhaps even tiresomely, at your side.' See also *Ratio* 283:34–284:2: 'Fortassis et a nobis nonnihil conferetur, si quando vacabit absolvere libellum olim coeptum de theologicis allegoriis.' Grünwald (4) finds a possible reference to Erasmus' start on *Ecclesiastes*: 'Die erste literarische Nachricht über den Ecclesiastes ist wahrscheinlich jene Notiz in der Ausgabe der Ratio seu Methodus aus dem Jahr 1518 ...'
40 Letter from Jan Becker of Borsele (Veere, 28 March 1519), Ep 932:25–38: 'It remains for you to lay down the right principles for a preacher of the Gospel, which will in fact be a benefit to a far larger public, not only to those who have

Erasmus moved to Basel to be close to the Froben press (where he would reside until 1529),[41] and in the following year Becker wrote Erasmus again, politely and less assertively, nudging him to apply himself to the task which he had promised three years previously.[42] Still the promise made to Becker may well have been merely a repetition of the same words given earlier to Fisher, and perhaps to others as well. Whatever the origin of such a promise, we find Erasmus jotting down some key ideas that would later appear in *Ecclesiastes* when he writes to Justus Jonas in the latter half of May 1519, though without signaling his intention of writing a work on preaching.[43] Only in January 1523, in his famous letter to Johann von Botzheim giving an expanded catalogue of his works for an eventual publication of his *opera omnia*, does Erasmus state his intention to compose *Ecclesiastes*: 'For a work on the theory of preaching I had only jotted down some divisions of the subject matter. And yet, if Christ grants me life and tranquillity, I have a mind to finish a work on preaching, which may do some good, especially as I am urged to do so by men whose opinion carries great weight.'[44] About the same time Erasmus writes to Christoph of Utenheim, bishop of Basel, stating the same.[45] Later, in September 1524 – at least four years after his 'promise' – Erasmus tells Fisher he has 'made a start on the book,' indicating the work was underway.[46]

* * * * *

imbibed your instruction and thereafter will preach better and with better results, but also to the public who in this way will listen to preachers more effectively and with much greater profit. Such a thing will be the greatest joy to me on behalf of us all and privately for my own use. Not long ago I was enrolled, as you know, among the shepherds of the Lord's flock, and what food can I find for my Lord's flock committed to my charge more nourishing and better for them than that provided by evangelists and apostles, if only I had been trained under your guidance and knew how to feed it to them with wisdom and skill? Say yes, I beg you, for two reasons: the very great and widespread benefits that will accrue and your own passionate devotion to the religion of Christ.'

41 For his reasons to reside permanently in Basel after November 1521 (to April 1529), see Halkin 160–1; Tracy (1) 128–9; Augustijn *Erasmus* 126 and his 'Reformation' 30–4.

42 Jan Becker to Erasmus (Louvain, 23 November 1522), Ep 1321:11–14: 'But I would not now dare to demand the book on the theory of preaching that you promised three years ago, since I see you beset on all sides by so many and such bitter diatribes and critical comments . . .'

43 Ep 967A to Justus Jonas, Antwerp, [c 20–6 May?] 1519

44 Letter to Johann von Botzheim (Basel, 30 January 1523), Ep 1341A:1334–8

45 Letter to Christoph von Utenheim (Basel, [early January?] 1523), Ep 1332:40–5; see 84 above.

46 Letter to John Fisher (Basel, 4 September 1524), Ep 1489:44

Despite Erasmus' natural aptitude and capacity for such a work, *Ecclesiastes* was anything but easy for him to compose.[47] He confesses anguish, loathing, and near despair over the seemingly endless years of *Ecclesiastes'* composition. In fact, for a long while the promised work remained little more than a velleity. Erasmus had other weighty problems such as the affair with Luther, which seems to have kept him perpetually 'swamped with work'[48] and drained of energy; he was urged by Lutheran, other reform-minded individuals, and papal adherents to state publicly his theological positions one way or the other, which at last he did only in 1524 with his *De libero arbitrio*. Nonetheless, *Ecclesiastes* seems still to have weighed much on his mind. In 1525, when concluding *Lingua*, he mentions again he is about to undertake the work: 'The progress of our speech has brought us to the tongue of angels, which is that of priests and bishops. We will investigate the nature of this gift of God in the books on the method of preaching, which we are now beginning . . .'[49] But then there were the numerous other works he was preparing during these years[50] as well as revisions of other works such as the *Novum Testamentum, Colloquia, De copia,* works on the Psalms, let alone his ongoing correspondence with individuals all over Europe and his changes of residence.[51] In these years too, as Erasmus found himself slowly losing his health, suffering numerous infirmities, and tormented by the sense 'his enemies were spying on him

* * * * *

47 Besides Erasmus' own statements on why it took so long for him to complete this work, especially those in his dedicatory letter to von Stadion, see Chomarat *Grammaire* II 1053–9.
48 Letter to Simon Pistoris (Basel, [c 2 September] 1526), Ep 1744:5–6
49 CWE 29 412 ('tongue of angels' [1 Cor 13:1])
50 *Exomologesis, Hyperaspistes* 1 & 2, *De civilitate, Institutio christiani matrimonii,* the Commentary on Origen, *Ciceronianus, Dialogus de recta latini graecique sermonis pronuntiatione, Paraphrasis in Elegantias Vallae, De pueris instituendis, De vidua christiana, De bello Turcico, Apophthegmata, Explanatio symboli, De concordia, De praeparatione, Precationes,* a revision of Jerome's *Opera,* the editions of Irenaeus', Ambrose's, Augustine's (Basel: Froben 1529), Chrysostom's, Basil's, and Origen's (Basel: Froben 1536, published posthumously) *opera,* and expositions of the Psalms, including *De puritate tabernaculi* (his last published work).
51 Letter to Paolo Bombace (23 September 1521), Ep 1236:124–6: 'I am entirely engrossed in revising the New Testament [third edition] and some other works of mine, slowly licking into shape the crude offspring of my brains like a she-bear.' For this image of the she-bear, see *De pueris instituendis* CWE 26 305. For a complete list of Erasmus' works, especially those produced while he was at work on *Ecclesiastes,* see Allen XII 30–4. See also Reedijk 46.

everywhere,'[52] he became embroiled in controversies with Edward Lee, Noël Béda, Pierre Cousturier, Frans Titelmans, Jacques Masson (Jacobus Latomus) and the theologians of Louvain, the Parisian theologians over his *Paraphrases in Novum Testamentum* and *Colloquia*, with Diego López Zúñiga and Alberto Pio, prince of Carpi, to name but a few.[53] Scattered references to the progress, and lack thereof, as well as to his intention to complete *Ecclesiastes* appear on occasion in Erasmus' correspondence between 1524 and 1535 as he bemoans his sporadic, desultory work and the rising pressure from a growing number of friends and followers urging him to complete it.[54] In late June 1531, he confides to Tielmannus Gravius, 'in my present circumstances there is neither time to complete *The Preacher* [*Concionator*] nor the willingness, nor is it expedient in this insane world.'[55] Add to this, as Jacques Chomarat and Robert Kleinhans opine, the fact that Erasmus may have had strong personal difficulties throwing himself into a work on preaching for which he would be criticized because he had not

* * * * *

52 Augustijn *Erasmus* 154; Reedijk 40
53 For these disputes, including those with Dominicans, Franciscans, and Carmelites, see Rummel *Catholic Critics*; for his troubles with the Dominicans at Louvain, see Wolfs; Marcel Gielis 'Leuven Theologians as Opponents of Erasmus and of Humanistic Theology' in *Biblical Humanism* 197–214; and Paolo Sartori 'Frans Titelmans, The Congregation of Montaigu, and Biblical Scholarship' in *Biblical Humanism* 215–23. See especially CWE 84 for his dispute with Alberto Pio, Prince of Carpi.
54 See eg Ep 1489 to John Fisher, Basel, 4 September 1524; and letter to Noël Béda (Basel, 15 June 1525), Ep 1581:742–3: 'John, bishop of Rochester, has been pressing me repeatedly for a work on preaching, threatening me, begging, and almost compelling me to comply.' In 1527, Becker writes Erasmus yet again, politely nudging him: 'I hope you will treat it more seriously than you treated the advice I gave you eight years ago, that you should write on the theory of preaching' (Ep 1787:43–5). See also the closing words of Erasmus' *Apologia adversus Petrum Sutorem*: 'Iam enim accingebar ad libros, olim a me promissos, et a multis flagitatos, de ratione concionandi, ni latrator iste de improviso prosilisset' (LB IX 804E, quoted by Kleinhans 18); his letter to Thomas More, Ep 1804:149–50: '... completing the long-awaited *On the Art of Preaching*'; letter to Henri de Bottis (Basel, 22 December 1527), Ep 1921:16–19: '*De ratione concionandi* has not been published yet; something always comes up to thwart our purpose and direct our attention elsewhere. And you can hardly imagine how much trouble the Augustine is giving.' See also his letter to Louis Ber (Freiburg, 22 October 1529), Allen Ep 2225:22–4: 'Aggredi cepi libros De ratione concionandi, sed animus semel elapsus e vinculis, veluti Proteus quispiam in omnia se vertit, ne rursus capiatur. Expugnabo tamen.'
55 (Freiburg, [?June fin. 1531]) Allen Ep 2508:6–8

preached since his days at the Collège de Montaigu.[56] And then there were the continuous reports of the deaths of so many good friends.[57] Whatever Erasmus' personal reasons for the untypical delay in bringing this work to production we can only speculate; yet it should be emphasized that during the years of *Ecclesiastes'* composition Erasmus was anything but inactive.[58]

It is only in August 1534 that we learn from Erasmus of his completion of book 1 and of his hopes to have the entire work finished by the end of the following autumn at the latest.[59] He tells us too that he contemplated having the treatise consist of three books (not four). Finally, in his letter of 7 May 1535 to Julius Pflug, just before his return from Freiburg im Breisgau to Basel to oversee the printing, we learn of his treatise's imminent completion,

* * * * *

56 See the letter to Jan (II) Łaski (Basel, 27 August 1528), Ep 2033:49–52: 'This winter, if the Lord grants me some free time, I will prepare my notes for the *De concionando*, and already magpies and jackdaws are squawking about it. "What?" they say, "Is he going to teach us how to preach when he has never preached in his life?"' Craig Thompson gives evidence that Erasmus preached at the Collège de Montaigu ('Better Teachers' 131); see eg the letter of Beatus Rhenanus to Charles V (Schlettstadt, 1 June 1540), Allen I 58:65–7 ('Ergo Scotista factus est, in collegio Montis agens; nam inter theologos disputatores Ioannes ille Dunsius Scotus ab acumine ingenii maxime praedicatur'); and, more important, Erasmus' letter to Johann von Botzheim (Basel, 30 January 1523), Ep 1341A:351: 'Very many things have fallen by the way which I do not regret; but I could wish that some speeches in sermon form still survived which I delivered long ago in Paris, when I was living in the Collège de Montaigu.' Erasmus did discourse publicly on at least one other occasion; see Erasmus' *Panegyricus* CWE 27 8–75, which he delivered on 6 January 1504 at Brussels. On Erasmus' desultory progress on *Ecclesiastes*, see Chomarat *Grammaire* II 1056–7; Béné *Érasme* 32–7; Halkin 'La pieté d'Erasme' *Revue d'histoire ecclésiastique* 79 (1984) 675: 'Il est alors pensionnaire du Collège de Montaigu et il y prononce quelques sermons' (See his footnote). See also Grünwald 12–4 (*Die Psychologie der Entstehung*).
57 See Halkin 257–8.
58 Erasmus took sixteen years to complete his edition of Jerome's works (1500–16), during which time he was also extremely active; see introduction, CWE 61 xvii.
59 Letter to Justus Decius (Freiburg, 22 August 1534), Allen Ep 2961:25–31: 'Est iam pridem in manibus Ecclesiastes, sed nescio quo pacto non favet genius. Tocies in manus recepi, toties deposui invita propemodum Minerva. Primum librum absolvi, secundum ac tertium orsus sum, nam tribus absolvere statui.Primus liber est plusquam iuste magnitudinis, metuo ne posteriores sint longiores. Si Deus dederit vitam et valetudinem mediocrem, hoc exibit autumno proximo ad summum.'

though not to his personal satisfaction.[60] Aware that his years were drawing quickly and painfully to a close, he tells Pflug he preferred to commit the work to his publisher if only in unpolished form than to have it finished by others after his death: 'I have handed over my *Ecclesiastes* to the printers. It is organized in four books, though it is still somewhat rough, lacking the final polish. But people were calling for the work, and when I thought about the weakness of my poor body, I preferred to send it out half-finished rather than allow it to make its appearance in the world as a posthumous child, for I know only too well how unscrupulously the works of dead authors are treated.'[61] Finally, on 24 August 1535, Erasmus writes to Bartholomaeus Latomus that his work is on its way.[62]

In late August 1535 (between 24–31 August),[63] Erasmus put the final touches to *Ecclesiastes*, and on 1 September, in collaboration with Hieronymus Froben and Nicolaus Episcopius, he oversaw publication of the *editio princeps* in folio (Edition A) at the Froben press. By October he had sent out the first copies to his friends Piotr Tomicki, bishop of Cracow, Paul Volz, Damião de Gois, Léonard of Gruyères,[64] archdeacon of Salins, and perhaps others. And as some 2600 copies of the treatise were being printed and sold,[65] Erasmus, Hieronymus Froben, and Nicolaus Episcopius were

* * * * *

60 Letter to Piotr Tomicki, Allen Ep 3049:67–8, especially 219: 'Tum erat excudendus Ecclesiastes, qui multis locis hiulcus et inchoatus vix potuisset absolvi, nisi praesens adfuissem.' See also Rhenanus 51; for Pflug see CEBR III 77–8 and letter to Julius Pflug (7 May 1535), Allen Ep 3016:25–30. For Erasmus' final years in Basel, see Thompson 'Return'; Schoeck (2) 350–61; and Reedijk.

61 Letter to Julius Pflug (7 May 1535), Allen Ep 3016:25–30

62 Letter to Bartholomaeus Latomus (Basel, 24 August 1535), Allen Ep 3048:75: 'Prodit Concionator meus, utinam bonis avibus.' For Bartholomaeus Latomus see CEBR I 303–4.

63 Letter to Leonhard von Eck (Basel, 5 August 1535), Allen Ep 3035:14–16: 'Ecclesiastes meus iam erat absolutus, nisi valetudo coegisset feriari praelum: at vel inabsolutus prodibit ad Calendas Septembris.'

64 Letter to Piotr Tomicki (Basel, 31 August 1535), Allen Ep 3049:187–9: 'Ecclesiastae volumen lubens ad te mississem, si quis voluisset sarcinam recipere; per negociatores isthuc perferetur.' Letter from Paul Volz (Strasbourg, 4 November 1535), Allen Ep 3069:1: 'S.P.D. Epistolium tuum, D. Erasme dilectissime, cum Ecclesiaste abs te mihi donato exultabundus accoepi.' Letter from Damião de Gois (Padua, 22 December 1535), Allen Ep 3078:36: 'Concionator tuus apud nos iam extat, opus dignum te, in quo non temere tam diu laborasti.' Letter to Léonard of Gruyères (Basel, 12 October 1535), Allen Ep 3063:11–12: 'Commitam opus Ecclesiastae Gilberto Cognato, amanuensi meo, si possit ferre onus.'

65 See letter to Damião de Gois (Basel, 15 December 1535), Allen Ep 3076:7–9: 'Ecclesiastes iam opinor isthic prostat. Excusa sunt duo milia voluminum et

engaged in preparing a second edition in octavo, which appeared in March 1536 (Edition B). This Erasmus edited with a few minor changes.[66] In August 1536, a month after Erasmus' death (11 July 1536), Froben and Episcopius published a third edition in octavo (Edition C), and in 1540 yet another one (Edition D), which is included in tome v of Erasmus' complete works published at Basel.[67] In the years following the first edition of *Ecclesiastes* many pirated editions ensued as well.[68]

Erasmus at first intended to dedicate *Ecclesiastes* to John Fisher, bishop of Rochester, but on 26 August 1535, having just completed it and days before its publication,[69] he received the painful report confirming the execution of Fisher (22 June 1535) and More (6 July 1535). He then dedicated the work to Christoph von Stadion, backdating his letter to 6 August 1535.[70] In this letter Erasmus describes the continuous physical and mental agonies he endured in bringing the work to completion, and he sketches a brief out-

* * * * *

sexcenta. Nunc denuo excusus est minore forma.' See also Allen's notes on the printing of *Ecclesiastes* in Allen xi 189–90.

66 See Chomarat 'Introduction' 22–7.

67 See the editions of *Ecclesiastes* that appear in Erasmus' collected works: *Opera omnia* (Basel: Hieronymus Froben 1538–41); LB v 769–1100; ASD v-4, v-5. Kleinhans gives a thorough history of the editions of *Ecclesiastes*; see 28–35, Appendix A 'Latin Editions of *Ecclesiastes*' (163–4), and Appendix B 'The First Froben Editions of *Ecclesiastes*' (165–7). See also Lawrence D. Green and James J. Murphy *Renaissance Rhetoric: Short-Title Catalogue 1460–1700* 2nd ed (Ashgate 2006) 190.

68 For a study of the printing history of the *Ecclesiastes*, see Kleinhans 31–5. Kleinhans lists the reprinted and pirated versions of *Ecclesiastes* (Antwerp: Martinus Caesar 1535; Antwerp: Michael Hillenius 1535; Basel: Froben, March 1536 and August 1536; Antwerp: G. Montanus 1539; Basel: Froben 1539; Basel: Froben 1540 [*Opera omnia* v 643–917]; Leiden: Sebastian Gryphius 1543; Basel: Froben 1544–5, 1554). See especially Allen's note for Ep 3036.

69 Letter to Bartholomaeus Latomus (Basel, 24 August 1535), Allen Ep 3048:53, where Erasmus speaks of the rumour that Fisher had been executed: 'Hic constans et verisimilis rumor est, ubi Rex cognovit Episcopum Roffensem a Paulo tertio cooptatum in numerum Cardinalium, eo maturius productum e carcere truncasse capite. Sic ille dedit rubrum galerum. Thomam Morum iam pridem esse in carcere, facultatibus in regium fiscum redactis, nimis verum est. Ferebatur et is ultimo affectus supplicio, sed nondum certum habeo'; and Letter to Piotr Tomicki (Basel, 31 August 1535) Allen Ep 3049:160–2: 'In Anglia quid acciderit episcopo Roffensi, ac Thomae Moro, quo hominum iugo nunquam habuit Anglia quicquam sanctius aut melius . . .'

70 See Kleinhans 23, who notes that Erasmus was also urged to dedicate this work to John III, duke of Cleves and Juliers.

line of *Ecclesiastes'* four books and explains his method of instructing the preacher.[71] The terse outline which Erasmus refers to as 'a rough sketch' does little to capture the substantial content and weighty significance of his work, let alone help to clarify its many organizational problems.

In his dedicatory letter to von Stadion Erasmus tells the bishop why he did not emend the *editio princeps* before its publication: 'To be quite frank, I could not face going over such a massive work again, for it was only with difficulty that I accomplished this much with my health growing weaker every day.'[72] The treatise's need for emendation, however, is evident in more than a few places. James Butrica notes that many parts of the work lack Erasmus' customary polish and care, and were obviously written in haste or in physical and emotional distress. Erasmus himself hints now and then that he had not thought through where all the parts of *Ecclesiastes* should go; he confesses to leaving 'gaps, repetitions, arguments that are incomplete or out

* * * * *

71 Von Stadion replied to Erasmus (Allen Ep 3073, Dilligen, 27 November 1535) with gratitude for the dedication of *Ecclesiastes* to him and concurred with the sentiments Erasmus expressed throughout *Ecclesiastes* about the need for good preachers and the timely importance of Erasmus' treatise: 'What could have been more spiritually wholesome for this age, more useful for teaching – indeed, more necessary? In my judgment there is nothing else to blame for such lukewarm faith among the common people than the shortage of good preachers.' Von Stadion also deplored Henry VIII's execution of John Fisher and Thomas More, and he sent Erasmus seventy crowns (*coronati*) and Gilbertus Cognatus (Gilbert Cousin), his amanuensis, ten. John Munro believes the money referred to could be either the French coin (the *écu au soleil à la couronne*) or the English coin, the crown, from which it was copied, from August 1526 (slightly revised in November 1526); the latter, known as the double-rose crown ('the crown of the rose'), was worth 5s (or 60d) and retained that value from November 1526 to 1542. If we take the wage of a master mason of Cambridge or Oxford in 1535 at 6d, the sum of 70 crowns (or 4200d) would have been equivalent to 700 days' wages; and with about 210 paid working days per year, that would mean 3.33 years' money wage income for said mason. Erasmus' choice of von Stadion for his dedication was indeed financially astute. For more information on these coins, see John H. Munro's Appendix E, 'Money and Coinage of the Age of Erasmus' CWE 1 311–47; 'Money, Wages, and Real Incomes in the Age of Erasmus: The Purchasing Power of Coins and of Building Craftsmen's Wages in England and the Southern Low Countries, 1500–1540' CWE 12 (appendix 551–699); and 'The Coinages and Monetary Policies of Henry VIII (r. 1509–47)' CWE 14 423–76, especially 440–50 and 476. See also 'Gilbert Cousin' CEBR I 350–2. My thanks to the late John Munro for his generous assistance with this footnote.

72 See 242–6 (dedicatory letter to Christoph von Stadion).

of place.'[73] In book 3, for example, when discussing the rhetorical device of similitude, he says, 'I forego an accumulation of examples, especially since we are giving the advice in this less pertinent place because it did not occur to me earlier.'[74] His decision not to revise and polish parts of the work is noteworthy, as is his admission of impatience with revision and correction. In a note to the reader (Basel, end of August 1535) he declares his reasons for the less-than-polished state of the text: 'Almost all the errors in this work must be attributed either to my amanuensis or myself. It is true that I was present during the printing, but because of my poor health I was unable to make a final revision, especially since the need to correct certain pages often coincided with the hours that had to be devoted to sleep or to the care of my poor body.' His words suggest how agonizingly close to death Erasmus felt by late August 1535, how greatly this work weighed upon him, and how determined he was to see it published in his lifetime.[75]

From its numerous editions and printings we can assume the work was as popular as it was timely and its reception and impact on preaching in both Roman Catholic and Protestant circles considerable. Robert Kleinhans sees the popularity of the work as lasting well into the decade after the appearance of the *editio princeps*. It was obviously read by many of Erasmus' close admirers,[76] and no doubt attracted the attention of numerous

* * * * *

73 See 243 (dedicatory letter to Christoph von Stadion); cf O'Malley 'Sacred Rhetoric' 18.
74 See book 3 CWE 68 879; see also Butrica 'Translator's Note' 239–40 above, and Hoffmann *Rhetoric* 39 for comments on the organizational problems with *Ecclesiastes*: 'The text is not readily analysable . . .'; see also Grünwald 2: 'Der Grund liegt im Ecclesiastes selbst, in seiner auffallend wirren Textlage. Das legte nahe, allem voraus nach der Geschichte und den persönlichen Umständen der Entstehung des Werkes zu fragen. Dabei stellte sich bereits der Character des Werkes als einer einigermaßen geordneten "sylva" d.h. Stoffsammlung heraus.' See also Grünwald 26–30 for the highly problematic nature of the work's organization.But see Chomarat's 'Introduction' 7–16, especially 7: 'Malgré ces flottements et ces néglences le plan général et l'idée directrice sont fort nettes.'
75 See 247 and 243 (dedicatory letter to Christoph von Stadion): 'my life (and what remains could easily lie in the palm of a small hand or within a closed fist) . . .'
76 See eg Wolfgang Faber Capito's comment to Bonifacius Amerbach, letter 1980 (Strasbourg, 20 September 1535) in *Die Amerbachkorrespondenz* ed Alfred Hartmann (*Die Briefe aus den Jahren 1531–1536*) (Basel 1943–8) IV 375: 'S. Lego Concionatorem Erasmi, quo non memini me hoc seculo legere librum his temporibus, adde et meo genio, fructuosiorem. Ambiguum reddiderat prefatio, quae invitum ad id muneris fuisse preseferebat. A quanta copia, quam appositus apparatus! Nihil scio, quo post lectionem Paulinam aeque afficiar, quia ubique ignaviam meam extimulat, incitat, impellit . . .' (quoted by Kleinhans 25 n4).

Reformers.[77] Though we have no conclusive evidence that the reform commission at the Council of Trent in 1545–6, which worked on the preparatory and final drafts of the conciliar decree on preaching, had a copy of *Ecclesiastes* to consult,[78] the considerable similarities in its document of 17 June 1546 (Session 5 *Decretum secundum: super lectione et praedicatione*) with *Ecclesiastes* in language, content, and recommendations strongly suggest that the commission found (or certainly should have found) the work squarely in line with its thinking on preaching reform.[79] Indeed, the often quoted comment by Hubert Jedin that this decree 'was the first, and we may add at once, the only successful attempt to combine church reform with whatever was sound in Christian humanism,'[80] expresses fittingly the impact (however unacknowledged) of Erasmus' life's work on Catholic reform at Trent and in the decades to follow.

We might well assume that Erasmus had many reasons for composing *Ecclesiastes* beyond the pressures put upon him by John Fisher, Jan Becker, and others. If we were to evaluate the state of preaching in Erasmus' day based on his comments in this text and elsewhere, we would find it hard to imagine that any members of the faithful remained in the church.[81] Erasmus himself no doubt believed there was a dearth of competent evangelists and that much had to be done to address the sorry plight of preaching. Like Jesus who asked that we pray to the lord of the harvest (Luke 10:2), Erasmus pleads that 'those who grieve sincerely over this should ask Christ with ardent and constant prayers to deign to send workers for his harvest or, to put it better, to send sowers to his

* * * * *

77 See the account of one crypto-Lutheran's reception of *Ecclesiastes* in John W. O'Malley 'Lutheranism in Rome, 1542–43 – The Treatise by Alfonso Zorrilla' *Thought* 54 (1979) 262–73; for the work's significance and wider impact see Debora K. Shuger *Sacred Rhetoric: The Christian Grand Style in the English Renaissance* (Princeton 1988) 58–64.

78 Tanner II 669. The text is also found in *Decretum secundum publicatum in ea quinta sessione super lectione et praedicatione* in *Concilium Tridentinum* V 241–3.

79 McGinness 'Erasmian Legacy' 95–8; see also Kleinhans 83–4.

80 Hubert Jedin *A History of the Council of Trent* trans Ernest Graf, 2 vols (St Louis 1963–) II 122–3. Jedin does not discuss the possible connection between the preaching-reform commission and Erasmus' *Ecclesiastes*, but he calls attention to the Erasmian influence on the commission.

81 See the important extensive note on the state of preaching in Erasmus' day in 'The Well-to-do Beggars' CWE 39 487–9 n46, which cautions against taking sweeping statements on the decay of preaching too seriously. The author calls attention to the large body of evidence suggesting 'an upsurge of interest in preaching' in the fifteenth century.

field.'[82] Lamenting the lands lost to Christ where preachers had failed – the East, Ethiopia, Palestine, Asia proper, Greece – Erasmus exclaims, 'Immortal God, how much land lies open in the world where the seed of the Gospel either has not yet been cast or else was cast in such a way that there are more weeds than wheat.'[83] Though Christendom had indeed suffered substantial territorial losses in the previous two centuries, behind Erasmus' laments and prayers lies the conviction that if enough clergy preached the word honestly and sincerely, God's grace would be virtually irresistible and the moral regeneration of society inevitable. Erasmus never explicitly attributes Christendom's territorial losses to the moral decline of society, but he evidently shares in this way of thinking.[84] To him the primary reason for the moral decline and abominations of the age was the want of good preachers to proclaim God's word 'in season, out of season,'[85] to the very ends of the earth. Christ's word was missing where it was meant to be.

Erasmus' remarks on the debased quality of preaching in his time, though illuminating, offer us little new information. The Roman church had for centuries been concerned about the poor quality of preaching. Long before Erasmus, major councils of the church had looked at the problem and called for reform. The tenth constitution of the Fourth Lateran Council (1215), 'On Training Preachers' (De praedicatoribus instituendis), was a milestone for the reform of preaching, and the contents of its constitution appear in Erasmus' and others' writings down to the Council of Trent (1545–63). Lateran IV declared the 'nourishment of God's word ... to be especially necessary, since just as the body is fed with material food so the soul

* * * * *

82 See book 1 357 below.
83 Book 1 358 below; see also Tracy (1) 88.
84 See eg letter to Ludwig Baer (Basel, 30 March 1529), Ep 2136:114–27 / Allen 2136: 117–27: 'How these stormy events will finally turn out is something we must leave in the hands of God. I am persuaded that a man who plants his foot on the immovable rock cannot perish. It may well be that, by these upheavals and disasters, the Lord wishes to correct our ways; for if we must admit the truth, our morals have fallen far, far short of true and genuine holiness, and this is especially the case with those who seemed to be pillars of the church. I make this judgment not by the demanding standard of the gospel spirit, but even in comparison with the decrees, issued by the popes of earlier times, on the proper conduct of priests and clerks, countless examples of which are recorded in a little work by Jean Gerson [And how greatly the morals of our age have declined even since the time of Gerson!]' Cf In psalmum 38 CWE 65.
85 Cf 2 Tim 4:2.

is fed with spiritual food ...' Recognizing that many bishops singly were unable to preach to their flocks because of the 'large and scattered dioceses' they administered, it mandated they appoint suitable individuals who could build up the faithful with their words and deeds. The document further instructed bishops to support these men 'with what is necessary' and that 'in both cathedral and other conventual churches' there be appointed 'suitable men whom the bishops can have as coadjutors and cooperators not only in the office of preaching but also in hearing confessions and enjoining penances and in other matters which are conducive to the salvation of souls ...'[86] The council refers to the decree of Lateran III (1179) that addressed the place of cathedral schools, recognizing their importance for advancing clerical literacy and mandating that each cathedral church provide an adequate benefice for a master of its school.[87] Erasmus' own recommendations follow closely these earlier conciliar pronouncements.

A comparison of Lateran IV's decree on preaching with that of Lateran V (1512–17) suggests that by the early sixteenth century the council fathers found even greater need for preaching reform. Though we have no evidence Erasmus himself examined either council's documents on preaching, just a few years before he began *Ecclesiastes*, Lateran V issued its decree on preaching (Session 11, *Supernae maiestatis praesidio*, 19 December 1516), which in its *dicta* and theology is strikingly similar to Erasmus' presentation of this office,[88] as well as in its castigation of the irregular practices of contemporary preachers. In unprecedented language for its denunciation of abuses in the pulpit, Lateran V reminded clergy that preaching is 'of the first importance, very necessary (*praecipuum ac pernecessarium*),'[89] and

* * * * *

86 Tanner I 239–40
87 Lateran III canon 18; see Tanner I 220.
88 Tanner I 634–8. There is much to suggest that Erasmus was familiar with Lateran V's document on preaching from Session 11 (19 December 1516), but much remains for scholarly investigation. See Nelson H. Minnich 'Erasmus and the Fifth Lateran Council (1512–17)' in *Erasmus of Rotterdam: The Man and the Scholar* ed J. Sperna Weiland and W.Th.M. Frijhoff (Leiden 1988) 46–60, who states, 'Although he seems never to have cited the conciliar decree on preaching, many of its provisions were in line with his own thinking ...' (52 and n24). We might add too that many of the words and images were as well, and that Erasmus recommends that preachers be familiar with papal and conciliar decrees (see book 4 CWE 68 1097).
89 Tanner I 634. Significant is the word *praecipuum* 'of the first importance, chief, principal, main, etc,' which is used throughout in reference to the teaching office of the preacher-bishop.

deplored the dereliction of those 'preaching many and various things contrary to the teachings and examples' of the apostles, 'a medley of fraud and error.'[90] The document conveys the impression that bad preaching was everywhere rampant: '[T]hese preachers, unmindful of their duty, are striving in their sermons not for the benefit of the hearers but rather for their own self-display.' It rebukes them for disregarding canon law, 'twisting the sense of Scripture in many places, often giving it rash and false interpretations,' 'preaching what is false,' 'merely following their own private interpretation,' putting forth apocalyptic nonsense as fact.[91] It urges that 'God's church suffer no scandal from their preaching' and that imprudent individuals refrain from attacking 'those who are honoured with pontifical rank and other prelates of the church.'[92]

To remedy these evils, Lateran v required that anyone with the duty to preach first be examined by his superior, and that wheresoever a preacher goes he should 'provide a guarantee to the bishop and other local ordinaries concerning his examination and competence . . .'[93] Ministers of the word are also commanded 'to preach and expound the Gospel truth and Holy Scripture in accordance with the exposition, interpretation, and commentaries that the church or long use has approved and accepted for teaching until now, and will accept in the future, without any addition contrary to its true meaning or in conflict with it. They are always to insist on the meanings which are in harmony with the words of Sacred Scripture and with the interpretations, properly and wisely understood, of the Doctors mentioned above.'[94] The council forbids 'predicting some future events as based on the sacred writings,' nor may preachers 'presume to declare that they know them from the Holy Spirit or from divine revelation . . . Rather, at the command of the divine word, let them expound and proclaim *the Gospel to every creature*, rejecting vices and commending virtues.'[95] And in

* * * * *

90 Tanner I 635
91 See Rosa Maria Dessì 'La prophétie, l'Évangile et l'État' in *Parole du praedicateur* I 395–444. See also the short account of preaching in Hans-Georg Beck et al *From the High Middle Ages to the Eve of the Reformation* trans Anselm Briggs, IV of *Handbook of Church History* Hubert Jedin and John Dolan (New York 1986) 574–8; and Walter Brandmüller '"*Traditio Scripturae Interpres*": The Teaching of the Councils on the Right Interpretation of Scripture up to the Council of Trent' *The Catholic Historical Review* 73 (1987) 523–40, especially 535–40.
92 Tanner I 636
93 Tanner I 636
94 Tanner I 636–7
95 Tanner I 637

sentiments Erasmus will later echo clearly, Lateran v insists that preachers 'foster everywhere the peace and mutual love so much commended by our Redeemer ...'[96] and 'not rend the seamless garment of Christ,' nor preach 'scandalous detraction' of their ecclesiastical or other superiors. Finally, the council directs that the ideas of those who believe they are endowed with the spirit of prophecy, 'before they are published, or preached to the people, are to be understood as reserved for examination by the apostolic see'; and if this is not possible, then to have the 'alleged inspirations' examined by the local ordinary who will appoint 'three or four knowledgeable and serious men to examine the matter carefully with him' to see whether such opinions may be published.[97] Violators of these canons would be subject to punishments and the penalty of excommunication, whose lifting was reserved to the Roman pontiff.[98] Individuals found violating these canons were to be informed that the office of preaching is forbidden to them forever. Despite such stern admonitions, Lateran v's decrees seem to have had little impact beyond the city of Rome.[99] The decrees, however, would be strikingly similar to the theology and positive recommendations of *Ecclesiastes*, as we note below.

The distressing picture Erasmus paints of contemporary preachers whom he heard personally or knew of by repute largely concurs with Lateran v's assessment.[100] It is extremely difficult, of course, to evaluate the level of quality in contemporary preaching solely on the basis of this council's decrees, Erasmus' own observations, or the comments of contemporaries, and we cannot pursue the question here. Certainly we should assume that many excellent preachers were also active in the years at the time of Lateran v, and not just men like John Colet (1467–1519) and Jean Vitrier (c 1456–d before 15 June 1521),[101] whom Erasmus knew personally, but others as well like Johann Ulrich Surgant (c 1450–1503),[102] who in 1503 offered

* * * * *

96 Tanner 1 637
97 On censorship by local bishops, see Minnich 50–1.
98 Tanner 1 638
99 Minnich 54
100 See eg his harsh comments on contemporary preaching in *Ratio* 299–305.
101 See Erasmus' profile of the Franciscan Jean Vitrier in his letter to Justus Jonas (Anderlecht, 13 June 1521), Ep 1211. See Godin 6–29; and his *Erasme: Vies de Jean Vitrier et de John Colet* trans and annot André Godin, introduction by Jean-Claude Margolin (Angers 1982); André Godin *Spiritualité*. See also CEBR III 408–9 and Tracy (1) 32–3.
102 *Manuale curatorum praedicandi* (Basel: M. Furter 1503). See Rudolf Hirsch 'Surgant's List of Recommended Books for Preachers (1502–1503)' *Renaissance Quarterly* 20 (1967) 199–210; and Dorothea Roth *Die mittelalterliche Predigt-*

preachers a handbook for improving their sermons. Moreover, the quality of preaching likely varied considerably from region to region, city to city, and village to village.[103] We might assume too, as Erasmus does, that in many places, even in a major city like Bruges, the quality of some preaching could be so low in its pastoral approach and theological content that the effect upon the faithful was deplorable. At the same time, however, we might also infer that Erasmus' ridicule of a fatuous 'man in very splendid vestments' at Bruges who concocts an absurd allegory about St Augustine as the spring from which flow the four mendicant orders and as a champion of confession suggests that Bruges had in fact sophisticated congregations that appreciated excellent preachers and had little patience for purveyors of such outlandish nonsense.[104] We might well assume that many competent preachers were indeed active in Bruges and in the lesser towns and villages of Brabant.

Before, during, and after Erasmus' writing of *Ecclesiastes*, some ecclesiastical synods, notable prelates, and humanists also took up the matter of preaching reform.[105] The Council of Sens (1527–8), the Council of Bourges (1528), and the First Council of Cologne (1536) addressed preaching reform in their dioceses. In Italy the noteworthy prelate Gian Matteo Giberti (1495–1543),[106] cardinal and bishop of Verona, and later Gasparo Contarini

* * * * *

theorie und das Manuale curatorum des Johann Ulrich Surgant Basler Beiträge zur Geschichtswissenschaft 58 (Basel 1956). Hirsch notes that Surgant's book 'is the earliest bibliography of books dealing with the art of preaching' (201).

103 See O'Malley *Praise and Blame* for the high quality of the sermons preached before the popes (1451–1521). For a brief but illuminating look at the authority, role, and influence of the church at this time, see Augustijn *Erasmus* 12–15.

104 See eg Erasmus' letter to Pieter Wichmans (Bruges, [c 29 August] 1521), Ep 1231:35–41: 'In ancient days hardly anyone preached a sermon without posting secretaries to take down what he said. If that were the practice today, heavens! What stories we should hear. Men who say things like that in the famous city of Bruges, which contains so many educated men, and so many men of lively wits and sound judgment even without academic education – what do you suppose they say in the villages, and across the dinner-table? And these are our pillars of orthodoxy.'

105 See McGinness *Right Thinking* 33–5.

106 For Giberti's *Constitutions*, after 1527, see Olin *Catholic Reformation* 145–6. Giberti's ideas fall squarely in line with Erasmus' recommendations: '... to preach and proclaim His Gospel sincerely to the people and to follow in His footsteps when He taught the Apostles 'Preach the Gospel to every creature ...' (146). See Adriano Prosperi *Tra evangelismo e controriforma: G.M. Giberti (1495–1543)* (Rome 1969) chapters 5 and 6.

(1483–1542),[107] cardinal and bishop of Belluno, focused on the problems of preaching in light of the challenges to Catholic doctrines brought about by the spread of Lutheran teachings, especially that on justification by faith alone. The urgency of the problem was no doubt recognized by many prelates, but a concerted, full-scale approach to renewing preaching throughout the dioceses of Europe could hardly occur without the reform of the episcopate itself, which would require a general council of the church. The need for preaching reform was also apparent to a few exceptional individuals who appreciated the potential of the classical authors for improving the quality of sacred oratory; among these were the Franciscan Lorenzo Guglielmo Traversagni, Johann Reuchlin, Philippus Melanchthon, Veit Dietrich, the German Franciscan Nicolaus Herborn,[108] and, of course, Erasmus.

Among the ancient pagan authorities on prescriptive rhetoric, none held greater status for Erasmus than Quintilian (Marcus Fabius Quintilianus, c 35–c 100), Roman educator and author of the *Institutio oratoria* on the grammatical and rhetorical training of the orator in the Ciceronian tradition.[109] Erasmus tells us he was 'the most painstaking of all rhetoricians,'[110] the supreme authority in the art of public speaking, and it is from the *Institutio oratoria*'s 'copious instructions' that he draws the bulk of his advice on speaking, as he had for his earlier works on education such as the *De ratione studii*, *De copia*, and *De recta pronuntiatione*.[111] Though following Quintilian closely, Erasmus (and following Reuchlin) underscores the infinitely different educational goal of *Ecclesiastes* from that of Quintilian's treatise. Whereas Quintilian considered being 'a good man, skilled in speaking' (*vir*

* * * * *

107 For Gasparo Contarini, see Elisabeth G. Gleason *Cardinal Gasparo Contarini: Venice, Rome, and Reform* (Berkeley and Los Angeles 1993) 260–76.

108 For Herborn see O'Malley 'Sacred Rhetoric' 8–9.

109 For the ancient rhetorical traditions, see James J. Murphy 'Chapter 1: The Four Ancient Traditions' in *Rhetoric in the Middle Ages: A History of Rhetorical Theory from St. Augustine to the Renaissance* (Berkeley 1974) 3–42. Murphy notes (22 n44) that 'this rhetorical portion of the *Institutio* ['Quintilian's treatment of *dispositio*, *actio*, and *memoria*'] apparently did not survive intact through the Middle Ages. The *Textus mutilatus* available to John of Salisbury (c 1159), for instance, had a great lacuna beginning at 1.i.6 and continuing to v.xiv.12, and a portion of VIII was also missing ... Although Petrarch knew the *Institutio*, the great post-classical popularity of the book came only in the fifteenth century.'

110 See book 3 CWE 68 877.

111 The *editio princeps* of Quintilian's *Institutio oratoria* appeared at Rome in 1470 and was based upon the manuscript of Quintilian found by Poggio Bracciolini at Sankt Gallen. Two editions of Quintilian's *Institutio oratoria* were printed by Aldus, the first in 1514, and the second edited by Andrea Navagero in 1521.

bonus dicendi peritus) as the greatest excellence in life and defined his purpose as 'the education of the perfect orator,'[112] Erasmus reformulates these qualities in terms of the preacher: 'a heart clean of all vices and human desires,'[113] or as he states elsewhere, 'a consummate purity, great strength of faith, a singular and burning love.'[114] The essential, infinite difference between the pagan orator and the Christian preacher Erasmus expressed succinctly in his *Apologia contra Latomi dialogum*: 'Orators agree on the definition of one of their number as "a good man, skilled in speaking." So why should we be dissatisfied with "A theologian is a pious man, skilled in speaking of the divine mysteries," or "Theology is piety linked to skill in speaking of the divine"?'[115] Quintilian and Erasmus both emphasize the crucial importance

* * * * *

112 For 'a good man skilled in speaking,' see Johann Reuchlin *Liber congestorum de arte praedicandi* (Pforzheim: Thomas Anshelm 1504) [Aiii], who modifies the phrase to 'a godly man skilled in speaking ...' (*Praedicator est vir religiosus, dicendi peritus, auctoritate superioris ecclesiastico pulpito praefectus*). See also Grünwald 72–5. The definition is attributed to Marcus Porcius Cato (the Elder); see Quintilian 12.1.1 ('But above all he must possess the quality which Cato places first and which is the very nature of things the greatest and most important, that is, he must be a good man ...') and 1. Pr. 9 ('The first essential for such an one is that he should be a good man, and consequently we demand of him not merely the possession of exceptional gifts of speech, but of all the excellences of character as well'). See also Cicero *De oratore* book 1. Erasmus understands Quintilian as sketching an 'ideal' or 'exemplar': see his comment in the letter to Paul Volz (Basel, 14 August 1518), Ep 858:361–3: 'Did Quintilian show contempt for the entire profession of orators when he composed the pattern of such an orator as had never yet existed?' Erasmus' admiration for and use of Quintilian for instruction in good Latin is well known; see eg *De copia* CWE 24 279–659; *De pueris instituendis* CWE 26 293–346; *De recta pronuntiatione* CWE 26 371 and passim. Murphy remarks on Quintilian's importance in Erasmus' day: 'After Cicero, the most important ancient rhetorical figure in this period was Quintilian. His *Institutio oratoria* was edited by five different scholars: J.A. Campanus ... Johannes Andreas de Bussis ... Omnibonus Leonicenus ... Andreas Ponticus ... and Raphael Regius who added his own commentary ... Finally, the text appeared with commentaries by Laurentius Valla, Pomponius Laetus, and Johannes Sulpitius Verulanus ...' *Incunabula* 14; see also idem *Rhetoric* 357–63.

113 See 284 below.

114 See 301 below.

115 *Apologia contra Latomi dialogum* CWE 71 55. See Georges Chantraine 'L'Apologia ad Latomum: Deux conceptions de la théologie' in *Scrinium* II 51–75. See also *Ratio* 193: 'But the chief goal of theologians is to expound the divine letters wisely, to give an account of the faith, not of frivolous questions, to speak seriously and effectually about godliness [*de pietate*], to produce tears, inflame hearts to heavenly things.'

of *ethos* – that unimpeachable character of the individual which lends credibility to everything he says – but Erasmus goes far beyond this in demanding that every preacher be like Christ, commended above all for his godliness (*pietas*), distinguished for teaching by word and example (*verbo exemploque*).

Aware that much of Quintilian's instruction focused on educating orators for the courts of Rome, Erasmus at times parries the objections of imaginary critics, declaring, 'Our business is with the preacher.'[116] 'Someone will say, "You are training an advocate, not a preacher"';[117] he rejoins, 'So I shall show what use comes to the preacher from this,' maintaining that 'these conjectures are often useful for proof' in certain types of sermons.[118] Erasmus may admit, however, that not everything Quintilian offers is of particular relevance for the preacher, but he never advises the reader not to pursue the author's thoughtful advice. Erasmus' purpose in using Quintilian is to offer as many methods and techniques as might be useful for instructing the aspiring preacher in oratorical rhetoric[119] without imposing rigid rules.[120] As the subject matter is vast and the field for invention virtually

* * * * *

116 See book 3 CWE 68 756: 'Nobis cum ecclesiasta res est.' Another formulation of Erasmus' purpose might well be that which he gives in his letter to Simon Pistoris (Basel, [c 2 September] 1526), Ep 1744:404. 'I have had no other aims than these: to join the study of languages and letters to more serious disciplines; to bring scholastic theology, which had often degenerated into mere sophistic wrangling, back to its roots in Holy Scripture; to have less ceremony in our practice, more piety in our hearts; to encourage bishops and priests to remember their office and urge monks to be true to what they are claimed to be; and, finally, to rid the minds of men of many wrong-headed and misguided ideas that have now plunged the world into confusion.' For biographical information on Pistoris, see Ep 1125 4n.

117 See book 2 CWE 68 638.

118 See book 2 CWE 68 599: 'I know that rhetoricians impart many other instructions regarding propositions, penetrating and not unpleasant to know, but we are training a preacher here, not a pleader of cases or a sophist or a declaimer.'

119 George A. Kennedy distinguishes between primary rhetoric (oratory) and secondary rhetoric (literary production); see his *Classical Rhetoric and Its Christian and Secular Tradition from Ancient to Modern Times* 2nd ed (Chapel Hill 1999) 1–5, but I follow Ronald G. Witt's 'oratorical rhetoric' to describe 'prose that aimed at public, oral expression.' See Witt *Footsteps* 1–30, especially 8–12; see also his 'Kristeller's Humanists as Heirs of the Medieval *Dictatores*' in *Interpretations of Renaissance Humanism* ed Angelo Mazzocco (Leiden 2006) 21–35.

120 One had to use rules of rhetoric judiciously, never letting the method subvert the very purpose for which one took up the practice of speaking in the first place; the same held true for the principles of dialectic. Erasmus had made clear this method of instruction in rhetoric in *De recta pronuntiatione* CWE 26 387: 'Rhetoric, within limits, must be studied with care, but it must not become a fetish: the point of it is to help in writing and speaking, not to instil

infinite, he maintains that almost everything Quintilian wrote can in some way assist the aspiring preacher. Whether it be instruction on the types of speaking, styles of speaking, decorum, rhetorical devices, gestures, delivery, the parts of oratory, handling the emotions, etc, Quintilian is eminently useful. However, accommodating Quintilian's 'science of speaking well'[121] to the practice of public (sacred) oratory does represent something of a shift in Erasmus, whose own pedagogical writings heretofore had focused primarily on the acquisition of good letters (*bonae litterae*) for writing, reading, conversation, and instruction in godliness (*pietas*), and not expressly for public oratory as such.[122]

Quintilian's theory of education offers Erasmus an uncommon benefit in plotting out the lifelong training of the preacher, who from the cradle onwards should advance programmatically in the four crucial elements that foster correct speaking: 'nature, art, imitation or example, and practice or exercise.'[123] Progressing through ever more complex disciplines, while never becoming too immersed in any one of them lest he lose the ultimate aim of his career, the preacher, with God's assistance, will strive throughout his life to embody the Christian model of the Roman *vir bonus dicendi peritus*.[124]

* * * * *

an anxious obedience to teachers' rules.' Hoffmann notes, 'It is clear that Erasmus freed himself from the rigid structure and strict terminology of rhetorical theory to pursue his theological intention' (*Rhetoric* 172).

121 Quintilian 3.3.12: 'The orator's task is to speak well, but rhetoric is the science of speaking well' ('Nam bene dicere est oratoris, rhetorice tamen erit bene dicendi scientia; vel, ut alii putant, artificis est persuadere, vis autem persuadendi artis').

122 See O'Malley 'Grammar' 81, 97–8; and 'Sacred Rhetoric' 21. For Erasmus' preference for written language over spoken language, see Hoffmann *Rhetoric* 79–80: 'According to J. Chomarat, he [Erasmus] gave the spoken word priority over the written word. And yet: "Erasme est l'homme des livres, en tous les sens: bibliothèques, écritoire, atelier de l'imprimeur." The humanist could not have been unaffected by what Cicero had said: "The pen is the best and most eminent author and teacher of eloquence, and rightly so." It is therefore plausible to assume that, despite his conventional appreciation for oration as such, Erasmus assigned to literature a higher value. He interpreted texts exclusively and showed no interest in delivering his work in public oratory.'

123 See *De copia* CWE 24 284; book 2 CWE 68 483; cf Pliny *Letters* 3.5.5.

124 For this theme, see Lausberg §§32, 1151. Quintilian gives a brief summary of this in 12.5.1: 'not merely of the art ... but of the orator himself. These are the weapons that he should have ready to his hand, this the knowledge with which he must be equipped, while it must be supplemented by a ready store of words and figures, power of imagination, skill in arrangement, retentiveness of memory and grace of delivery. But of all these qualities the highest is that loftiness of soul (*animi praestantia*) ...'

And although some humanist-trained clerics, especially in Italy, had already embraced classical rhetorical methods and classicizing techniques for sacred orations,[125] Erasmus' programme to transform the ancient Roman ideal of the perfect orator into the ideal Christian *ecclesiastes* (*orator christianus*) was his own creation, and one that would flourish over the next decades as a cultural model promoted by Catholic (above all Jesuit) and many Protestant teachers of rhetoric and authors of ecclesiastical rhetorics.[126] In Roman Catholicism, this ideal would be epitomized by the 'right-thinking' (orthodox) clergyman, above all the bishop, aflame with zeal, who combining Christian piety with eloquence and theological acumen fed his flock daily with the food of the gospel; the ideal would come to define Catholic clerical culture throughout the post-Tridentine era, 'the age of eloquence,' to use Marc Fumaroli's term.[127]

Before the publication of *Ecclesiastes* in 1535, clergy could find homiletic models and develop preaching techniques by turning to the many handbooks for preachers known throughout the Middle Ages as the 'arts of preaching' (*artes praedicandi*), which became widespread after the year 1200.[128]

* * * * *

125 See O'Malley *Praise and Blame* 36–122; John M. McManamon *Funeral Oratory and the Cultural Ideals of Italian Humanism* (Chapel Hill and London 1989) passim.
126 See McGinness *Right Thinking* 9–28.
127 Fumaroli. The author devotes only a few pages to Erasmus' *Ecclesiastes* (106–10) but calls attention to its later significance: 'Ce livre est le point de départ du long cheminement qui aboutira à l'éloquence sacrée "classique" en France' (109); 'L'*Ecclesiastes* d'Erasme nous apparaît comme la plus savante somme d'art oratoire de la Renaissance, le grand traité d'expressionnisme chrétien' (108); 'L'œuvre d'Erasme domine l'histoire de la rhétorique humaniste' (110). Following Charles Béné he refers to it 'avant tout comme une immense glose du *De Doctrina Christiana*' (106).
128 Unfortunately there is little room to list the many excellent studies on the *artes praedicandi*. Essential are: Th.-M. Charland, O.P. *Artes praedicandi: contribution à l'histoire de la rhétorique au moyen age* Publications de l'Institut d'Études Médiévales d'Ottawa VII (Paris and Ottawa 1936); Hervé Martin *Le métier de prédicateur en France septentrionale à la fin du moyen age (1350–1520)* (Paris 1988); Marianne G. Briscoe *Artes praedicandi* and Barbara H. Jaye *Artes Orandi* (Turnhout 1992); Murphy chapter VI: '*Ars praedicandi*: The Art of Preaching' in *Rhetoric* 269–355, especially 310–12; *Three Medieval Rhetorical Arts* ed idem, trans Leopold Krul (Berkeley and Los Angeles 1971); see now the useful publication, *Medieval Sermon Studies* International Medieval Sermon Studies Society (Leeds 1991–   ); Caplan; idem *Mediaeval Artes Praedicandi: A Hand-list* (Ithaca 1934); Gilson 'Michel Menot'; and idem *Sermons choisis de Michel Menot (1508–1518)* ed Joseph Nève (Paris 1924). For continuities between Erasmus and the tradition of *artes praedicandi*, see especially Kilcoyne and Jennings. See also Emile V. Telle ' "To every thing there is a season ...": Ways and Fashions in

At the same time many sermons of the mendicants and other clergy became widely available in manuscript, and later in printed editions, as examples of notable sacred discourse. Significantly, Erasmus neither refers to the *artes* in general nor makes mention of them in particular, nor does he recommend the sermons of his contemporaries, though we know of more than two hundred *artes* produced in the three hundred fifty years before 1500, many of which were in circulation, and we know of numerous published sermon collections that would surely have been available to him.[129]

The type of preaching prescribed by the *artes* is commonly called the thematic sermon because the preacher usually began his sermon by presenting a 'theme' (*thema*),[130] often a short passage – a verse or two – of Sacred Scripture, sometimes following this with a proposition, which he might divide into two or three parts to announce the principal parts of his discourse. Before proposing the theme, the preacher might also offer a 'protheme' (or 'antetheme') as a way to gain the audience's good will; this too might consist of a biblical passage, to which he sometimes added a short prayer for divine assistance. After these introductory elements he delivered an exordium, which he would follow up with a division (*divisio*) announcing the points he planned to cover; this in turn took him into the divisions and subdivisions of the narrative based upon the theme stated at the outset, each of which might consist of a central argument which, in log-

* * * * *

the Art of Preaching on the Eve of the Religious Upheaval in the Sixteenth Century"' ERSY 2 (1982) 13–24. For practical works for preachers on encouraging the laity to engender virtues and extirpate vices, see eg Thomas de Chobham *Summa de commendatione virtutum et extirpatione vitiorum* ed Franco Morenzoni (Turnhout 1997); and Alan of Lille.

129 See Murphy *Incunabula* (Units 22 and 23 Rhetoric, and Units 31, 23, 33, 73 Sermons), which contains printed treatises on preaching (*ars praedicandi*). Murphy notes: 'In a Christian society, especially one with a 350-year tradition of *artes praedicandi* that produced more than 200 separate medieval preaching manuals, one might expect that the revived European interest in classical rhetoric in the fifteenth century would have produced an immediate application to preaching. But this was not the case. In fact there were only two original works on preaching printed in this period (ie before 1500), and only five medieval treatises plus the fifth-century *De doctrina christiana* of St Augustine. The great age of Renaissance preaching theory was to be the latter part of the following century.' See also idem *Rhetoric* 275–6.

130 One recalls Chaucer's Pardoner telling his fellow pilgrims that when he preaches 'My theme is alwey oon, and evere was – Radix malorum est Cupiditas ...' (*Canterbury Tales* 'Pardoner's Prologue' lines 333–4) and then proceeds to describe his sermon's contents.

ical arrangement, he expanded by adding proofs or demonstrations from Scripture, authorities, reasons, discussions, questions, minor arguments, examples, analogies, or allegories. After completing the narrative he ended the sermon, often rather quickly, though sometimes he might include a conclusion (*peroratio, conclusio, epilogus*), which like the sermon's beginning also consisted of a prayer. The type of sermon following more or less this format also came to be referred to as a 'scholastic sermon' or 'university-style sermon' because its principles of organization were suggestive of the methods the scholastics used when expounding theological questions.[131] As Erasmus notes, these sermons, might sometimes vary with the addition of a silent prayer, the sign of the cross, an invocation of the Trinity,[132] a fuller statement of the theme or protheme, a brief discourse on the divisions, extended distinctions, formulized closings, and doxology ('Who live and reign, etc.').[133] The length of the thematic sermons could be brief or extended for hours, depending on the circumstances and the disposition of the preacher. Ideally this type of discourse had much to commend it; it was flexible, structurally clear, generally scriptural, and could be used to great effect depending on the preacher's talents.[134] Not surprisingly, perhaps, Erasmus' preferences in constructing examples of sermons in *Ecclesiastes* follow this format, though without rigidity, abstruseness, or the arid excesses of the scholastic preachers whom he was wont to lambaste, as we see below.

We know of many renowned preachers of the Middle Ages who preached according to the thematic format. Erasmus commends Bernard of Clair-

* * * * *

131 See Murphy *Rhetoric* 311; see also 325–6, where he suspects that this type of sermon might not have arisen in the milieu of a thirteenth-century university. See *Ecclesiastes* book 3 CWE 68 733: 'The addition of a question seems to have arisen from the ostentation of the scholastics ...'

132 See Erasmus' example of invoking the Trinity in his *De immensa Dei misericordia* CWE 70 77. See also his comment on the practice in his letter to Noël Béda, Ep 1581:149.

133 Book 2 CWE 68 554. The concluding doxology takes different forms, depending on which person of the Trinity is being addressed; if eg the Son is being addressed, the short form is *Qui vivis et regnas per omnia saecula saeculorum*; the long form *Qui vivis et regnas cum deo patre in unitate spiritus sancti deus per omnia saecula saeculorum*.

134 See Caplan 94: 'But while acknowledging the pedantry and concentrated formalism, we can find much to praise in the methodical ordering of the thematic sermon ... we can find much to laud, too, in the inventional scheme, and in the dexterity and practical variety of treatment, and can appreciate that the theory served its day well.'

vaux (1090–1153) for his skill in preaching,[135] and many of Bernard's sermons fall in line with the above schema of the thematic sermon, though with none of the obsessive divisions, distinctions, authorities, and subtleties that would characterize the sermons of many later scholastic theologians.[136] Apart from some negative general comments about the more novel elements, Erasmus does not call for an end to the thematic sermon; in fact most of his precepts are fully compatible with the format employed by various *artes praedicandi*, but he notes that such elaborately structured modern sermons have 'retreated from ancient precedents,'[137] and he appeals for a return to those simpler, more effective examples of sacred oratory of the church Fathers who offered a better way to preach and to move hearts.

The *artes praedicandi* in general sought to continue the preaching tradition of the church Fathers by providing instruction in the way Origen, Basil, John Chrysostom, Augustine, Gregory the Great, and other saintly bishops and clergy carried out the ministry of the word. Though aware that some early Christian writers were wary about using the classical authors because of their paganism, writers of the medieval *artes* did not reject the writings of the ancient grammarians and rhetoricians but rather drew lessons and

* * * * *

135 Book 2 494–5. See Bernard of Clairvaux *Sermones de tempore et de sanctis et de diversis* (Speyer: Peter Drach, between 1481–2); for his sermons, see Jean Leclercq 'Introduction to Saint Bernard's Sermons *De diversis*' *Cistercian Studies Quarterly* 42 1 (2007) 37–62.

136 See Robert of Basevorn's comment on Bernard in Murphy *Rhetoric* 345: 'The method of Saint Bernard is without method, exceeding the style and capability of almost all men of genius. He more than all the rest stresses Scripture in all his sayings, so that scarcely one statement is his own which does not depend upon an authority in the Bible or on a multitude of authorities. His procedure is always devout, always artful. He takes a certain theme or something in place of it and begins it artfully, divides it into two, three, or many members, confirms it and ends it, using every rhetorical color so that the whole shines with a double glow, earthly and heavenly; and this, it seems to me, invites to devotion those who understand more feelingly, and helps more in the novel methods which we are now discussing. No one has so effectively joined the two at the same time.' Erasmus notes however that Bernard's sermons are directed to a monastic audience, and for this reason are not as suited to those preaching to a mixed group of the laity (see book 2 CWE 68 495). Bernard regularly addresses his audience with *vobis, fratres,* or *charissimi,* referring to his monastic brethren; and his use of Scripture is often applied tropologically to living the monastic life. See eg *Sermones de diversis*.

137 Book 3 CWE 68 730

inspiration from them.[138] The *artes* ran a long course from the late twelfth century to Erasmus' day, and over the years their preceptive material tended to grow in technical complexity to accommodate the intricacies of theological subjects whether for discoursing on the Creed, Our Father, Ten Commandments, the vices and virtues, the Virgin Mary, the angels, and the saints, or for admonishing one's monastic community to fraternal charity, or urging Christians to crusade. To Erasmus these recent sermons fell short of the standards of excellent preaching that characterized the simpler sermons of the church Fathers, which extracted from the Scriptures lessons and inspiration for godly living. Sermons delivered at the medieval universities by doctors of theology, we know, could often sound more like disputations or lectures in theology than discourses on basic doctrines and exhortations to move souls to the love of God and dissuade from sin. Erasmus saw many preachers of these thematic sermons as incapable of giving a good sermon, unaware of their audience, and often rambling on without a point. His purpose now would be to show in a new key how effective communication should be done in the sacred ministry of the word.

It is not clear how many of the *artes praedicandi* Erasmus read, if any at all, as he never tells us, nor does he even mention the *genre*. With his penchant for reading good letters (*bonae litterae*), we might surmise he never found a preaching manual to recommend to others, though it is highly probable that he looked at some, if not many, available to him, and that he would find a goodly number of their precepts compatible with his own. It is also likely Erasmus approached writing *Ecclesiastes* as he did most everything else, by beginning in a fresh way, first going back to the sources (*ad fontes*) where preaching took its start – in the Sacred Scriptures – and examining the words of Christ and his apostles and those who came right after their time, such as Origen and the other church Fathers, to understand how they preached; it meant as well examining the best books on effective speaking, which of course were not the *artes* but the writings of Quintilian, Cicero, and other classical authors who had studied thoroughly the 'science of speaking' and instructed others in public discourse. It also meant examining the key works of later Christian authors who had given advice on preaching, such as Gregory of Nazianzus, Ambrose, and especially Augustine, whose *De doctrina christiana* greatly influences *Ecclesiastes*.[139] Though

* * * * *

138 See eg Caplan 85–6.
139 Béné *Érasme* 378–80. See book 3 CWE 68 972, where Erasmus especially commends Augustine as 'that most vigilant doctor of the Church' who 'has much to teach us in *On Christian Teaching*.' For Erasmus' lifelong involvement with

Erasmus maintains that Augustine's exposition needed to be done 'more simply and more plainly,'[140] his debt to the bishop of Hippo's treatise was considerable and went back many years. Charles Béné draws attention to Erasmus' involvement with the *De doctrina christiana* since 1497 as well as to the legion of borrowings from it he does not reference;[141] Marc Fumaroli concurs with Béné in seeing *Ecclesiastes* 'as an immense gloss on *De doctrina christiana*.'[142] Still, Augustine was not the only Father of the church to whom Erasmus owed so much for help on preaching; Origen, John Chrysostom, Basil, Gregory of Nazianzus, and Jerome also stand out prominently for their guidance, precepts, and inspiration for his treatise. And these Latin and Greek Fathers were themselves profoundly influenced by the type of educational programme espoused by Cicero, Quintilian, and other masters of Roman and Greek rhetoric.[143]

To Erasmus the thematic sermon was the customary, acceptable form for preaching as long as it was done 'purely and simply.' But he is quick to point out how dreadfully the scholastics had complicated the form with

* * * * *

Augustine and the church Fathers in general, see Jan den Boeft 'Erasmus and the Church Fathers' in *The Reception of the Church Fathers in the West from the Carolingians to the Maurists* ed Irena Backus, 2 vols (Leiden 1997) II 537–72; and John C. Olin *Six Essays on Erasmus and a Translation of Erasmus' Letter to Carondelet, 1523* (New York 1979). See also Grünwald 21–4 and 194–214 for commonalities and differences between *Ecclesiastes* and *De doctrina christiana*.

140 Book 2 CWE 68 496: 'The direction of my discourse requires that we sample some of the rhetoricians' precepts that seem appropriate to the preacher's office, something which St Augustine before us attempted in part in his work *De doctrina christiana*. Even if he had omitted nothing, nevertheless the very different nature of the times demands that some things be imparted more simply and more plainly.' For Erasmus' sometimes critical view of Augustine, see Tracy (1) 71–3. Note that Erasmus somewhat misrepresents Augustine's purpose; see *De doctrina christiana* 4.1.2: '... I must thwart the expectation of those readers who think that I shall give the rules of rhetoric here which I learned and taught in the secular schools. And I admonish them not to expect such rules from me, not that they have no utility, but because, if they have any, it should be sought elsewhere if perhaps some good man has the opportunity to learn them. But he should not expect these rules from me, either in this work or in any other.'

141 Béné *Érasme* 378–80

142 Fumaroli 106

143 See Murphy *Rhetoric* 21–3 and 21 n45: 'For example, Ambrose, Jerome, Augustine, Gregory of Caesarea [Nyssa (?)], Eusebius of Caesarea, John of Antioch (Chrysostom), and Basil of Caesarea. The influence of Roman education upon the medieval discourse modeled on these Fathers is surely incalculable.'

their many tedious and irrelevant accretions, such as their preference for
introducing a 'question' in sermons, which he suggests ought to be cur-
tailed or eliminated.[144] Noteworthy is his satire of the scholastics' sermons
in *Moria*, where Folly 'commends' contemporary preachers (mendicants),
wryly noting, 'It's absurd but highly enjoyable to see them observe the traditional rules of rhetoric.'[145] She does not attack their rote instruction in
oratorical rhetoric but pillories their complete misuse of it before a congregation where they fail to perform appropriately, whether in their gestures,
voice, exclamations, use of invocations, exordia or preambles or exposition.
These preachers introduce subtleties, novelties, irrelevant topics, displays
of theological arrogance, and 'let fly at the ignorant crowd their syllogisms,
major and minor, conclusions, corollaries, idiotic hypotheses, and further
scholastic rubbish.'[146] They 'trot out some foolish popular anecdote, from
the *Mirror of History*, I expect, or the *Deeds of the Romans*,[147] and proceed to
interpret it allegorically, tropologically, and anagogically. In this way they
complete their chimaera, a monstrosity which even Horace never dreamt of
when he wrote "Add to the human head" and so on.'[148] Erasmus does not
upbraid mendicant preachers for what (little) they learned from the grammarians or rhetoricians, but for how wretchedly they appropriated it, often
following the prescriptions of the rhetoricians so literally that Folly must
ask, 'Is there a comedian or cheapjack you'd rather watch than them when
they hold forth in their sermons?'[149] None of the preachers have words to
say on the Lord's Prayer, the Ten Commandments, the Apostles' Creed,
inculcating virtues, and shunning vice – the central topics at the heart of
the medieval preaching tradition.[150] If they appropriate classical rhetorical

* * * * *

144 See eg book 2 CWE 68 539–40.
145 *Moria* CWE 27 132
146 *Moria* CWE 27 134; see also *Ratio* 301.
147 For *Gesta Romanorum* (*Deeds of the Romans*), see book 2 CWE 68 544 n400. See
    Robert T. Lambdin 'Gesta Romanorum' in *Encyclopedia of Medieval Literature* ed
    Robert Thomas Lambdin and Laura Cooner Lambdin (Westport 2000); and
    Lynn M. Zott 'Gesta Romanorum' *Classical and Medieval Literature Criticism* 55
    (2003) 74–155.
148 Horace *Ars poetica* 1–5
149 *Moria* CWE 27 132
150 See Wenzel 'Preaching' 163: 'From roughly the Fourth Lateran Council on,
    priests were officially required and exhorted to preach the seven deadly sins
    together with other catechetical set pieces: the Creed, the Ten Commandments,
    the Lord's Prayer, and more.' See also his 'Vices, Virtues, and Popular Prea-
    ching,' in *Medieval and Renaissance Studies: Proceedings of the Southeastern In-
    stitute of Medieval and Renaissance Studies* Summer, 1974, ed Dale B.J. Randall
    (Durham, NC 1976) 28–54, especially 28–30 and notes on 51.

instruction for sacred eloquence, they should also learn how to handle those religious teachings of the church that every Christian needs to know for salvation.

As fundamental as speaking correctly is, *Ecclesiastes* puts before all else the requirement of godliness (*pietas*) in the preacher and defines the duties of the preacher within the Pauline categories of teaching, exhorting, rebuking, and consoling (cf 2 Tim 3:16–17 and 4:2), which Erasmus situates within the three classical 'types of speaking' (*genera dicendi*), particularly within the deliberative type (*genus deliberativum* or *suasorium*). It is here, Erasmus argues, 'the preacher is especially occupied.'[151] This adaptation of the classical *genera* to the explicitly Pauline duties of the preacher decisively breaks from the *artes praedicandi* tradition and marks the beginning of a new *genre* of preaching manuals, the ecclesiastical rhetorics,[152] which will appear widely after the Council of Trent (1545–63). Like *Ecclesiastes* these new ecclesiastical rhetorics place preaching intentionally within the *genera* of classical oratory (judicial, deliberative, demonstrative) and adapt their rhetorical precepts to speaking God's word. The significance of *Ecclesiastes* in creating this new direction in preaching is well summed up by John O'Malley, who observes that after the publication of *Ecclesiastes* the genre of the *artes praedicandi* disappears.[153]

As groundbreaking as *Ecclesiastes* was, applying the principles of classical rhetoric to preaching and epideictic orations at this time was not original with Erasmus. Besides the Fathers of the church, clergy trained in the *studia humanitatis* had already begun to accommodate classical rhetoric to sermons, panegyrics of saints, funeral orations, etc.[154] Erasmus might have been familiar with the sermons of some of the Italian preachers that John O'Malley analyzes in his study of sacred oratory at the papal court (c 1450–1521).[155] Many of these men adapted the classical *genus demonstrativum* ('the art of praise and blame') to discourse on God's marvellous benefits to humankind, the wonders of his creation, salvific deeds, angels, saints, and

* * * * *

151 Book 2 CWE 68 500
152 See O'Malley 'Content' and McGinness *Right Thinking* 49–61.
153 O'Malley 'Sacred Rhetoric' 13; see also Murphy *Incunabula* 15.
154 See John M. McManamon 'The Ideal Renaissance Pope: Funeral Oratory from the Papal Court' *Archivum Historiae Pontificiae* 14 (1976) 9–70; idem 'Innovation in Early Humanist Rhetoric: The Oratory of Pier Paolo Vergerio (the Elder)' *Rinascimento* n s 22 (1982) 3–32; and idem 'Pier Paolo Vergerio (the Elder) and the Beginnings of the Humanist Cult of Jerome' *Catholic Historical Review* 71 (1985) 353–71.
155 See also O'Malley 'Content.'

the mysteries of Christ's life. While at Cambridge, Erasmus might very well have looked into the Franciscan Lorenzo Guglielmo Traversagni's *Margarita eloquentiae* or *Rhetorica nova*, 'the first rhetorical text printed in England,'[156] which, among other things, situates preaching primarily in the *genus demonstrativum*; and he certainly must have seen Johann Reuchlin's brief treatise, *Liber congestorum de arte praedicandi* (1504),[157] which enumerated and defined the basic elements of classical rhetoric and demonstrated their place in preaching. It is very likely too that he was acquainted with the works of Reuchlin's grand nephew and pupil, Philippus Melanchthon, who beginning in 1519 followed up on Reuchlin's work with a flurry of his own works on preaching, which use the terms *concio* for the sermon and *concionator* for the preacher long before the appearance of Erasmus' treatise. Melanchthon's *De rhetorica libri tres* (later *Elementa rhetorices*) was published at Wittenberg and at Basel with Froben in 1519, and it too, like Reuchlin's work, addressed the matter of sacred oratory.[158] In 1521

* * * * *

156 Lorenzo Guglielmo Traversagni of Savona taught rhetoric at the University of Cambridge in the 1470s and 1480s, lecturing on the *Rhetorica ad Herennium*; his *Margarita eloquentiae* or *Rhetorica nova* was published by William Caxton during this time as a '"textbook" in the sense that each student was provided with a copy.' See Murphy *Incunabula* 15. See also O'Malley *Praise and Blame* 43–51; and idem 'Sacred Rhetoric' 6–7. Traversagni later published an abbreviated version of this work, which can be found translated and edited by Ronald H. Martin: *The* Epitoma Margarite Castigate Eloquentie *of Laurentius Gulielmus Traversagni de Saona* (Leeds 1986).

157 Pforzheim: Thomas Anshelm 1504. See O'Malley 'Content' and Lawrence D. Green 'Classical and Medieval Rhetorical Traditions in Traversagni's *Margarita Eloquentiae' Quarterly Journal of Speech* 72 (1986) 185–96. According to Green, Traversagni bases his treatment on the *Ad Herennium* ('a reworking of the *Ad Herennium* from an ecclesiatical point of view' 189) and Cicero's *De inventione*, not on Quintilian; and though Green does not discuss Erasmus' *Ecclesiastes*, he highlights a number of ideas in Traversagni's work and approach that also appear in Erasmus' treatment, such as the 'false dilemma,' the use of examples, deliberative and demonstrative oratory ('the only two *genera* which interest Traversagni' [188]), tropes, scholastics' mistakes in speaking (eg on division [190]), etc.

158 Even before Melanchthon the term *concionare* had been used for preaching; see the Franciscan handbook for preaching, erroneously ascribed to St Bonaventure, *Ars concionandi*, in *Opera omnia* Suppl. III (Trent: J.B. Monauni 1774) 385–417. Interestingly, the *Ars concionandi* borrows heavily from Cicero and Augustine (eg *De doctrina christiana* 4), which we discuss below. See Melanchthon's *De rhetorica libri tres* (Wittenberg: J. Grunenberg 1519) and (Basel: Johann Froben 1519). On 103–7 of the Froben edition he goes into the application of rhetoric to the matter of preaching (*De sacris concionibus*). Melanchthon followed this work up with

Melanchthon also published a treatise on theological commonplaces (*Loci communes theologici*,[159] which similarly positioned preaching squarely within the framework of classical rhetorical theory, though modifying the *genera* to fit the tasks he saw as essential to preaching. Melanchthon identified the preacher's primary duty as teaching, for which he invented the *genus didascalicum* (the genre for teaching),[160] a modification of the *ars recte docendi*, and the genre for teaching dialectics (*genus dialecticum*); he thought it crucial too that in teaching the preacher should move the affections.[161] To this Melanchthon added two other genres, the *epitrepticum* 'exhortation to believe' and the *paraeneticum* 'which urges moral reform,' both modifications of the classical *genus suasorium* (*deliberativum*) and all reflective of the *genera* given by St Paul.[162] Melanchthon's treatises find striking similarities in Erasmus' own method of fitting the classical *genera* to the specific tasks of the preacher as spelled out by St Paul in his Letter to the Romans and 2 Timothy (3:16–17 and 4:2), as we discuss below. As Erasmus' familiarity with Melanchthon's works suggests some debt to the

* * * * *

other treatises focused on preaching. For a complete list of Melanchthon's works on homiletics and modern editions of his works, see Uwe Schnell *Die homiletische Theorie Philipp Melanchthons* (Berlin and Hamburg 1968) 177–8, and 54–7 for background and analysis of Melanchthon's homiletic works and method. See also Mack *Renaissance Rhetoric* 104–22.

159 This treatise went into a second edition in 1535, a third edition in 1543, and a German edition in 1555. On Melanchthon's presentation of commonplaces, see Quirinus Breen 'The Terms "Loci Communes" and "Loci" in Melanchthon' *Church History* 16:4 (1947) 197–209; see too Lee A. Sonnino *A Handbook to Sixteenth-Century Rhetoric* (New York 1968); Sister Joan Marie Lechner *Renaissance Concepts of the Commonplaces: An Historical Investigation of the General and Universal Ideas Used in All Argumentation and Persuasion with Special Emphasis on the Educational and Literary Tradition of the Sixteenth and Seventeenth Centuries* (New York 1962). For Erasmus' knowledge of this work by Melanchthon and his final communications with Melanchthon, see Wengert. Wengert's article analyzes Melanchthon's subtle and cutting criticisms of Erasmus' *Ratio* and other writings.

160 See Schnell 39–44.

161 Schnell 87: 'Die Belehrung und die Bewirkung der Affekte sint nicht voneinander zu trennen. Sonst ist die Predigt fruchtlos und ohne geistlichen Nutzen für den Hörer.'

162 *De officiis concionatoris* (1529): 'Ex officiis concionatoris facile quod sint genera concionum colligi potest. Sunt enim haec tria, Didacticum, Epitrepticum, quod ad credendum: Paraeneticum, quod ad mores hortatur. Bona pars concionatorum solum hoc postremum genus tractat, quod qui sine fidei cognitione prosequuntur, tantum philosophantur, non tradunt Christi doctrinam . . .'

Reformer,[163] we might likewise assume that Melanchthon owed a sizeable debt to Erasmus as well.

In addition to theoretical works on classical and Christian discourse, Erasmus draws upon a wealth of personal experience of good and bad preaching, as his years of study and close observation allowed him to articulate what was in fact true sacred eloquence. His acquaintance with prelates and preachers throughout Europe, from his home monastery in Steyn to Utrecht, Paris, Rome, Canterbury, Oxford, Cambridge, Saint Omer, and elsewhere, furnished him with abundant memories of the good and poor preaching he had personally witnessed or heard about from others.[164] His familiarity with the ancient Greek and Latin poets, rhetoricians, and orators, above all Quintilian, Cicero, the author of the *Rhetorica ad Herennium*, and especially, with the biblical sources, the Greek church Fathers of the first centuries – Origen, Basil, John Chrysostom, Gregory of Nazianzus – enabled him to judge the merits of public religious discourse. The ancients Erasmus regarded as unsurpassed: 'Those ancient masters,' Erasmus noted to Jacques Masson (Jacobus Latomus), 'like Cyprian, Ambrose, Augustine, Victorinus, and Jerome were all products of the rhetorical schools, not the philosophical academies of the Stoa or the Lycaeum.'[165] And there were outstanding preachers of his own time, whom Erasmus knew personally and held in the highest regard – Jean Vitrier, John Colet, John Fisher, William Warham, Henry Bullock, to name but a few.

Erasmus' reflections on the preaching he witnessed personally run throughout *Ecclesiastes*. He will refer to preachers who made a lasting im-

* * * * *

163 See Schnell 16–17; see also Grünwald 51–4 and Wengert 18 and passim. On the other hand Erasmus alludes to 2 Tim 3:16–17, 4:2 in *Ratio* 280: 'Quod si quis sibi permittit in his ludere nonnunquam, huic plus erit veniae in exhortando, in consolando, in reprehendendo quam in asserenda veritate.'

164 See eg book 3 CWE 68 950: 'What I shall report now I have neither read nor seen myself but learned from a thoroughly serious man who heard it in person. The location will be suppressed so as not to offend anyone too fastidious.' For Erasmus' esteem of one's qualifications to preach, see also letter to Wolfgang Faber Capito, Ep 541. See of course Erasmus' biting words about the English Franciscan Henry Standish, 'one of those who preach in public,' in his annotations on letter 6 (Jerome to Paulinus) *Vita Hieronymi* CWE 61 218–9.

165 *Apologia contra Latomi dialogum* CWE 71 81. For Erasmus' view of the mischief Latomus (and Edward Lee) caused him, see his letter to Philippus Melanchthon (before 21 June 1520), Ep 1113. See also Marcel Gielis 'Leuven Theologians as Opponents of Erasmus and of Humanistic Theology' in *Biblical Humanism* 197–214, especially 202–3; Tracy (1) 834. See also *Vita Hieronymi* CWE 61 26 and 41–2 where Erasmus notes that Jerome refers to Gregory of Nazianzus as 'his teacher.'

pression on him, for better or worse. 'As a boy I heard a certain Dominican, endowed with an outstanding native grace of speech ...'[166] 'I have heard some preachers who were already so close to obvious delirium that they were abandoned by their congregation in derision.'[167] 'I myself have heard someone who used the same exordium to preach everyday throughout the whole of Lent.'[168] '[A preacher] used a similar fiction to lay the final judgment before their eyes, for he was endowed with a certain natural eloquence. I listened to these things with a certain pleasure, but as a child.'[169] Other incidents he passes on as reports from trustworthy witnesses: 'What I shall report now I have neither read nor seen myself but learned from a thoroughly serious man who heard it in person.'[170] Erasmus gives us the sense of having been attentive to every word he heard preached, being always the critical listener as he was the writer.

In general Erasmus has little good to say about the generations of preachers after the age of Augustine. Nevertheless he admired some contemporaries, though omitting their names. We know however of one important model preacher, his friend Jean Vitrier, a Franciscan whose exemplary morality as a monk and excellence in preaching commanded Erasmus' esteem. Erasmus alludes to him in *Ecclesiastes*, and we know of him from Erasmus' edifying profile of the man in his letter to Justus Jonas (13 June 1521), written about the time he began to jot down ideas for *Ecclesiastes*. Of Vitrier he writes that 'every sentence he produced was full of Scripture, nor could he utter anything else. His heart was in what he said. He was absorbed by a kind of incredible passion for bringing men to the true philosophy of Christ, and from labours of this sort he hoped to win the glory of martyrdom.'[171] We have in fact evidence that Vitrier was the inspiration for Erasmus' comments in book 3 of *Ecclesiastes*, for in the second and third editions of the work his name appears in the index in reference to this passage.[172] Doubt-

* * * * *

166 See book 2 CWE 68 508.
167 Book 1 282
168 See book 2 CWE 68 510; cf *Ratio* 282: 'I heard a certain Paris theologian who dragged out for forty days [*quadraginta*] the parable of the prodigal son so he could square it with the number of Lent [*quadragesimae numerum*] ...'
169 Book 3 CWE 68 862; cf *In psalmum 38* CWE 65 30–1.
170 Book 3 CWE 68 950
171 Letter to Justus Jonas (Anderlecht, 13 June 1521), Ep 1211:227
172 Chomarat believes that this 'someone of the same order' is the Franciscan Jean Vitrier (c 1456–before 15 June 1521); see ASD V-5 97 879n; see also Ep 1211:228. See especially Godin *Spiritualité*; CEBR III 408–9. Notably, this is the only instance in *Ecclesiastes* where Erasmus commends a Franciscan preacher.

less many other preachers Erasmus admired gave form to his work, though unfortunately they too remain anonymous.

Erasmus must have pondered often how a few individuals could preach so well while others failed miserably. How was it Jean Vitrier could speak 'as it were a continuous flow of language to connect the Epistle with the Gospel, so that his hearers went home not only better informed, but kindled with a new desire for a pious life'?[173] Erasmus admired the eloquence of certain Fathers of the church: What accounted for this? The question we might imagine had been begging an answer since his earliest years, and his experience of hearing many preachers – excellent and not – must have prodded him to inquire how one excelled in this most arduous of tasks, and how it was the Holy Spirit seemed to grace so few with true eloquence. Erasmus probes this question by considering the earthly ministry of 'the 'highest *concionator*,' Christ, whose divine nature and public life imparted to us a knowledge of God's expectations for future preachers, the nature of true eloquence, the theology of perfect communication, and the daunting training and personal holiness required to pursue this vocation worthily.

Ecclesiastes' theology of the word envisions Christ as mysteriously at work in the preacher's activity. Though the treatise does not advance deeply into the mechanics of how this happens, it places Christ as immediately – really, spiritually – present to all in the words and deeds of his human instrument, through whom he daily becomes reincarnated as the living word in God's ever continuing conversation (*sermo*) with humanity. In speaking God's word, the preacher is assisted by the Holy Spirit[174] as it was of old when God's Spirit mysteriously guided the words of the prophets and

* * * * *

For Erasmus' profile of Jean Vitrier, see Ep 1211:1–273. Vitrier's name appears in the index of the edition of *Ecclesiastes* published by H. Froben and N. Episcopius (August 1536), which would confirm Erasmus' attribution of these words to Vitrier. See also Kleinhans 153 n6 and Appendix B (165–7).

173 Letter to Justus Jonas (Anderlecht, 13 June 1521), Ep 1211:65–7. Cf Cicero *De oratore* 1.2–6.

174 Thomas Aquinas *Summa theologiae* IIa IIae q 177 a 1: 'Now the knowledge a man receives from God cannot be turned to another's profit, except by means of speech. And since the Holy Ghost does not fail in anything that pertains to the profit of the church, he provides also the members of the church with speech; to the effect that a man not only speaks so as to be understood by different people, which pertains to the gift of tongues, but also speaks with effect, and this pertains to the grace 'of the word.'' See *Summa theologiae* IIa IIae q 177 a 1 where he takes up prophecy under the general consideration of gratuitous graces.

apostles.[175] How this actually comes about Erasmus explains by saying that 'the person who is speaking is a man like you; but God is speaking to you through his mouth, and he is speaking God's words, not his own.'[176] Erasmus' statements beg clarification, but they consistently get at the idea formulated by Thomas Aquinas that 'the Holy Spirit makes use of the human tongue as an instrument, but it is he who perfects the work within us.'[177] Erasmus amplifies this by affirming that 'the tongue of the orator can be effective only if Christ's spirit inhabits his heart, moves the plectrum of his mouth, and imparts mystical force to the words that flow forth. The voice of the orator can strike the ears of his audience, but it is God alone who transforms their minds with secret inspiration.'[178] Nonetheless, even with a preacher's superhuman efforts there is no divine guarantee of spiritual change in hearers, for to each hearer is given the freedom to receive or reject God's word.[179] Though *Ecclesiastes* bypasses the question of the role of free will, we might well assume that Erasmus' thinking on this issue falls in line with his position in *De libero arbitrio* (1524), *Hyperaspistes* 1 (1526) and 2 (1527) that free will is somehow present in the listener and 'God does not withhold his grace from those doing what they can';[180] but at this moment in his life, revisiting this disputed question was

* * * * *

175 For the idea of 'inspiration' in biblical and patristic thought, see eg the article by Richard F. Smith 'Inspiration and Inerrancy' JBC II 499–514. For inspiration in the *artes praedicandi*, see Franco Morenzoni 'Parole du prédicateur et inspiration divine d'après les *artes praedicandi*' in *Parole du prédicateur* I 271–90.
176 Book 1 441
177 *Summa theologiae* IIa IIae q 177 a 1
178 Book 1 259; cf Rom 10:17 and Acts 20:32; *Paraphrasis in Acta* CWE 50 125; see especially *De concordia* CWE 65 152.
179 Erasmus does not explicitly take up the role of grace and human cooperation in *Ecclesiastes*, but one finds his thinking on this in his controversy with Luther; see *De libero arbitrio* (1524) CWE 76, and *Hyperaspistes* 1 (1526), and *Hyperaspistes* 2 (1527) CWE 76–7. Erasmus opened up the debate by responding to Article 36 of Luther's *Assertion of All the Articles of Martin Luther Which Were Quite Recently Condemned by a Bull of Leo X* (after 10 December 1520). Article 36 is found in CWE 76 301–9. In December 1525, Luther replied to Erasmus' first work with *The Enslaved Will* (*De servo arbitrio*), to which Erasmus responded with *Hyperaspistes* 1 & 2. See CWE 76 and 77, and Charles Trinkaus' introduction to these works in CWE 76 xi–cvi. See also Marjorie O'Rourke Boyle 'Erasmus and the "Modern" Question: Was He Semi-Pelagian?' *Archiv für Reformationsgeschichte* 75 (1984) 59–77; her analysis situates Erasmus' ideas on grace and free will within the rhetorical genre of the diatribe and refutes the opinion that Erasmus was a semi-Pelagian.
180 See Charles Trinkaus' introduction *Hyperaspistes* 1 & 2 CWE 76 xi–106, espe-

better left for another time.[181] Erasmus, however, is ever insistent that the preacher should not expect the power of the Holy Spirit to be so compelling that he need do nothing more. On the contrary, he must 'strive without pause, planting and watering and asking Christ's Spirit to give increase,[182] in short imitating that highest preacher in everything so far as his strength allows.'[183]

Christ promised his assistance to those he called to preach his word, but still the challenges of the office far surpassed those of any other. Like his dedicatory letter to von Stadion where Erasmus confesses having found nothing more difficult than writing this work, he similarly envisioned the preacher's instruction, toil, and commitment to the task as daunting and lifelong. Echoing Quintilian, he declares that 'among all the functions of human life none is more serious, none more noble, and none more dangerous than that of the preacher.[184] If you are wondering whence he has been sent, it is from that prince who created, sustains, and guides the universe; if you are wondering what his mission is, it is to teach his people the heavenly philosophy.'[185] Though Erasmus had only preached once or twice, he fully understood the momentous importance of oratorical rhetoric for the church, and perhaps even wished he had the natural disposition for public speaking and the calling to be a preacher.[186] In fact, as an *obiter dictum* in book 1 Erasmus expresses this sentiment in a poignant, personal way: 'That to which we urge you is difficult, but it is also the most beautiful and excellent enterprise of all; would that the Lord had given me such a spirit that I could earn death in so pious an activity rather than be consumed by a slow death

* * * * *

cially xciii–civ; see also 575: 'It is better ... to take a middle position than either to attribute nothing to our natural proclivity or else to attribute more to it than any pious person can tolerate.'

181 See Schoeck (2) 353–4.

182 Cf 1 Cor 3:6–8 and Matt 9:37–8. See Tracy (1) 24.

183 Book 1 259. Throughout *Ecclesiastes* Erasmus does not ask readers to imitate the great preachers in Christian tradition but urges them to imitate Christ, 'that highest Preacher in everything.'

184 For an illustration of the dangers to good preachers, see Erasmus' account of the near murder of Jean Vitrier in his letter to Justus Jonas (Anderlecht, 13 June 1521), Ep 1211:77–104; see also Taylor *Soldiers* and Larissa Taylor 'Dangerous Vocations: Preaching in France in the Late Middle Ages and Reformations' in *Preachers and People in the Reformations and Early Modern Period* ed Larissa Taylor (Leiden and Boston 2001) 91–124.

185 Book 1 330

186 For Erasmus' description of the physical torments he suffered while finishing *Ecclesiastes*, see Schoeck (2) 340–2.

in my present torments.'[187] 'The office of preacher, then, is very difficult,' one should expect, 'but also very beautiful; the contest is no ordinary one, but the prizes are outstanding.'[188]

Even with the Holy Spirit's assistance Erasmus envisions the instruction of the preacher as lengthy and arduous. Interestingly he sees the beginnings of a true reform of preaching in reversing society's negative judgment of the preacher and his profession, and in the preacher's diligent appropriation of those qualities that will lend him credibility. For this it is necessary first of all to correct the 'foolish judgments'[189] of the world (*mundus*), above all the judgments of those who should preach, by urging them to understand that 'foolish judgments, not only here but in pretty much every part of life, are the springs from which gushes all moral decay.'[190] The good preacher must first secure favour and authority, which can only happen by returning to the original simplicity of Christ, Paul, and the apostles, for only then will the world take notice of the sublime message presented; and at this the people will return to their original generosity. The preacher must embody the simplicity and interior sentiments of his conformity to Christ who inhabits his heart and follow the words and example of Paul, who instructs each Christian to 'keep himself from every appearance of evil, so as not to incur the suspicion of wrong in any regard';[191] for it is good example more than anything else that stimulates others to the pursuit of godliness. At the same time, it is vital that the preacher instruct his flock in the spiritual significance of his office and urge its cooperation in reversing their perception of preaching's fallen status. The reform of preaching, in effect, begins with the preacher himself, who with God's grace embarks upon the reformation of his own life, exercises himself in godliness (cf 1 Tim 4:7–8), and comes to understand the nature of his office that is 'more truly angelic than human.'[192] With this the preacher's audience will change its opinions, and

* * * * *

187 Book 1 364; cf *Adagia* II i 12 *Difficilia quae pulchra* 'Good things are difficult'; and *In psalmum 38* CWE 65 21.

188 Book 1 365

189 Book 1 404; see also the idea that foolish judgments 'in pretty much every part of life' lead to moral decay in *Moria* CWE 27 77–153.

190 Book 1 404; cf letter to Paul Volz, Ep 858:86: 'Nor is it easy to express what a decay in moral standards stems from topsy-turvy judgments like this'; and *Enchiridion* CWE 66 85: 'So Socrates in his discussion with Protagoras proves that knowledge has so great an importance in all virtue that sins arise solely from false opinions.'

191 See book 1 270; cf 1 Thess 5:22.

192 See book 1 327; cf 1 Tim 4:7–8 and *Enchiridion* CWE 66 78.

the preacher's credibility and effectiveness in the assembly of Christians will take hold.

Significant are Erasmus' choices of the terms *ecclesiastes* (*concionator*) for the preacher and *concio* (*contio*)[193] for his sacred discourse. The title of the work signals at the outset the central importance of public preaching in the life of the church and, as we shall see, in God's providential plan for our salvation.[194] Following St Jerome's commentary on the book of Ecclesiastes,[195] Erasmus informs us that '*ecclesia* means in Greek what *concio* does in Latin, that is, an assembling of the people to hear about state business'[196] or matters of the highest importance. 'The church (*ecclesia*) is called

* * * * *

193 The standard orthography of the word is *contio*; see L&S 451: '*contio* (less correctly *concio*).' Cf OLD 474 *contio*.

194 The idea that preaching was a public event is well established; see eg Alan of Lille 16: 'Preaching is an open and public instruction in faith and behavior, whose purpose is the forming of men ...'

195 Jerome *Commentarius in Ecclesiasten* CCSL 72 247–361; see 250: '1.1. *Verba Ecclesiastis filii David Regis Ierusalem. Tribus nominibus vocatum fuisse Salomonem scripturae manifestissime docent: pacificum, id est Salomonem; et Ididia, hoc est dilectum Domini; et quod nunc dicitur Coeleth, id est Ecclesiasten. Ecclesiastes autem graeco sermone appelatur, qui coetum, id est ecclesiam, congreget, quem nos nuncupare possumus concionatorem, quod loquatur ad populum, et sermo eius non specialiter ad unum, sed ad universos generaliter dirigatur.*'

196 Book 1 249–52. The word *concio* (*contio*) properly refers to the assembly called by an official to hear about state business, and the word takes on the meaning of the address spoken before that assembly. Erasmus purposely elects the Latin word *concio* rather than the common alternatives (*sermo, oratio, praedicatio, homilia*) to emphasize the public nature of preaching like its secular counterpart, where one 'speaks to an assembly' (*ecclesia* or *concio*) about matters of 'state business.' Erasmus can substitute *concio* for *ecclesia*; see eg *Credo sanctam ecclesiam*: '*Et te confiteor, sanctissima concio, qua gens* / *Christigena arcano nexu coit omnis in unum* / *Corpus & unanimis capiti sociatur Iesu,* / *Hinc proprium nescit, sed habet communia cuncta.*' *Christiani hominis institutum* LB V 1357E–F, quoted by Wilhelm Hentze *Kirche und kirchliche Einheit bei Desiderius Erasmus von Rotterdam* (Paderborn 1974) 2 n215. At Rome the term is used for a meeting called by a priest or a magistrate to hear an issue of common interest; *contionem habere* means 'to hold a meeting'; see L&S 451. But it can also refer to the oration given in such a meeting; see eg Cicero *De lege agraria* II 1.1 and 5.13. For the *contio* in the Roman world, see Lily Ross Taylor, *Roman Voting Assemblies from the Hannibalic War to the Dictatorship of Caesar* (Ann Arbor 1966). The Greek word *ecclesia* (Greek ἐκκλησία) meaning 'assembly' was used by the translators of the Septuagint to render the Hebrew word *qāhal* (קהל). Chomarat (*Grammaire* II 1102) notes that

a congregation (*congregatio*) or assembly (*concio*) which comes together to hear the word of God.'[197] The preacher, *concionator* or *ecclesiastes*, ἐκκλησιασ-τής (*ekklêsiastês*), like the Hebrew *qohelet* קהלת, is the man who addresses the *ecclesia* or ἐκκλησία (Hebrew *qahal*, קהל).[198] His counterpart in the external secular world is the ambassador (*orator* or ἐκκλησιαστής) of his prince who performs a similar function in 'pleading publicly before a crowd.' Indeed, the fundamental meaning of *concionare* or ἐκκλησιάζειν (*ekklêsiazein*) is 'to speak to the assembly.' The term *concio* is therefore not descriptive of the form or genre of the *ecclesiastes'* discourse but simply comes to mean the words delivered by the *concionator* at a public assembly (*in concione publica*).[199]

Because *Ecclesiastes* centres on the method of addressing the Christian assembly (*de ratione concionandi*), we should infer that the setting is generally a liturgical one, but not exclusively, for *contiones* could take place at various occasions outside the liturgy, and Erasmus recalls the commonplace that 'it befits the preacher to talk about Christ everywhere, not just in a church.'[200]

* * * * *

in this way the Greek word 'assembly' was Latinized to *ecclesia* to mean 'the church.'

197 Book 2 CWE 68 695: 'Ecclesia dicitur congregatio sive concio, quae convenit ad audiendum verbum Dei.'

198 See Jerome *Liber interpretationis hebraicorum nominum* CCSL 72 155: 'Clemens ecclesiastes sive concionator.' See too Augustine *Sermon 164, Sermons* WSA III 189: 'Delivering an address to the whole world from the platform, so to say, of his sublime authority, he cries out, "Listen, human race ..."' PL 38 896; (*concionator mundi, de quadam specula excelsae auctoritatis exclamat: audi, genus humanum*).

199 In the opening words of his commentary on the book of Ecclesiastes, St Jerome points out the meaning of the term *concio* (*contio*), as does Lorenzo Valla in his *Elegantiae* (1444). Erasmus includes this term in his *Paraphrasis in Elegantias Vallae*; see ASD I-4 238: 'Concio primo est congregatio multitudinis ad audiendum concionantem oratorem. Graeci concionem, id est conventum populi ἐκκλησίαν vocant. Secundo est oratio habita ad populum. Ubi fuisti? In concione.' Valla's work was reprinted in Basel in 1540. Erasmus had also employed the term for the discourse he wrote for John Colet's new school at St Paul's Cathedral in London and used it in his *Ratio*. O'Malley reviews Erasmus' use of this term in 'Sacred Rhetoric' 14–16. Sometime around 1510, Erasmus uses the term in his *Concio de puero Iesu*, translated as *Homily on the Child Jesus* (CWE 29 51–70), and in his *Concio de immensa Dei misericordia* of 1524 (CWE 70 69–139). Cicero often uses the term *contio* to mean the speeches given in an assembly; see eg *Ad Atticum* 2.20: 'Bibulus hominum admiratione et benevolentia in caelo est; edicta eius et contiones describunt et legunt.'

200 See book 3 CWE 68 883.

He refers, for example, to Peter's speech on Pentecost (Acts 2) as a *contio*, and indeed Erasmus labels some of his own compositions for special occasions as *conciones*.[201] Often he uses other Latin terms to convey the duty of speaking before the people, such as *praedicatio, praedicare, praedicator*, as these traditional words also aptly depict the public performative aspect of Christian preaching. Though often employing a variety of terms to describe the sacred discourse, such as homily (*homilia*), sermon (*sermo*), oration (*oratio*), panegyric (*laudatio*), he selects chiefly the words *concio, concionare, ecclesiastes*, and *concionator* to indicate that it is to the public assembly of Christians that the preacher addresses his words.[202]

Erasmus envisions the Christian assembly as a congregation comprised of all manner of individuals, from all backgrounds, and with varying levels of education, intellectual abilities, and moral worth. These Christ came to teach, a task fraught with enormous difficulty for any preacher. Although Erasmus recognizes the wide variety of individuals in a Christian assembly, he often views it in pejorative terms – as 'an untrained crowd inclined to yawn' or as 'souls ... rotting in sin as though in a tomb.'[203] The same might be said for his own view of Christian society; his comments suggest a world teeming with vice and sinfulness, and daily growing more alienated from God: 'But before whom does the preacher have to speak? I'm not

* * * * *

201 We have no *conciones* Erasmus delivered. His *Concio de puero Iesu* (*Homily on the Child Jesus*) (1511) was certainly a production of this kind, as were *Concio de immensa Dei misericordia* (1524), *In psalmum quartum concio* (1525; CWE 63), (*Concio*) for the *Virginis matris apud Lauretum cultae liturgia* (CWE 69), and *Concionalis interpretatio in psalmum 85* (1528; CWE 64). Though Erasmus never delivered any of these *conciones* or *conciunculae*, he constructed them with an imaginary audience in mind; they are addressed to 'brothers' and 'sisters' as if an audience were present. See O'Malley's discussion of this in 'Grammar' 90–3. Cynthia L. Polecritti gives a good picture of Bernardino da Siena's sermons after mass; see her *Preaching Peace in Renaissance Italy: Bernardino of Siena and His Audience* (Washington, DC 2000) chapter 1 'The Preacher and the Crowd' 67–83.

202 The Latin word *concio* (*contio*), with all its particular nuances for understanding this treatise, presents problems in English translation. There is no felicitous equivalent in our vocabulary to render *concio* in a way that would be true to Erasmus' linguistic and theological understanding. Lewis and Short (L&S 451) defines *contio* as 'a discourse, oration before a public assembly,' which gives only minimal help in expressing the idea of preaching to the congregation of the faithful as the bishop's principal duty; cf OLD 474–5 sv *contio*. Our decision therefore has been to render *concio* generally as 'sermon,' which here signals sacred public oratory, more commonly in a liturgical setting.

203 Book 3 CWE 68 773; book 1 396

talking now about a crowd of villagers and farmers but about a civic assembly with an indiscriminate mix of children, elders, maidens and whores, sailors, drivers, and shoemakers, among whom some are not much different from livestock so far as the capacity to be taught is concerned.'[204] And how might one's message touch all these persons of such diverse status, intelligence, and spiritual condition?[205] Erasmus has little to say about this;[206] yet he often emphasizes that the preacher does not address the spiritual elite to the neglect of the others, for it is the special universal character of a Christian assembly that no individual should be excluded from hearing God's word. This is all the more reason why the preacher, like Christ, must know how to accommodate his speech to everyone; and if done successfully, it effects marvellous social benefits: order, obedience, respect for the laws, domestic harmony, trust, honesty, chaste behaviour, alacrity in performing one's chores, upright commerce.[207] Good preaching brings about true social and spiritual reform.

If Quintilian and the other pagan authorities of antiquity maintained that the task of the orator was the most difficult of all, Erasmus takes this further, asserting that the task of the Christian preacher was incalculably greater than the pagans could ever have imagined, for nothing could be more challenging than calling sinners to their senses, bringing them to see their sinfulness and ingratitude to God, whose infinite love and goodness to humanity are beyond comprehension. If the duty of the Roman orator was arduous, how much more could this be said of the Christian preacher? In a world of folly and spiritual blindness, where 'in every class of men there are more bad than good' and 'every people is a beast of many heads,'[208] the challenge of calling humanity to godliness was never more difficult. It was therefore crucial that preachers have adamantine resolve and courage, for people may not be drawn to the good by clear, simple, and pure teaching; more realistically it is often necessary to awaken them from their moral

* * * * *

204 Book 3 CWE 68 791–2. Erasmus also often uses the word 'people' (*populus*) for the assembly of Christians listening to the preacher; see eg book 3 CWE 68 811.
205 For Erasmus' view of society as teeming with vice, see his letter to Paul Volz (Basel, 14 August 1518), Ep 858:166–90, 175–7: 'Is there any religious man who does not see with sorrow that this generation is far the most corrupt there has ever been?'; and Tracy (1) 87–103.
206 On this question see Murphy *Rhetoric* 284–97.
207 Dedicatory letter to Christoph von Stadion (246)
208 Book 1 267; cf Horace *Epistles* 1.1.76. Erasmus changes Horace's line from 'You are a beast of many heads' (*Belua multorum es capitum*) to '[Every people] is a beast of many heads.'

lethargy with stinging rebukes and by denouncing their vices. Erasmus in fact urges preachers, whenever appropriate, to dedicate a substantial part of their *concio* to attacking the vices prevalent in the community, and he sees the preacher's vocation as so profoundly dangerous precisely because of the wicked resistance of his hearers and the divine imperative to correct this.[209] Much of *Ecclesiastes* in fact centres on the moral reformation of society, which must start with the eradication of vices before virtue can be engendered, and the task as Erasmus saw it was more formidable in his age than ever. In comparing his world with that of John Chrysostom (another prominent *ecclesiastes* with a burning zeal to reform his vicious world), Erasmus utters the wish, 'If only the violence of princes, the rebelliousness of clerics, the insensibility of the people, the uproar of heresies were less today!'[210] No preacher should expect an easy life in this dangerous vocation.[211] *Ecclesiastes* in fact offers no words about bright prospects for a stable Christian peace, general tranquillity, and the cultivation of *bonae litterae*. In Erasmus' eyes, by the 1530s princes and bishops together, whose role it was to safeguard the Lord's vineyard for the cultivation of godliness, had so abandoned it that it was 'now almost destroyed.'[212] No doubt Erasmus' perception of his society's present moral abyss prompted him to impress upon the preacher the extreme difficulty he must expect in addressing Christian men and women and 'in trying to please all men in everything ... that they may be saved' (1 Cor 10:33).

Erasmus often uses terms other than *ecclesiastes* for the agents of this exalted ministry and for their message, such as 'heralds of evangelical philosophy' (*evangelicae philosophiae praecones*), 'teachers of heavenly wisdom' (*coelestis philosophiae doctores*), 'ambassadors' (*oratores*), 'evangelical preacher' (*concionator evangelicus*);[213] frequently too he refers to preachers as 'pastors' (*pastores*). Whatever terms used, it becomes evident early in book 1 that the

* * * * *

209 Book 1 330; cf Wenzel 'Preaching' passim.
210 Book 1 350
211 On the dangerous nature of the preacher's vocation, see eg Taylor *Soldiers* and her 'Dangerous Vocations: Preaching in France in the Late Middle Ages and Reformations.'
212 Book 1 370; cf *Ratio* 252: 'Annotandum interim et illud, quod Christus ubique fere miseretur turbae simplicis, in solos Pharisaeos, scribas et divites vae formidabile intonat, videlicet indicans in episcopis, theologis ac principibus esse situm, ut populi vigeat aut frigeat pietas. Ab illis omne malum oritur.'
213 Book 1 430, 309, 336; see also book 1 439: 'heralds of the word of salvation' (*Verbi salutiferi praeconibus*).

preacher (*ecclesiastes*) he envisions is first and foremost the bishop (*episcopus*) and by extension those to whom he delegates his pastoral authority. To the bishop-pastor belongs eminently the office of feeding – or teaching – the flock of Christians. He is the *ecclesiastes* in full, and all other sacred orators – pastors and others lawfully delegated – derive their authority and license exclusively from him. It is therefore the bishop's chief duty (*munus praecipuum*) to teach[214] and to move each one's heart to godliness. What the congregation hears from the dutiful bishop who 'expounds the edicts, promises, and will of the highest prince and persuades the people at large'[215] is nothing other than 'the evangelical philosophy,' those mysteries of the divine mind that have to do with our salvation.[216]

Erasmus' teacher-bishop (*ecclesiastes*) functions as the crucial link carrying on the earthly ministry of Christ, the Word (*sermo*) of the omnipotent God.[217] After Christ's ascension and visible departure, he serves as his representative, revealing to us the will of the Father that all human beings are to be enlightened in the truth, joined together into Christ's body, and united with the Father and Spirit to live as one people in perfect concord of hearts and minds.[218] Erasmus is emphatic that the bishop's teaching is altogether different from scholastic disputations and university lectures: 'However ingenious Duns Scotus' teachings about metaphysics, what do they have to do with the preacher?'[219] Nor should the 'subtleties of scholastic theologians,

* * * * *

214 See Tanner II 669, Council of Trent, Session 5, Decretum Secundum: super lectione et praedicatione: 'hoc est praecipuum episcoporum munus ...'
215 Book 1 251
216 Cf letter to Paul Volz (14 August 1518), Ep 858:219–24.
217 Erasmus makes clear the restorative role of Christ: his word repairs, reintegrates, and recreates what had been lost through Adam's sin and human sinfulness. God's word 'flows forth eternally without beginning, without end from the eternal heart of the Father; through it the Father created the universe, through it he rules all creation, through it he restored the fallen human race, through it he bound the church to himself, through it he desired to become known to the world in a singular and ineffable manner ...' (book 1 255). See also Ep 384:21–35, and Erasmus' words on bishops and their authority in *De esu carnium* ASD IX-1 38–42; and Augustijn *Erasmus* 149.
218 On St Jerome's authority Erasmus informs us that the 'spiritual reading' of the name *ecclesiastes* means that 'the pacific and beloved of God the Father and our *ecclesiastes* is Christ.' Jerome *Commentarius in Ecclesiasten* CCSL 72 251.
219 Book 2 CWE 68 482. From 1495–1500, during his years in Paris, Erasmus attended lectures on Scotus' theology at the Franciscan *studium*, and it appears it was then he conceived the idea of a new kind of theology that would bring the

who use various sophistries to dispute how the persons [of the Trinity] differ among themselves ... be presented to the congregation.'[220] The bishop's
concio on the other hand 'embraces both sound doctrine and the admonition,
rebuke, consolation, and refutation of those who carp at the truth of the
gospel' (cf 2 Tim 3:16–17, 4:2).[221] A further difference between the preacher-
bishop and the scholastic theologian is that the preacher speaking before the
congregation of the faithful is the true theologian,[222] for he instructs hearers
in 'that ineffable philosophy which the Son of God brought to earth from
the bosom of his Father.'[223] He carries on Jesus' earthly ministry in simple
and sincere speech. Notable examples of worthy prelates in this mission are
Gregory the Great (pontificate 590–604), who despite his innumerable responsibilities as pope 'preached before the people, sometimes several times
a day,'[224] Basil (330–79), John Chrysostom (347–407), and Augustine (354–
432). In teaching the heavenly philosophy, they followed the Lord Jesus,
'the perfect evangelist,' 'the teacher of all teachers.'[225] They embodied the
excellence of true bishops who 'promoted in every way what contributes to
godliness (*pietas*).'[226]

The exalted function of the preacher-bishop stands out even more strikingly in the ministry of Christ, the one on whose behalf he speaks. In his
earthly activity Jesus revealed to us the presence of the eternal Word from
before the beginning of creation until the consummation of the world, when
all will be in all. As the 'power and wisdom of God,'[227] the supreme teacher
brought 'the heavenly philosophy' to enlighten the minds of all people who

* * * * *

message of the gospel of Christ to Christians in their daily lives. See *Colloquia*
(*Convivium religiosum*) CWE 39 227–31 n190; cf *Ratio* 298–301.
220 See book 4 CWE 68 1078; cf letter to Paul Volz, Ep 858:35–119, and Augustine
De doctrina christiana 2.31.48; *Moria* CWE 27 132–5; and *Ratio* 297–8.
221 Book 1 402–3
222 Cf *Paraclesis* in Olin 145.
223 Book 1 320
224 Book 1 355; on Augustine's exemplary life as bishop, see the letter to Alonso
de Fonseca (Freiburg, [May] 1529), Ep 2157:74–82.
225 Book 1 418, 321; cf *Paraclesis* in Olin 95: 'He alone was a teacher who came
forth from heaven, he alone could teach certain doctrine, since it is eternal
wisdom, he alone, the sole author of human salvation, taught what pertains to
salvation, he alone fully vouches for whatsoever he taught, he alone is able to
grant whatsoever he has promised.'
226 Book 3 CWE 68 859
227 Cf 1 Cor 1:24.

would believe in him and thereby be saved.[228] Christ is the 'highest *ecclesiastes*,' 'that incomprehensible Word [*sermo*], the surest expounder [*enarrator*] of the divine mind and never in conflict with the model of perfect truth ...'[229] It is Christ 'who is never named more splendidly or more meaningfully in Holy Writ than when he is called the Word or Speech of God (*verbum sive sermo Dei*),'[230] for he mediates the mind of God through his continuous conversation with humanity.

Christ the *logos*, 'the way, the truth, and life,'[231] is the only model the preacher needs to imitate. He embodies eminently all precepts of the ancient writers on rhetoric, for as 'teacher of all teachers' he knew perfectly how to accommodate the divine word in different ways to persons of all stations in life.[232] His singular excellence was teaching (*docere*) us how everything spoken of or done in the Old Testament prefigured himself, the mediator of the heavenly philosophy, to instruct people towards godliness. As Erasmus states in *Paraclesis*, this philosophy was none other 'than the restoration of human nature originally well formed.'[233] Everywhere Christ went he went as teacher; whether sitting at the banquets of the Pharisees, in houses, on the mountain tops, in boats, Christ always taught by explaining to us through parables and allegories what had been foretold about him and our relationship through him with the Father. As mediator he spent his life recalling wayward humanity to the truth, which he himself was, and reversing the deceit of Satan, whose speech 'led the human race astray.'[234] Though Quintilian and the pagan rhetoricians had ably identified the rhetorical elements of persuasive speech, none of the pagans could ever have imagined that the perfect orator they idealized would be God's own Word made flesh, whose words by comparison rendered lifeless every artifice of human discourse.

* * * * *

228 Cf Ep 858:347–8: 'And there is only one goal: Christ, and his teaching in all its purity.'
229 Book 1 256
230 John 1:1. Book 1 253; Erasmus uses both terms for the 'Word of God.' See eg book 1 258: 'the highest orator, who was called the Word, that is, the image and voice, of God.' See *Paraphrasis in Joannem* CWE 46 13–21 and *Enchiridion* CWE 66 72. See also Kleinhans 102–6.
231 John 14:6: 'I am the way, and the truth, and the life.'
232 Cf *Paraclesis* in Olin 96: 'This doctrine in an equal degree accommodates itself to all, lowers itself to the little ones, adjusts itself to their measure, nourishing them with milk, bearing, fostering, sustaining them, doing everything until we grow in Christ ...'
233 *Paraclesis* in Olin 100
234 Book 1 259

Imparting an understanding of divine law was another crucial aspect of Jesus' mission that Erasmus places at the core of the preacher-bishop's ministry.[235] Law is nothing less than the expression of the eternal immutable will and mind of God, which all creation should hold dearest. In fact, Christ himself is the perfect expression of this law, and he came to us as ambassador of the Father to reveal it to us in its fullness. Erasmus announces this idea at the opening of *Ecclesiastes*, telling us that the sacred *ecclesiastes* 'expounds the edicts, promises, and will of the highest prince.'[236] The importance of order and the Law upholding it are paramount in Erasmus' thinking, as right order is crucial to peace, concord, and godliness.[237] The divine law moreover extends throughout all strata of creation, maintaining the salvific course of God's wisdom through every phase of human history from the time of Adam to the Second Coming of Christ. This law 'has been displayed in a variety of ways, taking account of differences in times and persons':[238] in dealing with human beings, God divided his communication of the Law into four major phases – '[man's] creation, his fall, his restitution, and his perfection.'[239] In moving from phase to phase, God's law remained ever fixed and immutable, though in the course of the history of our salvation the law was expressed and taught to us in different ways; hence humankind does not discard God's law in passing from one phase to the next, but learns in each new phase the deeper significance of God's teachings in light of what went before.

The crucial importance of God's law is further made clear in his providential plan for humanity's salvation. From the fall of Adam until the Law

* * * * *

235 See C. Douglas McCullough 'The Concept of Law in the Thought of Erasmus' ERSY 1 (1981) 89–112. This idea is also at the centre of the Council of Trent's decree on bishops; see Tanner II 763, Council of Trent, Session 24, Canon 4: 'Bishops are to announce the sacred scripture and the law of God in their own church ...' See also Hoffmann *Rhetoric* 156–62 and J.B. Payne *Erasmus: His Theology of the Sacraments* (Richmond 1970).

236 Book 1 251

237 On the conception of God's orderly creation, see also Philippus Melanchthon's discussion of Creation (Locus 2) in his *Loci communes*; see Philippus Melanchthon, *Heubtartikel Christlicher Lere: Melanchthons deutsche Fassung seiner* Loci theologici, *nach dem Autograph und dem Originaldruck von 1553* ed Ralf Jenett and Johannes Schilling (Leipzig 2002) 127–38 Cf Cicero *De legibus* 2.4.8–11.

238 Book 4 CWE 68 1031

239 See book 4 CWE 68 1031. Erasmus maintains that in this life no one reaches perfection, but each individual must strive; see *Ratio* 195: 'Nihil in rebus humanis vere perfectum, verum in suo cuique statu perfectionis studium adesse debet.

was given to Moses, the human race – including the many pagans living outside the Mosaic law – had some comprehension of the divine law as it was lived according to the law of nature; as Erasmus put it in *Hyperaspistes*, the Law was 'so deeply rooted in the mind of men, that even the pagans draw this conclusion: God is highly righteous and good';[240] and there were pagans of such natural virtue that they could with the light of reason understand the law God embedded within the natural order.[241] They grasped a considerable amount of the Law even without revelation, but little could they have imagined the New Law Christ would bring with the stupendous news of its insurmountable benefits to mankind, most of all the wondrous enjoyment of concord in the members of his body.

With Moses God gave the Law to Israel 'to show explicitly what was wrong, what right, and to use punishment to deter from the former, rewards to encourage proper behaviour.'[242] Until the time of Christ the Law had been the teacher, for whatever was written in the Old Testament was written to teach us about Christ.[243] Through the precepts of the Law, in shadows and veiled speech, and through the ministry of the ancient prophets, God slowly unfolded his plan over the ages until the time of John the Baptist, who,

* * * * *

240 *Hyperaspistes* 1 CWE 76 272–3; *Hyperaspistes* 2 CWE 77 737–8
241 See especially Erasmus' expression of this idea in *Colloquia* (*Convivium religiosum*) CWE 39 192–4.
242 Book 4 CWE 68 1032. The themes of vices and virtues, punishment and reward (or glory) lay at the heart of medieval preaching, especially that of the Franciscans. Erasmus notes that 'Glory could be subsumed under the heading of reward ...' (book 2 CWE 68 569). See chapter 9 of *The Later Rule* of St Francis, which uses 'glory' instead of 'reward,' in *Francis of Assisi* 1 104–5: 'Moreover, I admonish and exhort those brothers that when they preach their language be well considered and chaste for the benefit and edification of the people, announcing to them vices and virtues, punishment and glory, with brevity, because our Lord when on earth kept his word brief.' (105) See also Thomas Aquinas *Summa theologiae* IIa IIae q 6 a 1 rep obj 1: 'Fear of God cannot altogether precede faith, because if we knew nothing at all about him, with regard to rewards and punishments, concerning which faith teaches us, we should nowise fear him. If, however, faith be presupposed in reference to certain articles of faith, for example the divine excellence, then reverential fear follows, the result of which is that man submits his intellect to God, so as to believe in all the divine promises. Hence the text quoted continues: "And your reward shall not be made void."' Cf Plutarch *De liberis educandis* 12C–D.
243 See *Ratio* 210: 'Quemadmodum enim nihil gessit Christus, quod non adumbratum sit typis legis, quod non praedictum prophetarum oraculis, ita nihil factum est memorabile, quod non ante praedixerit apostolis suis, de morte sua ...'

standing at midpoint between the Old Law and the New, revealed to us the true light who enlightens every man coming into this world.[244] He disclosed to us Christ, the bringer of the heavenly philosophy, who baptized in fire and the Spirit, revealing at last God's New Law for our eternal blessedness. Becoming flesh among us, 'the perfect evangelist'[245] everywhere and at all times left 'memorials of his love and the seeds of the evangelical philosophy.'[246] His mission was to teach by leading us forth from the letter to the spirit, from 'shadows ... to the gleaming light of evangelical devotion'[247] and the perfection of the New Law.

As 'teacher of all teachers,'[248] Christ continually taught persons of every status and spiritual condition, and he actually spent the greater part of his ministry instructing his disciples, who would succeed him in his role as teacher. Little by little (*paulatim*), by word and example, he made known to them how they were to continue his ministry after his death and resurrection, for they and their successors would be to the men and women of their generations what Christ had been to them.[249] Slow learners that they were, they 'offered very attentive ears to Christ,'[250] all the while never grasping fully the sublime significance of his message until after his ascension when his Spirit opened their eyes at Pentecost, enlightened their minds, and bestowed upon them the power to proclaim and teach what they had heard and witnessed. Because of the slow pace of human understanding, the apostles and their successors would teach as Christ taught, knowing the right times and places for imparting truth, as Gregory of Nazianzus attests; 'In heavenly philosophy the most convenient method of teaching is if the highest things are not revealed immediately, but instead the listeners are led towards complete knowledge through distinct stages.'[251] Hearers of the word would be brought slowly to understand how God's eternal law has functioned throughout history and how under the New Law all persons of the earth have the chance to become members of Christ's body and share in the fellowship of the Trinity. Christ's example therefore provides the clearest

* * * * *

244 John 1:9; cf *Paraphrasis in Marcum* CWE 49 14–8.
245 Book 1 418
246 Book 3 CWE 68 881
247 Book 2 CWE 68 683
248 Book 1 321
249 On this motif of 'little by little' (*paulatim*) in Erasmus' theology, see Chomarat 'Grammar and Rhetoric' 60–1, 66.
250 Book 1 321
251 Book 3 CWE 68 963; see Gregory of Nazianzus *Oration* 31.37 (*On the Holy Spirit*); Nazianzus 138.

evidence of the content and method of preaching, its supreme importance, and how Jesus' own apostles were to provide for preachers in the generations after them.

The outpouring of the Holy Spirit at Pentecost represents the true beginning of the apostles' mission. Without ministers of the 'celestial philosophy' God's plan could not have continued; essentially God staked everything on them to carry on Christ's teaching as the church's first bishops. Accordingly, in the postapostolic age Christ the teacher continued his work in a very real way; and for this reason, godly Christians did not need to look for Christ in the relics of his earthly life – footprints, tunic, the wood of the cross, or in statuary representations – but could seek 'instead the living and breathing likeness of him'[252] in the gospel writings and listen to his teachers who interpret them for us. As Erasmus writes, 'After God himself the church has nothing more sacred, more wholesome, more venerable, and more sublime than the word of God, that is, canonical Scripture . . . ,'[253] and Christ's presence and mission in the church as the highest *ecclesiastes* continues daily through those whom he has called to interpret canonical Scripture. 'In church it is not Christ who is teaching, but it is the word of Christ that teaches; and the spirit of Christ speaks through the mouth of a man.'[254]

Erasmus' *ecclesiastes* functions therefore as Christ's vicar, upon whom Christ's ongoing earthly work depends. As Paul says, without preachers 'how then shall they call on him in whom they have not believed? Or how shall they believe him of whom they have not heard? And how shall they hear without a preacher? And how shall they preach unless they be sent . . . Faith then comes by hearing; and hearing by the word of Christ' (Rom 10:14–17). But much has changed since the apostolic age. That immediate infusion of Christ's spirit at Pentecost is not the experience of clergy

* * * * *

252 *Paraclesis* in Olin 105–6
253 See book 1 329. As in *Ratio* (211) Erasmus ranks the canonical books of the Bible according to 'some order of authority,' those of greatest weight being ones whose validity has never been questioned by the ancients: 'Isaiah is of more weight than Judith or Esther, Matthew's Gospel more than the Apocalypse ascribed to John, more to the Epistle of Paul to the Romans and Corinthians than the Epistle written to the Hebrews.' See also *Ratio* 294.
254 Book 3 CWE 68 883. The idea that we know Christ even more today through preaching Scripture than if we had lived with him during his earthly life finds a parallel in Erasmus' dedicatory letter to William Warham for the edition of St Jerome's works: 'If a man had lived in familiar converse with Cicero . . . for several years, he will know less of Cicero than they do who by constant reading of what he wrote converse with his spirit every day' (CWE 61 5).

in this era. The age of dazzling miracles ended[255] along with that primitive pentecostal fervour and the eloquence it engendered; the Holy Spirit now moves in different ways. Erasmus explains that 'miracles had their time, nor are there fewer miracles because the inspiration of the Spirit is silent; the altered nature of the times required this, and the gift of God is no less free because he determined to give it in this way. It is the same gift of the same Spirit but given differently according to the condition of the times, and it must not be doubted that it is given in a more perfect way.'[256] In fact, the new prophets who succeeded the apostles are far greater than the prophets of old: they have succeeded to the place 'of the apostles or rather, more truly, that of Christ himself.'[257] These are 'prophets of prophets' 'inasmuch as it is useless for the prophets to have written for us unless this new kind of prophet exists to interpret them.'[258] Erasmus illustrates the difference between the prophets of old and preachers of today in the new type of prophecy spoken of by Paul in 1 Corinthians (12:28–9), where we read that the prophets of the New Testament are teachers who 'enable us to understand the Scriptures by digging out the mysteries in them according to their spiritual meaning, offering the new and the old from their treasure stores'; they are 'trained to compare the spiritual with the spiritual.'[259]

Having set forth the ideal of the true *ecclesiastes* as embodied in Christ and a theology of God's love and plan for humanity, Erasmus embarks on

* * * * *

255 See book 1 283: 'Miracles have all but ceased.' On his day and age not depending on miracles, see Erasmus' letter to John Longland (Basel, 1 September 1528), Ep 2037:95–100. 'The Christian religion today does not depend on miracles, and it is no secret how many false beliefs have been brought into the world through men who are clever in procuring their own gain with the aid of fabricated miracles. We will believe much more firmly in what we read in the Scriptures if we do not believe in any old tales invented by men.'

256 Book 1 394

257 Book 1 372: 'Prophets I call those that announce the will of God to the people from the oracles of Scripture, so that they can legitimately use that preamble of the prophets, "The Lord says this."' Cf 1 Cor 14:37.

258 Book 1 397; cf 1 Cor 14:5; J. Vitrier 'Sermon de la Penthecouste' fol 209 verso in Godin *Spiritualité* 184 and n165.

259 Book 1 388; see also Erasmus' interpretation of this passage in *Annotationes in 1 ad Corinthios* 12:28 ASD VI-8 246–8, where he reads Paul to mean that God places first the apostles in the church to give the whole an order, then prophets, then teachers, and then powers. He does not mean by this that these are different groups of people, but that they are the same, though he ranks their functions in this way.

a programme to rehabilitate the fallen status of the preacher first by calling attention to the dismal state of preaching, where the social position of the preacher has been sadly demeaned – indeed, even scorned – not only by the faithful but even by so many whom Christ himself called to this office. Because of the clergy's widespread neglect of their pastoral duties, dissolute living, and the scandal these have caused, Erasmus envisions the rehabilitation of the preacher in the eyes of society as the necessary first step to reform the ministry of the word. To this end he begins by emphasizing the wondrous spiritual dignity of this office in order to correct society's foolish judgment of the preacher; from there he will address the instruction of the preacher. His goal is to impress upon clergy and laity alike the essence of the preacher's work so that everyone might understand 'the dignity, the difficulty, the purity, the courage, the usefulness, the reward of the faithful preacher.'[260] Once the preacher has grasped the profound significance of his role as dispenser of God's mysteries,[261] he will then strive zealously to reform his life and embrace his holy calling; in doing so, he will garner from his flock much favour along with the moral authority to compel others to embrace his message.

Erasmus' rhetorical display in book 1 to impress upon his readers the dignity of this office recalls the academic lectures that inaugurate the school year and those of new masters who received their *licentia docendi*, which essay to move students to pursue their subject by extolling its nature, usefulness, and importance.[262] Book 1 of *Ecclesiastes* is a tour de force, reminiscent of the *Paraclesis*, which he placed among the introductory writings to his Greek and Latin edition of the *Novum Instrumentum* (1516); it displays, in fact, many of the rhetorical devices he explains later in *Ecclesiastes* for preachers to render speech more forceful, and touches too on many themes Erasmus takes up later in greater detail. The design is to comment on the dismal condition of sacred oratory, reviewing the lamentable practices of many contemporary preachers while offering clergy a *paraenesis* to pattern their lives and ministry after Christ, the perfect *ecclesiastes*; such a man would not fear to take the message of the gospel to far distant lands or 'to give up

* * * * *

260 Book 1 443
261 Cf 1 Cor 4:1.
262 For the speaking styles (*genera dicendi*), see Quintilian 12.10.58–80. For an early example of an inaugural academic lecture, see that of Thomas Aquinas in Jean-Pierre Torrell, O.P., *Saint Thomas Aquinas* 1: *The Person and His Work* rev ed trans Robert Royal (Washington, DC c 1996, 2005) 50–3.

one's life for the gospel.'[263] Book 1 also cautions future preachers that before they open their mouths to speak 'there must be judgment before there is expression, knowledge before speech';[264] they must first become individuals of outstanding speaking ability and of good moral character. Long before they preach they should be required to devote extensive hours to perfecting their own spiritual lives and dedicate themselves entirely to the subjects comprising their *métier*. Such is the challenge.

To impress upon preachers the exalted status of their office, Erasmus employs numerous rhetorical devices (comparisons and contrasts, a fortiori arguments, enthymemes,[265] examples, amplification). In book 1, for example, he compares and contrasts the infinite difference between ambassadors (*oratores*) of princes and the ambassadors of Christ, the highest prince; if so much is expected of ambassadors of kings and potentates, 'how much greater are the qualities to be required of the evangelical preacher?'[266] If the requirements regulating the Aaronic priesthood were so strict under the Mosaic law, how much greater are those imposed on preachers of Christ under the New Law?[267] Erasmus draws upon comparisons from his earlier works: 'You listen carefully to someone who professes how a field, the nourisher of your body, should be cultivated, and do you not heed someone who teaches how the mind, which bears the fruit of eternal happiness, should be cultivated?'[268] In much of book 1 Erasmus deftly adapts these turns of speech to the traditional schemata contrasting the Old and New Testaments – type and antitype, shadow and substance, promise and fulfilment, Old Law and New Law, flesh and spirit, letter and spirit. The schemata in turn also allow him to amplify the contrast between the secular and the sacred, human society and the society of believers, pagans and Christians, body and soul, flesh and spirit. Having established the standard of moral excellence that should characterize the *ecclesiastes*, Erasmus then takes up the principles of oratorical artistry (*ars bene dicendi*), dialectic, biblical hermeneutics, preaching

* * * * *

263 Book 1 363
264 Book 2 CWE 68 473
265 Erasmus often speaks of the enthymeme; see book 2 CWE 68 716, where he defines it as 'a maxim with a reason adjoined.' See also book 3 CWE 68 867.
266 Book 1 319
267 Book 1 302
268 Book 1 441. Such techniques characterize the arguments in many of Erasmus' works, especially those on education; see eg *De pueris instituendis* CWE 26 313–4. See also Plutarch *De liberis educandis* 4A–B.

methods, and topics. Before we look at these, however, it is instructive to review some of the principal themes Erasmus addresses throughout this treatise, as well as the questions he anticipates readers raising. Many themes register important nuances and precisions in the development of Erasmus' thinking towards the close of his life; *Ecclesiastes* after all would be Erasmus' last major public statement on theological matters, in effect, his final word.

Among the misguided ideas about preaching that Lateran v singles out was the dangerous notion that a cleric, by virtue of his ordination, needed no further schooling to preach. Evidently there were also many self-appointed preachers at the time for whom even the question of ordination was irrelevant. Was it at all necessary for a zealous cleric or religious, or for one who suddenly felt inspired by the Holy Spirit, to be trained for years in liberal studies, oratorical rhetoric, or even sacred letters for that matter? Wouldn't the grace of the Holy Spirit suffice, as evidenced by the prophets of the Old Testament? On the contrary, Erasmus insists that instruction in grammar, rhetoric, scriptural languages, theology, and other germane disciplines was fundamental for preaching; like the pursuit of *pietas*, effective communication depended on constant human application, for 'that heavenly Spirit is so far from scorning our industry that it even demands it, and it does not disdain to have its gifts assisted in turn by our application ...'[269] Moreover 'the Holy Spirit works more fully if it finds a heart readied by the liberal disciplines,'[270] and of those disciplines genuine theology holds primacy of place, while grammar and rhetoric are its handmaidens.[271] The cleric must do all he can to preach well, which clearly includes the acquisition of languages. In *Apologia contra Latomi dialogum* (1519) Erasmus tells Jacques Masson (Jacobus Latomus): 'If we think that explaining the sacred texts is important to theology, if we judge it a sign of holiness to show wisdom in revealing the hidden mysteries of the Scriptures, which often lurk behind the formation of the very letters, then we must admit that no single subject is more dependent on languages than theology.'[272] These every preacher must strive to acquire. And what else is theology but 'piety linked to skill in speaking of the divine'?[273] Critical too, of course, is the spiritual disposition of the preacher who must humbly attribute every good result to the Spirit, all the

* * * * *

269 Book 2 CWE 68 470
270 Book 2 CWE 68 471
271 See the letter to Christopher Fisher (Paris [about March] 1505), Ep 182:94–6.
272 CWE 71 41
273 *Apologia contra Latomi dialogum* CWE 71 55

while praying constantly to the Lord of the harvest that there be an increase, for the Spirit 'requires our own effort so that through it the Spirit can work in us not less but more secretly.'[274] At the heart of the preacher's activity then lie the deep mystery of human cooperation with divine grace and the understanding that the Holy Spirit demands constant effort on our part.

Believing in the Holy Spirit's assistance, the godly preacher will also labour sedulously to accommodate himself to his audience. In this he reflects the sublime beneficence of God, who graciously accommodated himself to our humanity, above all in his gift to us of Jesus Christ, his Word, whose speech and life were perfectly tempered to engage humanity and invite it to godliness. The ancients' emphasis on the importance of accommodation could not be better illustrated than in the person and earthly ministry of Christ. The word 'accommodate' (*attemperare, temperare, accommodare*) runs throughout *Ecclesiastes*, as well as in Erasmus' other works;[275] with it he reminds preachers to adapt their ideas, words, and comportment to their listeners, as God does with humanity and as Jesus did throughout his earthly ministry.[276] Accommodation presupposes sound judgment and a sense of what is fitting (*aptum*); for learning is a slow process, and profound doctrines need to be unfolded gradually to those of limited capacity, as Jesus, Paul, and the apostles, Origen, Gregory of Nazianzus, and John Chrysostom attest.[277] As examples of such accommodation, Erasmus calls attention to the extraordinary thoughtfulness of Peter's speech on Pentecost (Acts 2:14–40)

* * * * *

274 Book 1 322; and Grünwald 96–8
275 See eg *Hyperaspistes* 1 CWE 76 172.
276 'One should consider throughout the address what is demanded by the case, the person, the time, the place, custom, and all the while what is appropriate as well'; see book 3 CWE 68 1002. See also Marjorie O'Rourke Boyle *Rhetoric and Reform: Erasmus' Civil Dispute with Luther* (Cambridge, Mass 1983); *Explanatio symboli* CWE 70 315 n102; McConica 'Grammar of Consent' 77–8, where 'Erasmus presents Christ himself as a kind of Proteus, whose variety of life and doctrine reaches out to men of all conditions, drawing them to himself and actually enhancing his essential harmony, as *omnia in omnibus*.' See of course Quintilian (passim) and Horace *Ars poetica* (passim); the theme runs throughout the ancient authors on literature and public speaking. For some uses of accommodation, see Lausberg §§258, 448, 808, 820, 823.2, 1058, 1084.
277 *Apologia contra Latomi dialogum* CWE 71 75–6: 'Both Origen and Chrysostom teach that the doctrine of God in man was not preached immediately and everywhere lest it should prove a stumbling-block to minds which were still not attuned to such a mystery and incapable of accepting it. In the Gospel itself the disciples are at first forbidden to proclaim Jesus as Christ.'

and Paul's preaching on the Areopagus (Acts 17:22–31),[278] where neither Peter nor Paul attempted to put the whole truth at once before their audiences, because they judged the need to disclose their teachings in such a way that listeners could absorb what they heard before moving on to more recondite truths.[279] With this kind of judgment also belongs the principle of decorum,[280] with which the preacher discerns what is appropriate to each person's station before attacking vices, praising virtues, and giving instruction in the necessary matters of the faith. Like judgment, a sense of what is fitting, the ancients say, comes only through experience, and even then, they remind us, some speakers never learn what is appropriate to say.

Because of the assistance of the Holy Spirit, the public speakers Erasmus instructs are in a qualitative sense infinitely different from the *oratores* Quintilian had in mind. The pagan rhetoricians believed that one's own experience brought judgment and discretion about what was appropriate,[281] 'skills that cannot be imparted by instruction but are derived from the orator's intelligence and are adopted from the circumstances of the case.'[282] But what the pagans attributed exclusively to human experience and sensitivity, Erasmus attributes in large measure to the mysterious activity of the Holy Spirit: 'The heavenly Spirit, by whose inspiration the preacher talks, does not disdain human effort, provided it be sober.'[283] Paul writes that 'the spirits of the prophets were subject to the prophets' (1 Cor 14:32),[284]

* * * * *

278 Book 1 301, 280; book 2 CWE 68 523; book 3 CWE 68 1006
279 Cf *Paraphrasis in Joannem* CWE 46 87: 'With such words our Lord Jesus instructed the unschooled and foolish crowd, wanting to draw them from the love of visible and physical things to the desire for things heavenly and eternal.' See also CWE 46 82: 'Jesus overlooked the people's ignorance and led them slowly to an awareness of spiritual matters in this way ...'
280 Book 3 CWE 68 1014: 'Moreover, one must everywhere have regard for decorum.' Cf 1 Cor 6:12.
281 Book 1 281–4. The ancients saw the appropriate (*aptum*) as divided into judgment (*iudicium*) and counsel (*consilium*), which define the *prudentia* of the speaker; see Lausberg §§258, 1055–62, 1074–7.
282 Book 1 281. On the idea of 'circumstance' (*circumstantia*), see Hoffmann *Rhetoric* 162–7, and Lausberg §§139 and 399.
283 Book 2 CWE 68 497
284 Book 2 CWE 68 497; Erasmus quotes 1 Cor 14:32; see *Paraphrasis in epistolam Pauli ad Corinthios priorem* CWE 43 170–3; and *Annotationes in 1 ad Corinthios* (14:31–40) ASD VI-8 282: 'πνεύματα Graecis plurativi numeri est, [E] quemadmodum citat Hieronymus prologo in Esaiam: *Spiritus prophetarum, prophetis subiecti sunt.* [A] Et "subiiciuntur" ὑποτάσσεται [B] verbum praesentis temporis,

which Erasmus interprets to mean that the Holy Spirit actively (however mysteriously) assists the preacher in finding what to say, arranging the matter, and delivering the sermon, though the full responsibility for speaking appositely lies with the man himself. Moreover, this preacher of the New Law is a prophet far different from that of the Old Law. Since the Holy Spirit no longer 'seizes' its prophets as it once did, for example, with Amos (Amos 7:15), today's preacher is to have his sermon under his own control (2 Cor 14:32), accommodating himself in a way that 'considers everywhere what is appropriate to each.'[285] In addition, the Holy Spirit acts differently with each individual,[286] for 'in a sacred orator judgment is a gift of the Holy Spirit;[287] but that Spirit tempers its force [*energia*] according to the organ that it has found, especially now that miracles have all but ceased,[288] so that a future preacher not only needs to be trained but must also be chosen for his obvious fitness for the office.'[289] Whatever the preacher's individual nature, talents, and suitability, the Holy Spirit engages uniquely and mysteriously with him as he labours to become a useful vessel of the Lord; as Solomon says, 'It is man's part to prepare the heart and the Lord's to guide the tongue.'[290] And it will be one of the bishop's special duties to select and prepare those seemingly best suited to preach.

* * * * *

[A] ne sentiamus hoc dictum de ipso Spiritu Sancto, sed dono Spiritus, quod ita datum esset singulis quibus contigit, ut in ipsorum esset arbitrio uti aut non uti, quod afflatis et lymphatis non item licet.'

285 Book 2 cwe 68 629
286 Cf Acts 2:4–13. Erasmus raises the complicated theological question here of the Holy Spirit's activity in assisting the preacher. Though he never analyzes this matter in *Ecclesiastes*, he provides numerous ways of considering what must be taken as a given; for even in the most deplorable situations, one cannot deny that the Holy Spirit is not somehow at work, as his example of Balaam's she-ass demonstrates (see Numbers 22).
287 Book 1 283. Erasmus refers to Isa 11:2–3, the locus for the theology of the seven gifts of the Holy Spirit: 'And the spirit of the Lord shall rest upon him: the spirit of wisdom, and of understanding, the spirit of counsel [*consilium*], and of fortitude, the spirit of knowledge, and of godliness [*pietas*]. And he shall be filled with the spirit of the fear of the Lord.'
288 Erasmus expresses his view that, after Jesus' earthly ministry and the age of the apostles, Christ's work continues in the church through the ministry of preaching; and for this God uses each preacher according to his nature and capacity. This treatise aims at identifying those who 'seem fitted by nature for this office' and providing direction.
289 Book 1 283
290 Prov 16:1; book 1 323

In the godly man preparing to preach well, Erasmus sees the grace of the Holy Spirit congruently perfecting his nature, allowing him to speak effectively in so far as his nature allows. The preacher mirrors Erasmus' view of the individual, the baptized Christian, the church, God's law – in short, his entire 'philosophy of Christ' and the path of *pietas*.[291] As the preacher progresses in virtue with God's grace towards godliness, he does not alter his physical characteristics; rather, his progress perfects that nature vitiated by Adam's sin and restores to its fullness what was originally there. In the measure the preacher cooperates with God's grace, the Holy Spirit transforms its vessel of clay into something stupendous, the mouthpiece of God's word, which spiritually vivifies all who receive the truth. Perfected in godliness, the preacher's body and spirit, his whole life and example, radiate him whose message he proclaims.[292] While the physical traits of the preacher do not change (for example, voice, physical size and shape, stamina), the divine Spirit now speaks through him 'as if through a living organ,'[293] making Christ present to the congregation through the preacher's word and life. In a spiritual sense, Erasmus' godly preacher receives in abundant measure the seven gifts of the Holy Spirit (*charismata*) that are imparted to all Christians at baptism – wisdom, understanding, counsel (*consilium*), fortitude, knowledge (*scientia*), godliness (*pietas*, εὐσέβεια),[294] and fear of the Lord[295] – each gift particularly vital for speaking God's word well.

The Holy Spirit's activity in the life and work of the preacher further underscores the enormous responsibility laid upon the teacher-bishop in his role within the church. The bishop not only should reside in his diocese and preach, to the extent he is physically able, but must provide good preachers, and, perhaps even more important, the right environment where aspiring preachers can work to perfect their native talents to assist him. As it is the

* * * * *

291 Cf *Ratio* 236: 'huc tendit universa Christi doctrina, ut ipsi pie sancteque vitam traducamus . . .'
292 See the opening passage of book 2 CWE 68 466 where Erasmus remarks on the transformed physical appearance of those who have embraced the spirit of Christ: 'The mind's interior appearance moves into the outer man and wholly transfigures him to its own image'; and 'How much more will the spirit of Christ alter a man's whole appearance if it inhabits his heart?'
293 Book 1 259
294 For Thomas Aquinas' teaching on piety as both a gift and a virtue, see *Summa theologiae* I–II qq 68 and 121.
295 Cf Isa 11:2–3. The Vulgate and Septuagint texts give seven gifts, the Hebrew text six.

bishop upon whom God places the weighty responsibility of 'feeding the flock of the Lord with zeal and joy out of the abundance of charity,'[296] so too must he judiciously select and continually assist his presbyters, who collaborate with him in carrying out God's plan of salvation. Bishops and religious superiors therefore should not presume to admit indiscriminately persons unsuited to this office but select only those who show both a natural aptitude and spiritual disposition for this mission, and provide the means for instructing them to carry out their pastoral duties.

The office of the bishop is therefore central to Erasmus' ecclesiology, for it is in the *synaxis* of the faithful that Christ becomes really present through his word. Erasmus further makes clear that in his earthly life Jesus established a visible, hierarchical structure in the church that is to remain until the end of the world,[297] and that he continues to be really present among the faithful in the teaching of the heavenly philosophy by the bishop, the successor of the apostles and Christ's legitimate representative.[298] 'The highest dignity in the ecclesiastical hierarchy' belongs to him because in the

* * * * *

296 Book 1 277. For the tradition of identifying 'feeding' (ie teaching the gospel) with the Eucharist, see Grünwald 93–4; cf Thomas à Kempis *Imitation of Christ* 4.11.

297 On hierarchy in Erasmus, see Rummel *Erasmus* (London and New York 2004) 54–7: 'Hierarchical order is the principle that informs Erasmus' definition of piety as well as his views on the best organization of society' (54). See also McConica 'Grammar of Consent' 89–97.

298 The apostle is in the bishop 'whose chief duty (*munus praecipuum*) is to teach the people.' For Erasmus' ecclesiology, see: Ernst-Wilhelm Kohls *Die Theologie des Erasmus* 2 vols (Basel 1966); Peter G. Bietenholz *History and Biography in the Work of Erasmus of Rotterdam* (Geneva 1966); J. Ijsewijn and C. Matheeussen 'Érasme et l'historiographie' in *The Late Middle Ages and the Dawn of Humanism outside Italy* ed Mag. G. Verbeke and J. Ijsewijn (Louvain 1972) 31–43; Hilmar M. Pabel 'The Peaceful People of Christ: The Irenic Ecclesiology of Erasmus of Rotterdam' in Pabel 57–93; Dominic Baker-Smith introduction CWE 63 especially lvi–lxiv; Myron P. Gilmore '*Fides et Eruditio*: Erasmus and the Study of History' in *Humanists and Jurists: Six Studies in the Renaissance* (Cambridge, Mass 1963) 87–114; Gogan; Harry J. McSorley 'Erasmus and the Primacy of the Roman Pontiff: Between Conciliarism and Papalism' *Archiv für Reformationsgeschichte* 65 (1974) 37–54; Stupperich; and István Bejczy *Erasmus and the Middle Ages: The Historical Consciousness of a Christian Humanist* (Leiden 2001). See also Cornelis Augustijn 'The Ecclesiology of Erasmus' *Scrinium* II 135–55; and Manfred Hoffmann 'Erasmus on Church and Ministry' ERSY 6 (1986) 1–30, who finds a 'remarkable consistency' in *Ecclesiastes* with Erasmus' many earlier 'statements on the church and its ministry' (5). See also Erasmus' *Inquisitio de fide* ed Craig R. Thompson (New Haven and London 1950).

fullest sense he carries on the work of Christ.[299] Repeatedly Erasmus insists that the bishop's role is to teach: 'However many the functions, chief among which are administration of the sacraments and spiritual instruction, he [the bishop] is at the pinnacle of his dignity whenever he feeds the souls of the people with the flesh and blood of Christ, which is the word of God.'[300] Preaching to instruct Christians towards godliness is his chief duty (*munus praecipuum*);[301] it the essence of the apostolic office,[302] as Paul attests at 1 Corinthians 1:17 – 'Christ sent me not to baptize, but to preach the Gospel ...' As successors of the apostles, bishops also perform other functions, but in rank of importance preaching is supreme. Moreover, Erasmus would allow no one to preach other than those delegated by the bishop, whose authority derives from Christ and passes to him through the apostolic succession.

Like the Lateran Councils, Erasmus describes the bishop's work of teaching as 'feeding,' which recalls Jesus' command to Peter, 'feed my sheep'

* * * * *

299 Book 1 328. Cf Thomas Aquinas: 'Preaching is the noblest of all ecclesiastical functions'; cited by Murphy *Rhetoric* 275 n8.
300 Book 1 403; and in this function too 'the prelate, though outstanding in everything, is absolutely at the peak of his dignity when he feeds the Lord's flock with sacred teaching from the pulpit and dispenses to them the treasure of evangelical philosophy.' Erasmus says next to nothing about the physical aspect of the sacrament of the Eucharist; he sets it rather in the context of preaching the word, which opens up the minds and hearts of the community to see in faith Christ who is among them. See Augustijn *Erasmus* 150–3; Hoffmann *Rhetoric* 101: 'What makes the Bible unique, universal, and final, however, is that Christ, the ultimate word of God, is incarnate in it as by a real presence ... Therefore, Christ is at once symbolically and really present in the sacred word, symbolically as to the human nature of the word and really in terms of the divine nature of the word ...'; and Grünwald 89–90.
301 Book 1 268. Erasmus made this point in Ep 967A to Justus Jonas (Antwerp, [c 20–6 May?] 1519) CWE 6 375: 'It may be splendid to move your hand in blessing over a multitude on its knees, it may be a great thing to administer the sacraments of the church; unquestionably the noblest office, the most truly worthy of apostle or of bishop, is to offer the doctrine of salvation to the people and make their thoughts and their life worthy of Christ.'
302 Cf Ep 1790:470, letter to John Longland (Basel, 3 March 1527), which is the preface to his *Chrysostomi lucubrationes* (1527), where he contrasts the eloquence of Athanasius as teacher with that of Tertullian, Jerome, Hilary, Augustine, Chrysostom, and Gregory of Nazianzus: 'Athanasius deserved to live in an age of peace and tranquillity; he would then have given us the marvellous fruit of his mind and of his eloquence, for he possessed that quality which Paul thought essential in a bishop – the ability to teach (*Habebat enim vere dotem illam quam Paulus in episcopo putat esse praecipuam*, τὸ διδακτικόν).'

and 'feed my lambs' (John 21:15–17). Preaching is the spiritual nourishment essential to the dispensation of the sacraments. As Jesus made manifest through preaching the spiritual significances of his earthly actions, the preacher does the same in the rites and ceremonies of the church. His words give life to the letter, ceremony, ritual, and events;[303] in fact, every sacrament, sacred rite, and religious observance would be meaningless without one to explain its spiritual significance.[304] 'What good is receiving the Lord's body and blood unless they have learned how this sacrament was instituted, what it effects in us, the faith and purity with which it should be received?'[305] Without the word, the sacraments and all other rites and ceremonies of the church remain blind and lifeless.

Erasmus' primary model of the church is Paul's image of the mystical body of Christ (cf Rom 12:5; 1 Cor 12:12–26), whose head is Christ, the paragon of godliness (*pietas*), and whose members are the faithful united in peace and concord, both those of the church triumphant in heavenly beatitude and those of the church militant plodding along the path of spiritual progress, persevering in godliness from the domination of the flesh to the freedom of the spirit.[306] Unlike those whose model of the church centred on

* * * * *

303 See eg Luke 24:31–3, and *Paraphrasis in Lucam 11–24* CWE 48 271–2, where Erasmus recounts Jesus' conversation with two disciples on the road to Emmaus after his resurrection: 'They did not recognize Jesus except in the house, that is, the church; they did not recognize him except when he himself offered them the bread of the gospel word. For that is what opens the eyes by which Jesus is recognized. He had broken and offered that bread mystically during the journey, when he unveiled the Scriptures to them. And what he had done there in spirit he afterward renewed in the bodily sign.' See Chomarat 'Grammar and Rhetoric' 52–3.

304 Godin refers to this idea in Jean Vitrier's *homiliare* (258r/v) in *Spiritualité* 209: 'Il est vray que c'est merveilleusement grand chose du sainct Sacrement, et je loue fort ce que je le vois fort honnourer, et admoneste chescun de le rechepvoir sainctement, et en grand reverence. Mais je dis cela que le sainct Sacrement ne prouffite non plus que on a de foi. Sainct Pol, premier hermitte, fut soixante ans en sa caverne sans le rechepvoir sacramentellement, et se fut sy très accepté de Dieu.'

305 Book 1 403

306 See *Enchiridion* CWE 66 especially the 'Fifth rule' 65–84: 'Perfect piety is the attempt to progress always from visible things, which are usually imperfect or indifferent, to invisible ...' (65); see also 83–4; and the 'Sixth rule,' 84–104, which presents Christ as the model of perfect piety. See Godin 34–76, which examines Origen's influence in the genesis of this work; see also Hilmar M. Pabel 'Erasmus' Irenic Vision of the Church' in Pabel 61–2. Cf *De puritate tabernaculi* CWE 65 217–67 and McConica 'Grammar of Consent' passim.

papal authority grounded in the Petrine texts (Matt 16:16–19; John 21:15–17; Luke 22:38),[307] Erasmus conceives of the church broadly as the congregation of the faithful that existed *ab initio*, much as Augustine viewed it: from the time of Abel, 'who belonged to the city of God,'[308] down to the patriarchs, through the history of the Hebrews to the time of Christ, and from then to the end of time. Where this 'church unknown to us'[309] is and who are those who belong to God remains always a mystery; it is Augustine's 'mixed church,' which embraces all Christians, the good and the bad alike, where 'even those who live impiously and heretics'[310] are tolerated and each baptized person is offered the grace to move from the bondage of the flesh to the liberation of the spirit. In the end, however, only God knows each one's eternal destination, but to each is extended the hope of eternal life, which is why preaching is of crucial importance in God's plan of salvation.[311]

* * * * *

307 On papal primacy and the papacy, see eg Johann Maier of Eck *Enchiridion locorum communionum adversus Luterum et alios hostes Ecclesiae (1525–1543)* Corpus Catholicorum 34 (Münster 1979); 'Papal Primacy' in *The Papacy: An Encyclopedia* ed Philippe Levillain 3 vols (New York and London 2002) I 1240–8; John E. Bigane III *Faith, Christ, or Peter: Matthew 16:18 in Sixteenth Century Roman Catholic Exegesis* (Washington, DC 1981) 15–68, who finds Erasmus' interpretation of the word *petra* in Matt 16:18 as referring to faith, not Peter or the church; Augustijn *Erasmus* 101; Tracy (1) 108; Bernhard Schimmelpfennig *The Papacy* (New York 1992); Michael Wilks *The Problem of Sovereignty in the Later Middle Ages: The Papal Monarchy with Augustinus Triumphus and the Publicists* (Cambridge 1963); Jared Wicks *Cajetan Responds: A Reader in Reformation Controversy* (Washington, DC 1978), and his 'Roman Reactions to Luther: The First Year (1518)' *Catholic Historical Review* 69 (1983) 521–62; Paolo Prodi *The Papal Prince: One Body and Two Souls: The Papal Monarchy in Early Modern Europe* trans Susan Haskins (Cambridge 1987).
308 Augustine *De civitate Dei* 15.1; see especially books 1–5. See also Tarsicius J. van Bavel 'Church' in *Augustine* 169–76; and the essays in Pabel. See *De puritate tabernaculi* CWE 65 228: 'The church of the just which is the body of Christ has existed from the very beginning of the world and so has the Christian message, that is, the remission of sins which was divinely revealed and has as its source the mercy of God freely given for Christ's sake; there has existed also the grace which has purified men's hearts by faith, although the incarnate Christ and the preaching of the apostles caused it to spread further and to shine forth more brightly. Indeed, what St Paul so often emphasized held true even then, namely that no one attains perfect righteousness through the Law or the works of the Law except by trusting in Christ . . .'
309 Book 3 CWE 68 994
310 Book 3 CWE 68 994
311 See *De concordia* CWE 65 152: 'There is a measure of truth in what some say, that the church is invisible. Only God can see into human hearts and know for

Erasmus similarly envisions the church in a dynamic way, where what had been prepared slowly by God teaching his people over time through crude ceremonies and types[312] as a method of progressive revelation at last became brightly manifest with the coming of Christ; as teacher of the heavenly philosophy, he made known to us what these previous things signified and finally at Pentecost revealed them abundantly through the Holy Spirit. As the church progresses through time, approaching the final age when Christ will be joined fully with his members, and as it becomes more perfected in love and concord,[313] it will more and more 'reflect the image of that heavenly one in which there is perfect order and perfect harmony,' until finally 'a new heaven and a new earth[314] are created not by the destruction of matter but by the removal of corruption.'[315] The eschatological age of a perfected church will be the result of a long and continuous process of ever more regular, diligent, and pure preaching.

In this vision of the church where the bishop functions primarily as teacher, Erasmus reminds us that Jesus neither baptized, anointed, nor administered the sacraments, but he taught continually.[316] Erasmus does not dismiss or discount the administration of the sacraments or the other functions that bishops and their coadjutors commonly perform, but he is emphatic

* * * * *

certain which are his own. But often we find that there are various methods which can be used to determine where we may find God's church, and where the synagogues of Satan; for the sins of many "run before them to judgment." But even this visible church, containing as it does wrongdoers together with the good, gives an extraordinarily imposing impression of zeal whenever it assembles for the ritual expression of devotion.' Cf book 2 CWE 68 695 where he describes the church by etymology: 'The church is called a "congregation" or "assembly" which comes together to hear the word of God; hence where there is no time for sacred learning, where there are discordant minds, there is no church.'

312 For types in Erasmus' exegesis, see Colloquia (Convivium religiosum) CWE 39 217 n117: 'Distinct from allegory in use though not always in name was typology, the interpretation of later events by earlier ones now perceived or believed to have prefigured them. Thus the preference of Isaac for Jacob prefigured the divine protection of Israel. The most characteristic typology found "types" of actions or persons in the Old Testament prefiguring those of the New; Adam and David prefigured Christ. Interpretation of much of the Old Testament by writers of the New Testament was inescapably typological ...'
313 Cf Eph 4:13–15.
314 See 2 Pet 3:13; Heb 12:22; Rev 21.
315 Book 1 255
316 Cf 1 Cor 1:17: 'For Christ sent me not to baptize, but to preach the Gospel ...' See also Ratio 199–200.

that it is in 'this supreme office of teaching' that the *ecclesiastes* 'should surpass himself.'[317] Teaching, after all, is the way God dealt with the children of Israel and Christ with those of his time; it should be the bishop's absolute priority. To emphasize this, Erasmus invokes the uncommon practice of John Colet, dean of St Paul's in London, who, unlike his contemporary priests in England who said mass every day, 'was content to celebrate on Sundays and festivals, or at least on very few days besides them; either because he was occupied with the sacred studies with which he used to prepare himself for preaching, and by the business of his cathedral, or because he discovered that he celebrated with more lively feeling if he did it at intervals.'[318] Like Colet, the good minister of the word knows that preparation for preaching is demanding, time-consuming, and must be foremost in his mind.

Erasmus acknowledges that at times the content of a bishop's teaching might clash with the teachings of his fellow bishops. Though he does not dwell on the relationship of bishops to one another, the relationship of bishops to the pope, or of the pope to universal councils of the church,[319] he identifies a singularly critical role for the supreme pontiff, the bishop of Rome, as judge. Because disagreements among teacher-bishops are inevitably bound to occur,[320] the universal church requires a single authority to whom all other bishops must submit their judgment; 'the existence of a single Roman pope to preside over all the churches is useful for fending off schisms.'[321] As the bishop exercises this role in his own diocese, so this expanded role befits the pope, 'the monarch of the church' and 'the pastor of the whole world,'[322] who serves as a catalyst of concord and a supreme

* * * * *

317 Book 1 403; see eg: 'How great, then, is the dignity befitting the ministers of the New Testament, who daily sacrifice that heavenly victim that merits the adoration even of the angelic spirits, who touch with their hands the flesh of the immaculate lamb!' Book 1 319.

318 Letter to Justus Jonas (Anderlecht, 13 June 1521) Ep 1211:240; for Colet see John Gleason *John Colet* (Berkeley 1989) and ER 2 36–8.

319 On Erasmus' view of the relationship of the pope to a general council of the church, see Minnich 52–3. Erasmus raises some of these questions in *Ratio* (206), though without taking a stand on them. See also his dedicatory letter to John Colet in *De copia* CWE 24 284: 'First, you observed that the richest rewards of charity lie in bringing Christ into the hearts of one's countrymen by continual preaching and by holy instruction.'

320 Cf 1 Cor 11:19.

321 Book 1 343

322 Book 1 360 'the monarch of the church' *monarcha ecclesiae*; book 1 359 *totius orbis pastor*

judge for the entire church, insuring that schisms do not occur and speaking out the consensus of bishops and the faithful everywhere. Erasmus tells Paul Volz (1518) that the pope is the 'principal teacher' of 'the heavenly philosophy of Christ.'[323] Though Erasmus neither asserts that this special power of the pope exists *de iure divino* (though arguably he strongly implies this), nor attributes to the pope the gift of infallibility, nor advances any type of anticonciliarist (or conciliarist) position,[324] he grants the pope this traditional ecclesiastical pre-eminence and jurisdictional prerogative because 'the Roman Pontiff, as he is the nearer to Christ whose role he performs,'[325] requires that ultimately all bishops submit to his judgment in obedience to Christ.[326] Without this prerogative, schisms and, even worse, heresies would resist every effort to resolve them, wherefore the pope alone enjoys the finality of judgment for the universal church.[327]

Erasmus does not directly entertain the question whether a pope might err in matters of faith and morals or whether a council may intervene to depose a pope teaching heretical doctrines. Words on these questions occur

* * * * *

323 Letter to Paul Volz (Basel, 14 August 1518), Ep 858:219–22: 'And yet no man more truly forwards the business of the pontiff than he who publishes in its pure form the heavenly philosophy of Christ, of which the pope is the principal teacher.'
324 See Stupperich 351–2.
325 Book 2 CWE 68 594 *vicinior est Christo cuius vices gerit*
326 See also Gogan 409. Cf Erasmus' letter to Arkleb of Boskovice (Louvain, 28 January 1521), Ep 1183:80–6: 'I cannot now discuss the source whence this authority [supreme authority of the pope] was originally conveyed to him; to say the least, just as in the early days out of many priests who were still all equal one bishop was chosen for the prevention of schism, so now it is expedient for one pope to be chosen out of all the bishops, not only to rule out divisions but to restrain the despotism of other bishops, should any one oppress his own flock, and of secular princes.' McSorley argues that Erasmus changed his view shortly afterwards: 'By June of 1524 Erasmus had, under the influence of his fresh awareness of the decrees of the Council of Florence, begun to make decisions about two questions that, until that time, had not really been clear in his mind: (1) is the Roman primacy of divine origin? and (2) is this still a matter for scholastic disputation or is it an article of faith?' (46–7). McSorley contends at this point Erasmus held the primacy of the pope as *de iure divino* and produces evidence to support his thesis. From the few statements in *Ecclesiastes* it is not possible to establish this argument as firmly.
327 Book 1 343. One steady refrain throughout *Ecclesiastes* is Erasmus' insistence on subordinating one's will to that of the church and refraining from stirring up rebellion and sedition against it, for this is great impiety.

only obliquely in *Ecclesiastes*. Yet, it seems to have become clear to Erasmus in the late 1520s and 1530s that only a hierarchical structure of authority could guarantee 'peace and concord' among the members of Christ's body in these years of worsening schism, despite the fact that historically some individual popes such as Julius II (1503–17) had been less than exemplary occupants of the chair of Peter.[328] True obedience and the need for Christian peace and concord, Erasmus repeatedly urges, compel one to submit to all legitimate authority, from councils to papal decrees, to legitimate secular authority; for without submission there cannot be lasting peace and tranquillity. Ultimately it is consensus among bishops that matters; so it is fitting 'to observe reverently what the public authority of the church has prescribed, especially in universal councils, and what has been approved by public and long-standing observance, nor should one scorn the instructions that popes have given on just grounds for the public good.'[329] Though Erasmus allows wide room for theological views that have not been defined by church councils, he maintains that once definitions have been made and judgments pronounced the limits of theological dissent have been reached.[330]

Erasmus is mindful that over the centuries the practical functions of bishops in their dioceses changed considerably, and to a large extent he concedes that the modifications in the original episcopal practices had been necessary. Looking historically at the evolution of the episcopacy, he observes

* * * * *

328 See eg *Julius exclusus* CWE 27 155–97; *Sileni Alcibiadis* in Olin *Catholic Reformation* 79: 'In the same way they call the priests, bishops and Popes "the Church", when in reality they are only the servants of the Church. The Church is the whole Christian people, and Christ himself says it is too great to lie down before the bishops who serve it ...'; and 'but pray tell me, if there is any pleasure in hating the enemy of the Church, could there be any enemy more pernicious, more deadly than a wicked Pope?'

329 Book 4 CWE 68 1035; see also Erasmus' letter to Simon Pistoris (Basel, [c 2 September] 1526), Ep 1744:17–23, where he declares, 'It is important to distinguish different kinds of church decrees. Some come from a general council, some from rescripts, some belong to the bishops, some to the Roman pontiff but have the character of a ruling, like the constitutions of the Camera. Again, some of the decrees of synods are permanent, some temporary. Similarly, some are inviolable – those, for example, that rest on Holy Scripture; some can be altered to suit the circumstances ...' For Pistoris, see Simon Pistoris CEBR III 96–7.

330 On the question of the limits of theological debate in Erasmus' writings, see Manfred Hoffmann 'Erasmus and Religious Tolerance' ERSY 2 (1982) 80–106; Myron P. Gilmore '*De modis disputandi*: The Apologetic Works of Erasmus' in *Florilegium Historiale: Essays Presented to Wallace K. Ferguson* ed J.G. Rowe and W.H. Stockdale (Toronto 1971) 62–88. See also Stupperich 354–7.

that in the early church only the bishop taught, but afterwards teaching was transferred to presbyters, 'outstanding ones,' however, 'and not indefinitely.'[331] St Augustine, for example, assumed this role for Valerian, his ordinary, who was not a native speaker of Latin; lacking Augustine's eloquence, the bishop prudently invited him to teach in his stead.[332] But historically much changed after the time of Augustine 'since today a single city requires several preachers,'[333] and 'this role is widely delegated to monks and presbyters.'[334] It has fallen therefore to bishops that they must not only be trained in Scripture and preach well but they must make it a principal concern to admit suitable people to that office and 'remove the unsuitable.'[335] Erasmus sees this new duty of the bishop as taking on an even greater importance than his regular preaching, for in this way the bishop can supply his diocese with good preachers in all his churches, something he himself cannot do personally, given the numerous parishes and other venues requiring continual pastoral attention.

Another reason for this historical change in the bishop's responsibilities, according to Erasmus, is the moral degeneration that has set in since the early church.[336] Once it was the bishop alone who preached daily; but

* * * * *

331 Book 1 328; see also Jedin II 646, where the Council of Vaison (529) 'presided over by Caesarius [of Arles], expressly gave to the priests in the country the right of preaching, which at the same time meant the duty of preaching ...'

332 Book 1 328. See Possidius *Life of St. Augustine* FOC 15 78–9. In the preface to the Froben edition of Augustine's *Opera* (1529), Erasmus singles out the bishop of Hippo as exceptionally notable for his dedication to the office of preaching. See the letter to Alonso de Fonseca (Freiburg [May] 1529), Ep 2157:26–31: 'But I do not think there is another Doctor whom that rich and generous Spirit has endowed so abundantly with all his gifts as Augustine. It is as though he wanted to paint on a single canvas a picture of the model bishop, complete with all the qualities that Peter and Paul, following Christ, the prince of bishops, demand of those who undertake to feed the Lord's flock.' See also lines 152–5: 'But especially in education, which is the most important function of a bishop, there was such a many-sided brilliance in him that there is no one, among either Greek or Latin writers, whom we could put alongside him in this role.'

333 Book 1 343

334 Erasmus' reference to monks includes above all the mendicant orders (Franciscans, Dominicans, Augustinians, and Carmelites); see book 1 443 and n1252.

335 Book 1 344

336 On Erasmus' view of the decay of church and society over time, see also Ep 858:530–632; and *Ratio* 249, where he compares the charity of the early

'after what belonged to one began to be distributed to many as human charity grew colder, that which was the chief function of a presbyter, namely teaching the people the precepts of the Lord, was now delegated to preachers.'[337] Erasmus sees the history of the church as a continuous descent from its spiritual apogee in the time of Christ, the early Christian writers, and first bishops of the church, after which 'sincerity decreased and luxury increased among evangelists,'[338] and most clergy not only lost the sense of the preaching office's tremendous significance but received no training in Scripture or skills in speaking. Whereas in the apostolic age the church 'grew strong and spread, flourished and reached the pinnacle of piety,'[339] afterwards it began its troubled decline, losing its fervour until at length 'religion became narrowly restricted and so devoid of passion that you would hardly say it was the same church.'[340] Erasmus notes caustically that today all one needs to preach is 'an ashen robe, a black or white mantle.'[341] Every sort of person – the young, the irresponsible, the ignorant – is admitted, sometimes even leaps up, to make sacred orations, as though nothing were easier than to expound divine Scripture to the people, and as though it were quite enough 'to put off all shame and set their tongue rolling.'[342] He gives Jan Becker the remedy for this disease: 'Make it your business to instill Christ pure and simple into the minds of your flock, for that we see done by very few.'[343] It is therefore one of *Ecclesiastes'* chief lessons that everyone teaching the Lord's flock 'must remember that he is occupied in an office that far surpasses the dignity of a king and that is primarily in a bishop, who is greater than any king, certainly in so far as the sublimity of his office is

* * * * *

church with charity of his day: where once there were no ceremonies, they now abound; then there was no mention of ceremonies, but now with ceremonies everywhere superstition thrives.

337 Book 1 149–50. For Erasmus' view of history, see the bibliography provided by *Humanismus und Historiographie* ed Hilmar A. Buck (Weinheim 1991); and see P. Bietenholz *History and Biography in Erasmus of Rotterdam* (Geneva 1966); *L'Histoire au temps de la Renaissance* ed M. Jones-Davies (Paris 1995).

338 Book 1 370; see also Ep 1334:384–407. Erasmus' view of the church's history is also succinctly treated below; see book 3 CWE 68 728–9 and n22. For this question, see Ralph Keen 'The Allure of the Past: Religious Reform and the Recovery of Ancient Ideals' ERSY 26 (2006) 16–28; and Augustijn *Erasmus* 84–6.

339 Book 3 CWE 68 728

340 Book 3 CWE 68 729. For the same 'Renaissance perspective' see introduction CWE 61 xxii–xxiii.

341 Book 1 327

342 Book 1 252

343 Letter to Jan Becker of Borsele (Louvain, 24 April 1519), Ep 952:51–2

concerned.'[344] All others who preach, whether mendicants, secular clergy, or suffragan bishops, assist the bishop as delegates in his office as teacher. And it falls upon the bishop to provide the best preachers possible; after all, he 'himself is in danger ... since he will render an account to the Lord for each sheep.'[345]

To prepare preachers, Erasmus envisions a kind of comprehensive *paideia*[346] commencing in the candidates' earliest years and continuing throughout life, much like the career of St Jerome.[347] Convinced that 'almost the whole corruption of character comes from a corrupted education'[348] and that 'we do most sucessfully what we have learned to do since childhood,' he advocates shaping the excellent preacher 'right from infancy.'[349] And because 'talent betrays itself by tokens right in earliest youth,'[350] he urges parents and bishops to identify early on those children with 'natural inclinations' for preaching that they might profitably employ the best years in life for memory retention, correct learning and pronunciation, and embracing 'the

* * * * *

344 Book 1 329
345 Book 1 345; see also Heb 13:17; John 10:11–16 and 21:15–17; cf Acts 20:28; 1 Pet 5:2–4.
346 See Erasmus *De pueris instituendis* CWE 26 291–346, which Froben published in September 1529 after Erasmus had moved from Basel to Freiburg im Breis- gau; it emphasizes the need for parents to undertake their children's liberal arts education as early as possible: 'You will see to it that your son makes his first acquaintance with a liberal education immediately, while his mind is still uncorrupted and free from distractions, while he is in his most forma- tive and impressionable years, and while his spirit is still open to each and every influence and at the same time highly retentive of what it has grasped; for we remember nothing in old age as well as what we absorbed during our unformed years' (297).
347 See *Vita Hieronymi* CWE 61 15–62.
348 Book 2 CWE 68 622. Erasmus notes in *Paraclesis* (in Olin 105): 'For that which the new earthen pot of the soul first imbibes settles most deeply and clings most tenaciously. Let the first lispings utter Christ, let earliest childhood be formed by the Gospels of him whom I would wish particularly presented in such a way that children also might love him.'
349 Book 1 297–8 and 326; see also Quintilian 1.1.1–36; and Plutarch *De liberis educandis* 3E: 'For youth is impressionable and plastic and while such minds are still tender lessons are infused deeply into them; but anything which has become hard is with difficulty softened.' See too Erasmus *Vita Hieronymi* CWE 61 25 and *Enchiridion* CWE 66 85: 'Children should imbibe convictions worthy of Christ, because nothing sinks more deeply into the mind or adheres to it more tenaciously than that which is instilled in it in early years, as Quintilian says.'
350 Book 2 CWE 68 484

precepts of living rightly.'[351] He supports this idea with examples from the lives of eloquent preachers: St Bernard's mother provided a model of schooling, for 'she educated her son as if she were preparing him for solitude, not the court';[352] and Athanasius was 'educated this way in the bishop's house, for bishops' homes were once schools of piety, whence they were also called monasteries.'[353] In good schools future preachers would meditate upon the law of the Lord, and 'if appropriate, careful, and correct instruction' were 'added to these natural inclinations, there is great hope that, with the protection of the Holy Spirit, we shall have suitable heralds of God's word.'[354] The preacher's career thus begins in the school of piety under careful parental and episcopal supervision.

The school Erasmus envisions is a bishop's collegium for generating qualified preachers to herald the good news of the gospel.[355] Responsibility for founding and maintaining it falls to the bishop, whose intention should be 'that chosen talents may be trained there not just for logical argument but much more for preaching.'[356] Erasmus may well have recalled the various colleges with which he was personally familiar at the universities of Paris and Cambridge, which trained clerics, but he certainly would have had more in mind the colleges supported by exemplary clergymen such as John Fisher, William Warham, David of Burgundy,[357] and John Colet.[358] His

* * * * *

351 Book 2 CWE 68 589; and *Vita Hieronymi* CWE 61 25
352 Book 2 CWE 68 622
353 Book 2 CWE 68 622; cf *Ratio* 256.
354 Book 2 CWE 68 485
355 A good view of the curriculum and purpose of such a collegium is found in Erasmus' *Apologia contra Latomi dialogum* (1518) CWE 71 33–84, which deals with Erasmus' understanding of 'the three [scriptural] languages and ... the approach to theological studies' (37).
356 Book 1 352
357 Book 1 345. David, formerly bishop of Utrecht, the natural son of duke Philip the Good (great-grandfather of Charles v), ordained Erasmus a priest in 1492; see CEBR I 226–7; see also Schoeck (1) 109–10. For Erasmus' esteem of Warham, see book 1 352–5 and Ep 326:124–9.
358 See also his dedicatory letter to John Colet in *De copia* CWE 24 especially 284: 'You founded a school that far excels the rest in beauty and splendour, so that the youth of England, under carefully chosen and highly reputed teachers, might there absorb Christian principles together with an excellent literary education for their earliest years. For you are profoundly aware both that the hope of the country lies in its youth – the crop in the blade, as it were – and also how important it is for one's whole life that one should be initiated into excellence from the very cradle onwards.'

experiences at the Collège de Montaigu, on the other hand, seem to have provided him with a useful corrective for how not to organize such an institution. More concretely, we get a glimpse of Erasmus' idea of the collegium if we examine the plans he shared with Jérôme de Busleyden for establishing at the University of Louvain a Collegium Trilingue for teaching Latin, Greek, and Hebrew, the three languages required for competence in Scripture and professional preaching.[359] Fisher, Warham, David of Burgundy, and Colet were in Erasmus' estimation true pastors who cared deeply that young men under their tutelage and destined for the priesthood become effective preachers. Since their dioceses had grown too large for them to preach in every church, they believed their weightiest responsibility was to provide their flocks with suitable preachers by carefully selecting young men 'who have given unambiguous evidence that they would one day be able to serve as a good preacher'; it should be 'first and foremost among their concerns.'[360] Neglecting this responsibility, Erasmus notes, has been 'the source from which the greatest part of the church's calamities flows.'[361]

Erasmus envisions this collegium as a rigorous religious and academic institution not only set apart from the vices and concerns of the world but differing from the type of (scholastic) education where 'those who receive long training in theological disputations come out clever in argument, very, very few suited to preaching.'[362] His episcopal school takes a refreshingly

* * * * *

359 See Schoeck (2) 194–5. See *Ratio* 181, where on Augustine's authority in *De doctrina christiana* (2.11) Erasmus attests to the importance of learning Greek and Hebrew. Erasmus also identifies Etienne Poncher, one-time bishop of Paris and then of Sens, who offered abundant rewards for teachers of these languages; see *Ratio* 181–2. On the Collegium Trilingue at Louvain, see Henry de Vocht *History of the Foundation and the Rise of the Collegium Trilingue Lovaniense, 1517–1550* Humanistica Lovaniensia 10–13, 4 vols (Louvain 1951–5) and his *Jérôme de Busleyden* Humanistica Lovaniensia 9 (Turnhout 1950) 4–8; see also M. Nauwelaerets 'Érasme à Louvain. Éphémérides d'un séjour de 1517 à 1521' in *Scrinium* 1 3–24, especially 9–10. See especially *Epithalamium* CWE 39 527 n19 and the introduction to CWE 63 xlvii: Erasmus' 'own efforts to tackle Hebrew do not appear to have been especially successful'; see also xlviii. Cf book 2 CWE 68 486: 'Though Hebrew occupies the first rank of these three, its usefulness is circumscribed by the narrowest of limits ...'

360 Book 1 344. Erasmus says of Fisher that he used the 'huge sum of money' given him by King Henry VIII's paternal grandmother for 'the training of preachers or on providing comfort for the needy.' See Ep 3036 to Christoph von Stadion, 6 August 1535 (244).

361 Book 1 344

362 Book 1 352

new direction. The programme would differentiate sharply between genuine theological training and training in dialectic for theological investigation and disputation. Excellent teachers would be retained whose loving care would render suitable pupils docile and instill in them a love of virtue and a solid foundation in Scripture and the humanities.[363] The future preacher would be trained to be, as it were, the wise generalist (very much the model orator of Cicero's and Quintilian's world), not one who had accumulated huge amounts of information or skills in dialectic but who had 'learned what is best and most necessary' – 'the most outstanding out of what is best';[364] the pupil's aim would be not to master everything comprehensively but handle competently 'those things that are most suited to the office of teaching.'[365] Dialectic would emphatically be an important part of this education, but only to a point. The future preacher would learn dialectic 'for making correct judgments about truth and falsehood'[366] and 'adapting the subtlety of dialectic to the capacity of the congregation and elevate to a loftier meaning whatever seems too humble';[367] he would also have a firm knowledge of the ancient sources, though he would 'have them learned rather than be learning them, and have them learned rather than thoroughly learned, in order to avoid the fate of those many who, as the study becomes more attractive day by day, grow old there as if at the Sirens' rocks; and, as

* * * * *

363 Book 1 370–1; cf Quintilian 2.3.10–12: 'The teacher should therefore be as distinguished for his eloquence as for his good character, and like Phoenix in the *Iliad* be able to teach his pupil both how to behave and how to speak.' (2.3.12). See also Plutarch *De liberis educandis* 4B: 'Teachers must be sought for the children who are free from scandal in their lives, who are unimpeachable in their manners, and in experience the very best that may be found.'

364 Book 1 326; book 2 CWE 68 481. Erasmus recognizes the need for learning dialectic but emphasizes that one should be moderate in doing so and not be like 'those who waste a good part, or indeed all, of their time in the labyrinthine intricacies of Aristotle or Averroes or Scotus and on sophistical hair-splitting and trivial questions which serve no useful purpose?' (letter to Noël Béda [Basel, 15 June 1525], Ep 1581:589–92, quoted by Mark Crane). For the difference between the scholastic and the humanist approach to church reform, see Mark Crane 'Competing Visions of Christian Reform: Noël Béda and Erasmus' ERSY 25 (2005) 39–57.

365 Book 1 326

366 Book 2 CWE 68 613

367 Book 2 CWE 68 714; see also book 4 CWE 68 1097 where Erasmus recommends scholastic disputes for assisting the preacher in teaching theological dogmas, but he advises that 'scholastic disputes ... should be conducted soberly and rely especially upon scriptural foundations.'

Augustine advises, one takes no pleasure in quarreling.'[368] All this recalls
Erasmus' earlier ideas and practice of education, as well as his description
of St Jerome's education. Because life was too short to master even a minute
amount of what was good and worthy of human investigation, why spend
all one's time on the modern scholastic theologians and neglect the study
of grammar, languages, and the orators?[369] It was imperative that one learn
to discriminate in this early on with prudent direction by teachers who can
bring forth the flowers of their subjects.

Ecclesiastes further recommends that essential texts be known thoroughly, beginning with Scripture and the best of the church Fathers, and in
these the preacher should be exercised continuously.[370] But good pedagogy
is not just a matter of excellent subject matter; it is even more how one keeps
a young man's heart centred on what is good so that his 'senses be trained
for the contemplation of the intelligible' and that he possess 'a mind pure
and untroubled by any human emotions.'[371] Here, of course, engendering
piety is the central ambition, for, as Erasmus argues in *Ratio*, a great part
of theological learning depends on the piety of the individual, and he who
does not love what he reads and says cannot truly be a theologian.[372] The
educator's goal then is to foster the right attitude towards his subjects; he
would not allow the aspiring preacher to engage in the rhetorical exercise
of speaking on either side of an argument or of treating frivolous or dis-
creditable subjects. Instead, future preachers would dwell on what is good
and useful as piety demands. In the end they are to be transformed by what

* * * * *

368 Book 2 CWE 68 612; Erasmus notes this of Jerome in *Vita Hieronymi* CWE 61 27;
cf Plutarch *De liberis educandis* 7A–F.
369 *Apologia contra Latomi dialogum* CWE 71 31–82. Erasmus emphasizes the point
repeatedly in this work; see eg 77–8: 'But I have heard the best theologians
making the same complaint as Pico, and lamenting not that they had spent
time on scholastic theology but that they had spent so much time on this one
field of study and this alone.' See *Ratio* 296–7.
370 Cf *Ratio* 296.
371 Book 4 CWE 68 1080. Erasmus does not condemn human emotions; as he notes
in *Ratio* 216, Christ had human emotions: 'quod [Christus] humanis affectibus
tangitur.' However he distinguishes between good and bad ones, those that
move us to the love of Christ and neighbour, and those needing to be removed
thoroughly from our hearts; see his discussion of these in *Ratio* 227–36.
372 Erasmus here adds a bold clarification to his statement in *Paraclesis* (in Olin
97–9) on who really can be called a theologian: 'And if anyone under the
inspiration of the spirit of Christ preaches this kind of doctrtine, inculcates
it, exhorts, incites, and encourages men to it, he indeed is truly a theologian,
even if he should be a common labourer or weaver . . .'

they learn, which, as Erasmus saw it, was the essential difference between the scholastics' schools and the bishops' seminaries of learned godliness.

Erasmus envisioned a school that would be dedicated to the practice and perfection of oratorical rhetoric: that is, delivery (*actio*), or, as Quintilian put it, *pronunciatio*,[373] and Demosthenes 'action' (ὑπόκρισις) – public speaking. There one would not merely learn soberly the mental dexterity for sound judgment to 'enable what has come into question to be explained more quickly and more easily through it,'[374] but acquire a facility in speaking before a congregation of persons of various backgrounds. Given the right conditions, in such schools the novice's native abilities would flourish; and 'when this ability has been acquired by human industry, the richer grace of the Spirit comes over it, and instead of depleting it completes it, instead of taking it away assists it.'[375] Given that, to the extent the preacher earnestly devotes himself to the task of preaching well, the Holy Spirit does not refuse its increment, a young man may be assured that God will somehow further in his own mysterious way every honourable measure that the preacher takes to improve his speaking abilities.

The collegium Erasmus proposes also promised considerable practical advantages for sacred oratory. Like the *paideia* of ancient Rome, which took place in practical settings where youth could witness their fathers, mentors, and notable orators hold forth in the courts and public gatherings,[376] Erasmus' collegium would expose youth to frequent sermons and other types of oratory. Away from the allurements of the city and the vices of society and severed from worldly business, they would 'spend time among those who speak purely and elegantly, listen to preachers valued for the grace of their language,' and 'pour over the books of those who have been valued for their eloquence in the vulgar tongue, like Dante and Petrarch.'[377] They could read the best literature of the Greek and Latin authors, and even enjoy authors writing in the vernacular. Students would learn to remember and recite what they had heard, analyze a sermon's structure, divisions, themes, handling of Scripture, apothegms, and so forth. Study and practice would

* * * * *

373 Quintilian 11.3 passim; see 11.3.1: '*Delivery* [*pronuntiatio*] is often styled *action* [*actio*], but the first name is derived from the voice, the second from the gesture. For Cicero in one passage speaks of *action* as being a *form of speech*, and in another as being *a kind of physical eloquence*.'
374 Book 2 CWE 68 614
375 Book 2 CWE 68 470
376 See Pliny *Epistles* 8.14.4–6. See also Cicero *Pro Caelio* 4.9–11 for his words on mentoring Caelius in the forensic arts.
377 Book 2 CWE 68 488

endow the student with the power to discriminate among preachers, criticize a sermon's shortcomings in a courteous and constructive way, identify what was excellent, and of course appropriate what was best. Like the patrician youth of ancient Rome, the school for preachers would be one where the practice of public speaking took prominent place.

As important as theological education was for the preacher's work, the pursuit of godliness (*pietas*) was paramount. Because the *ecclesiastes* was entrusted with the noblest calling of instructing others in godliness, so godliness had to be fostered in these *collegia* before all else so that the young man 'render his heart the purest possible source of speech';[378] for it is from the pure heart that divine knowledge is acquired and grows, and only with such a heart can one speak words of the divine Spirit and be 'instructed by God' (θεοδίδακτος).[379] The lifelong training of the preacher therefore would begin with acquiring that purity of heart which alone distinguished the perfect Christian orator. To this, Erasmus adds, the preacher must be like David, begging the Lord for a threefold spirit: 'an upright spirit against the attacks of temptations, a holy spirit to inflame the minds of others also and bring them over to sanctity, and a principal spirit, or "a powerful spirit" as Jerome translates it ... for the richness of perfection.'[380] This 'principal' spirit would provide courage lest the speaker succumb to flattering those in power or caving in to the pressures, influence, and threats of the mighty; it is what one might call today the courage to speak truth to power, as Peter and the other apostles displayed on Pentecost when 'strengthened now by the principal spirit, they were not frightened by any threats of the wicked or cast down by any afflictions or elated or puffed up by any honours ...'[381]

* * * * *

378 Book 1 260, 255 n36

379 1 Thess 4:9 (θεοδίδακτοι); cf Isa 54:13 and *Ratio* 179. See too the character Theodidactus in *Convivium religiosum* who gives brief words on whether one would wish 'to be a child again if he could ...' *Colloquia* CWE 39 193.

380 Book 1 263–4. Note the difference in Jerome's translation of Ps 50:14 according to the LXX: *et spiritu principali confirma me* and according to the Hebrew *et spiritu potenti confirma me*. Erasmus is obviously aware of both renderings, but prefers the LXX's rendering, πνεύματι ἡγεμονικῷ 'principal' as the word ἡγεμονικόν conveys the ancient philosophical idea of the power of self-control and self-mastery. DV translates the phrase as 'strengthen me with a perfect spirit'; RSV (Ps 51:12): 'uphold me with a willing spirit.' On the Stoic concept of ἡγεμονικόν, see *De libero arbitrio* CWE 76 61 n288.

381 Book 1 264; see too Erasmus' quotation about the silence of preachers in his day: 'About the most insane wars which for so many years now embroil everything sacred and profane the theologians are silent, the preachers say nothing. And here was the broadest field for straining every sinew' (CWE 61 xxxii).

It is in essence the fortitude to preach the word worthily; it is a gift of the Holy Spirit[382] and its nourishment constant: ardent prayers, good works, and 'the food of the gospel's teaching.'[383] The result of this education will be the worthy preacher whose 'sole pursuit, sole glory is to have felt that the Holy Spirit has set the people on fire with a love of godliness through himself as the instrument.'[384] The product of the new episcopal school is the reformed preacher – godly, learned, zealous, accommodating, yet uncompromising when speaking on behalf of his Lord who directs the universe.

Hubert Jedin and Jacques Chomarat have discerned in Erasmus' thoughts on the new episcopal school an outline of the Catholic seminaries that would emerge from the reform decrees of the Council of Trent. Perhaps it is not going too much further to say as well that the programme of clerical education Erasmus enunciates in *Ecclesiastes*, which envisioned providing churches with 'preachers endowed with the evangelical virtues,'[385] adumbrates the harvest of exceptional preachers to emerge from these 'seminaries' in the post-Tridentine world of the late sixteenth and seventeenth centuries.'[386] And it is perhaps not too much to say in addition that so much of the brilliance of preaching in the decades after *Ecclesiastes'* appearance and in the post-Tridentine years owes no small debt to this seminal work on sacred oratory.[387]

One other principal aim of *Ecclesiastes* is to provide preachers with a comprehensive strategy for calling fallen humanity – Christians, Jews, heretics, non-believers, schismatics – to the pursuit of godliness.[388] The treatise would have preachers make all persons understand their proper, rightly ordered hierarchical relationship to God, his church, society, and all legitimate authority, so that at the end of salvation history, as Erasmus makes clear in book 4, cosmic harmony would be restored through obedience to God's law, which all creation will then obey. This in turn would redound to

* * * * *

382 Cf Isa 11:2–3.
383 Book 1 268
384 Book 3 CWE 68 811
385 Important of course for Erasmus was staffing these colleges with 'learned and godly men capable of moulding the young and dropping the seeds of Christian devotion upon their tender minds. The reflowering of evangelical vigour in the people rests particularly with these persons' (book 1 370).
386 See Council of Trent, Session 23, Canon 18 in Tanner 1 750–3.
387 For the reform and revolution in sacred eloquence after the Council of Trent, see Fumaroli 116–423.
388 See John W. O'Malley's general introduction to Erasmus' works on *spiritualia*, CWE 66 ix–li, especially the section on *pietas* (xv–xxi).

God's glory, with all persons returning to their created purpose – to know, fear, and love the Creator.[389] The preacher's special activity thus lies in bringing minds to understand God's law in its many vestiges; for once they apprehend this, human beings will ardently cooperate with God's abundant grace to obey his commands and seek the reform of life. This strategy of reform for bringing about true godliness begins by engendering a hatred of sin and the personal and social disorders that result from it; it then promotes faith and charity until it culminates in the perfection of the virtues. Despite his disappointment at the religious dissension and the dissolution of society about him that he felt towards the end of his life, Erasmus continued to hold on strongly to his deep belief that God's invitation to godliness is offered to all persons, all races, men and women, clergy and laity alike, all religions, and that a reform will at some point come about. And for those who embrace this reform the rewards are beyond all measure: 'the peace of a mind at ease with itself, freedom of the spirit, having peace with God, communion with all the saints, becoming a child of God instead of the devil's slave, the spiritual solace that the prophet says cannot be conceived by man.'[390] Collectively, at the end of time the final result of the preacher's work will be a restoration of that pristine cosmic order as it was *ab initio*.

Erasmus gives most attention to godliness (*pietas*) in treating the vices and virtues, where he situates it under equity or (commutative and distributive) justice, 'the virtue by which we assign to each what is owed.'[391] This virtue conforms to the ancients' teaching on 'the honourable' (*honestum*), which 'includes right and wrong, whether according to nature or contrary to

* * * * *

389 Book 2 635. For 'fear of the Lord,' cf Isa 11:2–3; it is the last of the seven gifts of the Holy Spirit. Fear of God is fundamental in Erasmus' idea of spiritual progress, which ends in embracing *pietas* as fully as one can. See eg Erasmus' example of a sermon on the paralytic (Matt 9:2–8; Luke 5:17–26): 'Fear of God is a big step towards piety' (book 3 CWE 68 889). See also Jean Vitrier's Homily 19, in Godin *Spiritualité* 198: 'On peult demander: que esse de pieté? Sainct Augustin dit que c'est service de Dieu, car pieté est une vertu qui a compassion de aultrui. Comment y a ilz en Dieu quelque chose dont ilz faille avoir pieté? Non, mais la creature n'est jamais sy amollie, ne touchié en l'afection, que de considerer la bonté et magnificence de Dieu nostre createur, laquelle chose est appellee pieté. C'est une grande inpieté de sentir mal contre les parolle de Dieu et que on ne les croit, ne aime et que on ayme plus ung peu de bien qu'i donne en ce monde, que ce qu'ilz promet. Pieté dont est service de Dieu. Sainct Augustin dit que par foy, esperanche, et charité, on sert a Dieu.'

390 Book 3 CWE 68 783; cf Cicero *De officiis* 1 and passim.

391 Book 3 CWE 68 858; cf Rummel *Erasmus* 54–7.

nature, piety and impiety towards God and the saints, towards one's country, towards parents and children . . . all the categories of virtues and vices, which are countless . . .'[392] Under this consideration Christ provides us with 'the perfect model . . . of all the virtues in which there was no flaw or defect commingled.'[393] In the fullness of his virtues one may contemplate that perfect godliness that embraces 'every affection, adoration, and all the duties that we owe to those from whom we have received life.'[394]

Considering humanity in relation to God, Erasmus envisions an ideal hierarchical moral order measured in debts and obligations, where 'the highest devotion is owed to God, to whom we owe whatever we are, the next to our homeland, the third to our parents and children, the fourth to our teachers and catechists, who are in a sense the parents of our minds, the fifth to those by whose kindness we have been saved from death or otherwise very grave dangers. All these are categories of justice.'[395] True godliness therefore discerns the appropriate relationships in this divinely ordered moral world of multiple hierarchies – between ourselves and God, ourselves and those who have jurisdiction over our lives, ourselves and all other persons of our world. In this vision the powers of the church and society exist ideally in reciprocal relations determined exactly according to status, each created to serve its constituency, and each constituent to serve its designated authorities; for 'it has pleased God, out of his love for peace and concord, that inferiors should obey their superiors . . .'[396] With God's grace we give to each what each legitimately has a right to expect from us; and each of us in turn carries out his responsibilities to those he has been ordained to serve. The preacher will call his audience's attention to these lawful arrangements, urging each to give to the other his due; and as each person does so, each complies in godliness with the dictates of divine justice.[397]

* * * * *

392 Book 2 CWE 68 548; cf Plutarch *De liberis educandis* 7A–F; and the introduction to *De puritate tabernaculi* CWE 65 219.

393 Book 4 CWE 68 1039. Erasmus believes that a deficiency in one of the virtues suggests a corruption of all the virtues; see eg *De puritate tabernaculi* CWE 65 258–9: 'To walk without blemish, to do what is right, to speak the truth in one's heart, and all the other things which he enumerated. For they are all connected, and if any one of them is lacking then the rest are invalidated.' Cf Cicero *De amicitia* 22.83.

394 Book 4 CWE 68 1047

395 Book 4 CWE 68 1047

396 See book 3 CWE 68 907. For a look at Erasmus' view of Christian society, see Ep 858 to Paul Volz.

397 Book 3 CWE 68 906–8 and book 4 CWE 68 passim

Further underlying Erasmus' teaching on godliness is his awareness of the vast multiplicity of God's creation and that each person has a unique calling from God and unique relationships with others in this world; these define each individual in his or her own station in life, and maintaining these relationships properly is crucial to right order in church and society.[398] It must therefore be the preacher's aim to awaken in each person an understanding of that particular end for which he or she has been called, as he notes, 'Great happiness would accrue in human affairs if each person kept his eye upon his target, not the one that desire has proposed, but the one that God and honourable thought has put before him.'[399] Despite there being so many human beings adrift in the morass of sinfulness, each nonetheless has some recognition, however faintly, of his or her moral dislocation and sinfulness. Each person therefore is to be aroused from sloth and moved to godliness, to show fitting gratitude for the blessings God has given and the circumstances into which he or she has been placed in this world, no matter how rich or lowly one may be. Understanding one's divinely appointed station is therefore the first step towards correcting the disorder vis-à-vis God and neighbour; for this reason especially the preacher himself must first understand the profound importance of his own calling and be awoken from spiritual sleep that he might awaken others.

Among the ancients the axiom that one could only move another if he himself were moved first goes to the heart of Erasmus' understanding of what makes the excellent preacher. He tells Jacques Masson (Jacobus Latomus) that 'according to Quintilian "A man who is not ablaze himself will never set others afire, nor will one who does not feel grief himself succeed in arousing it in others." So a theologian who has not felt the touch of the Spirit does not touch others with his words. He does not inspire others unless he himself is inspired.'[400] Indeed, if Erasmus leaves his readers with one lesson, it is that each preacher should know that 'nothing is more effective for stirring devout emotions than having experienced godly feelings yourself and nothing more useful for calming evil emotions than having been foreign to them.'[401] The first step to being moved is the awakening

* * * * *

398 See book 4 CWE 68 passim.
399 Book 2 CWE 68 635
400 *Apologia contra Latomi dialogum* CWE 71 55; see Quintilian 6.2.26. For Jacques Masson (Jacobus Latomus), see CEBR II 304–5. See eg Horace *Ars poetica* 102–3: 'If you would have me weep, you must first feel grief yourself'; Cicero *De divinatione* 1.37.80.
401 Book 2 CWE 68 804

from spiritual death, as 'the source of all vices comes from the fact that human weakness obeys the flesh more than the spirit.'[402] For this the preacher must excel at impressing upon hearers' emotions and minds the infinite distance between the Supreme Good and their own sinfulness. He must 'stir the emotions,'[403] shake them so that sinners detest their disordered condition and vices, whether selfishness, greed, drunkenness, debauchery, indolence. Quintilian observed that 'it is in its power over the emotions that the life and soul of oratory is to be found';[404] and it is the preacher's special duty to drive out the baser emotions with ones of a noble sort, 'like a nail with a nail.'[405]

Stirring (*movere*) the emotions therefore is the preacher's craft, which is what so many of *Ecclesiastes'* instructions intend to refine; as Erasmus puts it, it must be the zealous preacher's goal 'to leave in the minds of his listeners barbs that hold fast and to scatter upon them, as it were, good seed on good ground, so that it exercises its power gradually until it bursts forth into the fruit of piety.'[406] The preacher's activity thus becomes an occasion of grace; moving the emotions over time, if done well (and not by using foolish gimmicks),[407] will impel hearers 'towards the characteristics of godliness, when they are inspired through the praise of harmony towards love of concord and hatred of schism, when by praise of alms they are inflamed towards generosity to the needy and scorn for greed, and when by praise of innocence they are kindled towards a zeal for piety and the love of a more reformed life.'[408] Preaching against vices and promoting the virtues fosters *pietas* (and is itself a work of *pietas*), for the elimination of vices and the acquisition of virtues are a society's key index of its right relation to God. For this reason too the preacher is directed especially to attack those vices that cause disorder in society rather than the persons who have fallen prey to them.[409] All this of course presupposes faith that, where preaching is done simply and sincerely, God's grace will be abundantly available for those who propose to amend their lives.

* * * * *

402 Book 4 CWE 68 1053
403 Book 3 CWE 68 766, 795
404 Quintilian 6.2.7
405 *Adagia* I ii 4 *Clavem clavo pelere* 'To drive out one nail by another' (CWE 31 148–9).
406 Book 3 CWE 68 806
407 Book 3 CWE 68 766
408 Book 3 CWE 68 722–3
409 See book 3 CWE 68 860, 1002–3, 1014.

If it is honourable and godly that each person render to others in the measure one has received, then in relation to God humanity is infinitely at a loss. Not only unresponsive and steeped in injustice, humanity also suffers from an even greater debt because to God and Christ is owed what no mortal could ever repay, as there exists no proportion between the infinite and the finite,[410] between the immensity of God's gift in Christ and what any human being, even one with the warmest, most generous heart, could possibly render in return. Here the preacher's task is to make listeners aware of the enormous chasm between God's infinite beneficence and their own contemptible forgetfulness of God, the giver and provider of all good things. It is here, too, the Christian must begin to grasp God's immeasurable gift in Christ, in whose body alone humanity can be reconciled with the Father. For only through membership in the body of Christ can humanity repay the gift of God's infinite mercy and transcend the divide between oneself and God's infinite goodness.

Erasmus' well known criticisms of pseudopiety abound in *Ecclesiastes*, but his attacks are moderate when measured against many of his earlier works. Frequently he gives vent to criticism of empty rituals, the lifestyles of monks, and pretentions of those whom he sees as claiming to have 're-nounced the world' (as if other Christians do not do so in their baptismal vows).[411] He may question whether Benedict or Francis ever prescribed a specific garment for their respective orders[412] and criticize the spiritual impoverishment of the monastic life where 'not a word [is said] about the pursuit of piety.'[413] Certain words appearing frequently in the Scriptures but distorted over time still provoke biting responses that can go on at length;[414] words like 'world,' 'religious,' 'brother' and 'obedience,' 'perfection,' 'the flesh,' 'concupiscence,' 'heretic,' 'apostate' often act as hair triggers firing off sharp comments.[415] Many of the old refrains we hear repeated, for example, that religious life was 'invented by men,'[416] and that in Benedictine monasticism 'it is not permitted to make time for the Bible, or to aspire

* * * * *

410 See book 2 CWE 68 714.

411 See book 3 CWE 68 901. For Erasmus on the original state of monasticism, see *Vita Hieronymi* CWE 61 29; *De concordia* CWE 65 164; and Rummel 'Monachatus' passim.

412 See book 3 CWE 68 905. For extensive criticism on monastic garb, see 'The Well-to-do Beggars, πτωχοπλούσιοι in *Colloquia* CWE 39 468–98, especially 481–2.

413 See book 2 CWE 68 623.

414 See eg book 3 CWE 68 909, 1014; see as well his comments in Ep 858 to Paul Volz.

415 See book 3 CWE 68 1014.

416 See book 3 CWE 68 909–10; *Ratio* 265.

to a purer piety if someone happened to want to.'[417] But as elsewhere Erasmus' purpose in calling attention to practices and institutions that deviate from true godliness is to reset human and spiritual values in proper perspective;[418] often he makes clear his intention, 'I am not attacking the word "monk," which would be popular with all good people if the character of many of them had not made it odious. Moreover I would tolerate monastic brotherhoods, commending their institution with invented origins ...'[419] 'Fasting in order to attune body to mind for the offices of piety is a holy work; fasting in order to be considered holy is hypocrisy.'[420] The increase of godliness – zealously pursuing an active spiritual life – therefore should ever be the proper end; whatever helps one pursue godliness effectively is good and should be judged on that basis. It is not the ritual, the fasting, praying, almsgiving, the pilgrimage, or the life of the monk as such, but how these dispose the heart and mind to carry out the obligations of true godliness (care for sick, love of neighbour, love of God, expansion of the heart ...) that we find the spiritual measure of the exercise. With the significance of the preacher's moral status, purpose, and duties made clear, Erasmus proceeds to the next two books of his treatise to take up the precepts of oratory that the *ecclesiastes* should learn as well as possible.

Erasmus' purpose in books 2 and 3 of *Ecclesiastes*, as he says, is to allow readers to 'sample some of the rhetoricians' precepts that seem appropriate to the preacher's office.'[421] At the outset he makes clear that he is not laying down rules of rhetoric that the learner must know by rote; it is rather but 'a sampling' as he says of the most useful rhetorical precepts that the reader might appropriate in his own way and in his own time, without passing through the rigours of a formal education programme (though this might well be the formal plan of a bishop's collegium). Book 2 begins by explaining what the art of rhetoric is and how the preacher can use it to preach well, and then reviews the disciplines with which the *ecclesiastes* should have some familiarity, above all grammar, whose fundamental importance Erasmus cannot emphasize enough; 'the art of speaking correctly'[422] is key to

* * * * *

417 See book 2 CWE 68 623.
418 Erasmus does this in Ep 858 to Paul Volz.
419 See book 3 CWE 68 752. On this saying in Erasmus and the controversy it generated, see Rummel 'Monachatus' passim.
420 See book 2 CWE 68 635.
421 Book 2 CWE 68 496; see also Erasmus' letter to Christoph von Stadion (243), where he states it is to 'accommodate to preaching the precepts of the rhetoricians, logicians, and theologians.'
422 Book 2 CWE 68 474: 'Grammar is the art of speaking flawlessly' (*grammatica sit ars emendate loquendi*). See Quintilian 1.4.1–2: 'As soon as the boy has learned

every discipline and vital for preaching. Without it every effort at communication falters. The study of grammar in Erasmus' Europe and throughout the Renaissance was far more broadly conceived than it is today.[423] Grammarians of antiquity and humanists of the Renaissance viewed the subject as embracing an extensive knowledge of philology, history, poetry, antiquity, and, for Erasmus in particular, the three ancient languages – Hebrew, Greek, Latin.[424] Ideally, the young man entering the bishop's collegium for training would come well prepared in the fundamentals of the Latin language for correct writing and conversation. By the time he took up the advanced study of grammar, he would have reached the stage where he could begin what was known as the *studia humanitatis* (grammar, rhetoric, poetry, history, and moral philosophy).[425] Each of these disciplines was similarly vast in compass and required extensive study, as Erasmus observes: 'History,' for example,

* * * * *

to read and write without difficulty, it is the turn for the teacher of literature (*grammaticus*) ... This profession may be most briefly considered under two heads, the art of speaking correctly and the interpretation of the poets ...' By this Quintilian primarily understands common speaking and not public oratory, which comes under rhetoric; see also *Apologia contra Latomi dialogum* CWE 71 81–2; and *De ratione studii* CWE 24 667–91. Speaking correctly means more than mere grammatical correctness; see Quintilian 1.6.27: 'It seems to me that the remark, that it is one thing to speak Latin and another to speak grammar, was far from unhappy' (*quare mihi non invenuste dici videtur, aliud esse Latine, aliud grammatice loqui*).

423 Book 2 CWE 68 480: Grammar 'embraces both history and poetry and knowledge of antiquity as well as knowledge of the three languages.' See also Henri Marrou *A History of Education in Antiquity* (New York 1956); Kaster *Guardians*; Black; Witt *Footsteps* 1–30; Grendler (1) 203–71, and Grendler (2) 199–205; see also his many pertinent articles in *Renaissance Education between Religion and Politics* Variorum Collected Studies Series CS845 (Aldershot 2006); O'Malley 'Grammar'; Stanley F. Bonner *Education in Ancient Rome: From the Elder Cato to the Younger Pliny* (Berkeley 1977) 189–211. See also O.B. Hardison 'The Orator and the Poet: The Dilemma of Humanist Literature' *Journal of Medieval and Renaissance Studies* 1 (1971) 33–44.

424 See book 2 CWE 68 485–6. Erasmus contended against Latomus that a knowledge of these languages was necessary for interpreting Scripture. See *Apologia contra Latomi dialogum* CWE 71 37–84, especially 41–56; and Georges Chantraine, 'L'Apologia ad Latomum: Deux conceptions de la théologie' in *Scrinium* II 51–75. See also *Ratio* 181–2. See also *De ratione studii* CWE 24 667–91.

425 See eg Hanna H. Gray 'Renaissance Humanism: The Pursuit of Eloquence' *Journal of the History of Ideas* 24 (1963) 497–514; William J. Bouwsma *The Culture of Renaissance Humanism* (Washington, DC 1973) passim; Black passim; Grendler (1) 203–71; W. Keith Percival 'The *Studia Humanitatis*: Renaissance Grammar' in Rabil III 67–83; John Monfasani 'Humanism and Rhetoric' in Rabil III 171–235.

'is simply blind without cosmography and arithmetic.'[426] The disciplines required time and diligence to acquire before one advanced to others.

For exercise in grammar Erasmus advocates reading the best of the ancient authors (*auctores*), those so advanced 'in the elegance of their language'[427] who demonstrated such correctness in speaking that all educated persons recognized their excellence. He advises boys to linger in grammar for some time, for in this one acquires an accuracy with words and in expressing their meaning; upon it every discipline depends, such as dialectic, which is 'blind without grammar,'[428] and above all the interpretation of Scripture. Erasmus demonstrates how particularly important grammar is by calling attention to the challenge words present as the names of (biblical) places and things have meanings that are often obscure, sometimes unknown, or have changed over time, 'as though nature's envy has taken care that there should be no sure knowledge of things that can be transmitted in writing to posterity with undoubtable fidelity, but require a particular experience of each of them.'[429] The exacting analysis of Scripture's obscurities demanded rigorous training in grammar and in languages, and even then one might never come to consensus, much less certainty, on what a passage – or even a particular word – of Scripture genuinely means, its true sense (*sensus germanus*). Yet it is the preacher's duty to strive to obtain a facility in determining the precise grammatical meaning of the words of the text, for in the end much of his success will depend upon how well he has understood the language of God's word as it was spoken to the patriarchs, prophets, and apostles long ago. With thorough instruction in Latin grammar – words, their ideas and metaphorical expressions, composition – the aspiring preacher will then seek to acquire other languages, especially Greek and Hebrew (and its relatives Aramaic and Syriac), to advance his understanding of biblical words and foster good judgment in speaking.

* * * * *

426 See book 2 CWE 68 474; see also *Ratio* 184–5. For Erasmus' insistence on establishing the historical accuracy of the text, see Hilmar M. Pabel 'Retelling the History of the Early Church: Erasmus' Paraphrase on Acts' *Church History* 69 1 (2000) 63–85, especially 69 for comments on the importance of geography.

427 See book 2 CWE 68 480. For the idea of *elegantia*, see Lausberg §460.1; it involves idiomatic correctness (*latinitas*) and clarity (*perspicuitas*), ornaments (*ornatus*) and appropriateness (*aptum*). See also Quintilian 8.1.2, 11.3.30.

428 See book 2 CWE 68 474; cf *Ratio* 185.

429 See book 2 CWE 68 476; cf Horace *Ars poetica* 46–72. Help for the problem of Hebrew names and places would come from Jerome's translation of Eusebius' *Loca hebraica* and Philo's *Nomina hebraica*, which appear in volume IV of Erasmus' 1516 edition of Jerome; see the introduction to CWE 61 xxviii; cf *Ratio* 184–5.

Erasmus' model of the aspiring preacher further demands that the candidate demonstrate a natural disposition for the office and advancement in the art of public speaking. The young man will need to listen to successful preachers whom he can imitate and with whom he can train continually.[430] Not surprisingly, Erasmus does not dismiss or denigrate the vernacular; he demands that the preacher know it well because it is principally in this tongue that he must make himself understood and draw people to Christ.[431] For this reason too it is crucial he be educated among those who excel in the vernacular language so that in 'the pulpit, where the greatest matters are discussed,' he might command 'a magnificent, appropriate, expressive, and ready supply of words (*verborum copia*).'[432] Likewise he must learn to pronounce correctly,[433] which was of paramount importance in the ancients' training of youth. Erasmus declares, according to what others have said, that the Italian, Spanish, and French vernaculars, 'however corrupted, contain a grace that Latin does not achieve,'[434] and possibly the same could be said for English and German. And he once noted in his brief sketch of John Colet's life that his study of the English authors 'who did for their own people what Dante and Petrarch did for the Italians' endowed him with 'a facility of speech ... to be a herald of the gospel message.'[435] Without attentive study of the vernacular language therefore, one lacked the linguistic dexterity to communicate with his audience and would likely produce tragic results.

Erasmus moves quickly into the matter of classical rhetoric by taking up 'the particular tasks of the orator,'often referred to as the five parts of oratory or duties of the orator (invention, arrangement, style, memory, delivery).[436] Although not immediately apparent to the reader, nor expressly stated by Erasmus, these five parts of oratory constitute something of a basic

* * * * *

430 See book 2 CWE 68 487.
431 See book 2 CWE 68 486–7.
432 See book 2 CWE 68 486–7.
433 See book 3 CWE 68 739–46. See also *De recta pronuntiatione* CWE 26 347–475, which deals with Latin and Greek pronunciation, but whose principles, in the matter of preaching, Erasmus would certainly admit applied to vernacular speech, despite the appearance of so many new 'barbarian languages,' 'the number of different dialects even within single countries ...,' and 'their tendency to being debased' (390).
434 Book 2 CWE 68 488
435 Ep 1211:307–9
436 See book 2 CWE 68 509; and Quintilian 3.3.1–15: 'The art of oratory (*omnis autem orandi ratio*), as taught by most authorities, and those the best, consists of five parts: invention, arrangement, expression, memory, and delivery or action ...'

structure for books 2 and 3 of *Ecclesiastes*.[437] Whether one addressed civic assemblies or sacred congregations, the speaker had to devote time to invention (*inventio*), that is finding the fitting subject or conceiving the idea (*res*),[438] and imposing an effective arrangement (*dispositio* or *ordo*) upon it.[439] He would then clothe it with his own words and style (*elocutio*), memorize what needed to be retained (*memoria*), and deliver it (*actio* or *pronuntiatio*). As important as these five parts are, Erasmus gives them somewhat unequal treatment: invention, he tells us, he treated extensively in book 2, largely subsuming arrangement under it (as well as treating it under division when he considers the parts of the oration – *partes operis*);[440] *elocutio* he covers throughout book 3, where he also addresses memory and offers advice on delivery.

Affirming as paramount the duty of the bishop to teach, and in doing so move listeners by stirring emotions and awakening hearts to embrace godliness, Erasmus situates the *ecclesiastes'* work squarely within the ancients' three tasks or functions (*munera*) of the orator – teaching, moving, and delighting (*docere, movere, delectare*). All of these fall under the more general task of persuasion (*persuasio*), which most ancient writers regarded as the essence of rhetoric – the art of persuasion:[441] teaching addresses the intellect, moving engages the will, delighting appeals to the senses. In Christian preaching, however, there is of course this difference: preaching is a work of *pietas* that must drive the preacher's words. As Erasmus notes, 'The most important thing for persuasion is to love what you are urging; the heart itself supplies ardour of speech to the lover, and it brings the greatest force to effective teaching if you display within yourself whatever you are teaching to others.'[442] Similarly Augustine, following classical rhetorical teaching in his *De doctrina christiana*, defined the preacher's goal with

* * * * *

437 For an analysis of the problematic 'internal structure' of *Ecclesiastes*, see Hoffmann *Rhetoric* 169–72.
438 Quintilian 3.3.1–2; see Hoffmann *Rhetoric* 135–67.
439 Quintilian 3.3.8: arrangement, 'the marshalling of arguments in the best possible order.' Important in this respect for the thematic sermon is Erasmus' instruction on 'division'; see book 2 passim.
440 See book 2 CWE 68 509: 'Invention, which supplies the subject matter, though really it embraces both expression and order ...'
441 See Quintilian 2.15.1–38, where the author gives many definitions of the ancients; eg Aristotle: 'Rhetoric is the power of discovering all means of persuading by speech.' Quintilian however sees it rather as 'the science of speaking well.' See Lausberg §§3–41.
442 See book 1 299.

the Ciceronian triad – 'to teach, to delight, to bend ...' (*docere, delectare, flectere*).[443] Of the three activities, however, the most important, according to Augustine and Erasmus, is teaching, for in the latter's words, 'By teaching we cause something to be understood and made persuasive ...'[444] Although, as Quintilian noted, 'There have been certain writers of no small authority who have held that the sole duty of the orator was to instruct,'[445] he and many others understood that teaching can be dry and unproductive if there is not present some charm or appeal that keeps one bound to the speaker's words. In a sermon one must feel moved or persuaded by the message; for if we do not desire to embrace the good, the words have not achieved their intended effect.[446] While understanding the importance of all three tasks, Erasmus maintains that teaching what needs to be known for salvation is the core of the preacher's work. Teaching the heavenly philosophy was after all the heart of Jesus' earthly ministry, but it was

* * * * *

443 The terms for this triad will vary. Usually the three components of persuasion (*persuadere*) are given as *docere, delectare, movere*. See Lausberg §§255–7. See Augustine *De doctrina christiana* 4.27: 'Therefore a certain eloquent man [Cicero] said, and said truly, that he who is eloquent should speak in such a way that he teaches, delights, and moves. Then he added, "To teach is a necessity, to please is a sweetness, to persuade is a victory"' (trans D.W. Robertson). See Cicero *Orator* 21.69: ... *ut probet, ut delectet, ut flectat. Probare necessitatis est, delectare suavitatis, flectere victoriae.*

444 Book 2 CWE 68 504

445 Quintilian 5. prf 1: 'In their view appeals to the emotions were to be excluded for two reasons, first on the ground that all disturbance of the mind was a fault, and secondly that it was wrong to distract the judge from the truth by exciting his pity, bringing influence to bear, and the like.' Quintilian and the others obviously have in mind speeches before law courts.

446 See also Thomas Aquinas *Summa theologiae* IIa IIae q 177, where he discusses the effect of the grace of the word: 'This happens in three ways. First, in order to instruct the intellect, and this is the case when a man speaks so as to teach. Secondly, in order to move the affections, so that a man willingly hearkens to the word of God. This is the case when a man speaks so as to please his hearers, not indeed with a view to his own favour, but in order to draw them to listen to God's word. Thirdly, in order that men may love that which is signified by the word, and desire to fulfill it, and this is the case when a man so speaks as to sway his hearers. In order to effect this the Holy Ghost makes use of the human tongue as of an instrument; but he it is who perfects the work within. Hence Gregory says in a homily for Pentecost (*Hom. 30 in Evangelia*): "Unless the Holy Ghost fill the hearts of the hearers, in vain does the voice of the teacher resound in the ears of the body."' Aquinas is aware that Augustine refers to this rhetorical triad in the *De doctrina christiana* (4.12); see *Summa theologiae* IIa IIae q 177 a 1 obj 1.

also his special charisma as teacher to move and delight the hearts of his hearers.

Ecclesiastes dwells but briefly on the three tasks of oratory, most likely because the matter was well known and needed little elaboration. Numerous passages from Scripture illustrate how these tasks were executed; those who heard Christ teaching, for example, could not help but be moved and take delight in his words, as the exclamation of the disciples on the road to Emmaus demonstrates: 'Did not our hearts burn within us while he talked to us on the road, while he opened to us the Scriptures?'[447] In *De doctrina christiana* (4.12) Augustine captures this succinctly when referring to Cicero's *Orator* (21.69): 'Of the three [tasks of the orator], that which is given first place, that is, the necessity of teaching, resides in the things which we have to say, the other two in the manner in which we say it.' Erasmus concurs with Augustine's remark that sometimes 'the matter itself is pleasing when it is revealed simply because it is true,'[448] and he praises the homilies of Origen because his teaching brought delight in the doctrine he presents.[449] *Ecclesiastes* likewise proceeds from this principle, that if one taught skilfully, the matter itself brought delight. Teaching therefore was of primary importance, but one did not on this account neglect the crucial obligations of moving (*movere, flectare*) and delighting (*delectare*). After all, the complaint Erasmus had with the scholastics was that their excessive focus on academic teaching did not take into account the emotional and spiritual needs of the congregation who had to listen to cold, lifeless words.[450]

* * * * *

447 Luke 24:32. See *Paraphrasis in Lucam 11–24* CWE 48 272: 'When he was explaining to us the puzzles of figures and prophecies from Scripture in personal conversation as we travelled, didn't we feel a kind of marvellous glowing in our heart, nothing like the feeling that the speeches of the Scribes and Pharisees regularly produce in the hearts of the hearers? But the speech of the Lord Jesus used to be just like that to those who listened to him with open minds. He pricked his hearers, moved them, carried them out of themselves, seared them, set them afire, left sparks and darts in their hearts.'

448 Augustine *De doctrina christiana* 4.12.27

449 See eg Erasmus' words on Origen's *Homilae in Genesim* 8 in *Ratio* 188–9 about Abraham's sacrifice of Isaac; he comments: 'Haec copiosius et elegantius ab Origene disseruntur, haud scio maiorene voluptate lectoris an fructu, cum tantum interim in historico sensu versetur' (189). See also *Ratio* 296 on Origen's teaching: 'nemo plus docet quam Origenes ...' See also his preface to *Fragmentum commentariorum Origenis in evangelium secundum Matthaeum* in Allen XI 338: 'Nusquam Origenes non ardet, sed nusquam est ardentior quam ubi Christi sermones actusque tractat.'

450 On the tension between humanists and scholastics, see Erika Rummel '*Et cum theologo bella poeta gerit:* The Conflict between Humanists and Scholastics Re-

Like Augustine, Erasmus also imagined that the preacher more often than not stood before benighted creatures who could scarcely appreciate the beauty of the celestial philosophy. The devout preacher therefore first had to move them – that is, to awaken, allure, stroke, cajole, and rebuke them. In this, as in the audience's delight that results from good preaching, the preacher would be guided by the goal that he apply everything to his hearers' benefit, 'striving in every way to render most pleasant to his audience that which is most wholesome,'[451] to persuade 'so that our hearer wants to embrace what is honourable and useful.'[452]

Though the preacher does in fact teach, move, and delight, at the general level the ancients believed the special power of eloquence lay in its ability to persuade others (*persuadere*), bending the listeners' will and emotions, turning them as it wishes, or winning over of the audience. Focusing on what is together inseparably honourable and expedient differs too from the aims of demagogues and crowd pleasers, for the preacher intends the emotional response of his hearers to be directed towards the highest end possible, namely that they understand why they should embrace the good and thereupon receive warmly the reform of life and pursuit of godliness. If the ancients focused on the benefit (*utilitas*) of public speaking, Erasmus, following Augustine, perceives an uncommon benefit since the message of the preacher deals with everlasting happiness.[453] It would therefore not be appropriate for preachers to tickle the ears of the crowd merely to please it; their task was to ensure that the crowd grew accustomed to take delight in those things of supreme importance.[454]

Since Aristotle's *Rhetoric* most classical authors held that there are three kinds of speaking (*genera dicendi*) – judicial or forensic (*genus iudiciale* or *forense*), deliberative or suasorial (*genus deliberativum* or *suasorium*), and demonstrative or encomiastic (*genus demonstrativum* or *encomiasticum*).[455] Quintilian observed that Aristotle, 'by his tripartite division of oratory into

* * * * *

visited' *Sixteenth Century Journal* 23 (1992) 713–26; and *The Humanist-Scholastic Debate in the Renaissance and Reformation* (Cambridge, Mass 1995).

451 See book 2 CWE 68 508–9.
452 Book 2 CWE 68 500; see also Cicero *De officiis* 3.3.11: 'Expediency can never conflict with moral rectitude.'
453 See book 2 CWE 68 510; Augustine *De doctrina christiana* 4.18.35: 'Everything we say, especially when speaking before the people, must be referred, not to the temporal welfare of man, but to his eternal welfare and to the avoidance of eternal punishment, so that everything we say is of great importance ...'
454 See book 3 CWE 68 850, 880–1.
455 The demonstrative genre is also often referred to as laudatory, encomiastic, or epideictic.

forensic, deliberative and demonstrative, practically brought everything into the orator's domain, since there is nothing that may not come up for treatment by one of these three kinds of rhetoric.'[456] Quintilian accepts this tripartite division, acknowledging the weighty authority of those who have held this classification of types of speaking, though he does not foreclose the possibility of other *genera* falling outside of these three. In book 3 of his *Institutio oratoria*, Quintilian takes up the question 'whether there are three kinds or more,'[457] noting somewhat impatiently and disparagingly that Cicero (*De oratore* 2.10.43–71) and someone else Quintilian refers to as 'the greatest authority of our time' (perhaps Pliny the Elder)[458] argued that 'there are not merely more than three, but that the number of kinds is almost past calculation . . .' Quintilian asks, 'If we place the task of praise and denunciation in the third division, on what kind of oratory are we to consider ourselves to be employed, when we complain, console, pacify, excite, terrify, encourage, instruct, explain obscurities, narrate, plead for mercy, thank, congratulate, reproach, abuse, describe, command, retract, express our desires and opinions not to mention no other of the many possibilities?' (Quintilian 3.4.3). 'As an adherent of the older view,' Quintilian takes 'the safest and most rational course,' reaffirming the tripartite division, 'following the authority of the majority' (Quintilian 3.4.12). His remarks however might have offered Erasmus inspiration for seeing in these three classical *genera dicendi* (judicial, deliberative, demonstrative), especially the deliberative *genus*, the specific oratorical types of Christian preaching enunciated by St Paul.

In his Second Letter to Timothy (2 Tim 3:16–17) Paul writes that 'all Scripture, inspired of God, is profitable to teach, to reprove, to correct, to instruct in justice, that the man of God may be perfect, furnished to every good work';[459] and he urges Timothy to 'preach the word: be urgent

* * * * *

456 Quintilian 2.21.23. These three *genera* are sometimes referred to as the art of accusing and defending (*ars accusandi et defendendi*), the art of persuading and dissuading (*ars persuadendi et dissuadendi*), and the art of praise and blame (*ars laudandi et vituperandi*); see O'Malley *Praise and Blame* Chapter Two: 'The New Rhetoric: Ars laudandi et vituperandi' 36–76.

457 Quintilian 3.4.1

458 Some commentators on Quintilian suggest Pliny the Elder (23/24–79), who according to Pliny the Younger (a student of Quintilian), wrote works on oratory; see Quintilian 3.1.21, 3.3.2, and OCD 845–6. Cf Cicero's remark to the jurors in *Pro Archia* 8.18.21–3: 'Quotiens ego hunc Archiam vidi, iudices – utar enim vestra benignitate, quoniam me in hoc novo genere dicendi tam diligenter attenditis . . .'

459 Erasmus quotes and alludes to these passages from Paul throughout *Ecclesiastes*.

in season and out of season, convince, rebuke, and exhort, be unfailing in patience and in teaching' (2 Tim 4:2).[460] To these duties Paul elsewhere adds consolation: 'He who prophesies speaks to men for their upbuilding and encouragement and consolation' (1 Cor 14:3, cf 14:5).[461] In line with Quintilian's position that 'all other species [of oratory] fall under these three *genera* ...,' Erasmus inventively situates the Pauline activities of the preacher chiefly within the classical *genus suasorium* (or *deliberativum*); at the same time he tells readers that many instructions for the judicial type also apply to the suasorial or deliberative,[462] as it is in this *genus* that 'the preacher is especially occupied' – 'with teaching, with persuading, with exhorting, advising, and admonishing.'[463] Citations and echoes of these Pauline passages defining the work of the preacher abound throughout *Ecclesiastes*; in Erasmus' view these activities constitute the essence of the preacher's work. Though in explaining these Pauline duties Erasmus gives most attention to teaching, he also offers methods of exhorting, reproving, correcting, entreating, consoling, and instructing in justice, with illustrations from the prophets of the Old Testament, Christ and Peter, and the Fathers of the church.[464] Scriptural preaching for Erasmus then chiefly follows the prescriptions of the classical *genus suasorium* (*deliberativum*). In the concrete context of the bishop's duties, the rhetorical prescriptions for this, as well as for the other two *genera*, find particular application.

* * * * *

460 RSV; see also 1 Cor 14:31; cf *In psalmum 38* CWE 65 20–1.
461 RSV
462 See book 2 CWE 68 585 where Erasmus sees some use for the judicial type: 'It is rare for a preacher to be occupied with the judicial type, but yet it is not much different from this sort when he speaks from his pulpit against Jews, heretics, schismatics, or even pagans.'
463 See book 2 CWE 68 500; later in book 2 CWE 68 545 Erasmus includes the encomiastic type: 'concerning the suasorial and encomiastic type, since the preacher is especially occupied with these ...' Cf 2 Tim 3:16–17, 4:2. Cf *Ratio* 280, 301. See also book 2 CWE 68 567: 'That leaves exhortation, which is a part of the suasorial type rather than a different one, except that someone who is persuading is teaching through arguments, someone who is exhorting is stimulating through emotions.'
464 Erasmus mentioned these duties of the preacher in passing in *Ratio* 280. Forty years after *Ecclesiastes'* publication the Spanish Franciscan Diego de Estella in his *Modo de predicar* (Salamanca: Joannes Baptista à Terranova 1576) moves decidedly beyond Erasmus' inspiration, bypassing the classical authorities altogether, and declaring that St Paul provided preachers with specifically Christian *genera*. Although Estella never acknowledges his sources, Erasmus' *Ecclesiastes* seems to have had a significant influence on his work.

Erasmus focuses attention mostly on the *genus suasorium* but shows how useful the other two *genera dicendi* can be to the preacher. Even though 'the forensic type (*genus iudiciale*) is far removed from the duty of the preacher'[465] because his work is quite different from that of a courtroom advocate, nonetheless 'many instructions imparted in this type are useful,' such as 'an argument has a main point' (*status*)[466] whose purpose is to give focus to the speech and make it 'internally consistent.' It is useful, for example, for the preacher whose work is 'especially occupied' in the suasorial and encomiastic genres to understand the idea and types of *status* (conjectural or negatory, characteristic, definitional) so he can focus every part of his sermon 'as though towards a target and not stray from the subject in pointless digressions ...'[467] In fact, 'everyone who speaks to the people in order to persuade, exhort, or console sets before himself some definite goal that he wishes to accomplish; at any rate it stands in the place of the status.'[468] Erasmus maintains that considerations of status emerge frequently in the themes of sermons as well as in private conversations, and thus can apply to all the activities defined by St Paul.

Using the ancients' teachings on public oratory, however, requires one to make crucial distinctions between speaking to deliberative assemblies like those of the Athenians and the Romans and preaching to an assembly of Christians.[469] In preaching, Erasmus notes, no real deliberation occurs because such takes place only when an issue is in doubt or one urges a more probable course of action whose outcome is not assured. In matters of faith and morality, on the other hand, there is no doubt, as they have been made abundantly clear in Scripture. Christians know what they must do,

* * * * *

465 Book 2 CWE 68 497

466 *status: quaestio, constitutio, caput,* στάσις 'status.' See Lausberg §§79–138, 149–97. Status means the issue in question, the basic issue; for 'a simple cause' it is 'that point which the orator sees to be the most important for him to make and on which the judge sees that he must fix all his attention. For it is on this that the cause will stand or fall' (Quintilian 3.6.9); yet questions may have 'more *bases* than one.' Cf Quintilian 3.6.1–104; *Rhetorica ad Herennium* 1.11.15–1.17.27; Cicero *Orator* 14.45. Each *genus* of oratory will have a status proper to it. See below where Erasmus defines the term: 'A status is the essential point of a case or question, to which the speaker refers everything and which the listener has particularly in view' (book 2 CWE 68 581).

467 Book 2 CWE 68 582

468 Book 2 CWE 68 582

469 Erasmus does however make clear that the preacher, though always urging only what is honourable, nonetheless often has an audience of persons of varying degrees of virtue; see eg books 2 and 3 CWE 68 714 and 1002.

and the preacher's task is to urge them 'to pursue more keenly what everyone agrees should be pursued . . .'[470] As Paul puts it, the preacher 'entreats'
(2 Tim 4:1–2) or 'urges' or 'exhorts' all to perform what they know is right.
Again, all this fits with Erasmus' understanding of God's revelation in his
law and *logos*, Christ, for in nature and in Jesus' teaching the matter of the
divine mind has been made known to us with brilliant clarity. It is not for
Christians to deliberate the merits of following God's law but to embrace
what God inscribed in our hearts and in nature and fully revealed to us in
his Son. To that end the preacher's *paraenesis* urges listeners to overcome all
fleshly resistance and willingly embrace godliness.

Erasmus' accommodation of the deliberative *genus* to preaching
presents the matter somewhat minimally. Surprisingly, it does not consider
those situations when persuasion to a course of action is not simply a question of sin versus virtue but of which course of action is more honourable according to circumstances. Such questions are particularly pertinent to Christian morality, but his treatise's purpose is not to offer advice on complex
pastoral principles of ethical decision making, rather to offer effective methods for preaching to an audience comprised of all manner of Christians, most
of whom in Erasmus' view are grossly steeped in sin. Erasmus recognized
that the types of assemblies Cicero and Quintilian had in mind for deliberative oratory no longer existed, but the ancients' teachings on the *genus suasorium*, mutatis mutandis, nonetheless offered the preacher extensive help
with sacred *conciones*.[471]

Similarly, with the *genus demonstrativum* (demonstrative or encomiastic) Erasmus distinguishes the aim of the preacher from the pagan pan-
egyrist, because Christian encomia should urge listeners to imitate, not
simply admire, the object of their praises. Contrary to pagan practices,
Erasmus advises that 'God's majesty must frequently be exalted,'[472] and
he tightly restricts this *genus* to extolling the praises of God, the Blessed
Mother, the saints, and angels. Preachers should use this genre for 'doxology and thanksgiving, partly in praise of the devout, especially of the
martyrs who have glorified God by their death';[473] however, he urges
caution on what is to be said about the saints, to avoid rashly adding

* * * * *

470 Book 2 CWE 68 546
471 See book 2 CWE 68 545–52.
472 Book 2 CWE 68 553
473 Book 2 CWE 68 501; see also book 2 CWE 68 553: 'The encomiastic type is generally occupied in extolling the praises of God or of the saints, since funeral
orations are not so much in use among ecclesiastics now as they once were.'

miracles[474] and various types of nonsense. Christian panegyrics, like the pagan panegyrics, should present something for us to admire, but go well beyond them by 'making admiration for them [the saints] sweep us into zeal for emulation.'[475] In fact, everything said about a saint should be put in such a way that 'God is thanked at the same time and the congregation is challenged to his example.'[476] Encomia ought to inflame people towards the love of godliness by putting before their eyes God's power in his saints that we might praise God by imitating the virtues of those holy men and women who themselves imitated Christ, each in his or her own unique way.[477] Erasmus notes that preachers may also use this genre for praising institutions such as marriage and monastic life,[478] though in doing so they should 'hunt out from everywhere what is conducive to living well, namely that we should revere the supremely powerful, above all that we should love the supremely good.'[479]

Although occasions abound for using the encomiastic genre Erasmus emphasizes that the particular purpose of the encomiastic genre is for frequently exalting the majesty of God,[480] which is to be done not merely for its own sake but for the greater purpose of urging others to godliness. In fact he provides readers with a brief outline of the parts of an encomiastic sermon (*laudatorium*) whose goal is to expound 'the generosity of the divinity towards the human race,'[481] which should engender thanksgiving in listeners and the desire to imitate Christ; for as Christ so loved us, so must we in gratitude turn to our neighbours in love. The sermon should then invite us to consider God's 'great power, wisdom, and goodness,' which 'shines in everything created, so that wherever we turn our eyes or mind we celebrate the craftsman in everything'; and it will tell 'how wondrously God has worked in holy men.' The entire oration thus begins and ends with a consideration of God's power and moves us not only to admiration but to imitation and the love of God in giving ourselves to others. In its function the encomiastic sermon replicates Erasmus' teaching on godliness in urging

* * * * *

474 Book 2 CWE 68 566
475 Book 3 CWE 68 798. See *Peregrinatio religionis ergo* in *Colloquia* CWE 40 624–5, 653–4 n25.
476 Book 2 CWE 68 566
477 Book 2 CWE 68 560
478 Book 2 CWE 68 588, 592. Erasmus of course praises monastic life where it is lived authentically, as it seemed to Erasmus was the case when St Jerome 'chose the monastic life'; see *Vita Hieronymi* CWE 61 29.
479 Book 2 CWE 68 554
480 Book 2 CWE 68 553
481 Book 2 CWE 68 554

the Christian always to be mindful of God's majesty and beneficence, because only with this interior disposition can one's heart open in justice with the will to reciprocate God's infinite love and mercy. It is therefore (characteristically Erasmian) to amplify and embellish the grandeur of God, as this device can awaken shame in the spiritually slothful who have received such benefits and are niggardly and ignoble in thanking the greatest giver. Erasmus observes that this method is also especially effective when the preacher deters from sin, 'so that it seems a more detestable crime to scorn him [God] by sinning or to prefer any created thing to him, whose greatness is such that there is nothing anywhere in heaven or in earth that can be compared to him ...'[482] The techniques of the encomiastic method thus focus on bringing listeners to the psychological awareness of their absolute finite contingency in the presence of the infinite supreme good; for this 'it is appropriate to stress the majesty that infinitely surpasses not only the eloquence but the understanding of all men.'[483] Having such emotions stirred, the heart is then moved to sorrow and love and can respond fittingly.

In principle Erasmus does not disallow the practice of publicly praising the saints, but he makes cautionary recommendations about it. The saints are secondary in the hierarchy of those to whom praises should be given; God the Father, Christ, and the Holy Spirit should be the ultimate term of all our praises. If one looks for a person who was perfectly praiseworthy in every way, a model for our lives, one finds it in Christ who alone should command our continuous praises; 'Christ is abundantly fertile ... a preacher could not lack a theme for speaking even if he wanted to preach four times every day ...'[484] So Erasmus advises those who preach on the saints that they dedicate the greatest part of the sermon to the Gospel and the Epistle and propose them for imitation rather than for praise.[485] Echoing the psalmist (Ps 113:9 [Vulg]), he reasons that praise should go to God alone whose power was alive in the saints, and that we should imitate the saints in so far as they were imitators of Christ.[486] For what we admire in these holy men and

* * * * *

482 Book 2 CWE 68 553
483 Book 2 CWE 68 553
484 Book 2 CWE 68 565; see also Ep 1211:105–6 for Erasmus' words on Jean Vitrier, who fits this perfectly: 'Sometimes he preached seven times in a single day, nor was he ever short of matter for a well-studied sermon, when Christ was his subject.'
485 See book 2 CWE 68 565.
486 Cf Ps 115:1 (Vulg 113:9–10): 'Not to us, O Lord, not to us; but to thy name give glory.' See also Colloquia (Convivium religiosum) CWE 39 203: 'Because all glory belongs to him, but especially ought we to praise him [Christ] by the

women is not the specific peculiarities or practices of their lives like the
types of austerities, clothing, or methods of prayer that matter, but their
dedication to follow Christ, which is what each one must do in his or her
own way.[487] Though we may praise these saints, we should at the same time
recall our purpose is to imitate them as they imitated Christ. Imitating the
saints therefore means the imitation of Christ who 'alone was the perfect
model ... of all the virtues.'[488]

Erasmus calls attention to some notable church Fathers who took from
the ancient orators techniques for praising the lives and deeds of great men
and applied them to praising living men and women imitating Christ. He
finds examples of these encomia in Basil of Caesarea, Gregory of Nyssa, Gregory of Nazianzus, and John Chrysostom;[489] but he cautions readers about
this and only with great reservation allows encomia of famous men and
praise of the living, a practice which he notes crept into the early church:
'I think that our preachers should be rather sparing in their imitation of
an example which the bishops of old derived from a public custom of the
heathen ...'[490] To be avoided, of course, is all manner of praising the living, especially in 'fawning orations that ambassadors or orators use before
the mighty in epithalamia' and other speeches.[491] Erasmus sharply criticizes

* * * * *

triple name ...' (203); and *Enchiridion* CWE 66 71: 'No devotion is more acceptable and proper to the saints than striving to imitate their virtues.' Cf *Ratio*
232–3.
487 See book 2 CWE 68 504 and book 4 CWE 68 1039: 'in uno Christo virtutum omnium absolutum exemplar ostensum est, in quo nihil vitii aut defectus fuit
admixtum'; and *Enchiridion* CWE 66 86: 'Our example is Christ, in whom alone
are all the patterns of the holy life. You may imitate him without any exception. From men of tried virtue you may take single qualities as a model according as they correspond to the archetype of Christ.' Similarly Erasmus does
not advocate the imitation of the church Fathers themselves but rather their
rhetorical, literary excellence in preaching and writing about the philosophy
of Christ. See eg Ralph Keen 'The Allure of the Past: Religious Reform and
the Recovery of Ancient Ideals,' ERSY 26 (2006) 16–28, especially 21–2.
488 Book 4 CWE 68 1039
489 See eg *Funeral Orations by Saint Gregory Nazianzen and Saint Ambrose* trans Leo
P. McCauley et al FOC 22 (Washington, DC 1968).
490 Book 2 CWE 68 503–4
491 Book 2 CWE 68 560. Erasmus might have in mind the panegyric he gave for
Archduke Philip of Austria (6 January 1504); see CWE 27 1–75. He concedes,
'It happens that some living man has to be praised'; if so, then 'we will shape
our praise in such a way that we speak of the gifts of God in him rather than
of the man himself.'

the preaching before the popes, lamenting that 'today, for shame, we have reached such a point of impudence that both the priest in the mass (*in ipso sacro*) itself and the preacher frequently flatter popes and princes abjectly in public assembly (*in concione publica*) . . .'[492] His personal experience in 1509 at a sermon preached before the pope (*coram papa inter missarum solemnia*) may have provoked this criticism, however unjust it might have been.[493]

After treating more generally the *genus deliberativum* (*suasorium*) and *demonstrativum* (*laudatorium*) in book 2, Erasmus turns to the specific tasks of the preacher as stated by Paul in his Second Letter to Timothy (2 Tim 3:16–17 and 4:2), promising to 'add in passing what seems particular to exhortation, consolation, or rebuke.'[494] In exhortation, which comes under the *genus suasorium*, he observes that those who persuade do so by teaching with arguments, but those who exhort do so 'by stimulating through the emotions.'[495] Paul's special skill in employing the *genus suasorium* elicits Erasmus' admiration: for Paul often beseeches, exhorts, and implores his communities ('I beseech you to walk worthily . . .'), which serves important functions, especially for supporting those needing encouragement to embrace godliness or to open their arms in love to their neighbours. Exhortation is most appropriate when, after urging listeners to acquire virtues and eradicate vices, the preacher can hold out the promise of rewards. For this the preacher must use psychology, as Christ did in promising Peter a hundredfold in this life and everlasting life in the world-to-come' (Mark 10:28–30). Rewards too can be understood diversely, for they can be promised for just merits in this life; and for a life of Christian godliness the preacher can promise the reward of eternal glory.[496] Like Paul, the preacher must therefore always be mindful of his listeners' human nature, which expects rewards for difficult undertakings.

* * * * *

492 Book 2 CWE 68 560
493 For Erasmus' attendance at the Good Friday sermon (likely delivered by Tommaso 'Fedra' Inghirami), see *Ciceronianus* CWE 28 384–7 and 562 n306 (Erasmus calls him Pietro Fedra). For a closer look at (and a positive evaluation of) Renaissance humanist preachers in Rome at the papal court in this time, see O'Malley *Praise and Blame* 29–31; see also Halkin 69–70.
494 Book 2 CWE 68 546; cf 2 Tim 3:16; see also *Lingua* CWE 29 410–11.
495 Book 2 CWE 68 567
496 Book 2 CWE 68 569. As we note below in regard to the Franciscan practice of preaching, Erasmus sometimes uses the term 'glory' for one's heavenly reward: 'Glory could be subsumed under the heading of reward . . .' See book 2 CWE 68 569 and n525.

To the preacher's activities also falls the Pauline injunction to console, the *consolatorium*, which on occasion is given a prominent place in the Christian assembly.[497] Citing Paul that 'he who prophesies speaks to men for their upbuilding and encouragement and consolation' (1 Cor 14:3),[498] Erasmus adds that one who consoles others needs to be well provided with specific topics and a method to address listeners at moments of public and private grief.[499] Again, unlike the pagan audiences that never knew Christ, Christians enjoy the benefit of a preacher who can speak of our temporal losses *sub specie aeternitatis*. Yet, far from discounting pagan writings, Erasmus maintains that the ancients' topics of the *genus consolatorium* will often be most appropriate when translated into a Christian context. Because God is the all-powerful source of good, the preacher will make clear to those who mourn 'that none of this is happening by chance but is sent divinely to purge us, or to call us back to a more moral life, or to exercise our patience and enhance our crown, so that in all of this we should thank God . . .'[500] It is the preacher's role, therefore, to place our sufferings within a wide Christian framework that allows listeners to see their losses in the light of God's providence and gain hope that he will reward them for their patience and acceptance of his will.

Finally, the preacher must 'rebuke' or 'reprove' his congregation, as Paul does with the Corinthians and Galatians, and as Jesus did with the scribes, Pharisees, and even with his own disciples. This activity, the *epitimêtikon* ('censorious' or 'critical') or *nouthetikos* ('monitory'),[501] however, requires discretion, for 'it suits the gentleness of the gospel that the preacher should admonish rather than rebuke, though sometimes the enormity of the crimes demands that a preacher do what Isaiah commands him to do: "Shout, do not cease, like a trumpet raise your voice and announce their crimes to the people and their sins to the house of Jacob"' (Isa 58:1).[502] It is of course a principal task of the preacher never to neglect the weighty

* * * * *

497 See book 2 CWE 68 571. For a broader picture of consolation in Christian tradition, see George W. McClure *Sorrow and Consolation in Italian Humanism* (Princeton 1991), especially 'Introduction: The Classical and Christian Traditions' 3–17. McClure notes that 'Paul largely proscribes the experience of sorrow as unbefitting the Christian,' but 'nonetheless, a tradition of Christian consolation does emerge, beginning with Paul's Epistles' (10–11).
498 RSV
499 Book 2 CWE 68 571–4
500 Book 2 CWE 68 573
501 See book 2 CWE 68 574–80.
502 Book 2 CWE 68 574; cf *Enchiridion* CWE 66 80.

obligation of calling the morally degenerate from their vices, for the preacher himself will be held accountable to God for those he failed to admonish of their sins and wickedness. Still, a prudential care is required when rebuking others. It is insufficient simply to rail against vices, as this often becomes counterproductive and can make a preacher look foolish. When rebuking, the preacher should also offer hearers salutary teaching and clear direction for the amendment of their lives, persuading them that 'the path of virtue all the way to perfection' is 'much more right and even pleasant' than the alternative.[503] Often, too, it is necessary to mitigate one's rebuke in order not to condemn the entire person or his work, but to praise what is good while singling out the specific errors that require charitable correction.[504] As in his treatment of the *genera*, Erasmus offers advice on employing discretion when speaking before a congregation, which might include souls who require sharp rebuke and others who have already set their hearts on friendship with Christ. Erasmus' many caveats further direct the preacher away from the abuses commonly committed by those who 'babble out before the congregation all the hideous crimes they have learnt in secret confessions'[505] or criticize certain crimes that are best left unspoken, especially those of a sexual nature – 'the bizarre forms of pleasure ... and countless other forms of abominable filth ...'; 'there is no need to depict them as though the intention were to teach them rather than to execrate them.'[506] Erasmus offers much practical advice for correction, all the while urging discretion, because 'very often a sober and moderate admonition accomplishes more than a furious outcry.'[507] Failing to observe decorum, especially in rebuke, can lead to faults far in excess of the moral lapses one seeks to correct.[508]

In explaining the *genera dicendi*, Erasmus also encourages freedom in mixing them in a single *concio*, as Quintilian allowed, 'for all three kinds (*genera*) rely on the mutual assistance of the other';[509] so in a single oration accusation, deliberation, and praise might occur as well, as seen in some speeches of the ancients. Erasmus further encourages preachers, whenever appropriate, to use more than one of the specific Pauline activities within

* * * * *

503 Book 2 CWE 68 575
504 See book 3 CWE 68 802, 886, 1015–17.
505 Cf *Moria* CWE 27 132; see also *Exomologesis* 39–40.
506 Book 2 CWE 68 575–6
507 Book 2 CWE 68 578
508 See book 3 CWE 68 574–80.
509 Quintilian 3.4.16

a single *concio*, assuring them that they need not feel constrained by the prescriptions of just one *genus*; it is appropriate to mix *genera* in so far as they contribute to the overall goal of the oration, which is the spiritual benefit to the congregation. With lengthy examples of preaching from Christ's teaching, Paul's letters, the prophets, the Acts of the Apostles,[510] and his own inventions, Erasmus lays out useful ways to teach, rebuke, exhort, and console that should both edify a congregation and win credibility for the preacher.

After instruction on the *genera dicendi* Erasmus moves on to the parts of an oration (*partes orationis* or *partes operis*),[511] which number will depend on the type of speech and the concrete circumstances. Those parts analyzed by the ancients and seen as most relevant to a sacred *concio* Erasmus identifies as exordium, narration (statement of facts), division (partition), confirmation (proofs), refutation, and conclusion (peroration).[512] He accepts Quintilian and others' teaching on them and demonstrates how these can be accommodated to sermons, sometimes by omitting one or more of the parts, as the ancients took the liberty of doing as well.[513] *Ecclesiastes* does not specifically recommend eliminating any of these parts, but it allows that one may modify them or omit one or more depending on circumstances; on the whole Erasmus affirms their usefulness for preaching, pointing out too how the Scriptures and the sermons of the Fathers employ them.[514]

It is important finally to emphasize that Erasmus' instructions on preaching do not reject the 'thematic sermon,' which developed more fully after 1200 and is regarded as emblematic of the sermon literature of the Middle Ages, but he urges that it be made more simple and that one not be enslaved to the rigid sermonic complexities in evidence among preachers of his day. Erasmus, in fact, fully embraces the thematic sermon and

* * * * *

510 For Erasmus' treatment of speeches in Acts, see Pabel 'Retelling the History of the Early Church' 63–85.
511 See book 2 CWE 68 509. For 'parts of the oration' see: Cicero *De partitione oratoria*; Quintilian 4–6; *Ad Herennium* 1.3.5–17, 1.27, and 2. Here Erasmus begins to instruct his readers on applying these traditional 'parts of oratory' to preaching; he begins with the exordium. For this see especially Quintilian 4.1.1; *Rhetorica ad Herennium* 1.4; Cicero *De inventione* 1.20.
512 See book 2 CWE 68 passim.
513 See book 2 CWE 68 510. The classic example of omitting or rearranging an important part of an oration is Cicero's *In Verrem*, where he foregoes his long opening consecutive speech in the *actio prima*, breaking it up instead into a number of short ones, each dealing with a specific charge.
514 See book 3 CWE 68 510–37.

gives advice on how to handle a theme correctly, that is, on how exordia and the other parts should be presented:[515] 'The practice by which men of more recent times begin a sermon from some line or other of Scripture (they call it a theme) is not inappropriate provided it is of such a sort as to embrace the whole of the theme because it has been taken from the very passage that he is interpreting.'[516] Erasmus observes that beginning a sermon this way is not without many examples among the Fathers. Basil, for example, when preparing to exhort a congregation to placate an angry God, follows the prophet Amos (3:8) by beginning, 'The lion has roared, and who will not fear? God has spoken, and who will not prophesy?'[517] Even the pagans delivered orations using similar conventions. But Erasmus concedes that since ancient times the practice of arranging sermons has changed: 'Some more modern authorities ... have devised other forms of order ... Some pray silently first, then stand straight and make the sign of the cross ... they then announce what they call the "theme," on which they make some general prefatory remarks ...'[518] Some preachers, after these preliminaries, repeat the theme, offer a division (a statement by the preacher of the principal points he plans to cover), and then begin the sermon proper. Significantly, Erasmus concedes validity to these changes in preaching practices: 'This does not merit disapproval so long as what they say inspires the listener with good will or attentiveness or willingness to learn.'[519] Erasmus also addresses the merits and faults of preachers who adopt the practice of appending an invocation to the deity when beginning or concluding their exordium, and he gives abundant guidance on ways to begin a sermon, emphasizing that a sermon's structure should allow for flexibility.

Though giving substantial instruction on exordia, Erasmus provides relatively little explicit help with narration (*narratio*), although he claims he

* * * * *

515 Erasmus treats the exordium in book 2 CWE 68 510–37. On Erasmus' continuities with the authors of the medieval *artes praedicandi*, see Kilcoyne and Jennings. For the thematic sermon in the Middle Ages, see especially: Th.-M Charland *Artes Praedicandi. Contribution à l'histoire de la rhétorique au Moyen Age* (Paris 1936); Gilson 'Michel Menot'; and Martin *Le métier de prédicateur* 236–51; Caplan; Murphy *Rhetoric* 215, 315, 320.

516 Book 2 CWE 68 511. For the theme in the medieval *artes praedicandi*, see Murphy *Rhetoric* 307–8.

517 Book 2 CWE 68 514; Basil *Homilia dicta tempore famis et siccitatis* PG 31 (1857) 303–28

518 Book 3 CWE 68 730–1

519 See book 3 CWE 68 731.

has given sufficient advice on the matter earlier in the treatise.[520] He does however make numerous comments and gives examples that illustrate narration, often echoing Quintilian's lengthy treatment of it.[521] Still, one might have expected Erasmus would have more to say on this topic since it lies at the heart of the preacher's work and is for Quintilian among 'the first subjects in which the rhetorician should give instruction.'[522] Erasmus does however take up 'partition' (*partitio*) with considerable attention,[523] analyzing its two aspects: first, the partition generally follows from the exordium and is the preacher's way of letting the audience know succinctly in advance the basic points of the sermon he plans to cover; second, 'it also sets forth the topics to be discussed, their precise number and sequence.'[524] Under this second aspect he also treats arrangement (*dispositio* or *ordo*), to which he will devote further, albeit cursory, treatment in book 3. In explaining the idea of partition, he lays down ways a sermon can best be structured to facilitate both the preacher's recollection as he delivers it and his audience's retention of it. But Erasmus cautions that partitions have their drawbacks; for example, important items often come spontaneously to mind, which do not fit the scheme promised; and he warns against emulating the scholastics in their excessive divisions and subdivisions of the matter to be propounded, which can cause annoyance.[525] Erasmus does not tell us much about how his own contemporaries partition their sermons; he refers them instead to the best of preachers – John Chrysostom, Gregory of Nazianzus, Basil, and especially Jesus and Paul – and provides examples of his own based largely on passages from Scripture. In general, he advises the preacher not to become obsessed with a sermon's partition but to divide it so it is 'clear and

* * * * *

520 See book 2 CWE 68 537 where Erasmus treats *narratio* in connection with the exordium; see Chomarat ASD V-4 305 363n; and Kleinhans 54.
521 See Quintilian 4.2.1–132 and 6.3.12, 14, 39.
522 Quintilian 2.4.1
523 Book 2 CWE 68 537
524 Book 2 CWE 68 537. For a clear example of this see Cicero *Pro Quinctio* 10.36, where first he announces briefly the three points he will prove and then succinctly repeats them; see also Cicero *Pro Murena* 5.11, cited by Quintilian 4.5.12; see book 2 CWE 68 545 n402.
525 See book 3 CWE 68 538–45. See also Erasmus' comment on Jean Vitrier's method of constructing sermons: 'As a rule he did not divide his sermons under heads as the common run of preachers do, as if it were not permitted to do anything else; which is often the source of very tedious subdivisions, though all that painstaking organization takes the warmth out of an address, and because it sounds artificial, it makes the speaker carry less conviction ...' Ep 1211:60–5. For the scholastics' excessive divisions, see *Ratio* 191.

brief' to allow hearers to retain the matter as well as possible.[526] Erasmus will return later to the principles of partition in book 2 when he takes up 'the discovery of parts or propositions.'[527]

Before delving into the discovery of propositions for winning the preacher credibility with his audience, Erasmus recalls Aristotle's observation that three things are crucial to credibility – 'practical wisdom, virtue, and good will'[528] – without all of which the preacher's words can become dangerous and deceptive. The discovery of propositions takes Erasmus into 'argumentation or proofs,' which 'induce belief in something doubtful.'[529] Here the skill or practical wisdom of the preacher is foremost, as the discovery of arguments rests partly on his native talent and partly on training.[530] Each invented proposition requires sufficient proofs to command the assent of one's audience. For authority on this Erasmus relies especially on the ancient rhetoricians, who divide proofs into two types of loci, nontechnical and technical,[531] and argue that every proof is taken either from the circumstances of persons or matters at hand. Under the nontechnical loci he lists precedents, rumours, the results of tortures, documentary evidence, oaths, and testimonies; along with these he lists signs, which are akin to them.[532] Among the technical he lists the accidental qualities of persons (family, nationality, country, sex, age, education, physical condition, fortune, etc), and those from the accidental qualities of the matter itself (cause, matter and form, the final end of an object of ultimate intention, place, time, ability, instrument, manner, etc). With abundant examples from Scripture, the ancients' writings, and human life, he demonstrates how these loci can be used by preachers in the various Pauline genres (teaching, encouraging, admonishing, rebuking, consoling etc)[533] that fall within deliberative and demonstrative oratory.

Erasmus maintains that some propositions 'are so obvious that they require no proof ... such as that God is to be loved and worshipped above all things.'[534] On the other hand, sometimes the matter does not require proof

* * * * *

526 Book 2 CWE 68 543
527 Book 2 CWE 68 585
528 Book 2 CWE 68 599
529 See book 2 CWE 68 599.
530 See book 2 CWE 68 600–15.
531 See book 2 CWE 68 645 and passim. For the idea of loci in *Ratio* and *Ecclesiastes*, see Hoffmann *Rhetoric* 151–6.
532 See book 2 CWE 68 607–9.
533 See 2 Tim 3:16.
534 Book 2 CWE 68 609

(for example, the social value of eradicating the vice of drunkenness) but can be treated by rhetorical amplification making people aware of 'the train of ills it brings with it.'[535] Asseveration and other devices too can similarly produce powerful rhetorical effects, and an adept use of them can help to confirm an argument; but one should be mindful that most arguments require sufficient, substantial, credible proof and cannot simply be stated as obvious, only to leave the audience in doubt. To create rhetorical proofs and arguments it helps if future preachers be 'trained in dialectic from childhood,'[536] most of all in the *Topics* and *Rhetoric* of Aristotle, and less so in those books constituting his *Organon*, which 'are more suitable for judging or for arguing in the schools than for preaching.'[537] The sensible study of dialectic enhances a preacher's natural capacity for 'making correct judgments about truth and falsehood' and for teaching.[538] A fast track to the discovery of arguments lies in the places (loci) where arguments can be sought,[539] and to sharpen one's ability for this, Erasmus urges readers to be as broadly read as possible in the ancient authors, especially the comic poets, historians, and philosophers who evince a profound understanding of the complexities of human nature and the vagaries of human affairs. Moving then to 'the common sources of arguments' or topics (Latin *loci*; Greek τόποι) Erasmus explains the four meanings of the term *locus*:[540] 1) 'commonplaces [*loci communes*]' because they are handled by either side; 2) maxims (*sententiae*); 3) the foundation of arguments, which are used in all three *genera* of speaking (for example, in the suasorial *genus* 'the honourable, the useful, the pleasant, the easy, the necessary';[541] in epideictic 'family, homeland, physical attributes, and mental attitudes'; in the judicial especially the negatory); and 4) 'the general *loci*, which show what as a whole are the accidental properties of each thing and how arguments both necessary and plausible are drawn from each.'[542] Erasmus dedicates his extended discussion of loci to the fourth meaning, which are employed by both orators and dialecticians, and recommends, in addition to Quintilian, the *Topics* of Aristotle for its precision, though he admits the work gets bogged down in minute

* * * * *

535 Book 2 CWE 68 610; for amplification, see Lausberg §§400–9.
536 Book 2 CWE 68 611
537 Book 2 CWE 68 612; for loci see Grünwald 112–31.
538 Book 2 CWE 68 613
539 See book 2 CWE 68 614–15.
540 Book 2 CWE 68 645–7
541 Book 2 CWE 68 646
542 Book 2 CWE 68 646

details. Important for the orator is to understand 'the general division of all questions,'[543] as well as definition, genus and species, difference and property, division and partition, comparison (*similitudo*), examples and analogies, comparison from an equal, a lesser, or a greater, opposites (*dissimilia* or *differentia*), efficient causes and effects, etc. After a thorough explanation and many examples of these loci at work in argumentations, Erasmus recommends that the 'preacher in general be advised to accommodate these loci to a broader use than do the dialecticians, whose examples are generally quite pedantic.'[544] With numerous illustrations Erasmus demonstrates the singular usefulness of these loci 'for digging out the wealth that Scripture contains hidden within it and that must be put before the eyes of the uninstructed congregation.'[545] 'With these methods the preacher can adapt the subtlety of dialectic to the capacity of the congregation and elevate to a loftier meaning whatever seems too humble.'[546]

After declaring he has treated invention 'with absolute thoroughness'[547] and said enough about expression (*elocutio*),[548] Erasmus begins book 3 by returning to 'arrangement or order,'[549] this time focusing on the four ways it is understood (to bring about clarity, a suitable arrangement of the principal propositions of a speech, organizing individual argumentations, and the general order of the whole speech). Finishing this up with observations on inept preaching practices, he moves on to memory (*memoria*), but treats it briefly as well, stating that he has given sufficient advice on the topic. The reader might have wished for more on this too, but Erasmus'

* * * * *

543 Book 2 CWE 68 647: ie 'whether it is, what it is, what sort it is.' See Quintilian 3.6.80: 'We must therefore accept the view of the authorities followed by Cicero, to the effect that there are three things on which enquiry is made in every case: we ask *whether a thing is, what it is*, and *of what kind it is.*'

544 Book 2 CWE 68 693 and 694 where he differentiates the preacher's use of definition from that of the dialectician: 'The dialectician adduces but one idea: the defined is predicated of the same thing of which the definition is predicated, and vice versa; but the preacher will find numerous ideas around each locus.'

545 Book 2 CWE 68 704

546 Book 2 CWE 68 714

547 Book 3 CWE 68 725; cf Quintilian 7.1. On Erasmus' disjointed presentation of the elements of oratorical rhetoric, see Hoffmann *Rhetoric* 169–72.

548 Book 2 CWE 68 509. Erasmus understands invention as also embracing elocution and arrangement: 'Invention, which supplies the subject matter, though really it embraces both expression and order: it is in a speech what bones are in an animal's body, that which must be firm to keep all the rest from collapsing.'

549 On arrangement (*dispositio, ordo*), see Hoffmann *Rhetoric* 142–8.

scattered comments elsewhere allow readers some sense of the role memory played in contemporary sermons.

Erasmus declares that the art of memory (*ars memoriae*) can often be more of an impediment than a help. Being overanxious about memorizing one's text 'blunts creativity and chills the ardour of speech, then chills the native power of memory.'[550] He points out that 'it is safer for those who mistrust their memory to propose only the gist of their theme, or at least to have the headings of their sermon to hand, written out on paper,' which seems to have been Augustine's method.[551] His comments suggest that contemporary preachers commonly did not commit the whole sermon to memory but only the principal outline, if even that, before its delivery; and from this the preacher, ideally, spoke forth from the heart what he had meditated upon beforehand.[552] When the time came to deliver the sermon (after prayer and meditation), experienced preachers like Jean Vitrier would ascend the pulpit and deliver it with spontaneity.[553] Consequently it was crucial that the preacher stepping into the pulpit have 'a magnificent, appropriate, expressive, and ready supply of words,' for 'if this is not at hand and in readiness, so to speak, as a result of much practice, the preacher is often at a loss.'[554] It was this quality of speaking from the heart – the ardour of speech – after diligent preparation that carried the preacher's words to the hearts of his hearers.[555] Erasmus' friend Jean Vitrier might well have been his inspiration for this manner of preaching, for he tells us that Vitrier 'brought his words out in such a way that you felt they came from a passionate and simple but yet sober heart ...'[556] If one needed to introduce lengthy passages from

* * * * *

550 See book 3 CWE 68 736. Memory is treated thoroughly in *Rhetorica ad Herennium* 3; see also Quintilian 9.
551 Book 2 CWE 68 538
552 See book 2 CWE 68 539. See also *De ratione studii* CWE 24 671: 'I do not deny that memory is aided by "places" and "images," nevertheless the best memory is based on three things above all: understanding, system, and care.'
553 See Erasmus' profile of the Franciscan Jean Vitrier in Ep 1211 to Justus Jonas, 13 June 1521. See also book 2 CWE 68 507 and book 3 CWE 68 814.
554 Book 2 CWE 68 486–7
555 Cf Ep 1211:57–60 to Justus Jonas, where Erasmus describes Jean Vitrier's preparation before his sermons: 'I asked him once ... how he prepared his mind when setting out to preach, and he replied that he usually opened Paul, and went on reading him until he felt his mind take fire. At that point he paused, praying to God with passion, until told that it was time to start.' See also Augustine *De doctrina christiana* 4.14.32; for a similar type of preparation before speaking to a court, see Cicero's description of the orator Galba in *Brutus* 22.87–8.
556 Ep 1211:69–70; cf Plutarch *De liberis educandis* 6c–7c.

Scripture or a long list of names, he should read them, as there is no shame in this. As in every other precept of oratorical rhetoric, Erasmus' advice on memory is based on much common sense and first-hand observation. Thorough preparation – not dominated by rigid rules of preceptive rhetoric – and prayer are the keys to simple, pure, effective preaching.

Arguably no words of Demosthenes are as well known as his response, 'Delivery ... delivery ... delivery,'[557] when asked what was the first, second, and third thing in oratory. By delivery (ὑπόκρισις, 'action') he meant the whole act of delivering the oration before an audience. This idea is often rendered by the word 'pronunciation' (*pronuntiatio*), that is, proclaiming publicly. Whatever the term, it is the crux of oratory. For Erasmus delivery consisted of the proper spiritual disposition and a set of well-coordinated rhetorical skills and harmoniously executed physical activities:[558] a natural temperance and modulation of one's voice, oral pauses, and physical motions; such would include artless movements of the face, head, brow, eyebrows, eyes, nose, lips, ears, as well as every gesture of the body made with the neck, arms, hands, fingers, together with laughter, exclamations, and the elevation or depression of the voice.[559] Action also included the general appearance of the preacher and required exhibiting an unaffected congruity with what he was about. Even one's clothing had to be appropriate, not ostentatious or shabby. The secret of such speaking, in effect, was to feign complete naturalness, as was said of Ovid's Pygmalion creating Galatea, 'So does his art conceal his art.'[560] Erasmus heaps scorn on preachers who used gimmicks in the pulpit (for example, waving the bloody shirt, putting dead men's skulls on the pulpit, having someone prowl through the congregation dressed as Satan, dressing up in strange costumes, etc). Performing in a perfectly natural manner accounted for everything when moving the emotions, the essence of the preacher's métier.

To endow the preacher with even greater help in moving the emotions, Erasmus proposes the study of commonplaces (*loci communes*), which he

* * * * *

557 See book 2 CWE 68 509–10; Plutarch *Moralia* (*Demosthenes* 845). Erasmus refers to this in *Enchiridion* CWE 66 85: 'In public speaking delivery was first, second, and third in importance, meaning that it was so essential that it was the whole of oratory'; see also Cicero *De oratore* 3.56.213, *Brutus* 37.142, *Orator* 17.56; Quintilian 11.3.6.

558 See book 3 CWE 68 passim.

559 See eg Erasmus' comment on Jean Vitrier: 'There was no purposeless gesticulation, no noisy ranting; he was entirely concentrated ...' (Ep 1211:68–9); cf *In psalmum 38* CWE 65 30–1.

560 Ovid *Metamorphoses* 10.252: *ars adeo latet arte sua ...*

defines as 'the frequently occurring sentiments that, when applied through amplification either for praise or for blame, assist in convincing people of our chosen point,'[561] and methods of amplification. Commonplaces allow one to understand how the emotions are distinguished – that is, gentler and tragic emotions – and the ways of stirring them by heightening the vigour of language.[562] Methods of amplification and developing the qualities of excellent speech (probability, clarity, vividness,[563] pleasantness, forcefulness, splendour or sublimity)[564] further enabled the preacher to appeal to the emotions by putting the narrative so vividly before the eyes of his hearers' imagination that they would feel wholly wrapped up in the drama as it played out, or as Erasmus puts it, 'unrolling Scripture itself like a fine tapestry and laying it open to view.'[565] These qualities of speech can be even further enhanced by figures of speech (*schemata*) such as repetition, conversion, complexion, exclamation, apostrophe, rhetorical questions, etc 'that contribute to the vigour and gravity of language.'[566] One need not feel uneasy about using these either; the Fathers of the church understood it as a matter of fact that God himself employed these figures of speech in his own word to us, using the medium of our human language, 'for that is how divine wisdom decided, so to speak, to babble to us in a most ordinary manner.'[567] Again, the Scriptures themselves offer the best demonstration of how this was done.[568]

* * * * *

561 See book 3 CWE 68 768. On 'commonplaces,' see Quintilian 5.13.57–60. For the history of the term, see Quirinus Breen 'The Terms "Loci Communes" and "Loci" in Melanchthon' in *Humanism and Christianity: Studies in the History of Ideas* (Grand Rapids 1968) 93–105; Joan Marie Lechner *Renaissance Concepts of the Commonplaces: An Historical Investigation of the General and Universal Ideas Used in All Argumentation and Persuasion, with Special Emphasis on the Educational and Literary Tradition of the Sixteenth and Seventeenth Centuries* (New York [1962]). On amplification, see Hoffmann *Rhetoric* 145–8.

562 See book 3 CWE 68 790–807; see also *Ratio* 187.

563 On vividness (*enargeia, evidentia*) see *Colloquia* (*Convivium religiosum*) CWE 39 211 n47.

564 Erasmus' main source for these many figures of speech are *Rhetorica ad Herennium* and Quintilian. See Lausberg §§552–754; see also *De copia* CWE 24 280–664.

565 See book 3 CWE 68 808; cf *Ratio* 188–9.

566 Book 3 CWE 68 847

567 See book 3 CWE 68 890. See also *Ratio* 197: 'Et quoniam totus ferme Christi sermo figuris ac tropis obliquus est, diligenter odorabitur theologiae candidatus, quam sustineat personam is, qui loquitur, capitis an membrorum, pastoris an gregis.'

568 See *Ratio* 259–66.

Ecclesiastes further draws heavily on Quintilian's extensive treatment of tropes such as pronomination, denomination, hyperbole, apostrophe, hypallage, enallage, and synechdoche. And as much as 'certain theologians who have been trained more in arguments than in Holy Writ' might deny it, Erasmus maintains that 'the whole of human language is packed with tropes.'[569] Understanding them not only makes the meaning of Scripture clearer and resolves difficulties in interpretation but helps one become a better preacher. By the same token, failing to recognize tropes and how they work in our speech can lead one mistakenly to reject the literal sense and resort to allegories instead. To apply tropes correctly preachers do well to study the ancient writers – poets, grammarians, rhetoricians, orators – who not only used them abundantly but identified, classified, and explained their literary purpose. No less an authority than Augustine, and many other church Fathers besides, recognized that God, the author of the sacred books, is also author of these tropes that move our hearts towards his word.[570]

Of all the rhetorical devices that appeal to the emotions Erasmus declares that metaphor[571] 'holds primacy among all the powers of language. Nothing persuades more effectively, nothing lays something more clearly before the eyes, nothing stirs emotions more powerfully, nothing contributes more dignity, charm, and attractiveness, or even eloquence ...'[572] It is 'the source of many tropes, of comparison, image and misuse [*abusio*], riddle, allegory, proverb and fable, and any others that are akin to this kind.'[573] Under metaphor he locates allegory, to which he dedicates extended discussion as a rhetorical device and later (under biblical interpretation) as one of the four

* * * * *

569 Book 3 CWE 68 829 and 890
570 Book 3 CWE 68 829–34; see Augustine *De doctrina christiana* 3.29.40.
571 On metaphor see Lausberg §§558–63 and CWE 68 871–932 above.
572 Book 3 CWE 68 871. See also ibidem: 'Examples have great power both for persuading and for inflaming minds with the emulation of virtue.' Here Erasmus repeats his fundamental belief in the power of example to move listeners to embrace virtue; the example par excellence is Christ in all his works and words. See Thomas Aquinas *Summa theologiae* 1 i 9 ('Whether Holy Scripture Should Use Metaphors?'): 'It is also befitting Holy Writ, which is proposed to all without distinction of persons – *To the wise and to the unwise I am a debtor* (Rom 1:14) – that spiritual truths be expounded by means of figures taken from corporeal things, in order that thereby even the simple who are unable by themselves to grasp intellectual things may be able to understand it ...' See Lausberg §§558–63; Quintilian 12.4.1; *Rhetorica ad Herennium* 4.49.62 (*exemplum*); and *De copia* CWE 24 606–20.
573 Book 3 CWE 68 930

senses of Scripture.[574] Taking readers through catachresis, similes, image, similitude, Erasmus proffers abundant examples of how these figures have been used effectively by sacred and other authors, and how they might be used by preachers of his day. Drawing upon Augustine's *De doctrina christiana*,[575] he demonstrates further how a preacher might take up the trope of similitude using the grand, middling, and humble styles of speaking[576] depending on the nature of the similitude, noting also many differences (for example, harsh and gentle, fiery and calm, etc) in the manner of speech. Tropes abound; some even 'have not yet found a name among rhetoricians or grammarians.'[577] If one will not acknowledge that these tropes in Sacred Scripture are the divine author's way to bring us to understand, he can never understand the lessons God inscribed there for our spiritual enlightenment.[578]

Because the study of language's rich complexities serves as the foundation for understanding God's word, it is imperative the preacher go about this diligently. Taking up the best authors will be of particular benefit for linguistic comprehension and power of expression.[579] Among the best, Erasmus gives the unqualified first place to the authors of Sacred Scripture who were divinely inspired to record God's word and whose eloquence renders all other writings pale by comparison. Erasmus invites preachers to ponder daily the fecundity of Christ's teaching, Paul's manifold ways of handling sacred themes, Peter's and Paul's speeches in Acts, and so forth. In

* * * * *

574 See *Colloquia* (*Convivium religiosum*) CWE 39 216 n117: 'For Erasmus, allegory is very often merely a synonym for "metaphor" or "figure." It is what is left, so to speak, when the "grammatical" (historical or literal) sense of a word or words is unintelligible or unacceptable to the reverent reader or commentator (for example in Gen 3:8, God "walking in the garden in the cool of the day" or in Gen 6:6 repenting that he had made man on the earth) . . .'

575 Augustine *De doctrina christiana* 4.17.34–4.28.61

576 See book 3 CWE 68 879–80; 'styles of speaking' (*tres orationis characteres*).

577 See book 3 CWE 68 890; cf Augustine *De doctrina christiana* 3.29.40; and *Ratio* 190: 'Poeticis figuris ac tropis scatent undique prophetarum litterae . . .' Erasmus understands the word 'trope' (τρόπος) in three ways: 'a figure of speech, a manner, and a person's life and character'; see book 3 CWE 68 934. The third sense of the word applies to the 'moral' or 'tropological' sense of Scripture, where 'the narrative itself indicates in passing whatever contributes to good character.' See book 3 CWE 68 934.

578 Cf *Ratio* 180.

579 See eg *De ratione studii* CWE 24 667: 'If the teacher is not available, then (as the next best thing) the best authors must certainly be used. Personally, I should like them to be very limited in number but carefully chosen . . .'

addition to Scripture, Erasmus provides a ranking of the most useful authors among the Greeks and Latins, whether Christian or pagan, prosaists or poets. For the sheer power of language his top selections among the pagans are also Quintilian's: 'There is no one to prefer, or scarcely even to compare, to Demosthenes and Cicero.'[580] One should not however neglect other distinguished pagan authors. Aristotle, for example, 'contributes a great deal to judgment and to knowledge, rather less to popular language';[581] Plato is commendable, for 'his comparisons lend one a sort of guiding hand towards knowledge of the truth.' Special mention goes to Plutarch, 'whose books deserve to be learnt word for word' and from whose writings Christians like Basil and Chrysostom drew heavily.[582] One can find excellent speeches in the Latin authors Livy, Tacitus, Seneca, and Sallust ('easily the most eloquent of all, with the exception of Cicero alone').[583]

Of the Greek and Latin church Fathers Erasmus recommends especially those regarded for their eloquence, sound exegetical methods, teaching, usefulness, propriety, and suitability for imitation. Among the Greeks he gives highest marks to Basil, who 'is crystal clear, devout, sound, pleasantly grave, and gravely pleasant, with not a trace of verbose affectation.'[584] Next to him stands Gregory of Nazianzus, and together with them John Chrysostom, to whom *Ecclesiastes* gives prominent attention. Other lights of the Eastern church follow: Athanasius is commended for his teaching and, Erasmus maintains, were his sermons extant, they would be as excellent as his teachings. Origen is eminently useful for his teaching but does not rank as high as the others; 'but as he calls his sermons "homilies," that is, conversations, his stylistic level hardly ever rises, but he is entirely occupied with

* * * * *

580 Book 2 CWE 68 489
581 Book 2 CWE 68 489
582 Book 2 CWE 68 490. Many editions of Plutarch's works were in circulation at this time. In March 1509, Aldus published Plutarch's *Moralia* under the title *Plutarchi opuscula* LXXXXII, edited by Demetrius Ducas, and in March 1531 Erasmus himself published the *Apophthegmata Plutarchi* with Froben. Erasmus draws much from Plutarch's works, especially *De liberis educandis*, which offers much practical advice that is reflected in *Ecclesiastes*; for example, it urges one 'to study knowledge at its source' (8B).
583 Book 3 CWE 68 777 and book 1 193. Erasmus recommends the speeches in Sallust, but Quintilian cautions his readers against imitating 'the famous terseness of Sallust (though in his case of course it is a merit) ...'; see Quintilian 4.2.45. Sallust's *Opera* were well known and available. Erasmus likely had access to the edition by Pomponius Laetus and Johannes Britannicus, printed at Venice in 1494–1500 by Christophorus de Pensis.
584 Book 1 193

teaching, and he touches none of the emotions except those that the subject itself stirs.'[585] Elsewhere Erasmus admits that Origen sometimes got carried away by excessive zeal in his exegeses, which were often immoderate in the use of allegories.[586]

Except for Jerome, Erasmus maintains that the Latin Fathers do not attain the level of eloquence of the Greeks, nor are they their equals in exegesis (for reasons noted below); they are nonetheless impressive and worthy of imitation. Jerome, by way of exception, 'is appropriate for acquiring every kind of speaking ability.'[587] Had he been a bishop, he would likely have left sermons of distinction, if not pre-eminence among the Latin Fathers.[588] As

* * * * *

585 See book 2 CWE 68 492. Origen, however, is given the highest rank for his exegesis; see Godin 139: 'Aux Grecs revient la première place.Dans ce classement préférentiel, non chronologique, Origène occupe un rang hors pair. Son statut est vraiment privilégié: il est en quelque sorte hors-concours, incomparable.' See also In psalmum 38 CWE 65 31–2.

586 Book 3 CWE 68 917; see also Ratio 284.

587 Book 2 CWE 68 494. See Erasmus' comments in his dedicatory letter to William Warham for the edition of Jerome's works, CWE 61 especially 6–7; and Hieronymi Vita CWE 61 57 on Jerome's eloquence and efforts 'to gain mastery of many languages'; '. . . he dealt with subjects that do not easily lend themselves to embellishment or take on rhetorical brilliance, and he even dictated a great deal. Despite this his eloquence proved to be of such high quality that there has been no one in our memory with whom we can compare him in this regard. And yet our age has seen outstanding men who would not have been deemed lacking in eloquence even in the time of Cicero. Chief among them are Lorenzo Valla, Ermolao Barbaro, Angelo Poliziano, Giovanni Pico, and our own Rodolphus Agricola.' Erasmus in fact declares: 'For indeed Cicero himself would have had to change his language if he were Jerome. The good qualities of style you admire in one author may be different from those you admire in another. Upon one person, Jerome, so many gifts were lavished at the same time that you find in him what you miss even in Cicero. Cicero speaks; Jerome thunders and fulminates. We admire the former's language; we admire the latter's heart as well' (58–9). 'Even Greece herself . . . has no one to compare with our Jerome' (59). For Erasmus and St Jerome, see especially John C. Olin 'Erasmus and Saint Jerome: The Close Bond and its Significance' ERSY 7 (1987) 33–53; idem introduction to CWE 61 xiii–xxxvii, especially xvi–xvii; idem 'Erasmus and the Church Fathers' in Six Essays on Erasmus and a Translation of Erasmus' Letter to Carondelet, 1523 (New York 1979) 35–8; Eugene F. Rice Saint Jerome in the Renaissance (Baltimore 1985); André Godin 'Erasme biographe patristique: Hieronymi Stridonensis vita' Bibliothèque d'Humanisme et Renaissance 50 (1988) 691–706.

588 In his Contra Rufinum (Apology Against Rufinus), Jerome states that he preached daily to the monks at Bethlehem. But until the nineteenth-century scholar Dom

much as Erasmus admires Jerome, at times he will disapprove of his con-
torted use of allegory (see below). He also criticizes the North African writers: Tertullian he finds 'harsh,' and to some degree Augustine who, though
commendable in many respects, suffered from his native land's penchant
for the florid style and for turning everything to a spiritual meaning[589] in his
often overworked allegories and in the devices he uses to win the attention
of his somewhat jaded congregation.[590] In general, however, Erasmus ap-
praises the North African Fathers as outstanding doctors of the church and
commends for their eloquence and benefit Cyprian and Lactantius, both of
whom seemed to have escaped the linguistic defects of North African Latinity. The Iberian Prudentius, though writing in verse, similarly receives
high praise. Yet on the whole, and with the exception of Jerome, Erasmus
does not warmly endorse the Latin Fathers for imitation; Ambrose, for example, was 'a great light of the church,' though 'not so suited to this age.'[591]
Nonetheless he encourages readers to read these and other authors like Leo
the Great (440–61), Maximus of Turin (d 408–23), and Fulgentius (c 468–
533), 'who have treated this kind of oratory with some success.'[592] After the
age of Augustine, Erasmus sees Latin in rapid decline, largely because of
the 'barbarian' influences that corrupted the language's purity. In Erasmus'
view of language we detect what one might call a natural entropy; Latin's
fate, much like that of Hebrew and Greek, was bound to degenerate ow-
ing to 'the corruption caused by ordinary people, who always turn everything for the worse.'[593] For this reason Erasmus advises against imitating

* * * * *

Germain Morin identified a series of homilies and attributed them to Jerome, no
one, including Erasmus, believed that any of Jerome's sermons were extant. See
the introduction to Jerome's homilies on Mark by Jean-Louis Gourdain: Jerome
Homélies sur Marc Sources chrétiennes 494 (Paris 2005) 9–21; *The Homilies of Saint
Jerome* 2 vols FOC 48 & 57 (Washington, DC 1966); *S. Hieronymi Presbyteri tractatus
homiliae in Psalmos, in Marci Evangelium aliaque varia argumenta* CCSL 78. See Erasmus' comments on Jean Vitrier's preference for Ambrose, Cyprian, Jerome, and
Origen in Ep 1211. On Jean Vitrier and Erasmus, see Godin *Spiritualité*; Godin;
and Godin 'Érasme et le modèle origénien de la prédication' in *Colloquia Erasmiana Turonensia* ed Jean-Claude Margolin, 2 vols (Toronto 1972) II 807–20.

589 Book 3 CWE 68 968; on his 'florid style' see book 3 CWE 68 494.
590 For Erasmus' preference for these other authors over Augustine, see Georges
Chantraine 'L'Apologie ad Latomum' *Scrinium* II 57.
591 Book 2 CWE 68 493
592 Book 2 CWE 68 495
593 Book 2 CWE 68 485–6. See *De recta pronuntiatione* CWE 26 390: 'It is no good
writing in the language of the man in the street if you wish your work to
stay fresh and to last for ever. Once upon a time a large part of Europe and

St Benedict[594] or Pope Gregory the Great, who though 'simple and devout in his sermons' suffers in his Latin from his contrived *clausulae*.[595] After him, with the exception of Bernard of Clairvaux, there is no one any preacher should wish to imitate, and even Bernard's value is diminished for he was 'a speaker more by nature than by art, witty and pleasant, yet ready to excite emotion'; but because his sermons were addressed to monks, they offer little to preachers today.[596] In fact, Erasmus finds little use for anyone after the mellifluent abbot of Clairvaux; since the twelfth century Europe has been awash in preachers of the worst sort.

For oratorical guidance and inspiration Erasmus finds little to commend among the 'modern' authors. Thomas Aquinas, by way of exception, he thinks probably would have been good at preaching; 'Scotus and his ilk,' on the other hand, 'are useful for a knowledge of ideas, useless for speaking.'[597] From Scotus' day to his own, Erasmus sees preaching in a wasteland,

* * * * *

Africa together with a smaller part of Asia spoke Latin or Greek. Now, look at the number of barbarian languages there are, which the common people have created out of Latin alone! Look at the number of different dialects even within single countries, as in Italy, France, and Spain. So it is important for scholars to confine themselves to those languages that have almost exclusively been used in learned writing. The reason is that they do not depend for their guarantee on ordinary people. The people are poor custodians of quality, whereas the guarantee of the integrity of the learned languages rests in the books written by good authors.'

594 Erasmus describes Benedict's Latin as 'grim' (*tetricus*); book 2 CWE 68 504–5.
595 Book 2 CWE 68 494. Steven M. Oberhelmann *Rhetoric and Homiletics in Fourth-Century Christian Literature: Prose Rhythm, Oratorical Style, and Preaching in the Works of Ambrose, Jerome, and Augustine* (Atlanta c 1991); and his *Prose Rhythm in Latin Literature of the Roman Empire: First Century B.C. to Fourth Century A.D.* (Lewiston, NY 2003) chapter 1, especially 9–11. On the Latin prose style of Gregory the Great, see Sister Kathleen Brazzel, *The Clausulae in the Works of St. Gregory the Great*, in Studies in Medieval and Renaissance Latin Language and Literature 11 (Washington, DC 1939). The author takes a more favorable stance towards Gregory's style than does Erasmus. See also Mary Borromeo Dunn *The Style of the Letters of St. Gregory the Great*, The Catholic University of America Patristic Studies 32 (Washington, DC 1931).
596 Book 2 CWE 68 494–5, 504. For Erasmus' views on Christian writers of middle Latin, see Paul Gerhard Schmidt 'Erasmus und die mittellateinische Literatur' in *Erasmus und Europa* ed August Buck, Wolfenbütteler Abhandlungen zur Renaissanceforschung 7 (Wiesbaden 1988) 129–37.
597 Book 2 CWE 68 495–6. Erasmus is likely referring to Scotus' writings in general, since there are no extant copies of his sermons, although apparently he did preach. See Schneyer 166; see also *Vita Hieronymi* CWE 61 57, where Erasmus comments on the moderns 'who lacked elegance of style. In this class we

for 'there came a type of preacher suited perhaps to the theatre of his time but quite ignorant of the art and displaying little wisdom';[598] but he gives scarce mention of any who achieved notoriety in their day, many of whom had printed sermon collections that would have been available,[599] such as Jordan von Quedlinburg (1300–80),[600] Jacopo da Varagine (c 1230–98),[601] Roberto Caracciolo (Fra Roberto da Lecce, O.F.M. c 1425–95),[602] Gabriel Biel

* * * * *

include Bonaventure, Thomas Aquinas, and Scotus; Jerome includes Jovinianus, Vigilantius, and Rufinus.' See Erasmus *Colloquia* (*Convivium religiosum*) CWE 39 171–243; see especially 230 n190 for the comment on J.-C. Margolin who 'perceives significant areas of agreement on certain major themes – liberty, love, individuality – between Scotus and Erasmus. He concludes that Erasmus was *un scotiste sans le savoir*.' See also Thompson 'Better Teachers' 128: 'In the vocabulary of Erasmus, "Scotus" and "Scotist" are generic terms for the whole catalogue of scholastic philosophers and theologians: the academic Establishment, from Thomas Aquinas to Erasmus' own day; typified in his pages by the Sorbonne. He is harder on Scotists than others, both because of his personal experiences with them and because of their Franciscan affiliations. To him the Scotists were always the worst of a bad lot.' See also book 2 CWE 68 612–13 and Ep 1211:24–7 for his comment on Jean Vitrier's view of Johannes Duns Scotus' teachings: 'The niceties of Scotist philosophy he had imbibed as a boy, and neither wholly rejected them (for there were clever things in it, he thought, though expressed in inelegant words) nor again did he set much store by them.' In *Ratio* 183, Erasmus views Thomas Aquinas as 'the most diligent of the recent [theologians].'

598 Book 2 CWE 68 496
599 For a bibliography of such works printed in 1503, which would have been available to Erasmus, see Hirsch especially 210: 'It is likely that most, if not all, the titles were available in the libraries of Basel and in nearby monasteries.'
600 Jordan von Quedlinburg, Saxon Augustinian monk, *Sermones de tempore* (Strassburg: [Printer of the Jordanus] 1483); see Schneyer 170; and 'Jordan of Quedlinburg' NCE 7 1032–3.
601 Sermons of Jacopo da Varagine, Dominican, author of the *Legenda sanctorum* (later known as *Legenda aurea*), *Sermones de tempore et de sanctis* (Basel: Johann Amerbach 1488). See 'James of Voragine' ODCC 861.
602 On Fra Roberto Caracciolo (Roberto da Lecce), see Telle ' "To every thing there is a season . . ." ' 13–24. Telle notes that 'Caracciolo's sermons were printed, *in his lifetime*, in about eighty editions – a prestigious number and all incunabula, that is printed before 1500 – which means that his fame became magnified and broadcast as an author all over Europe by the magic of the printing press' (20). Yale's Beineke Library has numerous collections of his sermons; eg *Sermones de adventu*, etc. (Strassburg: The R-printer (Adolf Rusch), not after 1475); *Hec est tabula o[mn]ium sermonum [con]tento[rum] in hoc volumine* (Venice: Gabriel de Grassis de Papia, between 1480–5). See also Cynthia L. Polecritti *Preaching Peace in Renaissance Italy: San Bernardino of Siena and His Audience* (Washington, DC 2000) 69–73.

(c 1425–95),[603] Johannes Herolt, O.P. (c 1380–1468),[604] and Girolamo Savona-rola (1452–98),[605] among others.[606] Surprisingly, except for the last two, many noted preachers who lived just before and during Erasmus' lifetime, such as Bernardino of Siena (1380–1444), Johannes Brugman (c 1405–73), Nicholas of Cusa (1401–64), Johann Tetzel (1465–1519), Michel Menot (d 1518), Johann Geiler von Kaysersberg (1445–1510), and Bernardino Ochino (1487–1564), to name but a few, merit not a word.[607] Erasmus does bring up Jean Gerson, but only to say he 'will help a preacher very little, at least in improving his ability to speak.'[608] Like the 'recent theologians' (neoterici) – William of Occam, Johannes Duns Scotus, William Durandus, Nicholas of Lyra, John Capreolus, Paul of Burgos – preachers of the recent past merit no praise.[609] In fact, Erasmus' anecdotes about Roberto Caracciolo's and others' antics make clear that their styles of preaching – though perhaps once popular among Italian audiences – are to be altogether avoided.[610]

While giving preference to the Latin church Fathers, Erasmus does not refrain from criticizing their Latinity, occasional lapses in judgment, and exegetical excesses especially in the use of allegory. He warmly en-dorses them as long as one exercises discretion in selecting what is valuable for preaching and rejecting what is not conducive to godliness. Apart from Scripture, the Fathers of the church are still the best guides, and the aspiring

* * * * *

603 *Sermones* (Tübingen: Johann Otmar for Friedrich Meynberger 1500)
604 *Sermones Discipuli de tempore et de sanctis cum promptuario exemplorum* (Reutlin-gen: Michael Greyff c 1479–82)
605 *Prediche de fra Hieronymo per tutto l'anno . . . sopra li Evanzelii, Psalmi & Propheti* (Venice: Cesaro Arrivabeno 1520)
606 See eg the list of published sermons given at the papal court between c 1450–1521 in O'Malley *Praise and Blame* 245–55.
607 Erasmus mentions an unidentified preacher ('Paradise') in book 2 496; per-haps he is mistaken, although he might be referring to a preacher from the Brigittine monastery of Paradiso in Florence.
608 John Gerson (1363–1429), theologian, chancellor of the University of Paris (1395), reformer, and strong proponent of conciliarism at the Council of Con-stance (1414–18), wrote numerous theological treatises and sermons. See G.H.M. Posthumus Meyjes *Jean Gerson, Apostle of Unity: His Church Politics and Ecclesi-ology* (Leiden 1999); 'Gerson, Jean le Charlier de' oDCC 669–70; and especially Christoph Burger 'Preaching for Members of the University in Latin, for Parish-ioners in French: Jean Gerson (1363–1429) on "Blessed Are They That Mourn"' in *Constructing the Medieval Sermon* ed Roger Andersson (Turnhout 2007) 207–20.
609 For a list of preachers active in the European lands at this time, see Schneyer 189–230.
610 See book 3 CWE 68 804–6.

preacher should learn to read them reverently, all the while being careful not to replicate their blemishes.[611] As for why one must be judicious in reading the Fathers, Erasmus explains that they sometimes stray into overallegorization, misinterpret the meaning of the text, or impose their own meaning upon a passage. He points out their aberrations, however, 'not to castigate men who have greatly assisted the Christian religion, whose memory we revere with very good reason as sacrosanct, but in order to make the preacher better trained to handle the Scriptures soundly.'[612] In essence when taking up the ancient Christian authors it all comes down to the principle of discrimination or good judgment, a quality in which even some Fathers were found wanting on occasion.

Because the marrow of the preacher's office is teaching 'the celestial philosophy,' Erasmus asserts that the preacher must be continuously exercised in understanding Scripture, for clerical membership itself bestows no qualification to preach or interpret Scripture. Unlike the apostles who were instructed by living with Christ and given the gift of his Spirit at Pentecost to infuse their preaching with divine force, clergy of the postapostolic age require rigorous methodical instruction. To this end Erasmus lays down numerous procedural rules throughout *Ecclesiastes* for interpreting Scripture, allotting to book 3 his most thorough exposition of hermeneutical principles, much of it recapitulating and expanding his teaching in *Ratio seu compendium verae theologiae* (1519),[613] as well as drawing heavily on Augustine's *De doctrina christiana*. He also culls material from other church Fathers like Origen, Gregory of Nazianzus, Jerome, and, of course, from Lorenzo Valla, whose *Adnotationes in Novum Testamentum* had earlier changed Erasmus' way of thinking about the interpretation of Scripture.[614] For handling Scripture in

* * * * *

611 See book 3 CWE 68 930.

612 Book 3 CWE 68 930

613 In February 1516, Erasmus published at the Froben press his *Methodus*, which was included with his *Paraclesis* and *Apologia* among the introductory writings of his first Greek and corrected Latin edition of the New Testament. Over the next years Erasmus revised and expanded *Methodus*, first renaming it *Ratio seu methodus compendio perveniendi ad veram theologiam*. This revision was published as a separate piece at Louvain in November 1518 at the press of Theodoricus Martinus (Dirk Martens). Two months later the same work was published by Froben, though with a slightly different title, *Ratio seu compendium verae theologiae*, and was included with Erasmus' newly and greatly emended edition of the New Testament, which he published with Froben in March 1519. See Holborn xiv–xv. For a comparison of *Ratio* with *Ecclesiastes*, see Hoffmann *Rhetoric* 55–60.

614 Erasmus had Valla's *Adnotationes* printed by Bade in Paris in 1505. See Erasmus' letter to Christopher Fisher and his edition of Valla's text in Laurentius

the pulpit Erasmus provides extensive instruction on the exegetical methods one should have mastered.[615] Acknowledging the current practice of interpreting Scripture according to the four senses (literal, tropological or moral, allegorical, and anagogical),[616] he favours the practice of the early church Fathers who distinguished only two senses: the literal (also referred to as the historical or grammatical sense) and the spiritual (often referred to by the Fathers as the tropological or allegorical or anagogical sense, 'but with no distinction between them').[617] Erasmus in fact shows with the story of

* * * * *

Valla *Opera omnia* ed Eugenio Garin (Turin 1962) I 801–95. See too Ep 182, especially 226–31; and Erika Rummel *Erasmus' 'Annotations' on the New Testament: From Philologist to Theologian* (Toronto 1986); Salvatore I. Camporeale *Lorenzo Valla: Umanesimo e teologia* (Florence 1972) 3–4, 23–4, 277–403; and his 'Poggio Bracciolini contra Lorenzo Valla. Les "Orationes in Laurentium Vallam"' in *Penser entre les lignes: Philologie et philosophie au Quattrocento* ed Fosca Mariani Zini (Paris 2001) 251–73; Bentley *Humanists* 32–69, 112–93; Christopher S. Celenza 'Renaissance Humanism and the New Testament: Lorenzo Valla's Annotations to the Vulgate' *Journal of Medieval and Renaissance Studies* 24 (1994) 33–52.

615 Erasmus sets forth the principles of allegorical exegesis in *Enchiridion* CWE 66 68–9 and *Ratio* 274–84. Many excellent studies have analyzed Erasmus' biblical hermeneutics in detail; see eg Hoffmann *Rhetoric* 32–9; Payne; John William Aldridge *The Hermeneutic of Erasmus* Basil Studies of Theology 2 (Zürich-Richmond [1966]); Chantraine 334–62. See also Thompson 'Better Teachers'; Albert Rabil Jr *Erasmus and the New Testament* (San Antonio 1972); Chomarat I 541–86; Bentley *Humanists* 112–93; Rummel *Erasmus' 'Annotations'*; Kathy Eden 'Erasmian Hermeneutics: The Road to *sola scriptura*' in her *Hermeneutics and the Rhetorical Tradition* (New Haven and London 1997) 64–78; see especially Godin 302–47; Béné *Érasme* 365–425; Augustijn *Erasmus* 89–106; Peter Walter *Theologie aus dem Geist der Rhetorik. Zur Schriftauslegung des Erasmus von Rotterdam* Tübinger Studien zur Theologie und Philosophie 1 (Mainz 1991) especially 194–8, 'Die Rolle der Kirchenväter.'

616 Book 3 CWE 68 932. See also Godin 323–7, and *Colloquia* (*Convivium religiosum*) CWE 39 216–19, 216 n117, for Erasmus' use of the four senses of Scripture: 'He has reservations about, but does not altogether reject, the conventional (medieval) fourfold distinctions . . .'

617 See book 3 CWE 68 933: 'The early doctors, however, recognize only two interpretations, the grammatical (or literal or, if you prefer, the historical) and the spiritual, which they call by a variety of names, sometimes "tropology," sometimes "allegory," sometimes "anagogy," but with no distinction between them.' For the four senses of Scripture, see Beryl Smalley *The Bible in the Middle Ages* (Notre Dame, Ind 1964) 1–26 and passim. See also de Lubac *Medieval Exegesis* I and II; CHB II chapter 6 155–279 and 492–505. See also Harry Caplan 'The Four Senses of Scriptural Interpretation and the Mediaeval Theory of Preaching' *Speculum* 4 (1929) 282–90; Augustijn *Erasmus* 98–100; Hoffmann *Rhetoric* 95–133, especially 101–6; and Grünwald 217–20. See *Vita Hieronymi*

Abraham's reception of the three men in Genesis 18 how a preacher can draw from the literal meaning of this passage a spiritual sense according to a tropological, allegorical, and anagogical interpretation,[618] and he demonstrates how the preacher can differentiate between rhetorical devices such as an allegory and a type. But more often Erasmus speaks of two senses of Scripture (literal and spiritual) as used by the church Fathers, the earliest and the most authentic interpreters of the word.

As a basic principle for the interpretation of Scripture, Erasmus demands that we believe that everything written in the Old Law teaches us about Christ.[619] Calling Christians to godliness and teaching the philosophy of Christ therefore demand that one first know the Old Law, its 'narration, precepts, types, ceremonies, and promises,'[620] and the New Law, which explains the old and contains 'narration, teaching, instructions, sacraments, the display of promises, grace, and the most perfect of all examples of godliness ...'[621] Similarly, the teaching of the New Law explains openly 'what was wrapped in riddles in the Old Law and draws out the mystical sense hidden in the letter of the Hebrew writings.'[622] The types and prophecies of the Old Law were fulfilled perfectly in Christ, who sometimes tells us himself when this occurred, as he did at the beginning of his public life in the synagogue at Nazareth when he explained the meaning of Isaiah's words, 'The spirit of the Lord is upon me ...' (Luke 4:18).[623] Finally, evangelists or persons in the Scriptures of the New Law often explain how Christ's words and activities fulfilled everything spoken of him and the types of him in the Old Law.[624]

* * * * *

CWE 61 53: 'Jerome makes no distinction between the first three [senses of Scripture].'

618 See book 3 CWE 68 934–9. See also Godin 327–9; cf *Ratio* 284: 'Porro in tractandis allegoriis felicissimus artifex est Origenes ...'

619 See book 3 CWE 68 1033, 1038. See *Ratio* 209; for this idea see also de Lubac *Medieval Exegesis* I 225–67, 'The Unity of the Two Testaments.' Cf *Ratio* 295, where Erasmus says of Origen: 'Inter quos praecipuus est Origenes, sic hanc Venerem exorsus, ut nemo post illum ausit manus apponere'; and ibidem 've-lut Origenem, qui sic est primus, ut nemo cum illo conferri possit ...'

620 Book 4 CWE 68 1033

621 Book 4 CWE 68 1036

622 Book 4 CWE 68 1037

623 Book 4 CWE 68 1038 (Luke 4:18)

624 See *Ratio* 209: 'There is almost nothing Christ did that those divine prophets did not describe'; 210: '... in the same way Christ did nothing that was not adumbrated by the types of the law, that was not predicted by the oracles of the prophets ...'

Contrary to some contemporaries, Erasmus contends that Scripture is not always easy to understand. Granted there are many clear teachings and sayings in Holy Writ, still not everything is obvious.[625] He recalls those Fathers of the church who testify that many passages continue to defy explanation and cause us to stumble when we try to make sense of them, such as Moses' injunctions in Deuteronomy against joining an ass to an ox when ploughing (22:10) and wearing clothing woven from linen and wool (22:11).[626] To assist the preacher with such mystifying passages, Erasmus lays down the principle that 'it is the custom of Scripture often to conceal mysteries that deserve worship beneath an unworthy covering.'[627] So we must believe that not a word of what we have fails in this regard; in fact 'in the canonical texts not even a point has been placed by chance.'[628] God encoded in the books of the Hebrews spiritual meanings that revealed his word from the very beginning, and if we seek earnestly in our prayers, with the assistance of the Holy Spirit, sometimes these meanings are made known to us. It is the divine plan too that we exercise ourselves continually to move from the literal sense to uncover deeper spiritual meanings.[629] Erasmus in effect envisions the Holy Spirit as progressively illuminating his church in the mysteries of his word. Though the spiritual significances of many passages may not yet be apparent, as surely as other meanings of Scripture have become clear to us over time, so we should expect hopefully that with prayer and meditation these too will become understood in the future as the church advances in godliness towards the final age. Moreover, it will be every preacher's duty to beg God daily through his prayers, work, and meditation to yield the meaning of these sacred passages, that he might become an evermore effective instrument in advancing our knowledge of his word and producing an abundant harvest of souls.

A further foundational principle for dealing with obscure passages in Scripture is to believe that Holy Writ's primary characteristic is its simplicity and that Scripture 'was prepared for simple people.'[630] This principle applies to preaching as well, for it too is to be done sincerely, simply, purely. Simplicity, in fact, distinguishes Erasmus' entire approach to laying

* * * * *

625 Cf *Ratio* 187 and 259–66.
626 Book 3 CWE 68 1000
627 Book 2 CWE 68 528
628 Book 2 CWE 68 528. See Hoffmann *Rhetoric* 118–26.
629 See also *Ratio* 259–62 on stories from Scripture that can be made fruitful with an allegorical interpretation; see also 275–7.
630 *Explanatio symboli* CWE 70 314

out Scripture, and it is this single quality he emphasizes repeatedly in his *Paraphrases* and in other writings dealing with the Bible.[631] God deals with us simply in his teaching; Christ did the same in his earthly life, and so should the preacher in speaking to his congregation. Unfortunately, Erasmus observes, with preaching, like monasticism, 'with the progress of time, little by little' that original simplicity and godliness of the church began to change for the worse with wealth and new ceremonies.[632] But in the beginning it was not this way, and even now God calls us back, speaking to us simply. For this reason the preacher should seek first to grasp Scripture's plain or humble meaning; for in dealing with benighted humanity, God's wont is to accommodate (*attemperat*) himself to his creatures, taking their times, circumstances, and needs into account,[633] reaching out to humanity in its ignorance and sinfulness.[634]

Much of what God communicates to us is straightforward and can be taken at the plain or literal meaning of the text, but at times he invites us to go beyond this to deeper spiritual levels. As God's communication with humankind in the Scriptures employs human ways of speaking, so like human speech his words often have a double meaning, 'one is more straightforward, the other allegorical and more sublime.'[635] The preacher's task is to understand both using his understanding of language. However, not all Erasmus' contemporaries conceded the usefulness of grammar and rhetoric to the detriment of dialectic, an attitude Erasmus blames on their almost exclusive training in scholastic method: 'Certain theologians who have been

* * * * *

631 See *Explanatio symboli* CWE 70 314 and n99: 'Simplicity: this represents Erasmus' standard for understanding Scripture in his *Annotationes*, his prefaces, and his controversy with Luther ...'

632 See the letter to Paul Volz, Ep 858:581–3, where Erasmus describes the process of degeneration in monastic life: 'Such were the first beginnings of monasticism, and such its patriarchs. Then gradually, with the passage of time, wealth grew, and with wealth ceremonies; and the genuine piety and simplicity grew cool.' See also *Ratio* 201, 203, 249, especially 201: 'Iam quintum tempus facere licebit ecclesiae prolabentis ac degenerantis a pristino vigore Christiani spiritus, ad quod opinor pertinere, quae dicit dominus in evangelio, quod abundante iniquitate refrigescet caritas multorum ...' See also Tracy (1) 102–3.

633 See *Explanatio symboli* CWE 70 315 n102.

634 See for example his dedicatory letter to Domenico Grimani for *Paraphrasis in epistolam ad Romanos*, Ep 710:195–9, especially 1965–7 where he describes his effort to accommodate the needs of his various readers. See also Marjorie O'Rourke Boyle *Rhetoric and Reform: Erasmus' Civil Dispute with Luther* (Cambridge, Mass 1983), and McConica 'Grammar of Consent.'

635 See book 1 316.

trained more in arguments than in Holy Writ ... think it ridiculous to mention hyperbole when expounding Scripture – as if all the tropes that the grammarians have gathered from the poets are not found in the divine books ...'[636] But it is only with the knowledge of the biblical languages, grammar, and rhetoric that the diligent preacher, with constant prayer and zeal, can unlock the genuine meaning of Scripture by comparing scriptural passages with each other and investigating how language is used by the biblical writers.[637] The *docta pietas* of the preacher therefore distinguishes itself from the dialectical techniques of the scholastic theologian in understanding grammar and rhetoric as foundational: biblical interpretation begins by establishing precisely the literal sense and factual details, and then probes for spiritual senses, if such appear warranted.[638]

Erasmus grows even more emphatic about the need for linguistic preparation, declaring that dialecticians who neglect to determine the literal or grammatical sense of Scripture, especially when interpreting Scripture allegorically, are simply wrong headed and prone to error. Additionally, they miss the opportunity to bring spiritual nourishment to their listeners. It is, after all, in the allegorical sense that the greatest spiritual benefits can be found because 'whatever is imparted through an allegory affects our minds more powerfully than anything related plainly.'[639] But Erasmus also advises caution; allegory is the most difficult rhetorical device to handle; 'no trope and no figure gives preachers more difficulty than allegory,'[640] and the dangers that lurk in allegorical interpretation can be considerable.

Erasmus adopts the ancient rhetoricians' definition of allegory as 'a continuous metaphor,'[641] but finds that the word in Sacred Scripture is given an even wider application and may include 'any trope at all.' It may even

* * * * *

636 Book 3 CWE 68 829; cf *Ratio* 268–70, where he discusses various hyperboles in Scripture.
637 See book 3. Erasmus might well have in mind his dispute with Jacobus Latomus (Jacques Masson), *Apologia contra Latomi dialogum* CWE 71 62–3. Contrary to Augustine (*De doctrina christiana* 2.11.16: '... because of the diversity of translators a knowledge of those languages is necessary'), Latomus seems to have rejected the idea that one any longer needed to know these biblical languages to determine the meaning of a scriptural passage.
638 See too Augustine *De doctrina christiana* 3.1; Chomarat *Grammaire* I 680; and Hoffman *Rhetoric* 101–33.
639 Book 3 CWE 68 962; cf *Ratio* 259–62. See also *Enchiridion* CWE 66 69, where Erasmus mentions that 'Theologians of the present day either practically despise allegory or treat it very cooly ...'
640 Book 3 CWE 68 896
641 Book 3 CWE 68 932

include a type, which brings forth a deeper spiritual meaning in the plain words of the biblical text, even where there is no trope, as Paul demonstrates in his exegesis of the story of Sarah and Isaac, Hagar and Ishmael (Gal 4:21–5:1), where 'the deeds themselves inherently signify a loftier meaning.'[642] Some spiritual meanings of these types we know because Christ and Paul and the sacred writers revealed them to us, such as the meaning of the bronze serpent Moses lifted up in the desert and the meaning of Jonah's triduum in the belly of the whale.[643] It is this deeper sense of Scripture that draws us closer to the philosophy of Christ for, as Erasmus explains, 'the more recondite something is, the more excellent it is and the more effective.'[644] Before one can grasp this deeper spiritual sense, however, he must not only determine the grammatical-historical sense as well as possible but then observe other procedural criteria, such as basing allegories especially upon those proof texts of Scripture (*scripturarum testimonia*) whose authority has never been doubted by the Hebrews, Greeks, or Latins,[645] and selecting those books of Scripture (for example, the Pentateuch) that 'have greater appeal' when introducing allegory and anagogy.[646]

Understanding the grammatical-historical sense requires above all that one establish the correct reading of the text, without which one might struggle endlessly to get an allegory to fit. Because of faulty, obscure, or ambiguous translations, and sometimes because the manuscript has been corrupted by careless scribes or even by perverters,[647] some Fathers interpreted passages of Scripture that simply made no sense; Erasmus illustrates this with the example of Augustine's exegesis of Psalm 34 (33 Vulgate), where David faces Abimelech, a text based upon a widely inaccurate Latin translation deriving from the Septuagint. Seeing Augustine 'turning everything into a spiritual meaning,' Erasmus exclaims, 'What strained allegories St Augustine uses in expounding the heading of Psalm 33, not through affectation but misled by an incorrect translation!'[648] Evidently Augustine's limited knowledge of Greek and ignorance of Hebrew accounted for his failure to grasp

* * * * *

642 Book 3 CWE 68 932
643 Book 3 CWE 68 959; see John 3:14–15 and Jon 2:1–10; see also book 4 CWE 68 1034.
644 See book 2 CWE 68 682.
645 Book 3 CWE 68 967
646 Book 3 CWE 68 968
647 Book 3 CWE 68 973. Erasmus makes this more precise a few lines later: 'The wickedness of interpolators never ceases, and the yawning of scribes never ceases.'
648 Book 3 CWE 68 921

the literal meaning of certain scriptural passages, hence his sometimes inapt allegories.

With his instruction on allegory Erasmus offers yet a further corollary, that 'unless the literal or grammatical sense on which the allegory is constructed has been understood and weighed accurately, for if there has been a mistake in the foundation, whatever you construct upon it cannot fit';[649] often the result is that the interpretation becomes ridiculous, 'since many props are needed to hold in place what has been twisted violently once one departs from the genuineness of Scripture.'[650] Here he adds that if one has found the plain meaning of a passage of Scripture and that meaning is consistent with other passages of Scripture, then there is no need to bring in a trope to explain the passage, unless of course that trope helps to clarify the plain meaning one has already established.[651] On the other hand, there are certain passages of Scripture containing tropes that need to be explained clearly lest hearers mistake what seems like the plain meaning for something bordering on blasphemy, as in Genesis 6:7 when God says 'I regret that I made man' (Gen 6:7).[652] Taking these words at face value makes the plain sense of Scripture look ridiculous; in this case one must turn to the other senses of Scripture to explain what God might have meant and dispel ambiguities. No less an authority than Augustine stated that tropes 'merit vigilant attention and memorization because "the knowledge of these is" especially "necessary for resolving the ambiguities of Scripture."'[653] Similarly, certain terms like 'law,' 'flesh,' 'spirit,' 'world'[654] also need careful

* * * * *

649 Book 3 CWE 68 919
650 Book 3 CWE 68 929
651 See book 3 CWE 68 943–52.
652 Gen 6:7 (*poenitet me fecisse hominem*); see book 3 CWE 68 955. See also Augustine *De diversis quaestionibus* LXXXIII (*Miscellany of Eighty-Three Questions*) WSA I-12 LII 65–6: 'The divine scriptures, which have lifted us up from their earthly and human meaning to one that is divine and heavenly, have stooped down to a language that is current even among the most learned ...' (65). Cf *Ratio* 292–3.
653 Book 3 CWE 68 895 and Augustine *De doctrina christiana* 3.29.40–1.
654 See book 3 CWE 68 898; cf *Enchiridion* CWE 66 101 where Erasmus makes clear how one should understand the meaning of 'world': 'What we read about the world in ancient theologians has now been made to refer to those who are not monks, according to some men of little learning. The "world" in the Gospel, in the writings of the apostles, Augustine, Ambrose, and Jerome is the name given to disbelievers, strangers to the faith, enemies of the cross of Christ, blasphemers against God.'

explanation since they have precise meanings in the Bible that are no longer current in our speech.

A typical, and perhaps the most striking, example in *Ecclesiastes* of Erasmus' method of allegorical exegesis is his elaboration in book 1 of the passage in Exodus 28 where the sacred author dwells on the divine directives for the liturgical vestments and other paraphernalia of the high priest Aaron.[655] Erasmus constructs his allegorical reading of this passage on Jerome's interpretation, extracting from the biblical text's myriad details a spiritual interpretation about the exacting standard of living required of the preacher of the New Law.[656] He affirms that this lengthy and otherwise wearying account, when read spiritually, reveals 'the endowments of the preacher in the priest Aaron' and 'offers us a picture to teach the spiritual priest of the New Testament that he should far surpass the ordinary person in all the adornments of the mind, purity of heart, chastity of body, sanctity of character, learning, wisdom, but above all eloquence worthy of the divine mysteries.'[657] In this respect Erasmus' pursuit of the spiritual meaning of the text is wholly traditional; in fact he manifests some reluctance in proffering new allegorical readings of Scripture, preferring to rely instead on interpretations of the church Fathers, especially those considered safe and widely accepted in Christian tradition. Aaron's vestments, like Scripture itself, 'reveal the interior ornaments of the spirit';[658] Scripture's words make known how it pleases God that we reform our lives in his image. The allegorical and tropological (spiritual) interpretation tells us far more than the dry exposition of Aaron's liturgical garb, and it illustrates the godliness we are called to embrace.

Erasmus proposes that preachers learn these rules thoroughly, almost by second nature, to avoid twisting Scripture's genuine meaning, which often happens if one tries to support the teachings of the faith with proof texts, especially when fighting heresies.[659] If he is fond of repeating one admonition, it is that the preacher should 'shun the emotion of those who

* * * * *

655 Book 1 301–20, 371–2. See Exodus 28 and 29; cf *Ratio* 261.
656 Book 1 314; see also Jerome *Ep* 64 (to Fabiola).
657 Book 1 302; cf *Moria* CWE 27 137, 140.
658 Book 1 310
659 See book 3 CWE 68 914, 916. See *Ratio* 287: 'And in fact hardly any one among the ancients does not at some point twist Scripture as often as he battles an opponent, and even Jerome himself does this, which he almost acknowledges in one place.' See also 288–91. Erasmus gives examples of Jerome's tendentious interpretations below.

lord it over Scripture, grabbing it by the neck and twisting it to the meaning that they themselves bring to it,[660] thereby accommodating it to their own personal feelings and agenda, 'a detestable impiety' that Christ's spirit does not forgive.[661] Twisting Scripture characterizes the heretic's exegesis, which is ultimately grounded in stubbornness and wickedness. Nonetheless, even well meaning, though sometimes overzealous, Fathers erred in this respect, falling prey to tendentious interpretations, as he illustrates with examples from Jerome's *Letter to Ageruchia* (Letter 123), where in pursuing his own agenda Jerome attempts to dissuade the woman from remarriage by his rendering of Jeremiah 3:3 ('You have made your own the face of a whore, you are shameless.').[662] Erasmus chides Jerome: 'What effrontery does it take then to twist such a cruel insult against a Christian woman who is engaged in lawful conduct, persevering in holy religion?'[663] Again, Erasmus censures Jerome's twisted use of 2 Timothy 2:20 in the same *Letter to Ageruchia*, where both text and context refer clearly to troublesome heretics of the church as wooden and earthen vessels:[664] 'How is it right, then, to compare a woman who marries twice to a chamber pot?'[665] But Jerome in 'his zeal for chastity' misappropriates Timothy's text and context for his own purposes, and his error can be observed in his departure from other church Fathers' allegorizations. Similarly Erasmus reviles those who do this for their own glory, or out of laziness or disregard for Scripture itself.[666] The guiding rule should be that 'it is more desirable never to depart from the genuine meaning of the Scriptures'[667] and that 'we must

* * * * *

660 See book 3 cwe 68 898 and book 1 372 ('Those who twist Scripture to human desires are lying . . .'); book 3 cwe 68 898, 949: 'to grab Scripture by the neck and force it to the remotest possible meaning.'

661 Book 3 cwe 68 900; cf Matt 12:32. See *Ratio* 284–7.

662 Erasmus follows Jerome's rendering of Jer 3:3 (*Facies meretricis facta est tibi, impudorata es tu*) in Ep 123:9. The Vulgate gives *Frons mulieris meretricis facta est tibi noluisti erubescere.*

663 Book 3 cwe 68 925. Erasmus refers to this woman as Gerontia, but Jerome gives her name as Ageruchia. Jerome also uses this rendering of Jer 3:3 Ep 22 and in his commentary on the minor prophets (*Commentarii in prophetas minores*) *In Osee* 1. See Jerome *Epistulae* csel 54 161. For background on Erasmus' views of widowhood, remarriage, sexuality, and the married and single states of Christian life, which obviously vary considerably with those of Jerome, see *De vidua christiana* cwe 66 177–257.

664 See book 3 cwe 68 926.

665 Book 3 cwe 68 926; cf *In psalmum 38* cwe 65 43.

666 Book 3 cwe 68 898

667 See book 3 cwe 68 930.

ensure in good faith, so far as can be accomplished by human effort, that our interpretation does as little violence and causes as little distortion as possible.'[668] The fundamental step in the method is establishing first the accurate and genuine meaning of the text by going beyond the narrow confines of the pericope, returning to the sources, studying the passage in its original language and context, noting what comes before and what follows.[669]

To handle the more recondite passages of Scripture, Erasmus advises preachers to consult the many commentaries of the ancient Christian authorities, comparing (*collatio*) their interpretation of passages with one another, and to take context into consideration as well as times and persons.[670] Because the church Fathers themselves often struggled with these same difficult passages, Erasmus advises preachers to consult their commentaries to understand how they read the passage and how they sought to resolve their difficulties with the text. If the Fathers shed no light, then the preacher should dwell at length upon the passage, praying in faith that God give light.[671] If it comes, the preacher should be careful not to grow proud or obstinate with his spiritual insight;[672] and if this new light is something he believes might benefit others, he should first refer the matter to the bishop to determine if it is consistent with the church's teaching.[673]

* * * * *

668 Book 3 CWE 68 919. See also *Ratio* 287 and *In psalmum 38* CWE 65 123.

669 Book 3 CWE 68 912: 'But in order to apply Scripture appositely and to the point, a preacher does not consider it enough to pluck snippets from collections or indices but must go to the sources themselves and search out the genuine meaning of Scripture from what precedes and what follows.' For this method, see also *Ratio* 285–6, and 292: 'Quandoquidem haec non Origeni tantum, sed et Augustino optima ratio est interpretandi divinas litteras, si locum obscurum ex aliorum locorum collatione reddamus illustrem et mysticam scripturam mystica, sacra sacram exponat.' Cf Augustine *De doctrina christiana* 3.28.39.

670 Book 3 CWE 68 983, where Erasmus treats allegories and their interpretation. He gives the reader no practical hint as to the editions he might consult, though by this time he had published numerous *opera* of the Fathers. He does not mention the *Glossa ordinaria*, though it was much in circulation, and in Erasmus' lifetime editions of it were printed at Strassburg (1480–1), Venice (1495), Basel (1498, 1502, 1508), Lyon (1520, 1528–29). See Lesley Smith *The* Glossa Ordinaria: *The Making of a Medieval Bible Commentary* (Leiden 2009) 241 and 187–91. Cf *Ratio* 295.

671 A good illustration of this method in practice is Erasmus' *In psalmum 2* CWE 63 65–146.

672 See book 3 CWE 68 1001.

673 Erasmus might here be referring to *Inter multiplices* (4 May 1515) of the Fifth Lateran Council, which, among its other provisions, mandated that bishops or

One premise of Erasmus' exegetical instructions is that the teachers of the early church had a greater grasp on the revealed truth of Christ and the teachings of the apostles because they stood closer in time to them than the 'moderns' and so understood God's message with an immediacy that was later blurred at times or even lost over the centuries.[674] In selecting the ancient authorities as guides, Erasmus prefers those who stood nearest to the time of the apostles, when the gospel was still fresh.[675] By the same logic Erasmus gives precedence to the Greek Fathers over the Latins, for 'the nation has always excelled in fertile intellects,'[676] and the more ancient of them – Clement, Papias, Ignatius, Justin, Irenaeus, Origen, (and Tertullian among the Latins) – stood closer in time and in language to the apostles themselves.[677] Their light guided the next generations of outstanding interpreters – among the Greeks, Athanasius, Basil, Chrysostom, and Cyril;[678] among the Latins, Ambrose, Jerome, and Augustine. Among these writers ('middle antiquity'), however, Erasmus assigns first place here to Augustine rather than Jerome 'on the grounds that he has given considerable assistance to the

* * * * *

their delegates examine 'any book or other writing of whatever kind' before its publication. Upon approval, a book would receive an *imprimatur* (*per eorum manu propria subscriptionem*). See Tanner 1 632–3; Stupperich 351.

674 See also *Ratio* 211.

675 See book 3 CWE 68 912; cf *Ratio* 211: 'Nec fortassis absurdum fuerit in sacris quoque voluminibus ordinem auctoritatis aliquem constituere, id quod facere non est veritus Augustinus. Nam primae debentur iis libris, de quibus nunquam fuit addubitatum a veteribus. Apud me certe plus habet ponderis Isaias quam Iudith aut Esther, plus evangelium Matthaei quam Apocalypsis inscripta Ioanni, plus epistolae Pauli ad Romanos et Corinthios quam epistola scripta ad Hebraeos. Proximum his locum tenent quaedam nobis ceu per manus tradita, vel ab ipsis apostolis ad nos usque profecta vel ab iis certe, qui vicini fuerunt temporibus apostolorum. Quo in numero cum primis pono symbolum in concilio Nicaeno, ni fallor, editum, quod vulgo dicitur apostolorum ...' This 'nostalgia for former times, for the golden age of the earliest Christianity,' according to Augustijn, appears first in *Moria*; see Augustijn *Erasmus* 63, and *Ratio* 284–5.

676 Book 3 CWE 68 912

677 Erasmus' preference is regularly for those authors who stood closest to Christ and the apostles; see eg *Ratio* 211.

678 Erasmus also refers at times to the commentary of the eleventh-century Bulgarian bishop Theophylact whose works he admired, although by the time he wrote *Ecclesiastes* he no longer believed him to be an early Greek commentator. See *Colloquia* (*Convivium religiosum*) CWE 39 225 n181. See also Augustijn *Erasmus* 97; and *Ratio* 271, where he refers to Theophylact's comment on Matt 26:45. See 'Theophylact' ODCC 1607.

schools of theology with his definitions.'[679] But the Fathers also often give different interpretations and sometimes even disagree among themselves as to the meaning of a passage in Scripture.[680] In such cases Erasmus advises readers to select 'the one that seems to come closest to the true meaning' and 'follow what seems to be more correct.'[681] It should be a guiding principle that Scripture itself is so rich in spiritual meanings that 'there never will be a lack of material for the devout application of scholars to pore over and dig out, provided always that the dogmas of the Catholic faith remain unshaken.'[682] But in using commentaries of the ancients, he counsels discrimination,[683] that one be mindful that the Fathers themselves were not without mistakes and occasional tendentious interpretations.[684]

Erasmus also advises preachers to approach the ancient commentators reverently and 'with greater forbearance than the more recent ones.'[685] Because, historically, doctrines often took ages to be clarified and then pronounced, he observes that in earlier ages the church 'had not yet pronounced explicitly on many topics, and it was not impious to hold doubts so long as it was done in such a spirit that the mistake or doubt would be put aside once the truth was revealed.'[686] Similarly, the preacher should have freedom to review what the ancients had written to see if perchance 'a truer and more genuine meaning of Scripture can be found,'[687] rather than being bound fast

* * * * *

679 Book 3 CWE 68 913. But see his letter to Johann Maier von Eck, Ep 844:132–291; also Tracy (1) 72. Erasmus refrains here from sharp comparisons made earlier between Jerome and Augustine; but see eg Erasmus' comparison of Jerome with Augustine in *Vita Hieronymi* CWE 61 54: 'The facts themselves proclaim that Jerome surpassed Augustine in dialectics no less than he outstripped him in eloquence and that he was no less Augustine's superior in learning than he was in excellence of style.' Cf *In psalmum 38* CWE 65 48, where he speaks of Augustine as 'the most intellectually able and careful of all the Fathers ...'

680 Book 3 CWE 68 913; cf *Ratio* 292 and *In psalmum 38* CWE 65 42–52, 121.

681 See book 3 CWE 68 964 and 913.

682 Book 3 CWE 68 913

683 See book 3 CWE 68 912–13. In *Ratio* 205 Erasmus cites Augustine's counsel that the books of other celebrated authors be read 'not with the necessity of believing but with the liberty of discerning' the truth of what they say.

684 See above for the instances of this in the exegeses of Jerome and Ambrose. See *In psalmum 38* CWE 65 42–54 especially 53: 'Not even the most distinguished men have been able to avoid committing occasional errors and no amount of circumspection has enabled them to escape the backbiting of their critics.' See also 53 n207.

685 Book 3 CWE 68 912; cf *In psalmum 38* CWE 65 42–53.

686 Book 3 CWE 68 912–13

687 See book 3 CWE 68 913; cf *Ratio* 215.

to the opinions of the ancients who not only often disagreed with one another but also were inconsistent in their own works.[688] The Holy Spirit, after all, does not cease to pour his light on those who prayerfully seek to understand the word of God. Moreover, as the Fathers themselves never insisted on the orthodoxy of their own opinions, so they would have concurred that later generations should also seek out other meanings of Scripture that might still lie hidden.[689]

As a further principle, Erasmus counsels readers to believe that Scripture is so perfectly consistent with itself that if we compare passages with one another the meaning of the pericope in question can often be drawn out.[690] However, when this and every other interpretative method fails, one should approach Scripture with the attitude of Augustine, who sometimes humbly confesses his bewilderment when he cannot understand a passage's meaning.[691] This approach Erasmus himself follows when confronted with passages that continue to puzzle him, such as 'The kingdom of heaven is suffering violence, and violent men are seizing it' (Matt 11:12), or Moses' command at Deuteronomy 22:10 'forbidding anyone ploughing with an ox and an ass' together.[692] One should also be of the same mind when approaching certain passages of the Old Testament that even seem to detract from the majesty of its author, such as God's command 'to destroy so many nations by killing and to shun them with everlasting hatred.'[693] In such instances, one should be like Paul who followed Christ's method of explaining these locutions as types and opening up their meanings with allegories. Yet even employing an allegory or a trope sometimes does not help to explain what Scripture is saying, and at times even the ancients failed badly in trying to do so. So we should also believe like Augustine that 'it was useful for the

* * * * *

688 Book 3 CWE 68 913
689 See Cornelis Augustijn 'Hyperaspistes 1: La doctrine d'Erasme et de Luther sur la "Claritas Scripturae"' in *Colloquia Erasmiana Turonensia* 2 vols (Paris 1972) II 737–48.
690 See book 4 CWE 68 1040: 'The New Testament is harmonious with the Old, and the whole of Scripture is so consistent with itself in all respects that there is never any conflict anywhere so long as it is understood correctly – something that is found in no human philosophy.' Cf *Hyperaspistes* CWE 77 749: 'Nothing could be more self-consistent than Scripture.' See too *Colloquia (Convivium religiosum)* CWE 39 188 and n150. Erasmus emphasizes this point in *Ratio* 209–11, 292; see also book 4 CWE 68 1039.
691 Book 3 CWE 68 914
692 Book 3 CWE 68 1000. Erasmus has a comment on Matt 11:12 in *De puritate tabernaculi* CWE 65 242–3.
693 Book 3 CWE 68 918–19; cf Num 21; Deut 3:1–7 and 7; Josh 10.

mysteries of heavenly philosophy to be veiled from the wicked.'[694] In instances where the meaning of Scripture still remains obscure, as in Ezekiel's words about the wheels and the dimensions of the temple (Ezekiel 40), it is best simply to confess our inability to grasp the passage's spiritual meaning, holding all the while in our hearts that there is a meaning, though God has not yet granted us the light of spiritual understanding.[695]

To aid readers in biblical interpretation, Erasmus offers additional advice on evaluating the ancient commentators' exegeses. He points out for example that in the past the Canticle of Canticles (Song of Solomon) was read spiritually as 'an allegory of Christ as groom and the church as bride.'[696] But the ages distorted this reading, adding a further interpretation that 'wrenched this [interpretation] to apply [the bride] to the most holy Virgin,' which runs 'contrary to the interpretation of all the ancients.'[697] So he advises the preacher to return to the interpretations of the early church Fathers, to prefer them to the more recent commentators' elaborations.[698] Still, this is not always the best solution, for sometimes even the Fathers erred in giving themselves some licence to twist the words of Scripture to their subject, especially when fighting heretics or exhorting to perfection.[699] Erasmus' hermeneutical approach offers a middle ground (*sobria mediocritas*): first ascertain the literal meaning of Scripture; if deeper senses suggest themselves, look at the interpretations of the Fathers; when their readings do not conflict, then one rests on solid ground; if they differ, one should prefer wherever possible those commanding greatest authority and consensus. And when the Fathers give no reading of the passage, one may proceed as long as one's own interpretation does not depart from solid doctrine and the sense is congruent with the words of the sacred text and 'seems to come closest to the true meaning.'[700]

* * * * *

694 See book 3 CWE 68 962; cf *De doctrina christiana* 2.6.7. See also *Ratio* 259–60.
695 Book 3 CWE 68 961
696 Book 3 CWE 68 919. For the exegetical history of *The Song of Songs* in the Middle Ages, see E. Ann Matter *The Voice of My Beloved:The Song of Songs in Western Christianity* (Philadelphia c 1990).
697 Book 3 CWE 68 920. See *Virginis et martyris comparatio* CWE 69 153–82 where in his devotional treatise to the Benedictine nuns of the convent of the Maccabees in Cologne Erasmus follows the traditional interpretation that he upholds here (CWE 69 164), but he also extends it to the virgins of the convent whose disposition 'thirsts after nothing but the glory of your Bridegroom' (159).
698 See also *Ratio* 283.
699 See book 3 CWE 68 914, 916.
700 Book 3 CWE 68 964

While writing *Ecclesiastes*, Erasmus found himself engaged in a two-front battle against what he saw as the extreme literalists and the incorrigible allegorizers, those on the one side who rigidly adhered to the 'literal,' 'grammatical' reading of Scripture, and those on the other side who saw everything written in Scripture as allegory.[701] Both extremes, he maintains, are problematic and can produce disastrous interpretative results. Referring to the first group, Erasmus declares that 'there is no lack today of people who walk with their loins girded because the Lord tells his people to have their loins girded.'[702] He calls these interpreters 'anthropomorphites' (attributing to God the physical characteristics of a human being) who read Scripture literally without extracting the spiritual meaning. This excessively literalist approach he labels as Judaism: 'People tend towards Judaism when they exclude tropes and allegories from the Scriptures, making a carnal law out of the Law that according to Paul is spiritual.'[703] Erasmus contends that literalism's effect suppresses the inner warmth and fire of Christ's teachings and his offer of universal salvation by making everything depend on an inflexible fidelity to blind ceremonies and to a strictly literal reading of the text. On the other hand, there are the allegorizers who 'reject the lowest [ie literal] meaning when no necessity so compels.'[704] Erasmus censures Origen for this in sometimes allegorizing too freely, noting that the result of excessive allegorizing can lead to a kind of free-for-all; without firm grounding in the text, whatever suggests itself becomes the foundation of the exegesis, which in turn can lead to unwarranted theological conclusions. With this also lurks the danger of misrepresenting the literal meaning of the scriptural text because of the sympathy and zeal of some commentators to exculpate certain biblical persons' behaviour. For this fault Erasmus reproaches Ambrose – 'a great light of the church, in whom nothing should be criticized unless it serves the instruction of

* * * * *

701 On these extremes in Erasmus' day see Kathy Eden 'Erasmian Hermeneutics: The Road to *sola scriptura*' in her *Hermeneutics and the Rhetorical Tradition* (New Haven and London 1997) 64–78, especially 73–8.

702 See book 3 CWE 68 940.

703 Book 3 CWE 68 943. For other comments on 'Judaism,' see *Declarationes ad censuras Lutetiae vulgatas* LB IX 889D–E, *Ratio* 200, and *De esu carnium* ASD IX-1 22. See also *Colloquia* (*Convivium religiosum*) CWE 39 222 n157; Augustijn *Erasmus* 80–1; and especially Dominic Baker-Smith's review and analysis of Erasmus' attitude towards Judaism in his introduction to CWE 63 xlix–lvi.

704 Book 3 CWE 68 943; see also *Ratio* 280, where Erasmus singles out Origen, Ambrose, and Hilary: 'Sometimes when there is no need they do away with the grammatical sense in their zeal to impose an allegory.'

preachers'[705] – for labouring to exculpate Peter after he denied Christ three times in the courtyard of the high priest Caiphas. However noble Ambrose's intention, his manipulation of the Johannine pericope was improper. Allegories and other readings based on the spiritual senses of Scripture must first find warrant in the literal sense, and it is a fault of those who do not understand tropes as used in the literal sense to have recourse to allegories.[706] These examples, of course, are merely cautionary. Erasmus urges preachers to learn how to use allegories expertly, as they are an exceedingly useful means of teaching –'truth that shines through an allegory delights us more'[707] – and when applied appositely yield much fruit. But he cautions as well against their overuse; they should instead be 'sprinkled like seasonings,' as Augustine suggests, for too much 'would easily become repugnant if served as foods.'[708]

To navigate the extremes of biblical interpretation Erasmus counsels 'a sober moderation.'[709] One should first accept the lowest level, the plain meaning of the text; often one needs to go no further than this. It is often on the plain meaning that we are called to dwell in many of the gospel narratives; therein lie riches enough to satisfy the heart. But at times Scripture is obscure and begs us to seek a deeper spiritual meaning. Erasmus observes that the historical account in Numbers 20 of Moses striking the rock is in itself not objectionable for pious consideration,[710] but often the possibly greater spiritual benefit one might bring one's listeners urges the preacher to probe for a deeper spiritual understanding.[711] There is also the practical benefit because allegories 'have considerable value for rousing the weary, for consoling the downcast, for instilling courage in the wavering, for

* * * * *

705 Book 3 CWE 68 943–4. Note Erasmus' harsh criticism of Ambrose's strained exegesis of Matt 26:69–75, Mark 14:66–72, Luke 22:54–62, and John 18:15–27, where Ambrose relates Peter's reaction to those in the court of the high priest 'in order either to excuse or to diminish the apostle's crime.' See also *Ratio* 278–80, where Erasmus notes he is 'sometimes excessive' (*immodicus esse nonnumquam*) (278); Jerome also chastises Ambrose. Erasmus notes that Origen, on the other hand, gives a much more responsible interpretation; see book 3 CWE 68 948, *Ratio* 278–80 and *In psalmum 38* CWE 65 43–4 and 44 n163.

706 Book 3 CWE 68 961–2; Erasmus notes that failing to understand tropes such as hyperbole can lead one to reject the literal sense and resort to allegorizing.

707 Book 3 CWE 68 962

708 Book 3 CWE 68 965

709 Book 3 CWE 68 952. See also Hoffmann *Rhetoric* 143–4 and passim. Erasmus gives the same counsel in *Ratio* 280.

710 Num 20:7–13; Exod 17:5–7

711 See book 3 CWE 68 953, 959, and book 4 CWE 68 1034.

attracting the hypercritical.'[712] Yet, like Augustine, Erasmus urges preachers, when expounding obscure passages of Scripture, to strive above all for
the clarity that produces spiritual understanding that leads to the reform of
life and the pursuit of godliness.[713] Likewise they should beware of those
who shun the lowest meaning; such 'subvert the foundation and strength of
Scripture, for they make it a matter of opinion, with the result that it is now
human rather than divine.'[714] Certainly it should be far from any preacher
to introduce contrived allegorical interpretations for fictitious dreams and
things false because he knows they bring pleasure to his listeners. Allegorizing is for the spiritual benefit of the congregation, not one's renown as
a theologian. In the end it is better to admit one does not know the meaning of a passage than introduce nonsense, to stick with the Scriptures rather
than 'contriving allegorical interpretations from things that are obviously
false,'[715] for then 'what is left except for the preacher in the pulpit to relate
and interpret his own dreams!'[716] If handling allegory is acquired slowly,
tropology, on the other hand, in the sense of finding ethical teaching in passages of Scripture, is entirely different; this type of moral teaching is abundant, although it too needs to be well understood. Erasmus contends that
these kinds of tropes abound so greatly in Scripture that there is never not
a place for tropology;[717] and it fits his understanding of the Pauline passage that 'all Scripture, inspired of God, is profitable to teach, to reprove, to
correct, to instruct in justice' (2 Tim 3:16).

Concluding his instruction on allegory, Erasmus declares that its use
all comes down to the judgment of the preacher, which is difficult to teach,
for it is a habit that comes with training and experience, one that almost
by second nature recognizes how the matter of Scripture can be useful for
teaching, moving hearts, and giving delight to one's listeners. The skill is
acquired over time, and as Quintilian noted of judgment, it 'can no more be
imparted by a manual than the sense of taste or smell, for all this proceeds
from nature and from an understanding of the matters at hand.'[718] It is in

* * * * *

712 Book 3 CWE 68 961
713 See also Augustine *De doctrina christiana* 4.8.22.
714 Book 3 CWE 68 943
715 Book 3 CWE 68 951
716 Book 3 CWE 68 952; cf *Ratio* 282.
717 Book 3 CWE 68 968; see also the introduction to CWE 63 xliv for tropology as
     'the dominant preoccupation throughout Erasmus' treatment of the Psalms . . .'
718 Book 3 CWE 68 passim. See Quintilian 6.5.1: '. . . personally I regard it [judg-
     ment, *iudicium*] as so inextricably blent with and involved in every portion of
     this work, that its influence extends even to single sentences or words, and it

essence this *prudentia dicendi*, which consists of *iudicium* and *consilium*, that sets apart the outstanding orator.

Finally, to deal with the most common difficulties in interpreting scriptural passages, Erasmus lays out a series of additional hermeneutical principles drawn from the Fathers and his own experience with the sacred texts. He cautions readers that even some biblical texts used in the liturgy of the hours for centuries are wrongly translated and need correction.[719] To avoid problems posed by defective readings, he urges preachers to consult the more correct editions of the biblical text, insist on correct translations, become acquainted with the idioms of the biblical languages, and know the historical circumstances of antiquity, so they can resolve various linguistic ambiguities (especially in the biblical languages).[720] Similarly preachers should know who the persons and places are that are often referred to by two or more names; they should observe scrupulously punctuation and pronunciation,[721] reject 'every statement that conflicts with the inviolable dogmas of the faith,'[722] understand chronological inconsistencies and duplicate narratives, learn how to harmonize apparent contradictions, explain seeming trivialities and absurdities. Above all, they should acquire facility in speaking about Christ in his divine and human natures and what we may predicate of each separately and together.

To augment these principles, Erasmus includes the seven 'Rules of Tyconius,'[723] which Augustine sets forth in book 3 of *De doctrina christiana*. The rules consist of methods for resolving common problems that arise in Scripture's *dicta* on Christ and his mystical body (which is the church), on the twofold body of Christ, on the promises and the Law, genus and species, grace through faith without works, the church, on the quantity of times and numbers, recapitulation (where Scripture returns to a subject it had left off), the devil and his body – topics Erasmus revisits in book 4.[724] Erasmus also repeats much of Augustine's teaching from *De utilitate credendi* (*On the*

* * * * *

is no more possible to teach it than it is to instruct the powers of taste and smell.'

719 See book 3 CWE 68 973.

720 Book 3 CWE 68 895 and passim; cf *Ratio* 266–72.

721 See book 3 CWE 68 895–9. See *Apologia contra Latomi dialogum* CWE 71 46: 'The whole sense of a passage often turns on the way one single syllable is written.'

722 Book 3 CWE 68 980–1

723 Book 3 CWE 68 993. Tyconius was a Donatist lay theologian; see 'Tyconius' in *Augustine* 853–5.

724 On Erasmus' use of Tyconius' rules, see Chomarat 'Introduction' 17 and Hoffmann *Rhetoric* 58.

Usefulness of Believing) on the fourfold interpretation of Scripture (literal, aetiological, analogical, allegorical).[725] The sum of *Ecclesiastes'* extensive instruction on methods for handling the literary and historical complexities of Scripture, exegetical traditions, and theological doctrine amounts to what one might rightly consider as the most advanced formulation of biblical hermeneutical principles to date. It is not just the mature product of Erasmus' many years in biblical and patristic studies but the harvest of a fertile field cultivated long ago by Origen, Jerome, Augustine and other church Fathers and enriched by biblical humanists from Lorenzo Valla down to the many scholars of Erasmus' own time.

In concluding his instructions on handling Scripture, Erasmus urges readers above all to approach Scripture devoutly. They should take up God's word with the same pious assumption Augustine expresses about the eternal value, veracity, and wholesomeness of Sacred Scripture: that we 'love the holy books before we learn them and be utterly convinced that there is nothing in them either false or trivial or written by a human mind but that, whatever appearance it displays, everything is full of the heavenly philosophy and worthy of the Holy Spirit if it is understood as it ought to be, and then to read the whole body of Scripture carefully with this in mind and to render it familiar by prolonged reflection.'[726] It should be each individual's conviction that the divine works are inspired by God and are his words spoken to us; they are not ours to suit our own agenda. If we do at times eek out some small new understanding that seems consistent with Scripture and the consensus of the ancients, we should lay it before those in authority so we know our interpretation is in harmony with the dogmas of the church and understood in the way the church believes. As Erasmus says of his comments at one point on the nature of the Trinity: 'I should like this said on the understanding that it was not said should the church not approve.'[727] With additional words and examples on judgment and counsel, Erasmus concludes his exposition of exegetical methods, having covered the last parcels of the vast campus of the preacher's proper instruction. To these three books of his grand treatise Erasmus now adds a fourth and somewhat

* * * * *

725 See this treatise in WSA I-8 105–48 *De utilitate credendi* (*The Advantage of Believing*).
726 Book 3 CWE 68 1001; see Augustine *De doctrina christiana* 1.35.39–1.40.44.
727 Book 2 CWE 68 693. Erasmus' comment follows his discussion of Augustine's handling of John 17:3, which he sees done in a manipulative way in refuting the Arians.

hastily composed inventory (*inventio*) of the doctrinal content of sermons, which he calls a *sylva*, a kind of rough outline of topics for the preacher.[728]

In September 1524, Erasmus wrote to bishop John Fisher that he could not avoid addressing several doctrines of the theologians in his forthcoming treatise on preaching.[729] Perhaps his idea then was to approximate his colloquy 'An Examination Concerning the Faith' (*Inquisitio de fide*, 1524).[730] Whatever his intention then, sometime towards 1535, in bringing *Ecclesiastes* to a close, he gives it as his purpose to provide 'a list or index of the subjects with which the preacher is especially concerned'[731] (God, the Father, the Son, the Holy Spirit, distinction of persons, God becoming known, the angels, vices and virtues); these he places within the grand framework of salvation history, from the rebellion of the angels, to the incarnation of Christ the teacher, and finally to the Last Judgment when the work of redemption shall have been completed. In providing these topics, Erasmus echoes many medieval *artes praedicandi*, but goes far beyond them by envisioning an extensive catechetical summa embracing everything that is necessary to know for salvation.[732] His topics recall the great summae of the Middle Ages, like those of Peter Lombard, Thomas Aquinas, and John Duns Scotus, but presented here in a more useful, modest, and digestable form. Perhaps, too, Erasmus had at one time anticipated giving preachers theological instruction in a kind of expanded catechism like the one he published with Froben in 1533, *Explanatio symboli* (*A Plain and Devout Explanation of the Apostles' Creed, the Precepts of the Decalogue, and the Lord's Prayer*).[733] Although book 4

* * * * *

728 See book 4 CWE 68 1055–6.
729 Ep 1489:369: 'But in a theoretical treatment of preaching I am obliged to point out some mistakes made by certain preachers and to touch on several of the theologians' favourite doctrines.'
730 CWE 39 419–47; see also Craig R. Thompson's other edition of this work with an extensive commentary: *Inquisitio de fide: A Colloquy by Desiderius Erasmus Roterodamus, 1524* Yale Studies in Religion 15 (New Haven 1950).
731 See book 4 CWE 68 1022. Erasmus does much the same in *De copia* CWE 24 635–48, especially 636, where he explains how one is to assemble 'an ample supply of examples' ('Assembling illustrative material'), which he arranges 'according to similars and opposites.'
732 See book 4 CWE 68 1040, 1042.
733 *Dilucida et pia explanatio Symboli quod apostolorum dicitur, decalogi praeceptorum, et dominicae precationis* (*Explanatio symboli*). For Erasmus' catechism within the context of early sixteenth-century catechesis, see John O'Malley's introduction to CWE 70 xx–xxvi, where he notes that after its initial enthusiastic reception, it 'began to sink almost into oblivion' (xxi), and Erasmus also suffered greatly

does not replicate the dialogic form of his catechism, it explicitly addresses the doctrinal and moral teachings to be expounded by the preacher-bishop, in accordance with Paul's words to Timothy that 'all Scripture is useful for teaching . . .,'[734] by taking up the Apostles' Creed and the Decalogue, and to some extent the Lord's Prayer (which Erasmus' catechism dealt with only cursorily), though without going into the articles in too much detail.[735] The arrangement of book 4, which also recalls some of the 'Rules of Tyconius' discussed in book 3,[736] presents the philosophy of Christ within the cosmic framework of divine law, the virtues, and their adversaries, the vices.

At some point early into book 4, Erasmus must have registered how exhausting it would be to cover all the theological subjects he envisioned treating comprehensively,[737] and there was no need to go further. After giving examples on how a list might be assembled, Erasmus leaves the task to the studious reader who after thorough private preparation and the systematic study of Scripture and doctrine would now be called to preach. Certainly Erasmus realized as well that, if he did not put an end to his writing, the book would far exceed the *vastum opus* it had become. Contemporary letters show, too, how ill and depressed he was. Still, he had done all he needed to do. His doctrinal teaching in book 4 had taken his readers to the heart of his philosophy of Christ and his teaching on godliness, and it expressed perhaps more comprehensively than any other work his unique theological vision whose ultimate hallmarks are godliness, order, tranquillity, peace, and concord (*pax et concordia*).

Believing that 'a fairly secure knowledge of the articles of the faith' is required both for one's spiritual life and eternal salvation,[738] Erasmus sees

* * * * *

from his many critics of the work, particularly Luther. See Luther *Tischreden* (Weimar 1921) III 3795, IV 4899. See also J.N. Bakhuizen van den Brink, introduction to *Explanatio symboli apostolorum* ASD V-1 177–200.

734 2 Tim 3:16: 'All Scripture, inspired of God, is profitable to teach, to reprove, to correct, to instruct in justice . . .' Cf Thomas Aquinas *Summa theologiae* Ia q 1 a 1.

735 Book 2 CWE 68 683 where Erasmus speaks of 'expounding in a sustained and continuous presentation some such theme as the Decalogue or the Apostles' Creed (*Symbolum apostolorum*),' topics comprising the core of the preacher's teaching, the matter necessary to know for salvation.

736 See book 3 CWE 68 993; see also Augustine *De doctrina christiana* 3.30.42–3.37.55.

737 Charles Béné believes that in book 4 'Erasmus sensed his own limits'; Béné *Érasme* 375: 'Erasme a senti ses propres limites.'

738 *certior cognitio articulorum fidei* book 2 CWE 68 639. For the importance of dogma and its correct apprehension in Erasmus' theology, see Vogel. In his *Symbolum*

it as each Christian's duty to know these teachings in a way commensurate with his or her natural intelligence and earthly circumstances. Such an understanding lay at the heart of the medieval preaching tradition from the time of Lateran IV (1215).[739] And eleven years after the publication of *Ecclesiastes* the Council of Trent would propose for itself the same ambition – perhaps even taking Erasmus' lead and inspiration – in its instruction to draw up a catechism on the 'necessary matters for salvation' (*res necessariae ad salutem*).[740] And the Roman Catechism of 1566, which was mandated by the tridentine decrees, would become the basic manual for Catholic preachers on 'the matters one needed to know for salvation.'[741]

Erasmus begins his presentation of the essential matters of the faith by returning to the vision of an orderly cosmos, society, and church that opened up book 1. Now, however, he widens his focus to consider the vast spiritual panorama consisting of God, his angels and the devil, and the visible world comprised of the church militant and human society, all seen in the light of salvation history. It will be the task of the preacher to 'consider first that there is according to [Pseudo-] Dionysius[742] a threefold hierarchy, the heavenly [composed of the angels and of the faithful departed], the ecclesiastical [the mystical body of Christ of the church

*****

or Catechism, *Inquisitio de fide*, *Antibarbari*, *Enchiridion*, *Ratio*, and *Paraclesis*, Erasmus earlier articulated what de Vogel calls 'formal principles of theology' or 'foundations' that are necessary for Christians to believe; see especially 114–5. De Vogel seems to have given only cursory attention to *Ecclesiastes* in his discussion of Erasmus and church dogma; otherwise he would certainly have seen the treatise as strongly supporting his thesis.

739 See Wenzel 'Preaching' 163.

740 See Tanner II 669: 'teaching ... what it is necessary for all to know with a view to salvation ... [*docendo ea, quae scire omnibus necessarium est ad salutem*]'; see also McGinness *Right Thinking* 30.

741 See *The Catechism of the Council of Trent Published by Command of Pope Pius the Fifth* trans J. Donovan (New York n d); see McGinness *Right Thinking* 37, 93.

742 Dionysius (Pseudo-Dionysius, the Areopagite, c 500) was believed to have followed St Paul after hearing his speech to the men of Athens on the Areopagus (Acts 17:16–34) and to have composed numerous works on mystical theology found in the *Corpus Areopagiticum* (or *Corpus Dionysiacum*): *De coelesti hierarchia* (*On Celestial Hierarchy*), *De ecclesiastica hierarchia* (*On Ecclesiastical Hierarchy*), *De divinis nominibus* (*On the Divine Names*), *De mystica theologia* (*Mystical Theology*). His works would have been available to Erasmus, such as the translation of Dionysius' *Opera* by Ambrogio Traversari, edited by Jacques Lefèvre d'Étaples (Paris: Johann Higman and Wolfgang Hopyl 1498–99). On hierarchy in Erasmus, see Rummel *Erasmus* 54–7. See also Pseudo-Dionysius *The Celestial Hierarchies* and Pseudo-Dionysius *The Divine Names*.

militant],[743] and the political [the public state of a city or region] ... '[744] To these Erasmus adds two more hierarchies: 'the monarchical [by which God as king and lord of all drives and guides the universe] and the spiritual [particular to each person].' Though 'presiding in all the hierarchies, but not in the same way,'[745] God stands at their centre as the incomprehensible, eternal, all-knowing, all-present being – 'that highest monarch, the creator, preserver, and governor of all'; 'he alone truly is.'[746] Having made known these cosmic hierarchies, the preacher will then convey an accurate understanding of the nature of God, to whom everything is to be referred: how he acts in nature, which is the mirror of his mind, and at times performs miracles by changing the 'ordinary course of nature';[747] and how Sacred Scripture can attribute to him 'eyes, ears, hands, arms' and ascribe the human emotions of 'anger, hatred, regret.'[748] Above all, the preacher will declare that God's 'ineffable majesty ... is believed through faith rather than understood': 'One understands by believing, interprets by worshipping.'[749] And in so far as he is able, he will speak about the Trinitarian nature of God, the distinction of persons, what is proper to each, how God presides through different agencies in the various hierarchies, and how all these hierarchies in some degree reflect the heavenly hierarchy, 'in which there is perfect order and perfect concord.'[750] He will relate further how in the heavenly hierarchy the Father, Son, and Holy Spirit exist in perfect unity, which is what the members of the body of Christ are, joined as far as possible in faith and charity, and drawn into the oneness of the Trinity – 'an example of perfect concord.'[751]

Of paramount importance in Erasmus' theological vision is order. God's original design of perfect concord ended the moment of the first great sin with the rebellion of the angels, when this cosmos split into two

* * * * *

743 Erasmus understands this 'in two ways: this word either embraces only the living and true members of Christ destined for blessed immortality that are known to God alone, or else for the whole congregation of those living in the communion of the sacraments of the church, which includes and tolerates the evil mingled with the good' (book 4 CWE 68 1023).
744 Book 4 CWE 68 1022–3; cf Erasmus' prefatory letter to the 1518 edition of *Enchiridion* CWE 66 14–6; see also McConica 'Grammar of Consent.'
745 See book 4 CWE 68 1027; cf Pseudo-Dionysius *The Divine Names*.
746 Book 4 CWE 68 1025
747 Book 4 CWE 68 1025
748 Book 4 CWE 68 1026
749 Book 4 CWE 68 1026. The author of this quotation is unknown.
750 Book 4 CWE 68 1028
751 Book 4 CWE 68 1029; see also Kleinhans 93–106 for a discussion of Erasmus' understanding of the Trinity.

great warring parties. Opposed to God's design stands his antithesis and antagonist, the tyrant Satan, Prince of Darkness.[752] And yet God dominates the cosmos absolutely while using Satan's malice 'for exercising the chosen and punishing the impious.'[753] Satan, who was created in goodness by God, by his own volition turned against his maker; as antagonist he now seeks to corrupt all that God has made and redeemed, turning the virtuous from the promise of heavenly life, persuading human beings to vices, sin, and bondage. Perversely, 'though he is one, he nevertheless reflects the three divine persons.'[754] With his impious demons, Satan in his 'supreme malice to lead astray and disturb good order'[755] seeks at every point to subvert the work of Christ, pitting his minions to work against Christ's angels, inciting rebellion in all the created hierarchies. As the great destroyer and seducer, 'he dissolves and scatters everything that he can.'[756]

At the heart of Erasmus' theology of our redemption and vision of cosmic hierarchical order lies God's eternal law,[757] 'than which nothing is more just, nothing more holy, nothing more beneficial.'[758] Conveying the importance of our knowledge of this law for every well-run polity therefore becomes paramount, and a knowledge of its importance for our eternal life indispensable. The preacher therefore must know how to explain the term 'law,' whose meanings in Scripture are various, as it can sometimes refer to the precepts of the Decalogue or to both Old and New Testaments; but in every instance God's law is 'always the same' though 'displayed in a variety of ways taking account of differences in times and persons.'[759] For in each epoch God dealt with humankind differently: at creation he spoke directly to Adam, commanding him not to eat of the tree of good and evil;

* * * * *

752 Book 4 CWE 68 1029; cf *De puritate tabernaculi* CWE 65 233.

753 Book 4 CWE 68 1029

754 Book 4 CWE 68 1029

755 Book 4 CWE 68 1030

756 Book 4 CWE 68 1030; see Augustine *De doctrina christiana* 2.23.36: 'The society of demons is to be feared and avoided, since they seek to do nothing under their leader the Devil but to block and cut off our return homeward.'

757 See book 4 CWE 68 1030 and passim. The Council of Trent (Session 24, Canon 4) will emphasize this part of the bishop-preacher's teaching: 'Bishops are to announce the sacred scripture and the law of God in their own church . . .' (Tanner II 763). For a broader understanding of the role of law in society at this time, see Gerald Strauss *Law, Resistance, and the State: The Opposition to Roman Law in Reformation Germany* (Princeton 1986).

758 Book 4 CWE 68 1030

759 See book 4 CWE 68 1031. For the idea of law in Erasmus, see C. Douglas McCullough 'The Concept of Law in the Thought of Erasmus' ERSY 1 (1981) 89–112.

after his banishment he inscribed an understanding of this law in nature to guide humankind in the knowledge of what was right and wrong; later he gave the written law to Moses to clarify and reinforce that law of nature;[760] and finally with humankind's redemption in Christ, 'the Law of the gospel was given in order to grant salvation through faith and grace.'[761] Under the New Law the *miles Christi* fights beneath the standard of Christ in the hope of everlasting triumph. In each instance God makes known how one should pursue godliness, but at the same time in each epoch human wickedness, prompted by Satan, seeks to break the restraints of the Law and turn to impiety. To thwart God's design, Satan established his own law 'in diametrical opposition to the divine laws. This is the law of the flesh; sin is its attendant, death its wages.'[762]

Erasmus' presentation of law stands in conscious opposition to the antinomian sentiments of Luther and of some other Reformers that the Law's only purpose was to reveal that humankind's weakness rendered it incapable of observance, and that the person justified through faith in Christ had no need of the Law and was free from its observance.[763] Erasmus rejects every notion that the Law has been abolished, maintaining that the preacher must make clear who the author of these laws is, their ministers, what all these laws looked to, namely Christ, 'the power [*vigor*] and perfection of all the laws,'[764] and how these different expressions of God's law contained various types that foreshadowed Christ, who 'revealed all truth both through himself and through the Holy Spirit.'[765] 'The New Law is both a clarification and a summary of the Old'; in it one finds 'what belongs to the spirit and to grace and renders one truly pious.'[766] Many prescriptions of the Old Law in fact 'pertain to kindness and fairness'[767] and are

* * * * *

760 Book 4 CWE 68 1031–3
761 See book 4 CWE 68 1033.
762 Book 4 CWE 68 1030; see Rom 6:23.
763 Erasmus' words reflect closely his *De libero arbitrio* and *Hyperaspistes* 1 & 2 against Luther's teaching in *De servo arbitrio*; see especially CWE 77 665–7. Cf Luther *Freedom of the Christian Man* LW 349: 'It is clear, then, that a Christian has all that he needs in faith and needs no works to justify him; and if he has no need of works, he has no need of the law; and if he has no need of the law, surely he is free from the law. It is true that "the law is not laid down for the just" [1 Tim 1:9].' For Zwingli's view on the Law, which is close to that of Erasmus, see Augustijn 'Reformation' 41–2.
764 Book 4 CWE 68 1033
765 Book 4 CWE 68 1033
766 Book 4 CWE 68 1036, 1037
767 Book 4 CWE 68 1036

eminently useful still; aspects of these laws support the Christian in his spiritual progress, and through them he comes to know the nature of the Law's precepts and how these should be understood today, as some have been abrogated, others modified, and still others reaffirmed with greater force: 'Those that prescribe rules for morals and piety are eternal; those that prescribe ceremonies have been abrogated according to the letter, they have not been abrogated according to their spiritual meaning.'[768] Erasmus maintains it is important to know that 'what the Lord or the apostles confirmed or changed must be observed as they prescribed.'[769] The preacher also needs to understand the meaning and function of ceremonies ('every external form of worship'),[770] how passages of the Old Law foreshadowed Christ's words and actions, how they give us shining examples of the virtues, and the many loci that arise from considerations of the Old and New Testaments, such as their authority, their authors, harmony, consistency, agreement, testimonies, pronouncements, the unanimous consent of the ages regarding their truth, their power to transform lives, and their fundamental accord with human nature.

Erasmus' considerations on the Law reflect his view of the individual's spiritual progress from impiety to piety, from flesh to spirit, the long progress of the church from the moment when 'charity cooled' in the postapostolic age to its slow but continual advancement in the spirit through the reform of its members over the ages, to the growing spiritual illumination of our minds as we return daily to the sources of Christian wisdom. In each consideration Erasmus posits no radical break from what went before or rejection of the past but sees rather a kind of conservation and sublimation of what had preceded into a more perfected spiritual reality. Consequently, considerations of the Old Law should draw us to appreciate more richly how it reflected and anticipated Christ, the fulfilment and perfection of the Old Law and our New Law (cf Rom 10:4). These spiritual realities further allow us to see more keenly the law of God existing throughout creation from its beginning to its consummation. Indeed, God's law has not been abrogated; rather, its hidden messages and types have been made manifest to

* * * * *

768 Book 4 CWE 68 1034; see book 3 CWE 68 919: 'The Old Law should not be rejected in the least but is holy and good if understood correctly.'
769 Book 4 CWE 68 1035
770 Book 4 CWE 68 1037; as in *Ratio* 252, Erasmus does not reject the church's ceremonies but does 'not approve that on the basis of human regulations nearly the whole life of Christians is burdened with ceremonies; because too much is given to them, very little to piety.'

us by Christ, 'the perfect model . . . of all the virtues,'[771] that we might know it, love it, and more willingly serve him whose eternal wisdom decreed it.

Considerations of the Old Law and the New Law give rise to numerous loci about Scripture – its mysteries, authority, authors, the perfect agreement of Scripture with itself, 'the consensus of so many ages and so many nations,' its efficacy.[772] Erasmus finds yet another locus in 'an examination of the meanings of the Scriptures,' but refers the reader back to book 3. Still further loci arise, such as the meaning of 'sin'[773] and the 'two kinds of death,'[774] which in turn draws him to present the virtues and the vices, starting with the 'heroic virtues' (faith, hope, and charity) and their contraries, to which Erasmus dedicates extended discussion.[775]

Having covered the theological virtues, Erasmus urges readers 'to assemble and arrange by loci a catalogue of all the virtues and vices.'[776] He notes that catalogues of this sort have already been drawn up by prominent theologians like Thomas Aquinas (one of his few references to the work of a 'modern' author),[777] and he encourages readers who cannot undertake

* * * * *

771 Book 4 CWE 68 1039
772 Book 4 CWE 68 1040
773 Book 4 CWE 68 1041
774 See Hoffmann *Rhetoric* 151–6.
775 Book 4 CWE 68 1041–6
776 Book 4 CWE 68 1046. For the idea of *loci communes* and in Aristotelian and Ciceronian traditions and their use by Philippus Melanchthon, see Breen 'The Terms' 197–209. In 1521, Philippus Melanchthon composed *Loci communes rerum theologicarum, seu, Hypotyposes theologicae* (Basel: Adam Petri 1521), a book for preachers that takes up *loci communes*. Breen argues that Melanchthon uses loci as Cicero, not Aristotle, used them (205); and he notes that 'Erasmus [besides seeking to 'reconstitute all knowledge' by the *loci*] . . . sought more particularly to reinterpret Christianity by *loci* belonging to ethics' (202). See also Paul Joachimsen 'Loci Communes: Eine Untersuchung zur Geistesgeschichte des Humanismus und der Reformation' *Luther-Jahrbuch* (Berlin 1926) 27–97. Breen also notes that a small treatise on the topical method appeared in 1531, 1532, 1533 in volumes that also contained Rodolphus Agricola's *De formando studio* and Erasmus' *Ratio colligendi exempla*. See also Quintilian 2.1.9, 11, 2.4.22 and 27; and Hoffmann *Rhetoric* 151–6.
777 See also Ep 858:74: 'Who can carry the *Secunda secundae* of Aquinas round with him? And yet the good life is everybody's business, and Christ wished the way to it to be accessible to all men . . .' See also CWE 66 272 n10: 'The second part of the second book of the *Summa theologiae* of Thomas Aquinas was often published separately as an authoritative manual of ethics.' For background on the genre of the treatise on vices and virtues, see Richard Newhauser *The Treatise on Vices and Virtues in Latin and the Vernacular* (Turnhout 1993) and

one on their own to make excerpts from them.[778] For each of these virtues a preacher will have a deep well of material from which he may draw lessons; such would include not only the many meanings of these terms but also their contraries, their effects, how they are nourished, those who have displayed these virtues pre-eminently, and those who have not. These lists would provide preachers with reliable loci drawn from the sacred books wherever they speak on matters necessary for salvation. Prominent among the virtues, after faith, hope, and charity, are the cardinal (philosophical or moral) virtues – prudence, justice, fortitude, and temperance – to which all *genera* of virtues can be referred. These virtues in turn correlate with the theological virtues; for example, 'prudence corresponds to faith, justice to charity, fortitude to hope; temperance is a species of justice that teaches how much should be assigned to the affections, how much to the body, how much to the mind . . .'[779] Significantly, at this point, just after considering temperance as a species of justice, Erasmus considers the many species of godliness (*pietas*), but without explicitly linking it first with justice. We know however that *pietas* also falls under justice and operates like temperance because after sketching an outline of the 'duties of godliness' he connects the two. At this point Erasmus constructs his locus (or 'compartment' [*nidus*]) for godliness (*pietas*) as a species of commutative and distributive justice.

A consideration of godliness begins at the summit of God's hierarchies. As God is owed our 'highest piety,' Erasmus starts with worship ($\lambda\acute{\alpha}\tau\rho\iota\alpha$)[780] and its many denotations, as well as the many loci and their contraries that arise from it, such as God's 'charity and generosity towards the human race'[781] and human impiety as manifested in idolatry, 'grumbling in adversity, forgetting God in prosperity, malicious arts, fortune telling, and whatever of this kind has either an obvious or a secret conspiracy with demons,

* * * * *

his edition of essays *In the Garden of Evil: Vices and Culture in the Middle Ages* (Toronto c 2005). See also *De copia* CWE 24 636: 'Each person should draw up a list of virtues and vices to suit himself, whether he looks for his examples in Cicero or Valerius Maximus or Aristotle or St Thomas.'

778 Besides Thomas' *Secunda secundae* Erasmus likely had access to other frequently published works on the subject: eg Gulielmus Peraldus *Summa de vitiis et virtutibus* (Venice: Paganinus de Paganinis 1497) and Jordanus von Quedlinburg *Tractatus virtutum et viciorum* (=*Sermones de tempore 439–441*) (Strasbourg 1483). See Newhauser *The Treatise* (n777 above) 35–6 and the essays *In the Garden of Evil* (n777 above) ed idem, especially Wenzel 'Preaching' passim.

779 Book 4 CWE 68 1047
780 More correctly $\lambda\alpha\tau\rho\epsilon\acute{\iota}\alpha$ ('service')
781 Book 4 CWE 68 1048

finally heresy.'[782] 'In general, every crime is connected with impiety, for whoever commits a crime is preferring some created thing to its creator and defecting from God to Satan ...'[783] Erasmus covers extensively all the additional species of godliness (*pietas*), beginning with how much we owe to our homeland, to the Catholic church, to our educators, 'above all those who shape tender minds towards godliness'[784] and those who have saved our lives, especially our spiritual lives by drawing us away from impiety or heresy and leading us to Christ. Such considerations bring us also to consider the demands of Christian charity, which extend even to mortal enemies, as shown us by Christ, especially when he died on the cross 'praying for those by whom he was being killed,'[785] and to all things contrary to these various stages of charity.

To systematize the theological doctrines he has presented Erasmus proposes fourteen headings on matters to be preached (*indicis capita sive titulos*).[786] These headings, beginning with God's nature or essence, he subdivides into parts covering those matters of the faith that each person should know under that entry; under most of these fall various loci. For each of the headings he starts out to provide a collection of pertinent material (*sylva*)[787]

* * * * *

782 See Book 4 CWE 68 1048. Erasmus here and elsewhere expresses his belief that 'malicious arts' (*artes maleficae*) are practised and that persons consort with demons; see also *De immensa Dei misericordia* CWE 70 80–1. For Erasmus on witchcraft and magic, see Chomarat *Grammaire* I 45–8. Heresy he lists in the final position, even worse than witchcraft. For Erasmus' changing attitude on heresy and heretics in the 1520s and 1530s, see Augustijn *Erasmus* 179–81.

783 See book 4 CWE 68 1049.

784 See book 4 CWE 68 1050.

785 See book 4 CWE 68 1051.

786 Book 4 CWE 68 1055

787 *sylva* or *silva*; see the note on this word by J.H. Mozley in *Statius* I: *Silvae-Thebaid I–IV* Loeb Classical Library (London and Cambridge, Mass 1982) xi note a: 'The word means literally "pieces of raw material," from *silva* = Greek ὕλη, i.e. pieces ready to be worked up into shape, or impromptu pieces; *cf.* Quintil. x.3.17 "diversum est eorum vitium, qui primum decurrere per materiam stilo quam velocissimo volunt, et sequentes calorem atque impetum ex tempore scribunt; hanc silvam vocant." "Their fault is different, who wish to run over their material first with as rapid a pen as possible, and write impromptu, following the inspiration of the moment: such work they call *silva*." *Cf.* also Aulus Gellius, *Noct. Atti.* Pref. 6.' Erasmus found this method in Jerome's scholarly activities; see *Vita Hieronymi* CWE 61 33: 'And to make his memory more reliable and his application more prompt he would organize whatever he read by topic, sorting all items on the basis of their affinity or their opposition.' See too *Ratio* 291 and the introduction to Angelo Poliziano *Silvae* trans and ed Charles

consisting of 'reasons, confirmations, witnesses, especially those of the Scriptures, types and figures, solutions of questions, parallels, examples, amplifications, epigrams, proverbs, and things like these' that can be used for preaching.[788] It seems however that Erasmus recognized quickly the enormity of the task of constructing a *sylva* for each of these headings; and rather than undertaking the entire project himself, he gives the reader a start by constructing *sylvae* on 'The Nature of God,' 'The Son,' 'The Holy Spirit,' 'The Distinction of Persons,' 'God Becoming Known,' and 'The Angels.' Appreciating the vast extent of this project, and perhaps the value in each one doing the work for himself, he leaves the remainder 'for the zealous to complete, so that each may examine the sacred books, choose for himself what he will judge useful for preaching, and arrange it in a convenient order ...'[789] Erasmus however provides some further assistance with an example of how a preacher might impose such an order on his material in the right theological sequence that demonstrates God's eternal plan in drawing us from carnality to spirituality by comparing carnal birth and propagation and the symbolic events as taught in the Old Testament (Gen 1:28) with spiritual birth and propagation and the significance of those events as proclaimed by the Gospel (Mark 16:15).[790] But he cuts short his example, making clear its purpose: preachers should 'select things of this sort to have at hand when speaking.'[791] From 'the gardens of the Scriptures' they will draw up lists and their *sylvae*, ready-to-hand topics or commonplaces for liturgical events and extraliturgical gatherings, such as panegyrics of saints, funeral orations, dedications of churches, catechesis, special commemorative moments, and

* * * * *

Fantazzi (Cambridge, Mass 2004) vii–xx, especially xi: 'In the introductory paragraphs to his commentary on Statius' poems, he [Angelo Poliziano] elaborates on the meaning of the word *silva*, which he says denotes *indigesta materia*, a sort of confused raw material that the poet has to re-work. It has the connotation of looseness of structure, a sense of spontaneity and discontinuity. Statius himself had emphasized these qualities in his prefatory letter to the *Sylvae*, using expressions that suggested rapidity of composition and improvisation. But it is a studied, controlled improvisation that is achieved by long labor. The flexible style of the *silva* allows for both epic grandeur and bucolic simplicity, varied stylistic artifice, multiplicity of themes, all seasoned with rare literary erudition.'

788 Book 4 CWE 68 1064; see *De copia* CWE 24 635–48, 672–3, where Erasmus shows the reader how to assemble illustrative materials for writing and speaking; and Grünwald 129–31.

789 Book 4 CWE 68 1090

790 Book 4 CWE 68 1090–1. See Gen 2:7 and John 3:5–6.

791 Book 4 CWE 68 1097

especially occasions for moral exhortations – for 'commending the virtues and execrating the vices' – teaching 'theological dogmas,'[792] and 'observing vigilantly the laws that the mystical books prescribe for human actions ...'[793] They will draw material not only from Scripture but from the commentaries on Scripture of those 'who by daily study have acquired a deep knowledge of the Scriptures and have won great authority in the church by the holiness of their life and the honesty of their judgments.'[794] Erasmus also advises the preacher to know the decrees of church synods and be familiar with the scholastic disputations that have been properly conducted, namely ones that 'rely especially upon scriptural foundations.'[795] With this, Erasmus refers his reader to the commonplaces, hermeneutical materials, and 'the remarkable occurrences in human life' that he proposed in book 3.[796]

Erasmus concludes *Ecclesiastes* by offering readers an example of how one might construct a *concio* commending concord, 'finished and complete with the entire paraphernalia of oratory.'[797] The approach follows the standard rhetorical divisions of an oration. His exordium sets forth a definition of true concord, and then follows a narration of the facts with definitions, reasonings, distinctions, illustrations, examples, confirmations, concord's author, and archetypal examples of concord, such as the Trinity, Christ in his church, the interassociation of the members of the mystical body of Christ,[798] the joining of male and female, the joining of body and soul, the concord of the heavenly bodies, the elements 'that serve each other in turn in a marvellous harmony,' and 'in brute animals and in their variety.'[799] His many examples of concord in inanimate things, like arrows bound together that resist force and serve to strengthen each other, further confirm the need for concord among human beings. Copious examples offer inventive ways to emphasize God's wondrous design that human beings should emulate the

* * * * *

792 Book 4 CWE 68 1097; see also Vogel. These two items, interestingly, are also the two identified by the Council of Trent in its decree on the reformation of preaching.

793 Book 4 CWE 68 1097; Erasmus often uses the term 'mystical books' for Sacred Scripture.

794 Book 4 CWE 68 1097

795 Book 4 CWE 68 1097

796 Book 4 CWE 68 1097

797 Book 4 CWE 68 1098. See Erasmus *Ratio*, which also concludes with words on avoiding contentions; see also *De concordia* CWE 65 125–216.

798 The symbol of the third and forth archetypes is the *synaxis* in the communion of the body and blood of the Lord. See book 4 CWE 68 1099.

799 Book 4 CWE 68 1100

harmony found not only in the Godhead but in even the lowest elements of creation, where every plant or rock evinces a harmonious dependence on others for survival and growth. These examples should prompt one to ask: If nature displays such a disposition to concord, by how much more should human beings strive for this among themselves, how much greater the benefits to all if people made it their constant duty to live in concord with one another? This argument then refutes the contrary evidence of the disorder in nature and society where Satan sows discord and works to impose his tyranny on the human race. And here one should take hope, for with the advent of Christ and his church, the enclosure separating us from God has been demolished.[800] Christ has made us 'children of God instead of enemies' and checks Satan's designs by re-establishing that primordial concord, seeking in his church 'an entire peaceful kingdom free from every rebellion.'[801] With this, the preacher then will make sure his audience understands what concord truly means by distinguishing the types of concord[802] – 'man with God,' 'man with man,' and 'each man with himself, which is provided by a mind at peace with itself and flesh that obeys the spirit.'[803] The types are so interconnected that they are either all present or all absent: 'No one has peace with himself if there is a tumult of thoughts in his breast accusing or defending each other. No one has peace with God if he has a quarrel with his neighbour.'[804] Erasmus would then have the preacher conclude with passages from Holy Writ and secular writings, selecting especially those 'passages that commend concord to us.'[805]

Erasmus' *concio* and the final passages of *Ecclesiastes* aptly recapitulate his life's teachings and his ideal of the purpose of good and sacred letters (*bonae ac sacrae litterae*). Like true education, preaching should promote the philosophy of Christ, who came to bring peace and concord, not just the kind that reigns in charity among individuals in society but that inner peace that individuals find with themselves, where flesh submits to spirit, and above all that persons find with God in faith and innocence. This, Erasmus contends, is the sum of the Law and the prophets, the essence of the *philosophia Christi*, Christian godliness. True concord generates perfect friendship and

* * * * *

800 See book 4 CWE 68 1101.
801 Book 4 CWE 68 1101
802 Book 4 CWE 68 1102; see also McConica 'Grammar of Consent' 96.
803 Book 4 CWE 68 1102; here Erasmus echoes Thomas Aquinas' teaching on 'peace' and 'concord'; see *Summa theologiae* IIa IIae q 29 a 1.
804 Book 4 CWE 68 1102; cf Matt 5:23–4.
805 Book 4 CWE 68 1103

harmony and peace among all members of Christ's body, of which there is nothing more in accordance with human nature, nothing more pleasing to God, and no greater sign that the *ecclesia*, Christ in his members, is truly present.[806]

In effect, *Ecclesiastes* gives preachers aspiring to excellence in their office a Christian equivalent of Quintilian's *Institutio oratoria* by offering all that is best in classical rhetoric and in the church Fathers to handle Scripture correctly and fruitfully, teach doctrine, and provide moral guidance. At the same time Erasmus hardly touches on the kinds of topics one might expect in the contentious climate of the Reformation; he says very little (but if so, often with a sting) about the theological subjects one regards as characteristic of the medieval church – hell, purgatory, holy images, saints' feast days and festivals, papal indulgences,[807] prayers for the souls of the departed, the Antichrist, and the end of the world. Nor does *Ecclesiastes* even hint that Scripture may be used as a key to interpret contemporary events or to indulge in apocalyptic speculation.[808] Erasmus' words on ceremonies and monks display hardly less restraint when compared, for example, with his *Ratio*,[809] but he is careful to mention why he makes such criticisms. Except for extolling the central importance of baptism, the treatise mentions mostly in passing and without provoking controversy the sacraments of penance, the Eucharist,[810] holy orders, matrimony,[811] and last anointing. It speaks but briefly of the primacy of the Roman pontiff,[812] the invocation of

* * * * *

806 The theme of harmony, concord, peace, and tranquillity runs throughout Erasmus' writings, especially in the final years of his life; see eg *In psalmum* CWE 65.

807 See book 2 CWE 68 701. Cf *In psalmum 38* CWE 65 30–1, where Erasmus calls attention to a preacher who vitiated his sermon by including words 'in commendation of papal indulgences ...'

808 See book 3 CWE 68 734.

809 See eg book 2 CWE 68 603, 622–3, 630, 635, 668.

810 Erasmus' discreet silence on the Eucharist or Last Supper would have been in keeping at this time with his life in the reformed city of Basel; see Reedijk 59.

811 Cf *Ratio* 207–8, where Erasmus takes issue with many ecclesiastical teachings regarding matrimony, eg that 'matrimony is indissoluble from consent alone'; he finds no scriptural support for the teaching. See also his comments there on contracting marriage. See especially *Institutio christiani matrimonii* CWE 69 203–438.

812 Cf *Ratio* 197–8, where referring to the Petrine text in Matthew (16:18–19) Erasmus gives the opinion of 'certain [theologians]' (and his own) that Peter's confession of faith 'belongs to the entire body of the Christian people' and not Peter alone; 'Peter responds with the voice and in the place of the entire

saints and angels, and mentions only in passing the virginity of Mary.[813]
Marian devotions,[814] the veneration of the saints and angels, liturgical feast
days, the divine office, relics, pilgrimages, the rosary and other sacramen-
tals, monastic vows, virginity, and celibacy are given minimal mention, if
at all. Nor does the treatise give us much of an idea how the *concio* might
be integrated with the Eucharistic liturgy, though the treatise strongly suggests that it is principally at mass that the preacher's discourse takes place.[815]
We might assume too that Erasmus took it as given that the bishop's preaching occurs both within and outside the liturgy, as St Paul insists (2 Tim
4:2); but still we hear scarcely anything about those times 'in season and
out of season.' Erasmus' focus falls almost entirely on the spiritual disposition and message of the preacher, who must assess the circumstances
for speaking and measure his words appropriately. Nor does he want the
preacher to go into the minutiae of specific theological doctrines; rather he
should set them out plainly, extracting their spiritual relevance and adding
no 'more ... than it is necessary to believe,'[816] as he once noted to Simon
Pistoris.

From the time Erasmus first conceived the writing of *Ecclesiastes* until its completion in August 1535, the Reformation advanced on a fateful
course, often with uncivil results, many of which Erasmus viewed first-
hand at Basel and which affected him personally, so causing him to depart

* * * * *

Christian people: "You are Christ, the son of the living God; for there is no
one in the body of Christ from whom that confession is not demanded ..."'
(198). Cf *Ratio* 206.

813 But see Erasmus' *Modus orandi Deum* cwe 70 141–230, especially 187–8, where
it is clear Erasmus understands 'the perpetual virginity of Mary' as a dogma
of the faith for the reason that 'it has been handed down to us by the consensus of early orthodox writers,' even though 'this is not a teaching based on
clear scriptural testimony ...' (187). See also *Explanatio symboli* cwe 70 231–387,
especially 289–93; and Vogel 118. Erasmus does not mention the theological
question of the immaculate conception of Mary.

814 Erasmus makes a few references to the Virgin Mary; for his views on the cult
of Mary, see L.-E. Halkin 'La Mariologie d'Erasme' arg 68 (1977) 32–54.

815 See book 2 cwe 68 565 where Erasmus says, 'Let the greatest part of the sermon nevertheless be given over to the Gospel and the Epistle.' See O'Malley
'Sacred Rhetoric' 22.

816 Ep 1744:68–9, where he objects to those 'who push more doctrine down our
throats than it is necessary to believe.' See also the prefatory letter to his edition of St Hilary (Ep 1334:253): 'This indeed is the mark of theological learning:
to define nothing beyond what is recorded in Holy Scripture, but to dispense
in good faith what is there recorded.'

for Freiburg im Breisgau on 13 April 1529.[817] In the years leading up to 1529 Erasmus had many dealings with individuals directly involved in the Reformation. Against his advice, his friend Johann Froben (d 1527) published Luther's works at Basel in 1518 and 1519, and Melanchthon's school companion, Johannes Oecolampadius, who assisted Erasmus at the Froben press with his 1516 edition of the Greek New Testament (*Novum instrumentum*), became a leading Reformer at Basel after 1522, where he emerged as the 'first Protestant preacher in the minster, the first head preacher (*antistes*) of the Basel reformed church.'[818] Erasmus' close proximity to the Reformation movement at Basel and his pleas for *concordia*, like his controversies with the Reformers, no doubt registered a deep impact on him; but he did not use his treatise to carry on controversies or settle theological questions. Nonetheless, certain passages do underscore Erasmus' final position vis-à-vis the various doctrines advanced by some Reformers, and they suggest a deliberate distancing of the author especially from Luther and his hostility towards the church of Rome.[819] Though Erasmus never mentions in this treatise the name of anyone associated with the Reformation,[820] it is hard not to imagine that behind some of his comments on preachers and their doctrines he is not merely calling to mind but stating his disagreements *sotto voce* with Martin Luther, Philippus Melanchthon, Guillaume Farel, Otto Brunfels, Huldrych

*****

817 See Augustijn 'Reformation'; Reedijk 34.
818 Thompson 'Return'; Erasmus did not subscribe to Oecolampadius' views on the Eucharist, as he made known to the town council of Basel; see Ep 1636:343–4; and Reedijk 36–7. See also Myron P. Gilmore 'Erasmus and the Cause of Christian Humanism: The Last Years 1529–1536' in his *Humanists and Jurists* (Cambridge, Mass 1963) 115–45; see also Augustijn *Erasmus* 173–83, and his 'Reformation' 38–9.
819 For Erasmus' even sharper differences from Luther's position not only on grace and free will but on basic theological issues such as Christology, which develop after their controversy, see Bengt Hägglund 'Erasmus und die Reformation' in *Erasmus und Europa* Wolfenbütteler Abhandlungen zur Renaissanceforschung 7, ed August Buck (Wiesbaden 1988) 139–47. Hägglund supports his argument on Manfred Hoffmann's *Erkenntnis und Verwirklichung der wahren Theologie nach Erasmus von Rotterdam* (Tübingen 1972), which considers Erasmus' Christology as 'a dualistic theory of accommodation,' meaning that the divine and human natures of Christ are 'unbridgeable. God and man in fact cannot become one' (Hägglund 143).
820 Erasmus ends his *Compendium vitae* commenting on 'the sad business of Luther'; CWE 4 410: 'The sad business of Luther had brought him a burden of intolerable ill will; he was torn in pieces by both sides, while aiming zealously at what was best for both.'

Zwingli, and others. Though touching on disputed theological questions but briefly, he affirms his own positions on justification by faith, faith and works, grace and free will, the Law and grace, how salvation occurs,[821] and how best to frame these teachings in *conciones*. Erasmus, for example might concur with Reformers that one is justified by faith, but he states emphatically that one who is justified must pursue good works, a position he finds solidly supported in the examples of the apostles and in the life of the early church.[822] Against the Reformers who teach that 'all our works are evil,'[823] he staunchly upholds the importance of good works, while affirming that piety consists in 'abandoning trust in human works, especially those that do not proceed from faith and charity.'[824] Without good works there could be no true religious reform of the church, and society would languish in immorality, believing everything has been predetermined by divine necessity. Horrible it would be if preachers disseminated the idea that because of our faith we are free of the Law and may do as we please.[825] Erasmus insists that religious rituals be performed, but preachers should emphasize at the same time the spiritual significance of these ceremonial actions. While Reformers assert that satisfaction is not necessary for sins committed, Erasmus underscores the importance of sacramental confession and 'satisfaction' (or

* * * * *

821 See eg book 3 CWE 68 585, 635, 955, 994–5, 1019, 1020–1 (faith and good works). Erasmus echoes the words from his *De concordia* CWE 65 201–3.

822 See book 3 CWE 68 995: 'Here the reader of the holy books ought to be careful and alert so that, when he sees that works are demanded, he does not judge that he can fulfil the instruction by his own strength, or that, when he reads that those who are of the faith are free from the Law, he is not obligated by any commandments of the Scriptures. The Law, which lights the way, shows what must be done, what avoided; grace allows us to have the ability to produce what we are commanded.' Cf *In psalmum 38* CWE 65 32, 49, and *De puritate tabernaculi* CWE 65 245–7 and n124.

823 Cf *Hyperaspistes* 2 CWE 76 284–5, where Erasmus takes issue with Karlstadt and Luther.

824 Book 3 CWE 68 1020. Perhaps what Erasmus would put more precisely here is what he expressed in his *De libero arbitrio* CWE 76 77: 'But when I hear people maintain that all human merit is so worthless that all human works, even those of godly men, are sins; when they claim that our will does no more than clay in the potter's hands, or attribute everything we do or will to absolute necessity, then I become exceedingly uneasy.' See also *Hyperaspistes* 2 CWE 77 746–7. For a concise analysis of the differences between Erasmus and Luther, see Augustijn *Erasmus* 135–45.

825 For the differences between Zwingli and Luther in their theology of the Law (and Erasmus' affinity with Zwingli on this question), see Augustijn 'Reformation' 41–2.

'compensation') as a vital part of it,[826] maintaining that one should not be permitted to sin with impunity but should feel motivated to make up for the crime out of love for God, who both avenges wicked deeds and forgives us our sins.[827]

Despite clear disagreements with the Reformers, Erasmus' words, on the other hand, can sometimes suggest a sympathy with them and a reaching out for open and honest dialogue. His remark on Hilary of Poitiers' comment, 'For faith alone justifies,' in reference to Matthew 9:6[828] prompts Erasmus to exclaim: 'And yet this statement, which is heard with reverence in Hilary, has been subjected to a long clamorous outcry in our age.'[829] In context this phrase is perfectly acceptable, but, to his dismay, his critics seemed ever prone to overlook context and make the words themselves touchstones of orthodoxy or heresy. Erasmus labours to make clear how his position on this doctrine differs from those who distort it by claiming, 'There is no righteousness from our works, and the nature of our works does not matter so long as we believe that Christ is our righteousness.'[830] It seemed tragic to him that learned men, Roman Catholic and Protestant alike, would be incapable of admitting their own limitations and fail to see Scripture and Christian tradition in its wider, complex historical development as an ongoing process of theological interpretation within the living community of believers, closing off honest scholarly exchanges, quickly denouncing one other as heretics because of certain words while missing the sincerity of each person's effort to express a belief, not working for that consensus of minds and hearts that is so vital for the life of the church.[831] It weighed heavily upon him that the time had passed when cooler minds 'might do the truth in charity' and 'in all things grow up in him who is the

* * * * *

826 See *Exomologesis* and Michael Heath's introduction above passim. In *Ratio* Erasmus shows greater willingness to express his opinion on the matter of confession than he shows here; see 205–6, where he criticizes those who teach as dogma its institution by Christ, not by the apostles.

827 See book 3 CWE 68 1021; cf book 2 CWE 68 610.

828 See book 3 CWE 68 967; cf Rom 4:5, 5:1; see Hilary of Poitiers *In Matthaeum* 21.15 SC 258 140–1: 'quia fides sola iustificat.' See also Erasmus' letter to Jean de Carondelet (preface to the edition of St Hilary), Ep 1334:969–70, which ends with a plea for reasoned, charitable restraint in theological discussion: 'Let the absence of furious contention, the bane of peace and concord, prevail everywhere.'

829 See book 3 CWE 68 967.

830 See book 3 CWE 68 1020.

831 See book 3 CWE 68 1016.

head, into Christ' (Eph 4:15). Ironically, among his generation of biblical humanists there were indeed a great many areas of unanimous agreement, but few it seemed worked for consensus; the majority insisted uncompromisingly on the unassailable correctness of their teachings. On the importance of instructing worthy preachers as heralds of God's word, for example, Erasmus would have found the Reformers in full accord with him; there was no debate either on the primary importance of preaching God's word or of Jesus' command to 'teach all nations' (Matt 28:19) as foremost among the duties entrusted to apostles and their delegates. Yet throughout the writing of *Ecclesiastes* we sense Erasmus viewing his contemporaries as bitterly fixated on theological questions, with each person unyielding in his insistence on having the truth, all the while missing the simplicity of Christ's teaching and example. Their intransigence would gravel him to the end of his life.

By 1534, the disruptive atmosphere of reformation Basel had largely subsided, and in the late spring or early summer of 1535 Erasmus returned there to see a few old friends and be close to the Froben press for the publication of *Ecclesiastes* and his edition of Origen's *Opera*.[832] We should surely assume that Erasmus' views of the Reformers' ideas or his own views did not change with his move, for he tells Conradus Goclenius of Louvain on 28 June 1536, in the last of his surviving letters, 'For although I am among the truest of friends here, which I did not have at Freiburg, nonetheless because of the dissension over dogma I'd prefer to end my life elsewhere. Would that Brabant were nearer.'[833] Erasmus never got his wish. He died in Basel close to midnight between 11 and 12 July 1536, having at last finished what would be the most influential work on sacred oratory after St Augustine's *De doctrina christiana*, and arguably the most important treatise of his life.

FJM

* * * * *

832 Erasmus did not live to see the publication of Origen's works; in September 1536, two months after Erasmus' death, Beatus Rhenanus finished the edition, added a preface, and published it with Hieronymus Froben and Nicolaus Episcopius; see *Origenis Adamantii eximii scripturarum interpretis Opera* 2 vols (Basel: Froben 1536).

833 Allen Ep 3130:26–9. For his difficult theological conversations with others at this time, see Reedijk 59–62. See also Allen's footnote for Erasmus' letter to Louis de Vers (Basel, 7 October 1535), Allen Ep 3062.

Translator's Note

For the text of *Ecclesiastes*, Erasmus' last and longest work, we are largely dependent upon the *editio princeps* (Basel 1535), its list of *errata*, prepared by Erasmus himself, and the corrections subsequently incorporated (whether or not at Erasmus' direction) in the two further editions issued in 1536 and the two issued in 1540, after the author's death. For a substantial portion of book 1, however, we have the additional authority of an autograph manuscript, G.K.S. 95 of the Danish Royal Library in Copenhagen. The editor is thus challenged chiefly in the portion of the text for which we have the conflicting authority of an autograph and a first edition; elsewhere there is little to do other than to identify possible errors, deciding whether they derive from Erasmus or from the printer, and whether they should be corrected or not. In the present version, book 1 was initially translated from the Leiden edition of 1706; then the translation was brought into conformity with the text of Jacques Chomarat[1] when it became available, and the remaining books were all translated directly from Chomarat; his copious annotations have often been consulted with profit.

While I have, in general, followed Chomarat's text, I have sometimes chosen to translate something other than what he has printed, and I have sometimes rejected his interpretation of the Latin; in revising the translation, I have also taken account of Nesselrath's reviews of the edition.[2] The disagreements with Chomarat's text or interpretations are indicated *ad locum* in notes to the translation: in some instances I reject his construction of the Latin to follow another; in some I reject an emendation he proposes; in some I propose (or even translate) my own suggested emendations; in some

* * * * *

1 ASD V-4, V-5
2 Heinz-Günther Nesselrath, review of ASD V-4 *Gnomon* 66 no 3 (1994) 221–7; and his review of ASD V-5 *Gnomon* 70 no 4 (1998) 313–7.

I repunctuate, an area where earlier editions are (by modern standards) particularly unreliable.

Once matters of the text have been settled, the translator must also decide how to translate, and must deploy the strategies that will best convey to Latinless readers what it is like to read Erasmus' original Latin.

Naturally the stylistic affections that are most prominently in evidence here need to be preserved. One of these is the use of plural subjects with singular verbs, sometimes because the subject is naturally compound or forms a hendiadys, sometimes because Erasmus simply strings a series of new subjects after the first one. Another is his fondness for asyndeton, which has been preserved wherever this can be done without creating some intolerable ambiguity in the English; this seems all the more appropriate given that Erasmus himself in book 3 commends asyndeton as a stylistic device to impart a certain ardour to language.

The broad range of Erasmus' vocabulary must be represented as well. Sometimes this requires the choice of word that is slightly exotic from the point of view of 'normal' Golden Age or Silver Age Latin prose (Erasmus of course was no strict Ciceronian – he is closer to Suetonius or Gellius – and in any case he did not write exclusively in a single style or stylistic register); again, examples have been indicated in the notes.

I have also tried to respect the stylistic register of Erasmus' vocabulary. For example, his preferred verb for expressing the idea of having relations with prostitutes is *scortari*. This is derived from *scortum*, originally 'skin,' a cruder term for 'prostitute' than the euphemistic *meretrix* 'wage earner,' and so the English verb 'to whore' seems the appropriate equivalent (especially since the OED notes that the noun 'whore' is 'confined to coarse and abusive speech': Erasmus uses the verb when attacking the men who engage in such activity). Erasmus also uses a variety of unflattering designations for 'ordinary people' or 'the common man.' They may be an ignorant mob, the common muck, or worse; no effort has been made to soften these terms. Erasmus' gift for satirical invective should be indulged wherever possible.

Very few concessions have been made to the concept of 'politically correct' or 'inclusive' language. Sometimes, where the context certainly warranted it, I have translated *homines* as 'people' or 'persons,' *filii* as 'children' rather than 'sons.' But these instances are outnumbered by those in which *homines* has been translated as 'men' or 'mankind'; to do so otherwise would be a betrayal of Erasmus. Equally, no attempt has been made to soften the language which Erasmus applies to Jews, however astonishing it may be to find someone saying, only a few decades after the expulsion of the Jews from Spain, that it is only thanks to Christian mercy that Judaism has survived so long.

Just as importantly, I have removed as little as possible of the syntactic awkwardness that sometimes intrudes; these blemishes reflect both the lack of final finishing touches and the very real mental and physical agony in which Erasmus found himself. These are not particularly apparent in books 1 and 4, which are fairly accomplished compositions, the former consistently eloquent and elevated, the latter a series of lists and headings followed by a few examples. Books 2 and 3, on the other hand, are simply a mess. There is a nightmarish welter of cross-referencing, as Erasmus constantly postpones topics for later discussion or resumes discussions interrupted earlier (or promises to). There is more syntactical irregularity here than elsewhere, to such an extent that one readily imagines Erasmus not only reluctant but even afraid to plunge in again and tidy up the confusion. Sentence fragments are commonplace here, as are errors in sequence of tenses. I have sought to preserve such errors in order to reflect the inchoate state in which Erasmus seems to have left these books.

JB

TO THE ILLUSTRIOUS PRINCE AND MOST REVEREND PRELATE,
CHRISTOPH VON STADION, BISHOP OF AUGSBURG, FROM
ERASMUS OF ROTTERDAM, GREETING[1]

Experience has taught me, dear Christoph, glory of the prelates of this age, that it was no empty maxim that the ancient oracles handed down to us when they said: 'Pledge your word, and ruin is close behind.'[2] Several years ago I promised a work on preaching. To tell the truth, I was not serious and did not really mean it. Later, people seriously demanded what I had not seriously promised. So not having the leisure to do what was being asked of me, I began jotting down a few notes at random for future use in case I found the will and the opportunity to tackle the subject. I did not proceed carefully and systematically, but sporadically, as something happened to come to mind. Later, when the demands became even more insistent, I began to collect my notes, which by this time were not just scattered, but torn and musty. When I examined them, my mind recoiled more and more from the project, though even earlier I had always had certain secret misgivings. I realized that the subject was vast and complex and that, if treated with the necessary care, would result in an immense volume. But when the demands continued without end, I put pen to paper against my better judgment, since I did not want anyone to think that I had reneged on a promise. When nothing worked out well, I rejected my first attempts. Time after time and at long intervals I took up the abandoned work to see if my interest could be rekindled. I fixed my mind on the task with chains as strong as those with which Virgil's Aristaeus bound Proteus, but his efforts succeeded and mine did not.[3] I kept hoping in the course of this long procrastination that someone would appear to relieve me of this responsibility, especially when I considered the rich harvest of talent that this age is producing and the great interest in printing new works. When no one appeared who was prepared to take over my role, and every day the numerous appeals, both spoken and written, grew more clamorous– now with an unmistakable undercurrent of reproach– I proceeded, almost against Minerva's will,[4] to put together a draft, which, though rough and disorganized, would prove that I did not lack the will to fulfil my promise, even if my abilities failed to match my intentions.

* * * * *

1 Ep 3036
2 *Adagia* I vi 91
3 Virgil *Georgics* 4.38–452, where Aristaeus binds with chains the wise but slippery Proteus to force him to answer his questions.
4 *Adagia* I i 42 *Invita Minerva* 'Against Minerva's will.'

However, even this I was not permitted to complete without interruptions. First ill health, then other responsibilities intervened to compel me to put aside the work, and it was only with difficulty and after long intervals that I was able to resume what I had begun. This explains what the learned reader will perhaps detect: gaps, repetitions, arguments that are incomplete or out of place. Someone will say, 'Why did you not make a final revision and correct what displeased you?' To be quite frank, I could not face going over such a massive work again, for it was only with difficulty that I accomplished this much with my health growing weaker every day. No one would find it easy to believe how desperately I longed in my soul to put aside these labours and withdraw into a world of peace and calm, and for the rest of my life (and what remains could easily lie in the palm of a small hand or within a closed fist) to speak only to him who cried out long ago and whose voice remains the same today, 'Come unto me all you who labour and are heavy laden and I will refresh you.'[5] For in this troubled, not to say tumultuous age, amid the many vexations that these times inflict on everyone and all the personal problems that come with age and failing health, there is no place where my spirit finds more rest and contentment than in this converse with the divine. When these thoughts occur to me, I feel more confident that the fair-minded reader will treat kindly what I offer now, such as it is. I do not make this appeal to you, most honoured bishop, for I know you are a man of such generosity of spirit that you always turn a blind and friendly eye to the failings of your friend Erasmus, and whenever my powers prove inadequate to the task, take the will for the deed.

I have divided the whole subject into four books. In the first I demonstrate the dignity of the office and what qualities the preacher ought to possess. In the second and third books I apply the principles taught by rhetoricians, dialecticians, and theologians to the practice of preaching. The fourth is a sort of catalogue, showing the preacher what ideas he should look for in Scripture and in what passages he will find them. However, with this I have done no more than point the studious reader in the right direction; otherwise the subject could not be fitted into a single short volume.

This rough sketch (for this is what I would prefer to call it rather than a work in the proper sense of the term) I had almost decided to dedicate to John Fisher, bishop of Rochester, a man of outstanding piety and learning, with whom I had enjoyed a long and close friendship, though I had made no promise to him but merely turned over the possibility silently in my mind.

* * * * *

5 Matt 11:28

He, more than anyone else, encouraged me by letter to take up this task, remarking that in the celebrated University of Cambridge, where he was permanent warden – the title they use is 'chancellor' – he was founding three colleges, which would graduate theologians who were not so much armed for the battles of words (λογομαχίαι) as trained for the sober preaching of the word of God.[6] He himself possessed a special grace of speech, which had long ago endeared him to the paternal grandmother of King Henry, who now rules over England.[7] God had given her a mind far above a woman's. While other princesses generally provide rich legacies for the building of monasteries (doing so, I fear, more out of pride than godliness), she, while she was still alive and in good health, had devoted herself enthusiastically to the holiest cause of all and was so little concerned with the breath of popular favour that her actions were almost kept a secret.[8] In several places, whenever she found men capable of passing on to the people the philosophy of the gospel, she arranged for them to be appointed at a generous salary, and for this same purpose she gave Bishop John a huge sum of money, all of which this most honourable man spent on the training of preachers or on providing comfort for the needy; far from taking anything for himself, he added liberally from his own resources. Here was a noble and saintly woman and a bishop of exemplary godliness, who rightly thought that nothing was more crucial for improving the behaviour of the people than to have qualified preachers to scatter the seed of gospel teaching. How is it that in many hearts Christ languishes or indeed is dead? How is it that so much that is pagan passes under the name of Christ, if not from a dearth of faithful preachers? It seemed to me that even the people of Italy (to say nothing of their princes) could be taught to live a godly life, were it not for a lack of teachers.

But these matters must wait for a more appropriate time. Now to continue what I began, when the bishop of Rochester was taken from me by a painful stroke of fate, it seemed right to me to launch this work, such as it is, under the happy auspices of your name, for your extraordinary compassion, more than anything else, is a consolation to me for the heavy loss of friends. When merchandise is lost in a shipwreck, there is weeping. But

* * * * *

6 'Battles of words'; Erasmus uses the Greek plural λογομαχίαι.
7 Henry VIII (149–1547). Henry VIII's paternal grandmother and the mother of King Henry VII was Margaret Beaufort (c 1441–1509). See Michael K. Jones and Malcolm G. Underwood *The King's Mother: Lady Margaret Beaufort, Countess of Richmond and Derby* (Cambridge and New York 1992) and CEBR I 109–11.
8 'Breath of popular favour'; Horace *Odes* 3.2.19; Virgil *Aeneid* 6.816

is there any merchandise so precious to be compared with a good friend? Could anything be more cruel than this recent tempest that has robbed me of so many distinguished friends: first William Warham, archbishop of Canterbury, then recently William Mountjoy and the bishop of Rochester and Thomas More, who was lord chancellor of his country, a man whose heart was purer than the snow, whose like England had never seen before, nor is likely to see again, and who, in addition to all this, was the father of a remarkably gifted family.[9] For so great a loss two things in particular ease my sorrow: first the reflection that we shall soon be reunited with Christ in a happier world, and secondly the thought of the remarkable band of friends that Augsburg has given me. You are first in rank among these and by far the dearest of my friends, unless the great Johann Paumgartner wants to take up the challenge.[10] Next to him is Anton Fugger, the world of learning's most generous supporter.[11] This is like a threefold rope, which Solomon says is not easily broken.[12] But it becomes stronger still if we add Johann Koler, who, like a fourth strand wound around the other three, makes the combination absolutely indestructible.[13] Your kindness does not of course guarantee that I shall not grieve, but it prevents me from succumbing to my grief. I must pray to God that he will keep safe for me such a precious treasure.

As for my hopes for the work, if it fails to win the approval of the learned world, my example may perhaps inspire some better scholar to accomplish what I wanted to accomplish and to produce not just a rough sketch but a work that is complete in every way, so that at last the Lord will send more true labourers into his harvest.[14] For just as, in the words of that amusing old proverb, 'Many can goad an ox, but few can plough,'[15] so, by the same token, it is easy to train a speaker to address the people but more difficult to find men to spread the word of God sincerely, fervently,

* * * * *

9 For William Warham, see CEBR III 42–31; see also book 1 352–5. For William Blount fourth baron of Montjoy, see CEBR I 154–6. For Thomas More, see CEBR II 456–8. See also John Guy *Thomas More* (London 2000). For Thomas More's family, see John Guy *A Daughter's Love: Thomas More and His Daughter Meg* (Boston 2009).

10 For Johann (II) Paumgartner, see CEBR III 60–1.

11 For Anton Fugger, see CEBR II 6–7.

12 Ecclus 4:12

13 For Johann Koler, see CEBR II 269–70.

14 Luke 10:2; Matt 9:38

15 *Adagia* I vii 9 *Multi qui boves stimulent, pauci aratores* 'Few men can plough, though many ply the goad.'

and faithfully. It is a gift of God that the seed sown by faithful ministers springs up. The world seems to have been in labour with Christ for a long time, but if he were truly formed in our souls, then, by a multitude of signs, the pure root of the heart will be revealed.[16] For the gospel is not just words, nor, as Flaccus says, is a forest merely firewood;[17] but whenever the seed of the living word has been received into good earth, it brings forth abundant fruit and as it grows, offers varied evidence of the inner purity of the mind. The people become more obedient to the government, more respectful of the laws, more desirous of peace, more averse to war. There is more harmony in the home, greater trust and honesty, and a stronger abhorrence of adultery. The husband becomes more gentle towards his wife, the wife more respectful of her husband. Children obey their parents with more trepidation, serfs obey their masters more willingly, domestic servants are more prompt in performing their duties.[18] Craftsmen and employees do their work more conscientiously. Businessmen do to no one what they would not like done to themselves. To sum it up in a word, everyone becomes more eager to serve and slower to take revenge or do an injury, less greedy and more thoughtful. In those whose behaviour does not show these qualities, but rather the opposite, it is to be feared that the good seed has not yet settled in their hearts.

But I must stop preaching so you may have time to read my *Ecclesiastes* if, that is, you will think it worth the attention of your eyes and ears. Farewell.

Basel, 6 August in the 1535th year since the birth of Christ

* * * * *

16 The image 'root of the heart' recalls Rom 11:16: 'And if the root be holy, so are the branches.'
17 Horace *Epistles* 1.6.32: 'Do you think virtue is a mere word and a forest only firewood?'
18 This ideal of family life is based on Col 3:18–23 and Eph 5:21–6:9.

ERASMUS OF ROTTERDAM TO THE READER, GREETING

Many authors like to blame their errors on the work of the printers. But here I frankly confess that almost all the errors in this work must be attributed either to my amanuensis or myself. It is true that I was present during the printing, but because of my poor health I was unable to make a final revision, especially since the need to correct certain pages often coincided with the hours that had to be devoted to sleep or to the care of my poor body. There was, however, no need for my help since that task was vigilantly carried out by Sigismundus Gelenius, a man of great learning and taste.[1] But when I had the leisure to read over some of the printed pages, I discovered several places that had slipped through my revision. There is not a huge number of these if you take into consideration the great length of the work, very few, if you discount trivial errors. I thought I should add a note here to this effect.

*****

1 For Sigismundus Gelenius, see CEBR II 84–5.

ECCLESIASTES,
OR THE EVANGELICAL PREACHER
BY DESIDERIUS ERASMUS OF ROTTERDAM:
ON THE DIGNITY, PURITY, WISDOM,
AND OTHER VIRTUES OF THE PREACHER[1]
BOOK ONE

Ecclesia means in Greek what *concio*[2] does in Latin, that is, an assembling of the people to hear about state business.[3] Those who convoke a crowd

* * * * *

1 On the frontispiece of the 1535 Froben edition, Erasmus gives the title of his treatise as *Des. Erasmi Rot. Ecclesiastae sive de ratione concionandi libri quatuor, opus recens, nec antehac a quoquam excusum*; just above the opening lines of book 1 he gives as the first book's title *ECCLESIASTES SIVE CONCIONATOR EVANGELICVS* [*ECCLESIASTES, OR THE EVANGELICAL PREACHER*]. To this Erasmus adds the subtitle: *DE DIGNITATE, PVRITATE, PRVDENTIA, CAETERISQVE VIRTVTIBVS ECCLESIASTAE LIBER PRIMVS*. Books 2, 3, and 4 will bear the titles *Ecclesiastae sive de ratione concionandi liber secundus* (*liber tertius, liber quartus*).

2 The word *concio* (or *contio*) properly refers to the assembly called by an official to hear about state business. The word takes on the meaning of the address spoken before the assembly. Erasmus purposely elects the classical Latin word *concio* (*contio*) rather than the common alternatives (*sermo, oratio, predicatio, homilia*) to emphasize the public nature of preaching like its secular counterpart, where one 'speaks to an assembly' (*ecclesia* or *concio*) about matters of 'state business.' As Erasmus presents it a few lines below, the preacher (*ecclesiastes*) is above all one who 'expound[s] the edicts, promises, and will of the highest Prince and persuade[s] the general public.' It is important to note as well that Erasmus will substitute *concio* for *ecclesia*; see eg 'Credo sanctam ecclesiam' ('Et te confiteor, sanctissima concio, qua gens / Christigena arcano nexu coit omnis in unum / Corpus & unanimis capiti sociatur Iesu, / Hinc proprium nescit, sed habet communia cuncta.' *Christiani hominis institutum* LB V 1357E–F, quoted by Wilhelm Hentze *Kirche und kirchliche Einheit bei Desiderius Erasmus von Rotterdam* (Paderborn 1974) [2].

3 At Rome the term is used for a meeting called by a priest or a magistrate to hear an issue; *contionem habere* means 'to hold a meeting.' See L&S 451; OLD II 44; and Francisco Pina Polo 'Procedures and Functions of Civil and Military *contiones* in Rome' *Klio* 77 (1995) 203–16. The Greek word *ecclesia* (ἐκκλησία), meaning 'assembly,' was used by the translators of the Septuagint to render the Hebrew word *qāhal*. For meanings of the word *ecclesia*, see *A Greek-English Lexicon*

for trivial matters are called ἀγύρται,[4] vagabonds and itinerant perform-
ers; those who do so against the state are termed seditious. Ἐκκλησιάζειν is
'to speak at an assembly,' and ἐκκλησιαστής 'someone who speaks publicly
before a crowd';[5] among the pagans too this office was always considered

* * * * *

of the New Testament and Other Early Christian Literature 4th ed, ed William F.
Arndt and F. Wilbur Gingrich (Chicago and Cambridge 1963) 240–1. For ecclesia and ecclesiastes as equivalents of the Hebrew words qāhāl and qōhelet, as
well as the problematic nature of the terms, see Thomas Krüger Qoheleth: A
Commentary ed Klaus Baltzer (Minneapolis 2004) 41: 'Yet it is not entirely clear
in what this consists: "The name Koheleth remains as enigmatic today as ever
before." ℭ translates קֹהֶלֶת qōhelet with ἐκκλησιαστής, "participant in a popular assembly" (Gk. ἐκκλησία Heb. קָהָל qāhāl), Jerome with concionator, "popular
speaker" (cf Luther: "preacher"). Thus there are two directions in which the
designation קֹהֶלֶת qōhelet from the Hebrew verb קהל qhl can be understood: (1)
a function that is defined in some way that is over against and in relation to a
popular assembly (however it might be more closely defined), or (2) a representation of this popular assembly or its participants themselves (and the two
possibilities do not have to be mutually exclusive).' Chomarat notes that in this
way the Greek word 'assembly' was Latinized to ecclesia to mean 'the church.'
4 'Prop. collector, esp. begging priest of Cybele' or 'vagabond' (LSJ); the religious
association of the former definition may be relevant to some of Erasmus' later
denunciations of certain behaviour among the clergy and religious of his day.
5 The book of Ecclesiastes (LXX Ἐκκλησιαστής; Qoheleth, from the Hebrew word
qāhal) receives its title from the word meaning 'leader of the assembly' or in
this case 'teacher of the assembly.' In this work of the Bible the 'Ecclesiastes'
identifies himself as having been 'the king of Israel in Jerusalem, who took it
to heart wisely to seek out and investigate everything under the sun' (Eccles
1:12). The Hebrew book consists of random topoi or various lessons and sayings for instructing a congregation in religious piety and practical wisdom (eg
piety towards God, the vanity of riches, obedience to authorities). The word
therefore is most appropriate for Erasmus' work because it captures his conception of the office of the preacher (concionator), which is publicly teaching
the heavenly philosophy. For Jerome's commentary on the book of Qohelet
(Ecclesiastes), see St. Jerome: Commentary on Ecclesiastes trans, ed, Richard J.
Goodrich and David J.D. Miller, Ancient Christian Writers in Translation 66
(New York; Mahwah, NJ 2012). Jerome employs the term frequently; see Commentarius in Ecclesiasten in S. Hieronymi Presbyteri Opera, Pars 1: Opera Exeget-
ica CCSL 72 247–361, especially 250 (1.1.1–9): 'Verba Ecclesiastis filii David Regis
Ierusalem. Tribus nominibus vocatum fuisse Salomonem scripturae manifestissime docent: pacificum, id est Salomonem; et Ididia, hoc est dilectum Domini;
et quod nunc dicitur Coeleth, id est Ecclesiasten. Ecclesiastes autem graeco
sermone appellatur, qui coetum, id est ecclesiam, congreget, quem nos nuncupare possumus concionatorem, quod loquatur ad populum, et sermo eius
non specialiter ad unum, sed ad universos generaliter dirigatur.'

especially lofty and honourable.[6] But just as there are two kinds of government, the secular (which some prefer to call the 'extrinsic' on the grounds that among Christians consecrated to God nothing should be secular) and the sacred (which today they call the ecclesiastical), so there are two kinds of *ecclesiastes*:[7] the secular, who proclaim the laws of princes and decrees of magistrates and persuade the people; and the sacred, who expound the edicts, promises, and will of the highest Prince[8] and persuade the people at large. Their functions, though differing in name, in no way conflict with each other; rather each serves the other, and they have the identical aim of ensuring that the state is peaceful and tranquil and that its tranquillity is dedicated not to pleasures and to luxury but to Christian devotion.[9] All Christians ought to bear this aim in mind above all in every action, both private and public. It is useless for a city to be safe against enemies, floods, or plague if its citizens' hearts are stained and disturbed by base desires.[10] No other kind of civil war is more deadly than when a man is at odds with himself. Likewise, having peace with your neighbours is useless if you are

* * * * *

6 See Quintilian 3.8.1.23–8: 'If I had to find a single object for them, I should have preferred Cicero's view that the essential feature of this type of theme is dignity [*dignitas*]. Not that I doubt that those who hold the former opinion also held the idealistic view that nothing that is not honourable [*honestum*] can be expedient [*utile*] either.' See Cicero *De oratore* 2.82.334 and *De finibus* 2.14.45.

7 In the course of the introduction to book 1, I retain *ecclesiastes* as long as Erasmus plays upon the sense of the word; otherwise it is simply 'preacher.' (J. Butrica)

8 In drawing parallels between secular and sacred 'government' (*politeia*), Erasmus will commonly use the language of the former in reference to affairs of the latter (eg 'edicts, promises, and will of the highest Prince'). In the church 'the highest prince,' Chomarat notes, refers to Christ, not the pope (ASD V-4 37 16n): Christ is also spoken of as 'the highest ecclesiastes.' In the state, 'the first and highest ecclesiastes is the king or prince'; in the sacred sphere, *ecclesiastes* is the bishop, who lawfully delegates this office to his pastors and others.

9 Erasmus articulates his idea of a constitution of the Christian republic, of secular and sacred realms, each independent in its own right, not conflicting but mutually serving each other, sharing the common aim of 'ensuring that the state be peaceful and tranquil' in accord with Christian devotion. Book 1 makes clear how infinitely exalted the 'sacred' is over the 'secular'; acknowledging this is a fundamental step in training the preacher.

10 Here Erasmus anticipates his vision at the end of book 4 of society at peace, where these 'base desires' have been eliminated and Christians dwell in peace and concord.

at war with God. Yet, just as physical condition and health frequently impede the pursuit of godliness, so external calamities of the state frequently hinder the discipline of religion and import a grievous moral plague: such are wars or the invasions of barbarian tribes.

Of the 'external' state, therefore, the first and highest *ecclesiastes* is the king or prince,[11] each in his own dominion, and under him governors, deputies, and magistrates; of the 'sacred' it is the bishop,[12] and under him pastors or others lawfully delegated to perform this office. We observe, however, that here too, as in many other matters, the business is handled wrong way round. No one rushes forward rashly to make a secular address about state business, nor is just anyone admitted to the platform; rather, out of the boundless mass of men, someone suitable is chosen, and whoever undertakes the task of speaking carefully studies the case about which he is going to speak to ensure that nothing is uttered that conflicts with the will of the prince or is not conducive to the good of the state. But persons of every sort – the young, the irresponsible, the ignorant – are admitted, sometimes even leap up, to make sacred orations, as though nothing were easier than to expound divine Scripture to the people, and as though it were quite enough to wipe away the blushes of shame and set the tongue rolling. The source of this problem is the failure to consider how great is the dignity and the difficulty and the utility of the ecclesiastical orator if he performs his duty correctly.[13] Therefore, desiring with the help of Christ's spirit to train the priestly *ecclesiastes*, we shall take our beginning from this point.

Many and varied are the gifts that divine goodness, in its eagerness for our salvation, has provided to the human race to obtain eternal life, but none among these is more splendid or more effective than to dispense the Lord's

* * * * *

11 Erasmus echoes the book of Ecclesiastes (1:1, 12) where 'the teacher' states he was 'the son of David, king of Jerusalem.'

12 The bishop is above all the teacher and therefore the most important agent in the ecclesiastical hierarchy, a point Erasmus repeatedly emphasizes.

13 Erasmus dedicates much of the first book to the theme of the 'dignity of the preacher.' The theme itself has a long history in homiletic literature. Erasmus, however, addresses it in a novel way by elaborating on contemporary abuses in the pulpit, contrasting these with the exalted office that preaching is divinely designed to be. He wastes no time excoriating deplorable preaching practices. His contrasts make the simple point that, if secular addresses in assemblies before kings are given such meticulous attention, those in sacred assemblies deserve immeasurably more. Erasmus' critique of preaching and preachers has a long history; see eg *Moria* CWE 27 132–5; *Ciceronianus* CWE 28 384–5; and *Colloquia* (*Concio, sive Merdardus*) CWE 40 938–62.

own word to his flock; and there is no other office in the whole ecclesiastical hierarchy either more outstanding in worth or more difficult to perform or more fruitful in application than to act as a herald of the divine will to the people and as a steward of heavenly philosophy.

Accordingly, that highest *ecclesiastes*, the Son of God, who is the most perfect image of the Father,[14] who is the eternal power and wisdom of his begetter,[15] through whom the Father decided to bestow on humankind whatever good he had determined to grant the race of mortals, is never named more splendidly or more meaningfully in Holy Writ than when he is called the Word or Speech of God.[16] This title, which can be shared with no creature, belongs specifically to his divine nature since the word 'Christ' and 'Jesus' is more in keeping with the human nature that he assumed; for the name of Jesus he has in common with many, and 'anointing of the Spirit' (a designation that he shares with kings and priests) applies only to a man. In fact all who are reborn in Christ and live piously in him are called 'children of God.'[17]

Is it not a superb commendation to be called 'light of the world'?[18] The Lord deemed his apostles worthy of the honour of this name: 'You are the light of the world, you are the salt of the earth.'[19] Yet the glory of this title

* * * * *

14 Col 1:15
15 Cf 1 Cor 1:24.
16 'Word or speech' (*verbum aut sermo*); John 1:1. Erasmus elsewhere dwells on the richness of the Greek word *logos* (λόγος), which denotes both 'word' and 'speech,' as well as many other meanings, eg reason, method, theory. For Erasmus' preferences for 'speech' (*sermo*) over 'word' (*verbum*), see *Paraphrasis in Joannem* CWE 46 15–16: 'And there is no other object that more fully and clearly expresses the invisible form of the mind than speech that does not lie' (15). Erasmus states: 'And I wonder why *verbum* pleased the Latin authors more than *sermo*'; see ASD VI-6 29–40, especially 30. See also Jane E. Phillips' extensive notes 16 and 17 in *Paraphrasis in Joannem* CWE 46 15 (notes appear on 234–5). See also 15 n19 (235) for Erasmus' preference for *oratio*. Erasmus returns to these favourite themes of his earlier writings: Christ as 'the Word' *verbum* or 'Speech of God' *oratio dei*. See *Apologia de 'In principio erat sermo'* LB IX 111–22. For Erasmus on 'the heavenly philosophy' and 'the philosophy of Christ,' see eg *Paraphrasis in Joannem* CWE 46 7, 14, 34 n131; *Enchiridion* CWE 66 xxii–xxv, 9, 11, 13 and especially letter to Paul Volz (14 August 1518), Ep 858. See also '*Mystère*' passim.
17 Luke 20:36; John 1:12; Rom 8:16; Gal 3:26, 4:5–6
18 Matt 5:14
19 'You are the light of the world, you are the salt of the earth' (Matt 5:13–14); 'gods' (Ps 82:6 [Vulg 81:6]; John 10:34). Erasmus reads in this psalm the terrifying reality of Christ, God, as judge of all 'gods' called to preach. See book 1 254 below and book 4 CWE 68 1069–71.

is owed to all who faithfully perform the apostles' role, just as they have succeeded to the apostles' place. It is even loftier to be called a 'messenger of God.'[20] Malachi uses this title to honour the priest who is learned and versed in the law of the Lord, saying, 'The lips of the priest guard knowledge, and men seek the law from his mouth, for he is the messenger of the Lord of Hosts.'[21] But more glorious even than this praise is to be called 'children of God'[22] and even 'gods';[23] this is how those pious men were addressed to whom God's Speech was directed and who communicated to the people in good faith what they had heard: 'I have said, you are gods and all sons of the Most High.' It is not right to equivocate about this testimony, which was spoken in the prophetic spirit in Psalm 81; the Lord himself cites and interprets it as irrefutable Scripture at John 10.[24]

In the midst of these gods stands the Redeemer[25] himself, the highest *ecclesiastes*, judge of those who dispense the word of God whether rightly or otherwise, for the Psalm reads, 'God stood in the council of the gods, in the midst he judges the gods.'[26] Just as we are made one in nature with Christ the head[27] through spiritual rebirth, so at the same time we are conveyed into the honour of his name and the sharing of his titles. He, the Son of God, has adopted us as his brothers; we have a common father, so that we too are already deservedly called the children of God, especially if we imitate the Son of God in preaching the gospel. He is God from God; if we remain in him, we too are rightly called gods, for what is born from God, what is made one and the same with God, must in some sense be God.[28]

Though I have said this to show the loftiness of the preacher's office, let us yet remember that the terms 'son' and 'god' are applied differently to us and to Christ. He is Son by nature,[29] we by adoption;[30] he was born God

* * * * *

20 'The lips of the priest ... messenger of the Lord of hosts' Mal 2:7
21 Mal 2:7
22 Luke 20:36; John 1:12; Rom 8:16; Gal 3:26, 4:5–6
23 Ps 82:6 (Vulg 81:6); John 10:34
24 See John 10:34– 5 and Ps 82:6 (Vulg 81:6).
25 Chomarat notes the rare occurrence of the word 'Redeemer' in Erasmus, whose view of Christ's salvific role is fundamentally that of the teacher who imparts heavenly wisdom, thereby restoring through his word the knowledge of things once known and necessary for salvation but lost through human dereliction. See ASD V-4 39 79n.
26 Ps 82:1 (Vulg 81:1)
27 Cf Eph 4:15.
28 Cf Rom 8:15–17, 5:5; John 17:21–2.
29 Cf John 1:1; Nicene Creed DS 125 (*de substantia Patris, Deum ex Deo*).
30 Rom 8:15–17

without beginning out of the substance of God, and we have been adopted mercifully through him into a share of immortality.[31]

There are likewise many other honorary titles with which Scripture dignifies the men who interpret the divine will, calling them 'heavens' that tell the glory of God.[32] They are called prophets,[33] a matter of which we shall speak later. Only Christ, who alone is God by nature, was called the 'Word of God';[34] according to this nature, he is designated by the title 'Word of God,' whose heralds are the preachers. A man's speech is the truthful image of his mind, reflected in his words as in a mirror;[35] 'for thoughts proceed from the heart,'[36] the Lord says. Christ however is the almighty Word of God, which flows forth eternally without beginning, without end from the eternal heart of the Father; through it the Father created the universe, through it he rules all creation, through it he restored the fallen human race,[37] through it he bound the church to himself, through it he desired to become known to the world in a singular and ineffable manner, through it he brings the dead to life, through it he bestows the gifts of the Holy Spirit, through it he imparts a mystical power to the sacraments of the church, through it he will judge the world when the goats are separated from the lambs[38] and a new heaven and a new earth[39] are created not by the destruction of matter but by the removal of corruption.[40] Through it the Father will intoxicate and sate the angels and the whole city of the heavenly Jerusalem with the abundance of his house, for a wise son is the joy and glory of his

* * * * *

31 Rom 8:15–17

32 Ps 19:1, 18:2 (Vulg 18). Erasmus interprets this verse allegorically.

33 For 'prophets,' see 322, 372, 386–98 below.

34 John 1:1 (*verbum Dei*)

35 Cf Col 1:15; see also *Paraphrasis in Joannem* CWE 46 15–16: 'Speech is truly the mirror of the heart, which cannot be seen with the body's eyes.'

36 Erasmus requires that the preacher's speech be filled with the spirit of God who animates his heart: 'As is the heart, so is the speech' (see 261 below). The preacher's model is Christ, the Word of God, who perfectly expressed his divinity; in imitation of Christ, the preacher 'must take care first and with the greatest effort to render his heart the purest possible source of speech.' The preacher's life, therefore, must be one of continuous attention to the virtues, to possess a 'clean heart.' 'For thoughts proceed from the heart' (Matt 15:19; Mark 7:21; Rom 10:8–10).

37 Erasmus makes clear the restorative role of Christ: his word repairs, restores, recreates what had been lost through Adam's sin and human sinfulness.

38 Cf Matt 25:32–3.

39 2 Pet 3:13

40 See book 4 for Erasmus' idea of the world restored in peace and concord.

father.⁴¹ This is that incomprehensible Word, surest expounder of the divine mind and never in conflict with the model of perfect truth; through this that eternal mind spoke wondrously to us at the creation of the world;⁴² through this it spoke in various ways to us in the prophets;⁴³ through this he told us quite openly that a man born of man had been sent to earth, so that now it not only tugged at our ears but could be perceived with all the senses, palpable even to our very hands.⁴⁴

But the word of man is not produced without spirit;⁴⁵ rather, as is our speech, so is our spirit.⁴⁶ But in divinity, just as the one that produces the Word is almighty, and the Word produced is equally almighty, so the Spirit too, which proceeds equally from each,⁴⁷ is almighty. However, just as nothing can be imagined above the sublimity of that divine mind (if indeed human imagination can reach it at all),⁴⁸ so there is nothing in man more outstanding than the mind, the part in which we differ most from the nature of beasts and reflect a kind of image of the divine mind.⁴⁹ It was surely wonder at this that led the greatest philosophers to suspect that human souls are like the sparks of that unchanging light;⁵⁰ imitating them,

* * * * *

41 Cf Prov 10:1.
42 Genesis 1
43 Heb 1:1
44 *Adagia* I vii 40 *Aurem vellere* 'To pluck by the ear'; 1 John 1:1–2
45 Erasmus is playing on the twofold and related senses of the Latin word *spiritus*, which means both 'spirit' and 'breath.'
46 Cf Matt 15:18–19; Mark 7:21; Rom 10:8–10.
47 Erasmus repeats the Latin phrase from the *Symbolum Constantinopolitanum* (DS 150), *Et in Spiritum Sanctum … qui ex Patre Filioque procedit …* which differs from the Greek, 'who proceeds from the Father' (τὸ ἐκ τοῦ πατρὸς ἐκπορευόμενον). See also DS 1300–2 for the Council of Florence's *Decretum pro Graecis* (*Laetentur caeli*, 6 July 1439): 'Spiritus Sanctus ex Patre et Filio aeternaliter est, et essentiam suam suumque esse subsistens habet ex Patre simul et Filio, et ex utroque aeternaliter tamquam ab uno principio et unica spiratione procedit.' For many reasons the Greeks later abandoned this formulation. Cf Jedin IV 479–82 and 496–8.
48 For the 'ontological argument' Erasmus possibly alludes to here, see Anselm of Canterbury *Proslogion* trans Thomas Williams (Indianapolis and Cambridge 1995/2001) especially chapter 15.
49 See Thomas Aquinas *Summa theologiae* I q 29 aa 1–9.
50 Erasmus expresses the classical topos of the exalted nature of the human mind, which differentiates human beings from brute beasts and reflects 'a kind of image of the divine mind.' 'The greatest philosophers' refers here to the Platonists, Neoplatonists, Stoics, and Pythagoreans. For Stoic beliefs, see Cicero *De natura deorum* 2, especially 2.6.18–2.8.22 and passim. Cf Sallust *Coniuratio Catilinae* 1.1–4.

Horace wrote: 'And fixes on the ground a particle of air divine.'[51] They are grossly mistaken indeed in thinking that anything created can be a part of God,[52] as if God were a physical thing that can be cut or propagated; but they realized correctly that nowhere does man approach nearer the nature of eternal divinity than in mind and speech, which the Greeks call νοῦς καὶ λόγος [mind and speech]. Mind is the source, speech the image that flows forth from the source. However, just as that singular Word of God is the image of the Father,[53] so thoroughly like its author that it shares with him the same indivisible nature, so speech is a sort of image of the human mind, the most marvellous or mighty thing that man possesses;[54] hence Hesiod calls it 'man's most excellent treasure.'[55] If it differs from the heart from which it proceeds, it does not deserve even the name of speech, no more indeed than a mask deserves to be called a face or rouge a person's complexion. Moreover, just as a wind blowing from a pestilential or a salubrious place brings with it the power of that place, so speech, as it flows forth from the heart, which is the source of speech, reflects its strength and disposition with remarkable power, so that there is no other part of himself in which man is more useful or more dangerous to man.

Moreover, those who have a double heart (the kind that Scripture criticizes by saying, 'They have spoken with a double heart,'[56] and likewise Ecclesiasticus, 'Woe to the double heart'[57]) have no heart at all and do not speak even when they say much, for the function of speech is to express in words what you have conceived in your mind.

Now, just as waters that bring intoxication, madness, disease, and death flow from certain springs, and just as exhalations that bring instant death to

* * * * *

51 Horace *Satires* 2.2.79: *atque adfigit humo divinae particulam aurae.* Erasmus takes this line somewhat out of context; but see Cicero *De senectute* 21.78 where he notes that Pythagoras 'never doubted that our souls were emanations of the universal divine mind.'

52 That the human soul is part of the divine substance Erasmus, of course, rejects because nothing created can be a part of God. The immortal soul is created, and God in the essential simplicity of his nature is indivisible. See also Thomas Aquinas *Summa theologiae* 1 q 3 a 7.

53 Cf Heb 1:3; Col 1:15.

54 Cicero *De natura deorum* 2.59.148–9: 'Then take the gift of speech, the queen of arts as you are fond of calling it – what a glorious, what a divine faculty it is!'

55 Hesiod *Works and Days* 719; Aulus Gellius quotes this line of Hesiod in *Noctes Atticae* 1.15.14.

56 Ps 12:2 (Vulg 11:3)

57 Ecclus 2:12. Erasmus explains below the meaning of 'double heart'; see 269.

those nearby blow from certain caves while others heal physical ailments, so there is nothing more wholesome than speech that proceeds from a sound and devout mind and, conversely, nothing more dangerous than speech breathed out by a heart corrupted and tainted by wicked opinions, base desires, and vices. People shudder at the hissing of a snake and flee quickly, fearing that it might breathe some poison upon them (for snakes harm in this way too, not by bite alone); but we should shudder much more at the conversation of a pestilential man who breathes out only the lethal venom of his soul. Physicians rightly warn us not to speak at close quarters with those infected with the pox commonly called 'French'[58] (though that form of leprosy, which spread from Italy, is, alas, common to all nations equally), since the contagion spreads most easily from drawing in the breath of someone tainted by this plague, but it is infinitely more dangerous to draw in the speech that flows out of an infected heart. A man's speech is like his heart. The man who has an earthly heart speaks earthly things, the one who has a heart of flesh speaks things of the flesh, the one who has the devil in his heart speaks the devil and breathes him on others: the man who has Christ's spirit in his heart speaks things heavenly, devout, holy, chaste, and worthy of God.[59]

To have Christ's spirit inhabiting the heart is in fact common to all Christians, but it especially befits the preacher, who could set before himself no more perfect model than that of the highest orator, who was called 'the Word,'[60] that is, the image and voice, of God. The tongue of the orator can be effective only if Christ's spirit inhabits his heart, moves the plectrum

* * * * *

58 'French' pox refers to syphilis, which was called different names at this time. Syphilis was commonly referred to as the 'sickness of Naples'; here Erasmus identifies it as spreading from Italy. Erasmus often mentions this disease (eg CWE 25 307, Ep 892, Colloquia ['Ιππεὺς ἄνιππος / sive Ementita nobilitas]). See The Great Pox: The French Disease in Renaissance Europe ed Jon Arrizabalaga et al (New Haven c 1997); and Medicine from the Black Death to the French Disease ed Roger French et al (Aldershot 1998). Erasmus' comparisons throughout this chapter draw attention to the vast difference between things noxious to the body and things noxious to the spirit; the phrase 'by how much more' (quanto magis) is a favoured rhetorical device for amplification, which signals his use of comparison moving from things of lesser importance to greater ones. Useful for Erasmus' general method of using rhetorical arguments of all kinds is his De copia, which lays out ways of arguing effectively (CWE 24 572–659). Cf Quintilian 8.4.9–12.

59 Cf Ps 12:6 (Vulg 11:7): 'The words of the Lord are pure words' (eloquia domini, eloquia casta).

60 John 1:1, 14. Erasmus uses the term sermo for 'the Word.'

of his mouth,[61] and imparts mystical force to the words that flow forth. The voice of the orator can strike the ears of his audience, but it is God alone who transforms their minds with secret inspiration.[62] Yet the preacher strives without pause, planting and watering and asking Christ's spirit to give increase,[63] in short imitating that highest preacher in everything so far as his strength allows.[64]

And what does he say about himself? 'I am the way, truth, and life,'[65] he says. Satan, speaking through the serpent, led the human race astray;[66] God, speaking through his Son, led back the straying sheep.[67] He deceived the founders of the human race with lies; Christ freed the world from error by speaking the truth.[68] Cast down from heaven, he dragged the world into ruin, trapped it into sharing his rebellion, and ensnared it into partaking of death; Christ, descending to earth from the bosom of the Father, won back the lost and restored the dead to life. The former drove out of Paradise those who trusted in him; the latter carries up into heaven those who have faith in him. The preacher has an example to avoid; he has one to follow. Let him shun the serpent that even today speaks through those who have Satan and the world in their heart; let him follow Christ in the apostles, who did not speak themselves but rather that divine Spirit spoke through them as if through a living organ.

And so anyone who is preparing for so excellent an office as this must be equipped with many things:[69] recondite knowledge of the sacred books, much proficiency in Scripture, varied reading of the doctors, sound judgment, uncommon prudence, a mind sincere and strong, the theory and

* * * * *

61 Cf Cicero *De natura deorum* 2.59.148–9; and Isidore *Etymologiae* 9.1.51.
62 Cf Rom 10:17.
63 1 Cor 3:6–8; cf Matt 9:37–8.
64 Throughout *Ecclesiastes* Erasmus refrains from urging preachers to imitate great preachers whether past or present; instead he recommends imitating Christ, 'that highest preacher in everything.'
65 John 14:6
66 Cf Genesis 3. Chomarat correctly notes that nowhere in Scripture is Satan identified with the serpent in the Garden of Eden; see ASD V-4 43 176n. In book 4 Erasmus takes up again the contrast between Satan leading away and Christ bringing back or restoring. Chomarat describes this as the opposition 'deduco-reduco' (cf Tob 13:2; Wisd of Sol 16:13; 1 Kings 2:6); see ASD V-4 43 176–7n.
67 Cf John 10:11–16; Matt 12:11.
68 Cf John 8:32.
69 Here Erasmus begins to enumerate the qualities and set forth the extensive preparation of the preacher, which is the substance of this treatise.

practice of speaking, and a ready fluency of speech with which he must
speak before a crowd, and others as well that I shall mention in their place.
In my opinion, however, the man who prepares himself for so high an office
must take care first and with the greatest effort to render his heart the purest
possible source of speech.[70] This advice is easily given 'by numbers,'[71] as
they say, but it is by far the most difficult of all to impart, and it requires
much extended practice. It is moreover pre-eminently necessary, not only
for teaching and inflaming the minds of the audience, not only for steadfastly protecting the truth against detractors, but also for acquiring knowledge of the heavenly philosophy that you are going to hand on to others.
Human disciplines can be learned even by the wicked; but this divine wisdom does not enter a mind contaminated by vice, and it does not deign to
dwell in a body prey to sin. Moreover, just as we learn more easily what
we believe to be most true and necessary for man's enduring happiness,
so we more effectively persuade others of that by which we ourselves are
strongly affected. Finally, we defend the cause more bravely if we remember that we are only the dispensers of God's mysteries,[72] that it is God who
gives the strength and bestows a happy outcome upon human endeavour.

Therefore the future preacher must strive right from his youth to obtain from the Lord a new heart and an upright spirit by a profound experience of Holy Scripture, a new heart in which there is nothing, or as little
as possible, of the old Adam,[73] and an upright spirit unbroken and erect
against all of Satan's wiles. For he alone can bestow what God promised
through Ezekiel, saying, 'A new heart I will give you, a new spirit I will
put within you.'[74] Only new wineskins hold new wine.[75] What Ezekiel calls
a 'new heart' David calls a 'clean heart.' He asks the Lord for this urgently
when intending to perform the office of a herald: 'Create a clean heart in
me, O God, and renew an upright spirit within me.'[76] After receiving it, he
promises to fulfil the duty of the preacher: 'I will teach transgressors your

* * * * *

70 These words recall the prayer inspired by the words of Isaiah (6:6–7) and
   spoken by the priest before reading the Gospel at the liturgy: *munda cor meum
   ac labia mea* ...
71 *Adagia* III vii 58. The phrase seems to mean 'fluently,' 'glibly.'
72 1 Cor 4:1
73 Adam means 'man'; Paul exhorts the Corinthians to be made new in Christ, the
   new 'man' ('Adam'); see 1 Cor 15:22, 45; cf Rom 5:12–21. See also *Paraphrasis
   in epistolam ad Romanos* CWE 42 34–6.
74 Ezek 36:26
75 Matt 9:17
76 Ps 51:10 (Vulg 50:12)

ways, and sinners will turn to you.'[77] After cleansing our eyes, we perceive more correctly the distinctive features of external objects: with a clean heart we have a more accurate view of God hidden in the coverings of Scripture.[78] He asks first for a clean heart, then for an upright spirit, for unconquerable vigour of spirit arises from sincerity of the heart; but God makes each anew. As is the heart, so is the speech; as the faith, so the courage. When the heart has been made anew, new tongues too begin to sound at once no longer what belongs to this world, no longer what smacks of the earth, but the magnificence of God. For what is so lofty in human affairs that it does not seem more base than mud when compared to that sublimity of the divine philosophy? That heavenly and truly fiery Spirit,[79] moreover, is not only an examiner of hearts[80] but also a creator and a renewer and has knowledge of speech as well. Hence anyone who believes that he can acquire true understanding of canonical Scripture without the inspiration of that Spirit whence they were produced is grievously mistaken; no less mistaken is the man who believes that he can act the true preacher without a draught of the heavenly Spirit, without which no one can say Jesus is Lord.[81] He bestows a fiery heart, fiery tongues.[82] What was more uninspired than the tongues of the apostles before they had drawn in fully that heavenly craftsman of new hearts? They said, 'We ask that one sit at your left hand, the other at your right in your kingdom.'[83] Thus James and John. What about Peter, who was to be the chief of the apostles? 'Perish the thought, Lord; let this not happen to you.'[84] But what was the reply? 'Your thoughts are not divine but mortal.'[85] An old and human heart shudders at death, seeks power and happiness in this life. From the same heart came that remark upon the mountain, 'Lord, it is good that we are here; let us make

* * * * *

77 Ps 51:13 (Vulg 50:15)
78 In later books, Erasmus takes up 'God hidden in the coverings of Scripture.'
79 Cf Acts 2:2–4.
80 Cf Rom 8:27; Rev 2:23.
81 'without ... Lord' 1 Cor 12:3; Erasmus' 1524 translation of the New Testament reads: ... & nemo potest dicere Dominum Jesum, nisi per Sanctum Spiritum.
82 Acts 2:1–5. Erasmus refers here to the Holy Spirit, 'the heavenly craftsman of new hearts,' whose descent on Pentecost gave the apostles force and the power of persuasion; before this they were 'rather uninspired' (frigidius).
83 Matt 20:20–8; Mark 10:35–45
84 See Matt 16:21–3. These words of Peter do not belong to the incident where James and John ask for the most prominent places in Jesus' kingdom; they belong rather to the pericope where Jesus foretells his death in Jerusalem at the hands of the elders, chief priests, and scribes.
85 Matt 16:23

three tents here.'[86] Still more uninspired, though shared by all the apostles, was when they said, 'Which of us will be first in the kingdom of heaven?'[87] But the most uninspired of all was when they said, 'Do you want us to bid fire come down from heaven and burn the city?'[88] And what is the reply? 'You do not know of what manner of spirit you are.'[89] Those were the words of a Jewish spirit thirsting for vengeance, though they professed themselves disciples of the most gentle Christ.[90] There are many other remarks of the apostles in the gospels with the full flavour of man and of the flesh, since they were not yet suitable heralds of the gospel; but as soon as that Spirit, which makes all things new, had slipped down from heaven into their breasts and fashioned in them a new heart, a clean heart, a heavenly heart, a fiery heart, they began to speak at once, with new tongues, words that were no longer human as before but worthy of the Spirit, which they had absorbed.[91]

If you want to see courage, the fisherman who earlier denied the Lord so many times when addressed by some woman now dares to come forward to speak with his eyes fixed upon the crowd,[92] in front of a huge and even riotous mob composed of various nations and tongues, and to raise his voice and preach Christ and him crucified.[93] If you are wondering about the result, some three thousand men were converted that day to faith in the gospel at a fisherman's extemporaneous and unstudied address.[94] Therefore, whoever desires to be διδακτικός in Paul's sense, that is, suited to imparting the teaching of God, let him strive first to be θεοδίδακτος, that is, divinely

* * * * *

86 Matt 17:4; Mark 9:5; Luke 9:33
87 Matt 18:1; Mark 9:34; Luke 9:46. Erasmus' quotation is not exact; he uses 'first' (primus) while the Synoptics use 'greater' (maior).
88 Luke 9:54
89 In the Vulgate Jesus does not utter these words in rebuking James and John (Luke 9:55); the words are found in some older manuscripts; see Nestle-Aland 190 n55–6 and Vulg 1627 n55.
90 Erasmus often contrasts the Jewish 'spirit' or 'toughness' with the Christian spirit, which corresponds to his structural antitheses of 'flesh versus spirit,' old man versus new man, shadow versus substance, earthly versus spiritual. These structural antitheses carry over into the ethical sphere; eg vengeance versus pardon, etc. See Colloquia ('Ιχθυοφαγία) CWE 40 724 n46; Paraphrasis in epistolam ad Galatas CWE 42 121–6. See also 324 below.
91 Acts 2:1–4
92 See Matt 26:69–75; Mark 14:66–72; Luke 22:54–62; John 18:15–18, 25–7.
93 Acts 2:1–14
94 Acts 2:41. Erasmus analyses the rhetorical merits of Peter's speech in book 3 CWE 68 1002–6.

taught.[95] The Lord Jesus had no need for a new anointing of the Spirit or for a renewer of the heart, for his Father had anointed him right from his very birth with every fullness of the Spirit;[96] nevertheless, marked from baptism with the sign of the dove sitting and abiding upon his head,[97] he presented in himself a pattern so that no one would rush to the office of teaching unless inspired by the heavenly Spirit.

But the operation of the Spirit has certain degrees in us, so that it is not enough for the future preacher to have drawn in just any little puff of the Spirit, but he must go right to the principal spirit.[98] David requests a threefold spirit from the Lord when intending to teach his ways: an upright spirit against the attacks of temptations, a holy spirit to inflame the minds of others also and bring them over to sanctity, and a principal spirit, or 'a powerful spirit,' as Jerome translates it,[99] or a 'munificent' or 'liberal' spirit,

* * * * *

95 See 1 Tim 3:2. Erasmus translates the Greek word (διδακτικός) as *appositum ad docendum, ad tradendam Dei doctrinam idoneus* 'suitable to pass on God's teaching'; the Vulgate gives *doctorem* 'one learned.' See *Paraphrasis in epistolam Pauli Apostoli ad Timotheum priorem* where Erasmus sketches the model bishop: 'There is a special quality which must be looked for in a bishop. He has to have an aptitude and inclination for teaching – not for teaching Jewish myths or the supercilious, inflated philosophies of this world, but the things which make us truly godly and truly Christian' (CWE 44 18–19). Erasmus singles out Basil 'in exposing the mysteries of the sacred books, wondrously διδακτικός, diligent, careful, transparent, and in no way at all violent' (Allen Ep 2611:76–8 to Jacopo Sadoleto, 22 February 1532, preface to Froben's Greek Basil); θεοδίδακτοι 'divinely taught' in 1 Thess 4:9.

96 Cf John 1:14–18.

97 John 1:32–3

98 Ps 51:10–12 (Vulg 50:12–14): 'cor mundum crea in me Deus et spiritum rectum innova in visceribus meis ne proicias me a facie tua et spiritum sanctum tuum ne auferas a me redde mihi laetitiam salutaris tui et spiritu principali confirma me' (Vulg). The RSV translates these instances of spirit: at Ps 51:10 the psalmist asks for 'a new and right spirit'; at 51:11 'thy holy spirit'; at 51:12 'a willing spirit.' This is the threefold spirit Erasmus interprets below.

99 Jerome translates the LXX word ἡγεμονικῷ (LXX Ps 50:14; RSV 51:12) as 'powerful' (*potentem*). Cicero explains this term in *De natura deorum* 2.11.29: 'I use the term "ruling principle" (*Principatum autem id dico quod Graeci ἡγεμονικόν vocant*) as the equivalent of the Greek *hêgimonikon*, meaning that part of anything which must and ought to have supremacy in a thing of that sort. Thus it follows that the element which contains the ruling principle of the whole of nature must also be the most excellent of all things and the most deserving of authority and sovereignty over all things.' For the meaning of this term in Stoic philosophy, see John M. Rist *Stoic Philosophy* (Cambridge 1969) 24: 'The ἡγεμονικόν is something of what we might call the "true self" or personality

as someone else has it, for the richness of perfection.[100] The Lord Jesus blew
upon the face of his apostles before he rose to heaven saying, 'Receive the
Holy Spirit,'[101] yet there still remained some trace of human weakness in
them when they said, 'Lord, will you be presented to us at this time, and
when will be the kingdom of Israel?'[102] They are still being reproached for
their hardness of heart and slowness to believe; but as soon as they drank that
munificent Spirit, which overflowed so torrentially that it filled the whole
house,[103] they stood now far above all human affairs and preached the gospel
with such confidence that, though beaten with rods,[104] they went rejoicing
from the council, rejoicing however not because they had been acquitted but
because they deemed it a singular glory to themselves to have been marked
with disgrace for Jesus' name.[105] Being strengthened now by the principal
spirit, they are not frightened by any threats of the wicked or cast down by
any afflictions or elated or puffed up by any honours; for this too is no mean
snare. For just as those who preach the word of God sincerely must meet the
varied storms of temptations, so the highest honour has always been paid to
those who preach the gospel worthily. On either side there is great danger:
on the one side threaten the rocks of Scylla, which entice towards arrogance,
on the other side Charybdis,[106] which sucks the mind down in a multitude

* * * * *

of each individual human being. It will therefore more aptly be rendered by
words referring to personality than by words referring to rationality.' See also
Jerome [*Commentarius*] *in Danielem prophetam* (chapter 1 ii 28c lines 330–2) CCSL
75A 791; and Tertullian *De anima* 14 ANF III 193; Augustine *De natura et orig-
ine animae* 4.5.6 NPNF 1st series 5 356–7. See also Ambrose *De apologia David
ad Theodosium Augustum* 15.72 CSEL 32 2 347–8; Origen (Origène) *Homélies sur
les Nombres* (trans Rufinus) SC 415 Homilia 6 par 3 35:2; see also *Homélies sur
le Lévitique* (trans Rufinus) SC 287 Homilia 8 par 11 66:161–2. Augustine also
uses the word 'principal' when citing Ps 50:14; see eg *Ennarationes in psalmos*
CCSL 38 Psalm 50 par 17 lines 8 and 13; par 18 lines 1 and 6; WSA III-16 424–5.
100 This commentator has not been identified.
101 John 20:22. John offers this passage, which suggests that Jesus bestowed the
Holy Spirit upon his apostles shortly after the resurrection; John does not give
an account of the ascension as do Luke and Mark. For the ascension, see Acts
1:9; Luke 24:51; Mark 16:19.
102 Cf Acts 1:6.
103 Acts 2:1–4
104 Acts 5:40; cf 2 Cor 11:25 (St Paul). Erasmus is conflating a number of scriptural passages, which, while adding force to his argument, creates problems
in historical sequence and fact.
105 Acts 5:41
106 Erasmus' allusion is to Homer's *Odyssey* 12.85–126, 222–59 and Virgil's *Aeneid*
3.420–32; see also *Adagia* I v 4; *De copia* CWE 24 611–2, which Erasmus lists as a

of afflictions and drags it into despair. The preacher must be thoroughly fortified against either peril, and I am not at all sure whether there is not more danger from what allures than from what terrifies. Paul boasts amid his afflictions and infirmities that the power of Christ dwells and reigns inside him;[107] concerning his revelations, he is afraid to boast.[108] In the former case he confesses his name, in the latter he is ἀνώνυμος,[109] anonymous: 'I know a man,' he says. He is Paul when beaten with rods, when bound in chains, when thrown to beasts, when pelted with stones; but when he is snatched up into the third heaven, he suppresses his name. At Philippi, with his clothes ripped, his body torn by the wounds of the rods, in chains, in the depths of a prison, starving, he sings at night with his colleague Silas;[110] but at Lystra, with his colleague Barnabas, when the ignorant and superstitious populace was preparing divine honours because of the healing of a lame man, he rent his garments and leapt forward declaring that he was only a mortal man like them.[111] Indeed, at Caesarea Peter does not tolerate the obeisance and worship of Cornelius but raises him up saying, 'Stand up; I too am a man,'[112] and he equates himself with the person to whom he would soon give the Holy Spirit;[113] so free was his mind from all desire for glory. The great veneration with which the believers are wont to receive Paul, the great honour with which they send him off is clear enough from the Acts of the Apostles; indeed he himself gives adequate evidence of this when he writes to the Galatians, 'You received me as an angel of God,' an outstanding honour, but he adds something loftier: 'like Jesus Christ.'[114] And soon after, in the same passage, 'I bear you witness that, if possible, you would have plucked out your eyes and given them to me.'[115] Yet he took on no air of haughtiness because of these honours, which he had earned in all the churches, but preaches to them through the weakness of the flesh,[116]

* * * * *

moral allegory for teaching on the virtues and vices. See eg Jerome Ep 125.2 NPNF 2nd series 6 245: 'For on one side is the Charybdis of covetousness, "the root of all evil"; and on the other lurks the Scylla of detraction . . .'

107 2 Cor 12:9
108 2 Cor 12:2–10
109 'Nameless'; 'anonymous' (J. Butrica)
110 Acts 16:22–5
111 Acts 14:7–17
112 Acts 10:24–6
113 See Acts 10.
114 Gal 4:14
115 Gal 4:15
116 Gal 4:13

displaying a frail presence[117] even though he had been armed by the Spirit against every arrogance that raises itself against the knowledge of God.[118] He witnesses the same thing about himself writing to the Thessalonians: 'We never used words of flattery, as you know, nor sought an opportunity for greed – God is our witness – and did not seek glory from men, neither from you nor from others, though we could claim for ourselves authority and a grave distinction as apostles of Christ; but we became babes in your midst, as if a nurse were tending her children.'[119] By his zeal for preaching, the same man made himself a slave to everyone though he was free of everyone.[120] This was not a mark of adulation or of hypocrisy; the goal proves that. 'In order to win more,'[121] he said; it was the Lord's profit, not his own, that he sought everywhere. Many marvel at St Paul's unfailing fortitude and alacrity in the midst of so many worries, dangers, afflictions, disgraces, deaths – and with excellent reason. But I think that his constant and unfailing modesty and humility of mind in the midst of his great strengths and the great glory of his accomplishments are more marvellous. On the model of this man, then, let the Christian preacher always remember, after he has been supplied with every kind of gift, that he has that treasure in earthen vessels,[122] so that the loftiness is the power of God and not from human strength: 'To the one who has, it will be given; from the one who has not, even what he has will be taken away.'[123] The man who seeks profit from them for himself or hunts his own glory does not know how to have the gifts of the Spirit; he truly has them who earnestly invests the talents entrusted to him, not for his own gain but for the profit of the Lord, to whom is owed both principal and interest, not expecting his reward here but content that, having done his work faithfully, he will hear that blessed and longed-for phrase, 'Enter into the joy of your Lord.'[124] To a man who has them in this way, then, more will be given; from a man who has them other than he ought even what was given free will be snatched away. If you hold it as another's, not as your own, then it truly becomes yours; if you hold as your

* * * * *

117 Gal 4:13; 2 Cor 10:10
118 Eph 6:11–17
119 1 Thess 2:5–7. Erasmus' rendering of these verses differs from the Vulgate, especially verse 7. He inserts 'and a grave distinction . . .' (*et gravitatis dignitatem nobis vindicare, tanquam*) to complete St Paul's thought. See LB VI 904A–906A.
120 1 Cor 9:19
121 1 Cor 9:19
122 2 Cor 4:7
123 Matt 13:12, 25:29; Mark 4:24–5; Luke 8:18, 19:26
124 Matt 25:21–3. Erasmus recalls Jesus' parable of the talents (Matt 25:14–30).

own what is another's, you do not have what you have, since you have it to your own sorrow. For if the famous maxim of the mime that 'the miser lacks what he has as much as what he has not'[125] has deservedly won praise from learned men because possession is pointless if you take no use from it, then much more will a man be said not to have if he has what he has to his own ruin. Actors who perform a play for the crowd, though they have omitted no kind of effort or attention to please the theatre, are nevertheless compelled to have a strong heart against the hissings and stampings of the people, who do not always like excellence; for truly, as the writer says, 'every people is a beast of many heads,'[126] not just the Roman. But the preacher must have the solid and unmovable spirit that David calls principal,[127] not only against the perverse judgments of the people, against the malice of those who slander even devout words, against the animosities of those whose corrupt life makes them hate the truth, but also against the acclamations and applause of those who praise them. 'It is typical of kings,' said some high-minded pagan, 'to have a bad reputation when one does good deeds.'[128] An actor endeavours to make his performance as pleasing as possible to the people; he thrives on applause, is dejected by hisses. The preacher aims to commend to the people things that are excellent in themselves. The only one who will be able to accomplish this is the man who has a clean heart,[129] pure from the love of wealth, pure from the thirst for earthly glory, pure from the ambition and other desires that frequently make us neither suitable to learn Christian wisdom nor strong enough to preach it steadfastly, inasmuch as we have not yet been strengthened by the principal spirit; this spirit places all its trust in the Lord so that it neither fears the world nor trembles at Satan nor shudders at a death threatened because of

* * * * *

125 Publilius Syrus 694. Erasmus published Publilius Syrus' mimes in *Disticha moralia titulo Catonis . . . Mimi Publiani (cum scholiis Erasmi) . . .* (London: Wynken de Worde 1514). See CWE 29 xxxviii–ix.
126 Horace *Epistles* 1.1.76. Erasmus changes Horace's line from 'You are a beast of many heads' (*Belua multorum es capitum*) to '[every people] is a beast of many heads.'
127 Ps 51:12 (Vulg 50:14)
128 Plutarch *Moralia* 181.32F, *Sayings of Kings and Commanders* (Alexander [the Great]): 'It is kingly to be ill spoken of for doing good.' This was a common aphorism in the ancient world. See also *Sayings Falsely Ascribed to Publilius* 112: *Est regium male audire et bene facere*, Eduardus Woefflin *Publilii Syri Sententiae. Ad fidem codicum optimorum primum recensuit Eduardus Woefflin. Accedit incerti auctoris liber qui vulgo dicitur de moribus* (Leipzig 1869) 123:112.
129 Ps 51:10 (Vulg 50:12); cf Isa 6:6–7.

the gospel, so long as the man preaches it with a good conscience. This then is the special source of the preacher's eloquence, a heart clean and fortified by the threefold spirit. That perceptive man Horace saw this as if through a cloud when he said, 'Wisdom is both the beginning and the source of speaking rightly.'[130] For knowledge is one thing, wisdom another. Even demons know much and have in fact taken their name from this (if we believe the grammarians), being called demons as if δαήμονες, that is, 'knowing'; yet no one says that they are wise.[131] The wise man is the one who has learned not everything but what pertains to true happiness, and is affected and has been transfigured by what he has learned. This happens whenever the food of the gospel's teaching,[132] taken with full faith, has been transported into the organs of the mind and has passed into an attitude and strength of spirit. It is right, therefore, that concern for this should be first [praecipuum] in accordance with its pre-eminence.[133]

* * * * *

130 Horace *Ars poetica* 309. Horace's line reads: 'Of good writing the source and fount is wisdom' (*Scribendi recte sapere est et principium et fons*), which Erasmus changes to 'Of good speaking' (*Dicendi*). This echoes Cato's definition of the orator as 'a good man skilled in speaking,' as related by Quintilian 12.1.1. The essence of eloquence therefore lies in the moral exemplarity of the speaker.

131 Cf *Moria* CWE 27 107, where demons are said to have been 'given their name because it means "those who know" [δάω] in Greek.' See also in this place the true wise man as opposed to those who 'know' or have knowledge. Chomarat notes that Erasmus' etymology is wrong; see ASD V-4 53 360n. Cf Plato *Cratylus* 397C–8C, especially 398B, where Socrates states it is his 'most entire conviction that he [Hesiod] called them daemons, because they were δαήμονες (knowing or wise) ...'

132 The alimentary metaphors for the philosophy of Christ, the word of God, for example, go back deep in biblical and Christian tradition and are used in conciliar statements on preaching and its reform; see eg the Fourth Lateran Council (1215) Canon 10 *De predicatoribus instituendis* in Tanner I 239: 'Among the various things that are conducive to the salvation of the Christian people, the nourishment of God's word is recognized to be especially necessary, since just as the body is fed with material food, so the soul is fed with spiritual food, according to the words, "Man lives not by bread alone but by every word that proceeds from the mouth of God."' Throughout this treatise Erasmus extensively selects such metaphors of nourishment, sweetness, and delight.

133 Erasmus applies the word 'pre-eminent' (*praecipuum*) regularly to the duty of preaching, greater than which there is none. Here Erasmus formulates the essence of the duty of preaching: that it does not involve learning everything, but 'those things that lead to true felicity'; elsewhere he gives as the content of preaching 'the things necessary for salvation' (*res necessariae ad salutem*). This is the true matter of preaching and the essential duty of the bishop. See 313–14, 344 below and book 4 CWE 68 1040 below. See also *Explanatio symboli* CWE 70

But human philosophy does not impart it, nor can humanity's native strength give it to anyone; it must be sought from him who alone dispenses true blessings, sought however not casually but with prayers at once constant and ardent. Nor must one request it only in prayers, but it must also be sought through good works so that what has been given may be kept and may daily increase. Someone who requests such a gift coolly is unworthy to receive it, and it is a kind of ingratitude to possess carelessly a gift that is both costly and received without payment; an ingrate, in fact, deserves to be deprived even of that which has been given. The Lord bestows a new heart, bestows a strengthening spirit; he likewise preserves and increases what he has given, but not for the careless, not for those with a double heart.[134]

Now to possess a double heart is to attempt to fight for the world and the gospel at the same time, that is, to try to mix an old heart with a new, the spirit of Adam with the spirit of Christ.[135] Those who fight for Caesar, men fighting for a man, are not entangled in cares that the Apostle calls βιωτικοῖ, that is, the cares of this life,[136] but leave off commerce, agriculture, manufacture, and other industries of this kind from which they were wont to earn their living, in order to be free from anxiety over their own property and to serve their emperor with all their heart,[137] content with their pay. How much more, then, should those who fight this glorious fight for God have an undivided heart and be untouched not only by luxury, pleasures, and other similar vices but also by those humbler concerns that, though they do not drag a man towards wrong, nevertheless do divert his mind from the loftiness that is required in a preacher. The warrior for Christ[138] is anyone

* * * * *

240 n24: '"*Praecipuum*": the original meaning of this term denotes that which is received from an inheritance before the general distribution.'

134 Ecclus 2:12, 1:28 *et ne accesseris ad illum duplici corde*

135 Cf 1 Cor 15:22, 45.

136 See Luke 21:34; see Nestle-Aland 231, where the reading in Greek is βιωτικαῖς.

137 Cf 2 Tim 2:3–4 'The soldier's aim is to please the enlisting officer.'

138 'Militat quidem Christo, quisquis illi dedit nomen in baptismo, sed *praecipue*, cui in alios commissus est gladius spiritus, quod est verbum Dei' (emphasis added); cf 2 Tim 2:3 'a good soldier of Christ Jesus.' For the currency of these metaphors in early Christianity, see Adolf von Harnack *Militia Christi: The Christian Religion and the Military in the First Three Centuries* trans David McInnes Gracie (Philadelphia c 1981). See of course *Enchiridion* CWE 66 1–127. Erasmus employs the Latin word *praecipue* in reference to this most important duty; the principle duty of the bishop is teaching (*in episcopo, cuius praecipuae partes sunt docere populum*), a crucial theme of *Ecclesiastes*.

who has signed on in baptism, but especially one to whom the sword of the Spirit, which is the word of God, has been entrusted against others.

Also relevant to pureness of heart is the fact that it is not enough for a herald of the divine word to be pure of every crime[139] unless, as St Paul advised, he also keeps himself from every appearance of evil, so as not to incur the suspicion of wrong in any regard. In a bishop, whose special role is to teach the people,[140] the apostle requires such purity of life and such prudence that he is approved even by the witness of those who are outside;[141] for outstanding virtue has the property of being venerated even by the wicked when closely inspected. Thus the wicked prophet Balaam[142] saw and praised the camp of the Israelites though paid to curse them; thus Pilate revered and, so far as he could, protected the innocence of Christ, which shone in his whole face;[143] thus the people of Jerusalem stood in such awe of Christ's disciples so that no one dared join them – though this was said particularly of those who had not yet believed.[144] Yet even then the people glorified them, not only because of their miracles but much more because of their admirable humility in such power, because of the astounding zeal they displayed amid such afflictions, because their minds showed no trace of greed or boastfulness but were open and ready to benefit everyone without charge.[145] Indeed we often read even in the histories of the heathens that certain people were honoured for an appearance of outstanding virtue. Diogenes, captured as a spy in the camp of King Philip of Macedon, not only was not punished for reproaching the armed king for his madness but was even sent away with a reward;[146] he also escaped punishment for not rising

* * * * *

139 Cf 1 Thess 5:22; Titus 1:7 'blameless.'
140 This phrase will appear in the Council of Trent's decree on preaching (*Decretum secundum publicatum in eadem quinta sessione super lectione et praedicatione*, 17 June 1546), which essentially reiterates Erasmus' teaching and emphasis on the fundamental role of the bishop as teacher (*hoc est praecipuum episcoporum munus*). See *Concilium Tridentinum* v 241–3, especially 242. See McGinness 'Erasmian Legacy' 98–100.
141 1 Tim 3:7
142 Cf Num 22–4. Balaam was a prophet called by the king of Moab to curse the Israelites, but his curses turned out as blessings. 2 Pet 2:15–16, Jude 11, and Rev 2:14 speak of him as typifying the false prophets who lead others astray.
143 Cf Luke 23:1–25; Matt 27:1–2, 11–26; Mark 15:1–15; John 18:28–19:16.
144 Acts 5:13
145 Acts 5:12–16
146 For this story of Diogenes and Philip, here somewhat modified by Erasmus, see Plutarch *Moralia* 606.16B, 70.30C; and Diogenes Laertius *Vitae philosophorum* 6.2.43. Neither author says that Diogenes was rewarded for his remark.

to meet and not answering respectfully Philip's son Alexander, a youth so ambitious that he had imagined an empire of the whole world.[147] Would it not have been thoroughly human if so mighty a monarch had scorned the Cynic in turn for revenge? He did not scorn him, but to those who urged him in this direction he replied, 'Were I not Alexander, I should wish to be Diogenes,'[148] assigning to the Cynic beggar a place of dignity next to himself. If the unreal shadow and false image of virtue has such power, how strong will be the heroic and true virtue of the divine spirit shining in the speech, life, and face of the preacher?[149]

There is one who said with supreme confidence, 'Who among you will convict me of sin?'[150] and again, 'The prince of this world has come and in me he has not found anything.'[151] And yet that purest lamb,[152] walking about and helping everyone without recompense, teaching with such mildness, did not escape the calumnies of men, was called a companion of publicans,[153] a drinker of wine, a seducer of the people, a Samaritan and a demoniac,[154] a blasphemer, and worthy of stoning:[155] by how much less[156] should this be hoped for by a mere man who, while reproving others' vices in accordance with his office, is himself not wholly pure of vice. Nevertheless, as far as human weakness can bear, the preacher must strive to come as near to the patience of Christ as he does to his purity and innocence. He was obedient to his Father to the point of death upon the

* * * * *

147 Plutarch *Alexander* 14.1–2; see Erasmus *Apophthegmata* CWE 37 279.
148 Diogenes Laertius *Diogenes* 6.32; Plutarch *Alexander* 14.3
149 Throughout *Ecclesiastes*, especially book 1, Erasmus often uses arguments from the greater and from the lesser as a method of amplification in calling attention to the infinite superiority of spiritual over temporal things: eg 'Since men of this world seek this thoughtfulness in cases of this world, how much more should it be required in a preacher; there one man's farm or rank is lost through an orator's lack of thoughtfulness, here countless souls are in danger.' For other methods of amplifying and attenuating, see Quintilian 8.4.1–14. Cf *De copia* CWE 24 377–8, 592–5, 616–20; and *De conscribendis epistolis* CWE 25 90–3.
150 John 8:46
151 John 14:30
152 John 1:29, 36
153 Matt 11:19
154 John 8:48
155 John 10:33
156 Erasmus gives an instance here of argument 'by the lesser' (*a minore*): 'all the less ... by how much less.' See Erasmus' exposition of various types of methods of this type and others in *De copia* CWE 24 572–659. See also Lausberg §420. Erasmus notes that 'there are just as many ways of toning down what we have to say as there are of building it up' (CWE 24 594 lines 31–2.)

cross;[157] let the preacher likewise strengthen his heart against all of Satan's devices, which are most numerous and most sharp against those who sincerely provide the thing that rescues the greatest number of people from his tyranny and claims them for Christ's domain. The Christian church has nothing more wholesome, nothing more useful, nothing more effective than the word of God, and there is nothing to which Satan is more hostile. But there is no reason for the preacher to become downcast. It is the Lord who gives the word to those who preach the Good News with great power;[158] it is he who grants that the good seed, cast in good faith, grows in its time,[159] he who grants that the strivings of the wicked brighten the glory of God and strengthen his teaching,[160] he who by his own power strengthens human weakness so that it is equal to or rather superior to all the storms of temptations.[161] The Lord indeed was completely pure of every blemish, even of the slightest fault;[162] while this should be desired by all preachers and striven for so far as strength allows, yet I do not think that it can be achieved by anyone (I always except the Virgin Mary, whom one should never mention when discussing vice).[163] With divine aid he will at least achieve purity from capital sins and vices;[164] but if human frailty has not always avoided even these, the next best thing is that it beware of those that the trumpet of foul repute[165] could betray to the people.

Such are luxury and daily drunkenness, notorious adultery, open debauchery, brawls, quarrels;[166] for these strip all credibility and authority from a preacher even though he teaches what is right. Who would believe that someone who lives this way is advocating virtue sincerely? Serving

* * * * *

157 Phil 2:8
158 Ps 68:11 (Vulg 67:12)
159 Cf Matt 13:24–30.
160 Cf 2 Cor 4:4.
161 Cf 1 Cor 10:13.
162 Heb 4:15
163 Erasmus follows Augustine closely; see Augustine *De natura et gratia* 42 [xxxvi] PL 44 267; NPNF 1st series 5 135: 'We must except the holy Virgin Mary, concerning whom I wish to raise no question when it touches the subject of sins, out of honour to the Lord; for from Him we know what abundance of grace for overcoming sin in every particular was conferred upon her who had the merit to conceive and bear Him who undoubtedly had no sin.' See also *De puritate tabernaculi* CWE 65 240 and n94.
164 Cf Titus 1:6–7.
165 See Juvenal *Satires* 14.152 *Sed qui sermones, quam foedae bucina famae!*
166 Cf Titus 1:6–9. Erasmus is expanding the prohibitions that Paul lists in his letter to Titus; cf 1 Tim 3:1–10.

Mammon[167] is no lesser vice than keeping a mistress, yet the latter incurs more contempt; ambition is a more dangerous evil than drunkenness, but among men the latter weakens a man's reputation more than the former. The wrongs of a past life reduce a teacher's authority also, except that those committed before baptism are usually neither defended nor taken into account unless there is a relapse, and sins committed in adolescence are more easily erased if adolescence is followed by a sober and strict early manhood.

Furthermore, the preacher must also consider that some things, because they present a bad appearance, are not free from the suspicion of wrong even though they do not involve wrong. The preacher must circumspectly beware of these as well, such as possessing wealth, building too lavishly, dressing too elegantly, dining too richly, growing merry over wine, having friendly relationships with women; these are not wrong in themselves, but to the common man, who is spiteful and more ready to rebuke than to submit, they offer matter for adverse suspicion and adverse talk. For this reason Paul does not admit to the office of bishop a man who, upon the death of a wife whom he had married before his baptism, married another woman after his baptism:[168] not because there is any wrong or blame here but because, since modesty wins a teacher the greatest authority, the second marriage offers some suspicion of incontinence. It is not remarkable if a man who has not experienced the unhappiness of wedlock aims at marriage and if someone who desires children and heirs seeks a wife with honourable motive; but, just as the comic poet says that 'It is shameless for one who is shipwrecked a second time to blame Neptune,'[169] so a man who seeks marriage again after experiencing wedlock and having children is somehow admitting his own incontinence; thus there is a danger of his marrying a third or a fourth wife and becoming a subject of humour and talk among the people without doing anything wrong (even among the pagans a plurality of wives always had a bad reputation) or of his hunting a cure for his incontinence in other men's wives if his own grows tiresome. Paul, in fact, instructs all Christians to refrain from every appearance of evil,[170] since in those days the novelty and rarity of Christians had the gaze

* * * * *

167 Cf Matt 6:24; Luke 16:13. Jesus speaks of Mammon as the personification of greed. Paul says, 'The love of money is the root of all kinds of evil' (1 Tim 6:10).
168 1 Tim 3:2; see *Paraphrasis in epistolam Pauli apostoli ad Timotheum priorem* CWE 44 18–19.
169 Publilius Syrus 331; see also *Adagia* IV v 62.
170 1 Thess 5:22

of the whole world turned upon it as though set upon a stage,[171] and so the wicked life of anyone who professed Christ did no small damage to the gospel; even today, of course, it does no small damage when, with the Christian religion reduced to such straits,[172] our own morals alienate still more from the fellowship of the Catholic church the Turks, Mohammedans, Jews, and other nations who either are completely ignorant of Christ or have embraced him in part. If only in the lands that are avowedly under ecclesiastical jurisdiction there were fewer who are more truly Christians in name than in fact, not to mention the great weakness that is nearly universal.

For these reasons the preacher, as he goes forth to this theatre and draws everyone's eyes upon himself, must be keener of sight than Argus[173] in order not to do through thoughtlessness anything that could diminish the profit of the Lord, who is very eager for this gain but wants it to increase day by day through his servants.[174] In fact, he can raise for himself the sons of Abraham from the very cobblestones of the streets,[175] and no one doubts that he is capable of still greater things than this; but his incomprehensible wisdom had decreed to bestow his gifts upon men through men, and no devout person asks why he so decreed, provided he believes that the author of this plan is infinite wisdom, infinite power, infinite goodness, so that it is wrong to doubt that whatever the Best wills is best, that whatever the Most Wise has determined is most wise, that the Almighty will achieve whatever he has determined howsoever he has determined it. And so the preacher who is in charge of the wealth of such a Lord must be free from all personal concerns and wholly intent upon the profit of him to whom everything is owed.[176]

* * * * *

171 Erasmus might have in mind here the story of Ananias and Sapphira (Acts 5:1–11), which is followed by the passage that 'among the people ... none of the rest dared to join them, but the people held them in high esteem ...' (Acts 5:11–13).

172 Erasmus elaborates on this below; see 357–8.

173 This is the mythological creature of one hundred eyes used by Juno to keep watch on Io after Jupiter had her turned into a heifer; Jupiter later ordered Mercury to kill him, and Juno (Saturnia) placed his eyes in the tail feathers of the peacock. See Ovid *Metamorphoses* 1.568–779; Plutarch *Moralia* 93c; *De copia* CWE 24 467; OCD 105.

174 Cf the parable of the talents in Matt 25:15–20 and Luke 19:12–24.

175 Cf Matt 3:9.

176 Cf Matt 25:15–20 and 1 Cor 9:19.

And there is no reason for him to say, 'Shall I teach the unteachable? Shall I labour for the ungrateful? Shall I sing to the deaf?[177] Shall I do good to the wicked?' After all, he who is infinitely greater than you did this, stretched out his hands all his life to an unbelieving and resistant people,[178] and never ceased sowing good seed, though he knew that it would not yield a harvest in everyone's heart.[179] He cultivated a vineyard that instead of sweet grapes brought forth bitter wild ones;[180] why are you slow to do this, when you do not know the outcome of your sowing? The business of casting seed, planting, and watering has been entrusted to you,[181] the outcome is in the hand of God; whatever it is like, he will never fail to reward you for performing in good faith the labour due to the Lord of the farm, though you are only a farmer casting another's seed into another's land.

As the Apostle says, 'The one thing desired in a steward is that he be found faithful.'[182] If among men this is required of those who have undertaken the management of lowly matters, how much more will God require this fidelity of those to whom he has entrusted the management of his mysteries![183] Someone who calls himself a steward knows that he is handling another's property, to be managed for the use of the household according to his master's expressed opinion. If he does not transgress from his lord's commands but completes his assignment zealously and in good faith, his own reward is secure even if what he does fails to succeed; the entire loss is his master's and cannot be imputed to the zealous steward. But if he does not pay out what he has received to pay out, or spends it otherwise than instructed (for each is an equal fault), far from receiving a reward, he will have to be summoned for punishment.[184] 'If I preach the gospel, it is no glory to me,'[185] says Paul: I carry on another's business under the Lord's auspices. I have escaped punishment, not earned praise, if I impart the teaching of the gospel to the Lord's flock only from fear of punishment and under the compulsion of necessity. 'Woe to me,' he says, 'if I do

* * * * *

177 *Adagia* I iv 87
178 Cf Isa 65:2; Rom 10:21.
179 Cf Matt 13:37.
180 Cf Isa 5:1–4.
181 Cf 1 Cor 3:6–9.
182 1 Cor 4:2; cf Luke 12:42–4.
183 Yet another instance of Erasmus' method of argument by comparison by moving from the lesser to the greater.
184 Cf Luke 12:35–48; Matt 24:45–51.
185 1 Cor 9:16

not preach the gospel! For if I do this of my own will, I have a reward; but if otherwise, I am entrusted with a commission.'[186] But who is it who serves willingly as a steward? He who eagerly, who urgently, who not from a love of reward but from an impulse of charity strives with all his might either to draw the greatest number of people to Christ with soft and comforting words, or to drive them to him with threats and accusations, or to lead them to him through instruction; he rejoices no less in his Lord's profit than in his own, if indeed we have any property of our own, we who are the servants of Christ[187] in more ways than one, being first created by him, then redeemed by him, from whose unselfish munificence comes whatever we possess or are.

The management of a household's property used to be entrusted to the slaves who seemed to surpass the rest in intelligence and trustworthiness, and Holy Writ rejoices in designating the ecclesiastical teacher with this term. Thus Paul, speaking about the church, which is the house of God,[188] says, 'of which I became a minister according to the dispensation of the grace of God, which was given to me among you, in order that I might fulfil the word of God,'[189] and again elsewhere, 'if you have heard the dispensation of the grace of God, which was given to me among you.'[190] However, describing to Titus the image of the good teacher, he says, 'A bishop, as God's steward, must be blameless, not arrogant, not quick-tempered, not a drunkard, not violent.'[191] And yet among men the mightier the luminaries they serve, the haughtier are their stewards. Of course man cheats man, and sometimes someone who is treacherous is taken for faithful, but no one can cheat God, who examines the recesses of the heart.[192] In addition, powerful men sometimes fear their own stewards because they are intimate with all their domestic affairs, and sometimes they are overthrown by them; but no one can either deceive or harm God, and no one can escape his vengeance, though here faithless stewards often take to flight seeking safety for themselves. But where will you run to escape the hand of God?[193] 'If you ascend

* * * * *

186 1 Cor 9:16–17
187 1 Cor 9:19
188 Col 1:24; cf Matt 16:18.
189 Col 1:25
190 Eph 3:2
191 Titus 1:7
192 Rom 8:27; 1 Cor 2:10, 14:25; Ps 7:10; Jer 17:10; cf Augustine *Confessions* 3.6.11: 'You though were more inward to me than my most inward self and higher to me than my highest' (*Tu autem eras interior intimo meo et superior summo meo*).
193 Wisd of Sol 16:15; Tob 13:2

to heaven, he is there; if you descend to hell, he is there too.'[194] There is then no reason why any steward under such a Lord should grow proud and arrogant. If you want to be safe, recognize that you are only the manager of another's property, and, the greater you are among men by the dignity of your office, the more humbly you should conduct yourself, not as a huckster but as an honest dealer in the word of God; but if you want to have praise, feed the flock[195] of your Lord with zeal and joy out of the abundance of charity, spending much above what necessity compels you. And so the Apostle liked the title of steward,[196] which urges modesty, deters pride, reminds one of the good faith that is due.

So too St Peter says, '... as every man has received grace, administering to you in turn, like good stewards of the manifold grace of God.'[197] But to understand that the title of steward is being emphasized in order to deter arrogance, listen to what follows soon after in Peter: 'Whoever speaks, let him speak as if speaking the words of God; whoever serves, let him serve as if from the strength that God supplies, in order that God may be glorified in everything through Jesus Christ, to whom belong glory and dominion for ever and ever, amen.'[198]

Again Paul, writing to the Corinthians, says, 'Let a man regard us as ministers of Christ and stewards of God's mysteries.'[199] That heavenly soul was content with the title of minister and steward.

In Luke a gospel parable presents an image of the faithful and the faithless teacher under the appellation of steward ('Who do you think is the faithful and wise steward' etc)[200] and calls 'blessed'[201] the one who performs his duty; the other – who has played tyrant instead of servant and starves those he had undertaken to feed with his master's grain and, not content with this, shows his rage in abusive language and beatings against his fellow servants, male and female, while he himself is well filled with food and drink – is cut into two parts when his master returns sooner than expected and is assigned to the lot of the hypocrites, for a man who behaves differently in his master's absence than in his presence is a hypocrite. Not that

* * * * *

194 Ps 139:7–8 (Vulg 138:7–8)
195 Cf 1 Pet 5:2 and John 21:15–17.
196 'Steward' *dispensator*; Titus 1:7–8; 1 Cor 4:1–2
197 1 Pet 4:10
198 1 Pet 4:11
199 1 Cor 4:1
200 Luke 12:42; Matt 24:45
201 Luke 12:43; Matt 24:46

God is ever absent, but wicked men abuse God's lenience to the point of rashly daring anything, as though he either did not know what men do or left unpunished what is committed against his own commands. If only we saw no ministers of this sort today, πλῆκται 'brawlers,' as the Apostle calls them,[202] fierce and rough in rebuke, looking only to wealth, to green and purple caps,[203] more like wolves[204] than like shepherds towards the Lord's flock.

It must be noted that the word of the gospel requires not only good faith but also good judgment in its steward.[205] Good faith belongs to dovelike simplicity, judgment to the caution of a serpent.[206] Good faith is shown by teaching the people only what the Lord has instructed, by everywhere considering sincerely his glory and the good of his holy flock; the role of judgment is to distinguish according to the circumstances of time, place, and person what is to be applied to whom, at what time, and with what discrimination.[207] Consider how Paul, in whom we see that the greatest simplicity was joined with equal judgment, adapts himself to every circumstance, not

* * * * *

202 1 Tim 3:3; Titus 1:7
203 These caps refer to the *galero*, the traditional green hat of Roman Catholic archbishops and bishops, and the red hat of cardinals. See *Concio, sive Merdardus* CWE 40 959 n75.
204 Cf Matt 7:15, 10:16; Luke 10:3; Acts 20:29.
205 Cf Luke 12:42. *Prudentia* is a favourite word of Erasmus and can take on many meanings depending on the context (thoughtfulness, good sense, prudence, discriminating judgment). Here Erasmus uses the word *prudentia*, rendered here as 'good judgment,' though the term includes a number of its other meanings; it conveys the idea that it is the particular virtue of the 'prudent' person to grasp what is fitting in each specific context. He explains this in the next few lines.
206 Cf Matt 10:16.
207 Erasmus introduces the crucial and recurrent theme of accommodation (*accommodare*), 'to speak aptly' (*apte dicere*), which is a product of the preacher's mature judgment, prudence or counsel that looks to 'circumstances of time, place, and person ...'; it intends what is 'apt' or 'fitting' (*aptum, decorum,* τὸ πρέπον) both as regards the relationship of the parts of the speech to each other and the external 'circumstances of time, place and person.' It also looks to the beneficial and honourable (*utilitas et honestas*). Quintilian considers this 'appropriateness of speech' as 'highly necessary'; see Quintilian 11.1 and passim; see also Cicero *Orator* 70–1. Erasmus returns to this idea in *Ecclesiastes*, often denouncing preachers' faults of 'decorum' as the fundamental error in the preaching of his day. In contrast, St Paul, like Jesus, displayed this excellence in his preaching; see below where Erasmus discusses Paul's preaching and letters (280 and book 3 CWE 68 1006–11). See also *Hyperaspistes* 1 CWE 76 209: 'There was nothing so recondite in Scripture that he [Paul] could not accommodate to proving the gospel.'

always pondering what is allowed but what is expedient,[208] how he at times abases himself,[209] then how he exalts his sublimity in Christ.[210] Sometimes he exercises his apostolic power and threatens the rod of severity,[211] but more often he implores, cajoles, and shows himself more a mother and nurse than an apostle.[212] Sometimes he scolds,[213] then mitigates[214] something that could seem too harshly spoken; some things he defers and puts off to say at a more convenient time.[215] How circumspectly he invites to counsel and perfection,[216] careful all the while not to lay a snare for anyone;[217] sometimes he does not have a commandment of the Lord, but he has nevertheless a useful counsel,[218] like a faithful steward. How cleverly he adapts the witness of Scripture to his present case; how wisely he opens the cloud of allegory when the letter has little significance for piety.[219] Among the perfected he speaks of wisdom hidden in secret;[220] among the weak he knows only Jesus Christ and him crucified.[221] He has milk with which to nourish children; he has solid food to offer adults.[222] He dares resist Peter, chief of the apostles, to his face,[223] supplicates Philemon, and pledges himself as surety for him to welcome back the runaway slave Onesimus.[224] Acting against those who assigned more than was right to the Mosaic rituals, he so exalts faith in Christ and the grace of the gospel in his words that he seems to neglect works of charity;[225] again, challenging those who were not renewing their life because they thought it sufficient to have been baptized and to profess

* * * * *

208 1 Cor 6:12, 10:23
209 Eg 1 Cor 15:9; 2 Cor 11:7, 12:7–11
210 Eg 1 Cor 15:10
211 1 Cor 4:21; 2 Cor 13:2
212 1 Cor 4:14; 2 Cor 6:13; Gal 4:19; 1 Thess 2:7–8
213 Rom 2:5–6
214 2 Cor 7:3
215 Cf 1 Cor 3:1–3.
216 Eg 1 Cor 7:25–40
217 Cf 1 Cor 7:35.
218 Eg 1 Cor 7:25
219 See for example 1 Cor 9:9–10, 10:1–11. See book 3 passim for Erasmus' treatment of allegory.
220 1 Cor 2:6–16
221 1 Cor 2:2
222 1 Cor 3:2
223 Gal 2:11; see Paul's report of this in Galatians 2.
224 Philemon; cf Col 4:9 where he is spoken of by Paul as 'a most beloved and faithful brother.' See *Paraphrasis ad Philemonem* CWE 44 69–74.
225 Galatians 3. Here Erasmus gently criticizes the Reformers' position on *sola fides*; below Erasmus will reiterate his position on 'faith and charity'; see book 3 CWE 68 1019–20.

the name of Christ, he urges them to works of devotion, preferring charity to all gifts, even faith,[226] of which he so often speaks so splendidly.[227]
When talking at Athens before the Areopagus, he takes his exordium from
an inscription on an altar and cites the witness of Callimachus,[228] a most elegant but pagan poet, speaking of Christ in such a way that he calls him
a man only;[229] but when he writes to those who had already received the
teaching of the gospel, how sublime and full of divine majesty is everything that he says about Christ.[230] In the course of accommodating himself
to everyone, then, he is so variable that he sometimes appears to be self-
contradictory and to speak inconsistencies,[231] though he is everywhere quite
consistent with himself; but this is the good judgment of the faithful steward
and manager,[232] as it were, of heaven's rich store.

　　With like judgment the Lord forbids that which is holy to be given to
dogs and pearls to be cast before swine,[233] speaking to the people in parables
which he sometimes did not trouble to explain to his closest disciples;[234]
and after the resurrection he entrusted the grace of the gospel to them for
dispensation in such a way that they preached first at Jerusalem, then in
Samaria, finally among the nations to the ends of the earth.[235]

　　Finally, what does the Scripture of the Old Testament present to us, as
it tempers its speech to the emotions of an unlearned people, now threatening external discomforts, now promising the comfort of this world, if
not an example of the thoughtful steward? Now, if we reflect how much
variety of sex, age, condition, intelligence, opinion, lifestyle, custom exists
within the same population, clearly a preacher must be endowed with great

* * * * *

226 1 Cor 13:1–13
227 See especially Romans 5.
228 Callimachus; see book 3 CWE 68 1009 n1715.
229 Acts 17:22–3, 16–34; see *Paraphrasis in acta apostolorum* CWE 50 107–111. Eras-
　　mus analyses Paul's speech in book 3 CWE 68 1006–11. For Folly's view of Paul
　　citing the words of the Greek poets in Acts 17, see *Moria* CWE 27 145.
230 Eg Phil 2:6–11; Col 1:15–20; Ephesians 1
231 Cf Rom 3:4 and 1 Cor 13:2; Rom 3:31 and Gal 5:2–4.
232 'Steward and manager' (*promus condus*) is a rare word, or rather two words:
　　promus 'one who takes out of storage,' and *condus* 'one who puts back into
　　storage.' Erasmus has borrowed it from comedy, where it refers to the slave
　　in charge of stores of food and wine (cf Plautus *Pseudolus* 608); hence the
　　subsequent apologetic 'as it were.' Cf Matt 24:45, 25:21, 23.
233 Matt 7:6
234 Matthew 13
235 Acts 1:8

judgment.[236] For he must so temper his speech that he does not give to some a handle for error while healing the errors of others, or teach vice while denouncing vice, or arouse sedition while boldly denouncing crime. Rhetoricians say that no one speaks well unless he speaks appropriately,[237] even though he also speaks elaborately, eloquently, and splendidly, and they demand that the rules of art should yield to good sense, which they divide into *iudicium* [judgment] and *consilium* [discretion], skills that cannot be imparted by instruction but are derived from the orator's intelligence and are adopted from the circumstances of the case.[238]

They deem, however, that there is not so much difference between *iudicium* and *consilium* – and no wonder, since to the ancients the verb *consulere* meant 'to decide,' hence the *consulta*, 'the decisions' of the Senate and also, if I am not mistaken, the title *consuls*.[239] Now, if there is any difference, it is that we apply 'judgment' to what is obvious and plain but use 'discretion' in more uncertain and doubtful matters which are sometimes brought in from far outside the case. For example, the art of rhetoric has instructed you to use an exordium to prepare the mind of your listener before the case, but the orator, after considering the circumstances of the case, sees that he should either forgo the exordium completely or make it through 'insinuation.'[240] That you may call judgment. But the fact that Cicero preferred to shorten his speaking time against Verres,[241] even though it otherwise served

* * * * *

236 Erasmus returns to the most important skills of the preacher, above all that of 'thoughtfulness' or 'prudence' or 'discretion,' which is central to accommodation; see n205 above.

237 Cf Quintilian 11.1.1–2: 'The appropriateness of speech (*ut dicamus apte*), which Cicero shows to be the fourth department of style, and which is, in my opinion, highly necessary.' Erasmus returns to this in book 3 CWE 68 1018.

238 Both judgment and discretion are the two components of *prudentia*, which here is often rendered as 'judgment.' The distinction between 'judgment' (*iudicium*) and 'discretion' (*consilium*) is explained by Quintilian 6.5.4. The former deals with evident facts; *consilium* is more a matter of strategy and tact, which takes into account the general circumstances of the case. It is difficult to find suitable English equivalents that fit all uses of these terms in this passage. See Quintilian 6.5.2–11 and 11.1.1–93; Cicero *Orator* 70–1.

239 On the derivation of *consul* from *consulo*, see Quintilian 1.6.32; OCD 286 *consul*.

240 'Insinuation' is a technical term in rhetoric meaning an indirect way of introducing a speech with the aim of gaining the favour of the judges. See Quintilian 4.1.41–50 and *Rhetorica ad Herennium* 1.4.6, 1.6.9–10.

241 Erasmus refers to Cicero's oration *In Verrem* (70 BC) but is following Quintilian 6.5.4. For Cicero's reasons for shortening his opening address, see L.H.G.

the building of his case to draw it out, rather than fall into the year in which Hortensius was going to be consul, since the authority of a consul as advocate would have helped Verres' case – that is considered an example of *consilium*. But it is enough for now to have touched on this briefly; an opportunity to say more will be given when we arrive at technical instruction.[242] Without judgment, however, the precepts of the art are so useless that some have thought that rhetoric is precisely judgment in speaking.[243]

But good judgment, though it is strengthened by both instruction and practice, nevertheless comes from nature above all; hence that true saying that the art of speaking is learned either quickly or never.[244] If that natural judgment is present, precepts are recognized rather than learned; if it is not present, art makes us speak worse and more tiresomely. Just as none reason more ineptly than those who are naturally slow and have learned dialectic by rote, so too none speak more ineptly than those who religiously observe the rhetoricians' instructions without Minerva's favour,[245] as the saying goes, for often the greatest art is to neglect art.[246] Since men of this world seek good judgment in cases of this world, how much more should it be required in a preacher; there one man's farm or rank is lost through an orator's lack of judgment, here countless souls are in danger.

Consider now, please, how dangerous it is when young men are admitted indiscriminately into the pulpit, who are sometimes more than half foolish by nature, with no experience of practical affairs, no judgment, trained neither in secular nor in sacred literature, sometimes (as we have not infrequently seen) laden with food and drink, and even if there is no hangover darkening their mental vigour, all that they bring to their speaking is their clerical garb and their impudence. I have heard some preachers who were already so close to obvious delirium that they were abandoned by their congregation in derision.[247] It is not enough, therefore, to know what must

* * * * *

Greenwood's introduction to *Cicero: The Verrine Orations* I Loeb Classical Library 221 (Cambridge, Mass and London 1928; repr 1989) ix–xix.

242 See book 2 CWE 68 510–37.

243 'judgment in speaking' (*dicendi prudentiam*); cf Cicero *Ad Brutum* 6.23: 'For no one can be a good speaker who is not a sound thinker.' See also *De oratore* 3.14.55; Quintilian 2.20.12–17.

244 Cicero *De oratore* 3.36.146

245 For 'without Minerva's favour,' see *Adagia* I i 42 (CWE 31 91, especially n42).

246 Cf *Rhetorica ad Herennium* 4.7.10; Cicero *Orator* 23.78; *De oratore* 2.41.177; Quintilian 4.1.56–7 and 4.2.58–60.

247 The impact of Erasmus' treatise relies partly on bringing to light the faults of contemporary preachers, as he does throughout. See above n13; see also *Moria*

be said unless you consciously distinguish when, before whom, how, with what words, in what order, with what figures, with what facial expression, with what gestures it must be said. This kind of good judgment[248] is so important that the same case earns applause if pleaded by one man, is hissed off if pleaded by another. Yet I do not deny that in a sacred orator judgment is a gift of the Holy Spirit;[249] but that Spirit tempers its force according to the organ that it has found, especially now that miracles have all but ceased,[250] so that a future preacher not only needs to be trained but also must be chosen for his obvious fitness for the office. No one is unaware that God can give a human voice even to a she-ass,[251] but no one would train as a preacher a person short of breath, with a poor voice or weak lungs or a hesitant and stumbling tongue, or someone of exceptional ugliness with no memory. But these flaws, which can still be repaired in part because they are external, affect us more strongly, while we overlook mental stolidity, poverty of judgment, anger, intemperance, stupidity, a runny and sieve-like memory, and other faults of this kind because they are not immediately obvious to the eye, though there is far more weight in the latter than in the former. St Chrysostom has much to say on this; he constantly draws attention to the good judgment and tactics of St Paul;[252] the Holy

* * * * *

CWE 27 132–5; *Colloquia* (*Concio, sive Merdardus*) CWE 40 938–62; and *Ciceronianus* CWE 28 384–5 for Bulephorus' disgust with a sermon at the papal court. But see especially John O'Malley who observes that Erasmus' judgment on the quality of the sermons at the papal court was 'simply wrong' (*Praise and Blame* 30–1).

248 Latin *prudentia*

249 Cf Acts 2:4. Erasmus raises the complicated theological question here of the Holy Spirit's activity in assisting the preacher. Though he never analyzes this matter in *Ecclesiastes*, he provides numerous ways of considering what must be taken as a given; for even in the most deplorable situations, one cannot deny that the Holy Spirit is not somehow at work, as his example of Balaam's she-ass demonstrates (see Numbers 22).

250 Erasmus expresses his view that, after Jesus' earthly ministry and the age of the apostles, Christ's work continues in the church through the ministry of preaching; and for this God uses each preacher according to his nature and capacity. This treatise aims at identifying those who 'seem fitted by nature for this office' and providing direction.

251 See Num 22:28 where 'the Lord opened the mouth of the [Balaam's] ass ...'

252 See eg John Chrysostom *De incomprehensibili dei natura homiliae* 1–5 PG 48 701–48; *On the Incomprehensible Nature of God* trans Paul W. Harkins FOC 72, *Homily* I 51–2, *Homily* V 137–8; *Homily* XXXIV (Acts 15.35) NPNF 1st series 11 212–19; *Homily* XXIX (1 Cor 12:1–2) NPNF 1st series 12 168–75.

Spirit did not take away this power, which was inborn in him by nature, but perfected it.[253]

The chief qualities[254] to be sought in a preacher are that he have a heart clean of all vices and human desires; that he have a life blameless and free not only from wrongdoing but also from any suspicion or appearance of wrongdoing; that he have a spirit strong, adamantine, and unshakeable against all of Satan's tricks; that he have a mind fiery and burning to benefit everyone; that he have the wisdom to season the folly of the people; that he have a wise and keen intelligence to distinguish readily what must be kept silent, what spoken, and before whom, at what time, in what way his speech should be adjusted: someone who, with Paul, knows how to change his voice and become all things to all people,[255] whenever he sees that this is expedient[256] for the salvation of his audience. For this should be the sole target to which the preacher directs all his considerations; if you deflect your gaze from it, the better trained you have been in speaking, the greater the danger you bring upon the Lord's flock. A voluble tongue, a melodious quill,[257] strong lungs, faithful memory, knowledge of Scripture are only wine blended with hemlock if sincerity of heart is absent, for this mixture makes the poison more potent. Therefore, as I began to say before, just as the most abundant profit comes to the church from devout preachers, so the greatest danger comes from wicked ones. But this outstanding ability is not given by man to man, and no one gives it to himself; it must be sought from God, and not only sought urgently in prayers but also solicited by pious works.[258]

* * * * *

253 See eg John Chrysostom *Homily* XXIX (1 Cor 12:1–2) for the idea of the Spirit perfecting our natural talents (NPNF 1st series 12 168–75).
254 Erasmus summarizes the qualities desirable in the preacher; cf Quintilian 1.Pr.9: 'My aim, then, is the education of the perfect orator. The first essential for such an one is that he should be a good man, and consequently we demand of him not merely the possession of exceptional gifts of speech, but of all the excellences of character as well.'
255 1 Cor 9:22
256 Cf 1 Cor 6:12. The rhetorical idea of 'the expedient' or 'beneficial' (*utilitas*), like 'the honourable' (*honestas*), falls under the category of 'the appropriate' (*aptum*); both go hand in hand in preaching.' See below books 3 and 4 passim. See also Quintilian 11.1.8–9: 'Whatever is becoming is, as a rule, useful . . .'; he concedes however that if the two are at variance 'expediency must yield to the demands of what is becoming.'
257 For the image of the tongue as a *plectrum* 'quill,' see 258–9 n61 above.
258 Another instance of Erasmus distancing himself from Luther's theology.

There are however two kinds of good works, of which one is akin to ceremonies and pertains to bodily exercise[259] (I gladly use Paul's term), the other bears more upon spiritual devotion. Of the former sort are abstention from the richer foods, frequent fasting, sleeping upon the ground, vigils, hair shirts, humble dress, enduring heat and cold, long prayers, the requirement to live according to a man's prescriptions, and other things like these that in a way bridle the flesh, which in a preacher should be vigorously tamed and subdued and, as Paul says, 'reduced to servitude'[260] to prevent it rampaging against the spirit. Of the latter sort are those with which that excellent fashioner of disciples[261] especially trained his own followers and from which a good tree is especially known.[262] And what are these? That the mind be strengthened and fortified against anger and hate, against desire for vengeance, against all human vainglory and shame alike, and against all the spiritual tricks with which Satan often casts down even outstanding men. Hence the preacher, before he enters this theatre, should particularly reflect upon the following: first, that he be poor in spirit,[263] opposed to all empty glory,[264] not hunting praise from men here but content with what the Lord promised when he said, 'For of such as these is the kingdom of heaven'; next, that he be meek in face of all the injuries of the wicked,[265] not regarding the prizes of this world but ignoring them all and hastening to the recompense that Christ promises to such men when he affirms that they will possess the earth, not this one that we hold in common with cattle and snakes but that solid and unchangeable, blessed immortality. And let him not think that it is enough to strengthen his mind so that he neither demands glory from men for his deserts nor seeks vengeance for his injuries, unless he remains keen even in affliction, content with the solace of the Spirit whose kindness even here sometimes softens the bitterness of temptations so that they can be borne until the coming of the joy that is soured by no bitterness of pain.[266] Let him hunger, let him thirst in this life for righteousness

* * * * *

259 Cf 1 Tim 4:8.
260 1 Cor 9:27
261 Ie Christ.
262 Matt 12:33; Luke 6:44
263 Matt 5:3. Erasmus' description of these excellent qualities in the preacher coincides with the beatitudes preached by Jesus in the Sermon on the Mount (Matt 5:1–12); Erasmus finds the embodiment of these qualities in Paul.
264 Gal 5:26; Phil 2:3
265 Matt 5:5
266 Matt 5:4

alone:[267] that is, let him desire the widest possible advancement of the fruit of gospel piety, in the knowledge that he will soon be satisfied to fullness with a heavenly banquet and the new wine that is drunk in the kingdom of heaven. It is a lofty soul that is touched by no desire for glory, is moved from its mental tranquillity by no human effrontery, is not only not dejected in exile, pillage, prison, torture, and death but remains ever eager, partly from the security of a good conscience, partly from the expectation of eternal happiness, and is slowed by no allurements or bogies of human life from the course of devotion and a most fervent zeal to help all mankind; but it is a loftier mind that returns good will for ill will, a friendly word for abuse, blessings for curses. At this point someone might say, 'Everyone knows that; give us something new.' I am aware that these sentiments are daily sung in the churches, recited in the monasteries, heard in sermons, read in the gospels; but those who practise these often-heard ideas carefully and conscientiously are, alas, too rare, though in fact it is these things that make a preacher truly great like the apostles, while it is possible to see not a few who conduct themselves diligently in the former sort. You may find many who are pale from eating beans and fish, wasted from fasting, worn out with vigils and toil, shabby in humble clothes, scarred from hard bedding and hair shirts; but how few you will find to preach the gospel without recompense, to bear insults calmly, to overcome their tormenter with kindness when provoked by an insult. This of course is the devotion that St Paul preaches is useful for everything, while exercising of the body produces little of use:[268] little, however, not in an absolute sense (let no one think that what tames the wantonness of the flesh should be neglected); they have little utility if they are not applied as though in a subordinate capacity to those proofs of true devotion, but considerable utility if they aim at this and prepare for it. Someone who leads an austere and ascetic life only in order to become accustomed to being content with little is accomplishing nothing of significance (philosophers who did not know Christ did the same); but someone who trains his body to endurance in order not to delay his spirit's rush towards those sublime duties of evangelical devotion is accomplishing something exceedingly useful.[269] Four things, however, should be avoided: haughtiness, superstition, perverse judgment, and neglect of moderation.

We see that both in the past and today people are most puffed up by those external tokens of righteousness that win favour in the sight of men.

* * * * *

267 Matt 5:6
268 'The devotion' (*pietas*); 1 Tim 4:8
269 Cf Phil 3:12–14; 1 Cor 9:24–7.

Superstition enters unseen in various ways, for instance when these things are observed in a Judaic spirit[270] (as if a kind of food of itself purifies or taints a man),[271] or when a man prescribes these things for himself not for use but for some superstitious feeling, just as there used to be some who in place of wine and water sipped (rather than drank) the juice of herbs, not from a cup but from a shell, though it is both simpler and more useful to drink plain water instead of wine. And it was not without superstition that some used to count their days of fasting, for three days, for a week, for forty days, sometimes for a whole lifetime; for fasting is not to be applied in accordance with a specified number, as in magic, but in accordance with what is useful to body and soul. Hence those who fast in this way behave no less foolishly than those who drain their cups not according to the measure of their thirst but to a specified number, now five, now three, now nine, when everyone should drink as much as suffices for slaking the thirst.

Errors are made through perverse judgment whenever more importance is assigned to what is of lesser moment and less to what is more pertinent to a subject. It is unnecessary to give examples of this since they are apparent everywhere, yet I shall point out one to clarify what I am saying. Many are deeply troubled if they have accidentally tasted meat on a Friday;[272] but the same people are not offended with themselves if by their slanders they have harmed the reputation of a neighbour and caused him sorrow. They tremble pathetically if they have had occasion to put off their sacred garment, but they do not tremble if through drunkenness, greed, hatred, envy they have cast off the white robe of the soul that Christ gave them in baptism and put on the black garb of Satan.

But perhaps not many err in this way since the mass of humanity is more drawn to the sweet than to the bitter. Here too, however, significant errors are committed, sometimes even by great men, Basil the Great and Gregory of Nazianzus among them, if it is true, as the latter relates, that each of them had brought ill health upon himself by fasts, drinking water, vigils, bedding on the ground, and other extreme forms of austerity; the result was that for Basil life was bitter and death desirable, while Gregory was compelled to resign the office of bishop because he lacked the physical strength to carry out a bishop's duties.[273] St Jerome does not hide

* * * * *

270 Erasmus opposes the spirit and the letter, as does Paul (1 Cor 8:8, 10:25–6); see eg *Colloquia (Convivium religiosum)* CWE 39 188.
271 Cf Matt 15:10–20; Mark 7:14–23.
272 Cf *De esu carnium* ASD IX-1 19–50.
273 Basil, bishop of Caesarea (c 329–79), one of the four doctors of the Eastern

the fact that among monks there were some who so damaged their health by the dampness of their cells, continual recitation of the Psalms, and excessive fasting that they had greater need of Hippocrates' poultices than of his own teaching.[274] In fact I myself know many others whom an excessively austere lifestyle has rendered useless for every important function, and in particular a certain theologian, a man otherwise good and uncommonly learned, who, after receiving his doctorate in theology at Paris, was given a canonry (or a preacher's prebend,[275] as they now call it) in a busy cathedral church; but this devout man determined, despite his change in station, to relax none of the former austerity in which he had trained. Within a few years he became so disabled that he contracted leprosy.[276] I know another[277] too who suddenly changed his habits when called from poverty to a similar station and began to feast, to pursue wealth, to keep a mistress, to stir rebellion against the bishop by whom he had been elevated, being scarcely tolerable even to the prince's court because of his arrogance. Each erred, the former with more honourable appearance than the latter, but the fruit of devotion withered in each alike, except that it did so still more in the former.[278] But there is a middle way between Scylla and Charybdis.[279] In the past it was those especially who were commended by the austerity of the life they led that were often summoned to the bishop's chair from the deserts in which the troops of monks led their harsh life,[280] for the unenlightened

* * * * *

church, along with John Chrysostom, Gregory of Nazianzus (329/30–389/90), 'the Theologian,' and Gregory of Nyssa (c 330–c 395). For Basil's austerities and condition, see Gregory of Nazianzus *Oration* 43 (*Panegyric on Saint Basil*) NPNF 2nd series 7 415. For Gregory of Nazianzus, see his *Oration* 42 (*The Last Farewell*) NPNF 2nd series 7 392; for John Chrysostom, see J.N.D. Kelly *Golden Mouth: The Story of John Chrysostom, Ascetic, Preacher, Bishop* (Ithaca 1995) 32–4, 113, 118–9.

274 See Jerome Ep 125.16 NPNF 2nd series 6 249–50.

275 An income or a stipend for a canon or college member that derives from the revenue of a cathedral or collegiate church.

276 Erasmus does not disclose the identity of this individual. Chomarat (ASD V-4 73 804n) notes it is impossible to determine what illness 'leprosy' (*lepra*) means here.

277 Erasmus does not disclose the identify of this individual.

278 The translator has rendered the literal meaning of Erasmus' text, which reads: ... *nisi quod magis etiam in priore*. Erasmus, perhaps in haste, wrote 'former' (*priore*) instead of 'latter' (*posteriore*).

279 See n106 above.

280 On monks' life in late antiquity, see Jerome Epp 22.7, 34, 125.7–17 NPNF 2nd series 6 24–5, 37, 240–50.

multitude judges godliness mostly according to these things. But St Chrysostom frankly confesses that it often happens that those who have been
called to the role of bishop from that kind of life are found to be more inept than others, as they give way to pleasure, swell up at the praise and
flattery of men, are upset even by minor wrongs, are difficult to approach,
sullen and harsh, unfit for every one of life's experiences, too bitter in rep-
rimanding vices;[281] while St Ambrose, though he was not yet reborn in the
sacred bath,[282] showed himself by turns a gentle, hardworking, strong, constant, and unwavering priest when he was called from the secular prefec-
ture to the office of bishop.[283] As to the conduct of Chrysostom, who was
summoned from the law courts,[284] or of Augustine[285] and Cyprian,[286] who
were summoned not from anchorites' cells but from the schools of rhetoric
and everyday life to guide the church, the facts speak for themselves.

I am not saying this as though persons to whom the office of teaching
the people may rightly be entrusted cannot be summoned from retreats and
monasteries (of course truly spiritual minds are found there as well), but in
order to show how different is the training given by John the Baptist and
that of our Lord Jesus Christ. The former, as he prepared his disciples for
their evangelical mission, prescribed fasts, long prayers, a spare and austere
diet, being himself a child of the forests, companion of the beasts, with a
robe woven not from wool but from camel hair, which would surpass the
roughness even of a hair shirt, girt not with a sash of silk or linen but a

* * * * *

281 See John Chrysostom *Treatise concerning the Christian Priesthood* (*De sacerdotio*)
    book 6 NPNF 1st series 9 74–83; PG 48 623–92.
282 Ie baptism.
283 See *Vita sancti Ambrosii* 41–5; Ambrose *De officiis* (*On the Duties of the Clergy*)
    1.1.4 CCSL 15, NPNF 2nd series 10 1; Ambrose *De paenitentia* (*On Repentence*)
    2.8.72 CSEL 73 117, SC 179, NPNF 2nd series 10 354. See Neil B. McLynn *Ambrose
    of Milan: Church and Court in a Christian Capital* (Berkeley and Los Angeles
    1994) especially chapter 1 'The Reluctant Bishop' 1–52.
284 See Chrysostom *On the Priesthood* 1.4 NPNF 1st series 9 33–4.
285 Augustine of Hippo (d 432), bishop, gives an account of this in his *Confessions*;
    see especially books 1–9. Erasmus draws on much of Augustine's teaching on
    rhetoric and Scripture in *De doctrina christiana*; see book 3 passim.
286 Cyprian, bishop of Carthage, former teacher of rhetoric and martyr (d 258),
    known for his eloquence in championing the rebaptism of schismatics who
    had lapsed during the persecution of Decian. Erasmus mentions Augustine
    and Cyprian again below in a similar passage; see 325. See *The Life and Passion
    of Cyprian, Bishop and Martyr* 2 ANF V 267; see also J. Patout Burns *Cyprian the
    Bishop* (London 2002). Erasmus published the works of Cyprian; see *Opera divi
    Caecilii Cypriani episcopi Carthaginensis* ... (Basel: Johann Froben 1520).

plain thong; if you are wondering about his diet, he fed on locusts and drank water,[287] and yet they envy the glory of this disciple of Christ and disparage his disciples. And what of Christ? He found fault neither with John nor his training[288] but inculcated in his disciples above all that they should place all their faith in him, scorn the world with all its delights or terrors, and through disgrace, affliction, and death seek their heavenly reward. This of course is the power of faith; the qualities of charity are that they should be so cleansed of anger, hate, envy, vindictiveness, and ambition that when provoked with evil they return good, love their enemies; that they should show equal benevolence to the worthy and the unworthy; that the greater they are, the more they should lower themselves to everyone in the love of Christ. 'But the disciples of Christ fled and hid when the Lord was seized and killed,'[289] you will say; 'one[290] denied him, and the others would have done the same had a like temptation occurred.' But this was before they had breathed in the principal Spirit[291] and under the duress of sudden fear, which often leaves even strong men senseless. Probably some among John's disciples shouted, 'Take him, take him; crucify him, crucify him';[292] fearing an evil that appears suddenly and inflicting death upon an innocent man are two quite different things. These things did not happen by chance, but a model for imitation was presented to us in them.

John's teaching was just like his baptism. Those who had been washed with John's baptism are baptized anew in the name of Jesus (Acts 19);[293] those who had been imbued with John's teaching need more precise teaching (as at Acts 18).[294] Though Apollo of Alexandria[295] had been taught the way of the Lord by John's disciples, spoke at Corinth burning in the Spirit, taught carefully those things that are God's, and conducted himself in the synagogue with great confidence, he is nevertheless taken away by Priscilla and Aquila and made a pupil instead of a teacher; he learns the way of the Lord more accurately and precisely and probably was rebaptized as well.

* * * * *

287 See Matt 3:1–4; Mark 1:2–8; Luke 3:1–20.
288 Matt 11:7–15; Luke 7:24–35; cf Matt 9:14; Mark 2:18; Luke 5:33.
289 Cf Matt 26:56; Mark 14:50; Luke 23:49.
290 Ie Peter; see Matt 26:69–75; Mark 14:66–72; Luke 22:55–62; John 18:25–7.
291 Acts 2:2–4
292 See John 19:6; Luke 23:21; Mark 15:13–14; Matt 27:22–3.
293 Acts 19:1–5
294 Acts 18:24–8
295 See Acts 18:24–6. Apollo seems to have known only the teaching and baptism of John the Baptist; he was educated by Priscilla and Aquila at Ephesus and then preached at Corinth. See 1 Cor 3:4–6; see also ODCC 86–7.

And in the next chapter the twelve disciples[296] whom Paul finds at Ephesus, who had been washed only in John's baptism, admit frankly, upon being asked by the Apostle whether they had received the Holy Spirit, that they had never even learned that there is a Holy Spirit. Not only do they learn of this Spirit from Christ's disciple, but they also receive it.[297] Let us too, like true and proper disciples of Christ, not be led by perverse judgment but recognize the gulf between the rudiments of devotion and the heavenly philosophy, between the beginning and the culmination, between the founding and the completion; and let us not neglect them through considerations of the moment but hasten with all our heart to the more excellent way that the Lord himself has paved, so that we may finish as heralds of the word such as the apostles were, becomingly adorned on the outside with modesty, sobriety, fasting, vigils, constant prayers, alms, and other good works, but strong on the inside and fortified by the might of the spirit of the gospel. The latter is the soul's sap, the former, so to speak, its flowers and leaves. In the mystical Song,[298] the bride hears the words, 'If you do not know yourself, O beautiful among women, depart and go after the flocks of your companions.'[299] Let the preacher believe that the same has been spoken to his soul: 'If you do not know the role you have taken on, do not be leader of the Lord's flock but rather follow the herdsmen.' The office that you undertake is by far the most difficult, but also much the most glorious.[300] We have already said a great deal about each aspect.

But, to review the same passages, divine Scripture declares openly at Daniel 12 the greatness of the preacher's rank and how much it differs from other functions: 'Those who are learned shall shine like the splendour of the firmament, and those who train many to justice like stars for everlasting eternities.'[301] The firmament itself has much light, but the stars shine conspicuously in it; these differ among themselves in brightness, as the Apostle teaches.[302] The source of all light is the sun, which brightens the whole world by itself, while different stars are visible to or hidden from different

* * * * *

296 Acts 19:7
297 Acts 19:1–7
298 The Song of Songs or The Song of Solomon
299 Song of Sol 1:8
300 Erasmus frequently repeats this theme that the office of the preacher is the most difficult; see eg 365 below: 'The office of preacher, then is very difficult but also very beautiful; the contest is no ordinary one, but the prizes are outstanding.'
301 Dan 12:3
302 See 1 Cor 15:41.

regions; among the lesser stars, moreover, the one with the greatest and most pleasing light is Hesperus, which we also call Venus and Lucifer.[303] I think that all who have believed in the gospel are called 'learned'[304] here; for why should they be called unlearned when from the Apostles' Creed they have learned, if nothing else, that transcendent philosophy[305] that not Pythagoras or Plato but the Son of God himself imparted to mankind, when they know the precepts of both laws, when they have been taught by Christ how they ought to pray, by what path they should strive towards what goal of happiness? How do those who have not learned this believe? On what pretext can those who have learned it and believe be called unlearned and seem to deserve the appellation 'rustic'? If we are willing to admit the truth, there is no holy rusticity, just as there is no rustic holiness; wherever there is true holiness, there is great wisdom and uncommon learning.[306] Yet among these outstandingly learned ones, the ones that excel are those who by the special munificence of the Spirit have received the gift of training many towards righteousness,[307] who have received from the Lord a heart clean in every way,[308] the principal and unconquerable spirit, a serpent's discretion combined with a dove's simplicity,[309] a tongue like the pen of a swiftly writing scribe,[310] lips upon which that persuasive Πειθώ [Persuasion][311] of the

* * * * *

303 Cf Job 38:32 (Vulg *luciferum, vesperum*; LXX ("Εσπερον). See Cicero *De natura deorum* 2.20.53: 'Lowest of the five planets and nearest to the earth is the star of Venus, called in Greek *Phosphorus* (the light-bringer) and in Latin Lucifer when it precedes the sun, but when it follows it *Hesperos*.'

304 Dan 12:3

305 Transcendent philosophy (*ultramundana philosophia*) is another of many variants for Erasmus' 'heavenly philosophy' or 'philosophy of Christ.' Erasmus often gives brief statements of the content of this 'heavenly philosophy'; see eg *Explanatio symboli* CWE 70 358: 'What are Christ's whole life, death, and resurrection, if not a very clear mirror of the philosophy of the gospel?'; and 237 n6; see *Paraclesis* in Olin: 'What else is the philosophy of Christ, which He himself calls a rebirth, than the restoration of human nature originally well formed?'; and Ep 1334:252: 'The sum and substance of our religion is peace and concord.' See also Chantraine passim.

306 Cf 1 John 2:20: 'But you have been anointed by the Holy One, and all of you have knowledge.'

307 Dan 12:3; cf Matt 5:20.

308 Ps 51:10 (Vulg 50:12)

309 Matt 10:16

310 Ps 45:1 (Vulg 44:2)

311 For Πειθώ 'Persuasion personified as a goddess,' see Cicero *De oratore* 2.44.187, and as goddess, Hesiod *Works and Days* 73. See also *Ciceronianus* CWE 28 343 and 545 n11.

heathen does not sit but upon which heavenly grace has been poured from the unction of the Spirit.[312] It is only fair, however, that someone who excels others in the honour of his rank should surpass them in his virtues as well, and it is not enough for him to be good among the bad unless he also appears to be better among the good, brighter among the bright. Unhappy is the condition of the state to which that saying of Isaiah applies, 'And as is the people so will be the priest, and as is the slave so will be his master,'[313] etc. The same prophet, however, marvels at the loftiness of preachers when he exclaims, 'Who are these who fly as clouds do, and like doves to their windows?'[314] Clouds fly aloft to moisten the earth below and render it fertile; teachers of the gospel, however, raised up far from earthly desires and near to heaven, imbue the lowly and infertile minds of man with the rain of the heavenly word, so that once the brambles have been torn out they can produce fruits worthy of God. For it is through them particularly that our earth is either fertile or sterile; they fly like clouds, scattering everywhere the grace of the gospel, but they also fly like doves to their cubbyholes, for they nest not upon the ground but in the clefts of lofty rocks; with their perpetual sighs and prayers they summon towards love of the heavenly life all that creep upon the ground. Joel also saw that the fertility of the church comes from these clouds, and he congratulates our earth when he says, 'Fear not, land, be glad and rejoice,'[315] etc, and later, 'Sons of Zion, be glad and rejoice in the Lord your God, for he has given you a teacher of righteousness, and he will make descend upon you the morning rain and the evening rain in the beginning, and the threshing floors will be filled with grain, and the vats will overflow with wine and oil.'[316]

From the same clouds comes 'the dew of Hermon that descends upon Mount Zion,'[317] from mountain to mountain of course, inasmuch as whoever is in the church is on a mountain, but someone who is to pour out the dew of gospel teaching here must be on a higher mountain. That is the mountain called Hermon, from 'dedication.'[318] 'Dedication' is the name given to

*****

312 Cf Acts 2:4; 1 John 2:20.
313 Isa 24:2
314 Isa 60:8
315 Joel 2:21
316 Joel 2:23–4
317 Ps 133:3 (Vulg 132:3)
318 The etymology of *anathemate* 'dedication' is interesting. Erasmus sees the Greek word ἀνάθεμα as coming from ἄνα 'up, above, from above,' etc and τίθημι 'to place,' thus meaning 'from setting aside or suspending': 'Such are the gifts called which dedicated to the gods are hung on the walls and columns of a

those things that are placed on high and preserved with veneration, are no longer touched by human hands and are not offered for common use as being already consecrated to divinity, are looked at only from afar and arouse reverence in those who see them; such ought to be the life of the preacher. In the tales of the poets[319] Prometheus is fixed upon Mount Caucasus and tormented constantly as an eagle gnaws his liver; but on this mountain there is an end to the grief that arises in human hearts over lesser things, as when a man is saddened by the death of a son, another is upset by the loss of money from theft, another by ill health, another by old age, which removes him from pleasures; for whoever professes himself to be a teacher of this heavenly philosophy, provided this indeed is what he teaches, is above all these emotions. It was upon this mountain that Abraham had ascended, who without hesitation, without sighs, with dry eyes sacrificed his only begotten son Isaac,[320] whom he loved: but perhaps there will be an opportunity elsewhere to speak of these mountains, which mystical Scripture mentions often, declaring to us the eminence of their powers. Let my discourse now return to its purpose.

Let the preacher recognize his worth, but let him remember ever and always that whatever is splendid here is the gift of God, not the excellence of man. Among the prophets of the Old Testament, Isaiah is by far the most eloquent, but he recognizes the author of his great office, saying, 'The Lord has given me a learned tongue that I may know how to sustain with a word him that is weary.'[321] I do not deny, and I am not unaware, that this

* * * * *

temple ...' He gives this explanation in *Annotationes in Lucam* (21.5) ASD VI-5 580: 'Et donis. Ἀναθήμασι. Ea dicuntur dona quae dicata diis suspenduntur in parietibus et columnis templi; cuiusmodi nunc visuntur potissimum iuxta monumenta divorum statuae argenteae, equi aurei, pocula, gemmata, dicta ab ἀναθῆναι, hoc est a seponendo sive suspendendo. Unde et ἀνάθεμα dicitur.' See LSJ 123 ἀνατίθημι for the idea of 'set up as a votive gift, dedicate.' See Jerome *Tractatuum in psalmos series altera* Ps 88:8 CCSL 78 411 209–10 *Hermon anathema interpretatur*; and *In psalmum xxxxi, ad neophytos* PL 40 1203. Augustine gives a different reading; see *Enarrationes in Psalmos* 88:13 CCSL 39 (1228:10–1229:15); and *Exposition 1 of Psalm 88* WSA III-18 283: 'Hermon is interpreted "anathema to him." The light came, and became anathema to him. To whom? To the devil – who else? To the wounded, proud one. By your gift we have been illuminated; by your gift it is that he who once held us prisoners in his error and pride has become anathema to us.'

319 Cf Hesiod *Theogony* 507–616; Aeschylus *Prometheus*.
320 Gen 22:1–10
321 Isa 50:4: 'The Lord hath given me the tongue of those who are taught, that I may know how to sustain with a word him that is weary.' Erasmus emphasizes this important quality in the preacher. Thomas of Celano's *Vita prima* (*The Life*

prophecy particularly fits Christ, but nothing forbids these words applying to the prophet and containing a prophecy about Christ in the character of a prophet; whatever was written about him was undoubtedly written for our instruction.[322] But in this chapter I am, so to speak, sketching the form of the proper preacher, so that it would not be out of place to pause awhile in contemplation of this passage. 'The Lord has given me':[323] you hear at once the irrefutable authority, then the modesty safe from all arrogance, for who would claim for himself what God has given without charge? What did he give? A good mind? All the devout share that. What then? A learned tongue, which is the special gift of preachers; nor does he say a tongue trained in philosophers' syllogisms or adorned with the embellishments of the rhetorician but learned in the speech of the Lord, as was written about Esdra.[324] For what use did he give it? 'That I may know,' he says, 'how to sustain with a word him that is weary.' When you hear 'that I may know,' you understand the knowledge and good sense of the preacher, of which I have said something already. 'That I may know how to sustain with a word him that is weary,' for there is more than one way of sustaining, and the divine word is applied in different ways to different people. And so a tongue has not been given to the preacher to win fame, wealth, and power for himself but to help as many people as possible: 'sustain,' not cast down, unlike the arrogant manner of the Pharisees, to sustain the weary as in the saying, 'On the road, a witty companion is like a carriage.'[325] We have no permanent city here, but we are temporary travellers hastening to our heavenly homeland.[326] The way that leads to life is narrow.[327] Through the wasteland

* * * * *

of Saint Francis, book 2 chapter 5) imputes this great gift to Hugolino, bishop of Ostia (later Pope Gregory IX), who became a close friend of Francis and a special patron of Francis' new order of lesser brethren (*minores*). See *Francis of Assisi: The Saint* I 269, where Thomas of Celano refers to him as 'the least among the lesser.'

322 Erasmus reiterates this as a fundamental principle of scriptural exegesis. Cf Jerome *Commentariorum in Esaiam libri XII–XVIII* 14 4/7 CCSL 73A 552–3. See also Rom 15:4, where Paul states that 'whatever was written in former days was written for our instruction ...'

323 Isa 50:4

324 2 Esd 7:65: 'a learned and skilled priest' (Vulg *sacerdos doctus et eruditus*)

325 Publilius Syrus 116 (*Comes facundus*), cited by Gellius *Noctes Atticae* 17.14.4 and Macrobius *Saturnalia* 2.7.11; see *De copia* CWE 24 643.

326 For 'no permanent city ... heavenly homeland,' see Augustine *De civitate Dei* 15.1 and passim; *Confessions* 10.5.6 and *Sermo* 255 in WSA III-7 158; and Erasmus *Colloquia* (*Convivium religiosum*) CWE 39 194; Luke 10:38–42 and 1 Cor 5:1–2.

327 Matt 7:14

of this world,[328] through spiritual way stations we hurry to that promised land; meanwhile much occurs that tires the travellers, who would surely fail were we not constantly sustained by a learned tongue. Moses led so many thousands of Hebrews out of Egypt; scarcely one would have reached the land flowing with milk and honey[329] had he not repeatedly propped them up with his learned tongue. According to physicians, physical weariness is a sign of imminent disease, mental weariness of fainting. The man who has a learned tongue knows how to head off approaching disease, knows how to sustain the weak in the faith, knows how to nurse infants with milk, knows how to restore to his footing with the spirit of leniency the man who has been caught by sin.

There follows in Isaiah, 'Morning by morning he pricks up, he pricks up my ear, that I may hear him as a teacher.'[330] What is the meaning of that ἀναδίπλωσις [anadiplosis],[331] 'He pricks up, he pricks up, morning by morning'? Human ears are by nature immobile; deer have very acute hearing when they raise their ears and are deaf when they lower them, but our mind has highly mobile ears, which have to be completely erect for it to hear the voice of the Spirit, and so the doubling is emphatic, as in 'morning by morning.' For human disciplines it does not matter how erect the ears are; for this learning the ears must be singularly erect. Yet the only one who can prick them up is God, and unless you learn your lessons from that teacher, it will be useless for you to profess yourself a teacher; as the psalm says, 'But you perfected my ears, then I said, "See, I am coming."'[332] It is useless for us to have ears if God does not perfect them, and they are perfected by faith and obedience. These are the ears of which the Lord says in the Gospel, 'He who has ears to hear, let him hear.'[333] No one says, 'See, I am coming' unless dragged by the ear; the Lord however does not tug at the ear except 'morning by morning,' that is, at the very break of day. Those who profess human disciplines choose the morning hours if they are preparing to teach something rather subtle, because bodies are better disposed at that time and the mind, being freer from intoxication, is more suited to perceive

* * * * *

328 For 'wasteland of this world' (*per desertum huius seculi*), cf Exod 16:35; Deut 2:7; see especially Jerome Ep 125.2 NPNF 2nd series 6 245: 'and the desert of this world is not untenanted by venomous reptiles.'
329 Exod 3:8; Lev 20:24
330 Isa 50:4
331 *Anadiplôsis* is a Greek rhetorical term meaning 'doubling' or 'repetition.'
332 Ps 40:7 (Vulg 39:8)
333 Matt 11:15, 13:9; Mark 4:9; Luke 8:8

subtleties; this is the reason they say that the noble Aristotle commonly lectured on the difficulties of physics only in the morning but taught rhetoric in the afternoon while strolling.[334] But it must be an outstanding morning to make us capable of learning that heavenly philosophy. The Apostle says, 'The night is far gone, the day is at hand, let us cast off the works of darkness';[335] behold the height of morning. 'Those who sleep sleep at night,' he says, 'and those who get drunk are drunk at night.'[336] If a human teacher is reluctant to teach human knowledge (logic or arithmetic, for example) to someone who is sleepy, nodding, or hungover, how much more will heavenly wisdom disdain to speak to men drunk with love for the pleasures of this world, nauseous in their neglect of the heavenly! Thus wisdom, more precious than all wealth, says in Solomon too, 'I love those who love me, and those who have kept watch for me in the morning shall find me,'[337] and a little later, 'Happy is the man who listens to me, and who watches daily at my gates, and who waits before the posts of my door.'[338] This is what lovers do at the door of their mistress, seeking a harmful pleasure that will soon turn to regret; do we then sleep while awaiting that wisdom than which nothing is more lovable? And what does it promise to its lovers? It says, 'He who finds me will find life, and will obtain salvation from the Lord.'[339] In addition, that 'morning by morning' also reminds us that the future preacher should begin right from his very childhood to ponder upon the law of the Lord in order to avoid what we see happen to many; after growing old in the study of secular philosophy or belles-lettres, they prove remarkably uninspired when they try to speak publicly or to write anything about religion.[340] We do most successfully what we have learned to do since

* * * * *

334 According to Gellius *Noctes Atticae* 20.5.1–6, Aristotle taught the 'exoteric' disciplines in the evening, 'which gave training in rhetorical exercises, logical subtlety, and acquaintance with politics ...'; the other subjects ('acroatic' training) were treated in the morning.

335 Rom 13:12

336 1 Thess 5:7

337 Prov 8:17

338 Prov 8:34

339 Prov 8:35

340 Erasmus later develops this idea that the preacher's training should begin very early in life; most important is his instruction in virtue and goodness, which should begin as early as possible; see *De pueris instituendis* CWE 26 318: 'Goodness, then, is best instilled at an early stage, for once a certain pattern of behaviour has been imprinted upon a young and receptive mind, that pattern will remain.' Erasmus praises John Colet who took on this task with the greatest diligence; see *De recta pronuntiatione* CWE 26 377, 379–80, 383.

childhood. Paul praises in Timothy the fact that he had learned Holy Scripture right from his very childhood,[341] that is, 'morning by morning.' It is
also necessary, therefore, to instruct a person destined for the preacher's office to keep watch at the door of hidden wisdom 'in the morning,' that is,
early, 'morning by morning,' that is, in full sobriety, and every day, so that
the Lord may deign to open his ear so that he can hear him as a teacher, not
as an idler hears an itinerant performer or a storyteller but as a true pupil
hears a teacher of the sublime wisdom: with fear, with attention, with obedience. Do you want to hear fear? 'The Lord God has opened my ear,'[342] he
says. Who would not fear such a teacher? Do you want to hear attention? 'I
am not rebellious, I turned not backward.'[343] When will someone who listens carelessly accept responsibility for what he hears? Now listen to obedience: 'I gave my body to the smiters and my cheeks to those who pulled
out the beard, but I did not turn away my face from those who rebuked
and spat upon me.'[344] Behold a heart ready for everything,[345] a heart obedient even unto death.[346] Now hear courage: 'The Lord God is my helper,
and therefore I have not been confounded, therefore I have set my face like
the hardest stone, and I know that I shall not be confounded. He who is to
justify me is at hand; who will contradict me? Let us stand together; who
is my adversary? Let him approach me.'[347] Remarkable confidence! He not
only does not fear his adversaries but even challenges them to meet. But on
what help does he rely? His own? Hardly. 'Behold,' he says, 'the Lord God
is my helper; who is there to condemn me?'[348] Likewise, when St Paul said,
'I can do all things,'[349] he spoke the voice not of confidence but of faith, for
he immediately added, 'in him who strengthens me.' This is the only safe
way to be bold.

The Lord gave a similar tongue and a similar confidence to Jeremiah as
well when he was about to preach to the people. 'And the Lord put forth his
hand and touched my mouth,'[350] he says; behold a clean heart, from which
arises a clean mouth, which only the hand of the Lord gives. There follows,

* * * * *

341 2 Tim 3:15
342 Isa 50:5
343 Isa 50:5
344 Isa 50:6
345 *paratum cor meum*; Ps 57:7 (Vulg 56:8)
346 Phil 2:8
347 Isa 50:7–8
348 Isa 50:9
349 Phil 4:13
350 Jer 1:9

'And the Lord said to me, "Behold, I have put my words in your mouth. Behold, I have set you this day over nations and over kingdoms to pluck up and to destroy and to scatter and to disperse and to build and to plant."'[351] He has embraced the sum of the pastoral office, which resides entirely in first pulling up from the minds of the audience the roots of wicked opinions and the evil seeds of impious doctrine from which bitter fruits grow, and in destroying the building constructed on an evil foundation, dispersing the weeds that have sprouted, scattering the structure badly begun, and sowing a good planting in place of what was torn up and destroyed, and erecting a structure that will give way to no storm. For all this the true preacher uses only the instrument of the tongue, but one that is trained in the word of God, which is 'the divinely inspired Scripture, useful' (as the Apostle says) 'for teaching, for reproof, for correction, for training in righteousness, that the man may be perfect, trained for every good work.'[352] But someone who handles heavenly Scripture with a polluted heart and a polluted mouth is told in the Psalms, 'Why do you relate my justices, and take up my testament through your mouth? You hate discipline, your mouth has overflowed with wickedness,'[353] etc.

The most important thing for persuasion,[354] then, is to love what you are urging; the heart itself supplies ardour of speech to the lover, and it brings the greatest force to effective teaching if you display within yourself whatever you are teaching to others. Consider the very beautiful compliment with which the man who was by far the most praised of all praised, John the Baptist, applies to the good preacher: 'He was a burning and shining lamp.'[355] Burning is first, shining second; fire belongs to the mind, light to teaching. Works too have their light, according to the Lord: 'Let your light shine before men so that they may see your good works.'[356] But just as the light of works without fire is hypocrisy, so teaching is weak and ineffective unless it proceeds from a burning spirit. For who will believe a man who praises modesty and sobriety but keeps concubines at home, who habituates unrestrained drinking parties? With what propriety or what credibility will

* * * * *

351 Jer 1:9–10
352 Cf 2 Tim 3:16–17. For the importance of this passage in Erasmus' understanding of the preacher's duties, see books 2 and 3 CWE 68 passim.
353 Ps 50:16–17, 19 (Vulg 49:16–17, 19)
354 The preacher's love of God's word is another fundamental principle for Erasmus; cf Quintilian 12.1.29.
355 John 5:35
356 Matt 5:16

he rebuke the vices of others if he is steeped in the same or even worse? Such reproof, even though it is severe, has no more force than 'lightning made by glass,'[357] as in the Greek proverbs; a sham lightning bolt grazes the eyes lightly but does not flatten or kill. Accordingly, a pure heart and blameless life lend the preacher both credibility and authority.[358] Even Isaiah trembles as long as he had his lips polluted; but as soon as one of the seraphim had cleansed his mouth with a burning coal, he answered with untrembling faith, 'Here I am, send me'[359] when the Lord said, 'Whom shall I send, and who will go for me?'[360] But just as the purity that a man makes for himself is false, false also is the confidence that a human purity engenders, for it yields whenever the storm of temptation strikes. False purity is that which certain people claim for themselves from external works, fasts, abstinence, vigils, masses, prayers, alms, clothing and the like, though their heart is impure and infected with a desire for money, a thirst for glory, love of themselves, hatred and envy of their neighbour, a hunger for revenge, sometimes the leprosy of heresy[361] as well. But he alone is truly pure who has been purified by the touch of a fiery and living coal, not from a secular hearth but from the altar of God; for true charity, the companion of a sincere faith, covers a multitude of sins[362] because it is the gift of God and knows neither dissimulation nor pretence. This purity is bestowed not by water poured upon the body but by him who alone baptizes the minds of men with Spirit and fire.[363] Just as every sacrifice that is burned in a common

* * * * *

357 The Latin form of this proverb given here is *fulgur ex vitro*, not *fulgur ex pelvi*. *Vitro* was Erasmus' mistaken translation of the Greek word πυέλιον 'a pan for feeding animals,' presumably a metal pan that reflected light. The history of this Greek proverb is related in *Adagia* II vii 90.

358 Erasmus emphasizes the importance of credibility (*fiducia*) in persuasion, which is grounded in the preacher's moral excellence. This parallels the Roman ideal of the orator as 'a good man skilled in speaking' (*vir bonus dicendi peritus*); see Quintilian 12.1.3: 'For I do not merely assert that the ideal orator should be a good man, but I affirm that no man can be an orator unless he is a good man.' See too 12.1.1: 'The orator then, whom I am concerned to form, shall be the orator as defined by Marcus Cato, "a good man, skilled in speaking."'

359 Isa 6:5-8

360 Isa 6:8

361 'Leprosy of heresy' (*haereseos lepra*); of all the vices Erasmus identifies as most loathsome, obstinately perpetrating heretical teachings takes first place since it is the antithesis of the philosophy of Christ. See book 3 CWE 68 961. See Chomarat *Grammaire* II 1129-39.

362 1 Pet 4:8

363 Ie Jesus; see Matt 3:11; Luke 3:16.

and secular fire is impure and hateful to God, so every work of man that has not been purified by celestial fire is unpleasing to God, for there is even a human charity, which produces works that will perish if tested through heavenly fire.[364] With this fire the Lord cleansed the apostles' lips on the day of Pentecost so that they could speak worthily the magnificent mysteries of God.[365]

But just as among the Jews an animal that was clean for eating was not immediately clean for sacrifice,[366] so not everyone who is clean in the sense of being innocent is automatically clean for the office of preaching the gospel; in our body, being an eye and being one of the limbs are different things. Outstanding endowments are required in an ecclesiastical teacher: a consummate purity, great strength of faith, a singular and burning love; and for that reason the Lord asked Peter three times for love, not any love, but love of himself: 'Do you love me, do you love me, do you love me more than these?'[367] teaching in the person of Peter all those who take up the office of priest. We dare not approach the Lord's table except fasting, and we are right to do this, but the preacher requires greater sobriety. We do not go to offer mass unless we have cleansed our conscience over and over with a detailed confession. I approve of what we do; but I do not approve of the fact that we do not show similar care when we are about to handle the word of God.

But because we are quite convinced, as we ought to be, that the Law is spiritual and that whatever was either written or done in the Old Testament was written and done to instruct us,[368] and because, according to Paul again, the spiritual must be compared with the spiritual,[369] mystical Scripture has portrayed for us as in a painting all the endowments of the preacher through the priest Aaron,[370] who was added to Moses in order to relate before the people not the stories of men but the commandments of God and to act as mediator and patron of the people[371] before the Lord of Hosts. And yet how like a preacher Moses himself is everywhere teaching, exhorting, accusing,

* * * * *

364 Cf 1 Cor 3:13.
365 Acts 2:4, 7
366 See Lev 22:18–24.
367 John 21:15–18
368 Rom 15:4
369 1 Cor 2:13
370 Erasmus proceeds to give a spiritual (allegorical) exegesis of God's prescriptions to Aaron in Exodus regarding his comportment, instructions, and clothing as high priest.
371 See Exod 4:14–16, 19:21–5, 28:1.

soothing, threatening, and above all restraining[372] with his tongue so great and so stiff-necked[373] a multitude, yet asserting nothing except from the authority of the Lord. Joshua and Samuel did the same.[374] But to return to the picture of Aaron. If these things did not have a hidden meaning, then what Moses related in such great and painstaking care about the method of consecration, about the regalia of the priest, about the sacrificial rites, about the return to be made to the priest from each creature, and about the whole way of life of the priest could seem dull and antiquarian; these are described so precisely in Exodus and other books of Scripture that if we do not look to their more recondite significance, they can hardly be read without tedium.[375] All of this offers us a picture to teach the spiritual priest of the New Testament that he should far surpass the ordinary person in all the adornments of the mind, purity of heart, chastity of body, sanctity of character, learning, wisdom, but above all eloquence worthy of the divine mysteries. But it is not my intention to delay the reader here by fitting the details of these things to an allegory, especially since commentaries of the ancients are available from which these things can be learned.[376] But since I am impatient to reach other topics, I shall touch upon some points in a rapid and cursory fashion.

First of all, though the whole people that worships God is rightly called holy,[377] nevertheless Aaron is consecrated in a special rite[378] so that you can understand that someone who is to take up the role of preacher must above all stand apart from worldly business, wholeheartedly devoted and dedicated to divine matters. For it was fitting that, just as the man through whom everyone's victims were consecrated should himself be specially consecrated, so the man who was appointed to call everyone's minds away from worldly cares towards the love of the heavenly should himself be pure of secular desires. The priest's hands were consecrated

* * * * *

372 Cf 2 Tim 3:16.

373 Exod 32:9, 33:3 and 5, 34:9; Deut 9:13

374 For Joshua, see Josh 3:9, 4:1–5, 20:1, 24:1–28; for Samuel, see 1 Sam 8:10, 10:17–18, 15:1–2, 16.

375 Erasmus states above that all Scripture is for our instruction (cf Rom 15:4); here everything depends on the interpreter's skill in discerning the spiritual significances of the letter. The idea is of fundamental importance for Erasmus' exegesis as well as for his programme for instructing the preacher.

376 For other comments on these passages among the Fathers, see eg Origen *Homily IX on the Tabernacle, Homilies on Genesis and Exodus* FOC 71 343–5; John Chrysostom *De sacerdotio* (Treatise concerning the Christian Priesthood) book 6 NPNF 1st series 9 46; and St Jerome Ep 64 passim.

377 *gens sancta*; Exod 19:6

378 Exod 29:1–6

also,[379] whose touch rendered the victim clean for sacrifice. The apostles used to give the Holy Spirit through the laying on of hands,[380] and today a priest who absolves after confession lays his hand upon the head, as if the person who was previously the slave of sin[381] were being manumitted and claimed as a free man. Moreover it is inappropriate that hands consecrated to God be polluted with blood to fight in war, or be impure so that they are a slave to unchastity, or be rapacious to be intent upon greed. For these are the two main sources of trouble for priests: luxury is the teacher of unchastity, greed is the mother and root of all ills,[382] and her firstborn child is accursed simony[383] – accursed it was at one time, but now it has almost become a joke.

His sons were consecrated too because, as St Paul taught, it is not enough for the bishop himself to be free of wrong unless his children and whole family are blameless as well.[384] People sometimes conceive an unfavourable opinion about a teacher from his family's faults, reckoning as follows: if those with whom he lives constantly and over whom he has power privately and whom he could quite easily shape to his own character and whom he is preparing to be the heirs of his office have such bad morals, he is either a hypocrite for favouring their worthlessness or else a careless guide.[385] When will a man who cannot control his own household effectively control the church effectively? Likewise also today it is not enough for a bishop to live purely and blamelessly himself unless he ensures that his presbyters and deacons are like him and are suitable to join him in his sacred function whenever circumstance demands or to succeed him upon his decease.

It was not, however, the hands alone that were consecrated but the head and feet as well.[386] Reason is in the head, feelings are in the feet.[387]

* * * * *

379 Exod 28:41, 29:35, 32:29; Lev 21:10
380 Acts 8:17–18
381 Cf Rom 6:6, 17–20.
382 'Greed' (cupiditas); 'the love of money is the root of all kinds of evil' (1 Tim 6:10).
383 Simony is the sale of ecclesiastical (spiritual) offices and by extension the sale of anything spiritual. The name derives from Simon Magus (Acts 8:18–24) who sought to purchase from Peter the power that came from the Holy Spirt. See *Paraphrasis in acta apostolorum* CWE 50 58–60. See 'Simony' ODCC 1504.
384 Exod 28:1–43; 29:4, 8–9, 28–9; 30:30. Cf 1 Tim 3:1–4.
385 Cf 1 Tim 3:1–5.
386 See Exod 29:7–21; Lev 21:10. There is no mention of an anointing of the feet with oil, but some blood of a ram is placed on the big toes of Aaron and his sons.
387 Chomarat calls attention to this same expression in *Paraphrasis in Joannem*; see ASD V-4 89 151n. See also *Paraphrasis in Joannem* CWE 46 161: 'his feet, that is,

Nor was the body alone consecrated by anointing; the robes too were conse-crated,[388] to signify that the preacher's life should be so pure of the taints of common men that even in his external actions, such as food, drink, groom-ing, face, carriage, habitation, and servants, there should appear nothing that does not bear witness to his holiness, so that everything he does is done for the glory of God.[389] Moreover oil, which lends cheerfulness, excludes the sadness of hypocrisy, for true holiness is joyful, not sad.[390]

Furthermore, none of this is done without the offering of a sacrifice, on the grounds that no one has the power to bestow this purity of life without divine assistance, and if anything is bestowed, it must not be claimed for our own strength but attributed to heaven's munificence, which enables us to mortify our animal desires and to serve the Lord in a pure spirit.

Today also priests' hands are consecrated, for they are going to han-dle the sacraments of the Lord's body and blood, as are the vestments and vessels, even the church itself, partly so that external ceremonies of this kind may provoke the people to reverence, partly so that those initiated in the holy rites may learn from external rituals what great purity of life is required of those who are assigned to sacred functions.

The consecration used to be carried out over seven days and in the tabernacle of God;[391] departure from that place during that time was pun-ishable by death.[392] Execrated, not consecrated, are those who are consecrated

* * * * *

the desires of his heart' and 315 n17: 'The *affectus* or *affectiones* are also the allegorical explanation of the feet given by Augustine *Tract in Joannem* 56.3–5, Hugh of St Cher (on 13:10) 366r, and Nicholas of Lyra (on 13:10) 225r.' See also *Ratio* 179: 'Quid pedes nisi affectus? Quid pedes liberi calciamentorum onere nisi animus nullis terrenis ac fluxarum rerum cupiditatibus oneratus?' See also *In psalmum 38* CWE 65 26–7: 'Faith undoubtedly has eyes while our emotions are the feet of the soul . . .' See also *In psalmum 38* CWE 65 55.

388 Exod 28:1–43
389 Cf Ps 115:1 (Vulg 113:9); John 8:50, 5:44, 7:18.
390 Cf Lev 21:10; Ps 45:7 (Vulg 44:8), 133:1–3 (Vulg 132:1–3), 23:5 (Vulg 22:5); cf Jerome *Breviaria in psalmos* 23.5 (PL 26 885); and Augustine *Exposition of Psalm 22* WSA III-15 244–5: 'because you have gladdened my soul with spiritual joy' (245).
391 Exod 29:35–7; Exod 26:30
392 Lev 8:35. Erasmus' allegorical interpretation of the consecration of Aaron un-der the Old Law emphasizes the weighty obligations of the priest of the New Law. If Aaron was forbidden to leave the sanctuary on pain of death, how much more should the true priest / preacher of the word of God understand his obligation not to leave the *sanctum* (the holy place / the spiritual life) on pain of spiritual death?

outside the church through simony or who consecrate themselves at home as schismatics do. In fact, throughout the entire period when he practices the religious rites, the priest is forbidden to depart from the sanctuary[393] and considers it wrong to approach even his wife, children, or kin,[394] not because a place or licit intercourse defiles a man, but because all of these are to be interpreted symbolically as relating to purity of mind. Whoever has decided to preach the word of the Lord sincerely must devote himself to constant and careful meditation upon his holy intention so that all the activities of his life are consistent. Someone who has departed from the sanctuary is not someone who goes out of the church but someone who after celebrating mass or preaching a sermon betakes himself to human and secular concerns, to joining or dissolving marriages,[395] to profit and business, to preparing banquets, to apportioning inheritances, to secular embassies, to conducting the business of the rich, to hunting and fowling, not to mention revels, dicing, wenches, warring. I grant that some of these things can be done with propriety, but not every function befits a priest, in the same way that the eye, ear, hand, foot have different functions in the body. The Lord refused angrily when asked to divide an inheritance among brothers,[396] not because dividing wealth among heirs is wrong but because something loftier befits a herald of the word. Likewise he recognizes neither Caesar's image nor his inscription,[397] not because the laws of princes are altogether deserving of criticism but because there are many things in them that are more to be tolerated than approved by devout men, some indeed that are to be neglected and almost ignored, as when Christ is asked by Peter who should pay tribute to kings, the children of the kingdom or foreigners?[398] Nothing whatsoever was hidden from Christ, but he wanted to indicate to his followers that the dignity of the evangelical office is so great that it should not rashly lower itself to mundane and pedestrian business. Someone who has undertaken the task of teaching Christians must first be a pupil of Christ

* * * * *

393 Lev 21:12
394 None of the books of the Pentateuch mention this prohibition; Erasmus perhaps infers this from the many sexual prohibitions enjoined upon the Israelites, especially in Leviticus 18.
395 On 'dissolving' marriages, see Erasmus' *Institutio christiani matrimonii* and Michael Heath's introduction CWE 69 207, 209, 210–11, 216, 221 and 221 n17. The Latin word 'dissolving' (*dirimendas*) can be interpreted widely (eg separate, dissolve, break off, etc).
396 Luke 12:13–16
397 Matt 22:17–22; Mark 12:13–17; Luke 20:21–5
398 Matt 17:24–5

himself; but the Lord says that no one is a pupil worthy of him if he does not for his sake hate father, mother, wife, children, neighbours, even his own life.[399] But the man who neglects all these from love of godliness hates them if on occasion they call him away from it; hence Aaron, while remaining in the sanctuary, does not recognize those related by a kinship of the flesh,[400] while Paul, as he professes to have known no one at all according to the flesh, adds that he no longer knew even Christ according to the flesh though he had once known him otherwise.[401] But human emotions, though no wrong attaches to them, frequently divert those who indulge in them from the single-mindedness required in a bishop. It is true that the Mosaic priests were not always occupied in the temple, since they served by turns, yet in a spiritual sense a bishop has a constant need to minister to holy things, and it is never right to depart from the holy place. Though he be in the court of a prince, at a banquet, on a ship or a carriage, he does not depart from the holy place if by his life and by his words he calls people to zeal for godliness. There alone the priest is safe, though doomed to perish elsewhere.

The same point is made when the priest is forbidden to participate in mourning for his sons and is not allowed to bare his head or rend his garments in the way that the Jews customarily do in bitter mourning.[402] It is harsh to forbid a father tears at the death of his sons, it is harsh not to allow brothers to groan at the sad demise of their brothers, and yet Aaron kept silent and obeyed Moses' commands along with his remaining sons because the Lord had so instructed.

In addition, an everlasting law is prescribed for the high priest at Leviticus 21: he must not attend the funeral even of his mother or father or of any deceased person at all but remain in the temple without interrupting his sacred functions.[403] The reason given is that holy oil has been poured upon his head, for it is not fitting that a head consecrated to God, the author of life, through spiritual unction should be bared or shaved because of carnal emotions. The greater the dignity of the office, the greater the purity of life required; the true death is sin, but the preacher ought

* * * * *

399 Luke 14:26; Matt 10:37–9
400 Cf Lev 8:35. Erasmus infers this from the prescriptions given to Aaron and his sons.
401 2 Cor 5:16; Erasmus *Paraphrasis in epistolam Pauli ad Corinthios posteriorem* CWE 43 231
402 Lev 21:10–12; cf Ezek 44:15–31.
403 Lev 21:10–15

to be pure and uncontaminated by the contagion of others' wrongs.[404] This law seems inhumane if interpreted literally; burying the dead is a work of charity, but mourning for the dead as the Jews used to mourn is an act of people who do not believe in the resurrection of the body. It is, however, most worthy of a priest to approach someone dead in spirit, but not in order to mourn someone wept over with useless wailing, 'to adorn the lifeless one with tears,'[405] as the poet says, but rather to recall him to life with the word of life, if he is able. This is not mourning the dead but waking the sleeper and giving medicine to the sick. For Christ even the dead were asleep;[406] for us, since it is uncertain whether an unburied sinner, however great his wrongs, will ever come to his senses, we must apply the word of salvation always but apply touch only to someone who is returning to life. Moreover, touch is an intimate practice in ordinary life; a preacher who employs this on those who live wickedly seems to be favouring their vices.

Indeed, the priest is commanded to abstain entirely from the touch of all carrion,[407] that is, from the contagion of all sin, even from the appearance of evil.[408] Otherwise touch is not to be denied entirely to those whose errors are slight and who have been caught in some mild offence, for even the Lord used to banquet with sinners[409] and extends his hand to the daughter of the ruler of the synagogue, but not without these words, 'Girl, I say

* * * * *

404 In the following exegeses Erasmus explains the allegorical meaning of the Old Testament priesthood's prohibition from joining in mourning for the dead or touching the dead and the meaning of Jesus' not touching the dead, not even the funereal stone at the tomb of his friend Lazarus. Here Erasmus is using death and sickness allegorically of sin, teaching that the preacher of the New Law ought to avoid physical contact with those steeped in sin. This sense of Scripture is not always consistent; in the case of Jairus' daughter, Jesus was careful to treat the case privately; so a recent sinner guilty of a not too serious offence should be dealt with in private. Cf Augustine *Tractate* 49 in *St. Augustine: Tractates on the Gospel of John 28–54* FOC 88 238–59, and John Chrysostom *Homiliae in Joannem* 63 (John 11:30–41) trans Sister Thomas Aquinas Goggin FOC 41 179–90. See the similarly elaborate interpretation of the story of the young man in Luke 7:11–17, where Jesus touches the bier; see *Paraphrasis in Lucam* 7:11 LB VII 352E.
405 Cicero *Tusculan Disputations* 1.48.117; *De senectute* 20.73 (Cicero citing Ennius: *Nemo me lacrumis decoret . . . nec funera fletu / Faxit!*).
406 Matt 9:24; Mark 5:39; Luke 8:52; John 11:11
407 Lev 21–2. See Jerome Ep 64.3 (PL 22 610).
408 Cf 1 Tim 3:1–7; Titus 1:7–9.
409 Matt 9:10–11; Mark 2:15–16; Luke 5:29–30

to you "Arise"' and only after dismissing the crowd.[410] It was a young girl who had fallen, her death was recent, and great care was taken for privacy: the crowd was dismissed, and only two disciples were admitted along with her father and mother. This is the first reproof, which the Lord commands us to make to a neighbour in private.[411] But we do not read of him touching the young man who was already being carried out for burial,[412] the mourning for whom had not remained within his household walls but was being conducted outside the city; rather he only touched the bier so that the bearers would stop, for the first step towards correction is to desist from vices before habit forms a callus and removes the awareness of wrongdoing. He touched him only when he was alive, as he handed him over to his mother, for a sinner who repents should be supported with kindness and courtesy, just as St Paul instructs the Corinthians to receive lovingly and to console in his affliction one that they had cast out for incest, lest he be swallowed up by a more grievous sadness.[413] The ejection of an incestuous person was granted to ecclesiastical discipline; the kindly reception of a penitent is an act of charity, which ought to prevail particularly in such assemblies. Jesus loved Lazarus but was unwilling to attend his funeral;[414] he wept, however, not so much for the dead man, who to him was asleep, as for the disbelief of the Jews, which he was still unable to cure with so many miracles.[415] He did not know the tomb of his friend, for Lazarus already prefigured those of whom it was said, 'He who does not know will not be known'[416] and 'He who is in filth, let him be in filth still.'[417] He does not touch the funereal stone, only applies his ringing voice; even after he was restored to life, he did not touch him but ordered that he be released by the others and that food by given him at once, so that he should give clear proof of his restored life by the natural motion of his body and by eating. And only under these circumstances do we read that Lazarus reclined at the same banquet where Jesus was present;[418] those who have lived all their lives in manifest and terrible wrongdoing should not be trusted immediately but watched until they certify their corrected attitude through unmistakable tokens.

* * * * *

410 Mark 5:22–43; cf Matt 9:23–5; Luke 8:41–55.
411 Cf Matt 5:23–4.
412 Luke 7:11–15
413 See 2 Cor 2:6–8.
414 John 11:5, 36
415 John 11:33–7
416 1 Cor 14:38
417 Rev 22:11
418 John 12:1–2

The following rules also illustrate the need for an exceptional purity of life: that anyone of Aaron's stock[419] who is affected by a discharge of blood is forbidden to approach the priest's table and to eat the holy loaves,[420] likewise that all who are disfigured by some physical flaw or mark are barred from the holy duties,[421] and that the priest himself is ordered to marry a virgin of his own race, to abstain from a widow, a divorced woman, or a prostitute.[422] What is permissible for people in general is not automatically permissible for the priest as well; many things are conceded to the multitude, but supreme purity is required from the priest in every aspect of his life.

The injunction that those who are to perform the rites not drink wine or *sicera* applies not only to the priest but to his sons as well,[423] for it is not appropriate that those who profess themselves teachers of heavenly wisdom should have their heart weighed down with intoxication and inebriation. And here the reason is added: it says, 'That you may have the knowledge of distinguishing between the holy and the profane, between the polluted and the clean, and that you may teach the sons of Israel all my ordinances.'[424] The teacher should be like his philosophy. As James says, this wisdom is chaste, peaceful, modest, open to reason, in harmony with the good, full of love and good fruits, judging without pretence;[425] but drunkenness and luxury beget immodesty, give birth to quarrels, teach violence, prattle secrets, rob all judgment.

In order not to weary the reader by discussing each of the many details, I shall treat briefly a few points concerning the priest's garb.[426] The whole consists of garments made of plain white linen[427] and of others dec-

* * * * *

419 Lev 22:4–6
420 Erasmus speaks of 'a discharge of blood' ('si quis de stirpe Aaron teneatur profluvio sanguinis, vetatur ad sacerdotis mensam accedere sacrisque vesci panibus . . .'), but Leviticus 22:4 (Vulg) renders 22:4 as 'a discharge of seed,' with the result that the man of the line of Aaron will be unclean: 'homo de semine Aaron qui fuerit leprosus aut patiens fluxum seminis non vescetur de his quae sanctificata sunt mihi donec sanetur . . .' See also Lev 15:2 (Vulg): 'loquimini filiis Israhel et dicite eis vir qui patitur fluxum seminis immundus erit.'
421 Leviticus 22
422 Lev 21:13–15
423 Lev 10:9; *sicera* (or *cicera*; LXX σίκερα), from the Hebrew word meaning 'a kind of spirituous, intoxicating drink'; see Jerome Ep 52.1; Isidore *Etymologiae* 20.3.16. The word is not used in the Vulgate (*vinum, et omne quod inebriare potest*).
424 Lev 10:10–11
425 James 3:17
426 Exod 28:4–42; Lev 8:13, 16:4
427 Exod 28:4; Jerome Ep 4.11–17 (to Fabiola) PL 22 613–17

orated with a variety of hues, adorned with the starry splendour of precious jewels,[428] brilliant with the gleam of gold, and marvellously woven throughout by the genius of the artisan. These things were appropriate for that people; for us, on whom has shone the truth of the gospel,[429] they signify the interior ornaments of the spirit, not the kind that dazzle the eyes of the ignorant with the costliness of things that the Lord commanded us to scorn,[430] but the kind that kindle the minds of those who see them towards love for that priceless treasure. Aaron's vestments were more than royal, but that true highest priest after the order of Melchisedech[431] wore none of these, nor did his disciples; but they had all these things within, and much more splendid, not from the skill of Beselehel[432] but from the power of the Holy Spirit.[433] To provide a more orderly account of the whole garb of the priest, we shall begin from the middle of the body, that is, from its most private part, and proceed from here to the lowest and highest parts.[434]

First of all, not only the high priest himself but also the other priests or assistants at the rites are commanded to wear linen drawers,[435] which, being drawn tight about the hips, thus cover the body's shameful parts, for they extend as far as the thighs, so that while the priests, in performing their sacred rites, bend their bodies to a variety of tasks, something that is more decently concealed does not happen to appear to the eyes of the people.

Over these 'breeches' was an ankle-length tunic [ποδήρης][436] not dissimilar, I think, to what we now commonly call a *camisia*,[437] of double linen,

* * * * *

428 Exod 28:9, 17–20
429 John 1:4–5, 9
430 Matt 6:19–24; Luke 12:15–34, 16:13; Mark 10:17–30
431 Ie Jesus. See Gen 14:18–20; Ps 110:4 (Vulg 109:4); Heb 5:6–10, 7 entire.
432 Exod 31:1–11, 35:30–5
433 Cf Acts 2:4.
434 Erasmus begins to interpret the spiritual meaning of sacerdotal garments worn by Aaron the high priest; see Exodus 28 and 39:1–30. For his understanding of the prescriptions addressed to Aaron and his sons Erasmus relies heavily on Jerome Ep 64.11–17 PL 22 613–17.
435 Latin *campestria linea* (Vulg Exod 28:40–3 *tunicas lineas*). To describe an article unfamiliar to the Romans, Erasmus uses the word *campestria* 'running shorts made for athletes,' so-called because they were used in sports at the Campus Martius. In the following paragraph this garment is called *bracae* 'breeches,' a word of Gallic origin. From its description in the sources, it is clearly not a loin cloth since it has separate parts for the legs. (A. Dalzell)
436 See Exod 28:4; Jerome Ep 64.11 CSEL 54 598; see Josephus *Antiquitates Judaicae* 3.153.3, 3.159.3.
437 A late Latin word for a long gown

deep blue in colour,[438] open at the top so that it could be put on by insert-
ing the head, but without a hood and fitting the whole body so neatly that
it had no folds, so that those who attended to the rites were not hindered
by flaps of cloth; this garment covered the arms as well.[439] Around the top
edge of this tunic was added a woven tape of the sort generally found on
the edges and fringes of garments to prevent their being torn easily. Moreover it came down longer than the breeches, indeed as far as the shins or
ankles.[440]

This tunic was drawn in from below the chest to the navel by a sash[441]
decorated with many colours and flowers,[442] of solid work, the width of a
hand – military style.[443]

A tiara[444] – that is, a kind of round cap – woven of linen covered the
head in such a way that it left some part bare above the brow; this was tied
at the back of the head to keep it from slipping off easily.

The features mentioned so far concerning Aaron's dress were shared
by the other priests with the high priest, but he had certain special features, such as the fact that around the bottom of his tunic, which we have
said clung to his whole body, were added pomegranates and bells with the
same variety of colours as the sash. The bells, moreover, were of gold, so arranged that one bell came between two pomegranates, with the result that
wherever the high priest went he made a sound as he moved.[445] He would
be punished with death if he walked without a sound. There were seventy-
two bells (and as many pomegranates) to make the sound louder and more
continuous.

* * * * *

438 Erasmus is wrong in suggesting that the long tunic was blue ('hyacinthine').
All priests, including the high priest, wore the white tunic. The high priest
wore a blue tunic over the white. Cf Exod 28:31–5. (A. Dalzell)
439 Jerome Ep 64.11 CSEL 54 598
440 Exod 28:32–3
441 Exod 28:4, 39, 40
442 The warp was white and the woof woven from blue, red, purple, and white
threads, giving a pattern that suggested flowers and jewels; see Jerome Ep
64.11 and Josephus *Antiquitates Judaicae* 3.154. (A. Dalzell)
443 Latin *gestamen militare*, literally 'military wear.' This comment seems to be
inspired by Jerome Ep 64.11, where he compares the priest's tunic to the
tightly fitted (*sic aptas membris et adstrictas corporibus*) tunic worn by soldiers.
(A. Dalzell)
444 Erasmus Latin *tiara*; Vulg *cidarim*; Greek LXX κίδαριν: see Exod 28:4, 36–9, 40;
Lev 8:9; Josephus *Antiquitates Judaicae* 3.7.157; Jerome Ep 64.13, 19 CSEL 54 599–
600, 609–10. See 313–14 below.
445 Exod 28:35

The *epomis*, which they translate *superhumerale*,[446] covered the shoulders; it was rather longer at the back, covering even part of the shoulder blades, but did not extend equally far over the chest, in order to leave a place for the most sacred ornament of all, which they call the 'rational.'[447] Jerome thinks that it was a mantle, not unlike a *caracalla* except that it lacked a hood;[448] if anyone wants a contemporary example, I suppose that it was not entirely unlike the shoulder capes with which German women modestly cover themselves today, except that the high priest's superhumeral was constructed with marvellous workmanship from little gold chains, rings, and hooks, and decorated with the four colours blue, scarlet, white, and purple, having on either shoulder an onyx set in gold. The ancients were uncertain whether the onyx ought to be counted among the gemstones;[449] for it is found in such large pieces that cups and ointment jars are carved from it. On the right stone were engraved the six names of the elder sons of Jacob, on the left the same number of the younger ones, and Scripture adds, 'And Aaron bore their names before the Lord upon both shoulders for a remembrance.'[450]

Over the chest another garment, lesser than the others in size but more sacred than all the rest, was joined to the *epomis* by little gold chains and rings; the Septuagint translated its name as λόγιον [oracular breastplate], Jerome as *rationale*.[451] It was woven from gold and decorated with the same colours as the superhumeral; also it was double for strength and was square,

* * * * *

446 The Vulgate rendering *epomis* of the LXX ἐπωμίς (see Exod 28:6 τὴν ἐπωμίδα), a word used of the upper part of a Greek woman's tunic, meaning literally 'on the shoulders,' is in turn literally translated into Latin as 'superhumeral' (*superhumerale*).

447 Exod 28:4,15. See Josephus *Antiquitates Judaicae* 3.7.163.

448 Jerome Ep 64.16 PL 22.616. *Caracalla*. L&S *caracalla* describes this garment as Celtic in origin: 'a long tunic or great-coat, with a hood, worn by the Gauls, and made of different materials.' The garment was introduced by the emperor (Caracalla) Marcus Aurelius Severus Antoninus Augustus (ruled 198–217), from which he received his cognomen. Erasmus is likely recalling here Jerome's reference to this in Ep 64.16 (to Fabiola) PL 22 615. OLD does not have an entry for *caracalla*.

449 See Pliny the Elder *Naturalis historia* 37.24.90–1.

450 Exod 28:12

451 Exod 28:15–30; see Jerome Ep 64.16 CSEL 54 602–3. In English translations of Exodus, this is variously rendered as 'breastpiece' or 'breastpiece of judgment' or 'breastplate of judgment' or 'rational.' The original Hebrew word meant 'pouch' for it held the Urim (doctrine) and Thummim (truth), two stones used as instruments for consulting the divinity; but the meaning of these two devices is obscure. It is likely they worked as oracular lots, which could provide a negative or affirmative answer; see eg 1 Sam 14:20–42, 30:7–8. See Jerome

each side having the width of a palm or of four fingers. On it were four rows
of precious stones, which Scripture lists by name. Each line had three stones,
so they were twelve in number; on each gem was engraved the name of one
of the patriarchs. I think that this chest covering is called δήλωσις or ἀλήθεια,
that is, 'manifestation' and 'truth,' on account of the wonderful brightness
of the gems, in which they think there was even a kind of divination.[452]

There remains the tiara,[453] which in the case of the high priest has this
special feature that it displayed, bound above his forehead with a blue cord,
a golden plate on which was written the tetragrammaton, the name of the
Lord;[454] this is why the high priest is forbidden to bare his head to anyone
lest the head of God, whose personage he bears, should appear subordinate
to a human person.[455]

It would be laborious indeed to explain what each of these reveals to
us according to its moral sense, since the mere reporting of the details as described by Moses is a highly troublesome task.[456] What is clear is that this
more than royal garb signifies, certainly in deacons and presbyters, a mind
adorned with every kind of heroic virtue and a perfect purity of life. But
still loftier gifts of the spirit than these are required of someone who has undertaken the office of preacher. In this respect all presbyters and bishops are
high priests; but after what belonged to one began to be distributed among
many as human charity grew colder,[457] that which was the chief function

* * * * *

Ep 64.16 CSEL 54 602–4; JBC I 63 (79), II 704–5 (6–8); William H.C. Propp *The
Anchor Bible. Exodus 19–40. A New Translation with Introduction and Commentary*
(New York 2006) 429–55.

452 Exod 28:30; cf Lev 8:8.

453 For 'tiara,' see Jerome Ep 64.16 CSEL 54 602–4 and 64.13 CSEL 54 599–600; see
also 311 n444 above.

454 On tetragrammaton, see Jerome Ep 64.16 CSEL 54 602–4: 'The golden plate,
that is, SIS ZAAB, on which the name of God is written with the four Hebraic
letters YHWH [JOD, HE, VAV, HE], which among them is called ineffable.' See
Exod 28:36, 39:30; Lev 8:9. The Vulgate translates these four letters as *Dominus*,
the Septuagint as Κύριος.

455 This explanation is neither in Scripture nor in Jerome's letter. Exodus 28:38
says only, 'It shall always be upon his forehead, that they may be accepted
before the Lord.'

456 Erasmus, like Jerome (*iuxta morem nostrum, spiritualis postea intelligentiae vela
pandamus*), now interprets the moral (or tropological) and allegorical senses
of these details about the vestments of Aaron and the Old Testament priesthood; see Jerome Ep 64.16 CSEL 54 602–4. For the four senses of Scripture, see
introduction 199–200 and n617.

457 Erasmus speaks here of the significant change that took place in the church
after bishops no longer assumed the duty of preaching exclusively but enlisted others to assist them. He sees this turning point occurring 'when human

[*quod . . . praecipuum erat*] of the high priest, namely teaching the people the precepts of the Lord, was now delegated to preachers. It is right, therefore, that those who claim the primary function of a presbyter should exhibit Aaron's whole adornment, not literally but allegorically, so that, wherever they turn, their light shines before men, their spiritual teaching sounds forth, and their whole life is one outstanding example of godliness.

On his head he wears the tiara[458] covered with blue linen because the mind, which is the highest part of a man, looks only at heaven and the heavenly, as the sky-blue colour of the headband demonstrates; the priest who is eager to please men, who abandons the truth of the gospel out of fear of the mighty, who twists Holy Writ to human desires,[459] is baring his head. On his forehead he carries the name of the Lord,[460] whose mysteries he dispenses, so that it is disgraceful for him to forget the one he professes as Lord and creator and to submit himself to any man, when Paul says that he will not yield even to an angel preaching from heaven.[461] In the same passage he says, 'Am I urging God or men? If I still pleased men, I would not be a servant of Christ.'[462] Someone who flatters the sins of men by laying bare, for example at a funeral, the gift of prophecy that he received from the heavenly Spirit or exposing it to men, corrupting the word of God from fear of the rich and mighty, is betraying and profaning his anointing.

Honour and love are owed above all to God,[463] whose name he bears atop his brow; next these are offered to the Lord's flock, and for this reason he carries on his shoulders the names of the sons of Israel,[464] which he carries not for human ostentation but before God, to whom, as Scripture has it, he will render an account for the sheep entrusted to him;[465] this is that

* * * * *

charity grew colder' (cf Matt 24:12); before this it was the bishop alone who preached, and it was the bishop's 'chief characteristic' to teach the people the precepts of the Lord (*id quod in pontifice praecipuum erat, videlicet populum docere praecepta Domini*). Erasmus' words anticipate the revived emphasis on the bishop by the Council of Trent; see Tanner II 667–70, *Decretum secundum: super lectione et praedicatione.* See n140 above.

458 See n444 above. Erasmus seems to be following Jerome exclusively for this interpretation of the colours of the sacred vestments.

459 Erasmus often rails against preachers who 'twist Holy Writ' to suit their own convenience or for profit; see book 2 CWE 68 513, 522; book 3 CWE 68 898–900.

460 Exod 28:36

461 Gal 1:8

462 Gal 1:10

463 Deut 6:5; Matt 22:37; Mark 12:29

464 Exod 28:36–7

465 John 10:11–16, 21:15–17; cf Acts 20:28; 1 Pet 5:2.

glorious burden that weighed upon the shoulders of Paul as well, the care of all the churches.[466] He carries them on his shoulders as he recognizes that the necessity of preaching the gospel[467] has been placed upon him and that to him has been enjoined the dispensation of the divine word,[468] which is the food of souls;[469] he carries on his breast, so that he cannot forget them, those whom he has adopted in the place of children and towards whom he ought to bear a parent's affection.[470] The Apostle bore all of them in his heart; whenever he sees his children advance in evangelical devotion, he so exults that he calls them his 'joy and crown'[471] in the Lord, 'rejoicing as they rejoice, weeping as they weep,'[472] as he burns if anyone stumbles, is tormented if any is weak,[473] gives birth a second time to those children lapsed to Judaism until Christ is formed within them,[474] wishes to be spent and overspent for their souls[475] and 'to be made anathema by Christ'[476] so long as he wins some as profit for Christ,[477] 'changes his voice'[478] among them and lowers himself 'like a nurse tending children,'[479] carries them all in his heart and in his bowels, as he himself writes.[480] The pastor, therefore, has no reason to say, 'What have I to do with a filthy tanner or with an abject beggar or with a two-bit drab?' No soul for which the Lord of glory[481] deigned to die should seem worthless,[482] and do not shrink from carrying about inscribed on gems those whose names have been written in heaven. But since you are not certain which names have been written in the book of life[483] and which have not, you will be vigilant for the salvation of them all as though they have been inscribed. If you have carried out your

* * * * *

466 2 Cor 11:28
467 1 Cor 9:16
468 1 Cor 9:17
469 Deut 8:3, cited at Matt 4:4; cf Luke 4:4.
470 Cf Rom 8:15; Gal 4:5; Eph 1:5.
471 Phil 4:1
472 Rom 12:15
473 2 Cor 11:29
474 Gal 4:19; see *Paraphrasis in epistolam Pauli apostoli ad Galatas* CWE 42 118–19.
475 2 Cor 12:15
476 Rom 9:3
477 1 Cor 9:19, 21
478 Gal 4:20; see *Paraphrasis in epistolam Pauli apostoli ad Galatas* CWE 42 118–19.
479 1 Thess 2:7
480 Phil 1:8
481 1 Cor 2:8
482 Cf Matt 8:8, 10:6, 15:24, 18:11; Luke 19:10; Gal 3:26–8.
483 Luke 10:20; Phil 4:3; Rev 17:8, 22:19

appointed function in good faith, the death of some will not be laid to your account; you owe your service to the Lord, the outcome is in his hand, not yours.[484] Unction is on the head, the λόγιον is on the breast because reason, by which we judge and which Paul calls spirit,[485] is the source from which flows whatever good is in us, if it is imbued with heavenly inspiration. From the head comes our knowledge of what constitutes sound teaching, out of the breast come voice and speech. For it is not enough that a priest knows what is right and devout unless the capacity to teach others is present.[486] Since that embraces knowledge of both Testaments, the λόγιον is twofold, pertaining to the Old, which is covered in the wrappings of figures and riddles,[487] and to the New, which uncovers the mysteries, offering manifest truth in place of shadows. It can also refer, however, to the double meaning of Scripture, of which one is more straightforward, the other allegorical and more sublime: the preacher should be versed in both. In explaining them, ἀλήθεια [truthfulness] should be present so that the preacher's teaching is not erroneous, since a perverse life arises from perverse opinions; then δήλωσις [manifestation] should be added so that whatever in Scripture has been hidden[488] should be made manifest by appropriate interpretation in order that it becomes clear even to the unlearned, so that, in other words, by removing the veil that had been placed over the face of Moses[489] those who believe in Christ may uncover their face and behold the glory of the Lord.

But we do not yet hear the sound of the golden bells that the bottom of the robe produces, for one must not leap forward immediately to the office of teaching unless the capacity to teach has first been created in the breast over a long period, nor must we teach others what they ought to believe, how they ought to live, unless what we are going to urge upon others first shines forth in our own life and behaviour. Jesus first began to act, then to teach, and the most effective kind of teaching is to show in one's own life what it is to live devoutly.

* * * * *

484 See 275 above.
485 See eg Gal 5:17.
486 This is the crucial skill and responsibility of the preacher; the bishop is primarily the teacher, like 'Christ, the teacher of all teachers.' See 321 below.
487 For the allegorical sense of Scripture ('wrappings and riddles') by which the Old Testament speaks of the things in the New Testament, see eg Gal 4:24 and book 3 CWE 68 919, 959.
488 For 'hidden,' see 2 Cor 3:7–18; Luke 24:27, 32.
489 Exod 34:33–5; cf 2 Cor 3:14–16.

In the middle are the linen breeches,[490] which restrain the loins and private parts to prevent any stain of turpitude either hiding in the soul or appearing in life.

There is also the double tunic of ordinary or fine linen[491] representing the innocence of body and mind, which we received in baptism when the white robe of the immaculate lamb[492] was given to us in place of the robe of skin[493] that we had received from Adam; the latter was stripped from dead animals, the former was born from the earth, brilliant and shining with the brightness of living, having nothing in common with dead things, for whoever is born of God does not sin.[494]

This is fastened by a sash. Girt with this, the soldier of Christ[495] stands in the truth; it binds his tunic lest it flow loosely, and it holds fast the 'rational' that adorns the breast to prevent it from puckering – for the 'rational' is connected from above to the superhumeral, from below to the sash. There are two things that protect innocence of life in the shepherd: fear and love of the highest shepherd, who, he believes, entrusted the flock to him, and unbroken sobriety of life, which brings with it watchfulness and prayer;[496] and so the Apostle writes to the Ephesians, 'Stand with your loins girded in truth,'[497] indicating that a chaste life is appropriate to chaste speech. For where there is pretence, there is no truth. He says to the Thessalonians, as if in explanation of this, 'We are not of the night or of darkness; so then let us not sleep as others do, but let us keep awake and be sober. For those who sleep sleep at night, and those who are drunk are drunk at night; but since we belong to the day, let us be sober, putting on the breastplate of faith and love,'[498] etc. What Moses called a tunic the Apostle calls a breastplate;[499] what the former called a sash, the latter calls sobriety and vigilance

* * * * *

490 Exod 28:42; see also Jerome Ep 64.10 CSEL 54 597–8; Augustine *Quaestiones in Heptateuchum* VII 2.122 CSEL 28(2) 171; Origen *Homiliae in Leviticum* 4.6 and 6.6 FOC 83 76–80.

491 'Double tunic of ordinary or fine linen' ($\pi o\delta\acute{\eta}\rho\eta s$); Exod 28:31; see Jerome Ep 64.11 CSEL 54 598. See n436 above.

492 Ie Jesus Christ. See Exodus 12:5 'lamb without blemish' and references in the New Testament to Jesus as the Lamb of God: John 1:29, 36; Rev 22:1, 3.

493 Gen 3:21

494 1 John 3:9, 5:18

495 For 'soldier of Christ' (*Christi miles*), see n138 above.

496 Cf Matt 26:41; Mark 13:33; Luke 21:36; 1 Pet 4:7, 5:8.

497 Eph 6:14

498 1 Thess 5:5–8

499 'Breastplate' (*lorica*); 1 Thess 5:8; Exod 28:31

in truth.[500] Soldiers carry provisions in their belt; purity is preserved in the
fear of God, which threatens from above and in unbroken sobriety of life.
'Fear is the beginning of wisdom,'[501] drawing us back from evil;[502] sobriety, as it girds the soft parts of a man, restrains concupiscence to prevent
our becoming enervated through luxury and negligence. Only in this way
do the golden bells, which are interspersed with pomegranates, ring out.[503]

Pomegranates have a bitter rind but a pleasantly refreshing juice
within; this is brotherly correction,[504] which tempers the harshness of rebuke with the juice of Christian consolation. They do not ring, because a
neighbour's vice is to be concealed so far as possible. Hence Paul suppresses
the names of the false prophets;[505] he did not wish us to know the name even
of the incestuous man,[506] and the Lord could not bear to reveal the name
of his betrayer[507] because he preferred that he be corrected rather than destroyed. The bells ring because general teaching helps everyone, harms no
one.

I have no doubt that far more mysteries than I have briefly indicated
here are concealed in the priests' garb, especially since mystical Scripture
has depicted them so carefully in several passages that outstanding Doctors
of the church, such as Origen, Tertullian, and Jerome, have not shrunk from
making exceptional efforts in explaining, though Tertullian's work was un-
available even to Jerome;[508] but for our present purpose, if types of this kind
indicate what purity is required in the priest of the Old Testament both in
his mind and in the whole of his life – the splendour of gold signifying the
wisdom of the gospel, the brilliant jewels indicating the principal virtues,
which they call heroic, the variety of the most precious colours, which seem

* * * * *

500 Exod 28:4; 1 Thess 5:6
501 Prov 1:7 'The fear of the Lord is the beginning of knowledge ...'; Ps 111:10
    (Vulg 110:10)
502 Cf Job 1:1, 8; 2:3.
503 Exod 28:33–4
504 Ecclus 19:13–15; Matt 18:15; cf Augustine De civitate Dei 1.9; Thomas Aquinas
    Summa theologiae IIa IIae q 33 aa 1–7.
505 2 Cor 11:13. Chomarat (ASD V-4 103 449–50n) notes that Erasmus adopts this
    way of concealing those he criticizes in his satire Moria, which he explains in
    Epistola ad Dorpium CWE 71 1–30, especially 18.
506 1 Cor 5:1
507 Matt 26:21–6; Mark 14:17–21; Luke 22:21–3; John 13:21–30
508 See Jerome Ep 64.23 PL 22 622, where he notes that Tertullian is said to have
    written a book on Aaron's vestments: 'A book on Aaron's vestments appears
    in the index of Septimus Tertullian, which for some time up to this very day
    I have not found.'

to indicate those moral virtues (for four are enumerated) and (not to go on too long) the careful and elaborate adornment of mind and of life – how much greater are the qualities to be required of the evangelical preacher?[509] The loftier the office, the greater the perfection demanded of him who performs it. Aaron used to lay his consecrated hands upon the victim to be slaughtered,[510] Aaron's sons slaughtered cattle,[511] stood by the cauldrons to lift with their fork the portion of meat owed to the sacrificers,[512] brought out and stored away the vessels, cleaned altars;[513] in sum, their work did not look very different from the similar activities of butchers, cooks, or tavern keepers, and nevertheless great honour was accorded those who ministered to these things. How great, then, is the dignity befitting the ministers of the New Testament, who daily sacrifice that heavenly victim that merits the adoration even of the angelic spirits, who touch with their hands the flesh of the immaculate lamb! So much for services; now let us consider the difference in learning.

What did Aaron teach? The laws of God. What are these? That the people know the difference between a clean and an unclean animal[514] and the difference between one clean for sacrifice and one clean for eating,[515] which animal ought to be sacrificed at what time, in what manner, with what rituals, when and how the unleavened cakes[516] should be cooked, from what things the incense (that is, the fumigant) should be made.[517] These, or certainly things of this kind, are the precepts that Aaron is commanded to teach the people of Israel. But what did he promise? That they would be well off and live long upon the earth,[518] have fertile wives, see the children of their children, have fruitful fields. Unsophisticated things suited the unsophisticated; and yet in the observance of these laws the discipline

* * * * *

509 Latin *quanto maiora requirenda sunt ab ecclesiasta evangelico*; this rhetorical comparison is fundamental to Erasmus' exegesis of the Old Testament, where what is adumbrated there is brought into full light in the New Testament.
510 Exod 29:9–10, 15; Lev 3:2, 8, 13
511 Exod 29:10; 2 Chron 29:21–4
512 Cf Exod 38:3.
513 Num 4:13
514 Lev 11:46–7
515 Deut 15:21–3
516 Lev 2:4, 7:12; Num 6:15; Exod 29:2
517 Exod 25:6, 30:34–8, 35:28
518 Leviticus 25–6 passim; Deut 11:14–15, 21, 23–5; 28:3–13. Chomarat (ASD V-4 105 482–4n) notes that Erasmus omits the promises about victory in war and the annihilation of enemies.

was so severe that two of Aaron's sons were consumed by a heavenly fire because they used secular fire for the rituals, contrary to the injunction of Moses.[519] King Ozias was stricken with leprosy for a similar wrong;[520] Oze, who tried to prop up the Ark with unanointed hands when it slipped, perished instantly.[521] How great, therefore, ought to be the awe of those who impart to the people that ineffable philosophy that the Son of God brought to earth from the bosom of his Father, and which that heavenly Spirit[522] inspired in the souls of the apostles, a wisdom that the world cannot comprehend. They promise neither long life on earth nor a country flowing with milk and honey, fecund wives, a numerous flock, fertile fields; but in this life they pledge remission of all sins through faith in Christ Jesus,[523] and in the resurrection they promise eternal life in heaven.[524] Those who either rashly usurp this holy office or administer it unworthily are not burned up by a heavenly fire, are not overwhelmed by sudden death, are not covered over by leprosy, but are cast body and soul together into everlasting fire.[525] The loftier the dignity, the more grievous the punishment of the delinquent. Someone might perhaps say at this point, 'If the danger is so great, and so many qualities beyond human strength are required of the preacher, it is better not to touch that Camarina.'[526] I would heed that warning if the business had to be done by human strength; as it is, the very one who delegates the office provides the strength and increases his gifts in accordance with the difficulty of the office, so much that we wholeheartedly place our trust in him and call upon his Spirit in constant prayers.

* * * * *

519 Lev 10:1–2, 16:1; Num 3:4, 26:61
520 2 Chron 26:16–21
521 2 Sam 6:6–7; 1 Chron 13:9–11
522 Acts 2:2–4
523 Matt 26:28; Acts 10:43; Eph 1:7; Col 1:14
524 John 6:40; 2 Cor 5:1
525 Matt 25:41. This is one of the few references to hell in *Ecclesiastes*.
526 See *Adagia* 1 i 64 *Movere Camarinam* 'To move Camarina.' 'To move Camarina,' Erasmus interprets, 'is to bring trouble upon oneself.' The most likely explanation is that Camarina, a town near Syracuse in Sicily, gave its name to a swamp that, when drying up, exhaled a pestilence. The townspeople consulted the oracle whether they should drain the swamp completely, which the oracle forbade. Nevertheless, they unwisely did so, with the result that 'their enemies came in across it, and they were well punished for not attending to the oracle' (107). Erasmus' introduction of this adage with the words 'Someone might perhaps say at this point ...' is an example of *anteoccupatio*, which he discusses in book 2 CWE 68 559–60; see Cicero *De oratore* 3.53.205.

And here again something else will occur to someone, and he will say, chiding me, 'If that ability depends upon the kindness of the deity, say no more: you have already done your duty by advising whence it must be sought – there is no further need for your instructions.' Let him again have the reply that anyone who has a mind or a tongue worthy of a preacher must simply ascribe it to the heavenly Spirit, but let no one now expect what was displayed in the apostles.[527] Miracles suited the beginnings of the nascent church, though not even the apostles were suddenly made heralds of the gospel out of ordinary citizens. For some years they offered very attentive ears to Christ, the teacher of all teachers; they fasted and prayed for ten days when about to receive the Holy Spirit and did the same constantly after receiving it,[528] and it is likely that they commonly spent some part of their time in reading the Bible. Certainly Paul asks to have books sent to him, especially those written on parchment;[529] these, I think, were not the books of Plato or of Pythagoras or cabalistic or Talmudic books, but those of the Old Testament. Paul, who wrote, 'I think that I too have the spirit of God,'[530] knew that its help would not fail him, but he also knew that that Spirit hates sloth,[531] loves industrious and alert minds, and so Paul does not disdain to be the pupil of Ananias[532] and does not shrink from comparing his Gospel with Peter and James.[533] Even supposing that none of this happened, yet the nature of our times is different, for no one would be heeded now who said, 'I received my gospel neither through a man nor from a man, but from Jesus Christ,' though even today, especially in Italy, there are some who claim openly before the public to have the spirit of prophecy:[534] certainly I have heard one with my own ears who did this

* * * * *

527 Ie after the experience of Pentecost (Acts 2 and Acts passim).
528 Cf Acts 1:14. Erasmus deduces this from two references to chronology: the 'forty days' after the resurrection and before the ascension when Jesus spoke to the apostles 'about the kingdom of God' (Acts 1:3), and Pentecost, the festival ending the paschal season and harvest festival (cf Lev 23:11); therefore fifty days after Easter and ten days after Jesus' ascension. At this time the apostles awaited the Holy Spirit promised by Christ (Acts 1:4–5). For their fasting, see Matt 9:15; Mark 2:20; Luke 5:35.
529 2 Tim 4:13
530 1 Cor 7:40
531 Cf 1 Tim 5:13; 2 Thess 3:10–11.
532 Acts 9:10–19
533 Galatians 2
534 Such claims were not uncommon. The Fifth Lateran Council (1513–17) prohibited preachers from making such claims and statements; see Tanner I 635: 'They [bad preachers] dare to claim that they possess this information from the light of eternity and by the guidance and grace of the Holy Spirit.' This

openly at Rome at a great popular gathering. I am not saying this because
the hand of God has been shortened; now as in the past it can give a human
voice to a she-ass.[535] The spirit of Christ works even today in the prophets,
for I call prophets those who explain the mysteries of arcane Scripture, and
the Apostle mentions this type of prophecy among the special gifts of the
Spirit;[536] but it requires our own effort so that through it the Spirit can work
in us not less but more secretly. But if, in the days when miracles were
in season, Peter urged his followers to heed the prophetic word as a lamp
shining in a dark place,[537] and Paul advised that whatever was written in
Sacred Scripture was written for our instruction so that by steadfastness
and the consolation of the Scriptures we might have hope,[538] all the more
should we in these days not sleep or nod off while awaiting the gifts of
the Spirit. For, as must be repeated often, he wants them to be requested
in prayers neither infrequent nor unimpassioned;[539] he wants them to be
sought through good works;[540] he wants them, as it were, to be purchased
by our labours, partly that he may give them to the worthy, partly that
he may give them more bountifully. Thus he lavishes them upon those on
whom he wishes and to the extent that he knows they are needed, and the
gift he gives is absolutely free,[541] so that we can claim nothing that comes
from it as our own,[542] lest we become puffed up[543] and fall into the devil's
snare;[544] but he imparts this munificence of his not to the sluggish, not to the
hostile, not to the resistant, but to those who ask it urgently with faith and
to those who accommodate themselves as wholly as they can to the divine
beneficence. The prophet exclaims, 'Make a clean heart in me, O God,'[545]
but if the Lord required no effort of our own here, he would not advise

* * * * *

suggests that Erasmus was familiar with the decrees of Lateran v. See Minnich.
535 Balaam's ass (Num 22:28–30)
536 1 Cor 14:1; see *Annotationes in 1 ad Corinthios* ASD VI-8 266–7, where Erasmus
    calls prophets those who 'explain the mysteries of arcane scripture' rather than
    those who give 'a prediction of things to come' (*Hoc loco Paulus prophetiam vocat
    non praedictionem futurorum, sed interpretationem divinae scripturae*). See also 1
    Cor 12:28 and *Annotationes in 1 ad Corinthios* ASD VI-8 246–8.
537 2 Pet 1:19
538 Rom 15:4
539 See Luke 18:1; Rom 12:12; Col 4:2–3; 1 Thess 5:17.
540 1 Tim 6:18; Titus 3:1, 8, 14; James 1:25
541 Eph 2:7–10
542 Cf 1 Cor 3:21; Eph 2:9; Gal 6:14; James 2:14.
543 1 Cor 4:6, 18, 19; Col 2:18; 1 Tim 3:6; 2 Tim 3:4
544 1 Tim 3:7, 6:9
545 Ps 51:10 (Vulg 50:12)

us through the prophet Ezekiel, 'Make yourselves a new heart and a new spirit.'[546] The heart is our means of understanding, the spirit our means of speech. Solomon would not say, 'It is man's part to prepare the heart and the Lord's to guide the tongue,'[547] nor would Scripture reproach Roboam because he had not prepared his heart to seek the Lord,[548] nor would the Baptist, Christ's πρόδρομος [forerunner], shout in the desert in accordance with the prophecy of Isaiah, 'Prepare the way of the Lord, make straight his pathways.'[549] From the Father of lights[550] comes every excellent and every perfect gift; from him as from the highest source flows all that is. But just as someone who has not obeyed his physician's advice is said to have caused his own illness, and just as someone who has implored a physician's help and handed himself over to him for treatment is said to cure his disease, similarly a man makes a new heart for himself when he does not retreat from the divine grace that calls him to better things,[551] when he opens for someone who stands before the door and knocks.[552] And he prepares the way for the Lord's coming when he recognizes the disease and gives the physician a kindly reception, when he obediently accommodates himself to the person who is offering the medicine, for this is in a sense helping the helper and cooperating with the operator. Just as someone who has rejected a physician is said to have destroyed himself, so whoever has entrusted himself to a reliable physician is said to have saved his own life, not because he could provide good health for himself but because he did not repulse someone who was willing to restore his health. But this obedience or petty effort of ours, if any of it is ours at all, is not so important that we should not ascribe everything to the munificence of divinity; but if this insignificant exertion of ours is not present, then the whole problem is

* * * * *

546 Ezek 18:31. Erasmus again brings up the complex theological question of the preacher's cooperation with the Holy Spirit for carrying out this ministry efficaciously.
547 Prov 16:1
548 2 Chron 12:14
549 Matt 3:3; Mark 1:3; Luke 3:4; John 1:23; cf Isa 40:3.
550 James 1:17
551 Erasmus gives hints here of his belief in the constant bounty of God's grace, which human beings continuously resist through idleness or perverse sinfulness. Human industry is required, but the initiative and result are fully God's. The whole issue of grace and human effort is discussed at great length in *De libero arbitrio* and *Hyperaspistes* 1 and 2 CWE 76–7; see also *Annotationes in epistolam ad Romanos* CWE 56 261, and *Paraphrasis in epistolam Pauli apostoli ad Romanos* CWE 42 55–9.
552 Rev 3:20; Luke 11:9–13; Matt 7:7–11

imputed to our idleness[553] for our having failed the divine goodness, which challenges us in so many ways on every side. Once when the Lord was consulted and, promising victory, commanded the Jews to attack their enemy, they armed themselves no less eagerly and made ready whatever contributed to winning the victory,[554] not because they distrusted the promises of the oracle or placed their hope of victory in their own strength but to ensure that their sloth did not render them unworthy of God's promises. For just as the Ninevites in submitting themselves to penitence compelled God, as it were, to sing a palinode[555] and to change his promulgated sentence, turning his anger to mercy,[556] so those who either reject or retain ungratefully God's prompt and welcoming kindness compel him, contrary to his nature, either to refuse or to reclaim his gifts and to direct threats in place of his spurned liberality, inasmuch as it is God's nature to benefit everyone. But if, in those ancient times when the hardness of the Jewish race or the infancy of the still suckling church required miracles, the Israelites did not withhold their own exertion from the divine promises, and if the Apostle, as was said, issues a call to the study of Scripture by innocently confessing that the spirits of the prophets are subject to prophets,[557] how much less appropriate it is in these times that we should nod off waiting for the grace of the Spirit to slip into us as we doze, now that faith in the gospel has grown up and reached maturity[558] and has no use for oracles or for miracles, since it regards canonical Scripture in place of oracles, faith instead of miracles, and according to the prophet Isaiah, 'The law of the Lord bound and sealed in our hearts is more precious to us than all the answers of the living and the dead.'[559] Our effort will not lessen the power of the Spirit[560] so long as we eschew self-confidence and attribute every

* * * * *

553 Erasmus singles out the vice of idleness (*inertia*) as a fundamental human failing and as resistance to God's constant promptings to embrace the philosophy of Christ. In this Erasmus falls in line with John Chrysostom's singling out 'idleness' (ῥαθυμία) as the greatest vice holding Christians back from eagerly embracing God's grace. See Carole Straw 'Chrysostom's Martyrs: Zealous Athletes and the Dangers of Sloth' *Studia Ephemeridis Augustinianum* 93 (2005) 521–54.
554 See eg Josh 10:7; 1 Sam 23:2–4, 30:8; 2 Sam 5:19–25.
555 *Adagia* I ix 59 *Palinodiam canere* 'To sing a palinode'
556 Jon 3:10
557 1 Cor 14:32
558 1 Cor 13:10–11
559 See Isa 8:16–19.
560 An important element of Erasmus' theology of grace is that the quantity of human effort in no way compromises or diminishes the activity of the Holy Spirit.

success to him who alone prospers human actions.[561] In fact, if heavenly grace comes upon us and finds in us some natural gift, such as physical health, a sonorous voice, an articulate tongue, a quick intellect, a reliable memory, or some ability obtained by human effort such as the adroitness in deduction that dialectic provides, the oratorical power that rhetoric confers, the knowledge of nature that science offers, it does not take them away but perfects them,[562] turning them to the promotion of godliness and to the glory of Christ. Paul, the persecutor of the church, learned the Law eagerly at Gamaliel's feet;[563] when the Spirit came upon him, it perfected this previously deadly knowledge and turned it into the most fertile fruit of the gospel. He seems to have been crafted by nature for speaking, having a quick mind, a burning intellect, a ready tongue; hence while Barnabas, who was taken for Jupiter, was silent, he was called Mercury because he was the leader in speech;[564] but the accession of the Spirit neither reduced the authority and dignity of Barnabas, which were displayed in his countenance, nor deprived Paul of his gifts. Cyprian's eloquence gave no faint lustre to the church, but he had acquired it while still serving idols instead of God; therefore the Spirit did not take it away but perfected it. Similarly St Augustine learned rhetoric and philosophy in paganism and exercised them in the heresy of the Manicheans; the Spirit took neither of these from him but completed what was imperfect, turning to the profit of the church even the very thing that was wicked in him, for if he had never been mad with the Manicheans, he would neither have revealed their insanity so plainly nor refuted it so effectively.[565]

* * * * *

561 2 Cor 3:4–5, 4:5–15

562 Erasmus expresses the scholastic principle that grace perfects nature: nature has, as it were, an 'obediential potency' (*potentia oboedientialis*) or fundamental receptiveness to the divine activity. See Thomas Aquinas *Summa theologiae* III q 111 a 4 on the relationship of gratuitous grace to nature and to persuading others to believe. Erasmus gives the examples of Cyprian and Augustine whose skills in pagan rhetoric were perfected by the Holy Spirit after their conversions to Christ. St Paul, of course, is the example par excellence.

563 Acts 22:3

564 Acts 14:11

565 See for example Augustine's anti-Manichaean writings *Contra Faustum Manichaeum* PL 42 207–518, *Answer to Faustus the Manichean* WSA I-19 and *The Manichean Debate* I/20, and in NPNF 1st series 4 3–365; Peter Brown *Augustine of Hippo: A Biography* (Berkeley and Los Angeles 1967; rev ed 2000) 46–60; James J. O'Donnell *Augustine: A New Biography* (New York 2005) 47–54. See also *Augustine* 'Mani, Manicheism' 520–4 and 'Anti-Manichean Writings' 39–41.

It is the duty of parents or teachers, therefore, if they have marked out
someone for the office of preacher, to prepare him right from infancy as an
instrument for the Holy Spirit, to train him in morals and especially in those
subjects that are most effective for the ability to teach.[566] For just as someone
once cleverly remarked that the person who should be called learned is not
someone who has learned the most but someone who has learned what is
best and most necessary,[567] so the future preacher must spend his effort and
his life – which is fleeting and brief, even if old age, which is not granted to
many, should be his lot – not with just anything at all, but must learn first
and foremost those things that are most suited to the office of teaching. We
have already characterized these to some extent elsewhere,[568] and will do
so to some extent in this work when it will be appropriate. People who are
being trained for athletics and for agriculture, for sailing, for soldiering and
for holding a magistracy, or for medicine, for legal cases and for service at
court are not all educated by the same methods; but if the children of this age
instruct their children with such care and thoughtfulness for common and
humble occupations, and if someone who thrusts himself forward for these
occupations without training is driven off with public derision, how careful
must be the preparation for the office of preacher, both the most beautiful
and the most difficult of all. If someone now puts his hand to the plough
without training in that skill, is he not pushed aside at once in mockery? If

* * * * *

566 Erasmus again emphasizes that education begins early, which holds true especially for the aspiring preacher. It is the duty of parents, bishops, and princes to
provide encouragement and the means by which young men can learn the liberal arts, study Scripture, and above all be instructed in the virtues. Erasmus
anticipates the canons of the Council of Trent (especially Session 23, Canon 18)
legislating the establishment in dioceses of houses of liberal arts and Scripture,
which would eventually lead to the Roman Catholic seminary system (seminary being a 'seedbed of the virtues'); see Tanner II 750–1. See also Quintilian 1.1.3 for the duty of 'a father' to 'devote the utmost care to fostering the
promise shown by the son whom he destines to become an orator.'
567 Here Erasmus anticipates the Council of Trent's Session 5, *Decretum secundum:
super lectione et praedicatione – ea, quae scire omnibus necessarium est ad salutem*
– the subject of the preacher's teaching; Tanner II 669–70. See 154, 268 above
where Erasmus reformulates this as 'those things that are most suited to the
office of teaching.' Erasmus promises elsewhere to discourse on these subjects;
see book 4 passim where he takes up these teachings of the faith.
568 See CWE 24 697–702 for the 1530 catalogue listing all of Erasmus' works; among
his works on literature and education of particular relevance for instructing
future preachers are: *De pueris instituendis* CWE 26 291–346; *De recta pronuntiatione* CWE 26 347–475; *De ratione studii* CWE 24 661–91; *De copia* CWE 24 279–659.

a storm comes up and someone without knowledge of the pilot's art seizes the rudder, does he not find himself being attacked immediately by angry passengers and in danger of being cast headlong into the sea? I shall turn to humbler matters to make my point. If someone goes to dance among the French ignorant of French steps, or among the Germans ignorant of German steps, or among the Italians ignorant of Italian steps, is he not met at once by general ridicule? Someone who plays at dice without knowing the rules and customs belonging to that 'subject' is also regarded as impudent, and someone who enters fencing school and errs through inexperience against the rules of the art is sometimes killed. How absurd, then, are the judgments of mortals who admit anyone at all to an office more truly angelic than human, men of untamed emotions, neither pure of vice nor trained in literature nor inspired by the Spirit nor steady in faith nor burning with charity, and not, I might add, either sober or sane; it takes only an ashen robe, a black or white mantle. And yet a man who wears a helmet or a breastplate is not immediately assigned to soldiering, nor is someone with a sailor's uniform straightway admitted to the helm, nor do we entrust the building of a house to anyone who has a saw or axe; rather we inquire carefully what sort of workman he is and what he has done. Now there leap up into the pulpit, that is, onto a more than royal seat, men who have been prepared for this office by no instruction, who put off all shame and set their tongues rolling, project their voices, thundering whatever comes into their mouths[569] or whatever has been prescribed to them by the unlearned or whatever human emotion has dictated; not to mention meanwhile those whom, alas, we hear too frequently, who speak in such a way that their words breathe only flattery, boasting, profit and, what is worse than these, hatred and envy of one's neighbour, and do it so obviously that sometimes the congregation, however dull and ignorant, gets up and leaves in midspeech. No wonder; in the theatre an actor is hooted off if his gestures suggest Thersites[570] when he is playing Agamemnon. Now leaving the church is all that is permitted to the crowd, since the custom of applauding, acclaiming, whistling off, and hooting off, which was derived from secular assemblies and from the theatres of the heathen and long persisted in ecclesiastical assemblies, has

* * * * *

569 Cf *Adagia* I v 73 *Quicquid in linguam venerit* 'Whatever may come on the tongue.'
570 A base warrior in the *Iliad* 2.212–14: 'Ugly was he beyond all men who came to Ilios'; Homer describes him as one 'whose mind was full of a great store of disorderly words ...' Thersites upbraids Agamemnon in the assembly but is shouted down and struck by Odysseus for being out of place. See *Lingua* CWE 29 270 and n5; *De virtute amplectenda* ibidem 5; *Adagia* IV iii 80.

long since been discarded. So all the more detestable are those who do not shrink from abusing the reverence of a holy place and the awed silence of the people and the authority of the divine word. It is one thing to speak from a wagon[571] or from a table but quite another to teach the heavenly philosophy from the sacred pulpit. The more sacred the function, the greater the dignity of him who performs it; and of course the greater the dignity, the greater the circumspection[572] with which the business must be conducted.

The first rank in the political hierarchy belongs to kings, but among the king's duties none is more noble than when he sits before a tribunal and examines cases, or urges before an assembly something pertinent to the tranquillity of the state. The highest dignity in the ecclesiastical hierarchy belongs to bishops;[573] however many their functions, chief among which are the administration of the sacraments and spiritual instruction, he is at the pinnacle of his dignity whenever he feeds the souls of the people with the flesh and blood of Christ, which is the Word of God.[574] The disciples of the apostles once used to perform baptism, just as the Lord Jesus did not himself baptize, but the apostles used to baptize in his name.[575] He himself used to teach personally, and for some time, as the church matured, no one preached in the churches except the bishop; afterwards the role of teaching was transferred to the presbyters, but to outstanding ones and not indefinitely, but only if they had a bishop who was insufficiently skilled in the vernacular but was otherwise a devout and learned man (as happened to Augustine under Valerian,[576] who was Greek by birth and

* * * * *

571 See *Adagia* I vii 73 *De plaustro loqui* 'Wagon-language.'
572 Latin *circumspectio*; similar to 'appropriateness'; see Cicero *De oratore* 3.210–12.
573 Erasmus takes up again this division between state and church, king and bishop; see 250–3 above. At the top of the ecclesiastical hierarchy stands the teacher-bishop, and teaching is his chief function in the church. Erasmus frequently emphasizes this fundamental distinction of orders.
574 Erasmus' words can be read to include both the bishop's teaching and his dispensing the Eucharist, though in this context and often elsewhere 'feeding' refers to the bishop's teaching office; as the passage below suggests, Christ's primary work was teaching, while the administration of the other sacraments (ie baptism) was left to the apostles. Erasmus holds nothing as more important than expounding 'canonical Scripture' by preaching. See 390 below: 'Mystical Scripture is a living bread descending from heaven, which bestows eternal life upon those who eat it: but someone is needed to break this bread appropriately and distribute it according to the Redeemer's example.'
575 Acts 8:12, 38; 9:18
576 Chomarat notes that Erasmus' memory failed him; the bishop in fact was Valerius; see ASD V-4 115 674n; see Possidius *Sancti Augustini vita scripta a Possidio*

therefore less fluent in Latin; but such honour was accorded Augustine, because of the dignity of the office, that he sat in the bishop's chair while the
bishop was still alive), or if the absence of a bishop, due to the pressures
of business or to illness, required the services of a substitute. Now, though
this role is widely delegated to monks and presbyters,[577] nevertheless anyone who steps up to that place ought to remember that he is occupied in
an office that far surpasses the dignity of a king and that is primary in a
bishop, who is greater than any king, certainly in so far as the sublimity
of his office is concerned. This statement is not made to make the preacher
conceited[578] but to make him put aside human desires and respond with
great awe and sincerity to the magnificence of his office. Epaminondas[579] so
conducted an insignificant and despised magistracy, which had been delegated to him by popular vote as an insult, that afterwards it came to be
sought as a splendid office: the heathen deservedly praise a heathen who
by his own ability added dignity to a despised function; but what praise
would a Christian earn if, by conducting it badly, he renders cheap and contemptible an office that is inherently most honourable?[580] After God himself
the church has nothing more sacred, more wholesome, more venerable, and
more sublime than the word of God, that is, canonical Scripture; but just as
the Lord complains in prophecy that his name becomes ignominious and has
a bad reputation among the nations because of the wickedness of those who

* * * * *

episcopo ed Herbert T. Weiskotten (Princeton 1919) 49 (with revised text, introduction, notes, and an English version): 'Valerius, a Greek by birth and less
versed in the Latin language and literature, saw that he himself was less useful for this end. Therefore he gave his presbyter the right of preaching the
Gospel in his presence in the church and very frequently of holding public
discussions – contrary to the practice and custom of the African churches. On
this account some bishops found fault with him.' See also Peter Brown *Augustine of Hippo: A Biography* (Berkeley and Los Angeles 1967; rev ed 2000)
138–40.
577 In Erasmus' day preaching was carried on extensively by members of the religious orders, above all by Franciscans and Dominicans, who frequently came
into conflict with local ordinaries. The Fifth Lateran Council and the Council
of Trent moved to reassert the authority of the bishop in all matters pertaining
to preaching; see Tanner I 636–8; and II 667–70, 763–4.
578 For 'become conceited' (*cristas sumat*), see *Adagia* I viii 69 *Tollere cristas* 'To raise
one's crest.'
579 See Plutarch *Moralia* 811B (*Precepts of Statecraft*), which says, 'Not only does the
office distinguish the man, but also the man the office'; cf Valerius Maximus
3.7 ext 5.
580 Another example of an argument by comparison.

avow it,[581] so he could complain with perfect justice that the faults of preachers make that sacrosanct office contemptible. Indeed, even the kings of this age think it an insult to them if their ambassadors have done something contrary to decorum. So the greater the one who sent them and the more serious the business being communicated, the more ambassadors are on their guard to ensure that they match both the dignity of the prince and the importance of the business delegated to them. But, as must be said often, among all the functions of human life none is more serious, none more noble, and none more dangerous than that of the preacher.[582] If you are wondering whence he has been sent, it is from that prince who created, sustains, and guides the universe; if you are wondering what his mission is, it is to teach his people the heavenly philosophy. It is not, therefore, a matter of arranging a marriage or claiming sovereignty or concluding a treaty between two powers; rather it is a matter of getting as many souls as possible espoused to Christ, who is so fervent a lover that he did not hesitate to die for them, a matter of keeping Satan from seizing what Christ redeemed with his own blood, of preventing wolves from devouring the Lord's flock, of keeping the Christian people from deserting their emperor, to whom in baptism they once and for all pledged their allegiance. This embassy, moreover, has been entrusted to the pastors on these terms, that if they omit no aspect of their office, they nonetheless claim from this no praise for themselves because whatever they do, they do in another's name, under another's protection and authority; but if they carry out their mission badly, all the loss is laid at their door. Through Ezekiel the Lord prescribed this law for the preacher:[583] if, through slackness in carrying out his delegated office, either a wicked man was not converted to penitence or a just man was turned away to impiety when the preacher should have won over the former and restrained the latter, both should die together, the wicked man for committing impiety, the preacher for his neglect of duty; and in the same prophet the Lord threatens that he will demand back his sheep from the hand of the shepherds who neglected the flock but fed themselves, shearing, milking, and slaughtering the sheep while taking no care of them.[584] What sort of paradise are those men promising themselves who take on the care of many sheepfolds and,

* * * * *

581 Ezek 36:20–3
582 See Larissa Taylor 'Dangerous Vocations: Preaching in France in the Late Middle Ages and Reformations' in *Preachers and People in the Reformations and Early Modern Period* ed Larissa Taylor (Leiden 2001) 91–124.
583 Ezek 3:18–21
584 See Ezek 34:1–10.

burdened with four or five bishoprics,[585] do not even think about pasturing their sheep, but become feeders on, not feeders of, their flocks and out of the yield of their sheep erect satraps' palaces, prepare Sicilian,[586] or rather Sybaritic,[587] dinners every day, keep warhorses, keep concubines, keep a more ostentatious retinue of servants than even secular princes?

An ambassador, moreover, errs in three ways: if he fails to perform what he has received in his commission; or if he does something else in passing that had not been commissioned; or if he otherwise displays anything in his behaviour that could bring disgrace upon the authority who entrusted his business to such a spokesman.

Someone who occupies the place of a teacher and accepts his fee but does not teach errs in the first way. Someone who teaches the word of God while intermingling some human doctrines, or who professes himself a soldier and general of Christ but is entangled in secular business, cultivating the courts of princes not in order to impart salubrious counsel to them but to offer himself as a constant companion[588] in banquets, gambling, dancing, hunting, and jesting, errs in the second way. Someone who preaches the gospel alertly enough and without error but abrogates the credibility of his teaching by an impure life errs in the third way.

The language of prophecy calls those who belong to the first sort 'mute dogs without the power to bark';[589] shepherd and dog are different in external features, but in this condition they are the same. They see a predator stalking night and day and hunting something to devour; they see wolves attacking the Lord's sheep pen and do not have a voice with which to drive away and reveal the thief, with which to frighten off the wolves – I only wish they sometimes lacked a voice with which to attract thieves and wolves! Zechariah calls shepherds of this kind 'idols,'[590] that is, statues and images

* * * * *

585 Erasmus criticizes the abuse of holding a plurality of benefices, ie where one man might be bishop and enjoy the revenues of two or more episcopal sees. This was one of many common abuses in Erasmus' day, but the greatest abuse he sees is in bishops who did not preach, even if they held only one see.

586 Erasmus' adage is actually *Syracusana mensa* 'A Syracusan table'; see *Adagia* II ii 68.

587 See *Adagia* II ii 65.

588 For 'a constant companion' (*omnium horarum socius*), see *Adagia* I iii 86 *Omnium horarum homo* 'A man for all hours.' See the preface to *Moria* (Ep 222:21, CWE 27 161–2) where the phrase is applied to Thomas More: 'You are both able and pleased to play with everyone the part of a man for all seasons.'

589 Isa 56:10

590 Zec 11:17

that display the perfect appearance of shepherds but are endowed with neither mind nor voice. If you were to examine their dress, if you were to observe their title, if you were to see them demanding tithes, you would say
that they were pastors; if for the healing of your conscience you were to require wholesome counsel for the soul, admonition, consolation, the nourishment of sacred teaching,[591] you would say that they were worse than statues,
which want to be worshipped but do not know how to be of use. A little
earlier in the same prophet the Lord says that there is no shepherd in Israel,[592] for someone who brings nothing useful to his flock does not deserve
the name of shepherd. The prophet describes the useless shepherd in these
words: 'Behold, I shall raise up in the land a shepherd who will not seek
out the lost, will not search for the scattered, and will not heal the maimed,
and will not nourish the sound, and will devour the flesh of the fat ones,
and will tear off their hooves,'[593] and at once the voice of the angry God
cries out against such a monstrosity: 'O shepherd and idol, and deserter of
the flock.'[594] The only charge against this foolish shepherd is his silence and
his failure to tend the flock, since he himself is fed from the yield of his
flock, not feeding it but feeding upon it. And yet hear the Lord's most terrible threats: 'The sword,' he says, 'is over his arm and over his right eye,
his arm will be withered by dryness, and his right eye will be darkened
by shadows.'[595] The prophet calls this shepherd 'foolish,'[596] for he thinks
that he is something though he is only an idol; he claims power for himself while he thunders against his subjects, he claims the wisdom of this
world, but he will be deprived of both, with his arm cut off and his eye
darkened.

In the second group belong those to whom the charge of παραπρεσβεία[597] [a false legation] applies, that is, conducting an embassy otherwise
than as it should. As I began to say before, error is committed here in more

* * * * *

591 Cf 2 Tim 3:16.
592 Zec 10:2
593 Zec 11:16
594 Zec 11:17
595 Zec 11:17
596 Zec 11:15
597 The Athenians held legates accountable for state embassies; those that failed
    or betrayed the *polis* were charged with conducting a 'faithless' or 'dishon-
    est embassy.' See LSJ 1322 παραπρεσβεία. Aeschines' *De falsa legatione* (*On the
    Embassy* and Demosthenes' *De falsa legatione* (*On the False Embassy*) give ac-
    counts of their joint embassy to Philip of Macedon. See also Quintilian 4.4.5
    and 7.4.36–7.

ways than one: first, if some part of the commission is passed over; next, if
the ambassador adds something on his own beyond his commission; finally,
if when a prince's embassy has been received, he does something inciden-
tally that is unworthy of the representative of a king or that is outside his
responsibilities and diverts him from attending to his commission. It is also
counted among the charges of παραπρεσβεία when someone receives a gift
from those to whom he was sent (apart from those minor presents that are
often given to ambassadors as a token of respect), such as accepting some
authority or a rich benefice or significant annual revenues.

The first kind of error is made by those who preach the law of God
strictly to the weak but to the powerful are silent or, even more disgracefully, fawning; Isaiah, in chapter 9, vents his anger against these under the
riddle of the head and the twisting and corrupting tail.[598] Before ordinary
folk they shout that the decrees of princes and bishops must be obeyed under penalty of Gehenna;[599] among princes they either keep silent or else
speak to win favour. The prince, they say, is above the law.[600] There is
nothing that the prince cannot do out of his sure knowledge and plenary
power; all the property of the citizens belongs to the prince, should he demand it, nor may the people inquire why he demands it. And yet Christ
cries out most harshly against the rich,[601] against the scribes and the Pharisees,[602] the governors of the people, though not unaware that there are
adulterers, misers, drunkards, and gluttons among the common people as
well. I would not say this because I think that those who trouble the minds
of princes with seditious and unseasonable clamourings deserve approval.
One thing suited the prophet of the Old Law, another befits the teacher of
the gospel, and things that were appropriate to Christ, to whom no blemish of wrong ever clung,[603] are not to be expected from a human evangelist as well, since he is a sinner admonishing sinners. Truth needs to be

* * * * *

598 See Isa 9:14–15.
599 Ie hell; cf Matt 5:29–30, 10:28.
600 *princeps est . . . supra legem*; proponents of royal absolutism argued that only a
    prince 'absolved from the laws' (*a legibus solutus*) could exercise full power to
    enforce the laws. See Erasmus' comment on the difference between monarchy
    and tyranny: *Tyrannicida* CWE 29 115 and Thomas Aquinas *Summa theologiae*
    1a–11ae q 96 a 5 ad 3. Royal absolutists, however, acknowledged that the prince
    was subject to divine law, which kept check on the king from becoming a
    tyrant. For the idea of the absolute prince, see 'Absolutism' ER I 2–4.
601 See especially Luke 16:19–31, 18:18–25; Mark 10:17–25.
602 See Matt 23:13–35.
603 Heb 4:15, 9:14; 1 Pet 2:22

revealed to different people in different ways according to the nature of the times and persons but should be withdrawn from no one when the case demands it,[604] so that one may boast with Paul, who bears witness as follows among the Ephesians: 'You know that I held back nothing that was useful to you and that nothing prevented my declaring it to you and teaching you publicly.'[605]

Those who add something of their own to the divine are no less seriously at fault than those who take something away; for sometimes it is right to conceal the truth when the hearer is unworthy or when he is yet unable to be taught the mystery. But mixing the human with the divine as though they were equals is a kind of sacrilege, for Scripture prohibits it many times, as in Deuteronomy 4, 'You shall not add to the word which I speak to you nor shall you take from it';[606] and also in Revelation the Holy Spirit threatens curses upon anyone who adds to or takes anything from the prophetic words.[607] But someone who keeps back some things for the present through discretion in finding the right moment is not diminishing, and someone who accommodates Scripture, which is naturally fertile, to various interpretations (a matter of which we will speak in its own place) is not adding so long as the interpretations are devout and useful. Someone who finds in the words of Scripture a meaning that is indeed devout but that perhaps the Holy Spirit did not express in those words is also not adding so long as he has an ingenuous spirit, which will yield readily if someone teaches him the true significance. Who is it then that adds? Someone who rates purely human enactments as equal to divine precepts, who knowingly twists the words of Scripture to a wicked or heretical meaning, who, among the untrained, quotes from canonical Scripture what is nowhere to be found there, who cites Plato or Aristotle with no less pride than Isaiah or Paul: not because the truth is not Christ's wherever it has been found, but because one may have doubts about human words, not so about divine. Aristotle teaches that a wife ought to be compliant to her husband, but this is right not because Aristotle taught it but because natural and divine law alike

* * * * *

604 Erasmus reiterates the fundamental rhetorical principle of accommodation; see 137, 278 above; see also Quintilian 11.
605 Acts 20:20. Erasmus mistakenly refers here to Ephesians. Chomarat cites this as 'a new proof that from one edition to another the text was reviewed neither by Erasmus nor by an attentive corrector' ASD V-4 121 788–9n.
606 Deut 4:2
607 Rev 22:18–19

so dictate; but whatever God instructs is right because it was instructed by the Lord.[608] A slave is asked in a comedy, 'Who ordered you to say this?'[609]

But if those who transact business or do something else of that kind when undertaking an embassy in the name of a prince or of a state are prosecuted, what should be said of those who undertake the office of the preacher, which requires the whole human heart and all the mind's strength, and not only transact their own business but even lend money and wage war and (I am ashamed to relate) lower themselves even to humble services, presiding over the kitchens of the rich for a scanty fee or tending constantly their hunting dogs and bird-catching fowl. 'But they are not preachers; they are only presbyters,' you will say; but teaching the gospel once belonged to all presbyters – surely they all ought to strive to qualify for admission to the office of teaching if occasion should demand. Does a man then who is toiling at such a great matter have time left over to spend on unessential business, which, though not disgraceful, is certainly harmful by virtue of calling him away from necessary concerns, inappropriate because those gestures do not befit this character, and criminal because those involved in these affairs do not give the Lord the work they owe and will be called worthless servants[610] when the time comes to exact a reckoning?

But if such integrity is required in human embassies that accepting a sumptuous gift from those to whom they are sent is subject to blame, what should be said of those who plunder the people they teach, who grasp at inheritances and wealth, who hunt the glory of the world even though Paul, so outstanding a preacher, says, 'Having food and clothing, with these we are content';[611] and yet among the Corinthians and Thessalonians he went beyond this, procuring food for himself with his own hands in order to preach the gospel without charge.[612] Scripture forbids 'tying the mouth of an ox that is threshing,'[613] and the Apostle recognizes that it is fair 'that no one be a soldier at his own expense.'[614] He admits that the worker deserves his reward, and writing to the Galatians he commands, 'Let him who is

* * * * *

608 Erasmus takes up these precepts on handling Scripture properly in book 3.
609 Terence *Phormio* 639
610 Matt 18:32; Luke 19:22
611 1 Tim 6:8
612 1 Cor 4:12; 1 Thess 2:9; 2 Thess 3:8
613 Deut 25:4; cf 1 Cor 9:9 and 1 Tim 5:18.
614 1 Cor 9:7

catechized' and instructed 'share with the catechist,' but adds 'in all good things';[615] but for the servant of God to grow rich in this world is not good, and for him to be charmed by the glory of the world is not good, and for him to be stuffed at splendid banquets is not good. To receive these things from the people, then, is wrong. In many places preachers have salaries prescribed for them, which suffice for a comfortable life provided they are thrifty and sober; the stipend is awarded to preachers, not to banqueters, not to satraps, not to keepers of whores or horses, and they should be content with it, especially since they are expecting an invaluable stipend, eternal life,[616] from him whose business they are transacting. Yet the Lord promised that on those who wholeheartedly seek the kingdom of God he would also bestow what pertains to physical necessity;[617] the kingdom of God is the yield of the gospel.[618]

Finally, if in the secular world those who had not been thrifty before and had lived rather dissolutely compose themselves when they undertake an embassy, summon up all the strength of their intellect, and, as it were, take on another personality to fulfil their delegated office, how much more should someone who performs an embassy for Christ apply the same attention in order to reconcile the world to the Father through him, as Paul writes to the Corinthians: 'All this is from God, who through Christ reconciled us to himself and gave us the ministry of reconciliation, because God was in him reconciling the world to himself, not counting their trespasses, and placed in us the word of reconciliation. So we are ambassadors for Christ, as if God were appealing through us.'[619] When you hear 'all this from God,' you recognize the stature of the sender; when you hear 'who through Christ reconciled us to himself,' you hear the sublime and indeed welcome theme of the mission; when you hear 'and placed in us the word of reconciliation,' you recognize the inescapable commission. You are sent by God the Father, on behalf of the Son of God; you bring the most joyful news, news of peace restored with God and with his Son. Your role is to persuade all and sundry who have placed their trust in Christ that through him all the sins of their past life are freely forgiven and that they are summoned to share as coheirs with Christ in the heavenly life[620] so long as they

* * * * *

615 Gal 6:6
616 1 Tim 6:12; John 12:25, 17:2
617 Matt 6:25–34
618 Matt 13:31–2; Mark 4:30–2; Luke 13:18–19
619 2 Cor 5:18–20
620 Cf Heb 9:15.

are resurrected through him and 'walk thereafter in the newness of life.'[621]
He writes similarly to the Ephesians with the prayer 'that utterance may be
given me in the opening of my mouth boldly to make known the mystery of
the gospel for which I am an ambassador in these bonds.'[622] And will not a
man who has undertaken an embassy so difficult, so splendid, and so gratify-
ing compose himself and summon every care to perform his delegated office
sincerely, fittingly, successfully? Or will he even offend, so as to destroy his
credibility by his behaviour and disgrace his office and provoke the anger
of the sender against himself and cheat Christ of his profit? Or will he rather
render his delegated function commendable by the holiness of his life?

Paul honours his Gospel: 'For I say to you gentiles, in so far as I am
apostle of the gentiles, I honour my ministry if I somehow provoke my flesh
to emulation and cause some of them to be saved.'[623] But how does Paul glorify his function? Not by the number of his horses, not by the clamour and
livery of his servants, as the ambassadors of this world commonly do, but
by becoming all things to all people[624] out of his zeal for gaining as many
converts as possible,[625] making himself everyone's servant because he administers the gospel free,[626] that is, to use his own word, ἀδάπανον [without
cost],[627] by being careful in every way not to place some stumbling block in
the path of the gospel,[628] and by preaching Christ with unflagging zeal in
the midst of so many afflictions, incarcerations, and deaths.[629] All preachers
should hasten towards this outstanding example so far as their strength allows, and those who are intended for this office should be educated towards
this goal from childhood.[630]

* * * * *

621 Rom 6:4
622 Eph 6:19–20
623 Rom 11:13–14; the phrase 'my flesh' (Vulg *carnem meam*) refers to Paul's blood
    kinship with the Jews: see *Paraphrasis in epistolam Pauli apostoli ad Romanos* CWE
    42 64–5: 'if somehow in this way, I might challenge my own people – for they
    are my people by blood relationship but strangers in the matter of faith – to
    emulate your piety, even by a kind of envy and jealousy, for the Jews are a
    jealous race.'
624 1 Cor 9:22
625 1 Cor 9:19–22
626 1 Cor 9:18
627 Latin *gratis*; 2 Cor 11:7; 2 Thess 3:8; *sine sumptu* (1 Cor 9:18)
628 1 Cor 9:12
629 Cf 2 Cor 11:23.
630 Erasmus once again emphasizes that the education of the preacher begins in
    childhood; here again the model of St Paul the preacher is put forward as the
    best for emulation (*egregium exemplar*), except for Christ, of course.

'But,' you say, 'rank should not be one's aim, nor should anyone undertake the task unless summoned like Aaron.'[631] It is one thing to seek after a rank out of a human desire, another to be aflame with eagerness to benefit as many as possible, yet another to prepare oneself for this most beautiful function in case he should be called, and another to usurp the task uncommissioned. The Apostle says, 'He who desires the office of bishop desires a noble task,'[632] inasmuch as 'bishop' is a title of office and not of rank, and bishop is a military word, so called because someone who professes himself leader of an army ought to ἐπισκοπεῖν, that is, 'look around,' to ensure that the soldiers of his banner lack nothing; hence Homer too calls Hector ἐπίσκοπος [overseer] and the commander Agamemnon ποιμὴν λαῶν,[633] that is, 'shepherd of the people.' Hence someone who desires this outstanding office is praised in Paul's mouth so long as he simultaneously looks to the things required for performing the office,[634] for a catalogue of these things is immediately appended: 'A bishop must be above reproach,' etc. Desiring a noble task is a mark of charity;[635] rank comes of its own, it is not striven for, and whatever rank falls to one's lot is turned wholly to the glory of Christ. Anyone who seeks a priestly office in order to receive fifteen thousand a year, to process surrounded by forty horses, to seize cities and fortresses, to be called duke or count, is desirous not of work but of wealth; but someone who mortifies his flesh with its vices and desires, who gathers the strength of the spirit by devout study, who instructs his heart with the doctrine of salvation, all with the object of being above reproach when he declares to the people the truth and law of the gospel, is truly desirous of a task that is the greatest of all and most pleasing to God but also the most difficult.[636]

It is exceedingly difficult not just because the philosophy it teaches is difficult, because the people is a beast with many heads,[637] because in every

* * * * *

631 Erasmus often employs this method of arguing in dialogic form, using a fictitious interlocutor; he explains this pedagogical device in book 3; see 852–4. For an extended example of this method, see *Explanatio symboli* CWE 70 231–387.

632 1 Tim 3:1

633 See *Iliad* 24.729 and 2.243.

634 1 Tim 3:2–7

635 1 Tim 3:1

636 Erasmus expands the Ciceronian idea that if the training of the orator is the most difficult occupation, how much more difficult is the training of the Christian orator? See *De oratore* 1.2.6–1.6.23; *Orator* 1.1–2.6, *Brutus* 49.181–2. This theme will be repeated frequently in many ecclesiastical rhetorics that follow Erasmus' *Ecclesiastes*.

637 Horace *Epistles* 1.1.76. Erasmus uses this saying, 267 above.

class of men there are more bad than good, because many are called, few chosen,[638] but much more because all this business of the preacher has to be conducted not with weapons, not with tortures or dungeons, but with the tongue, not with cruelty but with gentleness, not with violence but with persuasion, not by inflicting ills but by enduring them, not by killing but by dying for the sheep.[639]

Naturally this undertaking requires a lofty soul and a heart trained in a philosophy like no other; this clearly is what the prophet calls 'a learned tongue,'[640] what St Paul means by διδακτικὸς εἶναι,[641] that is, 'being suited to teach.' No one is suited to teach the divine unless divinely taught.

But it is a cause of grief that we absurdly devote much greater attention to trivial human affairs than to that on which eternal human happiness depends; I am compelled to complain about this rather often because errors are made without bound and restraint thanks to this fault. I know that it was said by the Lord that the sons of this age are more prudent in their generation than the sons of light,[642] but we Christians, on whom Christ, the 'sun of justice,'[643] has shone, on whom the truth of the gospel has beamed, 'we are not the sons of night or of darkness but the sons of day';[644] hence it is the more disgraceful that among us judgments are made that are equally perverse. Who assigns a field for plowing to a tenant farmer unless he first knows that he is trained for agriculture?[645] Who hires a vine

* * * * *

638 Matt 20:16, 22:14
639 Cf John 10:1–8, 11:47–52, 15:12–13.
640 Isa 50:4
641 1 Tim 3:2 (Vulg *doctorem*); 2 Tim 2:24 (Vulg *docibilem*). Erasmus translates 1 Tim 3:2 as 'skilled in teaching' (*aptum ad docendum*) and 2 Tim 2:24 as 'suited to teach' (*propensum ad docendum*); see the notes in LB VI 934D n8 for 1 Tim 3:2 (*appositum ad docendum*); and LB VI 957E n42 for 2 Tim 2:24 (*idoneum ac paratum ad docendum*). Erasmus speaks of this as 'a special quality which must be looked for in a bishop. He has to have an aptitude and inclination for teaching ... the things which make us truly godly and truly Christian ...' (*Paraphrasis in epistolam Pauli apostoli ad Timotheum priorem* CWE 44 19); see also *Paraphrasis in epistolam Pauli apostoli ad Timotheum secundam* CWE 44 48.
642 Luke 16:8
643 Mal 4:2
644 1 Thess 5:5
645 Erasmus demonstrates another variation on the rhetorical technique of argumentation, where, like Socrates, he uses questions that lead to an inescapable conclusion; here he argues that if we are careful in our choosing in matters of small importance, how much more should we be diligent in the matter of

dresser ignorant of tending vines? Who entrusts a wagon to someone untrained in driving? Who entrusts his horses to someone ignorant of this
skill? Why do I talk of horses? We do not entrust a herd of pigs just to anyone but require a dependable, vigilant, and practised swineherd. We choose
so carefully in frivolous matters, and we entrust the Lord's flock to anyone at all with no discrimination.[646] Similar folly is shown in the fact that
many powerful people pick the trainers of their horses with greater discrimination than the educators of their children,[647] and princes often assign
a magistracy with less careful attention than the tending of their falcons; but
what we have said about discrimination applies more to princes, bishops,
and patrons of benefices.

But others show a ridiculous modesty in taking up the divine functions. If someone were to say to a swordsman, 'Be a shipmaster,' he will answer, 'How can I? I've never seen the sea; the business is outside my arena.'
If someone were to say to a shipmaster, 'Be a doctor; cure the diseases of
the citizens,' he would refuse, asserting that he had not read Hippocrates or
Galen.[648] If someone were to say to a farmer, 'Build me a house,' he is going to answer, 'I learned to guide a plow, not a trowel, axe, or rule.' And
yet men thrust themselves to the priesthood, to the rank of pastor, who are
much less suitable for the task they undertake than a swineherd is for piloting a ship or a shoemaker for administering medicine. Who is so shameless
that he would desire to be considered a builder when he has never taken
a chisel in hand? Who dares call himself a painter when he knows neither
how to grind colours nor how to draw a brush? Who claims the role of
lutenist when he is absolutely ignorant of music? And yet men are found
who take up the office of a pastor, who claim the duties of a bishop though

* * * * *

choosing a preacher, which is of greatest importance? He uses this type of
argument throughout the treatise.
646 Erasmus often makes this point using similar comparisons; see especially John
Chrysostom *On the Priesthood* 4.2 NPNF 1st series 9 63–4.
647 See *De pueris instituendis* CWE 26 314. Erasmus employs the same arguments in
regard to the parents' selection of a teacher for youth.
648 Hippocrates and Galen were the two most eminent authorities on medicine in
the ancient world, whose authority was still uncontested in Erasmus' day. For
Hippocrates (the Asclepiad of Cos), see OCD 518; for Galen (of Pergamum), see
OCD 454–5. Erasmus emended the Greek text of Galen and translated three of
his treatises in the five-volume edition published by Aldus in 1525; Erasmus'
Latin translations were published by Froben in May 1526; see B. Ebels-Hoving
and E.J. Ebels 'Erasmus and Galen' in *Erasmus of Rotterdam: The Man and the
Scholar* ed J. Sperna Weiland and W.Th.M. Frijhoff (Leiden 1988) 132–42.

no more suited than 'if you put a psaltery on a tall slave,'[649] as the poet says.

I see that some will reply here, 'Anyone who acts through another is seen as acting for himself; it is in this sense that kings sail and rich men build.' I grant this, but the former are not called shipmasters and the latter are not called builders; yet some priests, though they have no quality worthy of a priest, still pride themselves on this title, demand the honour and the stipend due to priests, desire to be called and to be considered that which they are not. St Jerome, expounding Malachi, somewhere warns such men in these words: 'The priest who pleads a careful ignorance in other matters, a negligent one in the Holy Scriptures, boasts in vain of the high office whose works he does not show.'[650]

But some bishops do have an excuse in these times, a matter about which we shall say something a little later.[651] But I can hardly find a plea by which to excuse those who heap benefices upon benefices, and likewise the pastors who conduct their office through a substitute contractor, as does that substitute through a substitute down to the third or fourth: indeed, he does not conduct his office at all when the last substitute is the worst of all, as is frequently the case.[652] But this is an old complaint about bishops and priests, which is not part of my intention to revive here, especially in these days when bad priests are scorned to such an extent that even the good ones are despised by the laity. If warning helps, they have been warned enough in the canonical Scriptures and the writings of the church Fathers and in the very decrees of the popes.[653] Today one must urge rather that all the people change their lives for the better and ask God with constant prayers

* * * * *

649 See *Adagia* III v 43. The line is from Aulus Persius Flaccus (AD 34–62), Roman satirical poet, and summarizes Erasmus' point that one does not take up the office of bishop without full qualifications; see Persius *Satires* 5.95 *sambucam citius caloni aptaveris alto*.

650 Jerome *In Malachiam* CCSL 76A 918:217–19 (on Mal 2:7).

651 Erasmus concedes that bishops cannot do all the preaching themselves but must delegate this responsibility to competent preachers because of the changed conditions in the city; bishops can often do much better by providing their dioceses with suitable preachers than carrying out the duty of preaching by themselves; nevertheless, they too must be learned and able to preach; see 343–5 below.

652 On this abuse in England, see Robert C. Palmer *Selling the Church: The English Parish in Law, Commerce, and Religion, 1350–1550* (Chapel Hill, NC 2002).

653 See 320 above where Erasmus lists the terrifying punishments facing those negligent in the office of preacher. For the 'decrees of the popes,' see CIC 2.3.4 I 460, 3.5.5 465.

to turn the minds of princes and priests to what is both pleasing to Christ and salutary for the people.

If the people show themselves disposed to be taught, God will not allow a dearth of teachers. For it often happens that, because of the people's stubborness, God unleashes a tyrant instead of a prince, a hypocrite instead of a bishop, so that they may be scourged rather than healed through them;[654] so to the people of Israel, when they demanded a king to replace the very mild judge Samuel, he gave the tyrant Saul.[655] Holy Writ, though it does not approve of the speaker, does not disapprove of his statement that '[God] makes a hypocrite reign because of the sins of the people.'[656] What he calls a hypocrite Zechariah called an idol and a foolish shepherd,[657] whom the Lord professes he will rouse up, expressly because of the rebellion of the people; and, according to the prophecy of Micah, a lying spirit is sent by the Lord to deceive King Ahab.[658] Those unwilling to heed givers of good advice deserve to learn their own foolishness through affliction by the wicked.[659]

Those who turn the writings of the ancients against priests and bishops ought to remember that in certain countries the church now has a different status, perhaps brought on by compelling causes.[660] The ferocity of

* * * * *

654 Erasmus posits a God who demands docility in his people before he sends them worthy preachers, which somewhat contradicts the idea that God sends preachers in order to correct the vices of the people and foster docility to hearing the word. Erasmus supports his view by recalling God's punishment of the behaviour of the Israelites, who continuously proved 'stubborn' (eg Exod 32:9; Deut 9:13; Mic 6:16). Erasmus sees God's punishment on his age in princes and bishops who act as tyrants and hypocrites.

655 1 Samuel 8

656 Job 34:30. These words are uttered by Elihu, Job's friend, in his second discourse on God's justice, providence, and power. Erasmus judges Elihu harshly (persona non probata) because he is not a bad person, though he mistakenly believes Job impugned the absolute justice of God and brought on himself divine punishment. Erasmus is calling attention to certain locutions in Scripture where true utterances are spoken by the ungodly, like Balaam ('a base man' [homo reprobatus]) and Caiphas who says, 'It is expedient that one man die for the people' (John 11:50); Erasmus notes how true the utterance is though the speaker was not right with the Lord. See 389.

657 Zec 11:16–17

658 2 Chron 18:21–2

659 Cf Mic 6:16.

660 Erasmus takes a stand here against Reformers who would abolish bishops and priests, claiming they 'turn' (or 'twist' [torquent]) the Scriptures to demonstrate that bishops are not what they were at the time of Paul. Erasmus' view

the Germans has resulted in their bishops being fortified against popular uprisings by wealth, arms, fortresses, and secular authority, so that force and fear of trouble might restrain the common people, who were unwilling to obey salutary warnings. Among the English, bishops or abbots have no secular authority, though a good part of the wealth is in the hands of ecclesiastics; the same, I think, prevails among the Spanish. The Greeks still preserve an ancient frugality of which clear traces can be seen even today in Italy, despite the pomp and fanfare of secular authority that have long since made inroads there particularly among those who should have rebuked the desires of others. It would indeed be desirable that all bishops be only bishops, armed with spiritual weapons,[661] rich in spiritual wealth,[662] and that the greater each was in rank, the more free he would be from earthly cares; in turn, the people would be tractable and compliant to such bishops. But it is only fair that they should be more understanding of the German bishops on the ground that they did not invent that model themselves but received it by tradition from ancient times; moreover, the authority of many prelates extends so wide that if they were freed as far as possible from all earthly cares, they could still not preach in all their towns, since today a single city requires several preachers.[663] Hence I am all the more amazed that there was only one bishop and teacher at Milan or at Constantinople, Ambrose in the former, Chrysostom in the latter. And just as the existence of a single Roman pope to preside over all the churches is useful for fending off schisms,[664] so for the same reason it is appropriate to have many cities

* * * * *

is that the status (*status*) of bishops has been conditioned by the historical circumstances in which the episcopate developed among the various countries of Europe; though below he wishes that bishops truly be bishops (see 351 below), he does not advocate abolishing such configurations but acknowledges the historical result as being due to the specific temper of the peoples of Europe. Erasmus states below: 'Established usage can be excused and ought to be tolerated'; see 351.

661 Eph 6:11–17
662 Matt 6:20–1; Luke 12:33–4
663 Erasmus acknowledges the practical constraints on bishops of his own day; because they cannot possibly preach to the faithful in such large cities, they need to delegate this office to suitable clergy.
664 Here Erasmus gives another small, but important, clue to his ecclesiology; he views it as 'expedient' that the bishop of Rome 'preside over all the churches' to 'fend off schisms.' Papal authority therefore is crucial but restricted to working with fellow bishops for consensus in matters of doctrine and morality. The role of the bishop is, above all, to preach and to provide preachers who are 'suitable and διδακτικοί' (see 344 below) and to remove those unsuited. Erasmus

obey a single bishop. But he ought nevertheless to be trained in Scripture so that he too might preach on occasion and be able to admit other suitable people to that office; his example will stimulate some, his judgment will remove the unsuitable. And, in my opinion at least, such a bishop would make better use of his time if through himself and his staff he took constant and watchful care to ensure that pastors who are suitable and διδακτικοί [good at teaching] be put in charge of each church, that those who are clearly useless be removed from that office, than if he devoted himself wholly to the business of preaching.

It will be most conducive to providing a supply of such men if he ensures that youths of good potential are trained in public academies and if he admits to the rank of presbyter only those who have given unambiguous evidence that they will one day be able to serve as a good preacher; for this is the source from which the greatest part of the church's calamities flows.[665] A bishop cannot preach in all the churches, yet a single bishop can take care of all the churches by finding a reliable pastor. That perhaps cannot come about suddenly, yet it can happen slowly and gradually. If someone becomes a bishop who is more suited to administration than to teaching, by attending to this responsibility he will easily compensate for what he lacks, and he will devote himself to this with greater zeal[666] if he reflects that that supreme pastor will impute to him all the failings of those to whom he has delegated his role. Bishops then ought to make this first and foremost among their concerns.[667] Intelligent princes exercise the greatest care in acquiring

* * * * *

perhaps comes closest to articulating the function of the ideal pope in his description below of Pope Gregory the Great (590–604); see 355 below. For Erasmus' ecclesiology, see Cornelis Augustijn 'The Ecclesiology of Erasmus' in *Scrinium* II 135–56.

665 Erasmus' advice anticipates the central concern of the Fathers at Trent to emphasize the role of the bishop in instructing good preachers within the diocese and approving them before they preach. Erasmus speaks of training youth in 'public academies'; but in book3 CWE 68 passim he is more specific in describing the kind of programme most conducive to instructing youth for preaching. Erasmus' example of David of Burgundy, once bishop of Utrecht, suggests how far from that ideal many European dioceses were at the time of the Reformation. On David of Burgundy see CEBR I 226–7.

666 Zeal is the mark of an excellent bishop. This theme is echoed repeatedly after Trent in the numerous ecclesiastical rhetorics that follow *Ecclesiastes*. See McGinness *Right Thinking* 41 and 44.

667 Chomarat calls attention to Trent's use of Erasmus' words and ideas: 'Bishops then ought to make this first and foremost (*primam ac praecipuam*) among their concerns'; see ASD V-4 133 22–3nn. Erasmus' ideas and language are even more

trustworthy generals tested in war to whom to entrust their army, convinced that success in war depends upon them, and they do not consider it a serious loss if the common soldier and nameless ranks fall, so long as their energetic generals are unharmed; how much more care should be taken to ensure that the Lord's flock has appropriate shepherds. This is no light matter; so many thousands of souls are in danger, for whose freedom Christ shed his own blood when he handed himself over to death to give them life, but the bishop himself is in danger above all since he will render an account to the Lord for each sheep.[668] Accordingly, if a bishop ever allows himself any idleness, let him allow it somewhere else instead; if any laxness, let him be lax anywhere but in this business, which is by far the most perilous of all. It is not a sufficient excuse if a bishop says, 'I delegated that to my substitutes and officials,' since he must vouch for their integrity as well; if he punishes them when they are caught in embezzlement, so much the more justly should they be punished if they have conducted this work in bad faith.

It would not be out of place to relate here what befell David,[669] formerly bishop of Utrecht, the son of Duke Philip the Good.[670] He was a supremely learned man and trained in theology, something that is quite rare in nobles and in bishops, especially of that region, burdened as they are with their secular authority. He had heard that among the many admitted to holy orders very few were literate. He determined to investigate the matter more closely; he ordered a chair placed for himself in the hall where those to be examined were admitted, proposed questions personally to each according to the dignity of the rank that they sought: easier ones for those who were to be subdeacons, somewhat more difficult ones for deacons, theological ones for presbyters. Are you wondering how it turned out? He debarred

* * * * *

embedded in the decrees of the Council of Trent; see Session 6 *Decretum secundum publicatum in eadem quinta sessione super lectione et praedicatione.* Tanner II 669: 'This is the chief task of the bishops'; see also Tanner II 763 for Session 24, Canon 4. Significantly, *Ecclesiastes* uses the word *praecipuum* almost exclusively for this function of the bishops; see also McGinness 'Erasmian Legacy' 98–102.

668 See Heb 13:17; John 10:11–16, 21:15–17; cf Acts 20:28; 1 Pet 5:2–4.

669 David of Burgundy (c 1427–96), bishop in 1456. Chomarat notes that Erasmus knew this local anecdote because when he was ten years old he had been a choirboy at Utrecht. For David of Burgundy see CEBR I 226–7; see also Schoeck (1) 109–10.

670 Philip the Good, duke of Burgundy (1396–1467); see Richard Vaughan *Philip the Good: The Apogee of Burgundy* (New York 1970); and CEBR I 228–9.

all but three. Those who usually preside over these affairs thought it would be a great disgrace to the church if only three were admitted instead of three hundred; the bishop, who had an impetuous nature, replied that it would be a greater disgrace to the church if asses, and creatures more stupid than any ass, were admitted into it instead of men. Those who reap some profit from this urged him to moderate his opinion, bearing in mind that this age does not produce Pauls or Jeromes – instead, such men as the time does offer must be accepted; the bishop persisted, saying that he was not asking for Pauls and Jeromes but would not admit asses in place of men. Here they had to resort to their final trick; it was applied. What was it? 'If you are intending to continue as you are beginning,' they said, 'you must increase our salaries, for without these asses we have no other source of livelihood.' This battering ram beat down the prelate's noble soul; yet the ram could have been beaten back in many ways: 'Salaries are given to you not for luxury and ostentation but for a sober life; what we give is enough for this.' But this remark could perhaps be turned back against a bishop who receives a stipend from the church for a decent living, not for the noisy display of a satrap; it would therefore have been more noble to say, 'If anything is lacking to your needs, it will be made up from elsewhere, even from my own stipend, so long as the church is not tainted by such ministers.'

Generals experienced in war would rather lead out a small band suitable for combat than a huge crowd of useless soldiers; what does it matter whether the church has only a very few priests suitable for ecclesiastical service or an infinite crowd of useless ones who would sooner burden the church than support it? All desire the stipends of the church, few or none desire the church's work. They want to be fed, not to feed; take away the fodder, and you will see very few aspiring to ecclesiastical ranks.

Need I mention that the church would need fewer if each performed only his necessary and proper functions? Deacons would read aloud the sacred lections, presbyters would teach the gospel and assist the bishops in administering the sacraments. Now priests are consecrated for singing, which was once the role of the laity, and as mass priests; both would be more tolerable if they were confined strictly to public churches. In some regions individual houses now keep a chapel and priests privately,[671] and everywhere,

* * * * *

671 Erasmus refers here to the widespread practice of large wealthy landowners having private chapels and resident chaplains. This not only allowed family members to practice their devotions but kept them separate from the community church where regular religious services took place. Privatizing religious rites in this way de-emphasized the unity of the Christian community.

just as suffragan bishops[672] are created who could be hired by any bishop at all, so presbyters are consecrated who have no prescribed stipend but can be hired by the wife of any tanner to conduct his mistress to church, hand her the missal and genuflect three times, then lead her home again with a similar ritual. And they are created for this purpose at a jump,[673] as the saying goes, and before the legal age,[674] so long as a fee is paid out. Paul wants younger widows to marry and wants only those who are truly widows to be enrolled, in order to prevent the church from being burdened.[675] Why should what the Apostle established in women's ministries not be done in the higher orders that burden the church more, so that only those who are truly deacons, that is, ministers of the church, are received as deacons, only those who are truly presbyters, pure in life, grave in authority, salutary in learning, are admitted as presbyters? What a crowd of presbyters we now see in some places if the corpse of an ostentatious magnate is to be buried! You might see hundreds on hand to sing the dirges, to celebrate the rites. If the Gospel needs to be preached, how scarce they are; there you would hardly find one. How much more justly would those who wage war over the denying of tithes, angrily fulminating against those who cheat churches, be roused against those who by living luxuriously on ecclesiastical revenues burden and shame the whole church, not only among the Christian population but also among those who are outside the community of the church? For these people judge the whole church from the ministers of the church. Therefore, the bishop who genuinely favours the good of the church should be especially vigilant in this regard. If he does this, he will be readily forgiven the fact that he does not teach the philosophy of the gospel himself, and that old

* * * * *

672 Ie assistant bishops who receive their commission and stipend from the archbishop or bishop of a diocese.

673 'At a jump' (*per saltum*); Erasmus refers to the irregular practice of ordained individuals who skip over one or more of the required stages of advancement in the offices of the ecclesiastical hierarchy (subdeacon, deacon, priest, bishop).

674 Chomarat states that the canonical age was at least thirty years. The Third Lateran Council, however, fixed the age for ordination to the priesthood at twenty five. As Erasmus notes, there were many dispensations given that allowed younger males to be ordained earlier. See Tanner I 212, Third Lateran Council (1179), Canon 3; and Tanner II 766, Council of Trent, Session 24, Canon 12.

675 1 Tim 5:14–16. See 1 Tim 5:11–16 and Erasmus' understanding of Paul's counsel regarding young widows and the support of older widows in *Paraphrasis in 1 Timotheum* CWE 44 29–31. Also Luke Timothy Johnson *The First and Second Letters to Timothy: A New Translation with Introduction and Commentary*, Anchor Bible 35 (New York c 2001).

song of the lawyers will be valid, that 'whoever acts through others seems to act through himself,'[676] nor will the advice of the old man in the comedy seem absurd, who, when he saw an old neighbour constantly carrying something in a field, digging, plowing, and hoeing, advised him as follows: 'All that effort of your own that you spend in working, / You would get more done if you spent it in training them.'[677] Similarly, the bishop whose authority extends far will produce more profit if he devotes himself entirely to putting suitable pastors in charge of each church and to restraining those in office than if he carefully administers one or two churches himself.[678]

This attention would have to be applied not only to towns but also to villages and monasteries. The priests of villages and hamlets, I think, are called *corepiscopi*[679] in the ancient canons;[680] I believe that one should

* * * * *

676 The saying is one of many fundamental principles of law (*regulae iuris*), this one going back as far as Ulpian (c 170–228). Pope Boniface VIII (1294–1303) inserted eighty-nine such *regulae* in the last title (XII) of the sixth book of the *Decretals* (*Liber sextus decretalium*), which he published in 1298; in Erasmus' time the *editio princeps* was printed at Mainz by Johann Fust and Peter Schöffer in 1465. See *Regula* 68: *potest quis per alium quod potest facere per se ipsum*; and *Regula* 72: *qui facit per alium est perinde ac si faciat per se ipsum*. A similar *regula* appears in *The Digest of Justinian* ed Theodor Mommsen, Paul Krueger, and Alan Watson (Philadelphia 1985) 302: 'A person who has managed a tutelage through the agency of another is held to have managed it himself.' See also *Dokumente zur Causa Lutheri* ed Peter Fabisch and Erwin Iserloh 1 (Münster 1988–91) 162 75 verso–76 recto: 'Punctum 6: Pontifex indubitatus nedum a Concilio, sed neque a toto Mundo potest iure deponi. Cum enim ab eo in Ecclesia sit omnis auctoritas, si ab aliquo iuridice deponeretur, utique a seipso deponeretur, licet per alium, quia quod quis per alium facit, per seipsum facere videtur.'

677 Terence *Heauton timorumenos* (*Self-Tormentor*) 69, 73–4. The 'old man' is Chremes speaking to another old man, Menedemus. There is no mention in this passage of 'hoeing' (*sarrientem*); Erasmus is likely trying to recall it from memory.

678 Below Erasmus recalls his acquaintance with William Warham, archbishop of Canterbury, who excelled in this practice. See CEBR III 427–31.

679 *Corepiscopi, chorepiscopi* were fully consecrated bishops in country areas of the Eastern church in the fourth century but with restricted powers; they could only ordain the lower ranks of clergy and were subject to their diocesan. By the thirteenth century the position disappears. In the Western church they worked in missionary districts in Germany; they disappear by the twelfth century. See *chorepiscopus* in ODCC 331. Chomarat (ASD V-4 136:110–11 and 137 109n) notes that Erasmus' orthography is correct, though the etymology is inexact: χῶρα means 'place' and a *chorepiscopos* would hold the 'place' of the bishop; he is not a bishop of the country district.

680 See *Codex canonum ecclesiasticorum et constitutorum sanctae sedis apostolicae* (PL 56 709 A): *qui in vices et villis constitui sunt chorepiscopi*; CIC 1, 2, 68, 3, 254:

write *chorepiscopi*, because χῶρα in Greek sometimes means 'countryside' or 'field.' The more uneducated a farming community is, the more it needs someone to season it with the salt of the gospel,[681] and in ancient times monks and holy virgins used to hear the bishop teaching daily in common churches; now, since nuns are shut up and confined at home, care would have to be taken to ensure that they have people there to instruct them in sacred learning, to inspire them, to console and admonish them.[682] Why else do we see so much superstition instead of true devotion,[683] so much coldness and sloth instead of charity[684] even in well-regulated monasteries, if not because they do not feed daily upon the word of God?[685] From this, faith grows strong; from this, charity grows warm; from this, the desire for heavenly life wells up; without these, the choice of food, dress, songs, and other ceremonies tend more truly to superstition than to devotion.

Please consider here whether a man on whose shoulders weighs the care of so many cities and of so many churches has leisure for hunting, fowling, gambling, elaborate banquets, etc. Everyone will be able to judge at home what this is like. What a worrying business it is for the patriarch

* * * * *

chorepiscopi – in vices ordinarii possunt – minores tantummodo ordines tribuunt. See 'Chorbishop' NCE III 525–6.
681 Cf Matt 5:13; Mark 9:49.
682 Cf 2 Tim 3:16.
683 Erasmus makes clear that where the word is not preached competently the danger of superstition is always great, for believers mistake the forms for the substance or meaning that the ceremonies signify. Erasmus' criticisms of superstitious practices, external ceremonies, and ritualistic attitudes that have been so deeply embedded among Christians are well familiar; see eg *Moria* CWE 27 113–5 and *Enchiridion* CWE 66 73–83; see also Ep 1558 to Willibald Pirckheimer, especially line 66, and Jacques Chomarat 'Superstitio, religio et impietas' in *Moreana* 21 83/84 (Nov 1984) 151–6.
684 Cf Matt 24:12.
685 This idea will become a prominent theme at Trent; see Session 5 'Second decree: on instruction and preaching' no 11, Tanner II 669: 'Archpriests also, ordinary priests and any others who have some control over parochial and other churches, and have the care of souls, are to feed with the words of salvation the people committed to their charge. This they should do either personally or, if they are legitimately impeded, through others who are competent, by teaching at least on Sundays and solemn feasts, according to their own and their hearers' capacity, what it is necessary for all to know with a view to salvation, by proclaiming briefly and with ease of expression the vices they must avoid and the virtues they must cultivate so as to escape eternal punishment and gain the glory of heaven.'

of a modest household, with a wife, some children, and servants, to keep
this small household under control, though he has supreme authority over
them not only to command but also to confine and beat and disown,[686] while
a bishop, as bishop, has only the authority to teach, advise, reprimand, beseech, and console.[687] But St Chrysostom in his book *De sacerdotio* shows
with equal eloquence and erudition how difficult a business it would be if
today also individual bishops were in charge of individual cities.[688] Admit-
tedly he wrote when not yet a bishop, but once he had been dragged to
this office, he discovered in the event that his prophecy was quite true.[689]
If only the violence of princes, the rebelliousness of clerics, the insensibility
of the people, the uproar of heresies[690] were less today! How much trouble
then do we believe it is when twenty rich and populous cities, in addition
to towns and villages, owe obedience to a single bishop.[691] Even supposing
that burden to be light, four or five such bishoprics, with some added abba-
cies, are laid on the shoulders of a single man. Who would not acknowledge

* * * * *

686 On the authority of the father in the family, see Steven E. Ozment *When Fathers
Ruled: Family Life in Reformation Europe* (Cambridge 1983). Erasmus qualifies
the right of the father to beat a child; see *De pueris instituendis* CWE 26 326,
where he speaks of being flogged as a boy for an act he did not commit and
how this caused him to lose his love for studies.

687 See 2 Tim 3:16, 4:2.

688 See John Chrysostom *De sacerdotio* (*On the Priesthood*) NPNF 1st series 9 25–83.
Erasmus edited this work; see Ep 1558. Erasmus relies heavily on Chrysostom's *De sacerdotio* for much of his discussion of the priestly office. See PG 48
623–92.

689 John Chrysostom (c 347–407) became bishop of Constantinople on 26 February
398. He had written *De sacerdotio* probably while still a deacon (386), or possibly just after he was ordained a priest at Antioch (387). For the difficulties
one faces as bishop, see especially *De sacerdotio* book 2. And for his perils as
bishop of Constantinople, see J.N.D. Kelly *Golden Mouth: The Story of John Chrysostom, Ascetic, Preacher, Bishop* (Ithaca 1995), especially 104–44; Rudolf Brändle
*Jean Chrysostome, 'saint Jean Bouche d'or' (349–407): christianisme et politique au
IVe siècle* (Paris 2003) 79.

690 Erasmus speaks only generally of contemporary heresies. Here he is likely referring to what he sees as the proliferation of so many various 'errors' while
writing this treatise on preaching. 'Heresy' has a specific meaning for Erasmus; see book 4 CWE 68 1048: 'I use the term heresy not for any error at all
but for the willful malice that disturbs the peace of the church with perverse
dogmas for the sake of some advantage.'

691 Erasmus' solution to this problem is to remove the abuse of plurality of
benefices and the jurisdiction of a single bishop over numerous well-populated
towns, as well as insist that bishops regularly fulfil their divine duties as pastors of Christ's flock.

that this burden surpasses human strength? And yet these too are doubled by the addition of the secular authority. It is particularly difficult to be a good king; to be a devout prelate even to one city is much more difficult. How heavy then is the burden carried by a man who must be at the same time both a good bishop and a good prince to so many cities and so many regions? I do not make these remarks to castigate today's bishops but to show what sobriety and vigilance is required of them. Some of these things can be excused on honourable grounds; eagerness for concord and fear of sedition urged that several cities should be entrusted to one metropolitan, while the savagery of the population forced the addition of wealth and secular authority. The Irish are said to be like this even today,[692] and Germany was once more prone to warfare than to philosophy before she lowered her neck to Christ's yoke and was softened by liberal training – I only wish no traces of her ancient ferocity now remained! So far, then, established usage can be excused and ought to be tolerated; but I can hardly find grounds on which to excuse one man seeking several bishoprics, one priest seeking several benefices, unless we say that this proceeds not from avarice, not from ambition but from a certain abundance of charity by which they desire to benefit the greatest number.[693] But these things too are now done openly and with approval; nor am I unaware how powerful, how tyrannical a thing is a custom once received into public usage.

Accordingly, since it is better to leave this to the deity and to fate, all ought to take to heart that it should not be the last of their secular concerns to delegate to suitable men the duties that they cannot fulfil themselves. But favouritism and avarice, those worst of counsellors, should not be admitted to these deliberations. There is a relative who seeks a διοίκησις [diocese];[694] let love for the bride of Christ overcome the affection of kinship. If a prince puts forward a favoured candidate, let the interest of the highest prince take precedence with you. Finally, let the greatness of your power enable you to fend off those that try to break in, to expel those that have entered.

* * * * *

692 Erasmus never visited Ireland; it is likely his knowledge of the Irish church derives from what he heard while in England, much of which we might assume derives ultimately from Gerald of Wales. See the introduction to *Topographia Hiberniae* (*The Topography of Ireland*) (Middlesex repr 1982) 11–18, especially 13. For the Germans before the coming of Christianity, see Tacitus *Germania* 13–14; Caesar *Bellum Gallicum* 1.1.3–4, 1.27–52, 2.1–4, etc; Seneca *De ira* 1.11.3–4.

693 Cf 1 Tim 3:1; 1 Cor 9:15–18. The comment, we might suppose, is given with no small dose of irony.

694 An example of nepotism.

Let your wealth enable you to provide for some churches, on your own if necessary, to advance with kindness those who display a noble character, to found colleges for this very purpose,[695] to restore those that have failed, so that chosen talents may be trained there, not just for logical argument but much more for preaching;[696] for we see it happening now that the great part of those who receive long training in theological disputations come out clever in argument, but very, very few suited to preaching.

Here there comes to mind a man who deserves to be remembered for all time, William Warham,[697] archbishop of Canterbury, primate of all England, a theologian not in name but in fact, for he was a doctor of both civil and canon law,[698] grew famous from his successful conduct of several embassies, and became an intimate and friend of Henry vii,[699] a prince of great discretion. By these steps he rose to the pinnacle of the church of Canterbury, whose rank is first in that island. To this burden, quite heavy in itself, was added another more heavy; he was compelled to take on the office of chancellor, which among the English is positively royal. Out of respect he alone, when he went forth in public, was preceded by a royal crown with the royal sceptre placed upon it, for he was like the eye, the mouth, and the right hand of the king and was the highest judge in the whole British realm. He conducted this office for many years with such skill that you would say that he had been born to the business and was occupied by no other concern; but he was also so vigilant and alert in matters regarding religion and his ecclesiastical functions that you would say he was distracted by no other responsibilities. He had time enough to fulfil religiously his regular quota of prayers, to say mass almost every day, to hear two or three masses besides,

* * * * *

695 For Erasmus' idea of these colleges for training young men to preach, see 151–5.

696 Erasmus alludes to the importance of episcopal patronage for assisting worthy but indigent youth, and also insists upon the study of Scripture and the humanities as the educational purpose of such colleges. Elsewhere Erasmus emphasizes that such colleges should not be exclusively given over to dialectic for teaching theology, but the subject should be taught as part of the standard curriculum for future preachers. See book 2 CWE 68 468–74.

697 William Warham, archbishop of Canterbury (1450–22 August 1532), became lord chancellor and archbishop of Canterbury in 1503. Erasmus portrays Warharm as a model bishop. See CEBR III 427–31, and Colloquia (Peregrinatio religionis ergo CWE 40 669 n155. This part of Ecclesiastes therefore was written after 22 August 1532; see Allen III 631: 'for the passage occurs (f.35) in continuous composition and cannot be considered as an insertion.'

698 This is a doctor of both laws (utriusque iuris).

699 Henry vii, king of England (b 1457; ruled 1485–1509); CEBR II 117–18

to try cases, to receive legations, to advise the king if something of serious import had arisen at court, to visit churches as often as circumstances required an arbitrator, often to receive two hundred guests; finally, his leisure was devoted to reading. A single man had enough energy and time for such varied concerns because he gave no portion of it to hunting, none to gambling, none to idle stories, none to luxury or pleasure; for him some pleasant reading or a conversation with a learned man took the place of all these amusements. Though he sometimes entertained bishops, dukes, and counts, yet the meal was always over within the span of an hour. It is incredible to note how far he himself abstained from pleasures in the midst of the splendid pomp that that rank demands. He rarely tasted wine; but when he was in his seventies, he often drank a very weak fermented beverage that they call 'beer,'[700] and even that quite sparingly. Moreover, though he ate very little food, he nevertheless enlivened the whole party with his friendly countenance and jolly conversation; whether he had eaten or not, you would have seen the same sobriety. He refrained entirely from banquets, or, if some familiar friends had come (among whom we were counted), he did sit at table, but in such a way that he touched almost no food; if such friends were not available, he would spend on prayers or reading the time that was to be given to dinner. And just as he himself abounded in witticisms that were wonderfully pleasant but free from bite or frivolity, so he delighted in the freer jests of his friends; he shunned scurrility and insult as people do a snake.[701] In this way that excellent man made his days abundantly long, whose brevity many allege as an excuse; yet those who continually complain that they lack the time for serious business waste a good part of the day, sometimes of the night as well, in unnecessary activity. But to return to the point that led me to interject this digression, according to the custom of these times, he was required, besides the ample household that he was compelled to keep, to devote time also to the royal court and to the secular business of the entire kingdom. And although it is not customary there today for the highest prelates to preach, yet he abundantly made up for what had been lost in this part of his duty by a twofold vigilance, partly by ensuring that no useless person was ever put in charge of the Lord's flock, partly by using his own liberality to support in the study of literature many whom he hoped would eventually bear good fruit; his liberality towards them was so free that at his death he left no cash on hand at all but a considerable

* * * * *

700 'Beer' (*cervisiam quam illi biriam vocant*)
701 For 'he shunned . . . as people do a snake' (*tam horrebat quam quisquam ab angui*), see *Adagia* II ix 63 *Odit cane peius et angue* 'Hates worse than dog and snake.'

debt, though he provided the means of paying it off. I say this not at all in flattery; I loved him while he lived, no less do I love him dead, for what I loved in him has not perished. If I were to count up all that he was ready to give me, his liberality towards me was immense; if we were to calculate what I received, it is modest indeed. He conferred upon me but a single benefice; or rather he did not give it but thrust it upon me against my constant refusal, since it was of such a kind that the flock required a pastor, which I could not be because of my ignorance of the language. When he had changed it to a pension and sensed that I accepted that small sum grudgingly because it was collected from a population to which I was bringing no good, the outstandingly devout man consoled me, saying, 'What? Would you consider preaching to one small rustic congregation an important service? Now through your books you teach all pastors with far greater profit, and do you deem it unfair if a little of the church stipend returns to you? I take that anxiety upon myself; I shall see to it that the church lacks for nothing.' And so he did; for after removing the person to whom I had resigned the office (he was his assistant, a man distracted by various responsibilities), he put in charge another young man knowledgeable in theology, of proven and honourable character. He so loved, so venerated the Reverend Doctor John Fisher, bishop of Rochester,[702] because he showed himself a true bishop in all the offices worthy of a prelate but especially in his zeal for teaching the people,[703] that it seemed that Fisher was the metropolitan, he himself the suffragan. Now that my patron is deceased, I can offer this testimony without suspicion of flattery. He does not need my praise, and I expect no reward from him for my flattery. Rather, I have offered these recollections

* * * * *

702 John Fisher (Fischer), bishop of Rochester (1469–22 June 1535). John Fisher was made bishop of Rochester in 1504. At the time Erasmus was about to publish *Ecclesiastes* (July 1535), Fisher was executed by Henry VIII for refusing to accept the king's remarriage. See CEBR I 36–9. See also Edward L. Surtz *The Works and Days of John Fisher: An Introduction to the Position of St. John Fisher (1469–1535), Bishop of Rochester, in the English Renaissance and Reformation* (Cambridge, Mass 1967); *Humanism, Reform and the Reformation: The Career of Bishop John Fisher* ed Brendan Bradshaw and Eamon Duffy (Cambridge 1989). For Erasmus' knowledge in 1535 of Fisher's fate, see Schoeck (2) 339–40; see also Kleinhans 29–31.

703 'A true bishop ... especially in his zeal for teaching the people' (*tum praecipue studio docendi populum verum praestaret episcopum*); this is another instance of Erasmus' exclusive use of the word *praecipuum* 'special' or 'particular' in application to the teaching office of the bishop. 'Zeal' becomes the mark of the true preacher in the post-Tridentine era; see McGinness *Right Thinking* 41, 83–4; and 266, 277, 337, 344 above.

in order to present an example that the priests of today can follow[704] and easily make up the damage done to their office when the distraction of various duties leaves them no free time for preaching, and to show how they can make their days longer in order to have sufficient time and energy and good health for their varied concerns. Christian charity is an energetic and active thing; once it has seized someone, it is remarkable what varied responsibilities he can be equal to undertaking. For I fear that the mass of men, who are always complaining that they lack leisure, would find, if they made a true reckoning of their daily activity, that the better and greater part of their time was spent either on foolish pleasures or on frivolous trifles; since they have ample supply and surplus of leisure for these, it is a disgrace to plead lack of time as an excuse in the one responsibility for which they should have forgotten all other business and been wholeheartedly free.

But there is an example ready at hand, this one still more illustrious: St Gregory, the first pope of that name.[705] Though his frame was frail and his health unsteady, he was sufficient by himself to carry out so many duties: he celebrated holy rites, preached before the people, sometimes several times a day, sat to try cases, maintained a school of letters, composed rituals and chants for the church, wrote so many tomes, so many letters; he taught the catechumens, examined them after their instruction, initiated in the sacraments, scrutinized the candidates for initiation to test their suitability; he settled the conflicts of kings, opposed those causing schism, put suitable pastors in charge of each church, and, not satisfied with this, sent out men endowed with the apostolic spirit to distant regions to pacify savage and wild races and prepare them for the philosophy of the gospel and the discipline of the church;[706] meanwhile he was no more slack in his private duties, visiting the sick, rebuking the delinquent, goading the idle, consoling

* * * * *

704 Erasmus repeats his intention to present these two bishops as models of how prelates should live and carry out their divinely entrusted office. For models of the ideal bishop, see Hubert Jedin and Giuseppe Alberigo *Il tipo ideale di vescovo secondo la riforma cattolica* (Brescia 1985). Below Erasmus vividly describes the virtues of the good bishop, which likely had an impact on Trent's presentation of the holders of this most important office.

705 Gregory I, 'the Great,' pope (590–604). See Carole Straw *Gregory the Great: Perfection in Imperfection* (Berkeley 1988); and Robert A. Markus *Gregory the Great and His World* (Cambridge 1997). On his infirmities, see Gregory's letter to Leander of Seville in preface to the *Moralia in Iob* CCSL 143 1–7.

706 Erasmus' reference is to Pope Gregory I's mission of Augustine of Canterbury to King Ethelbert at Kent in 597. See Bede *Historia ecclesiastica gentis Anglorum* (*Ecclesiastical History of the English Nation*) 1.23–34.

the afflicted, encouraging the timid, aiding the oppressed, restoring quarrelling parties to concord, attending the dying. How did it happen that such a frail frame was equal to carrying out so many functions? Burning charity of course provided strength, and his time, truly the most precious resource, as someone has said, was dispensed so parsimoniously that no portion of it was wasted. This is how St Basil,[707] with his body diseased, how Chrysostom,[708] how St Augustine,[709] already in delicate health and burdened by old age, was sufficient to the church's many difficult tasks. The ancients said astutely that parsimony is a great source of revenue,[710] for it makes modest resources suffice a frugal man even to the point of liberality, while for the prodigal they would not be enough even for a modest living. The former bestows generously from moderate resources; the latter has not enough from ample funds to placate a creditor. Moreover, it is appropriate that just as nothing in human affairs is more precious than time, so nothing should be dispensed more circumspectly; but many now squander it as though there were nothing more worthless. If only all pastors would shape themselves to this image!

I know that today, because that lively and active charity has grown too chill[711] and the love of pleasures and the pursuit of secular authority and money have welled up, the various functions of the priest have been distributed among many persons, and sometimes absurdly, so that the highest function is delegated to the lowliest, the lowliest is reserved for the highest.

* * * * *

707 See 287 above for Basil, bishop of Caesarea (c 329–79), one of the four Doctors of the Eastern church, along with John Chrysostom, Gregory of Nazianzus, and Gregory of Nyssa. For details of Basil's condition, see Gregory of Nazianzus *Oration 43* 61 *Funebris oratio in laudem Basilii magni Caesareae in Cappadocia episcopi* (*Funeral Oration on the Great S. Basil, Bishop of Caesarea in Cappadocia*) in NPNF 2nd series 7 395–422 (especially 415); see SC 384 116–307 (par 61, 257–9). On Basil, see Philip Rousseau *Basil of Caesarea* (Berkeley and Los Angeles 1994); for Chrysostom see J.N.D. Kelly *Golden Mouth: The Story of John Chrysostom – Ascetic, Preacher, Bishop* (Ithaca 1995); and for Augustine, see Peter Brown *Augustine of Hippo: A Biography* (Berkeley and Los Angeles 1967; rev ed 2000).
708 See Sozomon 8.9 404–5: 'John had, by rigorous asceticism, rendered himself liable to pain in the head and stomach, and was thus prevented from being present at some of the choicest symposia' (405).
709 For Augustine's health, see Peter Brown *Augustine of Hippo: A Biography* (Berkeley and Los Angeles 1967; rev ed 2000) 109–10, 297, 299, 402, 410, 417.
710 See Cicero *Paradoxa Stoicorum* (*Paradoxes of the Stoics*) 6.49.
711 'That lively and active charity has grown too chill' (*refrixit illa vivida et operosa charitas*); Erasmus echoes Matt 24:12; see 313 above.

The person on whose shoulders the whole house leans and rests goes hunting or wages war; someone hired by him consecrates and ordains. He consecrates walls, vessels, robes, stones, and bells. A parish priest intones and administers the sacraments. A preacher is hired separately to speak on certain days and hours to the people of a single little town, though at one time a single man sufficed for all these ministries, in none of which was he more vigilant and busy than in teaching the people. Alas for our pleasures and the customs of these times![712] So too will you scarcely find anyone who would make a tolerable preacher, though this is such a great part of the priestly office. Hence it was our first wish that the Lord put in charge of his flock shepherds like himself, that is, truly good shepherds, who would not be reluctant to give even their life for their sheep,[713] who themselves know how and are willing to fulfil the delegated office and are anxious to enrol others who are able and willing to take on some part of the duties. If the best course is not available, one must, as they say, resort to second best.[714] And yet hardly anyone could fulfil this properly unless he is wise so that he knows how to choose, and devout so that he holds nothing more important than the welfare of his flock, and upright so that he desires what is right, and brave so that neither partialities nor enmities nor fear nor hope of human possessions can deflect him from the rectitude of his judgment.

We hear daily complaints from those who deplore that the Christian religion has collapsed and that the authority that once embraced the entire world has been reduced to these straits.[715] It is fitting therefore that those who grieve sincerely over this should ask Christ with ardent and constant prayers to deign to send out workers for his harvest[716] or, to put it better, to send sowers to his field. Immortal God, how much land lies open in the world where the seed of the gospel either has not yet been

* * * * *

712 Erasmus' words here (*Vae deliciis nostris et horum temporum moribus*) echo Cicero's laments in *In Catilinam* 1.2 (*O tempora, o mores!*) and *In Verrem* II 4 56 (line 11); *O tempora, o mores! nihil nimium vetus proferam*).

713 Cf John 10:11.

714 Erasmus might be recalling *Adagia* III iv 71 *Altera navigatio* 'The next best way to sail.'

715 These complaints, generally expressed, were not groundless: in addition to the turmoil of the Reformation and the Peasants War, wars continued between the Valois king of France and the Holy Roman Emperor, Turkish power menaced the eastern Mediterranean, especially after the loss of Constantinople (1453), Rome was sacked in 1527, etc.

716 Matt 9:38; Luke 10:2

cast[717] or else was cast in such a way that there are more weeds than wheat.[718] Europe is a very small part of the world; the most flourishing part of all is Greece and Asia Minor, where the gospel first emigrated from Judaea with great success,[719] but is this not almost completely occupied by Mahomed-dans and those who are hostile to the name of Christ? In all the length and breadth of Asia proper what part, I ask you, is ours, when Palestine itself, from which the light of the gospel first flowed forth, is in bondage to allo-phyles?[720] In Africa what is ours? Yet it must not be doubted that in such a vast area there are rude and simple peoples who could easily be attracted to Christ if men were sent out to make a good sowing, not to mention that regions hitherto unknown are being discovered every day;[721] it is said that there are others where none of our people has yet reached. I pass over now the boundless number of Jews commingled with us, I omit the many who are pagans cloaked under the name of Christ, I omit the great phalanxes of schismatics and heretics.[722] How much profit for Christ would there be in these if good and faithful workers were sent to cast good seed,[723] to tear up the weeds, to plant good seedlings, root out the bad, build the house of God, demolish the structures that do not rest on the rock of Christ,[724] and finally to harvest the mature crop but harvest it for Christ, not for

* * * * *

717 Erasmus seems to refer here to the recently discovered lands of the new world. For his awareness of these discoveries, see 359–62 below.

718 Cf Matt 13:24–6; see Ep 916: 236–50, especially 244–5.

719 See the Acts of the Apostles.

720 Those not belonging to the tribe or 'of another tribe' (ἀλλόφυλος): 'a gentile' (cf Acts 10:28 ἀλλοφύλῳ; cf Josephus *Antiquitates Judaicae* 4.8.2 ἀλλοφύλων), 'others,' 'foreigners,' 'heathen,' persons or groups with which one does not associate.

721 On preaching in the world's undiscovered regions, see Ep 1800, dedicated to John III, king of Portugal, *Chrysostomi lucubrationes* 'preface to some transla-tions from Chrysostom,' especially 513: 'How I wish we had such fine speak-ers [such as Paul or Chrysostom] today in every part of the Christian world, for it is on these that the education of the people in large measure depends. If we understand nothing of the philosophy of the gospel, if we flag in do-ing the work of charity, if our faith is weak where it should be strongest, it is because the people rarely hear preachers of the gospel, and competent gospel preachers are rarer still.'

722 For the schismatics Erasmus refers to the Christian churches of the East that have been divided from the West since the Great Schism of 1054; for who exactly is a heretic, see book 4 CWE 68 1048.

723 Erasmus refers here to the parables of the sower and the parable of the wheat and the tares (Matt 13:3–40).

724 1 Cor 10:4

themselves, and to collect souls for the Lord, not wealth for themselves?[725] Recently the king of Ethiopia, commonly called Prester John,[726] submitted himself to the Roman See through an ambassador, remonstrating somewhat with the pope because that race, though not alien to the Christian faith, was so long neglected by the pastor of the whole world.[727] Some good men zealous for the propagation of the faith complain that the Lapps,[728] a remarkably simple and uncultivated people of northern Scythia, are ruled by some Christian princes or other but are being oppressed by a harsh human yoke without having the sweet yoke of Christ[729] put upon them; they are being stripped of their secular possessions without being enriched by evangelical wealth. It would be most beautiful and most pleasing to God to give to, rather than take from, those whom we strive to win for Christ, and to receive them into our authority in such a way that they rejoice in being subject to princes under whose power they may live more comfortably than they lived before. Do we know

* * * * *

725 Cf 1 Cor 9:19–22.

726 Prester John (Pretre Jan): Otto of Freising's (c 1111–58) *Chronica de duabus civitatibus* mentions a Nestorian Christian king and priest living far off in Asia who supposedly advanced Christianity against the Muslims. After the twelfth century this legend was conflated with other reports of Prester John, which located him in Ethiopia. Erasmus' comment on Prester John refers to the king of Ethiopia, David IV (called Prester John), and the embassy he sent to Pope Clement VII in January 1533, who was then in Bologna. See C.E. Nowell 'The Historical Prester John' *Speculum* 28 (1953) 435–55. Viglius Zuichemus (Wigle Zuichem) wrote to Erasmus on 23 February 1533 from Padua about the event; see Allen Ep 2767:159–60: 'Interfui etiam cum ab Aethiopiae Rege, quem Pretioanem vocant, legatio in publico cardinalium consessu praesidente Pontifice audita est. Ea novam significabat illius religionem ac devotionem erga Sedem Apostolicam. A qua sese in obedientiam in filium ac Regem recipi petebat, multaque alia quae non lubet commemorare.'

727 Chomarat correctly notes that this information is not in Viglius Zuichemus' letter to Erasmus; it is probable he heard this from Damião de Gois (1501–74), who visited him in March of 1533, bringing with him his report, *Legatio presbyteri Ioannis*. See ASD V-4 149 325–6n. For Damião de Gois' account, see Allen Ep 2826:31.

728 'Lapps' (*Pilapios*); according to Chomarat this information also came to Erasmus from Damião de Gois in the letter written from Antwerp on 20 June 1533; Ep 2826:33–49. 'Scythia' is the word commonly used for the land in the extreme north of Europe; see eg Pliny *Naturalis historia* 2.50.51. 'Scythia' was historically a defined region with a distinctive people, but it vanished after the second century AD. See OCD 968.

729 Cf Matt 11:29.

how to tame wild and frightful beasts, either for entertainment or for ordinary use, and not know how to pacify men so that they serve Christ? Do
monarchs pay people to teach elephants to dance, to tame lions for sport,
to tame lynxes and leopards for hunting: and the monarch of the church[730]
cannot find how to entice men to the lovable service of Christ? I know that
hardly a beast is found more difficult to tame than a stubborn Jew and an
obdurate heretic, though no animal is so vicious that it may not be tamed by
kindness and gentleness, but I am speaking now of the heathen who wander
like sheep without a shepherd because none is sent them to teach the Christian philosophy; and not only is none being sent, but, if travellers to those
regions are telling the truth, those very Christian princes who have taken
control of these peoples prevent any evangelical teacher from approaching
out of fear that they will throw off the heavy yoke by which they are oppressed if they know a little more, for those satraps would rather rule over
asses than people. Moreover, what am I to say of those who sail past unknown shores in a fleet and sack and plunder cities that anticipate no hostility? Under what title are crimes of this kind celebrated? They are called
victories; and yet not even among the pagans did such victories earn praise
when people on whom war has not been declared are subject to surprise
attacks.[731] They say, 'But they favoured the Turk'; this is the only reason
offered for the destruction of the towns. I am not sure whether they themselves would accept this excuse if the Turk happened to sack a city and said,
'It favoured the Christians.' There is the greatest difference between ban-
ditry and a Christian war, between someone who propagates the kingdom
of the faith and someone who advances the tyranny of this world, between
someone who seeks the salvation of souls and someone who hunts the booty
of Mammon.[732] Gold is being brought from the regions discovered, and jewels, but it would be more deserving of a triumph to import there the wisdom
of Christ, which is more precious than gold, and the pearl of the gospel,[733]
which is well bought at the cost of all one's wealth. Among us there is too

* * * * *

730 Erasmus refers to the pope whom he criticizes here, as well as above, for not
    'sending workers for his harvest' (357). Princes, too, who rule those parts of
    the world are also especially to blame because of their oppressive practices
    and prohibitions against missionaries from entering those regions.
731 Erasmus expands his criticism of monarchs and rulers to include explorers
    and their methods of conquest and domination.
732 Luke 16:9, 13; Matt 6:24
733 Cf Matt 13:45–6.

much of what corrupts our minds. The Lord orders his people to ask the lord of the harvest to send out workers because the harvest was large, the workers few;[734] now too there is no less need to ask God to dispatch workers to such widespread fields.

But all give different excuses. And yet the Christian realm has so many myriads of Franciscans,[735] among whom are probably many that truly burn with a seraphic fire;[736] and no fewer are the myriads of Dominicans, and it is likely that there are many of a cherubic spirit among these.[737] From these

* * * * *

734 Matt 9:37–8
735 Chomarat (ASD V-4 151 366n) notes there were probably about thirty thousand Franciscans around the year 1500; in 1517 by papal decision the Franciscan order separated into Observants and Conventuals. In 1525 the newly reformed Capuchins separated from the Observants.
736 Isa 6:1–13 gives the account of a seraph touching the lips of Isaiah with a burning coal to prepare him to proclaim God's word. Pseudo-Dionysius the Areopagite places the seraphim in the highest rank of angels. Thomas of Celano's *The Life of Saint Francis* relates Francis' vision of 'a man, having six wings like a Seraph,' and gives the mystical meaning of the seraph's wings; see *Francis of Assisi* I 263–5 and 282–3. According to the *Legenda maior* of the Franciscan scholastic theologian St Bonaventure, Francis' 'vision of the Seraph winged after the likeness of the Crucified' accompanied his reception of the stigmata of Christ's wounds; Bonaventure 'The Major Legend of Saint Francis' in *Francis of Assisi: Early Documents* ed Regis J. Armstrong et al, 3 vols (Hyde Park, NY 1999–2001) II 630–9, chapter 13: 'The Sacred Stigmata.' Bonaventure himself came to be called the 'seraphic doctor' after his *Itinerarium mentis in Deum*, which speaks of the seraphim's six wings 'as six suspensions of illumination'; Bonaventure *The Journey of the Mind to God* trans Philotheus Boehner OFM, ed Stephen F. Brown (Indianapolis and Cambridge 1993) 3–4 (prologue 3), 5–7 (I 1–7), 37 (VII 1). Erasmus often criticizes Franciscans who 'defame' Francis 'by those who make a great parade of his name'; see eg *Ciceronianus* CWE 28 386. For Francis' stigmata, see now Augustine Thompson *Francis of Assisi: A New Biography* (Ithaca 2012) 116–19, 265–6.
737 Erasmus is playing on the phrase that suggests one given to mirth and fun – loving indulgence. The cherubim were not associated with the Dominican order as the seraphim were with the Franciscans, but Erasmus wittily makes the association; see also Allen Ep 2700:54–5: 'although he was neither a Seraphic nor a Cherubic (for they delight in being called by these names) . . .' Chomarat estimates that around 1500 the number of Franciscans and Dominicans was each roughly thirty thousand (ASD V-4 151 366n), a number much lower than the 'total membership of the Order in 1303 of about 20,650': see William A. Hinnebusch, O.P. *The History of the Dominican Order: Origins and Growth to 1500* (New York c 1966) I 331 and ODCC 'Dominican Order' 497–8. In 1517 the Franciscan order became divided, separating themselves into the Conventuals and

troops let men be chosen who are truly dead to the world, alive to Christ, to
teach the word of God sincerely among the barbarian races. Ignorance of the
language is given as an excuse; yet for human embassies princes find men
to learn different languages, and the Athenian Themistocles learned Persian well enough in a single year to be able to speak with the king without
an interpreter.[738] Will we not strive to achieve the same in an enterprise so
exalted? Among barbarous and unknown nations the apostles found food
and clothing,[739] and God has promised that those who seek the kingdom of
God will lack nothing;[740] but if they meet with a people so thankless that
they totally refuse bread, water, and shelter, there remains the outstandingly
beautiful example of that best of preachers Paul, who sewed hides together
with his own hands in order not to burden anyone.[741] He sewed together
the skins of goats, I say, with those very hands with which he gave the Holy
Spirit to believers,[742] with which he consecrated the body and blood of the
Lord.[743] Not even miracles will be lacking should the situation require them,
so long as sincere faith is present together with a seraphic charity; or at least
the place of miracles will be taken by a mind free from every desire for
the human, a constantly sober life, a zeal for helping everyone without recompense,[744] a patience firm against all injuries,[745] a constant cheerfulness
of spirit in afflictions,[746] and an affable modesty with no trace of haughtiness. Nor did the apostles produce miracles indiscriminately, but they attracted far more to Christ's realm with the things that I have mentioned
than with miracles, for many attributed the latter to magic while the former
demonstrated that the Spirit of God was working through men.[747]

* * * * *

the Observants, with the former declared 'the true Order of St Francis'; see
John Moorman *A History of the Franciscan Order: From Its Origins to the Year
1517* (Oxford 1968) 569–85; ODCC 'Franciscan Order' 634–6. For the mention of
cherubim in the Bible, see Gen 3:24; Exod 25:18–20, 37:7–9; Num 7:89; 1 Kings
6:23–35; Ps 18:10 (Vulg 17:11); Ezekiel 10.

738 See Plutarch *Themistocles* 29.3–4.
739 Rom 15:26–7; 1 Cor 16:1–4; 2 Cor 8–9
740 Matt 6:33
741 Acts 18:3
742 Acts 8:17
743 There is no explicit reference to this in Scripture. Erasmus might be alluding
    to 1 Cor 11:17–33.
744 See 2 Cor 11:7.
745 Gal 5:22; Rom 5:4
746 1 Thess 3:4, 7; 2 Cor 1:4, 8
747 Cf Acts 8:6–15.

There remains the final excuse, mortal danger. But, since all must die once,[748] what more attractive or what happier death could befall than for the sake of the gospel? Those who travel to Jerusalem from the farthest regions of the earth expose themselves to mortal danger, and all do not return home safe from that pilgrimage; yet every year such a multitude of men runs to Jerusalem to see some place or other, and is mortal peril offered as excuse here? What, I ask, is the importance of seeing the ruins of Jerusalem? But building a spiritual Jerusalem in men's minds is truly important. How many soldiers fearlessly commit themselves to battle, holding their life cheap for the sake of a mortal prince? And does that highest monarch, who promises in return for military service a crown of eternal glory,[749] not find soldiers endowed with a similar courage? How much more desirable to die as Paul died than to wither away from consumption,[750] to be tormented for many years by gout, to be twisted by paralysis, to die again and again from the stone.[751] Moreover, supposing death should come, it will not come before the day that the Father has appointed for his own. The apostles lived in a world of noisy confusion and reached a full old age; therefore there is no reason to fear death under the protection of Christ, who will not allow a hair to fall to the earth unless by his Father's will.[752] Finally, how is it proper that those who profess the apostolic life are deterred from the apostolic office by a love for life? To give up one's life for the gospel is perhaps truly apostolic.

* * * * *

748 Heb 9:27
749 See 1 Pet 5:4; 1 Thess 2:19; Isa 62:3.
750 Chomarat (ASD V-4 153 401n, 402) suggests that Erasmus has in mind the account of Paul's death from St Jerome; see Jerome *De viris inlustribus* PL 23 (1845) 603–726; *On Illustrious Men* trans Thomas P. Halton FOC 100 13. According to legend and Jerome, Paul was decapitated at Rome in the age of Nero (AD 67) on the same day that Peter was crucified, thirty-seven years after the death of Jesus; hence the celebration of Saints Peter and Paul (29 June). However, as Chomarat also suggests, it might be more likely that Erasmus is mindful of his own failing condition and painful infirmities; see eg his letter of 19 July 1530 to Johann Rinck, Allen Ep 2355:40–66. Note too Erasmus' words, 364 below: 'That to which we urge you is difficult, but it is also the most beautiful and excellent enterprise of all; would that the Lord had given me such a spirit that I could earn death in so pious an activity rather than be consumed by slow death in these torments.'
751 Erasmus often complains of the illness of the stone; see eg Ep 1558:65–75, especially 66.
752 See Luke 21:18; Acts 27:34; 2 Sam 14:11.

For Crates of Thebes and Socrates of Athens and Diogenes of Sinope,[753] along with many others, have scorned wealth though they knew neither Christ nor the apostles. Come on then,[754] you men of bravery, you glorious leaders of Christian soldiery, put on the helmet of salvation, the breastplate of devotion,[755] take up 'the shield of faith'[756] and 'the sword of the Spirit, which is the word of God,'[757] and 'girding your loins'[758] with the belt of modesty and with your feet shod, which represent the emotions, ready with the whole spiritual panoply to preach the gospel of peace,[759] gird yourselves up with fearless courage for the glorious enterprise; cast down, kill, slaughter – not men, but ignorance, impiety, and every vice, for to kill in this way is to save. Ensure not that you return home from them richer, but that you enrich them with a spiritual wealth; count it a rich booty if you snatch so many souls from the tyranny of Satan and claim them for the Redeemer, if you lead hordes of captives in triumph into heaven for him. That to which we urge you is difficult, but it is also the most beautiful and excellent enterprise of all; would that the Lord had given me such a spirit that I could earn death in so pious an activity rather than be consumed by a slow death in my present torments.[760]

But even though one does not go to barbarian nations, no one is suitable for the office of preacher who has not rendered his mind superior to

* * * * *

753 On Crates of Thebes (c 365–285 BC), see Diogenes Laertius *Vitae philosophorum* 6.5.4, where he writes that Crates divided up his fortune of two hundred talents among his fellow citizens; see Erasmus *Apophthegmata* CWE 38 831–2; OCD 296. On Socrates of Athens (469–399 BC), see Erasmus *Apophthegmata* CWE 37 221–51; Diogenes Laertius *Vitae philosophorum* 2.5.9; OCD 997–8. On Diogenes of Sinope (c 400–c 325 BC), see Erasmus *Apophthegmata* CWE 37 271–334; Diogenes Laertius *Vitae philosophorum* 6.2 passim; OCD 348.

754 Eph 6:14–17. Erasmus ends this part of book 1 by encouraging preachers to forego all earthly considerations and carry out the duty of proclaiming God's word. See St Paul's use of exhortation in Eph 6:14–20. Erasmus also echoes Tertullian *Ad martyras* 3; CCSL 1 1–8 ANF III 694; see also 365–7 below.

755 Eph 6:14; 1 Thess 5:8

756 Eph 6:16

757 Eph 6:17

758 Eph 6:14

759 Like Paul, Erasmus uses the metaphor of war for the spiritual combat of the individual Christian and of the preacher who in proclaiming 'the gospel of peace' battles against 'ignorance, impiety, and every vice.' See *Enchiridion* CWE 66 1–127; cf Prudentius' *Psychomachia*.

760 For Erasmus' description of the physical torments he suffered at the time he finished *Ecclesiastes*, see Schoeck (2) 340–2.

wealth, pleasures, and even life and death; the cross[761] is nowhere absent for those who preach the word of the Lord sincerely. There are certain powerful men today, not unlike Herod,[762] who mock Christ and his teaching; there are men like Annas and Caiaphas,[763] there are scribes and pharisees who would sooner confound heaven and earth[764] than suffer any loss to their authority and income; there are artisans not unlike those who among the Ephesians stirred up a mob against the apostles because their preaching reduced their own income;[765] and there is no lack of Judases[766] who, though they seem intimate with Christ, sell him and betray him to those who want him dead; and among the people some turn thumbs down[767] and shout, 'Crucify him, crucify him.'[768] Those who have experienced this freedom and the companion of freedom, the cross, will admit the truth of what I am saying.

The office of preacher, then, is very difficult but also very beautiful; the contest is no ordinary one, but the prizes are outstanding. In the games of princes men are found who willingly go through smoke and fire after a cap hung at the top of a pole, men who go forth to a dangerous single combat for a bull as the prize;[769] and does Christ – a master of the games[770] who promises everlasting triumph in heaven to those who compete faithfully – not find noble competitors? And yet a mortal master of the games does not always award whatever more or less worthless prize he is proposing to the person who has earned it but quite often transfers it to someone he favours more; and even if the judgment is free of all corruption, the person who

* * * * *

761 See Matt 10:38, 16:24; Mark 8:34; Luke 9:23, 14:27.

762 See Luke 23:6–12.

763 Matt 26:57; John 18:13–14, 19–24, 28

764 'Confound heaven and earth' (or, to mingle sea and sky); *Adagia* I iii 81 *Miscebis sacra profanis* 'You will mix sacred and profane.'

765 Acts 19:23–40

766 See John 13:21–30, 18:1–5; Matt 26:14–25; Luke 22:3–5.

767 For 'thumb down' (*verso police*), see Juvenal 3:36; cf *Adagia* I viii 46 *Premere pollicem. Convertere pollicem* 'Thumbs down. Thumbs up.'

768 See John 19:6; Luke 23:21; Mark 15:13–14; Matt 27:22–3.

769 For bull sports at Rome in the Renaissance, see Charles L. Stinger *The Renaissance in Rome* (Bloomington 1998) 57.

770 For 'master of the games' (*agonothetes*), see eg Tertullian *Ad martyras* 3 CCSL 1 5; ANF III 694: 'In like manner, O blessed ones, count whatever is hard in this lot of yours as a discipline of your powers of mind and body. You are about to pass through a noble struggle, in which the living God acts the part of superintendent (*agonothetes*), in which the Holy Ghost is your trainer, in which the prize is an eternal crown of angelic essence, citizenship in the heavens, glory everlasting.' Cf *De concordia* CWE 65 183 and n261.

proposes the prizes and invites to the contest does not give strength to the competitor. But our master of the games, who challenges you to win, also gives you the strength to win, and a defeated contestant does not take away disgrace instead of a prize; but each gets his full reward, if indeed in the gospel it is not only the one who had doubled five talents given as principal that is told, 'Well done, good and faithful servant,' but also the one who had doubled two: even the man who had received one would have been told the same had he not buried it in the ground despite knowing that he had a master who was quite eager for this sort of gain.[771]

Where then are those who profess apostolic perfection? Why do they not show apostolic courage? Why does none arise from among so many to claim Paul's glory,[772] to teach the gospel without charge and at his own expense?[773] If prizes inspire us towards strength,[774] all those that the world promises are nothing to these that Christ pledges. Whoever truly believes that such a reward awaits, whoever sighs for that unfading crown of heavenly glory[775] will readily make light of an effort that is neither lasting (for whatever is done here is ephemeral)[776] nor without effective relief. Wicked men plot an attack, but the good defend; the impious curse, but the devout pray for a blessing; evil men revile, but good men praise, and only the praise that the good offer to virtue is true praise; those whose minds the world has seized scorn, but those who cherish the glory of the Lord Jesus respect and revere. And yet meanwhile it is useless here to boast except in the Lord.[777] In place of the secular pleasures he has foregone, the preacher ought to be content with either a mind sure of its reward that is like an unending banquet[778] or the internal joy of the spirit that accompanies evangelical deeds.[779] These things the eye of man has not seen, nor has the ear heard them, nor have they ascended into the heart of man;[780] but

* * * * *

771 See the parable of the talents in Matt 25:14–30 and Luke 19:12–27.

772 See eg 2 Cor 3.

773 2 Cor 11:7; 1 Cor 4:12

774 *si praemiis accendimur ad virtutem*; prizes and punishments are two crucial components of the preacher's message; see especially book 4. 'Vices and virtues, punishment and rewards' are also central to Franciscan preaching and Christian preaching in general.

775 1 Cor 9:25; 1 Thess 2:19; 1 Pet 5:4

776 2 Cor 4:16–18

777 See 2 Corinthians 12 and Gal 6:14.

778 See Prov 15:15 'a cheerful heart has a continual feast.'

779 Cf Rom 14:17.

780 Isa 64:4 (cited by Paul 1 Cor 2:9)

they are perceived with a hidden sense of the mind[781] by those who have deserved to taste the sweetness of the Lord.[782] Someone who is only a man cannot grasp even with the fancy of thought how great this joy is; you must be greater than a man to look within, hear within, perceive within with the heart.[783] What joy, what exultation, what celebration must be in the heart of the faithful preacher when he considers how many souls the Lord has rescued from Satan's tyranny and claimed for himself by his ministry? How great is Paul's satisfaction, how great his triumph, whenever he recalls how widely he has spread the gospel, especially in places where it had not been sown.[784]

But I do not think that Christians are especially lacking here in strength of spirit and judgment, inasmuch as we see that in other matters many bravely scorn wealth and pleasures and other evils of a different sort to the point of scorning life. How many set out for Jerusalem through so many dangers, leaving at home their sweet children and dearest wife? How many – not only men but women as well – neglect homeland, parents, kin, comrades, property, together with all the pleasures of life, and hide themselves in a sort of everlasting imprisonment, professing the austere practice of the Brigittines or Carthusians,[785] whether to win remission of their sins or to lay up a greater treasure of glory for themselves in heaven?[786] There is one type of monk that wears an iron breastplate against the bare skin instead of a hair shirt, one that walks with shins and feet bare, one that takes the cold ground for his bed, one that drinks water instead of wine, eats dry bread instead of culinary delicacies; and there are even some who willingly tear their body with scourges and others who, covered only with a robe of hemp, walk about bareheaded, barefooted, sleep on no mattress, do not

* * * * *

781 Cf 2 Cor 12:4.
782 Ps 34:8 (Vulg 33:9)
783 Cf Augustine *De Trinitate* 13.2.5 CCSL 50A 386 10–11; NPNF 1st series 3 168: *nec foris est a nobis sed in intimis nobis* 'Nor is it without apart from us, but deeply seated within us.'
784 See Rom 15:18–20; 2 Cor 10:15–17.
785 'Brigittines' or Order of Our Saviour (or Bridgettine Order [*Ordo sanctissimi salvatoris*] was a congregation of cloistered religious women and men (double monastery) founded in 1346 by St Bridget of Sweden (1303–73) and noted for austerity; see ODCC 237–8. The Carthusians were a group of religious contemplatives founded by St Bruno in 1084 at the Grande Chartreuse. The Rule, the *Consuetudines Cartusiae*, received papal approval in 1122; additions were later made to it. See ODCC 293–4.
786 Matt 19:21; Mark 10:21; Luke 12:33, 18:22

cover themselves at night with cloaks but sleep upon the ground in the same garb in which they walk by day, taste neither wine nor ale, touch no kind of food but bread, raw vegetables, and fruit (a baked apple is an Easter treat for them), nor do they touch money or have anywhere a home or monastery or stewards from whom to ask anything. They fast on all the days on which the church has imposed it, and fast not as we fast at Lent but in such a way that for the whole day on which the fast has been imposed they touch neither food nor drink until lunch of the following day; and they never relax the austerity of their life at all, even when they travel in the coldest regions. Since so many do not refuse to adopt such harsh practices as these of their own free will in order to win Christ's favour for themselves, why do so few aim at the office of preacher, which is the most pleasing to Christ and the most effective for wiping out sins or winning a glorious crown? For it was not to drinkers of water or wearers of hemp or to the unkempt or to the goatish that the Lord promised a seat upon the twelve chairs,[787] but to the apostles and those who exercise the role of apostles; and to those who have received such a prophet in the name of the prophet he promises the reward of a prophet.[788] If alms extinguish sin,[789] no alms are more pleasing to God than acting as a good shepherd; if enduring hardships earns an increase of glory, no hardships are more pleasing to God than those that are borne for the sake of the gospel,[790] and there will be enough of these even if you do not bring them upon yourself. Why is it, I ask, that so many are found strong in these things that men prescribe for themselves, and there are so few to take on the rule of the perfect man,[791] where God challenges us with the highest prizes, especially when the world is everywhere full of people selling themselves under the label of the apostolic life and evangelical perfection? If they are truly dead to the world, let them show in this most beautiful enterprise that they truly are dead to the world.

In the cities there is no lack of people to preach the word of the Lord; it is most beautiful to sow the seed where no one sows, in solitary villages, in barbarous regions, where there is a full crop but no farmer. Not even here will there be a lack of people to offer, if not luxuries, at least vital necessities to those who live purely and teach sincerely. The sober are naturally content with little; what farmer, however slight his means, would be burdened by

* * * * *

787 Cf Matt 19:28.
788 Matt 10:41
789 See Luke 11:41 and Dan 4:24.
790 Mark 8:35
791 Eph 4:13

a guest who is content with pure water, coarse bread, and beets or turnips in place of meat? If a rich man invites of his own volition, let them go, by all means, but let them present a model of sobriety among the delights that are offered. If a poor man invites, let them go there too with equal eagerness. If no one invites, let them impose themselves nowhere but seek another town[792] without eating; the Lord will not allow his servants to die of hunger.[793] Finally, if going hungry is their excuse for not preaching because they may not carry around money in their belt [*zona*] to buy food, they can take along bread and cheese in a little sack [*sacculus*]; this is not an indignity but the pride of heralds, very pleasing to God.[794] So much for those who are said not to carry money about with them.

As for those who have belts, it is fitting that they should not only refrain from burdening the poor or thrifty but should share their own with the poor,[795] for it is the mark of the true shepherd to feed in three ways: with sacred teaching, with a saintly life, and with corporeal assistance. I know that it is not a great matter if those who sow their own spirituality reap the carnal harvest of others – I know that a worker is worthy of his reward[796] if it does not come from elsewhere; but though we read that this reward was given generously by willing donors,[797] we also read that it was never demanded by Christ nor by any of the apostles, nor did the Lord give them any such command. To Zacchaeus he said, 'I want to stay with you today.'[798] Zacchaeus had not invited the Lord aloud, but the Lord heard his heart and loved the modesty that kept him from daring to request what he most ardently desired; so in this instance the Lord did not impose himself upon his hospitality but relieved the bashfulness of one whose love was great. Judas received what was given willingly

* * * * *

792 Luke 4:43
793 Matt 6:25–6, 31–3; Luke 12:22–4, 29–30
794 See St Francis 'The Later Rule,' chapter IV in *Francis of Assisi* II 102: 'I strictly command all my brothers not to receive coins or money in any form, either personally or through intermediaries.' For the biblical basis of this command, see especially Luke 9:2–3 ('... and he sent them out to preach the kingdom of God and to heal. And he said to them, "Take nothing for your journey, no staff, nor bag [*pera*], nor bread, nor money ..."') and Matt 10:9–10 ('Take no gold, nor silver, nor copper in your belts [*zonis*], no bag [*pera*] for your journey ...'). Erasmus is presumably recalling Matthew's words, not Luke's.
795 Erasmus means bishops and clergy, as well as members of religious orders with financial resources.
796 Luke 10:7; 1 Tim 5:18
797 Cf Matt 20:1–16 (the parable of the eleventh hour).
798 Luke 19:5; see 1–10.

by friends, but from it gifts were made to the poor.[799] But today, they say, human generosity has cooled, and no wonder since sincerity has decreased and luxury increased among evangelists;[800] let them go back to their original simplicity, and the people will readily return to their original generosity. Let preachers therefore recognize the dignity of their function and strive with Paul to exalt their ministry,[801] not in order to create glory for themselves among men[802] but so that Christ may grow rich from the profit of souls[803] and God may be glorified in the saintly character of his servants.

But the Lord must be entreated to send such workers into the vineyard,[804] which is now almost destroyed. These responsibilities belong to everyone, but the salvation or damnation of the people at large depends most upon their princes and bishops.[805] The integrity of princes will ensure a minimum of warfare and brigandage, and will not allow powerful men to be permitted whatever they like; it will provide uncorrupted magistrates and judges. Bishops will provide clerics of a settled life, will provide preachers endowed with the evangelical virtues, will provide learned and godly men capable of moulding the young[806] and dropping the seeds of Christian devotion upon their tender minds.[807] The reflowering of evangelical vigour in the people rests particularly with these persons. One must pray

* * * * *

799 Cf John 13:28–30, 12:4–6.
800 Erasmus means those entrusted with the mission to preach the gospel. See *Moria* CWE 27 137–40.
801 Rom 11:13
802 1 Cor 9:16
803 1 Cor 9:19–22
804 Matt 20:1–7
805 Erasmus returns to this theme of princes and bishops bearing responsibility for ensuring peaceful and just conditions in which the gospel can be preached. Beside insuring freedom from turmoil, bishops and priests must promote education for training good preachers. Erasmus recommends in broad strokes what would become the Catholic diocesan seminary (*seminarium*) after Trent. See 151–8 and 326 above.
806 For 'men capable of moulding' (*formatores*), see Quintilian 10.2.20.
807 *semina christianae pietatis*; the word 'seminary' derives from this idea that the schools for young men who would become preachers would be 'seedbeds of virtue'; see the parallel idea in Quintilian 10.2.20, where he states that 'it is his [the 'director of the minds of others'] to foster whatever good qualities he may perceive in his pupils, to make good their deficiencies as far as may be, to correct their faults and turn them to better things.' See also Cicero *De finibus* 4.8.18, 5.7.18, 5.15.43, 5.21.59–60.

for them above all that God may impart to them the principal spirit[808] so
that each may glorify his ministry. However, just as God uses their ministry
to save the people, so he sometimes gives good or bad princes according
to the deserts or even the prayers of the people.[809] Paul himself, so outstanding an apostle, frequently asks that he be helped by the prayers of his
disciples when before God, saying, 'Brothers, pray for us, that the word of
God may have free course and that we may be delivered from perverse and
wicked men.'[810] Since a witless people does not know what should be requested or how, the Apostle prescribes what he wishes to be sought from
God through them, namely the greatest thing of all, that the gospel have
free course, that is, that Christian devotion spread quickly and widely. With
loud shouts we ask God for a successful harvest of grain, but we should
ask with louder ones that the evangelical crop produce an abundant harvest. The common people wish longevity, victories, and triumphs for their
prince, things that God would give even unasked if this best suited the
state. It is more correct to ask from God on behalf of monarchs those things
that Solomon, that wisest of kings, asked for himself,[811] and for this prudent
request he was praised by the Lord; and what he sought by name he received
in abundance, while wealth and glory and other advantages, which he had
not sought, were given in addition. 'A wise prince is the salvation of his
people,'[812] says Scripture. In fact, in every kind of affair what is paramount
should come first in our prayers. Let someone who is commending a secular state to God in his prayers seek for his prince the wisdom that sits
by the heavenly throne, judgment, an upright mind, fear of God, love for
the state, and the other virtues that render a prince truly great and beneficial to his people. But we must pray much more fervently that the Lord
give to the shepherds of his flock a heart pure of all earthly desires, a mind
thirsting for the profit and honour of the Lord Jesus, a spirit fearless against
all terrors, a learned tongue,[813] a heart packed with the treasure of heavenly learning[814] – in short, that they be all equipped on every side with

* * * * *

808 Ps 51:12 (Vulg 50:14). See 263–4, 267, 290 above for Erasmus' discussion of
'principal spirit.'
809 2 Chron 18:21–2; Mic 6:16
810 2 Thess 3:1–2
811 Wisd of Sol 7–9
812 See Wisd of Sol 6:26 (Vulg *multitudo autem sapientium sanitas est orbis terrarum
et rex sapiens populi stabilimentum est*). Erasmus' quotation does not follow the
Vulgate exactly.
813 Isa 50:4
814 Cf Col 2:3.

the mystical adornment of Aaron,[815] and that other prophets under them be found faithful.

Prophets I call those that announce the will of God to the people from the oracles of Scripture,[816] so that they can legitimately use that preamble of the prophets, 'The Lord says this';[817] for false prophets[818] also used to shout, 'The Lord says this' even more insistently than the true ones, and they have always been greater in number. Whoever interprets the meaning of Scripture in good faith can rightly begin, 'The Lord says this.' These are the main hinges upon which hangs the condition of the Christian commonwealth. Accordingly, it would be right for them to have first place in prayers, first concern in appointments. It would scarcely be possible to express in words how much influence a prince brings upon either correcting or corrupting the public character, but the primates of the church are much more influential, since they are the teachers even of princes, at least in what pertains to religion and devotion. But sometimes it happens that enduring a harsh and wicked prince is good for the people,[819] so that the savagery of one may restrain the many and drive them to penitence through their affliction in external things; but a wicked shepherd can only bring the greatest misery to the multitude, and yet he too is sometimes given because of the people's stubborn rebelliousness. Hence the Lord's frequent indignation, hence the angry threats against bad prophets who adduce prophecy from their own heart, saying, 'The Lord says this' though the Lord has not spoken to them.[820] Those who twist Scripture to human desires are lying, however much they shout, 'The Lord says this,' because they do indeed have the label of Scripture but put forward a spurious sense. Such men are the more dangerous because they conceal human desires under divine authority and import the destruction of devotion under an image of devotion. Accordingly, the Lord in the gospel does not order them to be avoided, does not order them to be killed, but warns us to beware of them.[821] They are intermingled,

* * * * *

815 See 301–20 above where Erasmus explains the spiritual significance of Aaron's vestments.

816 Cf 1 Cor 14:1. Erasmus' definition of a prophet fits his definition of the preacher; see 322 above.

817 'The Lord says this' is the customary exordium of the prophets when they delivered God's word to his people. See eg the repetitions of this phrase in Amos 1–2: 'Thus says the Lord' (*Haec dicit Dominus*); see also Ezek 13:7.

818 Cf Matt 24:11, 24; 1 John 4:1.

819 Cf Mic 6:16.

820 Ezek 13:7

821 See Matt 16:6, 11–12; Mark 8:15; Luke 12:1. Erasmus' description of the false

like darnel with wheat,[822] in such a way that it is not expedient that they be torn up outright; a warning is enough to prevent them from deceiving anyone. For occasionally they even prove profitable, when they strengthen the chosen in their faith,[823] when they sharpen the devout to the knowledge of Scripture; were there no fire, gold would not shine.[824] The furnace tests the potter's vessels, and the trials of affliction test just men.[825] While great care must be taken in appointment to public and private functions, so the greatest care is necessary in selecting those to teach the people.

As has been said, all human emotions, which blind the judgment of the mind, must be banished far from these elections, for through them it happens that there is either no judgment or an absurd one (for what must never be forgotten needs to be driven home often). Is it not ridiculous to examine the reliability and skill of someone to whom you have decided to entrust your cattle or horses and give no consideration at all to those to whom you entrust the souls of men, for which Christ died?[826] Do you remove a farmer who cultivates your fields carelessly or ignorantly and not a pastor who casts bad seed into the Lord's good crop? Is it not ridiculous when sailing to entrust the oars to just anyone, to assign to the helm not just anyone but one who is experienced in piloting, while entrusting the care of the church to anyone at all indiscriminately? If someone were to say there, 'Let this man sit at the helm; he comes from a good family, is quite rich and has money to give and gives generously, has favour with the prince, is a close relative of yours and a friend,' would you not object at once, 'What does it matter to me what kind of person he is in other respects? This storm requires a trained and energetic pilot; otherwise everyone is in danger'? And does this occur to no one in a case where the danger is far more serious? In a shipwreck, cargo is at risk, bodies are at risk, though when a ship is smashed, many swim away unharmed, and the sea itself throws up much cargo onto the shore; in this shipwreck it is the souls, the cargo dearest to Christ, that face the greatest danger.

* * * * *

prophets fits that of heretics, and he makes clear that Christ did not order false prophets (heretics) to be killed, as happened to many condemned as 'heretics' in Erasmus' own day.

822 See the parable of the wheat and the tares (Matt 13:24–30).
823 See 1 Cor 11:19; Acts 3:16.
824 *Adagia* IV i 58 *Aurum igni probatum* 'Gold tested in fire.'
825 See Ecclus 27:6 (Vulg *vasa figuli probat fornax* ...); see eg Job passim.
826 Erasmus often uses this type of argument *a minore* in his writing; see eg *De pueris instituendis* CWE 26 313–4; see especially *De copia* CWE 24 61–2, where he gives such examples of similes in arranging illustrative material.

This concern then pertains principally to monarchs, popes, bishops, and colleges of canons, or any others entrusted with the care of conferring ecclesiastical posts, since the right to choose a prelate has long since been removed from the people.[827] I do not condemn this removal (the present state of the times has required it), so long as those upon whom the power of selection has devolved consider sincerely, in making their choice, what is useful to the Lord's flock, for in some places the will of the prince alone creates bishops or abbots. But by whom they are created does not matter so much as the judgment and the sincerity with which they are created. Many kings think that they have obliged God with a great favour by funding some masses, by building a new monastery. I do not deny that what they are doing is a pious work if their mind is upright, but, in my opinion, they would bind God to themselves by no lesser merit if they were to apply both a Christian mind and Christian judgment in selecting the leaders of the church, and if they were to pay due honour and show obedience to these leaders when they perform their office correctly, so that the people too might heed them more readily.

Moreover, it is important that the person selecting and the person selected both understand the dignity, difficulty, and danger of the office. Let the person who has entrusted the priestly office to a worthy man congratulate himself and rejoice in his heart since he has accomplished successfully something difficult and splendid; let the person to whom the task has been assigned consider how magnificent, how sublime and excellent an office he has received, but at the same time how arduous and difficult. Let him weigh what ample rewards have been prepared for the person who, in carrying out his responsibilities, has demonstrated his fidelity and his service to the Lord, whose place he takes, and what a grave judgment, what a fearsome punishment awaits those who turn ecclesiastical power into tyranny, who neglect the Lord's profit and hunt their own gain.

Moreover, all that has been said here concerning bishops (for they are the true and first shepherds of the sheep) applies also to those who are now called *parochi* [parish priests], their name derived from the fact that they have undertaken the task of 'providing' spiritual nourishment to the

* * * * *

827 Erasmus refers to the practice in the early church of congregations choosing their bishops; notable is the case of Ambrose; see *Vita sancti Ambrosii* 41–5. The Second Lateran Council (1139) ended this practice. See I.S. Robinson 'The institutions of the church, 1073–1216' in *The New Cambridge Medieval History* IV *c 1024–c 1198* ed David Luscombe and Jonathan Riley-Smith (Cambridge 2004) 368–460, especially 455.

laity.[828] And they should not act less diligently because they have taken on
the care of a flock that is small or rural or composed of women; it is a great
thing to be a good shepherd, even of a tiny flock. Others perhaps are more
bishops by virtue of titles, mitres, crooks, and the pallium, but they excel
only if they present in reality what they profess in their external garb. I admit that in the eyes of men the dignity is not the same; in the eyes of God the
dignity of someone who faithfully tends his flock, however small and humble, is greater than those who commend themselves to the eyes of men with
jeweled crowns, golden crooks, a jeweled pallium, and other hoopla. Listen
then, you pastor of a small and rustic village; listen, you prior or abbot gov-
erning a single small monastery; listen, you father entrusted with the care
of a few cloistered maidens: recognize your dignity, not so that you swell
up with pride, but so that you do not spoil the glory of your office by the ad-
mixture of something lower. What matters is not how numerous or splendid
is the flock assigned to you but that you bring profit to the Lord, the mon-
eylender, in proportion to the principal entrusted to you.[829] Consider not so
much what has been entrusted as who has entrusted it; it is for him to evaluate what he has invested. Those who have managed a numerous flock well
are going to get a greater prize, but no one who is going to gain eternal life
should regret his reward. Listen, then, to the dignity of your office so that
you do not underrate yourself, but listen also to its difficulty and danger,
not so as to become dejected but to be more attentive and vigilant. It takes
a fine kind of wisdom to be neither exalted by the dignity of an office nor
dejected at its difficulty. If the honour excites you, reflect that you are only
a steward;[830] if the difficulty frightens, reflect that the highest pastor, who
does not fail his flock up to the end of time, still lives.[831] Paul, though in
general unassuming, boasts that he can do all things through faith in him.[832]
Finally, this too requires a great kind of heart, to turn a tiny flock into a
great one, a humble one into a distinguished one, for that is to do honour
to your ministry. No king deems himself humble even if a less widespread

* * * * *

828 A *parochus* is a parish priest who has the care of souls (*cura animarum*). Erasmus
bases his explanation of the term upon the folk etymology of this word from
the Greek παρέχω 'to provide, furnish, supply,' πάροχος 'a provider.' Cf Horace
Satires 1.5.46 and 2.8.36; Cicero *Ad Atticum* 13.2.2.
829 Cf the parable of the talents in Matt 25:14–30; Luke 19:11–27.
830 For 'steward' (*dispensator*), cf Titus 1:7; 1 Cor 4:1–2; 1 Pet 4:10. See *Paraphrasis in
epistolam Pauli ad Corinthios priorem* CWE 43 60–1, *Annotationes in 1 ad Corinthios*
(1 Cor 4.2) ASD VI-8 80, and *Paraphrasis in epistolam Pauli ad Titum* CWE 44 58–9.
831 Cf Matt 28:20; 2 Cor 13:4.
832 Phil 4:13

domain has fallen to his lot; he is great by the very fact of administering as king the Sparta that which has befallen him.[833]

Wonderful indeed is the splendour of royal distinction, which is called by a term that signifies something divine and greater than man: majesty.[834] To violate this in any way is punishable by death;[835] I do not at all diminish it. The Apostle orders that due honour be paid to kings for their eminence;[836] but, if we weigh the things themselves in a true scale, no king, in so far as he is a king, is so magnificent that he is not beneath the dignity, I shall say not of a bishop but of a village pastor in so far as he is a pastor.[837] If this seems paradoxical, the proof is at hand if you consider the content and aim of each office. What is the object of a king's concern? That the wicked be restrained by the laws, that the others be allowed to live their lives in peace, that is, that the property and persons of their citizens be safe. But how much loftier is the aim of the evangelical pastor, who ensures that there is peace in the minds of all by lulling and restraining the desires of this world. The king procures the establishment of peace with his neighbours; the priest provides that each has peace with God, and whoever has been reconciled to him has peace with himself[838] and plots no ill against another. The king provides that walls, houses, and fields along with their flocks are safe from bandits; you see the humble content of his royal duty. What of the preacher? That the property of the mind – faith, charity, sobriety, modesty, whose retention makes men happy, whose loss makes them miserable – is safe from the attack of Satan. What does royal liberality bestow? Stipends, salaries, honorary titles, all fleeting and prey to fortune's mockery. What of the preacher? Through the sacraments of the church he supplies heavenly grace; through baptism he makes heirs of the heavenly kingdom out of the sons of Gehenna;[839] through holy unction he gives strength of mind against the power of demons; through the Holy Eucharist he both joins men among

* * * * *

833 See *Adagia* II v 1 *Sparta nactus es, hanc orna* 'Sparta is your portion; do your best for her.'
834 *maiestas*; the word majesty is from the Latin meaning 'greater' (*maior, maius*).
835 The crime against majesty Erasmus refers to is *lèse-majesté* (*maiestas laesa*).
836 Rom 13:7; 1 Pet 2:13–14
837 Erasmus recalls the opening of this work where he sketches out the vast difference between sacred and secular assemblies; here he explains the infinitely higher and qualitatively different value of ecclesiastical duties and their benefits.
838 Cf Eph 2:16; Col 1:16; 2 Cor 5:19–20.
839 For 'sons of Gehenna' (*ex filiis gehennae*), see Matt 23:15 (singular 'son of Gehenna').

themselves and, binding them in harmony, joins them with God so that they now become one with him; through the sacrament of penitence he makes living men out of dead, free men out of slaves. Finally, from the storehouse of Scripture he daily sets out the morsels of salutary teaching with which souls are nourished and invigorated; he brings forth the spiritual wine that truly gladdens the heart, brings forth the medicine with which truly deadly diseases of the mind are healed, brings forth the antidotes effective against the poison of the ancient serpent. In sum, whatever falls properly under the care of a king is earthly and temporary, but what a priest handles is divine, is heavenly, is eternal. The gulf between the royal and the pastoral office is just as great as that between heaven and earth, between body and soul, between the transient and the eternal.

In this evaluation please consider not what man assigns to man but what the nature of the office itself merits. I know that a royal sceptre is more highly valued than a bishop's crook, a crown than a mitre; yet the fact that we see pastors generally held in contempt these days derives for the most part (if we want to admit the truth) from their own fault. It is clear from ancient literature that bishops were once valued most highly, not only in the eyes of the people but also in the eyes of monarchs, and were customarily all but worshipped. The kissing of hands, knees, and vestments bears witness to this; I do not recall reading of the kissing of feet among ancient writers, though the sinful woman of the Gospel planted kisses on Jesus' feet,[840] and devout women grasped his feet when he had returned to life after the resurrection.[841] That was not the obligation of respect but the emotion of warmest love, though the Lord is greater than any honour we may pay him. The elder Theodosius[842] shows this when he obeyed

* * * * *

840 Luke 7:36–50
841 Matt 28:9
842 Theodosius the Great (379–95) made Orthodox Christianity the state religion, outlawing Arianism and all other non-Orthodox sects. Erasmus' likely source for this historical information and what follows are Beatus Rhenanus' three editions (Basel 1523, 1528, and 1535) of the histories of the early Christian writers: see eg *Autores historiae ecclesiasticae Eusebii Pamphili Caesariensis libri novem, Ruffino interprete. Ruffini presbyteri Aquileiensis, libri duo. Item ex Theodorito Episcopo Cyrensi, Sozomeno, & Socrate Constantinopolitano libri duodecim, versi ab Epiphanio Scholastico, adbreviati per Cassiodorum Senatorem: unde illis Tripartitae historiae vocabulum. Omnia recognita ad antiqua exemplaria Latina, per Beatum Rhenanum. PRAETEREA NON ANTE EXCUSA Nicephori ecclesiastica historia, incerto interprete. Victoris episcopi libri III De persecutione Vandalica. Theodoriti libri v graece, ut sunt ab autore conscripti* (Basel: Froben 1535); he also published an edition at Basel in 1539. Beatus Rhenanus dedicated these works to Stanislaus

Ambrose's exclusion of him from the church;[843] when ordered to go away into the place of penitents, he obeyed, he put aside his royal majesty and lay upon the ground in public, tear-stained he asked forgiveness and did not oppose him when he prescribed the rules for reparation, and finally, when commanded to leave the sanctuary, he complied, excusing himself modestly. But how did the bishop of a single city get such authority? Because he was a true bishop, and that severity of his displayed no pride or arrogance but rather an authority worthy of a priest, to such an extent that the emperor was not ashamed to bear witness before others that he had found but one bishop, Ambrose, from whom he had learned how great is the difference between emperor and priest. The man who dictated laws to the world received from a priest the law that no edict of Caesar had force before the thirtieth day;[844]

* * * * *

Thurzó, bishop of Olmütz (1471/2–1540). See Martin Rothkegel *Der lateinische Briefwechsel des Olmützer Bischofs Stanislaus Thurzó: Eine ostmitteleuropäische Humanistenkorrespondenz der ersten Hälfte des 16. Jahrhunderts* (Hamburg 2007) 70–3, 159–71, 193–200. The sixth-century disciple of Cassiodorus, Epiphanius Scholasticus, compiled and translated into Latin from the Greek these early Christian authors (Theodoret of Cyrus, Sozomen, and Socrates of Constantinople), later revised by Cassiodorus under the title *Tripartite History*. The specific information given in Beatus Rhenanus' edition occurs in Theodoret of Cyrus' history, chapters 30–2 522–4; see NPNF 2nd series 3 book V chapters 17–19 142–4. For Beatus Rhenanus' edition, see: Stéphane Ratti 'Beatus Rhenanus éditeur de l'*Historia Tripertita* de Cassiodore-Epiphane' in *Beatus Rhenanus lecteur et éditeur des textes anciens*, ed James Hirstein (Turnhout 2000) 299–326; John F. D'Amico *Theory and Practice in Renaissance Textual Criticism: Beatus Rhenanus between Conjecture and History* (Berkeley 1988) especially chapter 5: 'From Text to Context I: Beatus Rhenanus and Ecclesiastical History' 143–72.

843 The significance of Ambrose prevailing over Theodosius is made clear by Theodoret of Cyrus (c 393–466) *Ecclesiastical History* chapters 30–2 522–4 (Beatus Rhenanus edition) and NPNF 2nd series 3 book V chapters 17–19 142–4. Theodoret relates that Ambrose 'forbade him to step over the sacred threshold' and demanded that Theodosius do public penance after 'multitudes were mowed down like ears of corn in harvest-tide' (143) in reprisal for a great sedition at Thessalonika in which several magistrates were killed. Ambrose made clear to the emperor 'the differences between an emperor and a priest'; Theodosius confesses that 'Ambrose alone deserves the title of bishop' (145). See Theodoret of Cyrus 5.17 NPNF 2nd series 2 143–5. See also the account by Paulinus *Vita sancti Ambrosii* chapter 8 section 26 66–7 and 141 n6. Ambrose delivered the funeral oration for Theodosius *De obitu Theodosii oratio* (*On the Death of Emperor Theodosius*), found in *Funeral Orations by Saint Gregory Nazianzen and Saint Ambrose* trans Leo P. McCauley et al FOC 22 303–32.

844 According to Theodoret, Ambrose required that Theodosius, as a condition of his penance, enact as law the provision that thirty days elapse before

this law helped the people of Antioch when they had committed a more grievous offence than had the Thessalonians.[845] Not only Theodosius but many other monarchs as well have submitted the royal sceptre to a priest's authority. Why so? Because they saw virtues worthy of a bishop shining in them. For outstanding virtue has a remarkable power of impelling human minds to love and admiration of itself. With it St Basil scorned Modestus,[846] the emperor's prefect, with impunity, and not only with impunity but he impelled that truculent man to admiration of Christian fortitude; with it he cast down Eusebius,[847] the prefect of Pontus, when he was swollen with anger, and soon after helped him in his dejection. With it he had a startling effect on the emperor Valens, who was hostile to the Catholics and favoured the Arians, for as soon as he entered the church, he was struck by the general scene, the man's physical appearance, his steadfast gaze and dignified countenance; then Basil deterred him from his intended cruelty by his wise conversation and would even have called him back from the Arian faction, which he loved with a mad passion, had not the stubborn wickedness of others later overturned what the bishop's authority had convinced him of. The fearless constancy of the Christians whom he had ordered to be executed so moved the wicked Julian,[848] born for the subversion

* * * * *

executing the law when a death sentence or proscription had been signed against anyone, after which time the case would be brought to the emperor to review in tranquillity (144); see *Ecclesiastical History* 5.17 NPNF 2nd series 2 143–5.

845 The troubles occurred in Antioch three years earlier as a result of a new tax to pay for the war; this was years before the revolt in Thessalonika. Again Erasmus is following Theodoret: *Ecclesiastical History* 5.19; cf Sozomen 7.23 392–3.

846 Flavius Domitius Modestus, praetorian prefect of the East (369–77) under Emperor Valens (364–78). See Allen Ep 2611:438 (preface to Froben's Greek Basil *Opera*). See Gregory of Nazianzus *The Panegyric on S. Basil* 43.48–52 NPNF 2nd series 7 411–12; and Gregory of Nyssa *Contra Eunomium* NPNF 2nd series 5 49; see especially Theodoret *Ecclesiastical History* 4.16 NPNF 2nd series 2 119–20.

847 For Basil and Eusebius, prefect of Pontus, see Gregory of Nazianzus *The Panegyric on S. Basil* 43.48–52 NPNF 2nd series 7 413; for Valens see ibidem 410–12. For Basil's conflict with Valens, see Gregory of Nazianzus *The Panegyric on S. Basil* 43.48–52, 55–7 NPNF 2nd series 7 395–422 and Theodoret *Ecclesiastical History* 4.16 NPNF 2nd series 2 119–20.

848 Julian the Apostate (361–3); see ODCC 910. For Basil and Julian, see Sozomen 5.4 328–9. For Erasmus and Julian, see Jean Larmat 'Julien dans les textes du xvie siècle' in *L'empereur Julien: De l'histoire à la légende (331–1715)* 2 vols, ed Renè Braun and Jean Richer (Paris 1978) I 303–5.

of the Christian religion, that he recalled his cruel edict. What of the fact that Allebichus,[849] master of the imperial palace, so honoured the saintliness of the monk Macedonius,[850] a simple mountain dweller ignorant of all literature, that he heeded his advice quite willingly, abandoned his savage commission, and turned the emperor to a different opinion? What a fashionable and eloquent ambassador would not have secured, he secured, or more truly demanded, a despicable old man, uneducated, unsophisticated, and covered in the cheapest rags. What moved Allebichus? What moved the emperor? Truth unalloyed and a piety ignorant of pretence. If priests today showed this, and showed it constantly and without pretence, men's minds would not yet have so degenerated that they are disinclined to honour outstanding piety.

Now if, as the Greek proverb has it, the more difficult anything is, the fairer it is,[851] see how much easier it is to be a good king than a good bishop. The king uses fear and punishments to compel to obedience those he cannot persuade. He has an armed escort, he has troops, he has prisons, sacks, swords, and countless forms of death; he can kill with a nod whomever he pleases. But it is much easier to compel by force than to persuade by speech; it is simpler to kill the body than to turn the mind to goodness. And yet this very thing, which is inherently most difficult, the preacher does mainly with the tongue; instead of weapons he has sacred teaching, tears, prayers, and a blameless life. As Isaiah teaches, 'And he shall smite the earth with the rod of his mouth, and with the breath of his lips he shall slay the wicked, and righteousness shall be the girdle of his loins and faithfulness the girdle of his reins.'[852] These are the weapons of justice, armed with which on the right and left the preacher accomplishes such difficult deeds, by leading rather than by compelling. Bodies can be compelled; minds must be turned, since they cannot be compelled. How much sweat do you think must be expended here by the priest so that he can heal with the word those who are

* * * * *

849 Allebichus (Allobich, Allobichus, Elebichus). See Theodoret *Ecclesiastical History* NPNF 2nd series 3 book v chapter 19 145–6, who calls him *magister militum* 'a military commander.' Erasmus refers to him as *aulae magister* 'master of the imperial palace.' See J.R. Martindale *The Prosopography of the Later Roman Empire* II: AD 395–527 (Cambridge 1980) 61.

850 For the life of Macedonius (the Barley-eater), see Theodoret of Cyrrhus (Cyrus) *A History of the Monks of Syria* trans R.M. Price (Kalamazoo, Mich 1985) 100–7; for the incident here see 102–3 and Theodoret *Ecclesiastical History* NPNF 2nd series 3 book v chapter 19 145–6.

851 *Adagia* II i 12 *Difficilia quae pulchra* 'Good things are difficult.'

852 Isa 11:4–5

ailing not with one but with many illnesses, prop up someone who is slipping, recall to life someone who is without life and lacks even an awareness of evil? By giving money, the king easily enriches whom he wishes; but to convince a miser to scorn gold, to convince someone accustomed to robbery to be kind to the poor, to persuade someone who before did not so much possess wealth as be possessed by it to impoverish himself by spontaneous generosity in order to grow rich in spiritual wealth, that indeed takes great and persistent effort. The king ties a thief in a noose but does not remove the flaw in his mind; he stretches the robber upon the wheel but does not cure the disease of robbing; he punishes adultery and incest but does not implant the love of chastity. The priest does not have the right to kill, but his work is to call back to life with his effective voice minds that have been buried long since in vices, not for four days, but sometimes for forty or sixty years. He often deals with vipers who close up their ears; they push him away when he teaches, do not suffer his warnings, threaten him when he rebukes. This wise enchanter must use effective enchantments[853] to turn the asp into a lamb. But if someone should exaggerate the dignity of princes (which I certainly am not diminishing), let him consider that the priest is father and nourisher and teacher and judge of monarchs too;[854] through him they are Christians, through him they have been imbued with the sacraments of the church, through him they have learned the law of the Lord and the way of salvation, through him they are called back from error if ever they tend towards ill-judged schemes. And that this must be so has been shown in examples from the Old Testament also; at 4 Kings 22 the priest Hilkiah sends to King Josiah through the scribe Shaphan a book that was read out in his presence and warned him of what had been overlooked.[855] Again at Chronicles 23 the priest Jehoiada in the temple hands a book of law to the king who is to be anointed;[856] the same thing that I mentioned a little earlier occurs at 2 Chronicles 24.[857] If the only Christian king is one who administers his realm according to the divine laws, it is a priest who presents, reads, and explains the text; if anointing makes a king, it is a priest who administers it. But if those who administer external unction to a king are regarded as being of the highest dignity, how much loftier is it to bestow

* * * * *

853 On vipers and enchantments, cf Ps 57:5–6 (Vulg), 58:5–6.
854 This again is the lesson of Ambrose's rebuke of Theodosius the Great; see 377–8 above.
855 4 Kings 22 (= 2 Kings 22:8–20)
856 2 Chron 23:11
857 2 Chron 24:20

a spiritual unction on the minds of kings? Which then is more outstanding, the one who gives birth or the one who is born, the one who nourishes or the one who is nourished, the teacher or the pupil, the one who corrects or the one who is corrected, the one who anoints the skin or the one who anoints the mind? The king owes honour to those from whom he was born to this world according to the body, but how much more honour does he owe to the one through whom he was reborn in the spirit to God and heaven! A prince owes to a priest the best thing he has according to the better part of himself, and he is subject to him according to the nobler portion of himself, not to mention that, as was just said, he learns from a priest how to administer correctly this very realm that has become his lot.

From this learn at least how difficult is the office of the preacher, who owes counsel, teaching, and correction[858] not only to the people but to monarchs as well. For he is, as the Apostle says, debtor to the wise and to the foolish,[859] in fact to boys and girls, to youths and maidens, to husbands and wives, to old men and old women, to magistrates and merchants, to sailors and cobblers, to soldiers and farmers, and finally to pimps and prostitutes; to the lowest and to the highest he is debtor. The shepherd of sheep tends only one kind of creature, whose nature is not so difficult to know; the cowherd easily learns the nature of his animal, as do the swineherd and the sheepherder as well; those who tend elephants learn the nature of a single animal with no great trouble. But in this flock there are so many kinds of animals, so many hybrids, that Africa scarcely produces more.[860] Moreover, it requires no little effort to learn the nature of all and to apply to each what is suitable, especially since there is no animal more wily and more changeable than man;[861] his heart is fraught with caves and recesses, and he turns every colour like an octopus or chamaeleon,[862] more changeable even than Proteus[863] himself. Bulls are enraged by red, elephants by white, tigers driven to madness by the noise of drums, lions provoked if someone

* * * * *

858 Cf 2 Tim 3:16.
859 Rom 1:14
860 See *Adagia* III vii 10 *Semper Africa novi aliquid apportat* 'Africa always produces something novel'; cf Pliny *Naturalis historia* 8.17.42. See book 2 CWE 68 476–7.
861 Cf Sophocles *Antigone* 332–74. On the changeable nature of man, see 'Proteus' n863 below.
862 For 'octopus' (*polypi/polypus*), see *Adagia* II iii 91 *Polypi* 'Polyps.' For 'chamaeleon,' see *Adagia* III iv 1 *Chamaeleonte mutabilior* 'As changeable as a chameleon.'
863 'Proteus': Greek mythological character capable of changing appearance at any time. See *Adagia* II ii 74 *Proteo mutabilior* 'As many shapes as Proteus,' which also explains 'changeable.'

regards them with sidelong glances, raging horses calmed by the sound of smacking lips. It is not so difficult to observe in individual animals the features that are common to each; but in a single human being you will find whatever exists in all types of animal, though you add the monstrosities of Libya as well.[864] What of the fact that bears are shut up in pens, lions behind bars, and animals likely to harm are restrained by force? This shepherd of ours has only the power of persuasion.

But I return to princes, whose ears are often tender, accustomed to flattery (not to say corrupted by adulation), intolerant of frank advice, arrogant from Fortune's indulgence, crippled by luxury. Do you think it a matter of slight skill to handle temperaments of this sort and to use persuasion to send under Christ's yoke[865] those whom you could not compel? Not everyone is competent to apply his hand to a noble and naturally fierce horse; but it requires much greater skill to teach a prince in such a way that you convince him of what is best, advise him so that he obeys, rebuke him without his blazing anger turning him to the worse, and finally to censure the faults of princes in public in such a way as not to provoke the people to sedition and rebellion.[866]

A certain special praise was earned in the past by those who scorned the world with all its ceremonies and pleasures, retreated far away into the rugged wastelands, lived a rough life in the haunts of beasts or in caves, separating themselves from all contact with men and imposing a harsher regimen upon themselves than that suffered by those deported to a desert island.[867] But, in the opinion of Chrysostom, the man who provides a good pastor to a congregation provides something that is both much more difficult and much holier.[868] His very solitude renders a monk safe from the

* * * * *

864 Libya was known for its exotic creatures. See *Adagia* III vii 10 *Semper Africa novi aliquid apportat* 'Africa always produces something novel,' where Erasmus quotes Pliny *Historia mundi* 8.17.42: 'Libya always brings forth something new.' See 382 and n860 above.

865 Cf Matt 11:29–30.

866 In book 2 CWE 68 637 and book 4 CWE 68 1049 Erasmus repeats this salutary admonition that preachers are not to provoke sedition and rebellion but encourage obedience and submission, even when princes act in godless ways. Chomarat suggests that Erasmus has in mind here certain inconsiderate preachers whose words inflamed the people in the Peasants War, see ASD V-4 177 852n. For preaching at the time of the Peasants War, see Justus Maurer *Prediger im Bauernkrieg* (Stuttgart 1979).

867 Erasmus' picture calls to mind Athanasius' *Vita Antonii* and Jerome's *Vita S. Pauli* and *Vita S. Hilarionis*; see NPNF 2nd series 4 188–221; 6 299–315.

868 John Chrysostom *De sacerdotio* 6.2–10 NPNF 1st series 9 75–80.

many provocations and temptations of vice, and it is not so great a matter to manage the care of a single animal, though this too is a great matter;
but as the pastor maintains his solitary watch over everyone, as he tends
his flock composed of so many different personalities, as he is compelled to
have dealings with the honest and dishonest alike, to attend banquets, to see
every day what he is not allowed to desire, as he is assailed by the scorn of
some, soothed by the flattery of others, attacked by the accusations of others,
frightened by the threats of others, tempted by the largesse of others, as he
humours the violence of princes, in short, as he is shaken on all sides by so
many siege engines, how, I ask, could he stand firm, unless he has a heart of
adamant[869] fortified on all sides by much learning, much philosophy, and
many gifts of the mystical Spirit?

   And so, since the priest bears so heavy a burden upon his shoulders,
since he holds so outstanding an office, how great is the ingratitude of certain
congregations who as an insult call 'common' the one through whom they
are Christians, whom they have as their teacher of devotion, by whose intervention they are reconciled to God. How seriously misguided are princes
who contemptuously misuse bishops as servants. On the other hand, how
ignorant of their own dignity are bishops who deem it a wonderful stroke
of fortune to become the servants of kings, whose teachers and guides they
ought to be! Finally, how greatly mistaken are monks, however austere, who
prefer their own way of life to the order of bishops and pastors. The pastor
of a single little town, of a single village who performs his office correctly
is to be preferred to many Carthusians and Brigittines.[870] Let no one take
this as an expression of contempt for monks; it is not an insult to be less
esteemed than your betters, but it is arrogance, when you are inferior, to
wish to be regarded as the equal of those more outstanding. Yet the flocks
of monks owe to their superiors the honour that a congregation owes to its
parish priest, nor should there be pride or haughtiness among the members
of the same body. Each has his own gift from the same Spirit[871] and has it
for the benefit of all, but there must be rank among the members of the body
in order to avoid sedition. Domination, ambition, insolence, and the sedition that arises from these must be kept at bay. Let the one who is greater

* * * * *

869 *adamantinum*; cf Ezek 3:9; cf also Zec 7:12, where the prophet uses 'the heart
   of adamantine' in a contrary sense, castigating the people of Israel for the
   hardening of their hearts 'in order not to hear the law and the words that the
   Lord of hosts had sent by his spirit through the former prophets.'
870 On Carthusians and Brigittines, see n785 above.
871 See 1 Cor 12.

surpass the inferior in honour; let the one who is lesser reverently acknowledge his superior, inasmuch as according to Christ's teaching he who is first in rank in the hierarchy of the church[872] is especially the servant of all. He who will stoop lower from love of Christ and a zeal to help his neighbour is truly the greater for it, and the more honour is owed him the less honour he claims for himself. Certainly a custom that we have seen among the Italians merits no approval: an ordinary monk, of no worth or learning, takes first place at dinner though uninvited, with the polite excuse, 'You won't mind; you know this is my place,' as he points to his habit.[873] What? Do you wear a humble garment in order to be the more esteemed?[874] On the other hand, the custom that we see in certain families of the powerful also deserves no approval: a priest with a towel over his shoulder carries a basin and pours the water for those who are about to eat and stands bareheaded throughout the banquet ministering to the laity who are seated at table. But priests themselves are largely at fault for their becoming cheapened in this way. When they show themselves more like the laity than like priests, they are scorned by the laity, as in the words of Hosea, 'Because you have rejected knowledge, I shall reject you from performing as a priest for me.'[875] Moreover, it requires no ordinary prudence to be gentle towards everyone while nevertheless maintaining the authority of your office, to be familiar, modest, and friendly towards subordinates without familiarity and gentleness breeding contempt. The priest must therefore be advised to preserve the decorum of the role that he has undertaken; the congregation must be advised to remember what it owes to those entrusted with the care of their souls and not to consider how much Conrad or Walter is worth but the function he is performing and whose place he is taking. Whatever honour is paid to a man out of respect for Christ is paid to Christ, not to the man.

But I hear some objecting, 'They do not perform the role of Christ properly.' That is very difficult for a man to judge, and even if it is clear,

* * * * *

872 *ecclesiastica hierarchia*; Erasmus means here the concrete institution of the church and its various offices, where the bishop as head is 'the servant of all' in his diocese. Erasmus might be alluding to the title popes have used since the papacy of Gregory the Great (590–604), 'servant of the servants of God' (*servus servorum Dei*). See also Matt 23:11 and Pseudo-Dionysius the Areopagite *De ecclesiastica hierarchia* (*The Ecclesiastical Hierarchy*) trans Thomas L. Campbell (Lanham, Md 1981).

873 Erasmus refers to this as an Italian custom; he might have come across examples of such behaviour in his visit to Italy in 1506–9.

874 See Matt 20:26–7, 23:11–12.

875 Hos 4:6

nevertheless some honour is due to the office itself for the sake of public tranquillity, since the Apostle teaches us to pay due honour to those placed over us, even idolaters, until the Lord himself gives a clear sign that they are to be removed.[876] This sign is not always given by a miracle through good men, but it is also frequently given through bad men; for example, he abolished the sacrifices of the Jews through Titus by the complete destruction of the temple and the carrying off of the monuments on which their religion rested (they formerly boasted of the tablets of Moses, the Sacred Ark, the rod of Aaron, and certain other things of this kind).[877] Likewise he showed through the Goths and other barbarian tribes that the Romans were to be deprived of their empire,[878] which at the beginning happened to serve the gospel, but its destruction was expedient afterwards since the remnants of ancient paganism could not otherwise be wholly uprooted.[879] But let us leave aside these tangential subjects and return now to explaining the dignity of the preacher's office.

The loftiness of the prophets whom God has thought worthy of his personal address and through whom as intermediaries he wanted his inscrutable will[880] to be unlocked for men approaches nearest to the authority of divinity.[881] Moreover, as we began to say earlier, there are two kinds of

* * * * *

876 See Rom 13:1, 7; Heb 13:17. Scripture does not say, 'Until the Lord himself gives a clear sign that they are to be removed.' Erasmus likely means that it is God's work to remove those he no longer wishes to rule, as the examples below illustrate. See especially *Annotationes in Romanos* CWE 56 346–53; Erasmus states that the only exception Paul makes is 'for the interests of faith and piety'; otherwise Christians 'should comply even with tyrants and bear with them' (347).

877 For the account of the Roman general Titus (son of Vespasian) and the destruction of the temple of Jerusalem, see Josephus *De bello Judaica* books 5–7; for the triumph at Rome featuring the spoils from the war with the Jews, see 7.5–7.

878 For the invasions of the Goths, Erasmus might be drawing on Jerome's preface to his commentary on the book of Ezekiel, written after hearing news of Alaric's sack of Rome in 410; and certainly on Augustine's *De civitate Dei*, written in response to this event. See Jerome's preface to his commentary on Ezekiel NPNF 2nd series 6 499–500; and Ep 127.12–14, 257–8.

879 Erasmus' brief comment on the fall of Rome suggests a view of church history similar to Augustine's as developed in the *De civitate Dei*. Erasmus does not continue his exposition of God's providential direction of history, nor does he give readers topics for preaching on God's hand in history.

880 Cf Rom 11:33. Erasmus defines 'prophet' as God's spokesman to interpret his 'inscrutable will.'

881 See 1 Cor 14:1–3, where Paul puts 'prophets' in the first rank, that is, those who can expound the mysteries of God and 'speak to others for their edification, exhortation, and comfort'; cf 2 Tim 3:16, 4:2.

prophecy, one which opens the past or predicts the future, another which explains present mysteries or reveals secrets without reference to time.[882] In the Gospel of John, the Lord is told, 'You are a prophet'[883] because he had revealed his mysteries to the woman of Samaria. But the Jews deemed worthy of this name only one who was distinguished by greater than human powers, and so those who had the highest opinion of Christ honoured him at that time with the name of prophet.[884] In fact when the Lord himself wanted to implant in the minds of the Jews, who had a high regard for John the Baptist, some understanding of his special and even more than human qualities, he pronounced John to be more than a prophet.[885] But if those to whom God has spoken, namely the prophets, have been called gods,[886] what great praise it is to be called more than a prophet! Yet he who was lesser in the kingdom of heaven was infinitely greater than this man,[887] since by his splendour he obscured the glory of all the prophets, though to be obscured in this way is to be illuminated. But, just as the power of miracles has flourished only occasionally ever since the time of this heavenly prophet, so this type of ancient prophecy was not removed gradually at the light of the gospel but grew cold or, to speak more correctly, was changed into another loftier kind. Once people ran to the oracle and to the ephod,[888] seeking a sign; now the Scriptures take the place of oracles, faith the place of miracles. Isaiah 8 shows this, saying, 'To the law rather and to the witness.'[889] If we believe in the Scriptures correctly understood, what need for miracles?

Moreover, the prophets of the New Testament, trained to compare the spiritual with the spiritual,[890] enable us to understand the Scriptures by

* * * * *

882 This twofold meaning of prophet is crucial in Erasmus: the Old Testament prophets spoke of things to come and especially of Christ. But prophets of the New Testament interpret the mystical sense of what had been predicted: John the Baptist identified Jesus, as do Paul and Philip, the apostles; and since their time it has been the role of the *ecclesiastes* to carry on this lofty role. Therefore, without Scripture interpreting Scripture, which is what the prophet does, the message is lost. As Erasmus presents it, the Jews hold on to the first form of prophecy without accepting the second, thereby closing off recognizing what was signified by the prophets of the Old Testament.

883 John 4:19

884 Matt 16:14, 21:11, and 46; Mark 6:15, 8:28; Luke 7:16 and 39, 9:8 and 19, 24:19; John 4:19, 6:14, 7:40, 9:17; Acts 3:22–6, 7:37

885 Matt 11:9

886 John 10:34–5; cf Ps 82:6 (Vulg 81:6).

887 Ie John the Baptist; Matt 11:11

888 Exod 25:7; see n426 above and Exod 39:2–7.

889 Isa 8:20

890 Cf 1 Cor 2:13.

digging out the mysteries of the Scriptures according to their spiritual meaning, offering 'the new and the old' from their treasure stores.[891] What good
does it do the Jews that they have memorized their prophets? Those prophets
need other prophets; otherwise what St Paul writes about the philosophers
of the world can truly be said of the Jews, that 'though they professed themselves wise,' they became 'foolish' and 'vain in their thoughts.'[892] The Jews
have become more foolish; though they read so many allegories, so many
prophecies about Christ every day, they nevertheless not only do not recognize the one designated by these but even pursue him with an implacable
hatred. What is responsible? The fact that they lack this new and loftier kind
of prophecy to open the mystical meaning of Scripture.

Christ held first place in this kind of prophecy, after him the apostles inspired by the spirit of Christ, and among them especially St Paul,
then the other doctors of the church. Now, since it is admitted that the Holy
Spirit poured out its gifts more generously and widely after the Lord was
received into heaven[893] than it had done in the Old Testatment, Paul bestows
his highest commendation among all the gifts of the Spirit on prophecy,[894]
without which he deems a gathering of Christians to be virtually useless.
Moreover, he means by prophecy not a precognition of the future but skill
in digging out the mystical meaning that is hidden and buried, so to speak,
in the Holy Scriptures.[895] No one who is without the spirit of Christ can be
truly suited to this office; for just as only an artist can judge about art, so no
one but a spiritual person pronounces truly about spiritual Scripture. There
is indeed less obscurity in the New Testament, yet here too there is need
of prophets; and there will be need until the end of the world, for through
them the church flourishes or fails, grows or shrinks.

Now consider, please, which kind of prophet is by its own nature more
lofty. Among the less lofty was Balaam,[896] a base man, and it is also attested
in the proverbs of the Hebrews that Saul was counted among the prophets.[897]
Indeed in a gospel parable those who have given out prophecies in Jesus'

* * * * *

891 Matt 13:52
892 Rom 1:21–2
893 Acts 2:4; cf Heb 9:24.
894 1 Cor 14:4–5. See *Annotationes in 1 ad Corinthios* 14.1–3 ASD VI-8 266–8.
895 Here Erasmus identifies the new prophet as one skilled in exegesis and who
     in preaching can reveal the hidden meaning of Scripture, teaching this to the
     faithful.
896 Num 22:20–2; see also Josh 13:22.
897 1 Sam 10:11–13

name are told by him, 'I do not know you.'[898] In addition, even in the
Gospel itself Caiaphas pronounces a true prophecy concerning Christ.[899]
Why am I speaking of Caiaphas when demons speak the truth about
Christ in evangelical literature,[900] and in Acts the possessed girl gives true
witness to the apostles?[901] Finally, even today astrologers, palm readers,
'belly talkers,'[902] and wizards predict many future occurrences, but there
is no particularly great profit in this foreknowledge; for if what they predict is going to come to pass, precognition of the inevitable is the height
of misery: if it does not, the very fear of misfortune is a great part of
misfortune.[903]

But enough of the unpraiseworthy; let us discuss the praiseworthy.
Those sixteen prophets admitted by canonical Scripture[904] who undoubtedly prophesied about Christ were enveloped in such obscurities that they
were not understood even after what they had predicted was revealed so
clearly to view. Their prophecies seemed riddles, or rather dreams, until that heavenly Spirit whose inspiration has been the source of all truth
flowed more bountifully into the minds of the new prophets, expounding
the riddles of types and undoing the wrappings of prophecy.[905] Which is
more important, the temporary or the eternal? 'The Law and the prophets

* * * * *

898 Matt 7:22–3
899 John 11:50–2. The high priest Caiaphas' prophecy stated: 'You do not understand that it is better for you to have one man die for the people than to have
the whole nation destroyed' (11:50). Though an evil man and urging what was
politically expedient, he did not grasp the profound spiritual significance and
truth of his ironic utterance.
900 See Mark 1:23–4, 5:2–7; Luke 4:33–5, 8:27–8.
901 Acts 16:16–19
902 Latin *ventriloqui*. One today does not associate ventriloquism with the phe-
nomenon of those who appeared possessed of a spirit speaking from the belly
and predicting future events. Erasmus might well have been reminded here
of this kind of fraud given in Lucian's *Alexander*; cf *Adagia* II iv 21.
903 Cf Cicero *De divinatione* 2 passim; Gellius *Noctes Atticae* 14.1.36.
904 See DS 179, *Decretum Damasi seu De explanatione fidei* (AD 382).
905 For allegory and typology in Erasmus, see especially CWE 39 n117, which gives
an extensive discussion of allegory, typology, the senses of Scripture, and principles of biblical interpretation in Erasmus' writings; see also *Augustine* 'Typology' 855–7; M.F. Wiles, 'Origen as Biblical Scholar' in *The Cambridge History
of the Bible* I: *From the Beginnings to Jerome* ed P.R. Ackroyd and C.F. Evans
(Cambridge 1976) 454–89, especially 482–5; and Gerard E. Caspary *Politics and
Exegesis: Origen and the Two Swords* (Berkeley 1979) chapter 1 'The Sword and
the Letter' 11–39.

until John,'[906] says the Lord, designating types by the word 'law' and predictions produced about Christ by the term 'prophets.' So, while that kind of prophecy was necessary before the coming of the Redeemer, it largely ceased after the brilliant light of the gospel shone forth, not because the church has been deprived of this gift but because the nature of the times is different. What the prophets had promised would come has all been revealed, has been laid out for all the senses; nothing is left but that final day[907] when the church is complete and each will receive his reward according to his deserts.[908] We do not need prophets to convince people of this, since the Lord himself foretold all this so clearly that no one can doubt unless he distrusts the canonical Scriptures. He wanted the fact to be well known to us; those who had seen him alive were told, 'He will come just as you saw him going into heaven.'[909] He wanted the day to be uncertain,[910] hence those people have always been ridiculous who have tried to appear prescient in a matter that the Lord did not want known beforehand and that, if it could be known beforehand, is more profitably left unknown. But this second kind of prophecy will be necessary for all parts of the globe until the world's last days; human souls can no more survive without it than their bodies without food and drink,[911] inasmuch as mystical Scripture is living bread descending from heaven, which bestows eternal life upon those who eat it:[912] but someone is needed to break this bread appropriately and distribute it according to the Redeemer's example.[913] It is a spring of water leaping up to eternal life:[914] but people are needed to draw it from its hidden channels and proffer it to those that thirst for righteousness.[915] Finally, the flesh of Christ is truly food,[916] the blood of Christ is truly drink; unless the hearts of the congregation are fed and refreshed daily with these through preachers, they cannot maintain life, true life I mean, for the life of the body is a shadow of life rather than life:[917] only true food and drink

* * * * *

906 Matt 11:13
907 Matt 24:3–50; Mark 13:4–8; Luke 21:6–36
908 See Matt 25:32–46.
909 Acts 1:11
910 Matt 24:36
911 Cf Matt 4:4; Luke 4:4; Deut 8:3.
912 John 6:33, 50–1
913 Matt 26:26; Luke 24:30–2; 1 Cor 10:16
914 John 4:14
915 Matt 5:6
916 John 6:56
917 Cf Matt 10:26–31.

can give true life.[918] The teachers of the church and ministers alike dispense both to those at the table; it is the Lord himself who gives the banquet, who through the hands of his disciples bestows upon the hungry multitude the food, that is, the word of life, whose stewards are bishops and those that fulfil the function of bishops.[919] Through it those who do not exist are born to God, through it infants are nourished in Christ with milk until they grow and can take solid food,[920] through it they are strengthened against the woes of this life,[921] through it they are stirred to hope of heavenly life,[922] through it they are strengthened when weak,[923] healed when sick,[924] restored to life when dead.[925] This is the ministry of preachers. Who could not see that its dignity is no longer royal but more than angelic? For it is more to be an evangelist than to be an angel; an angel merely announces, but bad things also are announced –what an evangelist announces is happy and peaceful.[926] The former says, 'Take the boy and his mother and flee into Egypt, and stay there until I advise you.'[927] What does the latter do? He causes Christ to be born in us, to grow up, to be kept, to be perfected,[928] which is man's true and complete happiness. Those who spoke in tongues were themselves prophets as well,[929] for the Spirit spoke mysteries in them; yet in the church this type is so useless in itself that if some unbeliever or outsider entered the gathering, he would say at once, 'Those men are mad.'[930] I think that we would say the same if we saw Saul dancing and prophesying naked all day among the naked prophets.[931] On the other hand, when a prophet of the second kind speaks,[932] that mocker is transformed into an admirer, and he falls

* * * * *

918 Cf John 6:31–5. When speaking of dispensing the word of God, Erasmus often follows Johannine theology, presenting as virtually indistinguishable the word of God as preached and the sacrament of the Eucharist.

919 For 'those that fulfil the function of bishops,' see 328 above.

920 1 Cor 3:1–2

921 Eph 3:16

922 Titus 1:2, 3:7

923 Rom 1:11

924 Matt 14:14; Mark 6:13

925 Matt 11:5

926 Erasmus is playing on the Greek word ἄγγελος 'angel, messenger' and 'evangelist' (evangelista, ie bringer of good news [εὐαγγέλιον 'good news, gospel']).

927 Matt 2:13

928 See Gal 4:19 and *Paraphrasis in epistolam Pauli apostoli ad Galatas* CWE 42 118.

929 See 1 Cor 14:1–5.

930 See 1 Cor 14:23.

931 1 Sam 19:24

932 Ie the prophet of the New Testament, one who interprets Scripture.

upon his face[933] and acknowledges that God speaks in those who relate the mysteries of Scripture thoughtfully and sincerely. It is the same Spirit that dispenses its gifts according to the condition of the times for the salvation of the human race. If you consider the source, the dignity is equal; if you consider the quality of the times, the need for the latter prophecy is greater and its utility more fruitful. There is a very great difference between the synagogue and the church; so there is no small difference between a prophet of the synagogue and a prophet of the church. How few children the synagogue has borne for the Lord, but to what a numerous progeny the church has given and continues to give birth every day – and through whom but through preachers?[934] Once there was catechism before baptism, and that from the Lord's instruction, 'Go, teach all nations, baptizing them.[935] Behold at once, at the very beginning, the office of the evangelist. The catechist teaches[936] and imparts the fundamentals of the faith to the unlearned, and through him mother church conceives fetuses, as it were, and gives birth to them in baptism by the same man's ministry.

Now weigh the difference in content. What does the prophet of the synagogue promise? 'You will live well and long in the land that the Lord will give you;[937] your sons will be as shoots of olive around your table, your wife will be as a fruitful vine on the sides of your house.'[938] What of the prophet of the church? 'If you believe in the Lord Jesus, all your sins will be forgiven free,[939] you will receive his spirit,[940] you will be placed in the rank of the children of God,[941] having already become a brother of Christ[942] and coheir of the heavenly kingdom,[943] and you will receive meanwhile a hundredfold in this world for what you have left.[944] And indeed it is not only a hundredfold but a hundred times a thousandfold, that joy of a clean and hopeful conscience, if it is compared to all the comforts that the

* * * * *

933 See Matt 17:6; Luke 5:12, 17:16; 1 Cor 14:25.
934 See Rom 10:17.
935 Matt 28:19
936 See Gal 6:6.
937 Deut 5:16
938 Ps 128:3 (Vulg 127:3)
939 See Matt 9:2; Luke 5:20, 7:48–9.
940 John 20:22–3
941 Matt 5:9; Luke 20:36; see also Rom 8:14.
942 Matt 12:50
943 Rom 8:17
944 Matt 19:29

world promises, and not even that in good faith.[945] Again, what does the old prophet threaten? "If you do not keep the laws of the Lord, the Lord will give your wife a sterile womb and dry breasts;[946] you will till the field and another will gather the fruit from it, you will plant a vineyard and you will not taste the wine from it." '[947] What of the new? 'Unless you are reborn from water and the Holy Spirit,[948] you will be dead even while you live in this world,[949] and in the time to come the eternal death of Gehenna awaits your soul and body.'[950] We have already touched to some degree upon the differences in the manner of teaching.[951]

But if so much honour was accorded the prophets of the synagogue, who used to forecast a future happiness as if from afar and did it under a veil, what is owed to the prophets of the church, who show a happiness that is here and now, and not only show it but also confer it where it is right, and do so clearly with no veils or riddles? What is simpler than to say, 'Have faith in the Lord Jesus'?[952] Further, what is more helpful than to use a washing[953] with water to turn a son of wrath into a son of love, an heir of eternal life?[954] Hence they are called not only prophets but, more appropriately, evangelists.

By the Lord's testimony John the Baptist was preferred to the ranks of the prophets because he did not predict Christ's coming in ambiguous oracles but pointed him out with his finger as he came.[955] But whom did he point out? The son of Mary and of a carpenter,[956] a mortal living among mortals like one of many, not yet celebrated for his miracles and teaching, not yet restored to life after defeating Satan, not yet taken back to heaven,[957]

* * * * *

945 See Acts 23:1, 24:16; Rom 9:1; 2 Cor 1:12, 4:2; 1 Tim 1:5, 3:9; 2 Tim 1:3; Heb 9:14, 10:2, and 22; 1 Pet 3:21.
946 Hos 9:14
947 See Hos 9:14; Deut 28:30 and 33.
948 John 3:5
949 1 Tim 5:6; cf Rev 3:1.
950 Matt 5:29; Mark 9:42
951 See eg 387–92 above.
952 See Eph 1:15; Phil 1:5; Acts 20:21; Col 1:4; cf Prov 3:5: 'Trust in the Lord with all your heart' (*Habe fiduciam in Domino ex toto corde tuo*).
953 That is, baptism. See Eph 5:26 where baptism is referred to as 'the laver of water in the word of life' (*aquae lavacrum*).
954 Col 1:13; Rom 8:17
955 John 1:29, 36; Matt 3:3, 14
956 Matt 13:55
957 Acts 1:11

not yet scattering most generously from on high his heavenly gifts[958] by sending the Spirit of the Father,[959] not yet sitting at the right hand of the Father in an equal share of power and glory.[960] If what John showed was great, what the prophets of the church show is greater, as they now show him triumphing in heaven, show him reigning in the souls of the faithful,[961] presiding over his church. The Baptist showed a Christ still of the flesh to the physical eyes of men, but now prophets show him in spiritual guise to the eyes of faith. Many then saw him and, being offended by his external appearance, scorned or even hated the sight of him;[962] but these point him out in such a way that those who gaze upon him are restored to life.[963] The Baptist showed what Paul in a way rejected, saying, 'Even if we once knew Christ according to the flesh, now we no longer know him.'[964] As a Jew, he knew the Lord according to the flesh; made spiritual, he knows him much more happily by faith. The Galatians had not seen Christ, and yet the Apostle affirms that Christ had been portrayed before their eyes because they had believed those who revealed him.[965] What is handled by the spirit is more evident than what is handled with the touch, and the tongue points more successfully than the corporeal finger.

The faithful prophets of this age should not be valued less because this power does not seem to be given, as it once was, by the inspiration of the Spirit[966] or by an obvious miracle but is, so to speak, bought with much sweat. Indeed, the greater the labour, the larger the reward. Miracles had their time, nor are there fewer miracles because the inspiration of the Spirit is silent; the altered nature of the times required this, and the gift of God is no less free because he determined to give it in this way. It is the same gift of the same Spirit but given differently according to the condition of the times,[967] and it must not be doubted that it is given in a more perfect way. It was expedient for the perfection of faith that the external signs that had been given to the unbelieving and unsure should be taken away from

* * * * *

958 See Eph 4:8.
959 Acts 2:2–4
960 Mark 13:26; Luke 4:6; Matt 26:64; 1 Pet 4:14
961 Luke 17:21; Rom 5:17, 21; Rev 22:5
962 See Isa 52:14–53:5; John 7:7, 15.
963 See John 3:14; Deut 5:12–15.
964 2 Cor 5:16
965 Gal 3:1
966 Cf John 3:8, 20:22 (insufflavit); Acts 2:2–4.
967 Erasmus often emphasizes that the times have changed greatly and that accommodations have to be made accordingly.

the senses. Moreover, who administers his office more perfectly, the teacher who uses beatings and terror to coerce a boy or the one who uses counsel to guide a boy placed under his control?[968] The Law was the teacher up until Christ;[969] the ancient prophets are its ministers. John the Baptist is midway between the Old and the New. Some traces of the already aging old prophecy remained for a time in the beginnings of the youthful church until the lights produced by lesser bodies were gradually obscured as the sun of evangelical truth shone throughout the whole world. No miracles occur in the sky, where everything seen is a miracle, for we call miracles things that happen outside the common run of human affairs; no one marvels at everyday things, even if they are more miraculous. It is called a great miracle that the Lord summoned a few lifeless people back to life, and no one marvels that living men are born every day from dead liquid.[970] The Lord once or twice multiplied loaves with his hands so that a very few sufficed for many thousands,[971] and no one marvels that every day an ear pregnant with sixty grains rises from a single dead grain of wheat.[972] To Matthew presiding at the custom house he said, 'Follow me,'[973] and he was changed on the spot and obeyed the call; we all marvel at this because it was displayed to the senses. But we marvel more that he called Lazarus, who was dead four days already, back to a life[974] that had soon to be exchanged again for death; how much more marvellous is it that so many weeds are turned into the Lord's excellent wheat at the voice of a single man,[975] that every day the mystical energy of the Spirit restores sixty-year-old corpses[976] to eternal life through the ministers of the church? We admire and gape at what is shown to the external senses; we do not admire something much more

* * * * *

968 Erasmus' rhetorical question here is thoroughly treated in *De pueris*, where he condemns physical punishment in the education of youth; see *De pueris instituendis* CWE 26 326–31.

969 Gal 3:15–29

970 *liquor mortuus*; Chomarat states that this is 'sperm, dead because it is inert!'; see ASD V-4 193 111–12nn.

971 Matt 14:17–21, 15:32–8; Mark 6:35–44, 8:1–9; Luke 9:10–17; John 6:1–13

972 See John 12:24.

973 Matt 9:9

974 John 11:1–45

975 See Matt 13:25–30.

976 Chomarat states that Erasmus chose this adjective to symbolize a great age; according to Roman usage, at sixty years electors lost the right to vote. See ASD V-4 193 120n. At the time he wrote this part of *Ecclesiastes*, Erasmus himself was likely over sixty years of age. For the idea of 'the energy' (or 'action') of the Holy Spirit, see *De concordia* CWE 65 152 n82.

extraordinary that is done within. Peter prays, and Dorcas lives again in the body:[977] we are amazed; a good preacher speaks and rouses many souls from death, but we do not marvel to the same degree. He who raises Dorcas and he who converts the sinner is the same; but what God works in the soul of a sinner returning to his senses is greater than what he works in a corpse returning to life. The fact that Peter used to preach in everyone's language seemed a miracle to everyone,[978] and it was; how much more marvellous that about three thousand men were transformed into a new creature at a single speech of a fisherman![979] This is far more stupendous than the idea that Nebuchadnezzar was changed from a man into the shape of a bull, then changed back again from a bull into a man.[980] But it is characteristic of a commonplace and dull mind to admire more what is perceived with the eyes, ears, and touch; the spiritual man[981] judges otherwise. And so if Peter prayed long on bended knees, in response to the supplications of many women, to restore one mere woman to the life of the body (where being restored was only a double death), what must be done by the devout preacher, whose task is to recall to true life as many souls as possible that are rotting in sin as though in a tomb? Surely such considerations seem not to be weighed by those who mount the pulpit tipsy from lunch or dulled in the morning by the night's hangover, then break off, rather than complete, their sermon and run off to bouts of drinking. Come then, if someone were to declare a preacher the equal of those ancient prophets, would everyone not admit that a high rank has been assigned to him? And yet the thing itself convinces us that someone who administers the food of evangelical teaching to the Lord's flock is more excellent on many accounts, so long as he performs his duty sincerely and in good faith. If anyone is not persuaded of this, a cruder proof will be offered from which he may reach this conclusion. Which were in greater esteem in the beginnings of the church, Agabus with his companions, and the daughters of Philip,[982] or Peter and Paul? Even stones, I think, would admit that there is no comparison; nor, I think, is it unclear which brought greater benefit to the church. What did

* * * * *

977 Acts 9:36–42
978 Acts 2:4–12
979 Acts 2:41
980 Dan 4:30–1. Erasmus uses this same example to make a similar point in *Concio, sive Merdardus*, which he published in 1531; see *Colloquia* CWE 40 953.
981 Cf 1 Cor 2:13–15; 1 Cor 2:15: 'The spiritual man makes judgments about all things, but he himself is not subject to any man's judgment.'
982 Acts 11:27–8, 21:8–15

Agabus provide? He foretold a coming famine and advised that the emergency be met with timely provision, not quite according to the perfect teaching of Christ, who had forbidden his followers to be concerned about tomorrow.[983] Again, when he took Paul's sash and bound his own feet at Caesarea, predicting that the owner of the sash would be bound at Jerusalem by the Jews and handed over to the heathen, what good did he accomplish?[984] Only that the Apostle left his saddened companions a sadder man, not because he feared the chains, since he was ready even to die for the name of Jesus, but because that blessed soul, all afire with love of his neighbours, was tormented by his friends' tears. But as to the prophecy, that is, the preaching of Peter and Paul, how great was the profit to the church! Agabus and those like Agabus had succeeded to the place of the ancient prophets; you, parish priest, and you, preacher, to whose place have you succeeded? Not to that of Agabus but to that of the apostles or rather, more truly, that of Christ himself, to whom the dignity of the apostolic name most applies. Let someone else hold the title of apostolic lord or apostolic legate;[985] the real meaning of the term and the dignity belong to everyone who, by virtue of the authority delegated to him,[986] proclaims Christ by interpreting Scripture. The person who does this is not simply a prophet but a prophet of the prophets, inasmuch as it is useless for the prophets to have written for us unless this kind of prophet exists to interpret them.[987] For it is truly a sealed

* * * * *

983 Matt 6:31–4
984 Acts 21:10–15; cf Acts 5:40–1.
985 Chomarat believes that Erasmus must have had Girolamo Aleandro (1480–1542) in mind when he wrote this; Erasmus pointedly exalts the humble preacher far above someone who bears the title 'apostolic.' Erasmus had encouraged Aleandro in Greek and humanistic studies; Aleandro later became rector of the University of Paris and was chosen by Leo x as envoy to Martin Luther to present the bull of excommunication (*Exsurge domine*), at which point Erasmus refused to side with Aleandro and the pope and turned down all invitations to dine with Aleandro. See Schoeck (1) 225–7. See also CEBR 'Aleandro, Girolamo' I 28–32.
986 Of crucial importance is the belief that only the bishop can delegate this authority to preach; it is not an authority one assumes on one's own, as was often the practice in the years before and during the Reformation. See the Fifth Lateran Council, Session 11 (19 December 1516) *Circa modum praedicandi* in Tanner I 634–8; and McGinness *Right Thinking* 33–4.
987 Again Erasmus makes this crucial distinction between prophets of the Old and New Testaments, for the latter can interpret the meaning of the prophecies (Scripture interpreting itself), whereas the prophets of the Old Testament did not know the true spiritual term and significances of their utterances as the

book that is understood neither by a man who is literate in the worldly sense because it is sealed nor by an ordinary man because he is illiterate. It was Jesus Christ who held first place in this order, who beginning from Moses and the prophets opened the Scriptures to his disciples;[988] and so their hearts, which were previously cold to the words of the prophets, were set on fire.

There are moreover two kinds of prophecy in the Old Law, the spoken and the unspoken. Types and figures belong to unspoken prophecy,[989] predictions about Christ to spoken. The Lord explains an unspoken prophecy in the Gospel when he says, 'Just as Moses lifted up the serpent in the desert, so must the Son of Man be lifted up';[990] likewise, 'Just as Jonah was in the belly of the whale for three days and three nights, so the Son of Man will be in the heart of the earth.'[991] More frequently he was occupied with the other kind, in general when he says, 'If you believed Moses, you would likewise believe me as well, for he wrote about me,'[992] specifically when he secretly shows the scribes and Pharisees that the prediction of the Psalm, 'The Lord said to my Lord,'[993] applies not to Solomon but to himself; again when, after reading in the temple the passage of prophetic Scripture that is in Isaiah chapter 61, he adds, 'Today this Scripture has been fulfilled in your ears.'[994] He showed that the manna that flowed down for the Hebrews in the desert had been a type of the heavenly teaching that he brought to earth from the bosom of his Father,[995] or is his own body and blood with which we are restored in the Eucharist;[996] finally, reciting Psalm 21 on the cross, he shows that the very events that were then taking place had been predicted in it.[997] Similarly, the evangelists also show many predictions advanced about Christ, such as when John shows that what was written in Exodus about the paschal lamb was foretold of Christ,

* * * * *

full revelation of Christ had not yet come. See *Annotationes in 1 ad Corinthios* (14:1–3) ASD VI-8 266–8.
988 Luke 24:27
989 On 'types and figures' see de Lubac *Medieval Exegesis* I 225–67, II passim; Raymond E. Brown 'Hermeneutics' JBC II 605–21, especially 611–13. See book 3 CWE 68 896, 952–3.
990 John 3:14
991 Matt 12:40
992 John 5:46
993 Ps 110:1 (Vulg 109:1), which Jesus cites in Matt 22:41–6; Mark 12:35–7; Luke 20:41–4.
994 Isa 61:1–2
995 John 6:31–5
996 John 6:56–9
997 Matt 27:46; Psalm 22 (Vulg 21)

such as, 'You will not break a bone of him';[998] but it is not appropriate to pursue this here. In either kind of prophecy no one explained more allegories than St Paul, such as when he fits to the Old Testament and the New the story about Hagar the maidservant cast out with her son and about Sarah's son Isaac, likewise about Mount Sinai and Zion;[999] he teaches that the rock from which the water flowed in the desert for the thirsting Hebrews was a figure of Christ.[1000] Peter shows in a sermon that the prophecy, 'You will not give your holy one to see corruption,' does not apply at all to David, who was corrupted in the tomb like other men, but to Christ, who rose with his body whole;[1001] he also indicates that the Flood was a type of baptism, the ark of the believing church.[1002] Indeed Paul shows that Christ's entire life is crowded with mystical types, expounding what it is to die with him,[1003] to be buried with him,[1004] to rise again, to ascend into heaven.[1005]

Preacher, you now know the dignity of your office, you now know its burden and its reward; what remains is to have always ringing in your ears the words that Paul bids be relayed to Archippus, 'See that you fulfil the ministry that you have received from the Lord.'[1006] Nothing is more honourable than a faithful prophet, nothing more detestable than a pseudo-prophet, nothing more precious in the eyes of God than sincere evangelists, nothing more abominable than pseudevangelists.[1007] If you acknowledge its dignity, take care to glorify the office you have undertaken; if you recognize its difficulty, cast off sloth and be vigilant; if you understand its danger, beware of swerving to the right or to the left;[1008] if you consider its reward, let no difficulty deter you. Wherever you turn your eyes, there is something to stimulate your concern. If you look upward, you see who it is that has delegated that office to you, you see the reward that awaits; if you look about at what surrounds you, you see the sheep of Christ entrusted to your good faith; if you cast your eyes downward, you see the horrible vengeance for mishandling your office; if you penetrate into yourself, you recognize how

* * * * *

998 John 19:36; Exod 12:46
999 Gal 4:22–6
1000 1 Cor 10:4; Exod 17:6; Num 20:11
1001 Acts 2:27, 29–31; Ps 16:10 (Vulg 15:10)
1002 1 Pet 3:20–1; Genesis 7–8
1003 2 Cor 7:3; Col 2:20
1004 Col 2:12
1005 Rom 10:6–13
1006 Col 4:17; cf Philem 2.
1007 Cf 2 Cor 11:13–15.
1008 Cf Deut 17:11.

much purity of soul, how much learning, how much judgment, how much ardent charity, how much courage this office demands: if you know that you are not prepared, either keep away from it or else acquire what you need.

If a man has decided to enter an Olympic competition, what does he not do and endure in order to win the prize? With what care does he prepare everything? And yet what is all that but play, just as the rewards too are playthings – the applause of the stupid mob, the oaken crown that more likely points to a fool than an intelligent or a brave man? Though we are so careful in trivial matters, does someone yet dare to approach the office of preacher with no more training than a farmer at the lyre, a sailor at the plow? And, instead of the many outstanding virtues that the dignity of the office demands, does he bring nothing but exceptional shamelessness and impudence, taking no account of what rewards await the victor, what punishment the vanquished? It is a small thing to be hissed off the stage by a single crowd, but to be hooted off by the whole company of holy angels and pious souls is the height of misery. So let those who undertake this contest heed the Apostle when he urges, 'Run so that you may gain the prize,'[1009] so that they can boast along with him, 'I have finished the course, I have kept the faith; now the crown of righteousness has been laid up for me.'[1010]

Now, if it is sufficiently agreed that the dignity of the priest, if compared with any kind of mortal honour, is greater by many parasangs,[1011] as the saying goes, and is in some respect superior to the very angels, it remains for us to compare the priest with himself in order to clarify in what part of himself he is greatest. The principal offices of priests, that is, of bishops,[1012] are five: they administer the sacraments of the New Law, they pray for the people, they judge, they ordain, and they teach. There is none of these that does not surpass the excellence of kings. For no sacrament is conferred except through priests, apart from baptism, which in fact is not repeated when duly conferred by a lay person;[1013] but though it is

* * * * *

1009 1 Cor 9:24
1010 2 Tim 4:7–8
1011 See *Adagia* ii iii 82 *Multis parasangis praecurrere* 'To be many parasangs ahead.' Erasmus explains that 'parasang' is the Persian name for a distance of thirty stadia (one *stadion* = 606.75 English feet) and is applied to 'a man who is a long way in front of the rest and is in many respects superior.' See LSJ 1631.
1012 The fullness of the priesthood is the bishop who alone can carry out all five duties Erasmus enumerates here (the power of ordination, for example, belongs exclusively to one already invested with the office of bishop).
1013 Anyone may baptize another in extreme circumstances (*in causa autem necessitatis*) as long as it is done according to the form of the church and the person

not annulled, only necessity excuses doing this – an excuse that does not apply to other sacraments. Moreover, baptism seems to have been introduced to replace circumcision, but circumcision required neither a priest nor a Levite. But in the past the Holy Spirit was given through the laying on of hands to someone sprinkled with sacramental water;[1014] this was reserved to bishops alone. Then, with the advance of time,[1015] the body and blood of the Lord was given even to baptized infants, and this required the mouth and hands of the priest. In place of animal victims[1016] and other ceremonies, more spiritual sacraments were introduced: baptism, the Eucharist, confirmation, penitence, and extreme unction.[1017] Moreover, none of these is done without praying, but praying is common to both the priests of the New Law and the sacrificers of the Old Testament. For when a fire was raging against the people because of God's anger, Aaron took the thurible, stood midway between the dead and the living, and by his intervention turned the Lord's fury to mercy.[1018] The priest prays for a woman who has borne a child, and she is cleansed;[1019] he prays for a house contaminated by the stain of leprosy, and it is purified;[1020] he prays for the sins of those sacrificing, and their sins are remitted.[1021] In addition, he judges between case and case, between leprosy and

* * * * *

baptizing intends by it what the church does; see DS 1314 (Council of Florence 1439).

1014 Acts 8:14–18
1015 See Erasmus *Apologia adversus monachos* LB IX 1066B where he refers to Augustine's *Sermo* 174.7 WSA III-5 261: 'They are infants, but they share in his table, in order to have life in themselves'; and *Contra duas epistolas Pelagianorum* PL 44 (1865) 576 (*Answer to the Two Letters of the Pelagians*) WSA I-24 146: 'You see, Pope Innocent of blessed memory says that little ones do not have eternal life without Christ's baptism and without partaking of the body and blood of Christ.' See Chomarat ASD V-4 201 242n.
1016 See Leviticus 1–7, 23; Numbers 28–9.
1017 Erasmus does not mention ordination and marriage, but he strongly implies that ordination is a sacrament; see 402 and book 4 CWE 68 1056 n210. Although the Council of Florence affirmed marriage as the seventh of the seven sacraments (DS 1327), Erasmus' position on marriage as a sacrament is problematic, as is 'his attack on the indissolubility of marriage, which was what gave matrimony its sacramental quality in the eyes of Augustine'; see *Institutio christiani matrimonii* CWE 69 203–438, especially 'Introductory Note' 205–6, 212.
1018 In Num 16:35 it is Eleazar who 'took the thurible ...'; in a similar event at Num 16:46–50 it is Aaron who does the same, so causing God's wrath to cease.
1019 Lev 12:6–8
1020 Lev 14:34–57
1021 Lev 19:20–2

nonleprosy,[1022] between clean and unclean;[1023] and if any more serious controversy occurred, they are ordered to go to a priest, who is to end the dis-
agreement with his judgment.[1024] Now, if a difficult question should arise –
whether it is right to undertake a war or not, whether a marriage is valid
or not, whether this or that is permitted to a prince and magistrate or not
– where should one go but to a priest trained in the law of the Lord? It
would be expedient for the conflicts of kings and the quarrels of spouses to
be settled through them and for those involved in an acrimonious conflict
to be reconciled through them. If that happened, there would be no need
of so many soldiers for war, there would be no need of so many lawyers
and advocates for settling disputes, and there would not be such complaining about corrupt judgments. The Hebrews lived in the greatest tranquillity
for forty years under Samuel as judge and prophet.[1025] But the holier are
the mysteries of the New Law and the more abundant its grace, so much
greater is the dignity of the person who administers them; likewise, the
greater the things that are sought and the firmer the confidence in receiving
them through Christ, the greater is the authority of the person who inter-
cedes. Again, the fuller the knowledge we now possess of the Lord's law,
the more splendid is the office of judging. Add to this that the more sublime is the office of preaching, the more excellent is the power of ordaining,[1026] especially when the ability to confer the gift of the Spirit through
the sacrament has been added. The people create a magistrate, the king creates a governor, but neither the one nor the other bestows the strength to
carry out the office correctly. Therefore, since in what we have hitherto related the priest of the New Law far surpasses both the rank of the Mosaic
priests, which was nonetheless held in high esteem in those days, and the
excellence of kings, he greatly surpasses himself in this final function, which
consists in teaching the Lord's flock.[1027] The word 'teaching' embraces both

* * * * *

1022 Deuteronomy 13
1023 Lev 14:57, 11:47; Ezek 44:23; cf Matt 8:1–4; Mark 1:40–4; Luke 5:12–14.
1024 Deut 17:8–11; Ezek 44:24
1025 See 1 & 2 Samuel.
1026 Erasmus implies that ordination is a sacrament, for it is an outward sign of an
     invisible grace; here (below) the grace given 'bestows the strength to carry it
     [ie the office] out correctly.'
1027 Erasmus notes that it is in 'teaching the Lord's flock' that the *ecclesiastes* sur-
     passes the excellence of kings, and 'to fulfil the office of teaching is both the
     most difficult by far and also the most beautiful by far ...' (below). In this
     'supreme office of teaching' he has his 'greatest dignity.' 'Teaching' has a spe-
     cific content and definition, as Erasmus goes on to note; see 2 Tim 3:16: 'All

sound doctrine and the admonition, rebuke, consolation, and refutation of those who carp at the truth of the gospel.[1028] A lay person baptizes too; the congregation prays in turn for the priest; the administration of the other sacraments is not difficult; but to fulfil the office of teaching is both the most difficult by far and also the most beautiful by far, since its effectiveness is the most far-reaching. The priest is not always baptizing, not always anointing or absolving, but the office of teaching, without which the others are useless, is continuous. For what good is it to adults to have been baptized unless they have been taught through a catechist what baptism means, what they ought to believe, how they ought to order their life according to their Christian faith? What good is receiving the Lord's body and blood unless they have learned how this sacrament was instituted, what it effects in us, the faith and purity with which it should be received? Lest I become too wordy by naming every one, a similar opinion should be held about the rest. Therefore, just as an actor, though he strives to please the crowd in each scene of a play, applies all the art he has in the final act, so the Christian preacher, though he ought to apply great care to please the Lord in his other functions, should surpass himself in this supreme office of teaching. The offices of kings are numerous and splendid, though they are all inferior to the priestly office, but kings are never occupied in a more kingly duty than when they speak before an assembly and urge peace, settle sedition, exhort to obedience of the laws, or sit before tribunals and hear cases and render a fair judgment to the people; even so the prelate, though outstanding in everything, is absolutely at the peak of his dignity when he feeds the Lord's flock with sacred teaching from the pulpit and dispenses to them the treasure of evangelical philosophy.[1029]

All the more deplorable is the perverse judgment of some who relegate the right of ordaining to certain factitious and venal bishops,[1030] entrust the power of baptizing and absolving to the untried, and grant authority to consecrate the Lord's body and blood to people they sometimes would not

* * * * *

Scripture, inspired of God, is profitable to teach, to reprove, to correct, to instruct in justice, that the man of God may be perfect, furnished to every good work.' See also 2 Tim 4:2. See the introduction 172–5.

1028 See 2 Tim 3:16.

1029 Erasmus states his thesis most affirmatively here: teaching is the apex of the bishop's office; it is in this that he most fulfils the ministry of Christ the teacher. Trent's decrees on preaching will echo this clearly; see Tanner II 669 and 763–4.

1030 Erasmus refers here to the practice of creating stipendary bishops, ie bishops consecrated to assume the duties of absentee or nonfunctioning diocesan bishops in exchange for fees.

deem worthy of sharing their own table or conversation. The most excellent duty of all, teaching, they sometimes toss to the least respected priests and monks, the sort to which perhaps they would be unwilling to entrust the care of their stable or kitchen (I am not criticizing monasticism or the priesthood but the foolish choice). Meanwhile, what part of the priestly dignity do they keep for themselves? They take charge of cavalry, occupy fortresses, keep bodyguards, supervise accounts, serve monarchs, and only in this way regard themselves as outstanding prelates. But though these things do not deserve rebuke, yet they should be entrusted instead to the lowliest servants, being unworthy to be delegated even to subdeacons; they are ashamed of what is most honourable, glory in what is meanest.

Foolish judgments,[1031] not only here but in pretty much every part of life, are the springs from which gushes all moral decay. How rare is the man who does not value more highly the external goods that are attributed to luck than those of the body![1032] What do men not endure to turn out rich, to win the honours of this world! They sail, travel, wage war; there is no kind of danger that they do not scorn. But are those who do not value the gifts of the body above those of the mind, the temporary above the eternal, any fewer in number? Could you find anyone who does not fear a mortal prince more than God? Who does not value a relation or a friend according to the flesh[1033] more than Christ? What other reason is there except that we are of flesh and therefore come nearer the nature of animals, which are ruled by their feelings, than that of the angels and recognize neither the dignity of our condition nor the loftiness of the office undertaken?

An ancient and profane oracle advises that each man should know himself.[1034] Once King Philip of Macedon,[1035] otherwise an intelligent man, ran dancing through the midst of his army when quite drunk himself, together

*   *   *   *   *

1031 Erasmus' best illustration of this thesis that foolish judgments 'in pretty much every part of life' lead to moral decay is *Moria* CWE 27 77–153.

1032 'Luck' (*fortuna*); Diogenes Laertius identifies some of the benefits: 'wealth, good birth, reputation and the like'; see *Vitae philosophorum* 5.1.30, where he attributes to Aristotle the ranking of 'goods': 'in the highest order are the goods of the soul, then goods of the body, then external goods' (ie 'attributed to luck'). See also Cicero *Tusculan Disputations* 5.8.24, 25, where he attributes this ranking to Theophrastus.

1033 Cf 2 Cor 11:18; Phil 3:3–7; Gal 6:12; 2 Cor 5:16; John 8:15.

1034 The Greek oracle at Delphi. For the oracle's words 'know yourself' (γνῶθι σεαυτόν; *nosce teipsum*), see *Adagia* I vi 95.

1035 Philip of Macedon (King Philip II, ruled 359–36 BC), father of Alexander the Great.

with other inebriates, and was rebuked as follows by the Athenian orator Demades:[1036] 'What are you doing, king? Fortune has placed upon you the mask of Agamemnon, and you adopt the mask of Thersites.'[1037] The pagan king, warned by a man whom no one praised, reformed himself to a more virtuous state. If only priests would heed the voice of Christ, who threatens in the mystical Song, 'If you do not know yourself, O beautiful among women, go out and follow the tracks of your flocks.'[1038] Regard this as having been spoken to the soul of the pastor who, though he professes himself a leader of churches, forgets the task he has undertaken and lowers himself to gain, to idleness, to pleasures. So, it appears, he is commanded to change his course, and since instead of leading his flock he is leading it astray, he has to walk behind the tracks of the flocks so that he may become a pupil instead of a teacher and learn to obey before he commands. This self-ignorance causes a man, though he is close to an angel in status, to be compared to 'the witless beasts'[1039] and to become 'like them'; it causes him to delegate to the lowest what is highest in his ministry, to reserve for himself as highest what is lowest. Tell me, whoever you are, distinguished with your holy mitre, while you listen to confessions, while you console the suffering, are you ashamed to serve your prince Christ by serving his members[1040] and not ashamed to serve a mortal prince in the business of his palace, not to say his war camp? Do you consider yourself demeaned if you teach the people the way of the Lord[1041] from the pulpit and take pride in riding armed among soldiers – I almost said scoundrels?

In Holy Writ humility was praised,[1042] pride condemned;[1043] but there is a kind of humility than which nothing is more detestable, and there is also a kind of pride than which nothing is more laudable.[1044] Humble in the

* * * * *

1036 See *Apophthegmata* CWE 38 702. The anecdote is from Diodorus Siculus *Bibliotheca historica* 16.87.1–3.

1037 See 327 n570 above.

1038 Song of Sol 1:7. Cf Origen *The Song of Songs: Commentary and Homilies* trans R.P. Lawson ACW 26 128–39; *Commentarium in Cantica Canticorum* to 2:15 trans Rufinus of Aquileia, ed W.A. Baehrens *Origines Werke* VIII GCS 33 (1925); *Homiliae in Cantica Canticorum* to 2:14 trans St Jerome, ed W.A. Baehrens *Origines Werke* VIII GCS 33 (1925) 26–60.

1039 Ps 49:12 (Vulg 48:13)

1040 1 Cor 6:15; Eph 5:30

1041 Matt 22:16; Luke 20:21

1042 Prov 11:2; Col 3:12; 1 Pet 5:5; Luke 1:48

1043 Prov 11:2

1044 Erasmus contrasts a wrong kind of humility with the right kind of pride, using the parable of the prodigal son and the words of St Paul. In the first case the wrong way was the prodigal son who left the house of a wealthy and kindly father and became the swineherd of a foreigner,[1045] once a citizen now an exile, once a free man now a servant, feeding upon the husks thrown to pigs instead of delicacies; but he happily regained his self-esteem after he began to recognize his worth: 'How many hired men there are in my father's house who have bread aplenty, and here I die of hunger.'[1046] On the other hand, there is a certain laudable pride that makes a man conscious of the dignity to which he has been raised through God's mercy and judge it unworthy of himself to sink into dishonourable behaviour, so as to become the servant of Satan though adopted into the company of the children of God,[1047] to stain himself with vice though purified in the sacred font, to hunt after worldly comforts though called to a heavenly reward. This pride especially befits a priest and preacher, for others, I think, scarcely deserve this claim to distinction. Hear in Paul an example of the common kind of pride (for he is not speaking there in his own person): 'Shall I take the limbs of Christ and make them the limbs of a harlot?'[1048] But again hear the voice of the proud teacher: 'It is better for me to die than to empty out my glory, which I have in the gospel of Christ.'[1049] He does not glory in palaces, wealth, attendants, horsemen, but grows proud because he had illuminated the gospel by his labours and trials, because he carried about Christ's

* * * * *

worldly young man who has debased himself as the lowliest of servants in a far-off land comes to his senses in recognizing the lost status he once enjoyed in the house of his father and seeks to regain it; so, rising from his humble station, he sets out to return to his father by begging forgiveness and hoping for an amelioration of his impoverished condition. Erasmus sees this as a 'detestable' example of humility and contrasts it with Paul, who so mightily values the exalted status of the preaching ministry entrusted to him that he would never consent to allow it to be diminished in any way through any failing on his part. Paul exemplifies good pride; he is humbly aware of the extraordinary gift he, though altogether unworthy, has received from God and his obligation to carry out the Lord's mission faithfully. See also Erasmus' interpretation of this passage in *De libero arbitrio* CWE 76 72, where he gives the prodigal son's repentance as an example of the working of 'prevenient grace.' See also *Paraphrasis in Lucam* (15:11–32) CWE 48 74–88 and accompanying footnotes.

1045 Luke 15:11–32
1046 Luke 15:17
1047 Rom 8:15
1048 1 Cor 6:15. Paul follows up his rhetorical question in this passage with 'God forbid!' 'Pray God, may such a thing never happen!' (*Id quidem avertat Deus*). See *Paraphrasis in 1 ad Corinthios* LB VII 877 C / CWE 43 83.
1049 1 Cor 9:15

triumph[1050] in every place. Therefore, he forgets those things that are behind and hastens on towards those that lie ahead in order to seize the crown,[1051] so far is he from degenerating to lower levels. Now, how great is the shame if someone who was a physician becomes a surgeon or a pharmacist, or someone who was a courtier becomes a farmer, or if someone who was the steward of a powerful man becomes a common cook! Anyone driven to such a fate would want to hang himself, so great is the pride we take in things of little consequence, so great the nobility of soul, while great indeed is our humility and dejection in matters that are of the highest importance. Christ should be especially implored that all bishops recognize their worth so that they imitate the pride of the apostles. Surely you, pastor, to whom a bishop has delegated the responsibility of tending the flock in his place, you, preacher, to whom the office of teaching the people has been entrusted, recognize the dignity of your position, recognize that what is greatest and fairest in all the functions of a bishop has been channelled into you. Take pride, then, take a pride worthy of your office, and believe that you should be deeply ashamed if you are a slave to gain, to luxury, to shameful pleasures, to the other vices of the common herd; but honour your ministry,[1052] mindful of whose sheep you have undertaken to tend,[1053] whose treasures you dispense,[1054] to whom you will soon render an account of the conduct of your duty, what rewards await the faithful steward, what punishments the faithless.[1055]

How could anyone who reflects upon this be free from worry? If someone is unaware of it, what is more stupid than he? If someone understands but ignores it, what is more pitiable than he? Let consideration of the worth of your function[1056] raise your mind from earthbound cares; let the severity

* * * * *

1050 2 Cor 2:14
1051 Phil 3:13–14
1052 Rom 11:13
1053 Cf John 21:17.
1054 2 Cor 4:7; Matt 13:44; Luke 12:42
1055 Cf Matt 25:14–30; Luke 19:11–27.
1056 The unanimous reading of the sources here, *consideratae functionis dignitas*, presents a difficulty that Chomarat resolves by taking *consideratae* in the non-classical sense 'en vue,' 'qui attire les regards'; ASD V-4 207 383n. This is certainly possible; but if *consideratae* is not simply a slip for *considerata*, it is also possible that it is a feminine plural form intended to modify each of the nouns in the series, all of them feminine (*dignitas, severitas, difficultas, magnitudo*). Erasmus' point would be: 'Let consideration of the dignity, etc and consideration of the severity, etc and consideration of the difficulty, etc and consideration of the magnitude, etc' have the specified effects rather than the dignity, the

of the one who commissions you deter you from prevarication; let the difficulty of the office undertaken exclude sloth; let the magnitude of the reward,
which will have to be expected not from men but from God, rouse your industry and vigilance: it is for him you serve as a soldier, he will pay you an
everlasting wage. Do not say, 'What? Am I to serve the people without pay?'
You do not serve the people, good fellow, but serve Christ in the people;
and lest you scorn any of the common folk, all are members of Christ;[1057]
or if any are not that yet, your purpose is to make them that.

Imagine that what the Lord commands through Isaiah was said to
you by name: 'Get up upon a high mountain, you who bring good tidings to Zion; lift up your voice in strength, you who bring good tidings to
Jerusalem.'[1058] A magnificent mission has been entrusted to you, an argument difficult to make convincingly to those who love the world. What is
it? 'All flesh is grass, all its glory like the flower of the grass.'[1059] What is
left then but for us to cast off the flesh and turn into spirit? Let our grass
wither at the rising of the sun, which illuminates every man coming into
this world;[1060] let our flower fall before the shining glory of the gospel,
for there follows, 'But the word of the Lord remains forever.'[1061] The preaching of this word has been entrusted to you; do not speak humbly, do not
creep upon the ground, but speak lofty things from aloft. Zion embodies
a type of the church,[1062] inasmuch as it is itself the mountain supporting
the temple of God, which is the church. He who brings good tidings to this
is commanded to rise onto another higher mountain; thus the Lord, when
he was about to teach those lofty things, ascended a mountain and sat.[1063]

* * * * *

severity, the difficulty, and the magnitude themselves. The clash between the
plural adjective and the singular verb is awkward but perhaps not impossible.
(J. Butrica)

1057 1 Cor 6:15, 12:27; Eph 5:30
1058 Isa 40:9
1059 Isa 40:6
1060 John 1:9. Erasmus substitutes the word 'sun' (sol) for the word 'light' (lux and
    lumen). 'Sun' recalls Plato's Republic 6.507D–508E: it is the metaphor for the
    'reality ... that gives their truth to the objects of knowledge and the power of
    knowing to the knower ... the idea of good ... the cause of knowledge, and
    of truth in so far as known' (508E).
1061 Isa 40:8; 1 Pet 1:25
1062 Cf Gal 4:22–6.
1063 Matt 5:1; see Erasmus Paraphrasis in Mattheum CWE 45 83: 'And so when he
    reached the top of the hill Jesus sat down, not out of weariness, but because
    he was about to teach difficult and serious things that required an attentive
    listener.'

The mountain shows the heroic strengths in the evangelist, the sitting his constancy and his heart untroubled by any confusion of carnal desires. On Zion we gaze at the heavenly; in Jerusalem is the vision of peace.[1064] Therefore, you, whoever you are, who teach love for the good things of heaven and scorn for the things of earth, who announce good news, who preach the peace that passes all understanding, ascend the mountain,[1065] shout[1066] from it. The word 'shout' here does not indicate a straining of the voice but the fire of emotion and the urgency of preaching. 'There is no peace for the wicked,' shouts prophecy.[1067] Whoever teaches piety is summoning us towards peace. There is a great serenity in having God's favour, a great joy always in having before one's eyes that heavenly peace that neither the malice of the wicked nor the envy of Satan nor any iniquity can disturb. This is that heavenly church of all the saints,[1068] which is built as a city[1069] that is compact together. That peace is seen here too, but from afar, partially and in a riddle;[1070] there it will be seen perfect and present. The church militant is a city placed upon a mountain,[1071] as the word of the gospel has it; the evangelical philosophy that he who came from heaven[1072] brought is sublime, and just as he, according to the Baptist, is over all, so he speaks heavenly things. And so how will it be possible for a man to preach the sublime to the sublime if he himself is sunk in the muck of pleasures, somnolence, luxury, and greed? Go up, therefore, upon the mountain, evangelist, whoever you are, not with your feet but with your emotions; for to ascend to a rank of dignity and not ascend to lofty virtues is more truly a descent than an ascent. But what follows, 'As a shepherd feeds his flock,'[1073] shows abundantly that this passage of prophecy pertains to pastors.

In chapter 52 the same prophet saw such evangelists with prophetic eyes, saying, 'How beautiful upon the mountains are the feet of him who announces and proclaims peace, of him who announces the good news, proclaims salvation.'[1074] What are 'lovely feet'? Emotions free of the desire for

* * * * *

1064 See Revelation 21.
1065 Isa 40:9
1066 Isa 40:6–9
1067 Isa 48:22, 57:21
1068 Ps 149:1 (Vulg 149:1); cf Ecclus 31:11, 44:15.
1069 Ps 122:3 (Vulg 121:3)
1070 Cf 1 Cor 13:12.
1071 Matt 5:14
1072 John 3:31; see Erasmus *Paraphrasis in Joannem* CWE 46 52.
1073 Isa 40:11
1074 Isa 52:7

what is base. What are 'feet upon the mountains'? What else but residence in heaven[1075] and a mind that knows what is above and seeks what is above. What does that repetition mean, 'announcing, announcing' and 'proclaiming peace, good news, and salvation'? What else but insistence and constancy in the business of the gospel, which Paul wants to be announced in season and out of season.[1076] We announce the new, we publish what is public; the voice of one who announces new and joyful things earns applause, the voice of the herald penetrates to everyone's ears. The voice of the synagogue was thin; it barely sounded throughout a single region, while it has been said of the heralds of the gospel that 'their sound has gone out into every land and their words to the ends of the earth.'[1077] The Law was given to a single people; Christ's grace is extended to all the nations of the world.[1078] The herald of the gospel is told, 'Shout; do not cease; be not afraid,'[1079] and again in chapter 58, 'Shout; do not cease; lift up your voice like a trumpet.'[1080] At the music from this sort of trumpet fell the walls of Jericho,[1081] a word that in Hebrew means 'moon.'[1082] The moon is near the earth, wandering and changeable like those who are stuck to the lowly and the unstable, but lunatic desires of this sort collapse at the music of the priestly trumpets. Sacred are those who play, sacred are the trumpets, which were used at the Jubilee, as you read at Joshua 6.[1083] Freedom of the spirit follows the destruction of the earthly emotions that reduce us to slavery. These trumpets do not sound the secular, the lowly, and the lunatic, but that lofty sun of righteousness,[1084] Christ, who never changes; for, as Paul says, 'He is yesterday and today, the same for all time.'[1085] Victory is assured when the armed multitude shouts to the noise of the priestly trumpets.[1086] This happens whenever the voice of the preacher, thanks to the energy of the Spirit,[1087] penetrates into the hearts

* * * * *

1075 Cf Phil 3:20 *conversatio in caelis* and Col 3:1–2.

1076 2 Tim 4:2

1077 Ps 19:4 (Vulg 18:5); see Rom 10:18; Matt 28:19–20; Acts 1:8.

1078 Matt 28:19

1079 Chomarat notes that this line is not in Scripture. Erasmus constructs this by connecting Isa 40:6 and 9. See ASD V-4 210 439n.

1080 Isa 58:1

1081 Joshua 6

1082 Erasmus appears to have taken this reading from Augustine; see Augustine *Enarratio in Psalmum 60* CCSL 39 770 (*Exposition of Psalm 60*) WSA III-17 199.

1083 Josh 6:4

1084 Mal 4:2

1085 Heb 13:8

1086 Josh 6:5

1087 Cf Rom 15:13, 19; 1 Corinthians 12.

of his listeners, just as in St Paul the outsider who hears the prophet speaking in plain language falls upon his face and glorifies God,[1088] and in the Gospel the Jews, moved by the trumpet of John the Baptist, shout, 'What shall we do to be saved?';[1089] and in Acts, at Peter's first bugle (for we read that he raised his voice),[1090] they shout, cut to the heart, 'What shall we do, brethren?'[1091] and nearly three thousand men embraced the gospel.[1092]

But to return to the earlier passage of Isaiah. It says, 'The voice of your watchmen, they have raised their voice, they will praise together.'[1093] Whoever wishes to be considered a herald of the gospel should be in a watchtower[1094] so that he can keep watch from on high, not only for himself but for others too. Instead of 'watchmen' the Septuagint has 'guards,'[1095] that is, those who stand guard upon the walls of the church. Therefore remember, herald of the gospel, whoever you are, that according to the language of the prophet you must stand guard by day and by night,[1096] so that if a voice is heard from Seir, 'Watchman, what of the night? Watchman, what of the night?,'[1097] you may have a ready answer. What is 'they will praise' or 'they will rejoice together'?[1098] It shows the harmony of the preachers in their teaching, which in these times, alas, we miss in many of them; we hear the cry of their exultation, but it is dissonant and discordant. What sound does the herald of the Law make? 'The soul that sins shall die,'[1099] and unless you abide by what is written in this book, all curses will befall you.[1100] The Mosaic herald announces laws and strikes terror with threats;

* * * * *

1088 1 Cor 14:24–5
1089 Luke 3:10
1090 Acts 2:14
1091 Acts 2:37
1092 Acts 2:14–41
1093 Isa 52:8
1094 Cf Isa 21:8. See *Paraphrasis in acta apostolorum* CWE 50 13. Erasmus explains that 'Mount Sion, which in Hebrew means "watchtower," from which all things earthly are looked down upon, all things heavenly are, through faith, observed as though nearby.'
1095 φυλασσόντων, Greek genitive plural
1096 Isa 62:6
1097 Isa 21:11. Seir, eponymous ancestor of the Edomites and the ancient name of Edom, designates the location of these gentiles in the mountains south, southeast of the Dead Sea; the name is also associated with Esau. See Gen 36:20–30 where Seir's genealogy is given.
1098 Cf Isa 65:14.
1099 Ezek 18:4
1100 Cf Deut 27:26; Gal 3:10.

what about the herald of the church? He announces to all nations living under whatever sky that remission of all sins has been secured through faith
in Jesus Christ;[1101] with the angels he announces peace to men on earth,[1102]
not through the works of the Law but through the free will and gratuitous
kindness of God, who was in Christ reconciling the world to himself;[1103]
he announces goodness instead of vengeance, salvation instead of the death
that is due the sins of man. To whom are these things preached? To Zion,
which is now the church scattered throughout the entire world, for so goes
the prophecy, saying, 'Zion, your god will reign.'[1104] Where sin reigns, there
is not the kingdom of God; where the flesh reigns, there the Spirit does not
reign; where superstition reigns, there true devotion does not reign. And
so the church prays daily, 'Thy kingdom come';[1105] if God reigns within us,
we too reign with him in the freedom of the spirit.[1106] This reign was illuminated when the Spirit came upon the apostles on the day of Pentecost.[1107]
The Law had been given on Mount Sinai on the same day;[1108] thunder was
heard, lightning was seen, all shuddered at the smoking mountain[1109] and
at Moses' face, which all but flashed,[1110] but upon no one did that Spirit descend that forgives sins freely through faith,[1111] conferring righteousness[1112]
and liberty.[1113]

That each prophecy in fact speaks of grace made through Christ is
shown in the fact that one professes, 'The Lord has comforted his people,
he has redeemed Jerusalem; the Lord has prepared his holy arm in the eyes
of all nations and all the ends of the earth will see the salvation of our
God,'[1114] and the other begins, 'Be comforted, be comforted, my people;
speak to the heart of Jerusalem.'[1115] 'It is with the heart that one believes

* * * * *

1101 Acts 13:38
1102 Luke 2:13–14
1103 2 Cor 5:17–21; Eph 2:16; Col 1:20
1104 Isa 52:7
1105 Matt 6:10; Luke 11:2
1106 Cf Rom 8:21; 2 Cor 3:17.
1107 Acts 2:1–4
1108 Erasmus develops this figurative interpretation in *Paraphrasis in acta apostolo-*
      rum CWE 50 13, 23; see 168 n1 and 179 n111.
1109 Exod 19:16, 18
1110 Exod 34:29–30
1111 Matt 9:2
1112 Rom 3:22
1113 2 Cor 3:17
1114 Isa 52:9–10
1115 Isa 40:1–2

in righteousness,'[1116] which promises salvation through faith in Christ and speaks to the heart because it speaks of the things of the spirit. Moreover, no one can speak to the heart of the people unless he speaks from the heart;[1117] but the Law, which demanded works from the Jews, frightened those who did not provide them[1118] and did not add grace: it spoke not to the heart but only to the ears of the body. But after the prophecy that we cited in the first passage there follows an obvious prediction about Christ: 'He was wounded for our transgressions, he was bruised for our iniquities; the chastisement of our peace was upon him, and we have been healed by his bruising. All we like sheep have gone astray, everyone has turned to his own way, and the Lord has laid on him the iniquity of us all.'[1119] Different passages of Scripture apply to different persons, with some instruction for husbands,[1120] some also for wives,[1121] some for virgins,[1122] some for commoners,[1123] some for kings,[1124] some for priests;[1125] this proclamation pertains to everyone, and no man has any hope of salvation unless it reaches his heart.

In the same prophet the watchman is also instructed to announce whatever he sees.[1126] What does a secular watchman announce? From the tower he sees cavalry or a fleet in the distance; immediately he gives the signal with a bell so that danger does not overwhelm without warning. It is therefore the duty of the good pastor to see far off, to see through darkness, to train his eyes in every direction, so that he not only remedies present ills but rushes to forestall the dangers that threaten trouble from afar: schisms, heresies, wars, paganism, Judaism.[1127] Whoever guesses wisely about the future

* * * * *

1116 Rom 10:10
1117 Matt 12:34; Luke 6:45
1118 See eg Exod 22:20, 31:13–15, 35:2; Num 18:3; Deut 21:21; Lev 20:13–14.
1119 Isa 53:5–6
1120 Matt 5:32; Col 3:19
1121 1 Cor 7:39–40; Col 3:18; 1 Pet 3:1
1122 1 Cor 7:1, 8, 25–38; 7:32–4; see also 1 Cor 7:36–8.
1123 Rom 13:1–7; Titus 3:1; 1 Pet 2:13–14; Heb 13:17
1124 Rom 13:4
1125 1 Tim 3:2–3; Titus 1:7–9
1126 Isa 21:6
1127 Erasmus calls attention to the duty of pastors to protect their flock against all manner of false doctrine that would adulterate the 'heavenly philosophy' and so lure the faithful away from Christ. Again his central point is that the heavenly teaching (safe, pure, and solid doctrine) is constantly endangered by all manner of pseudoprophets. If Christ's teaching is perverted, that is, by killing him in human minds, the consequence to the Christian who willingly

has the eyes of a prophet, and whatever evil befalls will be accounted to his silence if he does not give the signal clearly to the sleepers with his ringing. It is punishable by death if someone who keeps watch in the tower either has not seen or has not told in advance of an approaching enemy; but no enemies are more dangerous than the deadly vices, which destroy souls and which kill Christ in his members. What penalty, therefore, awaits a watchman if he has been silent?[1128] A dull-witted watchman sees someone plotting treachery and is condemned if he does not denounce him in time; and do you see Satan digging tunnels and keep silent? The most vigilant watchman was Habakkuk, who said, 'I will stand upon my guard and fix my step upon the fortification, and I will watch in order to see what will be said to me and what I may answer to the one who accuses me.'[1129] The prophecy that is in Isaiah also addresses preachers: 'Upon your walls I have set guards, all the day and all the night perpetually they will not be silent. You who remember the Lord, do not keep quiet and do not give him silence.'[1130] Preacher, do you hear? You should be on the walls, not in the taverns, if you want to perform your duty, nor is it right for you to keep quiet at any time, neither by night nor by day. For danger threatens God's people on either side: in adversity they are tempted through affliction to blasphemy, despair, and desertion from God, and in prosperity they are enticed through the blandishments of the flesh to forgetfulness of God. Or understand the night as when Satan openly tempts to drunkenness, luxury, adultery, and whoring, which are the works of night and of darkness,[1131] the day as when the midday demon[1132] lays its snare under the mask of religion and piety; the guardian of Jerusalem must be absolutely alert in either case.

Nor must anyone be heeded who replies, 'All this squares with the prophets of the first kind who foretold the coming of the Redeemer; what need for such shouting now, when it is agreed that he has already come?' No, Christ has not yet come for all. He has not yet come for the Jews, who are still awaiting their Messiah; he has not come for those who do not believe

* * * * *

follows the false prophet is the loss of his immortal soul. More detail about some of these dangers appears below.
1128 Ezek 33:6
1129 Hab 2:1
1130 Isa 62:6–7
1131 Rom 13:12–13
1132 Ps 91:6 (Vulg 90:6)

that he redeemed the world by his death; he has not come for those who imagine him other than as he is, such as the Arians,[1133] the Eunomians,[1134] the Sabellians;[1135] finally, he has not yet come for those who profess him with their mouth but deny him with their acts. He has truly come only for those who live and are moved by his spirit and for all who can say with the Apostle, 'It is no longer I who live, but Christ who lives within me.'[1136] Some cried out against those who announced Christ's coming, nor are there fewer now who resist his gospel. Some killed Christ when he was dwelling in the flesh; I only wish there were none now who more dangerously kill him in the minds of men![1137] Whoever draws a true believer into heretical error kills Christ; whoever has coaxed a simple girl to turn her zeal for modesty into lust has killed Christ in her. Accordingly, there is no less work and no less danger today than there was in the past for those who announce Christ sincerely. Christ is killed particularly through the tongue; through the tongue he is born and reborn in us: 'Base conversations corrupt good character.'[1138] He is born again in those who are regenerated by the word of life and whenever he is formed anew in the minds of men by learned correction. Even when the Lord wore a mortal body on earth, he was pierced and slain by tongues. Those who accused him before the priests,[1139] before

* * * * *

1133 Arians did not accept the eternal consubstantiality of the Son with the Father, and therefore denied his divinity; the heresy was condemned at the Council of Nicea (325); see DS 125, 126 (anathematizing the Arian position). See 'Arianism' ODCC 99–100.

1134 Eunomians, followers of Eunomius (d 394), took an even more extreme position than the Arians by holding that Christ was not of the divine substance but only a being immediately produced by the Father and in that way resembled him. Eunomius' teachings were condemned at the Council of Constantinople (381); see DS 150, which condemned the teaching of many types of 'Arianizers'; see 'Eunomius' ODCC 572–3.

1135 Sabellians, also known as Monarchians, believed in the oneness of the single monarchical godhead without distinctions of persons; the persons, rather, were different manifestations of God at various events or moments in various modes. Their condemnation came at Nicea and Constantinople. See ODCC 1434.

1136 Gal 2:20

1137 Erasmus speaks here of schismatics, heretics, and Jews who would deter someone from the teaching of Christ or corrupt the gospel with the result that one loses everlasting life.

1138 1 Cor 15:33. Paul cites Menander; see *Adagia* I x 74 *Corrumpunt mores bonos colloquia prava* 'Evil communications corrupt good manners.'

1139 Matt 26:60–2; Mark 14:55–9; Luke 22:66–71; John 18:12–14, 19–24

Pilate,[1140] those who shouted, 'Take and crucify him,'[1141] used tongues in place of sharp swords; whatever was done then at the level of human feeling is done daily at the spiritual level, and with greater danger as the spiritual is higher than the physical. Therefore, what Solomon said in Proverbs, 'Death and life are in the hands of the tongue,'[1142] applies especially to them. Some bear a poison in their tongue more effective than the venom of asps;[1143] but some, on the other hand, heal with the tongue those wounded by the tongue and with a healing tongue cure those infected by a pestilent tongue, as he also teaches: 'The tongue of the wise man is health.'[1144] It is attested even in pagan proverbs that 'speech is a physician to an ailing soul';[1145] likewise the Psalm goes, 'He sent forth his speech and healed them.'[1146] The great power of the human tongue is shown abundantly in ancient literature, and we see it every day as the tongue of a single man stirs to war an entire city or a whole region that was peaceful before or compels troops drawn up and thirsting for blood to lay down their arms, overthrows states by ruinous counsel and saves them, if it wishes, by wholesome counsel, arranges alliances of princes and puts asunder those arranged, strengthens the bonds of marriage and tears these bonds asunder. If the human tongue has such power, how much more potent is the force of the preacher's tongue, which is the instrument of the Holy Spirit. Truly death is in the hands of this tongue, as is life; it is life when it turns sinners towards penitence, it is death when it kills the old Adam in them along with his deeds.[1147] This of course is the treasure from which the wealthy householder brings forth new and old things,[1148] that is, he is instructed in the writings of both Testaments.

There are dogs that Paul detests and orders us to guard against, namely workers of iniquity;[1149] there are also praiseworthy dogs that by

* * * * *

1140 Matt 27:2–24; Mark 15:1–15; Luke 23:1–24; John 18:29–19:15
1141 John 19:15
1142 Prov 18:21
1143 Ps 140:3 (Vulg 139:4)
1144 Prov 12:18
1145 *Adagia* III i 100 *Animo aegrotanti medicus est oratio* 'To a sick spirit speech is a physician.' Erasmus imprecisely remembers the adage. In the text he gives it as *animae aegrotanti medicum esse sermonem.* He finds versions of this in Plutarch, Aeschylus, Horace, the Stoics, Terence, Isocrates, and in 'the Hebrew sage' (Prov 15:1).
1146 Ps 107:20 (Vulg 106:20)
1147 For 'Old Adam ... deeds' cf Col 3:9–10.
1148 Matt 13:52
1149 Phil 3:2; see *Paraphrasis in epistolam Pauli apostoli ad Philippenses* CWE 43 378.

their barking deter nocturnal thieves who try to break into the house, whence the Greeks call them οἰκουροί [oikouroi], that is, 'guards and watchers of the house,'[1150] not like the dog that the Psalm accuses, 'If you saw a thief, you ran with him.'[1151] Moreover, just as thieves are wont to silence dogs by tossing them some morsel,[1152] so those who love their own private gain more than the public gain of the Lord's flock toss money or a bishopric into their maw like a tidbit when preachers begin to bark, so that they are silent and betray God's house to the thieves. But the faithful watchman who stands upon the walls of Jerusalem must be silent neither by night nor by day,[1153] and he does not check his voice at the tossing of food as ill-bred dogs are wont to do and will not forego his heavenly reward for a piece of bread. Dogs of this kind are suited to hunting souls, for they know when they should change their voice and the tricks to drive a wild beast into the Lord's nets. Finally, this animal is said to have the power in its tongue to heal wounds;[1154] they lick out the gore and keep the wounded place from putrefying. The tongue of the good preacher should be such that no one departs from a talk with him without being cleaner; with gentle warnings and mild correction he should bring healing to good people who have fallen through weakness and with his faithful barking drive away the incurable. Lest anyone be offended by this designation, these dogs have great dignity in the eyes of God, for in the mystical writings those who are called dogs are also called gods;[1155] they are called prophets, as we have shown, and they are also called kings (if a majestic title appeals to anyone).

For it is clear that heralds of the gospel are the subject at Psalm 67, wherein we read, 'You will set aside a gracious rain, God, for your inheritance';[1156] this of course is the rain of heavenly teaching that makes our

* * * * *

1150 Οἰκουρός means 'watching' or 'keeping the house'; LSJ 1205. Cf Aristophanes *Wasps* 970: 'That other Cur is a mere stay-at-home.'
1151 Ps 50:18 (Vulg 49:18)
1152 See Seneca *De constantia* 2.14.2 and Virgil *Aeneid* 6.417–23.
1153 Isa 62:6; see also Isa 56:10 for Israel's watchmen who are like 'mute dogs.'
1154 Aelian *De natura animalium* 8.9
1155 See John 10:34 (citing Ps 82:6 [Vulg 81:6]). References to dogs in Scripture are commonly negative, and no passage suggests that 'dogs have great dignity in the eyes of God' (cf Tob 11:9 as a possible exception). Dogs were considered unclean animals who fed on carrion (cf Exod 22:31). But see Luke 16:21 where Erasmus says the dogs who lick Lazarus' wounds 'rebuked the inhumanity of the self-indulgent rich man, for they would come and lick Lazarus' sores'; see *Paraphrasis in Lucam* 11–24 CWE 48 99 and n28.
1156 Ps 68:9 (Vulg 67:10)

land fertile. And there follows, 'The Lord will give the word to those who preach good tidings with great power.'[1157] These are the ones who sleep amidst unknown dangers,[1158] resting securely through faith in the writings of both Testaments,[1159] who have the silvered wings of the dove,[1160] namely evangelical innocence[1161] joined with purity of life and splendour of character,[1162] not without the pleasant ringing of salutary teaching that rings out not the sounds of earth but those of heaven. And although silver also shines if you work it properly and gives delight by its ringing tone, it is nonetheless liable to tarnish if you neglect it. If a preacher attends to the letter, his teaching takes on a tarnish; hence there follows, 'and his hinder parts covered in the paleness or the greenness of gold.'[1163] The letter is first, the mystical sense[1164] comes after; it is not corrupted but is green with perpetual authority. But from what author does all this come? Of course from the king of hosts of the beloved,[1165] the beloved who gives the word to those who bring good tidings with great power,[1166] from the king of hosts whom Paul calls the king of the ages.[1167] The Jews have the ringing of silver, but spoiled by much tarnish; comparing the spiritual with the spiritual, we have gold. The perfect evangelist was the Lord Jesus; the Father loved him uniquely[1168] as his only begotten.[1169] What is carnal is first, then what is spiritual; but what is spiritual is far more outstanding, inasmuch as

* * * * *

1157 Ps 68:11 (Vulg 67:12)
1158 Ps 68:13 (Vulg 67:14 *inter medios cleros* 'amidst unknown dangers'). Here the Latin word (accusative plural) *cleros* must be taken over from the Greek κλῆρος meaning 'lot,' either a lot of land or one's destiny; here 'destiny,' 'fate.'
1159 See Prov 3:24; Isa 30:15; 1 Tim 2:2.
1160 Ps 68:13 (Vulg 67:14)
1161 Cf Acts 2:46; Rom 12:8; 2 Cor 1:12, 8:2, 9:11 and 13; Eph 6:5; Col 3:22.
1162 Cf 1 Tim 3:9, 2:8; 2 Tim 1:3. See *Paraphrasis in epistolam Pauli apostoli ad Timotheum priorem* CWE 44 16.
1163 Ps 68:13 (Vulg 67:14). The reference is to pale gold. Erasmus has chosen to call it 'green' perhaps because the Septuagint version of the Psalm uses the word χλωρός (ἐν χλωρότητι χρυσίου), meaning both 'pale' and 'green.' This then allows him in his 'mystical' interpretation of the verse to understand greenness in the sense 'verdant,' 'flourishing.'
1164 That is, the spiritual sense; for Erasmus' distinction between the literal and spiritual sense of Scripture, see introduction 201–5 and books 2 and 3 CWE 68 passim.
1165 Ps 68:12 (Vulg 67:13 *Rex virtutum dilecti dilecti*)
1166 Ps 68:11 (Vulg 67:12)
1167 1 Tim 1:17
1168 Luke 3:22; Matt 3:17; Mark 1:11
1169 John 1:18

according to the Greek proverb as well τὰ δεύτερα [second things] are called
ἀμείνω [best].[1170] Perhaps this image depicts the Christian preacher for us.
Wings are needed to fly up in the spirit to the heavenly and to draw others
up to the same place, but a dove's wings are needed[1171] either because no
bird is swifter in flight or because none is simpler or more innocent. But a
double ringing is needed, of silver and of gold, in order to be candid and
open in explaining the humbler meaning, then to reveal to the more advanced the gold of hidden wisdom, which Paul speaks of in symbols, not to
any at all but to the trained.[1172] Earthly wisdom professes great and wonderful things on its surface,[1173] but if you were to penetrate more deeply
you would simply find coals instead of treasure.[1174] The nature of evangelical philosophy is different; it has far more in depth than it shows on its
surface, and the more deeply you enter, the more magnificent the wealth
it shows. How unseemly it would be then if, professing to be a preacher,
you were a hog rolling in the muck of vulgar pleasures[1175] instead of a
dove, with clay in your heart instead of silver, coals instead of gold. A vessel of clay gives only the sound of clay, and the man of earth speaks the
earthly.

There are many other things in Holy Writ that show the dignity, the
utility, the difficulty of the preacher's role, and the greatness of the reward
awaiting those who carry out their assigned task in good faith, but greater
horrors are threatened for those who wear the mask of shepherd[1176] but in
fact act like wolves or betrayers of the Lord's flock;[1177] we, however, have
preferred to collect the things that attract rather than those that terrify, for
one who is driven to his duty by fear can scarcely play the part of an evangelical preacher sincerely. There is faith, which shuns no danger; there is
charity, which shuns no toil.[1178] If these two are present, terrors are unnecessary; if they are not, cheap threats give little help, and if they do help,
they help the ignorant. The preacher should not be ignorant, since he has
undertaken to instruct the ignorant.

* * * * *

1170 See *Adagia* I iii 38 *Posterioribus melioribus* 'Better luck next time.'
1171 Ps 68:13 (Vulg 67:14)
1172 1 Cor 2:6–7
1173 *Adagia* I ix 88 *Prima facie. Prima fronte* 'At first sight. On the face of it.'
1174 *Adagia* I ix 30 *Thesaurus carbones erant* 'The treasure consisted of coals.'
1175 2 Pet 2:22. See *Adagia* IV iii 62 *Sus in volutabro coeni* 'A swine in a wallowing
      hole of filth.'
1176 Cf Matthew 23.
1177 Cf Matt 7:15.
1178 Cf 1 Cor 13:1–13.

We have shown how dignity need not entail hauteur or the difficulty sloth or the danger despair.

And so this volume appears to be just about full enough if we give some brief advice about how a preacher can secure both favour and authority with the people and keep them once he has them, inasmuch as love for a teacher and the teacher's authority are the two chief stimuli to learning;[1179] love makes us listen gladly and without boredom, while authority makes us believe the truth of what is imparted. When I say love, I understand Christian love, not the ordinary kind; when I say authority, I understand that which is won by virtue, not by bluff. But if someone happens to have these from some other source, the wise man will turn to the profit of piety those human emotions that congregations feel, provided they are neither immoderate nor associated with vice. Many win favour by their pleasant appearance or a common homeland or kinship or some other human feeling; let the preacher seize this opportunity, turning what is human to spiritual profit. Some follow the disciples of St Francis with marvellous zeal, others more eagerly favour the Dominicans. This emotion is purely human and often differs among equally devout persons, and therefore this kind of favour should not be sought; but if it is present on its own, it should be accommodated to the good of the audience. Likewise, many win authority through the actual appearance of their person and the dignity of their countenance, distinguished family, holy dress, title, age, or something else like these; it is alien to Christian perfection to judge someone from external qualities of this kind, for St Paul rebukes those who do so for seeing only what is according to appearance,[1180] since those who value a man highly for these things scorn him for different ones. But because he is compelled to become all things to all people[1181] on account of human weakness, the preacher will use this emotion of the simple as a bait to lure the souls of the inexperienced until they advance to something better. This happened to the Lord, the prince of preachers: his appearance and the lowliness of his life offended many Jews, the weakness of the cross offended even his closest disciples,[1182] yet for a time the Lord allowed himself to be loved by his followers according to the flesh until they advanced to the spiritual.[1183] Similarly Paul's

* * * * *

1179 Cf *De pueris instituendis* CWE 26 334.
1180 See 2 Cor 10:7.
1181 1 Cor 9:22
1182 Matt 16:21–5, 26:56; Mark 14:27; John 16:32
1183 That is, until they received the gift of the Holy Spirit on Pentecost; see Acts 2:1–4.

chains scandalized many,[1184] and so he thanks the stronger ones because they had not recoiled from the gospel, offended by their teacher's afflictions. The Lord bids us judge a teacher by his works;[1185] sometimes a mind worthy of heaven is hidden under a filthy cloak in a loathsome and foul body.[1186] And yet Moses forbids anyone blind or lame or hunchbacked or ruptured or marked by any physical blemish at all to approach the altar,[1187] though born of Aaron's stock, or to enter within the veil, not because such things contaminate the Lord's temple but because outer appearance is often an impediment for the weak. Moreover, after the darkness of the Law was abolished,[1188] Roman popes established that no lame, one-eyed, feeble or defective persons, or those below a prescribed age would be admitted to ecclesiastical ministry,[1189] not because there is respect of persons in the eyes of God (for in the Gospel parable beggars, the blind, and the lame are summoned to the royal banquet)[1190] but because the mass of men are influenced to scorn the spiritual by what lies exposed to their physical vision. This emotion of ordinary people should be indulged for a time, but only in such a way that they are gradually enticed to seek a greater perfection; and so a teacher tolerates a pupil who is still a beginner, cajoling him, as it were, with little gifts and compliments lest he recoil from his intention.[1191] Otherwise, it would be unnecessary to mention this; for both authority and general favour will readily attend whoever has been endowed with the virtues that I mentioned earlier, provided he perseveres in them. For approval by everyone's votes has so far been the lot of no mortal man; the preacher must strive as far as possible to please all persons in all things and to get himself good report even among outsiders,[1192] always bearing in mind that saying of Paul, 'Everything is permitted me, but not everything is useful.'[1193]

* * * * *

1184 Phil 1:12–15
1185 See Matt 7:15–20.
1186 Cf James 2:1–5.
1187 Lev 21:17–24
1188 Cf Heb 8:5, 10:1; Col 2:16–17.
1189 See Code of Canon Law (1917), c.984 (2) for 'Irregularities by Defect'; after the 1983 revision, virtually all irregularities of the type Erasmus gives are removed (cf cc.1040–9 'Irregularities and Other Impediments').
1190 Luke 14:12–15
1191 For another statement of these pedagogical practices, see *De pueris instituendis* CWE 26 334–5.
1192 1 Thess 4:12
1193 1 Cor 6:12, 10:22; cf *Colloquia* (*Convivium religiosum*) CWE 39 189–91.

Therefore, in order to gain authority both more quickly and among more persons, let the preacher carefully avoid those things that bring a man into contempt, and let him exhibit within himself those that the common man esteems. Luxury, drunkenness, somnolence, pleasures (especially lust), silly and foolish chatter, idleness and excessive familiarity, vanity, inconstancy, fawning, grasping after gifts, admiration for the trivial and commonplace render a man contemptible and diminish his authority. On the other hand, authority is secured by sobriety, a frugal life, vigilance, a chaste character, restrained speech seasoned with wit, the ability to keep a secret, seriousness of character, truth in speech, affability tempered by an appropriate gravity, association with all the most serious men, either no or infrequent dealings with men who are worthless or of unchaste reputation, and only for the purpose of admonishing them, not drinking with them, but dealing with them as a doctor deals with the sick.[1194] Let him have such conversations with the wealthy that he neither provokes them to anger by an inappropriate severity nor falls into an appearance of flattery by saying only what they want to hear. Let him accept gifts casually from no one, but let him be courteous in refusing. Let him preserve his liberty intact in all respects, for whoever accepts a gift loses somehow a portion of his trustworthiness, and the giver has less esteem for the receiver. This fault is revealed by its consequences. When a preacher admonishes the giver rather freely, then anger grows hot, and he is called ungrateful, though for a trivial kindness he is returning a far greater. Understanding this, the Apostle does not think it right to take from the Corinthians but preferred to sew skins together rather than lose some part of his apostolic freedom,[1195] not because he hunted glory from men but because this was useful for the gospel.[1196] And so those who willingly run to the tables of the rich and go hunting after rich banquets given by powerful men act to the detriment of their authority; but far worse is the behaviour of those who sit the great part of the day in the public inns of the taverners, among men who are hardly sober, and joke with them about anything at all, drinking up the prescribed measure of wine[1197] themselves

* * * * *

1194 Cf Matt 9:12; Luke 5:31.
1195 1 Cor 9:1, 12, 15, 19; cf Acts 18:3.
1196 1 Cor 9:23
1197 See references to this custom of prescribed measure of wine in Plato *Symposium* 176A–E; Catullus 27.3; Horace *Odes* 2.7.25; and Cicero *In Verrem* 2.5.11 (§28) ('all the laws prescribed for the drinking of wine'). The playwright Eubulus (Euboulos) also gives this information; see *Eubulus: The Fragments* ed R.L. Hunter (Cambridge 1983) 186. The Latin word *hemina* for a portion of wine is attested to in Pliny the Elder, Plautus, Seneca, Aulus Gellius, and

and encouraging others in turn. Sometimes too they play cards and dice far into the night and dance in awkward movements; finally the pastor of the sheep returns home so affected that he has to be propped on the arms of those whose souls should be propped up by him. Add now to this a concubine taking the place of a wife,[1198] and not just one, or if it is just one, a licentious and domineering woman. Who will heed his words, or who will revere him, if he sees that some wretched woman rules him? I ask you, if a man always lives in such a way that he is one of the dregs of the mob, the most abject among the abject, what authority will he have in teaching, what weight in admonition? Or who will dare reveal the drama of his life in confession to a man he sees every day soaked with wine or ale blubbering out even his own secrets? I know that these things are not at all seemly to speak of; I only wish they did not occur everywhere (which is more unseemly still), and not only in villages but in the cities also! In discussing this subject, however, I hope that I shall always be indulged to the extent that if there is occasion to say something by way of admonition, the good people to whom it does not apply will not be offended and those who are subject to these vices will not be angered, for we do not want to expose them to scorn but to render them more acceptable to Christ.

Now, since people everywhere have certain particular follies of their own, such as clubs and drinking parties in churches, superstitious processions of saints like Lieven and Winnoc[1199] in Flanders, and ridiculous festivals, which have become so established by long-standing custom that they

* * * * *

M. Porcius Cato among others; see also *The Rule of Benedict* chapter 40 (On the Measure of Drink): 'Nevertheless, bearing in mind the needs of the weak we believe that a *hemina* of wine each day is sufficient for each person.' See OLD I 868 'hemina,' where the measure is given as 'a liquid or dry measure, one half of a sextarius.'

1198 See *Paraphrasis in epistolam Pauli apostoli ad Timotheum priorem* CWE 44 12–22, where Erasmus describes the ideal behaviour of bishops and priests; and CWE 44 16–18 for views on the proper behaviour of women: 'to follow and not to take the lead or to put on a display of authority in the presence of their husbands, to whom they should be subject in every way.'

1199 Chomarat notes that St Lieven (or Liévin) was martyred in Belgium in the seventh century, and each year on 28 June a procession carried his statue to Ghent, where he is particularly revered (ASD V-4 227 735n). See H. Nowé 'Gentsche voorgeboden op de Sint-Lievensbedevaart' in *Miscellanea Jean Gessler* I ed K.C. Peeters and R. Roemans (Deurne, Drukker 1948) 967–9; *Bibliotheca sanctorum* (Rome 1961–70) VIII 74. For St Winnoc (or Gwynnog), founder of Wormhoudt and of Bergues-Saint Winnoc near Dunkirk in the eighth century, see *Bibliotheca sanctorum* XII 1199.

cannot easily be abolished without commotion, and if they are abolished
there is danger of more foolish ones taking the place of those abolished, let
the pastor remove himself from such entertainments if only to show in this
way that he does not approve the practice. Since there are different forms
of such festivals in different regions, I shall present one or two as examples so that the reader may understand what I mean. Among the English
it is the custom at London that on a certain day the people bring into the
main church, dedicated to St Paul,[1200] the head of a wild animal impaled on
a long spear – some there call them *damae*,[1201] most people call them *capri*,
though in fact it is a sort of *hircus* [he-goat] with palmate antlers, abundant
on that island – all this to the accompaniment of the unlovely sound of hunting horns. In this solemn procession they advance to the high altar; you
would say that they were all inspired with the frenzy of Diana.[1202] What is

* * * * *

1200 St Paul's Cathedral was the seat of the bishop of London. See *A History of Saint
      Paul's Cathedral and the Men Associated with It* ed W.R. Matthews and W.M.
      Atkins (London 1957). Erasmus might have have observed this custom when
      he was in London in 1498–9 or 1505–6, or heard of it from John Colet or others.
      For his six visits to England, see Schoeck (1) 223–34. This example must be a
      reference to the yearly ceremony ('The Offering of a Buck and a Doe') on 29
      June (feast of Saints Peter and Paul) when a buck was presented at the high
      altar. The story is told by William Camden (1551–1623) that in 1328 a certain
      Sir William le Baud, in return for a favour granted by the chapter, gave a
      doe to the dean and canons of the cathedral on 25 January (the Conversion
      of St Paul) and a fat buck on 29 June. The later date was the occasion for
      the special procession with bugles. Camden cannot be Erasmus' source, but
      may provide some hint about its origin. See William Benham *Old St. Paul's
      Cathedral* (London 1902) 62–3.
1201 It is next to impossible to identify precisely the animals referred to here as
      damae, capri, and *hircus,* so they have been left in Latin. *Dama* according to L&S
      refers generically to 'beasts of the deer kind'; *hircus* is a 'he-goat' or 'buck';
      there is no other meaning for *capri* but 'goats,' but goats do not have palmate
      antlers. We might guess that the animal in question was a male roe deer (*capre-
      olus capreolus*) and that it was vulgarly and mistakenly called *caper.* (A. Dalzell)
      For *dama* (*damma*), see also OLD I 530: 'the general name of various, usu. small,
      members of the deer family (red or fallow deer, gazelle, antelope, etc.).'
1202 Diana (Greek Artemis) was the Roman goddess of the hunt. It is likely Eras-
      mus takes this aspect of Diana from Phoenix's words to Achilles in Homer's
      Iliad 9.530–49, which tell of the huge, fierce boar that Diana (Artemis) set loose
      in her rage upon the land and people of Calydon in revenge for the insult she
      received from King Oeneus for not offering her the first fruits of his land's
      harvest. See also Plutarch's likely reference to this and other aspects of Di-
      ana's frenzied nature in *De superstitione, Moralia* 170A–B. See also the Homeric
      Hymn 27 'To Artemis,' which celebrates her mastery as archer in the violence
      of the hunt.

the pastor to do in this situation? If he were to protest, custom is a powerful thing, and he might sooner stir up a revolt than remedy the problem. Elsewhere the body of the Lord is carried about through the fields, all the more disgracefully because it is borne by a priest on horseback.[1203] In villages and even in some towns the guilds of artisans have their own processions.[1204] Poles are carried erect by many men who sweat and would faint if they were not continually refreshed with drink; at the top is a saint, the patron of each craft. The people have other festivals and processions as well, in which stage shows are brought around, maidens in marvellous costumes are led about, and many things are said and done that are more to be concealed than approved. Such also are the bull contests among the Italians, and the races of asses, buffaloes, and horses.[1205] It is not seemly that those whose

* * * * *

1203 Erasmus is likely referring to the Feast of Corpus Christi, which had been inspired by St Juliana of Liège (d 1256) and made an official feast of the Roman church under Pope Urban IV (1261–4); held on the Thursday after Trinity Sunday, it often featured a procession in which the Eucharist was carried through the town and surrounding area. For a thorough look at the feast of Corpus Christi, see Miri Rubin *Corpus Christi: The Eucharist in Late Medieval Culture* (Cambridge and New York 1991).

1204 Erasmus speaks of processions held by guilds and confraternities; in many European cities processions of this kind can still be observed today. On confraternities in Italy at this time, see Christopher F. Black *Italian Confraternities in the Sixteenth Century* (Cambridge 1989; repr 2003); and especially his 'The development of confraternity studies over the last thirty years' in *Politics of Ritual Kingship: Confraternities and Social Order in Early Modern Italy* ed Nicholas Terpstra (Cambridge and New York 2000) 9–29; and Christopher F. Black 'Confraternities, Hospitals and Philanthropy' in his *Church, Religion and Society in Early Modern Italy* (Houndmills, Basingstoke, Hampshire; New York 2004) 130–48.

1205 For the kinds of violent games and sports Erasmus alludes to here, see his *In psalmum 38* CWE 65 103 and n420; and his letter to John Choler (Basel, August 1535), Ep 3032:417–31 where he speaks negatively of the bullfight he witnessed at the palace of Julius II: 'Huiusmodi spectaculum risimus in palatio Iulii Secundi, quo ad taurea ab amicis quibusdam eram pertractus: nam ipse nunquam cruentis illis ludis ac vetustate paganitatis reliquiis sum delectatus'; Martine Boiteux 'Chasse aux taureaux à Rome' in *Les jeux à la Renaissance: Actes du XXIIIe Colloque international d'études humanistes, Tours, juillet 1980* ed Philippe Ariès and Jean-Claude Margolin (Paris 1982) 33–53; and Charles L. Stinger *The Renaissance in Rome* (Bloomington and Indianapolis 1985) 57–8 and n160. In *Supputatio* LB IX 516C–517A Erasmus speaks of bullfights he saw just before Lent in Siena (*ex prisco ritu agebantur taurea, veteris Paganismi vestigia*). Widely known today is Siena's *palio*, whose origins go back to the Middle Ages; see *The Palio and Its Image: History, Culture and Representation of Siena's Festival* ed Maria A. Ceppari Ridolfi, Marco Ciampolini, Patrizia Turrini; texts

authority should recall the people from such follies should attend shows of this kind. The same opinion should be held about similar shows that occur on occasion, such as when a wealthy bride is wed or when princes put on their own productions at funerals[1206] or victory celebrations,[1207] to which the ignorant masses run with foolish enthusiasm. Only with difficulty did Christians remove the contests of boxers and gladiators;[1208] but when this ill cannot be uprooted utterly, the wise preacher will temper the licence, if he can, or at least not show the multitude his apparent approval by watching.

Furthermore, just as excessive familiarity breeds contempt,[1209] so a man's homeland sometimes diminishes his authority, as happened to the Lord Jesus, who learned himself by experience the validity of that proverbial expression that says that a prophet is less esteemed in his own land.[1210] There are two remedies against this human attitude: the preacher may do as the Lord did, leave his neighbours and relatives and betake himself elsewhere to teach the gospel,[1211] or he may withdraw to some far distant region especially celebrated for its reputation in religion and studies, and after a

* * * * *

by Raffaele Argenziano et al; with the collaboration of Sonia Corsi, Laura Vigni; photography by Andrea and Fabio Lensini; trans Anthony Brierley et al (Florence 2003). For sports of this kind in general, see also Julius R. Ruff *Violence in Early Modern Europe* (Cambridge 2001), especially chapter 5: 'Ritual group violence' 160–83, where the author takes up the violence 'inflicted on animals' (173) in games involving bulls, cocks, dogs, badgers, bears, geese, roosters, and cats.

1206 See Erasmus' description of a funeral cortege ('pompous funerals, which border on insanity') in *Paraphrasis in Marcum* CWE 49 72–3 (Mark 5:40).

1207 Erasmus himself witnessed Julius II's triumphal entry into Bologna on 11 November 1506 after the pope's victory over the Bentivogli; see ASD I-1 573 and Ep 205:42–3: 'Pope Julius is waging war, conquering, leading triumphal processions; in fact, playing Julius to the life.' See also *Julius exclusus* CWE 27 172, 174. For this aspect of Julius II and his pontificate (1503–13), see Christine Shaw *Julius II: The Warrior Pope* (Oxford and Cambridge, Mass 1993).

1208 See Ep 1400 to Francis I (preface to *Paraphrasis in Marcum*, Basel, 1 December 1523) where Erasmus discusses the suppression of gladiator contests by the emperor Honorius after hearing that the monk Telemachus had been stoned by the mob for trying to stop a gladiator match. See CWE 10 120–1. This story is from the *Tripartite History* of Socrates, Sozomen, and Theodoret, translated by Epiphanius and edited by Cassiodorus; see *The Ecclesiatical History of Theodoret* 5.26 NPNF 2nd series 3 151.

1209 This is a common saying (*nimia familiaritas parit contemptum*), one Erasmus does not include in his *Adagia*. See eg Walther and Schmidt 38823c (II 688).

1210 Luke 4:24: Matt 13:57; Mark 6:4; John 4:44

1211 Matt 4:13

long stay there return at last as a foreigner, excitedly and eagerly awaited now by many.

In addition, both ages, youth and quite advanced old age, also sometimes breed contempt; the former is scorned for its inexperience, the latter is despised as having no sense. A remedy will be found for both problems: let the youth obey the advice of the Apostle, 'Let no one despise your youth.'[1212] 'How will that happen?' you say. If he arranges his life, his speech, his expression, and all his gestures in accordance with sobriety, modesty, gravity, and constancy so as to reveal in himself the truth of what that famous wise man said, 'Venerable old age is not in length of days nor calculated by the number of years.'[1213] Age brings grey hair and a wrinkled brow even to the foolish and feeble-minded, but only the greyness that shines in a character free from all appearance of levity and youthful desires is venerable. Old men will protect their authority if they are always sober, if they are seldom difficult or irascible, and if they avoid useless chatter but are sparing and careful in their words so that they speak only after forethought either what is necessary or what is useful and allow nothing to slip out that is silly or too trivial to mention or altogether unworthy of their grey hairs, especially when in the company of young people; and let him not be harsh or grumpy in scolding when the situation requires rebuke but temper the bitterness of his admonition with Christian gentleness, and not involve himself in every kind of business (not all roles of a play suit every actor) but leave certain things to others. In sum, let him govern all his actions in such a way that old age seems to have brought him only greater experience, more perceptive judgment, more reliable counsel, a more forgiving mind. Thus it will happen that just as Paul bids widows who are truly widows to be honoured, so the people revere elders who are truly elders.[1214]

But to return to what we said about giving, we admit that it is quite fair for those who minister at the altar to live off the altar,[1215] but only to live, not to live in luxury; yet it would be highly desirable if more were to imitate the shining example of the apostle Paul, who preached the gospel without fee not because he did not know what was due but because he gave more consideration to what served the spreading of Christ's religion and the protection of apostolic authority, especially among the Corinthians, who

* * * * *

1212 1 Tim 4:12
1213 Wisd of Sol 4:8
1214 1 Tim 5:3
1215 Cf 1 Cor 9:13.

were both wealthy and eager for profit.[1216] If only people like the Corinthians were not everywhere these days, since you will find nobody like Paul! Someone might say that introducing this model would inevitably prove useless, because at present when people are required to bring their carnal offerings to the sower of spiritual seed, you see very few who pay what they owe in good faith; so what would happen if they learned through an unpaid preacher to give nothing? Once they had a taste of these guts[1217] they would never be pushed away, and so it would soon come to pass that, with salaries abolished and none being found who were willing to teach unpaid, the churches would be stripped entirely of pastors. But this reasoning in no way deterred Paul from boasting that he served as an unpaid evangelist,[1218] and he did not fear a lack of heralds of the word but was more afraid that the generosity of the people might invite wolves instead of shepherds;[1219] for all hasten towards profit, but only the truly devout can rise to unpaid labour. But if there were no lack of people to support apostles and elders of their own volition in those days when there was such a scarcity of Christians and no prescribed salaries that could be demanded, how is it that we are now afraid that good and faithful pastors will lack food and clothing? Those like the Corinthians will not give, but those like the Macedonians will give the more generously;[1220] there is no population that does not combine both kinds, and Paul's example, if exhibited once or twice, would perhaps inspire more to emulation. Why should we not hope for the same thing here that we see happening every day in other situations?

In antiquity someone, half covered by a robe, started to walk about with a staff and to live by begging and curse those in his way. Not only was there no lack of people to imitate this practice, but a school of philosophers arose from it called the Cynics.[1221] Likewise among the Christians there was someone who went about wearing an iron breastplate,[1222] though otherwise unclothed; far from there not being an imitator, a new order was added to

* * * * *

1216 Cf 1 Cor 4:8–13; 2 Corinthians 9.
1217 See *Adagia* II iv 22 *Periculosum est canem intestina gustasse* 'It is risky for a dog to taste guts.'
1218 2 Cor 11:7; 1 Cor 9:18
1219 Acts 20:29
1220 Cf 2 Cor 11:9.
1221 Erasmus refers to the philosopher Diogenes of Sinope (c 400–325 BC), called 'the dog' because of the thoroughly unconventional style of life he and his followers adopted. The word 'Cynic' derives from the Greek word 'dog' (ὁ κύων). See OCD 348; and Diogenes Laertius *Vitae philosophorum* (*Diogenes*) 6.20–81.
1222 See Rev 9:7–9: 'In appearance the locusts were like horses arrayed for battle ... they had scales like iron breastplates ...' Cf 1 Thess 5:8 and Eph 6:14.

the swarms of monks. There was another who walked about through summer and winter alike covered with a tunic of hemp but with the rest of his body bare, carrying a wooden cross and having no home to which to betake himself and touching no money and feeding only upon bread and greens or raw fruits and drinking only plain water;[1223] we see that there has been no lack of imitators. Who would have believed that there would be people to imitate the practice of St Francis? The world is everywhere full of them. Indeed, I think that if there were someone who covered his genitals with fig leaves instead of a loincloth but was otherwise nude, walked about in bronze sandals as Empedocles did,[1224] and fed upon beans instead of wheat, common grass, or hay instead of vegetables, there would be no lack of imitators. How much more must we hope that, if someone were to revive the example of so illustrious an apostle, there would be many to imitate it, especially since there is no need today for a preacher to wander through various regions of the world, and there is no one to strip priests of their patrimony or snatch away the resources gained by their industry.

But if it seems too ungracious to reject the voluntary generosity of good people, let the preacher adopt this compromise. Let him excuse himself politely to those who have people at home in greater need of such assistance or to those who do not seem to be giving sincerely but either for ostentation or for some other human reason, hoping perhaps that by tossing a morsel they can stop up the mouth of those who preach the truth of the gospel sincerely. Such was the kindness of Balaac, king of the Moabites,[1225] who hired Balaam to curse the people of Israel. Let him point out to the former those on whom they could better bestow what they have determined to put into the temple treasure;[1226] let him take away from the latter their hope of

* * * * *

1223 Erasmus is recalling stories of monks similar to those related by Theodoret of Cyrrus in his *Historia religiosa* (*A History of the Monks of Syria*) trans Richard M. Price (Kalamazoo 1985).

1224 Empedocles (c 492–32 BC), Greek philosopher who postulated that the entire universe consists of only four basic elements – earth, air, fire, and water; all existents are comprised of these in some combination, if not in their pure element. His bronze sandals are mentioned by Diogenes Laertius *Vitae philosophorum* (*Empedocles*) 11. See OCD 382.

1225 See Num 22:1–40.

1226 See Matt 27:6; Mark 7:11. The Latin *corbona* renders the word *corban* (*korban*, *qorban*) from the Hebrew, meaning 'a gift' to the temple treasury. See JBC II 36–7 (42F). Erasmus addresses this in his *Paraphrasis in Marcum* CWE 49 91, where he presents it as a perversion of the Mosaic law when the priests promoted giving to the temple treasury by allowing children to avoid caring for needy parents in dedicating their money to the temple treasury, which restricted it to exclusively sacred purposes.

corrupting a tongue that has been dedicated to preaching Christ. Let him accept, if he so decides, what has been offered willingly by others, but accept it in order to dispense it to others; let him not lose his own glory, in which he glories not according to the flesh but in the Lord.[1227]

I know that the Levites and priests and high priests of the Old Testament, who lived off tithes,[1228] victims,[1229] and gifts,[1230] will be cited in objection to us; but they were provided for in this way because they had no other lot in sharing the Promised Land.[1231] Yet the author of the New Law, who calls his people to the example of the sparrows and the lilies,[1232] removed rather than confirmed this provision. Without doubt it is characteristic of evangelical perfection to deserve more and demand less, and to refrain from the appearance of hawking the word of God such that you impart sacred teaching even to the rich without compensation in order to do it to greater profit and give assistance to the poor even from your own resources. In addition, the ministers of the Mosaic religion sustained not only themselves together with their assistants[1233] but also their wives and children and slaves and serving girls out of what Moses had granted them; now, however, being the less encumbered by such burdens, priests need that much less. The former nourished their descendants, who were to succeed to the ministry; in place of wives and children, let ours nourish – but nourish more with spiritual teaching than with money – those that they know will turn out suitable heralds of evangelical philosophy. Some make the following invalid syllogism: if those who sacrificed calves and goats lived off tithes, how much more is owed to those who handle more sacred things.[1234] I am not disputing now what is owed, but what it is seemly to demand: the loftier the evangelical office is, the purer it ought

* * * * *

1227 1 Cor 1:31; 2 Cor 10:17
1228 Num 18:21; Deut 18:1–5; Gen 14:20
1229 Exod 29:28–35
1230 Num 18:29–31
1231 That the Levites did not have a 'lot' in the Promised Land is contradicted by Num 35:2–8 where Moses assigns cities and their territories to the Levites; Joshua carries out Moses' directive (Joshua 21).
1232 Matt 6:26–9, 10:29–31
1233 Latin *diaconi*. The 'assistants' here must surely refer to the lower ranks of the Levites, 'the brothers of the tribe of Levi' (Num 18:2), since they received 'their portion of the tithe' according to Num 18:21–32.
1234 Erasmus calls this an 'invalid syllogism,' which it is; as Chomarat notes, it is a syllogism only so in the wide sense of 'argumentation'; it is properly a comparison *a maiore*.

to be from temporal profit. Besides, if they find the enthymeme[1235] from Levites to evangelists appealing, they will on the same basis reason as follows: they had wives, much more is the same permitted to us.[1236] Invert the enthymeme, and it will be valid: The priests of the Old Testament were not permitted to possess wealth,[1237] much less is it permitted to ours;[1238] they were not permitted to keep a concubine,[1239] much less is the same permitted to ours;[1240] they were not permitted to have relations with their wife, at least when they were serving the temple, much less is it permitted to ours.

Because they were given freely and gladly, the things that were once given to the heralds of the gospel were called εὐλογίαι, that is, 'blessings,'[1241] because the giver considered himself more blessed than the recipient. In some places now, since personal, predial, and windfall tithes[1242] are extorted with imprecations and threats from people who baulk and curse, they are more truly κακολογίαι [curses] than εὐλογίαι. While that is hateful in itself, the resentment is doubled if those who so scrupulously[1243] demand what they think is owed them are utterly forgetful of their own duty, but we see it happen that none demand more insistently than those to whom the least

* * * * *

1235 Quintilian 5.10.1–3 gives a few definitions of enthymeme: 'a proposition with a reason ... a conclusion of an argument drawn either from denial of consequents or from incompatibles ... a rhetorical syllogism ... an incomplete syllogism ...' Erasmus deals at length with this form of rhetorical argumentation for preaching; see book 2 CWE 68 passim.

1236 Though not making this argument, St Paul does argue that he has the right to take a Christian wife with him as do Cephas and the other apostles (1 Cor 9:5).

1237 Deut 18:1–2

1238 Matt 19:21; Mark 10:21; Luke 18:22; cf Matt 5:3, 19:23–4; Luke 6:20.

1239 Lev 21:7

1240 1 Cor 6:12–20

1241 The word εὐλογίαι means 'praise,' 'speaking well,' 'the act of blessing.' Erasmus means here the idea of 'a bountiful gift,' 'bounty' (2 Cor 9:5; cf Heb 6:7) bestowed upon the evangelists by the community.

1242 'Tithes' had their foundation in the Old Testament; see Gen 14:20; Lev 27:30–1; Num 18:24, 28 and 28:21; Deut 12:6, 11 and 14:22. The Christian church understood the giving of tithes as a divine obligation. The three types of tithes noted by Erasmus concern the tithe on the annual crops (predial); on what has been nourished by the land such as sheep and cattle (mixed); and the work of one's hands (personal). The 'windfall' tithes may refer to the produce of the land or revenue of inherited property, which would be subject to tithing; see 'tithes' ODCC 1626; 'tithes' NCE 14 90–2; 'Tithes' DMA 12 62–5.

1243 For 'scrupulously,' see Adagia I v 91 Ad unguem 'To the fingernail.'

is owed; for 'to presbyters a twofold honour'[1244] is due, as the Apostle says, but he adds, 'to those who rule well.' Suppose a layperson offers as excuse his poverty, the need to support his wife and children; he is not heeded. Suppose someone offers as excuse a shipwreck or fire or similar catastrophe; he is not heeded but is told, 'God wants to lose nothing.' We have not read of anything similar happening even among the Jews. I am not acting now as an advocate for ingrates but looking out for the preacher's authority.

In later centuries certain bishops used to accept what was offered but with the intention of dispensing for the support of the needy what remained from their temperate lifestyle. But St Cyprian bids the poor be supported from his own money;[1245] St Basil fed the poor from his own resources.[1246] Augustine, who allowed nothing to be forced upon him that could not pass into common use,[1247] departed very little from the Apostle's freedom; in what words then does he beg from the people? 'Brothers, I have nothing to give the poor; let your charity help them.'[1248] He refused some things offered by those who seemed to have people at home needing help; to someone who had repented his generosity he gave back some things that had already been given and signed over to the church's authority, though not unaware that what has once been dedicated to God should not be demanded back, but the lofty-minded man preferred to reduce the authority of the church rather than appear acquisitive or a greedy seagull.[1249]

The situation is much less squalid in some lands where the pastor demands nothing from the congregation but has a salary set for him from elsewhere, enough to suffice for a frugal and temperate man. He has a comfortable house, a small garden that provides various delights for his table, a little vineyard that bears enough wine for someone who drinks it well diluted and sparingly, and he has a coop that supplies an egg and sometimes even a chicken; if twelve ducats[1250] are added to this, there is already

* * * * *

1244 1 Tim 5:17
1245 Cf Cyprian *On Works and Alms* ANF V 476–84 passim.
1246 See Gregory of Nazianzus *Oration* 43.35 (Funeral Oration on the Great St Basil) NPNF 2nd series 7 407.
1247 The Rule of Augustine is from his *Letter* 211. See WSA II-4 19–28. For this letter see especially George Lawless *Augustine of Hippo and His Monastic Rule* (Oxford 1987).
1248 This exact phrase (*fratres non habeo quod dem pauperibus, subveniat illis charitas vestra*) does not appear in Augustine; Erasmus might be recalling this from memory.
1249 For 'sea-gull' (*larus*), see *Adagia* II ii 33 *Larus* 'Seamew.'
1250 The ducat was a coin issued under the Holy Roman emperors representing the

something left over beyond his simple life to relieve the poverty of a few. But to what depths of squalor some have now sunk! Begging takes place during the very act of worship, and the sacristan, jingling a tin plate and calling loudly again and again, invites – not to say compels – the congregation to give; the priest all the while stands by disgracefully observing who gives, who does not. Some do the same during sermons; a collection plate is passed around and a subsidy sought – demanded, rather – for the preacher. I am not objecting to these practices if need should require, but I am showing how far they are from that apostolic pride that I should like to see imitated by as many as possible. One pious and unlettered man was discovered to have written, 'Let them go confidently for charity, nor should they be ashamed, since the Lord made himself poor for us in this world,'[1251] and behold, we see the world full of those who willingly profess begging.[1252] But that illustrious evangelist, who says, 'I want all to be as I am,'[1253] boasts so often that he obtained his own livelihood with his own hands[1254] in order to teach the gospel without charge, that he worked night and day so as to burden no one[1255] – he has found hardly a single imitator.

As excuse many offer necessity, a hard weapon[1256] indeed, but the source of that necessity must be considered. The actual pastor[1257] delegates

* * * * *

value of a little more than three and a half grams of gold; see CWE 1 314, 332–47, especially 336–7, 'Money and coinage of the age of Erasmus,' for the table of monies in Erasmus' times. The Habsburgs minted many ducats throughout Erasmus' lifetime; see also Arthur L. Friedberg and Ira S. Friedberg *Gold Coins of the World: From Ancient Times to the Present* 7th ed (Clifton, NJ 2001) 92–7.

1251 Erasmus refers here to St Francis of Assisi. See *Francis of Assisi* I, *The Later Rule* (1223), chapter VI 103: 'Let the brothers not make anything their own, neither house, nor place, nor anything at all. As pilgrims and strangers in this world, serving the Lord in poverty and humility, let them go seeking alms with confidence, and they should not be ashamed because, for our sakes, our Lord made Himself poor in this world.'

1252 Erasmus refers here to the number of religious belonging to the mendicant orders, ie Dominicans, Franciscans, Carmelites, Servites, and Augustinians; cf ODCC 'Mendicant Friars' 1070.

1253 Erasmus refers here to St Paul; see 1 Cor 7:7.

1254 See 1 Cor 4:12; Acts 20:34.

1255 1 Thess 2:5–10; 1 Cor 9:16–19

1256 See *Adagia* II iii 40 *Ingens telum necessitas* 'Necessity's a mighty weapon.'

1257 For 'actual pastor' (*verus pastor*), cf John 10:11–16. If translated literally as 'true pastor,' Erasmus surely means this ironically. Such individuals, as Erasmus notes elsewhere, delegate their offices to others but keep the tithes for themselves.

his roles to another, doling out a little something from the tithes; he in turn hires it out to another, leaving him nothing but the gleanings after the harvest[1258] is already over. The same complaint is made about some monasteries and about colleges[1259] that have curacies incorporated (for that is the language these people use): the money, that is, the wool, they keep for themselves, the sheep they hand over to a hungry man, often an ignorant and shameless fellow, who will skin them.[1260] And are we surprised that a pastor lacks the authority that he should have with the people? The role of bishops or princes here should be to force those who receive compensation to perform their duty. So much concerning authority.

What is it pertinent to say about gaining good will?[1261] Nothing wins true love more effectively than serving everyone cheerfully and without compensation; even ferocious animals are tamed by kindness and enticed to friendship. Imagine now for me such a preacher as we are seeking, the sort who makes himself completely available for helping everyone, keeping watch for the salvation of each with more than fatherly or motherly concern, teaching the ignorant, gently calling back those who stray, cheering the sick, consoling the bereaved, aiding the afflicted, assisting the oppressed; who entrusts the newborn to Christ, attends the dying, buries the dead, comforts the needy, prays and makes offering for the salvation of all; who, in sum, leaves no one untouched by his kindness and does this both constantly and gladly, asking no reward at all from anyone in return for these services, not money, not

* * * * *

1258 Cf Lev 19:9–10. Erasmus' allusion to the divine command to provide for the poor is obviously to be taken ironically.

1259 Latin *collegia*; Erasmus refers to the colleges at a university, such as the Collège du Montaigu at Paris, Balliol at Oxford, Queens' College at Cambridge, where stipends were paid to their curates, ie priests with the care of souls (*cura animarum*). Chomarat notes that the chapel of the college is also a parish church; ASD V-4 235 925n.

1260 See *Adagia* III vii 12 *Boni pastoris est, tondere pecus, non deglubere* 'The good shepherd shears the sheep; he doesn't skin them.'

1261 Erasmus refers to the importance rhetoricians place upon garnering 'good will'; this comes from *ethos*, whereby '[the calm and gentle passions] persuade and induce a feeling of goodwill'; see Quintilian 6.2.8–19, especially where he discusses the difference between *pathos* and *ethos* and what it is in the orator and in his speaking that generates good will in his listeners; he observes that 'the chief merit in its [ethos'] expression lies in making it seem that all that we say derives directly from the nature of the facts and persons concerned and in the revelation of the character of the orator in such a way that all may recognise it.' See Lausberg §§257.2a.

subservience, not glory. Who, I ask, is so hardened that he would not both love and revere a man like this as some deity come down from heaven? Such charity compels even the wicked to a mutual love; but if there are some who could bear to hate such a man obstinately, what would they gain except to be judged by everyone more bestial than any beast? These are much the most effective charms, the most potent philtres for winning – and not just winning but even wresting – good will from men.

The others are more trivial but have no little force when added to these. For the heroic virtues[1262] do not reject the services of whatever human endowments have been instilled by nature or training and effort, rather they courteously embrace, purify, and perfect them;[1263] yet it happens sometimes that men endowed with those outstanding virtues seem careless about these lesser matters, just as nothing is entirely happy in the affairs of mortals.[1264]

Socrates, a man highly praised among the heathen,[1265] occasioned no little hatred for himself by a familiar irony in all his conversation, which in him, however, was not a flaw but nature;[1266] Plato was accused of arrogance, though in him this was not τύφος [arrogance] but σεμνότης [solemnity], for what I mean is better said in Greek.[1267] Diogenes' sharp and witty outspokenness was mocked by many;[1268] Xenocrates' austerity troubled some;[1269] Stilpo's affability, which took everything in a good way, even

* * * * *

1262 Erasmus' understanding of the 'heroic virtues' and his brief sketch of the self-less preacher anticipate the marks of 'heroic sanctity' characteristic of Counter-Reformation saints in the decades to come; see Romeo DeMaio 'L'ideale eroico nei processi di canonizzazione della Controriforma' in *Riforme e miti nella Chiesa del Cinquecento* (Naples 1973) 257–78; and DS 7 337–43 'Héroïcité des vertues.'

1263 See Thomas Aquinas *Summae theologiae* I IIae q 61 a 4.

1264 See *Adagia* III i 87 *Nihil est ab omni parte beatum* 'Naught is at all points blest'; and Horace *Odes* 2.16.27–8.

1265 See nn131 and 645 above. Erasmus refers here to Socrates' inner 'daemon,' which prompted him to search for the truth; see Plato *Apology* 31C–D, 40A; cf *Symposium* 202D–203A.

1266 Cicero frequently refers to Socrates' irony, sometimes calling him an εἴρων 'dissembler'; see *De officiis* 1.30.108; *Brutus* 85.292, 87.299; *Academica* II (*Lucullus*) 2.5.15.

1267 Ie solemnity, dignity, or seriousness rather than arrogance. See LSJ 1591 σεμνότης.

1268 See Diogenes Laertius *Vitae philosophorum* (*Diogenes*) 6.2 passim; and Lucian *Vitarum auctio* 8–11.

1269 Diogenes Laertius *Vitae philosophorum* (*Xenocrates*) 4.2.6–15

what tends to give great offence to the mass of men, seemed hardly worthy of a philosopher.[1270] In Scipio Africanus there was a natural majesty;[1271] in Lucius Crassus the orator possessed a modesty that added grace to his speech rather than obscuring his talents;[1272] Cicero lost some authority from his fondness for jesting;[1273] the elder Cato's censorial severity towards everyone won him considerable resentment,[1274] and the famous Cato of Utica seemed unfairly harsh.[1275] You could also find similar differences of character among the men made famous by the commendation of religion. Ambrose is everywhere easy-going and pleasant rather than powerful,[1276] Augustine charming and firm, Jerome powerful, frank, sometimes rather austere too. Chrysostom was rebuked by his rivals because he liked to take food alone.[1277] This characteristic sobriety of his was criticized as inhospitality; his diction shows that he was a man nicely suited to teaching. In Basil you could sense an outstanding loftiness of soul tempered by a thoughtful affability; Gregory of Nazianzus is rather shrewd; Athanasius had an admirable ability in getting things done; in Cyprian you would marvel at his natural speaking ability. Why should I say more? There is no less variety in men's talents than in their face and voice.

It is not always safe to change into a different character the way that Demea[1278] in the comedies suddenly becomes quite unlike himself, but one must try to correct towards virtue what nature has sown deep within us, if it is associated with vice.[1279] If the natural condition is simple, one must beware of it degenerating into a kindred vice, that, say, a natural gravity does not turn into harshness, cruelty, and meanness, or a placid temperament

* * * * *

1270 Plutarch *Moralia* 5F (*De liberis educandis*); *Demetrius* 893
1271 See eg Livy 26.18–19; cf Cicero *Brutus* 87.299.
1272 Cicero *De oratore* 1.26.122
1273 Quintilian 6.3.2–3
1274 Plutarch *Cato Censor* 18–19
1275 Plutarch *Cato of Uticensis* 1
1276 See Erasmus' preface to *Ambrosii Opera*, Ep 1855:257–63. See especially Paulinus of Milan *Vita sancti Ambrosii*.
1277 See *Sozomen* 8.9 404–5. See J.N.D. Kelly *Golden Mouth: The Story of John Chrysostom, Ascetic, Preacher, Bishop* (Ithaca 1995) 126–7.
1278 Demea is the country-dwelling father in Terence's *Adelphi* who allowed one of his two sons to be raised by his brother Micio, an Athenian city dweller. Demea's method of education was severe, Micio's gentle and indulging. Chomarat observes that the Demea and Micio brothers represent two opposing models of education: force and severity, sweetness and indulgence; ASD V-4 238 and 976–7n.
1279 Erasmus provides an extensive treatment of vices and virtues in book 4.

turn into carelessness and contempt, or flattery into fawning. Moreover, there must be no pretence in correcting these things. What is feigned cannot endure, and the sorts of thing that you try against Minerva's will[1280] generally turn out unsuccessfully; if we do not struggle against her, it is still possible for different personalities to win equal authority and favour. Let the man who is naturally obliging and merry avoid the appearance of flattery and frivolity; let the man who is too talkative try to speak only when the need arises; let one who is too quiet and gloomy temper his native austerity with affability for the real benefit of his neighbours; let charity and zeal for piety stimulate one who is too easy-going. Nature's faults are easily corrected if the habit is not of too long standing. Yet it is profitable to be open to advice in these matters, for we see others' business more clearly than our own.

Now, both age and homeland cause no small difference in character. Adolescence abandons itself to pleasures and wantonness if it is not restrained; youth is impetuous and unthinking; old age is generally gloomier, more irritable, more careful, and slower to forgive. Out of each we should take what utility it contains, correct what tends to vice. Let the playfulness of our tender years be tamed by liberal studies; let the ardour of youth be tempered by the precepts of philosophy; let the weakness of age be propped up by reason, counsel, and carefulness. Likewise, the German will strive to be strong while avoiding cruelty and will not be easily pushed into impiety. Let the Spaniard thirst for the glory of Christ; let the Italian show in other things too the temperance that he displays in food and drink; let the Frenchman direct his natural facility to the service of God; let the Guelderlander turn his natural shrewdness into evangelical wisdom; let the Hollander season his natural simplicity with evangelical wisdom. Lest I make myself a bore by multiplying examples, let each one make a similar evaluation about others for himself in his own mind.

Therefore, by knowing and noticing these differences of character, age, and region, let each prescribe rules for himself by which both to correct what tends to vice and to promote what displays the quality of virtue. These things, I admit, are rather trivial and related to human weakness, but they are still not to be neglected if they serve those sublime endowments of the Holy Spirit, in so far as we are engaged men with men, the weak with the weak. May the Lord be pleased to inspire qualities more effective than these

* * * * *

1280 *Adagia* I i 42 *Invita Minerva* 'Against Minerva's will'; see CWE 31 91 n42. The following sentence then must mean: if we do not try to alter our character, we may still win favour and influence.

in the minds of his shepherds so that they may all despise the cheap rewards of this world and apply themselves wholeheartedly to this most beautiful campaign of all, to receive after a short time – for what is more fleeting than this life? – the eternal crown of blessed immortality. And if any labour is to be expended here (for nothing important is accomplished without effort), let them consider how great a solace it will be to hear the beatific words, 'Well done, good and faithful servant; enter into the joy of your Lord; come, valiant leader, and celebrate a heavenly triumph, take your share of joy since you did not refuse to share afflictions for my sake.'[1281] What a celebration there will be, what applause, what a glad acclamation when you see many there who will attribute to you the receipt of their happiness, of their salvation, whom you led to godliness, whom you recalled from error, whom you inflamed with a love for the blessings of heaven. Indeed, since perfect charity makes everything there common to all, what will be more fortunate, more splendid, or more glorious than you when the countless myriads of heavenly orders will congratulate you on every side with one mouth, with harmonious voice, and will give thanks to Christ the prince, who deigned to increase through you that blessed company that for perfect beatitude needs only to have the number of the elect filled up, and happiness will be full and absolute in every respect after the resurrection of bodies!

But the consideration of what I mentioned above ought rightly to stimulate not only teachers to teaching but also their audiences to zeal for learning and readiness in obedience, for how alertly and vigorously someone teaches depends in no small part upon his pupils. How few could you find whose temper is so patient that they could long retain zeal, eagerness, and passion in teaching if they saw that out of so many so few come to the sermon, then that among these few there are so few on whom their effort is not wasted, as some, heavy with drink, though hearing do not hear, others show boredom in their whole face and whole body, nodding, spitting, belching, coughing, others listen to the preacher with the same expression as they do an actor performing in the theatre, many sleep, and some even snore loudly because they come to the sermon with distended belly, coming only to while away the day and shake off the tedium of the house, are deaf to the rest, and wait only for something witty or amusing to occur that they can recite over dinner to their fellow drinkers. And yet still worse than these are the ones who do not come to learn but to catch something to find fault with and do not mask this intention but betray it by laughs and grins,

* * * * *

1281 See Matt 25:21–3 (parable of the talents); 2 Cor 2:14.

sometimes even whistling and grumbling. I pass over now the wailing children, the barking dogs, the disruptive gossips. And are we surprised if we have preachers who are less than conscientious? Or do we forget that they are human too? Actors of comedies complain about the spectators and beg them by their attentive silence to assist them to act correctly; otherwise the acting is uninspired. Is what an actor rightly demands denied to heralds of the word of salvation? You attend the theatre to see trifles, and you listen; but at the sermon you sleep, though you would hear something to make you both better to yourself and dearer to God. If the preacher starts up a tale about the wool of a goat or about the shadow of an ass[1282] (for some deliberately mix in such things), you wake up, rub the sleep from your eyes, prick up your ears, summon your attention; and do you have no ears for what contributes to true and eternal happiness? A preacher would rightly be dispirited if he saw that the congregation listened attentively indeed to what was being taught but that no fruit of his teaching appeared in their character; how much more justly would he feel dispirited if he saw that the scorn of the crowd was so great that they could not even endure the words of the teaching that brings salvation? They listen eagerly to the entertainer in the marketplace chattering ridiculous, sometimes even obscene, trifles; and do they not extend the same hearing to the teacher of heavenly philosophy? We support the actor so that he will not have learned his part in vain, should he be hissed off the stage; how much more justly should we support the preacher, who has spent his life preparing with the utmost effort and labour to improve the people. As well, even if the actor is hooted off, that occasions no loss to the spectators; on the other hand, if the preacher tells his story to deaf ears,[1283] all the loss falls on the people, but he himself will be held excused in the eyes of God since he carried out his delegated task in accordance with his ability. But what sort of loss? Not of flocks or of money, not of health or of physical sensation, but the most destructive of all: ignorance of the truth, mental blindness, impiety, the deadly afflictions of the soul. If someone were to scatter presents into the crowd, such as coins or biscuits, how eager, how large a throng would gather from

* * * * *

1282 See *Adagia* I iii 53 *De lana caprina* 'About goat's wool.' The adage is applied to inconsequential disputes and to bad-tempered persons ready to argue with friends 'on the slightest pretext.' See also *Adagia* I iii 52 *De asini umbra* 'About an ass's shadow.' The adage, like the previous one, refers to a matter of no moment.

1283 See *Adagia* I iv 87 *Surdo canis, surdo fabulam narras* 'You are singing, or telling a story to the deaf.'

everywhere; but how much more precious are the things that the preacher takes from the treasure house of heavenly philosophy and scatters from the pulpit. The riches that are scattered are those of the wisdom that, by the witness of Solomon, is more precious than all riches;[1284] the gems of ecclesiastical virtues are scattered to enrich and adorn your mind forever, and you do not come running, do not snatch what is thrown, especially when the condition for the gatherers is better here than there. There what another has grabbed before you cannot be yours; here each one, if he so desires, can have in its entirety the gift that is thrown out in common. Another's gain does not become your loss, but each one's gain becomes everyone's joy. We see that people come running in great numbers with extraordinary eagerness if some peddler sets up a table and promises skill in removing stains set in garments or remedies for toothaches, inflammation of the eyes, and quartan fever; and we are reluctant to listen to someone who shows how to wash out stains from the mind, to drive away greed, immodesty, insane love, hatred, and envy, threatening afflictions of the mind. St Paul inveighs against those who dined in an unbecoming manner in the assembly of Christians, scorning the church of God, and asks them whether they do not have homes where they may eat as they choose and drink even to intoxication if they like.[1285] I think that he would inveigh still more sternly if he saw our sermons and would exclaim, 'Why do you thus scorn the church of God?' If it pleases you to belch out your hangover, to sleep off your drunkenness, a private home and bedroom are more suited for that than a church. If you have decided to relax, there are ball courts where that can be done without insulting the church; if it pleases you to trifle, there are barbershops, markets, and porticoes where those things are done, I shall not say becomingly (for what is foolish is nowhere becoming), but at least less disgracefully. When invited to dinner you prepare yourself according to the rank of your host, you ready your appetite so as not to appear a fussy guest, and you encourage your host with much civility since he has expended money and effort to provide you with an elegant dinner; and do you sadden with your indifference and your nausea the one who feeds your mind with heavenly bread, who passes you wine that gladdens the heart? What is the source of this perverse estimation of things in us? At least we should have proceeded from lowest to loftier. A courier comes to a town saying that he has been sent, I shall not say now from the emperor, but from some governor; he receives a respectful hearing, not because of his own merits but

* * * * *

1284 Prov 3:15
1285 1 Cor 11:22

because of the authority of the one who sends him: and is the preacher, the representative of God, despised, thus causing an affront to the one who sends him? Do not judge according to appearance.[1286] The person who is speaking is a man like you; but God is speaking to you through his mouth, and he is speaking God's words, not his own. The person who is teaching about Christ therefore deserves to have you hear him as Christ. You heed a man sent by a man reciting edicts that burden you and reduce your possessions; and do you not heed someone who expounds the commands of God that make you blessed? If it is right to venerate in an ambassador the person of whoever sends him, nothing is more exalted than God; if it is right to receive with applause and favour what is said to our benefit, nothing is more excellent than the salvation of souls, nothing more gracious than the gospel. You listen carefully to someone who professes how a field, the nourisher of your body, should be cultivated, and do you not heed someone who teaches how the mind, which bears the fruit of eternal happiness, should be cultivated? In order to recover from a disease of the body you offer attentive ears to a physician, who will demand a reward for his bitter remedies; and are you loath to hear someone who at no cost treats diseases of the soul with agreeable words? Moreover, who of us does not have his soul torn by many wounds or does not suffer under many deadly diseases? Or, if he is not suffering, it is at least a risk shared by us all. It is best to learn from a physician how a disease is to be avoided before you catch it; whatever sins mankind has ever committed can befall you. And so if the laity consider how great is the dignity of the preacher, how laborious and how dangerous a task he performs, whose place he is taking, the business he is conducting, the great benefits he brings, how sublime his teachings, how magnificent his promises, they will of course venerate him more reverently and listen to him more carefully and obey him more willingly. If any human weakness in him gives offence, he must not at once be scorned insolently but rather supported humanely. How, you will say, is he to be supported? If you listen cheerfully to his teaching, listen patiently to his criticism, if you retain what he has taught, if you correct what he has rebuked, if under his teaching you turn out every day better than yourself. By these goads, as it were, he will be stimulated to become more vigilant in his study of Holy Writ, more ardent in his teaching, more frank in his admonition. In fact, he should be supported by everyone's prayers. God must be implored to bestow better things every day upon his flock through

* * * * *

1286 John 7:24; 2 Cor 10:7

his ambassador. When the people pray for this, they pray on their own behalf, and because they ask in the name of Jesus, God will not show himself deaf to such prayers.[1287] The preacher in turn prays that the spirit of
Christ may render everyone's mind susceptible to teaching and prepare the
ground so that the good seed cast may produce a successful crop.[1288] The
Lord exclaims through Jeremiah, 'Break up your fallow ground, men of Judah and of Jerusalem, and do not sow upon thorns; circumcise yourselves
to the Lord and remove the foreskin of your hearts.'[1289] The men of Judah
are all those who confess and acknowledge their own unrighteousness; the
men of Jerusalem are all those who persevere in the Catholic church, pursue the side of peace towards God and towards their neighbour alike, for
only these can be taught the evangelical philosophy. Someone who does not
acknowledge his own disease cannot be treated by the physician's art, and
'if someone is contentious, we have no such a custom,'[1290] says the Apostle.
New teaching loves new fields, sober loves sober minds, pure loves pure
minds. Cut out the thorns of earthly cares, uproot the useless stalks of evil
desires, tear out the burrs, thistles, briars, and whatever harmful emotions
have taken hold of your mind; thus will you prepare a good field for good
seed: 'Circumcise the foreskin of your heart, cutting away pleasures, luxury, and delights.'[1291] The Holy Spirit urges likewise through Hosea, saying,
'Sow for yourselves in righteousness and harvest in mercy; break up your
fallow field. It is time moreover to seek the Lord, who will teach you righteousness when he comes.'[1292] He who thirsts for righteousness[1293] sows in
righteousness; he who achieves what he thirsts for, not by his own strength
but by the Lord's kindness, harvests in mercy; he who prepares his heart
for the teaching of the gospel breaks up his fallow field for himself. For
this is the new wine that the Lord does not want to be put into old wineskins;[1294] this is the new patch that fits badly on the old robe.[1295] I think that
I have given each side admonition enough; but if each performs its duty –
the preacher by dispensing the treasures of his Lord in good faith, carefully,

* * * * *

1287 John 14:13, 15:16, 16:23 and 26
1288 Matt 13:27, 37, 38
1289 Jer 4:3–4
1290 1 Cor 11:16. See *Annotationes in 1 ad Corinthios* (11.16) ASD VI-8 224:221–4; see
     also JBC II 270 (51:69).
1291 Deut 10:16; Jer 4:4
1292 Hos 10:12
1293 Cf Matt 5:6.
1294 Matt 9:17; Mark 2:22; Luke 5:37–8
1295 Matt 9:16; Mark 2:21; Luke 5:36

eagerly, lovingly, unbendingly, the congregation by receiving the gifts with devout and eager minds – there is no doubt that that heavenly farmer will give a rich and abundant increase.

And so we have included in this volume what seemed to need saying about the dignity, the difficulty, the purity, the courage, the usefulness, and the reward of the faithful preacher; since it has grown large enough, we shall reserve the rest for the next book.

WORKS FREQUENTLY CITED

SHORT-TITLE FORMS
FOR ERASMUS' WORKS

WORKS FREQUENTLY CITED

This list provides bibliographical information for the publications referred to in short-title form in introductions and notes. For Erasmus' writings see the short-title list following.

ACW
Ancient Christian Writers: The Works of the Fathers in Translation ed Johannes Quaesten and Walter J. Burghardt (New York 1946–)

Alan of Lille
Alan of Lille *The Art of Preaching* [*Summa de arte praedicatoria*] trans Gillian R. Evans, Cistercian Studies Series 23 (Kalamazoo 1981)

Allen
Opus epistolarum Des. Erasmi Roterodami ed P.S Allen, H.M. Allen, and H.W. Garrod (Oxford 1906–58) 11 vols and index vol by B. Flower and E. Rosenbaum (Oxford 1958).

Anal. hymenica
Analecta hymenica medii aevi ed Guido Maria Dreves and Clemens Blume (Leipzig 1886–1922; repr New York 1961)

ANF
The Ante-Nicene Fathers ed Alexander Roberts and James Donaldson (Buffalo 1886–96; Peabody, Mass repr 1994) 10 vols

ASD
Opera omnia Desiderii Erasmi Roterodami (Amsterdam 1969–)

Augustine
Saint Augustine *On Christian Doctrine* trans D.W. Robertson (New York 1958)

Augustine
Augustine through the Ages: An Encyclopedia ed Allan D. Fitzgerald (Grand Rapids, Mich 1999)

Augustijn *Erasmus*
Cornelis Augustijn *Erasmus: His Life, Works, and Influence* trans J.C. Grayson (Toronto 1991)

Augustijn 'Reformation'
'Erasmus und die Reformation in der Schweiz' *Basler Zeitschrift für Geschichte und Altertumskunde* 86 (1986) 27–42

AV
The Holy Bible ... Authorized King James Version (London 1611; repr 1969)

Béné *Érasme*
Charles Béné *Érasme et saint Augustin ou influence de saint Augustin sur l'humanisme d'Érasme* (Geneva 1969)

Bentley *Humanists*
Jerry H. Bentley *Humanists and Holy Writ: New Testament Scholarship in the Renaissance* (Princeton 1983)

Biblical Humanism	*Biblical Humanism and Scholasticism in the Age of Erasmus* ed Erika Rummel (Leiden 2008)
Bibliotheca sanctorum	*Bibliotheca sanctorum* (Rome 1961–70)
Black	Robert Black *Humanism and Education in Medieval and Renaissance Italy: Tradition and Innovation in Latin Schools from the Twelfth to the Fifteenth Century* (Cambridge c 2001)
Bowersock *Late Antiquity*	*Late Antiquity: A Guide to the Postclassical World* ed G.W. Bowersock, Peter Brown, and Oleg Grabar (Cambridge, Mass 1999)
Caplan	Harry Caplan 'Classical Rhetoric and the Mediaeval Theory of Preaching' *Classical Philology* 28 (1933) 73–96
CCSL	*Corpus christianorum, series Latina* (Turnhout 1954–)
CCCM	*Corpus christianorum, continuatio mediaevalis* (Turnhout 1966–)
CEBR	*Contemporaries of Erasmus: A Biographical Register of the Renaissance and Reformation* ed Peter G. Bietenholz and Thomas B. Deutscher (Toronto 1985–7) 3 vols
CHB	*Cambridge History of the Bible:* I *From the Beginnings to Jerome* ed P.R. Ackroyd and C.F. Evans (Cambridge 1970); II *The West from the Fathers to the Reformation* ed G.W.H. Lampe (Cambridge 1969); III *The West from the Reformation to the Present Day* ed S.L. Greenslade (Cambridge 1963)
Chantraine	Georges Chantraine *'Mystère' et 'philosophie du Christ' selon Érasme: étude de la lettre à P. Volz et de la 'Ratio verae theologiae' (1518)* (Namur 1971)
Chomarat 'Grammar and Rhetoric'	Jacques Chomarat 'Grammar and Rhetoric in the Paraphrases of the Gospels by Erasmus' ERSY 1 (1981) 30–69
Chomarat *Grammaire*	Jacques Chomarat *Grammaire et rhétorique chez Erasme* (Paris 1981) 2 vols
Chomarat 'Introduction'	Jacques Chomarat 'Introduction' in ASD V-4 (Amsterdam 1991) 3–28
CIC	*Codex iuris canonici*
Classical Tradition	*The Classical Tradition* ed Anthony Grafton, Glenn W. Most, and Salvatore Settis (Cambridge, Mass 2010)

Clavasio   Angelus de Clavasio *Summa angelica* (Lyon: J. de Cambray
                            1523)

CLCLT   Library of Latin texts (online) [CLCLT = CETEDOC] (Turnhout
                            2005–   )

Colloquia Erasmiana   *Colloquia Erasmiana Turonensia: douzième stage international
                            d'études humanistes, Tours 1969* ed Jean Claude Margolin
                            (Toronto 1972–   ) 2 vols

Concilium Tridentinum   *Concilium Tridentinum: diariorum, actorum, epistularum,
                            tractatuum nova collectio* ed Societas Goerresiana (Freiburg
                            im Breisgau 1901–2001) 13 vols

CPG   *Clavis patrum Graecorum* ed Maurice Geerard (Turnhout
                            1974–87) 5 vols

CPL   *Clavis patrum Latinorum* ed Eligius Dekkers (Steenbrugis
                            1995)

Crichton   J.D. Crichton *The Ministry of Reconciliation* (London and
                            Dublin 1974)

CSEL   *Corpus scriptorum ecclesiasticorum Latinorum* (Vienna
                            1866–   )

CWE   *Collected Works of Erasmus* (Toronto 1974–   )

de Lubac *Medieval*   Henri de Lubac *Medieval Exegesis* I: *The Four Senses of
   Exegesis*   Scripture* trans Mark Sebanc (Grand Rapids, Mich and
                            Edinburgh 1998); and idem II trans E. M. Macierowski
                            (Grand Rapids, Mich and Edinburgh 2000)

Denzinger   *Enchiridion symbolorum, definitionum et declarationum de rebus
                            fidei et morum* ed H.D. Denzinger and A. Schönmetzer 33rd
                            ed (Barcelona 1965)

DMA   *Dictionary of the Middle Ages* ed Joseph R. Strayer (New York
                            c 1982–c 1989) 13 vols, 1 Supplement

DS   *Dictionnaire de spiritualité ascétique et mystique: doctrine et
                            histoire* ed Marcel Viller, F. Cavallera, J. de Guibert (Paris
                            1937–95) 17 vols

DV   Douay-Rheims Version (Bible)

ER   *Encyclopedia of the Renaissance* ed Paul F. Grendler (New
                            York 1999) 6 vols

ERSY	*Erasmus of Rotterdam Society Yearbook*
Escobar	Andreas de Escobar *Modus confitendi* (n p c 1520) British Library C 32 a 39 [8]
Exomologesis 1524	Erasmus of Rotterdam *Exomologesis sive Modus confitendi, per Erasmum Roterodamum, opus nunc primum & natum & excusum cum aliis lectu dignis, quorum catalogum reperies in proxima pagella* (Basel: Ioannes Froben 1524)
Exomologesis 1530	Erasmus of Rotterdam *Exomologesis, per Des. Erasmum Roterodamum recognita diligenter & aucta* ... (Basel: Froben 1530)
FOC	*The Fathers of the Church* (Washington, DC 1947–) 127 vols
Francis of Assisi	*Francis of Assisi: Early Documents* I ed Regis J. Armstrong et al (New York 1999)
Fumaroli	Marc Fumaroli *L'Age de l'éloquence: rhétorique et 'res literaria' de la Renaissance au seuil de l'époque classique* 3rd ed (Geneva 2002)
Gabbay	*Handbook of the History of Logic* II: *Mediaeval and Renaissance Logic* ed Dov M. Gabbay and John Woods 1st ed (Amsterdam and Boston 2004–)
GCS	*Die griechischen christlichen Schriftsteller der ersten drei Jahrhunderte* (Leipzig 1897–1969) 53 vols
Gilson 'Michel Menot'	Étienne Gilson 'Michel Menot et la technique du sermon médiéval' in *Les Idées et les Lettres* (Paris 1932) 93–154
Godin	André Godin *Erasme, lecteur d'Origène* Travaux d'humanisme et Renaissance 190 (Geneva 1982)
Godin *Spiritualité*	André Godin *Spiritualité franciscaine en Flandre au XVIe siècle: l'homélaire de Jean Vitrier. Texte, étude thématique et sémantique* preface by Alphonse Dupront (Geneva 1971)
Gogan	Brian Gogan 'The Ecclesiology of Erasmus of Rotterdam: A Genetic Account' *Heythrop Journal* 21/1 (1980) 393–411
Grendler (1)	Paul Grendler *Schooling in Renaissance Italy: Literacy and Learning, 1300–1600* (Baltimore c 1989)
Grendler (2)	Paul Grendler *The Universities of the Italian Renaissance* (Baltimore 2002)

Grillmeier	Aloys Grillmeier *Christ in Christian Tradition* trans John Bowden 2nd rev ed (Atlanta 1975) I *From the Apostolic Age to Chalcedon (451)*; idem II *From the Council of Chalcedon (451) to Gregory the Great (590–604)*; Part 2: *The Church of Constantinople in the sixth century* trans John Cawte and Pauline Allen (London and Louisville 1995)
Grünwald	Michael Grünwald 'Der "Ecclesiastes" des Erasmus von Rotterdam: Reform der Predigt durch Erneuerung des Predigers' (Diss. University of Innsbruck 1969)
Halkin	Léon-E. Halkin *Erasmus: A Critical Biography* (Oxford 1993)
Hirsch	Rudolf Hirsch 'Surgant's List of Recommended Books for Preachers (1502–1503)' *Renaissance Quarterly* 20 (1967) 199–210
Hoffmann *Rhetoric*	Manfred Hoffmann *Rhetoric and Theology: The Hermeneutic of Erasmus* (Toronto 1994)
Holborn	Desiderius Erasmus Roterodamus *Ausgewählte Werke* ed Hajo Holborn with Annemarie Holborn (Munich 1933; repr 1964)
JBC	*The Jerome Biblical Commentary* ed Raymond E. Brown, Joseph A. Fitzmyer, and Roland E. Murphy (Englewood Cliffs, NJ 1968) 2 vols
Jedin	*Handbook of Church History* ed Hubert Jedin and John Dolan ([New York] [1965–70]) I, III, IV; *History of the Church* ed Hubert Jedin and John Dolan (New York 1980–2) II, V–X
Jungmann	Joseph A. Jungmann *The Mass of the Roman Rite: Its Origins and Development (Missarum Sollemnia)* trans Francis A. Brunner (Westminster, Md 1986) 2 vols
Kaster *Guardians*	Robert A. Kaster *Guardians of Language: The Grammarian and Society in Late Antiquity* (Berkeley 1988)
Kennedy	George Kennedy *The Art of Rhetoric in the Roman World, 300 B.C.–A.D. 300* (Princeton 1972)
Kilcoyne and Jennings	Francis P. Kilcoyne and Margaret Jennings 'Rethinking "continuity": Erasmus' *Ecclesiastes* and the *Artes praedicandi*' in *Renaissance and Reformation / Renaissance et Réforme* n s 21/4 (1997) 5–24

Kleinhans

Robert G. Kleinhans 'Erasmus' Doctrine of Preaching, a Study of "Ecclesiastes Sive de Ratione Concionandi" ' (diss. Princeton Theological Seminary 1968)

Lampe

G.W.H. Lampe *A Patristic Greek Lexicon* (Oxford 1961)

Lausberg

Heinrich Lausberg *Handbook of Literary Rhetoric: A Foundation for Literary Study* ed David E. Orton and R. Dean Anderson, foreword by George A. Kennedy (Leiden 1998)

LB

Erasmus *Opera omnia* ed Jean Leclerc (Leiden 1703–6; repr Hildesheim 1961–2) 10 vols

Legenda aurea

Jacobus de Voragine *The Golden Legend: Readings on the Saints* trans William Granger Ryan (Princeton 1993)

L&S

Charlton T. Lewis and Charles Short *A Latin Dictionary* (Oxford 1962)

LSJ

Henry George Liddell and Robert Scott *A Greek-English Lexicon* 9th ed (Oxford 1990)

LW

Luther's Works (American Edition) ed Jaroslav Pelikan and Helmut T. Lehmann (Philadelphia and St Louis 1955–86) 55 vols

LXX

Septuaginta ed Alfred Rahlfs (Stuttgart 1935; 1979) 2 vols in one

Mack

Peter Mack *Renaissance Argument: Valla and Agricola in the Traditions of Rhetoric and Dialectic* (Leiden 1993)

Mack *Renaissance Rhetoric*

Peter Mack *A History of Renaissance Rhetoric 1380–1620* (Oxford and New York 2012)

Manifesta mendacia

Manifest Lies trans Erika Rummel CWE 71 115–31

Mansi

Giovanni Domenico Mansi *Sacrorum conciliorum nova et amplissima collectio* (Florence and Venice: Antonius Zatta 1758–98; repr Graz 1960–2) 54 vols in 59

McConica 'Grammar of Consent'

James K. McConica 'Erasmus and the Grammar of Consent' in *Scrinium* II 77–99

McGinness 'Erasmian Legacy'

Frederick J. McGinness 'An Erasmian Legacy: Ecclesiastes and the Reform of Preaching at Trent' in *Heresy, Culture and Religion in Early Modern Italy* ed Ronald K. Delph, Michelle M. Fontaine, John Jeffries Martin (Kirksville, Mo 2006) 93–112

McGinness *Right Thinking* — Frederick J. McGinness *Right Thinking and Sacred Oratory in Counter-Reformation Rome* (Princeton 1995)

McNeil — J.T. McNeil and H.M. Gamer *Medieval Handbooks of Penance* (New York 1938)

Methodus — *Ratio seu Methodus compendio perveniendi ad veram theologiam* in Holborn 150–62

Minnich — Nelson H. Minnich 'Erasmus and the Fifth Lateran Council (1512–17)' in *Erasmus of Rotterdam: The Man and the Scholar* ed J. Sperna Weiland and W.Th.M. Frijhoff (Leiden 1988) 46–60

Murphy *Incunabula* — James J. Murphy *Incunabula: The Printing Revolution in Europe 1455–1500. A Guide to Units Twenty-two and Twenty-three of the Microfiche Collection. Incunabula Units 22 & 23: Rhetoric Incunabula: Parts I & II* (Woodbridge, Conn 1998)

Murphy *Rhetoric* — James J. Murphy *Rhetoric in the Middle Ages: A History of Rhetorical Theory from Augustine to the Renaissance* (Berkeley 1974)

Myers 'Humanism' — W. David Myers 'Humanism and Confession in Northern Europe in the Age of Clement VII' in *The Pontificate of Clement VII: History, Politics, Culture* ed Kenneth Gouwens and Sheryl E. Reiss (Aldershot and Burlington, Vt 2005) 363–83

Myers *Sinning* — W. David Myers *'Poor Sinning Folk': Confession and Conscience in Counter-Reformation Germany* (Ithaca and London 1996)

Nazianzus — St Gregory of Nazianzus *On God and Christ: The Five Theological Orations and Two Letters of Cledonius* ed Frederick J. Williams and Lionel R. Wickham (Crestwood, NY 2002)

NCE — *The New Catholic Encyclopedia* (New York 1967–79) 17 vols

Nestle-Aland — Nestle-Aland *Novum Testamentum Graece* 27th ed (Stuttgart 2001)

Noonan *Church Visible* — James-Charles Noonan Jr *The Church Visible: The Ceremonial Life and Protocol of the Roman Catholic Church* (New York 1999)

NPNF — *Nicene and Post-Nicene Fathers* series II (= NPPF series II)

NRSV — *The Holy Bible New Revised Standard Version* (New York 1989)

OCD
    The Oxford Classical Dictionary ed N.G.L. Hammond et al 2nd ed (Oxford repr 1984)

ODB
    The Oxford Dictionary of Byzantium (New York and Oxford 1991) 3 vols

ODCC
    F.L. Cross *The Oxford Dictionary of the Christian Church* ed E.A. Livingstone 3rd ed (Oxford 1997)

ODS
    The Oxford Dictionary of Saints ed David Hugh Farmer 5th ed (Oxford 2003)

OED
    The Compact Edition of the Oxford English Dictionary: Complete Text Reproduced Micrographically (Oxford 1971) 2 vols

OLD
    Oxford Latin Dictionary ed P.G.W. Glare 2nd ed (Oxford 2012) 2 vols

Olin
    John C. Olin *Christian Humanism and the Reformation: Desiderius Erasmus, Selected Writings* (New York 1965)

Olin *Catholic Reformation*
    John C. Olin *The Catholic Reformation: Savonarola to Ignatius Loyola* (New York 1969)

O'Malley 'Content'
    John W. O'Malley 'Content and Rhetorical Forms in Sixteenth-Century Treatises on Preaching' in *Renaissance Eloquence: Studies in the Theory and Practice of Renaissance Rhetoric* ed James J. Murphy (Berkeley and Los Angeles 1983) 238–52

O'Malley 'Grammar'
    John W. O'Malley 'Grammar and Rhetoric in the *Pietas* of Erasmus' *The Journal of Medieval and Renaissance Studies* 19 (1988) 81–98

O'Malley *Praise and Blame*
    John W. O'Malley *Praise and Blame in Renaissance Rome: Rhetoric, Doctrine, and Reform in the Sacred Orators of the Papal Court, c. 1450–1521* Duke Monographs in Medieval and Renaissance Studies 3 (Durham 1979)

O'Malley 'Sacred Rhetoric'
    John W. O'Malley 'Erasmus and the History of Sacred Rhetoric: The *Ecclesiastes* of 1535' ERSY 5 (1985) 1–29

Origenes Werke
    Origenes Werke: Homilien zum Hexateuch in Rufins Übersetzung part 1: *Die Homilien zu Genesis, Exodus und Leviticus* ed W. Baehrens GCS 29 (Leipzig 1920)

Opuscula
    Erasmus *Erasmi Opuscula: A Supplement to the Opera Omnia* ed Wallace K. Ferguson (The Hague 1933)

Otto   A. Otto *Die Sprichwörter und sprichwörtlichen Redensarten der Römer, gesammelt und erklärt von A. Otto* (Leipzig 1890; repr Hildesheim and New York 1988)

Pabel   *Erasmus' Vision of the Church* ed Hilmar M. Pabel, Sixteenth Century Essays and Studies 33 (Kirksville, Mo 1995)

Parole du prédicateur   *Parole du prédicateur ve–xve siècle* ed Rosa Maria Dessì and Michel Lauwers, Collection du Centre d'études médiévales de Nice (Nice 1997)

Pastor   Ludwig Pastor (Freiherr von) *The History of the Popes, From the Close of the Middle Ages* ed Frederick Ignatius Antrobus (London 1923) 40 vols

Payne (1)   John B. Payne *Erasmus: His Theology of the Sacraments* (Richmond 1970)

Payne (2)   John B. Payne 'The Hermeneutics of Erasmus' in *Scrinium* II 13–49

PG   *Patrologiae cursus completus … series Graeca* ed J.P. Migne (Paris 1857–1912) 162 vols

PL   *Patrologiae cursus completus … series Latina* ed J.P. Migne (Paris 1844–1902) 221 vols

Poeniteas cito   [?Peter of Blois] *De poenitentia* PL 207 1153–6

Porter 'Fisher and Erasmus'   H.C. Porter 'Fisher and Erasmus' in *Humanism, Reform and the Reformation: The Career of Bishop John Fisher* ed Brendan Bradshaw and Eamon Duffy (Cambridge 1989) 81–102

Pseudo-Dionysius *The Celestial Hierarchies*   Pseudo-Dionysius the Areopagite *The Celestial Hierarchies* 15 (London 1935)

Pseudo-Dionysius *The Divine Names*   Pseudo-Dionysius (the Areopagite) *The Divine Names and the Mystical Theology* trans John D. Jones (Milwaukee 1999)

Quintilian   Marcus Fabius Quintilianus *Institutio oratoria*

Rabil   Albert J. Rabil Jr *Renaissance Humanism: Foundations, Forms and Legacy* (Philadelphia 1988) 3 vols

Rahner   Karl Rahner 'Forgotten Truths Concerning the Sacrament of Penance' in *Theological Investigations* II trans K.H. Kruger (Baltimore and London 1963) 135–74

Ratio   *Ratio seu compendium verae theologiae per Des. Erasmum
                        Roterodamum* in Holborn 175–305

Reedijk   Cornelis Reedijk 'Das Lebensende des Erasmus' *Basler
                        Zeitschrift für Geschichte und Altertumskunde* 57 (1958) 23–66

Reeve and Screech (1)   *Erasmus' Annotations on the New Testament: Acts, Romans, I
                        and II Corinthians: Facsimile of the Final Latin Text with All
                        Earlier Variants* ed Anne Reeve and M.A. Screech, Studies
                        in the History of Christian Thought 42 (Leiden 1990)

Reeve and Screech (2)   *Erasmus' Annotations on the New Testament: Galatians to the
                        Apocalypse: Facsimile of the Final Latin Text with All Earlier
                        Variants* ed Anne Reeve, introduction by M.A. Screech,
                        Studies in the History of Christian Thought 52 (Leiden
                        1993)

Rhenanus   Beatus Rhenanus *The Life of Erasmus* (in Olin)

Rosemondt   Godschalk Rosemondt *Confessionale* (Antwerp: M. Hillen
                        1518)

RSV   *The Holy Bible Revised Standard Version* (New York 1974)

Rummel *Catholic   Erika Rummel *Erasmus and his Catholic Critics* Bibliotheca
Critics*   humanistica & reformatorica 45 (Nieuwkoop 1989) 2 vols

Rummel *Monachatus*   Erika Rummel *'Monachatus Non Est Pietas*: Interpretations
                        and Misinterpretations of a Dictum' in Pabel 41–55

SC   *Sources chrétiennes* ed H. de Lubac and J. Daniélou (Paris
                        1941–   ) 564 vols

Schneyer   Johann Baptist Schneyer *Geschichte der katholischen Predigt*
                        (Freiburg c 1969)

Schoeck (1)   R.J. Schoeck *Erasmus of Europe: The Making of a Humanist,
                        1467–1500* (Savage, Md 1990)

Schoeck (2)   R.J. Schoeck *Erasmus of Europe: The Prince of Humanists,
                        1501–1536* (Edinburgh 1993)

Scrinium   *Scrinium Erasmianum* ed J. Coppens 2nd ed (Leiden 1969) 2
                        vols

Seidel Menchi *Erasmus Silvana Seidel Menchi *Erasmus als Ketzer: Reformation und
als Ketzer*   Inquisition im Italien des 16. Jahrhunderts* (Leiden 1993)

Sozomen   *The Ecclesiastical History of Sozomen* trans E. Walford NPNF series II (Peabody, Mass 1994) 2 179–427

Spykman   Gordon J. Spykman *Attrition and Contrition at the Council of Trent* (Amsterdam 1955)

Stupperich   Robert Stupperich 'Erasmus und die kirchlichen Autoritäten' *Annuarium historiae conciliorum* 8 (1976) 346–64

Tanner   *Decrees of the Ecumenical Councils* ed N.P. Tanner (London and Washington 1990) 2 vols

Taylor *Soldiers*   Larissa Taylor *Soldiers of Christ: Preaching in Late Medieval and Reformation France* (New York 1992)

Tentler 'Forgiveness'   Thomas N. Tentler 'Forgiveness and Consolation in the Religious Thought of Erasmus' *Studies in the Renaissance* 12 (1965) 110–33

Tentler *Sin*   Thomas N. Tentler *Sin and Confession on the Eve of the Renaissance* (Princeton 1977)

Thomas à Kempis   Thomas à Kempis *Thomae Hemerken a Kempis Opera omnia* ed Michael Iosephus Pohl (Freiburg im Breisgau 1902–22) 7 vols

Thompson 'Better Teachers'   Craig R. Thompson 'Better Teachers than Scotus or Aquinas' in *Medieval and Renaissance Studies: Proceedings of the Southeastern Institute of Medieval and Renaissance Studies, Summer, 1966* ed John L. Lievsay, Medieval and Renaissance Series 2 (Durham, NC c 1968) 114–45

Thompson 'Return'   Craig R. Thompson 'The Return to Basel' CWE 40 1122–36

TLG   *Thesaurus Linguae Graecae: Canon of Greek Authors and Works* ed Luci Berkowitz and Karl A. Squitier 3rd ed (New York and Oxford 1990)

Tracy (1)   James D. Tracy *Erasmus of the Low Countries* (Berkeley 1996)

Tracy (2)   James D. Tracy *Erasmus: The Growth of a Mind* (Geneva 1972)

Vita sancti Ambrosii   Paulinus of Milan *Vita sancti Ambrosii* trans Sister Mary Simplicia Kaniecka (Washington, DC 1928)

Vogel   C.J. de Vogel 'Erasmus and His Attitude towards Church Dogma' in *Scrinium* II 101–32

Vulg   *Biblia sacra iuxta vulgatam versionem* ed Robertus Weber et al 4th ed (Stuttgart 1994)

Walther and Schmidt   *Proverbia sententiaeque Latinitatis medii ac recentioris aevi: Lateinische Sprichtwörter und Sentenzen des Mittelalters unter frühen Neuzeit in alphabetischer Anordnung aus dem Nachlass von Hans Walther* ed Paul Gerhard Schmidt, n s (Göttingen 1982–6) 3 vols

Wengert   Timothy Wengert 'Famous Last Words: The Final Epistolary Exchange between Erasmus of Rotterdam and Philip Melanchthon (1536)' ERSY 25 (2005) 18–38

Wenzel 'Preaching'   Siegfried Wenzel 'Preaching the Seven Deadly Sins' in *In the Garden of Evil: The Vices and Culture in the Middle Ages* ed Richard Newhauser (Toronto 2005) 145–69

Witt *Footsteps*   Ronald G. Witt *In the Footsteps of the Ancients: The Origins of Humanism from Lovato to Bruni* (Leiden 2000)

Wolfs   S.P. Wolfs 'Erasmus von Rotterdam und die Dominikaner zu Löwen' in *Xenia medii aevi historiam illustrantia oblata Thomae Kaeppeli O.P.* ed Raymundus Creytens and Pius Künzle (Rome 1978) 787–808

WSA   *The Works of Saint Augustine, A Translation for the 21st Century* (Hyde Park, NY 2000–   )

SHORT-TITLE FORMS FOR ERASMUS' WORKS

Titles following colons are longer versions of the short-titles, or are alternative
titles. Items entirely enclosed in square brackets are of doubtful authorship. For
abbreviations see Works Frequently Cited.

Acta: Acta Academiae Lovaniensis contra Lutherum *Opuscula* / CWE 71
Adagia: Adagiorum chiliades 1508, etc (Adagiorum collectanea for the primitive
  form, when required) LB II / ASD II-1–9 / CWE 30–6
Admonitio adversus mendacium: Admonitio adversus mendacium et obtrecta-
  tionem LB X / CWE 78
Annotationes in Novum Testamentum LB VI / ASD VI-5–10 / CWE 51–60
Antibarbari LB X / ASD I-1 / CWE 23
Apologia ad annotationes Stunicae: Apologia respondens ad ea quae Iacobus Lopis
  Stunica taxaverat in prima duntaxat Novi Testamenti aeditione LB IX / ASD IX-2
Apologia ad Caranzam: Apologia ad Sanctium Caranzam, or Apologia de tribus
  locis, or Responsio ad annotationem Stunicae … a Sanctio Caranza defensam
  LB IX / ASD IX-8
Apologia ad Fabrum: Apologia ad Iacobum Fabrum Stapulensem LB IX / ASD IX-3 /
  CWE 83
Apologia ad prodromon Stunicae LB IX / ASD IX-8
Apologia ad Stunicae conclusiones LB IX / ASD IX-8
Apologia adversus monachos: Apologia adversus monachos quosdam Hispanos
  LB IX
Apologia adversus Petrum Sutorem: Apologia adversus debacchationes Petri
  Sutoris LB IX
Apologia adversus rhapsodias Alberti Pii: Apologia ad viginti et quattuor libros
  A. Pii LB IX / ASD IX-6 / CWE 84
Apologia adversus Stunicae Blasphemiae: Apologia adversus libellum Stunicae cui
  titulum fecit Blasphemiae et impietates Erasmi LB IX / ASD IX-8
Apologia contra Latomi dialogum: Apologia contra Iacobi Latomi dialogum de
  tribus linguis LB IX / CWE 71
Apologia de 'In principio erat sermo': Apologia palam refellens quorundam
  seditiosos clamores apud populum ac magnates quod in evangelio Ioannis
  verterit 'In principio erat sermo' (1520a); Apologia de 'In principio erat sermo'
  (1520b) LB IX / CWE 73
Apologia de laude matrimonii: Apologia pro declamatione de laude matrimonii
  LB IX / CWE 71
Apologia de loco 'Omnes quidem': Apologia de loco taxato in publica professione
  per Nicolaum Ecmondanum theologum et Carmelitanum Lovanii 'Omnes quidem
  resurgemus' LB IX / CWE 73
Apologia qua respondet invectivis Lei: Apologia qua respondet duabus invectivis
  Eduardi Lei *Opuscula* / ASD IX-4 / CWE 72
Apophthegmata LB IV / ASD IV-4 / CWE 37–8
Appendix de scriptis Clithovei LB IX / CWE 83
Appendix respondens ad Sutorem: Appendix respondens ad quaedam Antapologiae
  Petri Sutoris LB IX
Argumenta: Argumenta in omnes epistolas apostolicas nova (with Paraphrases)
Axiomata pro causa Lutheri: Axiomata pro causa Martini Lutheri *Opuscula* /
  CWE 71

Brevissima scholia: In Elenchum Alberti Pii brevissima scholia per eundem
 Erasmum Roterodamum ASD IX-6 / CWE 84

Carmina LB I, IV, V, VIII / ASD I-7 / CWE 85–6
Catalogus lucubrationum LB I / CWE 9 (Ep 1341A)
Ciceronianus: Dialogus Ciceronianus LB I / ASD I-2 / CWE 28
Colloquia LB I / ASD I-3 / CWE 39–40
Compendium vitae Allen I / CWE 4
Conflictus: Conflictus Thaliae et Barbariei LB I / ASD I-8
[Consilium: Consilium cuiusdam ex animo cupientis esse consultum] Opuscula /
 CWE 71

De bello Turcico: Utilissima consultatio de bello Turcis inferendo, et obiter enarratus
 psalmus 28 LB V / ASD V-3 / CWE 64
De civilitate: De civilitate morum puerilium LB I / ASD I-8 / CWE 25
Declamatio de morte LB IV
Declamatiuncula LB IV
Declarationes ad censuras Lutetiae vulgatas: Declarationes ad censuras Lutetiae
 vulgatas sub nomine facultatis theologiae Parisiensis LB IX / ASD IX-7 / CWE 82
De concordia: De sarcienda ecclesiae concordia, or De amabili ecclesiae concordia
 [on Psalm 83] LB V / ASD V-3 / CWE 65
De conscribendis epistolis LB I / ASD I-2 / CWE 25
De constructione: De constructione octo partium orationis, or Syntaxis LB I /
 ASD I-4
De contemptu mundi: Epistola de contemptu mundi LB V / ASD V-1 / CWE 66
De copia: De duplici copia verborum ac rerum LB I / ASD I-6 / CWE 24
De esu carnium: Epistola apologetica ad Christophorum episcopum Basiliensem de
 interdicto esu carnium (published with scholia in a 1532 edition but not in the
 1540 Opera) LB IX / ASD IX-1 / CWE 73
De immensa Dei misericordia: Concio de immensa Dei misericordia LB V / ASD V-7 /
 CWE 70
De libero arbitrio: De libero arbitrio diatribe LB IX / CWE 76
De philosophia evangelica LB VI
De praeparatione: De praeparatione ad mortem LB V / ASD V-1 / CWE 70
De pueris instituendis: De pueris statim ac liberaliter instituendis LB I / ASD I-2 /
 CWE 26
De puero Iesu: Concio de puero Iesu LB V / ASD V-7 / CWE 29
De puritate tabernaculi: Enarratio psalmi 14 qui est de puritate tabernaculi sive
 ecclesiae christianae LB V / ASD V-2 / CWE 65
De ratione studii LB I / ASD I-2 / CWE 24
De recta pronuntiatione: De recta latini graecique sermonis pronuntiatione LB I /
 ASD I-4 / CWE 26
De taedio Iesu: Disputatiuncula de taedio, pavore, tristicia Iesu LB V / ASD V-7 /
 CWE 70
Detectio praestigiarum: Detectio praestigiarum cuiusdam libelli Germanice scripti
 LB X / ASD IX-1 / CWE 78
De vidua christiana LB V / ASD V-6 / CWE 66
De virtute amplectenda: Oratio de virtute amplectenda LB V / CWE 29
[Dialogus bilinguium ac trilinguium: Chonradi Nastadiensis dialogus bilinguium
 ac trilinguium] Opuscula / CWE 7

Dilutio: Dilutio eorum quae Iodocus Clithoveus scripsit adversus declamationem suasoriam matrimonii / *Dilutio eorum quae Iodocus Clithoveus scripsit* ed Émile V. Telle (Paris 1968) / CWE 83

Divinationes ad notata Bedae: Divinationes ad notata per Bedam de Paraphrasi Erasmi in Matthaeum, et primo de duabus praemissis epistolis LB IX / ASD IX-5

Ecclesiastes: Ecclesiastes sive de ratione concionandi LB V / ASD V-4–5 / CWE 67–8

Elenchus in censuras Bedae: In N. Bedae censuras erroneas elenchus LB IX / ASD IX-5

Enchiridion: Enchiridion militis christiani LB V / CWE 66

Encomium matrimonii (in De conscribendis epistolis)

Encomium medicinae: Declamatio in laudem artis medicae LB I / ASD I-4 / CWE 29

Epistola ad Dorpium LB IX / CWE 3 (Ep 337) / CWE 71

Epistola ad fratres Inferioris Germaniae: Responsio ad fratres Germaniae Inferioris ad epistolam apologeticam incerto autore proditam LB X / ASD IX-1 / CWE 78

Epistola ad gracculos: Epistola ad quosdam impudentissimos gracculos LB X / Ep 2275

Epistola apologetica adversus Stunicam LB IX / ASD IX-8 / ASD-8 / Ep 2172

Epistola apologetica de Termino LB X / Ep 2018

Epistola consolatoria: Epistola consolatoria virginibus sacris, or Epistola consolatoria in adversis LB V / CWE 69

Epistola contra pseudevangelicos: Epistola contra quosdam qui se falso iactant evangelicos LB X / ASD IX-1 / CWE 78

Euripidis Hecuba LB I / ASD I-1

Euripidis Iphigenia in Aulide LB I / ASD I-1

Exomologesis: Exomologesis sive modus confitendi LB V / CWE 67

Explanatio symboli: Explanatio symboli apostolorum sive catechismus LB V / ASD V-1 / CWE 70

Ex Plutarcho versa LB IV / ASD IV-2

Formula: Conficiendarum epistolarum formula (see De conscribendis epistolis)

Hyperaspistes LB X / CWE 76–7

In Nucem Ovidii commentarius LB I / ASD I-1 / CWE 29

In Prudentium: Commentarius in duos hymnos Prudentii LB V / ASD V-7 / CWE 29

In psalmum 1: Enarratio primi psalmi, 'Beatus vir,' iuxta tropologiam potissimum LB V / ASD V-2 / CWE 63

In psalmum 2: Commentarius in psalmum 2, 'Quare fremuerunt gentes?' LB V / ASD V-2 / CWE 63

In psalmum 3: Paraphrasis in tertium psalmum, 'Domine quid multiplicate' LB V / ASD V-2 / CWE 63

In psalmum 4: In psalmum quartum concio LB V / ASD V-2 / CWE 63

In psalmum 22: In psalmum 22 enarratio triplex LB V / ASD V-2 / CWE 64

In psalmum 33: Enarratio psalmi 33 LB V / ASD V-3 / CWE 64

In psalmum 38: Enarratio psalmi 38 LB V / ASD V-3 / CWE 65

In psalmum 85: Concionalis interpretatio, plena pietatis, in psalmum 85 LB V / ASD V-3 / CWE 64

Institutio christiani matrimonii LB V / ASD V-6 / CWE 69

Institutio principis christiani LB IV / ASD IV-1 / CWE 27

[Julius exclusus: Dialogus Julius exclusus e coelis] *Opuscula* ASD I-8 / CWE 27

Lingua LB IV / ASD IV-1A / CWE 29
Liturgia Virginis Matris: Virginis Matris apud Lauretum cultae liturgia LB V /
    ASD V-1 / CWE 69
Luciani dialogi LB I / ASD I-1

Manifesta mendacia ASD IX-4 / CWE 71
Methodus (see Ratio)
Modus orandi Deum LB V / ASD V-1 / CWE 70
Moria: Moriae encomium LB IV / ASD IV-3 / CWE 27

Notatiunculae: Notatiunculae quaedam extemporales ad naenias Bedaicas, or
    Responsio ad notulas Bedaicas LB IX / ASD IX-5
Novum Testamentum: Novum Testamentum 1519 and later (Novum instrumentum
    for the first edition, 1516, when required) LB VI / ASD VI-2, 3, 4

Obsecratio ad Virginem Mariam: Obsecratio sive oratio ad Virginem Mariam in
    rebus adversis, or Obsecratio ad Virginem Matrem Mariam in rebus adversis
    LB V / CWE 69
Oratio de pace: Oratio de pace et discordia LB VIII
Oratio funebris: Oratio funebris in funere Bertae de Heyen LB VIII / CWE 29

Paean Virgini Matri: Paean Virgini Matri dicendus LB V / CWE 69
Panegyricus: Panegyricus ad Philippum Austriae ducem LB IV / ASD IV-1 /
    CWE 27
Parabolae: Parabolae sive similia LB I / ASD I-5 / CWE 23
Paraclesis LB V, VI / ASD V-7
Paraphrasis in Elegantias Vallae: Paraphrasis in Elegantias Laurentii Vallae LB I /
    ASD I-4
Paraphrasis in Matthaeum, etc LB VII / ASD VII-6 / CWE 42–50
Peregrinatio apostolorum: Peregrinatio apostolorum Petri et Pauli LB VI, VII
Precatio ad Virginis filium Iesum LB V / CWE 69
Precatio dominica LB V / CWE 69
Precationes: Precationes aliquot novae LB V / CWE 69
Precatio pro pace ecclesiae: Precatio ad Dominum Iesum pro pace ecclesiae LB IV,
    V / CWE 69
Prologus supputationis: Prologus in supputationem calumniarum Natalis Bedae
    (1526), or Prologus supputationis errorum in censuris Bedae (1527) LB IX /
    ASD IX-5
Purgatio adversus epistolam Lutheri: Purgatio adversus epistolam non sobriam
    Lutheri LB X / ASD IX-1 / CWE 78

Querela pacis LB IV / ASD IV-2 / CWE 27

Ratio: Ratio seu Methodus compendio perveniendi ad veram theologiam (Methodus
    for the shorter version originally published in the Novum instrumentum of 1516)
    LB V, VI

Responsio ad annotationes Lei: Responsio ad annotationes Eduardi Lei LB IX /
    ASD IX-4 / CWE 72
Responsio ad Collationes: Responsio ad Collationes cuiusdam iuvenis geronto-
    didascali LB IX / CWE 73
Responsio ad disputationem de divortio: Responsio ad disputationem cuiusdam
    Phimostomi de divortio LB IX / ASD IX-4 / CWE 83
Responsio ad epistolam Alberti Pii: Responsio ad epistolam paraeneticam Alberti
    Pii, or Responsio ad exhortationem Pii LB IX / ASD IX-6 / CWE 84
Responsio ad notulas Bedaicas (*see* Notatiunculae)
Responsio ad Petri Cursii defensionem: Epistola de apologia Cursii LB X /
    Ep 3032
Responsio adversus febricitantis cuiusdam libellum LB X

Spongia: Spongia adversus aspergines Hutteni LB X / ASD IX-1 / CWE 78
Supputatio: Supputatio errorum in censuris Bedae LB IX
Supputationes: Supputationes errorum in censuris Natalis Bedae: contains Sup-
    putatio and reprints of Prologus supputationis; Divinationes ad notata Bedae;
    Elenchus in censuras Bedae; Appendix respondens ad Sutorem; Appendix de
    scriptis Clithovei LB IX / ASD IX-5

Tyrannicida: Tyrannicida, declamatio Lucianicae respondens LB I / ASD I-1 / CWE 29

Virginis et martyris comparatio LB V / ASD V-7 / CWE 69
Vita Hieronymi: Vita divi Hieronymi Stridonensis *Opuscula* / CWE 61